The Role of AI in Economic and Financial Forecasting

Sara Elouadi
https://orcid.org/0000-0001-5412-2714
Hassan II University, Morocco

Hicham El Bouanani
https://orcid.org/0009-0002-5211-9831
Univesite Hassan II, Morocco

IGI Global
Scientific Publishing
Publishing Tomorrow's Research Today

Vice President of Editorial — Melissa Wagner
Director of Acquisitions — Mikaela Felty
Director of Book Development — Jocelynn Hessler
Production Manager — Mike Brehm
Cover Design — Jose Rosado

Published in the United States of America by
IGI Global Scientific Publishing
701 East Chocolate Avenue
Hershey, PA, 17033, USA
Tel: 717-533-8845 | Fax: 717-533-7115
Website: https://www.igi-global.com E-mail: cust@igi-global.com

Library of Congress Cataloging-in-Publication Data

Names: Elouadi, Sara, 1983- editor | El Bouanani, Hicham, 1979- editor
Title: The role of AI in economic and financial forecasting / [edited by] Sara Elouadi, Hicham El Bouanani.
Description: Hershey, PA : IGI Global Scientific Publishing, [2027] | Includes bibliographical references and index. | Summary: "The book aims to achieve a comprehensive encapsulation of these recent breakthroughs as well as the anticipated further developments, their methodological innovations, and practical implementations"-- Provided by publisher.
Identifiers: LCCN 2025013535 (print) | LCCN 2025013536 (ebook) | ISBN 9798337330532 hardback | ISBN 9798337330549 paperback | ISBN 9798337330556 ebook
Subjects: LCSH: Economic forecasting | Artificial intelligence
Classification: LCC HB3730 .R645 2026 (print) | LCC HB3730 (ebook) | DDC 330.01/12--dc23/eng/20250820
LC record available at https://lccn.loc.gov/2025013535
LC ebook record available at https://lccn.loc.gov/2025013536

British Cataloguing in Publication Data
A Cataloguing in Publication record for this book is available from the British Library.

Table of Contents

Detailed Table of Contents

Big data has transformed economic crisis detection by analyzing vast datasets from financial markets, macroeconomic indicators, and alternative sources like satellite imagery and social media sentiment. The surge in global financial transactions, reaching $12.6 trillion daily in 2023, underscores the need for real-time analysis. Traditional forecasting models (ARIMA, VAR, GARCH) often fail to capture nonlinear trends and disruptions. Machine learning (ML) and AI models, including RNN, LSTM, and transformers, enhance predictive accuracy by detecting financial anomalies. AI-driven models, such as deep learning-based credit risk analysis, have improved prediction accuracy by up to 30%. Economic indicators like GDP contraction, inflation volatility, and VIX index trends aid crisis detection. NLP-based sentiment analysis of financial news further enhances predictions. Challenges persist in data privacy and regulatory compliance, but advancements in distributed computing and ethical AI will strengthen economic forecasting and crisis mitigation.

This study compares statistical, machine learning (ML), and deep learning models for forecasting NIFTY stock index prices under normal and crisis conditions. Using ARIMA, Random Forest, XGBoost, SVM, RNN, LSTM, and blended models, predictive performance is evaluated through recursive forecasting, test data, and exogenous variables such as gold prices and USD/INR rates. Results show that while ML and deep learning models perform well in stable periods, they falter during high volatility. The Rolling ARIMA model consistently outperforms others due to dynamic retraining. Exogenous variables yield marginal gains, and synthetic noise experiments reveal overfitting in complex models like XGBoost. The study underscores the importance of model simplicity, adaptability, and methodological rigor in financial forecasting, challenging the EMH and supporting the Adaptive

to compare classical and AI-based models, and to propose an adapted methodology suited to local market .

The finance and economics sector has significantly influenced society over the past century. Forecasting is a crucial activity in this field, systematically applied for decision-making and predicting future events. Since Mincer's seminal paper in 1969, the use of forecasts by financial analysts has been increasing. The transition from traditional to algorithmic forecasting is gaining attention in academia and real-world applications, driven by the rise in algorithmic trading and digitalized social interactions that provide extensive signals to describe asset price behavior. This change, powered by the recent big data revolution, led to widespread adoption in the financial arena necessitating a thorough examination of relevant literature.

This study examines the evolving role of Artificial Intelligence (AI) in economic and financial forecasting, highlighting its capacity to process complex, high-frequency data and enhance predictive accuracy. Findings reveal that around 75% of professionals—particularly data scientists and technical experts—acknowledge AI's effectiveness in real-time and crisis forecasting. However, adoption remains uneven, with skepticism among policymakers and academics due to concerns over model transparency, interpretability, and data privacy. Respondents emphasized the ethical risks posed by biased algorithms and called for regulatory. The study also found strong support for hybrid forecasting models that integrate AI with traditional econometric approaches, offering a balanced framework that meets both computational and governance demands. Stakeholders identified accuracy, transparency, and ethical accountability as top priorities for AI adoption in forecasting.

This chapter studies the potential of improving business forecasting with the help of artificial intelligence, more precisely TimeGPT, a generative pre-trained transformer for time series. The chapter emphasizes the practical points of view, including computational efficiency, scalability, and challenges of roll-out from the point of view of explainability. Results from two cases of business forecasting that include revenue forecasting for an IT company and cost forecasting for a state-owned company are presented and the results are comparatively analyzed against more traditional forecasting methods utilized for the same purpose. This chapter contributes to the literature on using AI in business forecasting by providing comparative empirical studies that highlight the potential of these new forecasting opportunities and to practice by showcasing real-world experiences.

Agriculture remains a critical pillar of the Indian economy, employing 42% of the labour force and representing 18% of the nation's Gross Domestic Product (GDP). Although it holds great value, the sector grapples with countless hurdles within the supply chain, involving both production and market flow. Weather variability and the market conditions cause price volatility which is a source of uncertainty to both farmers and policymakers. The authors in this chapter analyse major Indian crops - Wheat and Maize using price prediction models using machine learning approaches such as Linear Regression, Decision Tree, Random Forest, XGBoost and K-Nearest Neighbours. The chapter establishes that the Random Forest algorithm outperforms the other ML models in predicting crop prices. These findings offer valuable insights for policymakers, enabling the development of more effective, data-driven price stabilization strategies and risk reduction measures to support India's agricultural economy.

Preface

Artificial intelligence (AI) has emerged as a major driver of transformation in economic, financial, and organizational systems. In just a few years, it has profoundly revolutionized fields as diverse as credit risk assessment, financial governance, macroeconomic forecasting, crisis detection, stock market analysis, and business competitiveness. Through machine learning, deep learning, natural language processing, and stochastic simulation models, AI now offers unprecedented capabilities for handling complexity, capturing non-linearities, leveraging massive amounts of data, and generating actionable insights in near real-time.

This book is at the heart of this revolution. It offers a comprehensive and multidimensional exploration of the role of AI in finance, economics, management, and organizations. Its chapters address issues ranging from the transformation of financial decision-making systems to algorithmic ethics, from risk modeling to sentiment analysis, from macroeconomic resilience to the impact of AI on public policy, supply chains, marketing, and SME governance. The diversity of approaches—empirical studies, theoretical models, case studies, field surveys, and systematic reviews—reflects the richness and scope of the phenomenon under study.

In a world marked by uncertainty, successive crises, and the accelerating pace of technological change, AI plays a central role in the pursuit of robustness, transparency, and efficiency. However, its integration into financial and economic systems raises major challenges: model reliability, interpretability, algorithmic bias, data protection, regulatory requirements, and societal implications. This book is situated precisely at the intersection of technological innovation and these ethical and strategic challenges. It highlights not only methodological advances and successful applications, but also the limitations, risks, and conditions for responsible and sustainable adoption, both in developed countries and emerging economies, particularly in Morocco and India.

This book is aimed at a broad audience concerned with the digital transformation of economic and organizational systems. It is primarily intended for researchers, doctoral candidates, and students interested in AI applied to finance, economics, or management. It is also a valuable resource for professionals: financial analysts, risk managers, public policymakers, data scientists, consultants, SME executives, and corporate managers seeking to understand the opportunities and constraints associated with AI integration. Finally, it offers regulators, international organizations, and institutional stakeholders rigorous analyses to inform their decisions in a constantly evolving environment.

CHAPTER OVERVIEW

Chapter 1. Big Data and Advanced Time Series Analysis for Economic Crisis Detection

Big data has transformed economic crisis detection by analyzing vast datasets from financial markets, macroeconomic indicators, and alternative sources like satellite imagery and social media sentiment. The surge in global financial transactions, reaching $12.6 trillion daily in 2023, underscores the need for real-time analysis. Traditional forecasting models (ARIMA, VAR, GARCH) often fail to capture nonlinear trends and disruptions. Machine learning (ML) and AI models, including RNN, LSTM, and transformers, enhance predictive accuracy by detecting financial anomalies. AI-driven models, such as deep learning-based credit risk analysis, have improved prediction accuracy by up to 30%. Economic indicators like GDP contraction, inflation volatility, and VIX index trends aid crisis detection. NLP-based sentiment analysis of financial news further enhances predictions. Challenges persist in data privacy and regulatory compliance, but advancements in distributed computing and ethical AI will strengthen economic forecasting and crisis mitigation.

Chapter 2. Evaluation of forecasting methods for the Indian Stock Market: A comparison of Statistical and Machine Learning techniques

This study compares statistical, machine learning (ML), and deep learning models for forecasting NIFTY stock index prices under normal and crisis conditions. Using ARIMA, Random Forest, XGBoost, SVM, RNN, LSTM, and blended models, predictive performance is evaluated through recursive forecasting, test data, and exogenous variables such as gold prices and USD/INR rates. Results show that while ML and deep learning models perform well in stable periods, they falter during high volatility. The Rolling ARIMA model consistently outperforms others due to dynamic retraining. Exogenous variables yield marginal gains, and synthetic noise experiments reveal overfitting in complex models like XGBoost. The study underscores the importance of model simplicity, adaptability, and methodological rigor in financial forecasting, challenging the EMH and supporting the Adaptive Market Hypothesis by highlighting exploitable inefficiencies and the robustness of Rolling ARIMA during crises.

Chapter 3. The Role of Predictive Models and Machine Learning in Macroeconomic and Financial Forecasting

Machine learning (ML) has become a transformative tool in improving forecasting accuracy in both macroeconomics and finance. Traditional forecasting models face limitations in handling complex, non-linear data and adapting to sudden economic shifts. ML overcomes these challenges by analyzing large datasets, detecting hidden patterns, and providing real-time, dynamic predictions. Applications such as stock price forecasting, credit scoring, and economic trend analysis showcase its superior performance over conventional methods. Moreover, the integration of alternative data sources, like social media sentiment and satellite imagery, enhances forecasting capabilities. The use of hybrid models combining traditional econometrics with ML, along with explainable AI for transparency, ensures broader acceptance. As ML evolves, it promises more accurate, scalable, and adaptive models for future economic and financial forecasting.

Chapter 4. The Evaluation of Financial Product With Models That Involve Artificial Intelligence

This chapter explores the development of a methodological framework for the evaluation of derivative products in the specific context of the Moroccan financial market. While derivatives are widely used in developed markets for hedging and speculation purposes, their deployment in emerging economies remains limited due to structural and regulatory constraints.The literature review highlights the traditional valuation models—such as Black-Scholes, binomial models, and discounted cash flow methods—and discusses their limitations in emerging markets like Morocco, where issues of market liquidity, data availability, and institutional maturity prevail. A critical assessment of the Moroccan legal and regulatory environment is provided, followed by a discussion on how machine learning models, particularly Random Forest, can enhance pricing accuracy in the presence of incomplete or noisy financial data. The empirical study, based on real financial data from Moroccan institutions, aims to compare classical and AI-based models, and to propose an adapted methodology suited to local market.

Chapter 5. The Evolution of Algorithmic Forecasting in Finance: From Traditional Models to AI-Driven Insights

The finance and economics sector has significantly influenced society over the past century. Forecasting is a crucial activity in this field, systematically applied for decision-making and predicting future events. Since Mincer's seminal paper in 1969, the use of forecasts by financial analysts has been increasing. The transition from traditional to algorithmic forecasting is gaining attention in academia and real-world applications, driven by the rise in algorithmic trading and digitalized social interactions that provide extensive signals to describe asset price behavior. This change, powered by the recent big data revolution, led to widespread adoption in the financial arena necessitating a thorough examination of relevant literature.

Chapter 6. The Role of AI in Economic and Financial Forecasting

This study examines the evolving role of Artificial Intelligence (AI) in economic and financial forecasting, highlighting its capacity to process complex, high-frequency data and enhance predictive accuracy. Findings reveal that around 75% of professionals—particularly data scientists and technical experts—acknowledge AI's effectiveness in real-time and crisis forecasting. However, adoption remains uneven, with skepticism among policymakers and academics due to concerns over model transparency, interpretability, and data privacy. Respondents emphasized the ethical risks posed by biased algorithms and called for regulatory. The study also found strong support for hybrid forecasting models that integrate AI with traditional econometric approaches, offering a balanced framework that meets both computational and governance demands. Stakeholders identified accuracy, transparency, and ethical accountability as top priorities for AI adoption in forecasting.

Chapter 7. Artificial Intelligence in Economic and Financial Forecasting: A Paradigm Shift in Predictive Analytics

Sudden economic problems can have a severe impact on people and nations alike. However, the speed of development of Artificial Intelligence in anticipation has now taken on an increasingly vital role. The capacity of Artificial Intelligence to forecast the economy is not flawless. However, the notable increase in the pace, volume, and significance of financial and economic quotation analysis by Artificial Intelligence is currently evident. More knowledge about economic and financial forecasting, as well as the increased processing capabilities of Artificial Intelligence, widens the area for directional forecasting in the future. Technological advancements also facilitate the growth of more predictive instruments in various places. There has been a notable increase in the use of Artificial Intelligence (particularly Machine Learning and Neural Networks) in financial and economic forecasting for defining the contemporary market, which is a phenomenon developing in markets, primarily in India.

Chapter 8. AI-Powered Economic Policy for Enhancing Growth, Stability, and Crisis Management

This Chapter explores the transformative role of Artificial Intelligence (AI) in economic policymaking and governance. AI enhances economic forecasting, public financial management, taxation systems, crisis response, and sustainability efforts. It enables real-time analytics and smarter decision-making, supporting inclusive and resilient growth. Drawing on global case studies, the study highlights AI's applications in smart governance, trade optimization, infrastructure planning, and credit risk assessment. While AI offers immense benefits, it also raises critical concerns around data privacy, algorithmic bias, and transparency. The Chapter emphasizes the need for robust, ethical, and inclusive governance frameworks to ensure accountability and fairness. Overall, AI is positioned not just as a technological advancement but as a strategic enabler for sustainable and equitable economic development in the digital era.

Chapter 9. Improving business forecasting with AI: Cases of revenue- and cost-forecasting

This chapter studies the potential of improving business forecasting with the help of artificial intelligence, more precisely TimeGPT, a generative pre-trained transformer for time series. The chapter emphasizes the practical points of view, including computational efficiency, scalability, and challenges of roll-out from the point of view of explainability. Results from two cases of business forecasting that include revenue forecasting for an IT company and cost forecasting for a state-owned company are presented and the results are comparatively analyzed against more traditional forecasting methods utilized for the same purpose. This chapter contributes to the literature on using AI in business forecasting by providing comparative empirical studies that highlight the potential of these new forecasting opportunities and to practice by showcasing real-world experiences.

Chapter 10. Crop Price Prediction Using Machine Learning Techniques - An Indian Case Study of Wheat and Maize: ML-Based Crop Price Forecasting in India

Agriculture remains a critical pillar of the Indian economy, employing 42% of the labour force and representing 18% of the nation's Gross Domestic Product (GDP). Although it holds great value, the sector grapples with countless hurdles within the supply chain, involving both production and market flow. Weather variability and the market conditions cause price volatility which is a source of uncertainty to both farmers and policymakers. The authors in this chapter analyse major Indian crops - Wheat and Maize using price prediction models using machine learning approaches such as Linear Regression, Decision Tree, Random Forest, XGBoost and K-Nearest Neighbours. The chapter establishes that the Random Forest algorithm outperforms the other ML models in predicting crop prices. These findings offer valuable insights for policymakers, enabling the development of more effective, data-driven price stabilization strategies and risk reduction measures to support India's agricultural economy.

Chapter 11. Artificial Intelligence and Migration Forecasting: Adapting Predictive Models to Sudden Economic and Humanitarian Shocks

This chapter examines the role of artificial intelligence (AI) in forecasting migration during sudden crises such as wars, pandemics, and climate disasters. Traditional models struggle to anticipate rapid changes due to reliance on stable historical data. AI approaches—like machine learning and hybrid systems—can process diverse, real-time data (e.g., social media, mobile tracking, satellite images), offering better adaptability. Case studies (Syria, COVID-19, climate migration) show promising results but also highlight ethical and practical challenges: data quality, algorithmic bias, and lack of transparency. The chapter calls for explainable AI (XAI), strong data governance, and interdisciplinary collaboration to ensure fair, responsible, and effective migration forecasting.

By bringing together research covering a broad spectrum – from credit to financial markets, from macroeconomic forecasting to public policy, from management systems to societal challenges – this book aims to provide a clear, critical, and practical overview of the contribution of artificial intelligence. It thus opens up avenues for reflection and action to build more efficient, transparent, and resilient financial and economic practices in a world where AI is becoming an essential driver of transformation.

Sara Elouadi
Hassan II University, Morocco

Hicham El Bouanani
Hassan II University, Morocco

Chapter 1
Big Data and Advanced Time Series Analysis for Economic Crisis Detection

Harshit Mishra
http://orcid.org/0009-0000-1951-7278
Acharya Narendra Deva University of Agriculture and Technology, Kumarganj, India

ABSTRACT

Big data has transformed economic crisis detection by analyzing vast datasets from financial markets, macroeconomic indicators, and alternative sources like satellite imagery and social media sentiment. The surge in global financial transactions, reaching $12.6 trillion daily in 2023, underscores the need for real-time analysis. Traditional forecasting models (ARIMA, VAR, GARCH) often fail to capture nonlinear trends and disruptions. Machine learning (ML) and AI models, including RNN, LSTM, and transformers, enhance predictive accuracy by detecting financial anomalies. AI-driven models, such as deep learning-based credit risk analysis, have improved prediction accuracy by up to 30%. Economic indicators like GDP contraction, inflation volatility, and VIX index trends aid crisis detection. NLP-based sentiment analysis of financial news further enhances predictions. Challenges persist in data privacy and regulatory compliance, but advancements in distributed computing and ethical AI will strengthen economic forecasting and crisis mitigation.

DOI: 10.4018/979-8-3373-3053-2.ch001

INTRODUCTION

Crisis detection in economics has evolved significantly with the advent of big data and advanced time series analysis techniques. The global financial crisis of 2007-2008, which led to a 1.7% contraction in global GDP in 2009, underscored the necessity for more sophisticated tools to foresee and mitigate economic downturns. Traditional economic models, often limited by smaller datasets and linear assumptions, struggled to predict such crises, highlighting the imperative for integrating big data analytics and advanced modelling approaches (Li, 2024). Big data in economics refers to the vast and complex datasets generated from diverse sources, characterized by high volume, velocity, and variety. These sources encompass financial market data, macroeconomic indicators, social media sentiment, high-frequency trading information, and alternative data like satellite imagery and web-scraped content (Zhang *et al.,* 2022). For instance, the European Central Bank (ECB) has utilized high-frequency data to monitor economic activity in real-time, enhancing their ability to detect early signs of economic stress. The integration of such diverse datasets allows for a more comprehensive understanding of economic dynamics, facilitating the early detection of anomalies that may signal impending crises.

Advanced time series analysis techniques have become instrumental in processing and interpreting these large datasets. Classical models like Autoregressive Integrated Moving Average (ARIMA), Vector Autoregression (VAR), and Generalized Autoregressive Conditional Heteroskedasticity (GARCH) have been foundational in economic forecasting. However, the complexity of modern economies necessitates more robust models (Rezaee *et al.,* 2018). Machine learning approaches, including Recurrent Neural Networks (RNNs) and Long Short-Term Memory (LSTM) networks, have demonstrated superior performance in capturing nonlinear patterns and temporal dependencies in economic data. For example, a study employing LSTM models to predict stock market trends during the post-COVID-19 period revealed that the U.S. stock market continued to exhibit volatility, emphasizing the model's capability to adapt to rapidly changing economic conditions.

The integration of artificial intelligence (AI) and big data has also enhanced the development of early warning systems (EWS) for economic crises. Machine learning algorithms, such as decision trees, random forests, and support vector machines, have been applied to predict financial downturns with notable accuracy. A comprehensive evaluation of these models across 18 OECD countries from 1875 to 2020 indicated that advanced machine learning techniques could effectively identify periods of financial instability, offering a significant advantage over traditional logistic regression models (Škare and Porada-Rochoń, 2020). Moreover, natural language processing (NLP) techniques have been utilized to extract sentiment from financial news and central bank communications, providing real-time insights into market perceptions and potential stress points. For instance, during the COVID-19 pandemic, the analysis of social media and news sentiment helped in assessing the economic impact and public response, thereby aiding in timely policy interventions (Qadir *et al.,* 2016).

Despite these advancements, challenges persist in the application of big data and AI for economic crisis detection. Data quality and reliability remain critical concerns, as inaccuracies can lead to misleading forecasts. The complexity of AI models often results in overfitting, where models perform well on historical data but fail to generalize to unseen scenarios. Additionally, the interpretability of AI-driven forecasts poses a challenge for policymakers who require transparent and understandable models to make informed decisions. Ethical considerations, including data privacy and the potential for algorithmic bias, further complicate the deployment of these technologies in economic monitoring. For instance, reliance on biased data sources can perpetuate systemic inequalities, leading to skewed policy responses.

The fusion of big data and advanced time series analysis has substantially improved our ability to detect and respond to economic crises. By leveraging diverse data sources and sophisticated modelling techniques, economists and policymakers can identify early warning signals and implement preventive measures more effectively. However, it is imperative to address the inherent challenges associated with data quality, model interpretability, and ethical considerations to fully harness the potential of these technologies. Ongoing research and collaboration among data scientists, economists, and policymakers are essential to refine these tools and ensure they contribute positively to economic stability and resilience. Considering the above aspects, the objectives of this chapter are:

- To explore the integration of big data and advanced time series analysis techniques in enhancing economic crisis detection methodologies.
- To critically assess the challenges and limitations inherent in applying AI-driven models for economic forecasting and policy formulation.

FUNDAMENTALS OF BIG DATA IN ECONOMIC ANALYSIS

Economic analysis has traditionally relied on structured datasets such as GDP figures, inflation rates, and employment statistics. However, the advent of big data has revolutionized economic modelling by integrating vast, complex, and high-velocity datasets from diverse sources. The ability to analyse large datasets using advanced computational techniques has significantly improved economic forecasting, especially in detecting financial and economic crises. This section explores the fundamental aspects of big data in economic analysis, including its definition, sources, importance, and challenges (Peña and Tsay, 2021).

Definition and Characteristics of Big Data

Big data refers to extremely large and complex datasets that cannot be processed using traditional data management techniques. It is characterized by the five Vs:

1. **Volume** – The scale of data is enormous, often measured in terabytes or petabytes. Economic and financial data come from various sources, including stock exchanges, central banks, and social media platforms.
2. **Velocity** – The speed at which data is generated and processed is critical, especially in financial markets where high-frequency trading occurs in milliseconds.
3. **Variety** – Data originates from structured sources (e.g., official statistics, financial transactions) and unstructured sources (e.g., social media, satellite images).
4. **Veracity** – The reliability and accuracy of data must be ensured before incorporating it into economic models.
5. **Value** – The ability to extract meaningful insights from data to improve decision-making and policy formulation.

Big data in economic analysis provides a more comprehensive understanding of market behaviour, economic trends, and financial stability. The integration of real-time and alternative data sources allows for more accurate crisis detection and economic forecasting.

Sources of Big Data in Economics and Finance

Big data in economics and finance is derived from multiple sources, ranging from traditional economic indicators to non-traditional sources such as social media and satellite imagery. These sources provide real-time insights into market behaviour, economic trends, and financial stability.

Financial Market Data

Financial markets generate a vast amount of data every second, including stock prices, trading volumes, interest rates, and foreign exchange rates. This data is used for real-time monitoring of market trends and forecasting economic downturns. High-frequency trading algorithms analyse this data to make split-second investment decisions, while policymakers and researchers use it to assess market volatility.

Macroeconomic Indicators

Traditional macroeconomic indicators, such as GDP growth, inflation, unemployment rates, and industrial production, remain critical in economic analysis. These indicators are typically released periodically by government agencies and international organizations. However, incorporating big data techniques enables real-time tracking of these indicators through alternative sources, such as online job postings for unemployment trends and retail sales data for consumption patterns.

Social Media and Sentiment Analysis

Social media platforms like Twitter, Facebook, and LinkedIn generate vast amounts of data that can be analysed for sentiment trends in the economy. Public opinions, consumer confidence, and investor sentiment can be extracted using NLP techniques. For instance, a surge in negative sentiments about a financial institution may signal an impending crisis, allowing regulators to take pre-emptive measures (Mishra, 2025).

High-Frequency Trading Data

High-frequency trading (HFT) involves automated trading strategies executed within microseconds. The data generated from HFT includes bid-ask spreads, transaction logs, and market liquidity measures. Analysing this data can reveal market anomalies, liquidity crises, and flash crashes, which are critical for understanding financial instability.

Alternative Data Sources (Satellite Data, Web Scraping)

Alternative data sources have gained prominence in economic analysis due to their ability to provide real-time and granular insights. These include:

- **Satellite Data:** Used to monitor industrial activity, agricultural output, and urban expansion. For example, nighttime lights data from satellite images can serve as a proxy for economic activity in developing regions.
- **Web Scraping:** Extracting data from websites, including online sales, housing listings, and corporate filings, to generate real-time economic indicators. This method is widely used in e-commerce analysis and real estate market forecasting.

The integration of these diverse data sources enhances the accuracy of economic forecasting and crisis detection models.

Importance of Big Data in Crisis Detection

The application of big data in economic crisis detection has transformed traditional forecasting methodologies. Some advantages include:

- **Early Warning Systems:** Machine learning models trained on big data can detect patterns indicating potential economic downturns before they materialize. For example, an unusual decline in consumer sentiment on social media combined with a sudden drop in financial liquidity could signal an impending crisis.
- **Real-Time Analysis:** Unlike conventional economic indicators that are published monthly or quarterly, big data sources provide near-instantaneous updates, enabling policymakers to respond quickly to economic shocks.
- **Enhanced Risk Assessment:** By integrating multiple data sources, risk models can assess vulnerabilities in financial institutions, corporate sectors, and government policies.
- **Predictive Modelling:** Advanced time series analysis techniques, such as deep learning and neural networks, improve the accuracy of economic forecasts by recognizing complex, nonlinear relationships in data.

To illustrate the role of big data in crisis detection, Table 1 compares traditional economic analysis methods with big data-based approaches.

Table 1. Traditional vs. big data-based economic crisis detection

Feature	Traditional Methods	Big Data-Based Methods
Data Sources	Official statistics, surveys	Financial transactions, social media, web data, satellite imagery
Speed of Data Collection	Delayed (monthly, quarterly)	Real-time or near real-time
Analytical Techniques	Regression analysis, time series models	Machine learning, deep learning, NLP
Predictive Accuracy	Moderate	High due to real-time inputs and large datasets
Application in Crisis Detection	Limited	Strong, with early warning capabilities

Source: Author's compilation

Big data enhances economic crisis detection by providing high-frequency, diverse, and granular information that can improve forecasting accuracy and policy responses.

Challenges in Handling Big Data for Economic Forecasting

Despite its advantages, big data presents several challenges in economic forecasting:

- **Data Quality and Reliability:** The accuracy of big data depends on the quality of its sources. Inconsistent or biased data can lead to misleading conclusions.
- **Computational Complexity:** Processing large-scale economic data requires significant computational resources and specialized algorithms.
- **Privacy and Ethical Concerns:** The use of financial transactions and social media data raises concerns about individual privacy and data security.
- **Integration with Traditional Models:** Combining big data with established economic theories is challenging, as many machine learning models function as black boxes without clear economic interpretations.
- **Legal and Regulatory Issues:** The use of alternative data sources, such as web scraping and satellite images, may raise legal and compliance challenges, particularly regarding data ownership and usage rights.

Overcoming these challenges requires interdisciplinary collaboration between economists, data scientists, and policymakers to develop robust, transparent, and ethical big data-driven forecasting models.

ADVANCED TIME SERIES ANALYSIS TECHNIQUES FOR ECONOMIC FORECASTING

Economic forecasting is a crucial tool for policymakers, financial analysts, and businesses to anticipate future trends and make informed decisions. Traditional statistical methods have long been employed to model economic data, but the emergence of advanced computational techniques, particularly machine learning and AI-driven models, has revolutionized time series analysis.

Fundamentals of Time Series Data in Economics

Time series data consists of sequential observations recorded over time at equal intervals, such as daily stock prices, quarterly GDP growth rates, or annual inflation figures. Unlike cross-sectional data, time series data exhibits temporal dependencies, meaning that past observations influence future values (Ali *et al.,* 2016). Table 2 presents some characteristics of economic time series data:

Table 2. Characteristics of economic time series data

Characteristic	Definition	Example in Economics
Trend	Long-term movement in data	GDP growth over decades
Seasonality	Regular, periodic fluctuations	Retail sales peak during holidays
Cyclic Patterns	Recurrent fluctuations over years	Business cycles (booms & recessions)
Stationarity	Constant mean and variance over time	Interest rates under stable monetary policy

Classical Time Series Models

Traditional time series forecasting relies on statistical models that assume linear dependencies among data points. These models have been widely used due to their interpretability and solid theoretical foundations.

Autoregressive Integrated Moving Average (ARIMA)

The ARIMA model is a widely used technique for univariate time series forecasting. It combines three components:

$$ARIMA(p,d,q) \;=\; AR(p) + I(d) + MA(q)$$

Where:

- p represents the number of autoregressive (AR) terms,
- d represents the degree of differencing needed to achieve stationarity, and
- q represents the number of moving average (MA) terms.

Figure 1. ARIMA model process

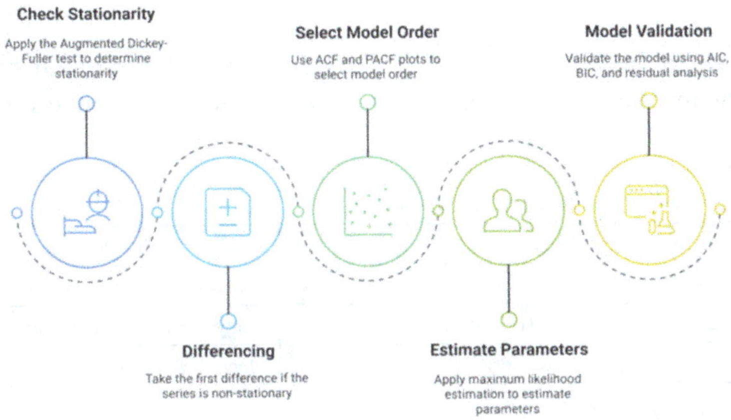

(Source: Author's compilation)

As illustrated in Figure 1, the ARIMA model process involves identifying the appropriate values of p, d, and q based on the characteristics of the time series data. The general equation for an ARIMA model is:

$$Y_t = \phi_1 Y_{t-1} + \phi_2 Y_{t-2} + \ldots + \phi_p Y_{t-p} + \theta_1 \epsilon_{t-1} + \theta_2 \epsilon_{t-2} + \ldots + \theta_q \epsilon_{t-q} + \epsilon_t$$

where ϕ and θ are the model parameters, and ϵ_t is white noise.

Applications of ARIMA in Economic Forecasting:

- Predicting GDP growth rates
- Inflation rate modelling
- Stock price movements

Vector Autoregression (VAR)

VAR extends the AR model to handle multivariate time series, where multiple economic variables influence each other. A VAR model of order p is defined as:

$$Y_t = A_1 Y_{t-1} + A_2 Y_{t-2} + \ldots + A_p Y_{t-p} + \epsilon_t$$

where

Y_t is a vector of economic variables,

A_i are coefficient matrices, and
ϵ_t is the error term.

As shown in Table 3, VAR models are widely applied in economic analysis to examine the interactions between key financial and macroeconomic variables.

Table 3. Example of VAR model applications

Economic Variables in VAR Model	Purpose
Inflation, Interest Rate, GDP	Assess monetary policy impact
Exchange Rate, Foreign Reserves, Trade Balance	Analyse currency market stability
Stock Market Index, Gold Prices, Oil Prices	Model financial market dynamics

Source: Author's compilation

Applications of VAR in Economics:

- Forecasting interest rates and inflation
- Examining the impact of monetary policies on economic indicators
- Modelling global trade dynamics

Generalized Autoregressive Conditional Heteroskedasticity (GARCH)

Many economic time series, such as stock market returns, exhibit volatility clustering—periods of high or low variance. The GARCH model captures this dynamic variance structure:

$$\sigma_t^2 = \alpha_0 + \sum_{i=1}^{q} \alpha_i \epsilon_{t-i}^2 + \sum_{j=1}^{p} \beta_i \sigma_{t-j}^2$$

where σ_t^2 represents conditional variance, and α and β are model parameters.

Example: Stock market volatility prediction using GARCH. Figure 2 illustrates volatility clustering.

Figure 2. Concept of volatility clustering in financial markets

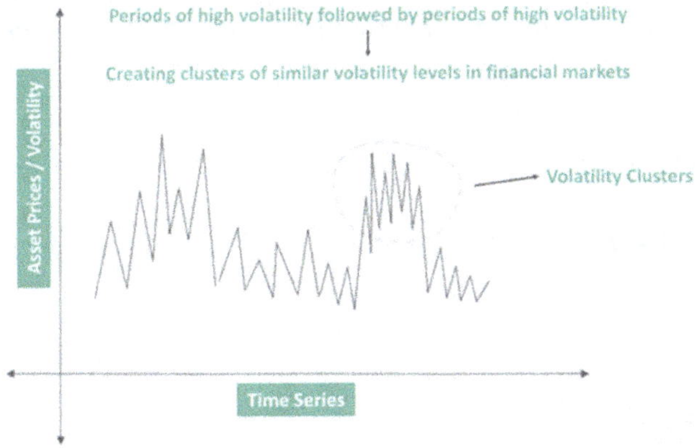

(Source: Suthar, 2025)

Applications of GARCH:

- Stock market risk assessment
- Exchange rate volatility analysis
- Inflation rate forecasting

Machine Learning and AI-Based Time Series Models

With advancements in computational power and data availability, AI-driven models have significantly improved economic forecasting by capturing complex patterns in data.

Recurrent Neural Networks (RNN) and Long Short-Term Memory (LSTM)

Traditional neural networks struggle with sequential data due to the vanishing gradient problem. RNNs address this by maintaining a hidden state that preserves memory across time steps:

$$h_t = f(W_h h_{t-1} + W_x x_t)$$

where h_t is the hidden state, W_h and W_x are weight matrices, and x_t is the input at time t.

However, RNNs face limitations in handling long-term dependencies. As shown in Table 4, LSTM networks overcome this with a gating mechanism that selectively retains or forgets information, making them more effective for extended sequences. The LSTM model is defined as:

$$f_t = \sigma\left(W_f[h_{t-1}, x_t] + b_f\right)$$

$$i_t = \sigma\left(W_i[h_{t-1}, x_t] + b_i\right)$$

$$\widetilde{C}_t = \tanh\left(W_c[h_{t-1}, x_t] + b_c\right)$$

$$C_t = f_t \times C_{t-1} + i_t \times \widetilde{C}_t$$

where f_t, i_t, and C_t represent forget, input, and cell states, respectively.

Table 4. Comparison of RNN vs. LSTM in time series forecasting

Model	Strength	Limitation
RNN	Captures sequential dependencies	Struggles with long-term memory
LSTM	Handles long-term dependencies	Requires high computational power

Applications of LSTM in Economic Forecasting:

- Stock price prediction
- Economic growth modelling
- Demand forecasting in financial markets

Transformer Models for Time Series Forecasting

Transformers, originally designed for natural language processing, have recently been adapted for time series analysis due to their self-attention mechanism. The Attention Mechanism computes the weighted sum of input features:

$$Attention(Q, K, V) = softmax\left(\frac{QK^T}{\sqrt{d_k}}\right)V$$

where Q, K, and V are query, key, and value matrices, respectively.

Transformers, such as Temporal Fusion Transformers (TFTs), outperform traditional models by capturing both short- and long-term dependencies in economic time series.

Applications of Transformers:

- Macroeconomic forecasting
- Global supply chain modelling
- Real-time economic monitoring

Hybrid Models Combining Traditional and AI Approaches

Hybrid models leverage the strengths of both classical statistical methods and machine learning. A common hybrid approach integrates ARIMA with LSTM:

1. ARIMA captures linear patterns and removes seasonality.
2. Residual errors are fed into an LSTM network for capturing non-linear relationships.
3. The final output combines both predictions.

Another hybrid model combines GARCH with RNNs for volatility forecasting. GARCH captures variance dynamics, while RNNs model complex dependencies in residuals. As shown in Table 5, hybrid models outperform classical and AI-based approaches by combining statistical rigor with deep learning flexibility.

Table 5. Comparison of classical, AI, and hybrid models

Model Type	Example	Strength	Weakness
Classical	ARIMA, GARCH	Strong theoretical basis	Struggles with non-linearity
AI-Based	LSTM, Transformers	Captures complex patterns	High computational cost
Hybrid	ARIMA-LSTM	Combines strengths of both	Complex implementation

Applications of Hybrid Models:

- Enhanced financial risk modelling
- Multi-step economic forecasting
- Predicting market crashes

Advanced time series analysis techniques are crucial for understanding and predicting economic crises. While traditional models like ARIMA, VAR, and GARCH provide a strong statistical foundation, machine learning approaches such as LSTMs and transformers enhance forecasting accuracy by capturing intricate temporal patterns. Hybrid models that integrate classical and AI-driven methods offer the best of both worlds, ensuring robust economic forecasting frameworks (Picoli *et al.,* 2018).

Comparative Evaluation of Classical vs. AI Models

The comparative evaluation of classical and AI-based time series models in economic forecasting has evolved into a central area of research, especially after the increasing availability of large-scale, high-frequency economic data. Classical models such as ARIMA, VAR, and GARCH have long provided the foundation for time series analysis in macroeconomics and finance. Their mathematical rigor, transparency, and interpretability made them the preferred choice for policymakers and financial institutions throughout the twentieth century. However, as data complexity grew and nonlinear dependencies became more evident, researchers began to question whether these traditional approaches could adequately capture the dynamic and volatile nature of modern economies. Empirical studies over the last decade consistently show that artificial intelligence models, particularly RNN, LSTM, and Transformer-based architectures, often outperform traditional models in terms of predictive accuracy when dealing with non-linear, multi-dimensional data. For instance, when forecasting exchange rate volatility or inflation under conditions of market turbulence, AI models tend to capture hidden temporal dependencies that linear models fail to represent. These capabilities stem from their data-driven learning process, which allows the model to automatically identify complex structures without explicit model specification (Chae *et al.,* 2012).

Nevertheless, the performance advantage of AI models is not universal. Comparative evidence suggests that classical models remain robust in short-term forecasting tasks with well-behaved data or limited historical volatility. In contrast, AI models tend to excel in long-horizon forecasting, where long-term dependencies, regime shifts, and structural breaks dominate the data-generating process. For example, a 2024 study comparing ARIMA, LSTM, and Transformer models for GDP growth forecasting across OECD countries found that while ARIMA provided lower short-term errors during stable periods, Transformer-based models achieved significantly better performance during economic shocks, such as the 2020–2022 pandemic period and subsequent inflationary waves. In financial markets, hybrid models combining GARCH with LSTM architectures have also demonstrated substantial gains in volatility prediction accuracy. These hybrids integrate the strengths of statistical specification with the adaptability of neural networks. Case studies on cryptocurrency markets, where data exhibit extreme volatility and non-stationarity, confirm that such hybrid frameworks reduce forecast errors and better capture tail-risk events. Similar findings are reported in studies analysing sovereign bond yields and energy market prices.

However, one of the major challenges that emerge from this comparative evaluation concerns computational cost and model stability. While ARIMA or VAR models can be trained and validated within minutes using standard statistical software, deep learning architectures require significant computational resources, careful hyperparameter tuning, and large datasets to avoid overfitting. Moreover, AI models' performance can deteriorate under data scarcity or in low-frequency macroeconomic series, where limited observations make parameter estimation difficult. Empirical evidence thus points toward a complementary relationship rather than a strict substitution between classical and AI approaches. The best-performing models often combine the statistical discipline of classical econometrics with the adaptability of AI. In policy and crisis detection applications, this integrated perspective allows analysts to balance interpretability with predictive power. The ongoing trend, reflected in recent literature, moves toward such hybrid or ensemble frameworks as the optimal paradigm for economic forecasting in complex and data-rich environments (Nahar *et al.,* 2024).

Explainable AI and Model Interpretability in Economic Forecasting

As AI-driven models increasingly influence economic forecasting and policy decision-making, the demand for explainability and interpretability has grown substantially. Traditional econometric models like ARIMA and VAR have long been valued not merely for their forecasting performance but for their ability to convey clear, interpretable relationships among variables. Economists could identify causality, elasticity, and lag effects directly through coefficients and impulse response functions. However, AI-based models—especially deep neural networks—operate as complex, non-linear function approximators, often described as "black boxes." This opacity raises legitimate concerns regarding accountability, transparency, and trust in economic analysis. Explainable AI (XAI) seeks to address these challenges by providing mechanisms through which model predictions can be understood, visualized, and rationalized (Shawon *et al.,* 2024). In the context of economic forecasting, interpretability involves not only understanding which variables influence a prediction but also how those variables interact over time and under different market conditions. Techniques such as SHAP (SHapley Additive exPlanations), LIME (Local Interpretable Model-Agnostic Explanations), and attention-weight visualization in Transformer architectures have emerged as valuable tools for this purpose.

For example, SHAP values can decompose a model's forecast—say, of inflation or exchange rate volatility—into the contribution of individual input features, such as consumer spending, interest rate differentials, or oil prices. This decomposition enables economists to identify which drivers most strongly influenced a model's prediction, enhancing the interpretive transparency of AI systems. Similarly, in Transformer models, attention scores can reveal which temporal patterns or economic indicators the model "attends to" when forming its forecasts, providing an intuitive sense of causal relevance even without explicit structural equations. Explainability has become especially critical in policy-sensitive domains such as crisis prediction, where forecasts influence regulatory decisions, monetary interventions, or fiscal stimulus measures. Decision-makers must be able to justify forecasts to stakeholders and the public. Thus, an accurate but opaque model may be less useful than a slightly less accurate but interpretable one. Recent developments in interpretable deep learning, such as monotonic neural networks and symbolic regression hybrids, aim to reconcile this trade-off by embedding interpretability into the model architecture itself.

Another important strand of research involves causal interpretability—moving beyond correlation-based explanations toward models that reflect underlying economic mechanisms. The fusion of causal inference methods with AI-based forecasting allows analysts to simulate counterfactual scenarios, such as the impact of interest rate changes or commodity shocks on GDP. By combining the predictive flexibility of AI with the structural interpretability of econometrics, these methods bring AI models closer to the explanatory standards long expected in economic research (Lanari *et al.,* 2020).

ECONOMIC INDICATORS AND CRISIS DETECTION METRICS

Economic crises, whether in the form of recessions, financial market crashes, or debt crises, have significant socio-economic implications. Early detection of such crises is essential for policymakers, financial institutions, and businesses to implement preventive measures. Big data and advanced time series analysis play a crucial role in identifying patterns, anomalies, and leading indicators that signal potential economic downturns. This chapter section explores various macroeconomic and financial market indicators used for economic crisis detection, with a focus on real-time data and early warning systems.

Macroeconomic Indicators for Crisis Detection

Macroeconomic indicators provide a broad view of a country's economic health and help assess the likelihood of a crisis. These indicators reflect structural economic conditions and are essential for economic modelling and forecasting. The key macroeconomic indicators include GDP growth rates, inflation measures, interest rates, unemployment trends, and public debt levels.

GDP Growth Rates and Recession Indicators

Gross Domestic Product (GDP) growth rate is one of the primary indicators used to assess the overall economic performance of a country. A declining or negative GDP growth rate over consecutive quarters typically signals a recession. The National Bureau of Economic Research (NBER) defines a recession as a significant decline in economic activity across multiple sectors, lasting for a sustained period (Zamanzadeh Darban *et al.,* 2024).

Mathematical Representation of GDP Growth Rate

The GDP growth rate can be expressed mathematically as:

$$GDP_{growth} = \left(\frac{GDP_t - GDP_{t-1}}{GDP_{t-1}}\right) \times 100$$

where: GDP_t represents the current period GDP, and GDP_{t-1} represents the GDP of the previous period.

A prolonged decline in GDP growth rate, combined with other macroeconomic indicators, provides strong evidence of an impending economic crisis.

Inflation and Hyperinflation Measures

Inflation, defined as the rate at which the general price level of goods and services rises over time, is a critical factor in economic crisis detection. Moderate inflation is normal in a growing economy, but excessive inflation (hyperinflation) or deflation can indicate economic instability.

Consumer Price Index (CPI) and Inflation Rate Calculation

Inflation is often measured using the Consumer Price Index (CPI), which tracks the price changes of a basket of goods and services over time:

$$Inflation_{rate} = \left(\frac{CPI_t - CPI_{t-1}}{CPI_{t-1}}\right) \times 100$$

where: CPI_t represents the consumer price index at time t, and CPI_{t-1} represents the CPI at the previous time period.

Hyperinflation, often defined as inflation exceeding 50% per month, is a severe crisis indicator that disrupts economic stability.

Interest Rates and Yield Curve Inversion

Interest rates, set by central banks, influence borrowing, lending, and overall economic activity. A key indicator of economic downturns is the inversion of the yield curve, which occurs when long-term interest rates fall below short-term interest rates. This inversion signals investor pessimism and is historically linked to recessions.

Yield Curve Spread Formula

$$YCS = r_{10y} - r_{2y}$$

where: r_{10y} is the 10-year government bond yield, and r_{2y} is the 2-year government bond yield.

A negative yield curve spread (i.e., $YCS<0$) has predicted most recessions over the past decades.

Unemployment and Labor Market Trends

Unemployment rates are fundamental indicators of economic distress. A rising unemployment rate suggests weakening economic activity, reduced business confidence, and declining household income levels.

$$Unemployment_{rate} = \left(\frac{Unemployed}{Labour\ force}\right) \times 100$$

where: Unemployed refers to individuals actively seeking work, and Labor Force includes both employed and unemployed individuals.

Sudden spikes in unemployment, particularly in key economic sectors, serve as early warning signals for economic crises.

Public Debt and Fiscal Deficits

Public debt and fiscal deficits indicate a government's financial health and its ability to manage economic downturns. A high debt-to-GDP ratio reduces a country's ability to respond to economic crises effectively.

$$Debt\ ratio = \left(\frac{Public\ debt}{GDP}\right) \times 100$$

A persistently high debt ratio (>100%) suggests fiscal vulnerability and increases the risk of sovereign debt crises.

Climate-Related Financial Risks (e.g., Carbon Pricing, Climate Shocks)

In recent years, the growing recognition of climate change as a systemic economic risk has significantly altered the framework through which economists and policymakers assess financial stability. Climate-related financial risks have become an essential component of macroprudential analysis, reflecting the complex interactions between environmental stressors, policy transitions, and market behaviour. These risks can be broadly classified into two interrelated categories: physical risks and transition risks. Physical risks refer to the direct economic consequences of climate events such as floods, droughts, hurricanes, wildfires, and rising sea levels. These events disrupt production systems, damage infrastructure, and erode asset values. For instance, prolonged droughts can severely affect agricultural output, leading to food price volatility and income losses in rural economies. Similarly, frequent hurricanes can impair energy supply chains and housing markets, thereby affecting GDP growth and employment levels. The cumulative economic impact of such events is often nonlinear, meaning that repeated shocks can magnify financial vulnerabilities over time. In macroeconomic terms, physical risks can reduce potential output, strain fiscal balances through increased disaster relief spending, and destabilize insurance and reinsurance markets.

Transition risks, on the other hand, emerge from the policy and technological shifts required to move toward a low-carbon economy. These include changes in carbon pricing mechanisms, the introduction of emissions trading systems, regulatory interventions on fossil fuel industries, and the rapid expansion of green technologies. For example, the implementation of higher carbon taxes may alter the profitability of energy-intensive sectors, leading to asset revaluations and changes in investment behaviour. Financial institutions exposed to carbon-intensive portfolios could experience sharp declines in asset values, while markets may reprice climate-related risks unevenly across sectors. The sudden repricing of "stranded assets" — those whose value diminishes due to regulatory or technological changes — can have cascading effects on credit markets and banking stability. Another dimension of transition risk involves carbon pricing, which has become a central policy instrument for internalizing the external costs of greenhouse gas emissions (Chinta, 2023). Carbon pricing schemes, including carbon taxes and cap-and-trade systems, serve not only as environmental tools but also as economic signals. They influence production costs, consumer prices, and investment decisions across industries. However, the degree of uncertainty surrounding carbon prices can itself be a source of market instability. When firms and investors are unsure about future carbon costs, they may delay or misallocate investments, contributing to economic inefficiency and volatility. In this way, climate policy uncertainty becomes an implicit financial risk factor.

From an analytical perspective, the integration of climate-related data into economic forecasting models represents a major advancement in crisis detection research. With the advent of big data and machine learning, it has become feasible to incorporate high-resolution environmental indicators — such as satellite-based temperature anomalies, emissions data, and disaster frequency — into macro-financial models. Time series analysis of such data can reveal subtle correlations between climate stressors and economic variables. For example, temporal clustering of extreme weather events can be linked to fluctuations in agricultural commodity prices or regional GDP contractions. Moreover, structural break tests in time series models can help identify regime shifts triggered by major climate events or policy changes. Central banks and financial regulators are increasingly developing climate stress tests to evaluate the resilience of financial institutions under various climate scenarios. These tests simulate the effects of prolonged droughts, carbon taxation, or abrupt shifts in energy markets on credit risk, capital adequacy, and liquidity positions. When combined with large-scale economic datasets, such models enable a probabilistic assessment of crisis likelihood under different climate trajectories (Chinta *et al.,* 2024; Shu *et al.,* 2024).

Indicators by Risk Type and Predictive Horizon

The analysis of economic crisis detection metrics benefits greatly from a structured synthesis of indicators according to their risk type and predictive horizon. Such a synthesis helps researchers, policymakers, and analysts understand not only which variables are most relevant to specific types of crises but also how far in advance they can reliably signal distress. The construction of summary figures and classification tables is, therefore, a methodological necessity in both empirical research and policy modelling. In practice, indicators can be grouped into four primary risk categories: macroeconomic, financial market, fiscal, and environmental or climate-related risks. Each of these categories captures distinct transmission channels through which vulnerabilities evolve into full-blown crises. For instance, macroeconomic indicators such as GDP growth, inflation, and unemployment rates typically reflect medium-term structural weaknesses. Financial indicators — including stock market volatility, credit default spreads, and interbank liquidity measures — often provide short-term, high-frequency signals of market stress. Fiscal indicators like public debt ratios and fiscal deficits reveal longer-term sustainability concerns, while environmental indicators capture the emerging dimension of climate-induced instability (Wang *et al.,* 2025).

When plotted along a predictive horizon, these categories reveal important temporal patterns. Short-term indicators (ranging from daily to quarterly data) are most effective in detecting market-based distress, such as liquidity shortages or sudden capital outflows. Medium-term indicators (typically quarterly to annual data) tend to reflect cyclical downturns and policy transmission effects, making them valuable for identifying early signs of recessions or stagflation. Long-term indicators (spanning several years or decades) are more relevant for structural risks such as demographic shifts, technological transformations, and climate change. A well-designed summary figure might therefore display a two-dimensional framework: the horizontal axis representing time horizons (short, medium, and long term), and the vertical axis organizing indicators by risk type (Malempati, 2022). For example, in the short-term cell of financial risks, one might find measures like daily stock market volatility or interbank lending spreads. In the medium-term section for macroeconomic risks, GDP growth rates, output gaps, and inflation expectations could appear. The long-term environmental risk cell would include metrics like cumulative carbon emissions, climate vulnerability indices, and green investment ratios.

Another layer of sophistication in such figures arises when predictive accuracy or signal strength is incorporated as a visual dimension. Indicators can be color-coded or ranked according to their historical forecasting performance, based on back-testing or machine learning validation. For example, yield curve inversions may be highlighted as strong early predictors of recessions, while climate risk measures might show rising predictive power as data availability improves. In this way, the summary figures become dynamic research tools, not just static tables. From a methodological viewpoint, these figures also serve as bridges between qualitative interpretation and quantitative modelling. They help translate large volumes of heterogeneous data into an intelligible structure, guiding the selection of variables for time series modelling and machine learning applications. In academic settings, they allow for transparent communication of complex relationships among variables, helping to validate model assumptions and interpret empirical results (Saba *et al.,* 2021).

Furthermore, such visual summaries are particularly valuable in policy contexts, where decision-makers must quickly grasp which, indicators warrant attention in real time. By mapping indicators to predictive horizons, policymakers can prioritize data monitoring according to urgency. For instance, a sudden spike in short-term market volatility might trigger immediate liquidity interventions, while a long-term rise in climate vulnerability could prompt strategic investment in green infrastructure.

Financial Market Indicators

Financial market indicators offer real-time insights into investor sentiment, liquidity conditions, and systemic risks. These indicators include stock market volatility, credit default swaps, and banking sector stability metrics.

Stock Market Volatility

Stock market fluctuations are early indicators of financial instability. The most widely used measure of stock market volatility is the VIX Index, which represents expected market fluctuations over the next 30 days.

$$VIX = \sqrt{\sum_{t=1}^{n} (r_t - \bar{r})^2}$$

where: r_t is the daily return, and $\bar{r}$ is the mean return.

Spikes in the VIX index indicate heightened market uncertainty and potential crises.

Credit Default Swaps (CDS) and Bond Yields

CDS represent the cost of insuring against default on government or corporate bonds. Rising CDS spreads indicate increasing default risks and financial stress. Similarly, bond yield spreads between safe assets (e.g., U.S. Treasury bonds) and risky assets (e.g., corporate bonds) serve as crisis indicators.

$$Spread = Yield_{corporate} - Yield_{treasury}$$

An increasing spread suggests heightened credit risk and investor concern about economic stability.

Banking Sector Stability Indicators

The stability of the banking sector is crucial in preventing financial crises. Main banking stability indicators include:

- **Non-Performing Loan (NPL) Ratio**: Higher NPL ratios indicate stressed banking conditions.
- **Capital Adequacy Ratio (CAR)**: A lower CAR suggests weaker bank solvency.

$$CAR = \frac{Bank\ capital}{Risk\ wieghted\ assets} \times 100$$

A declining CAR signals financial distress and potential banking failures.

Role of Real-Time Data in Early Warning Systems

Real-time economic data enhances crisis detection accuracy by providing continuous monitoring of macroeconomic and financial indicators. Advanced time series models such as:

- ARIMA
- GARCH
- Machine Learning Models (e.g., Random Forest, LSTMs)

These models enable policymakers to identify early warning signals and implement timely interventions. The integration of big data, real-time economic indicators, and advanced time series analysis significantly enhances economic crisis detection. Understanding macroeconomic trends, financial market indicators, and leveraging AI-based forecasting tools can help mitigate economic downturns and ensure stability (Wanckel, 2022).

AI-DRIVEN APPROACHES FOR ECONOMIC CRISIS DETECTION

The detection and prediction of economic crises have long been critical challenges in financial and economic research. With the advent of big data and AI, sophisticated computational techniques are increasingly being employed to analyse vast and complex economic datasets. AI-driven approaches enhance traditional econometric methods by integrating ML, NLP, and reinforcement learning (RL), allowing for a more nuanced understanding of financial stability (Bukar *et al.,* 2022). These approaches enable early detection of crisis indicators, provide real-time monitoring of economic conditions, and support policymakers in making informed decisions. The following sections discuss various AI-driven methodologies that are instrumental in economic crisis detection.

Machine Learning Algorithms for Crisis Prediction

Machine learning techniques are widely used in financial time series analysis, offering robust predictive capabilities for economic crises. Unlike conventional econometric models, which rely on predefined functional forms, ML methods can identify complex, nonlinear relationships within economic indicators, making them highly effective in detecting early warning signals of financial distress. The subsections below elaborate on specific ML techniques used for economic crisis prediction.

Decision Trees and Random Forests

Decision trees are supervised learning models that recursively partition a dataset into smaller subsets based on feature importance, ultimately forming a tree-like structure. These models are particularly useful for economic crisis detection as they provide interpretability and allow for rule-based decision-making. However, individual decision trees are prone to overfitting, making them unreliable for large and noisy financial datasets (Mishra, 2024).

To address these limitations, Random Forests (RF)—an ensemble learning technique—are employed. Random forests consist of multiple decision trees trained on different random subsets of data (Vogiazas and Alexiou, 2017). The final prediction is determined by aggregating the outputs of all trees, reducing variance and improving robustness. Random forests are effective in crisis detection as they:

- Handle high-dimensional economic data efficiently.
- Identify important macroeconomic variables influencing financial stability.
- Provide feature importance scores, enabling policymakers to understand critical risk factors.

Mathematically, a random forest prediction for a given input X is computed as:

$$\hat{y} = \frac{1}{N}\sum_{i=1}^{N} f_i(X)$$

where $f_i(X)$ represents the prediction of the ith decision tree, and N is the total number of trees.

Random forests have been successfully applied in forecasting stock market crashes, currency devaluations, and banking crises by analysing economic indicators such as GDP growth, inflation rates, credit spreads, and liquidity ratios (Mahmoud and Mohammed, 2021).

Support Vector Machines (SVM)

SVM are powerful classification algorithms used to detect financial distress by separating crisis and non-crisis periods in economic time series data. SVM works by finding an optimal hyperplane that maximizes the margin between different classes, ensuring robust classification. Main advantage of SVM in crisis detection lies in its ability to handle high-dimensional data and capture nonlinear relationships using kernel functions (Ali and Thakkar, 2023). The decision function for an SVM classifier is given by:

$$f(X) = sign\left(\sum_{i=1}^{N} \alpha_i y_i K(X_i, X) + b\right)$$

where:

$K(X_i, X)$ is the kernel function (e.g., radial basis function, polynomial kernel).
α_i are Lagrange multipliers.
y_i are class labels (e.g., crisis or non-crisis).
b is the bias term.

SVMs have been widely used in predicting stock market crashes, banking crises, and bond market collapses, outperforming traditional econometric models due to their adaptability in complex financial environments.

Deep Learning for Time Series Anomalies

Deep learning techniques, particularly RNNs and LSTM networks, have revolutionized financial time series analysis by capturing long-term dependencies in sequential data. These methods are particularly effective in identifying anomalies in macroeconomic indicators that precede financial crises. LSTMs are designed to mitigate the vanishing gradient problem associated with traditional RNNs by introducing memory cells that selectively retain or forget information (Shu and Zhu, 2020). The LSTM cell operations are defined as:

$$f_t = \sigma\left(W_f \bullet [h_{t-1}, x_t] + b_f\right)$$

$$i_t = \sigma\left(W_i \bullet [h_{t-1}, x_t] + b_i\right)$$

$$\widetilde{C}_t = \tanh(W_c \bullet [h_{t-1}, x_t] + b_c)$$

$$C_t = f_t \bullet C_{t-1}, i_t \bullet \widetilde{C}_t$$

$$o_t = \sigma(W_o \bullet [h_{t-1}, x_t] + b_o)$$

$$h_t = o_t \bullet \tanh(C_t)$$

where f_t, i_t, o_t are forget, input, and output gates, respectively.

LSTMs have demonstrated high accuracy in crisis prediction by detecting patterns in GDP fluctuations, currency volatility, and credit default swap spreads, making them a powerful tool for economic forecasting.

Comparative Case Studies: Performance Across Markets (ECB, RBI, IMF)

Comparative analyses of AI-based economic crisis detection models across different institutional and market contexts provide essential insights into the robustness and adaptability of machine learning frameworks. Examining how these models perform within the operational structures of organizations such as the ECB, the Reserve Bank of India (RBI), and the International Monetary Fund (IMF) reveals both the universality of algorithmic techniques and their sensitivity to contextual data environments. Within the ECB framework, AI-driven models are primarily integrated into macro-financial surveillance systems that focus on systemic risk indicators within the Eurozone (Gallego and Font, 2021). The ECB's approach emphasizes data harmonization, where cross-country banking and credit datasets are standardized for training machine learning algorithms. Random forests and RNNs have been applied to forecast sovereign risk levels, liquidity shocks, and contagion patterns across member economies. The models demonstrate strong predictive accuracy when supplied with high-frequency financial data, yet their performance tends to fluctuate in response to regulatory heterogeneity and country-specific fiscal policies. This reflects the challenge of generalizing AI models across multiple jurisdictions within a single monetary union.

In contrast, the RBI operates within a more data-diverse and policy-sensitive environment, where machine learning systems must accommodate a mixture of structured and unstructured data. India's financial ecosystem, characterized by high volatility in credit markets and complex monetary-fiscal linkages, necessitates adaptive algorithms capable of learning from dynamic and non-stationary time series. The RBI's pilot applications of gradient boosting machines and LSTM networks for currency fluctuation detection and credit default prediction have shown promising results, particularly when combined with sentiment indices extracted from financial media. However, data quality, incomplete reporting, and limited data depth across sectors continue to constrain the accuracy and generalizability of AI models in emerging markets. The IMF, as a global surveillance institution, adopts a more integrative perspective (Murri *et al.,* 2024). Its AI-based economic crisis prediction frameworks are designed to analyse cross-country macroeconomic indicators, capital flow dynamics, and policy interventions at a global scale. Here, machine learning models are calibrated to detect early warning signals of financial distress by analysing multidimensional datasets that include both macroeconomic fundamentals and textual information from country reports. The IMF's experimentation with ensemble learning—where multiple algorithms such as decision trees, neural networks, and Bayesian models are combined—has improved the detection of crisis precursors. The comparative findings suggest that model interpretability remains a key concern, particularly when AI predictions are used to inform policy discussions with national authorities (Tan *et al.,* 2019).

Across these three cases, one observes that while AI systems consistently outperform traditional econometric models in identifying non-linear relationships and early warning signals, their effectiveness is contingent on institutional data infrastructures, governance standards, and model transparency requirements. The ECB benefits from a stable data environment, the RBI demonstrates flexibility under uncertainty, and the IMF exemplifies scalability across borders. Together, they illustrate how the same class of algorithms can yield diverse outcomes depending on local data realities and policy objectives (Metawa *et al.,* 2021).

Natural Language Processing (NLP) for Economic Forecasting

NLP is increasingly used to extract valuable economic insights from unstructured textual data, including news articles, financial reports, and central bank communications. The subsections below discuss various NLP applications in economic crisis detection.

Sentiment Analysis from Financial News and Reports

Sentiment analysis uses NLP techniques to evaluate the sentiment conveyed in financial news, central bank statements, and earnings reports. Lexicon-based and machine learning-based sentiment analysis approaches are commonly used to assess economic confidence and detect early warning signs of instability.

A sentiment score S is often computed as:

$$S = \frac{\sum_{i=1}^{N} w_i \cdot f_i}{N}$$

where w_i represents the weight of a financial term, and f_i is its frequency.

Higher negative sentiment in financial reports has been correlated with increased market volatility, credit tightening, and economic downturns.

Text Mining from Central Bank Communications

Text mining techniques extract critical economic insights from central bank reports and monetary policy announcements. Topic modelling algorithms such as Latent Dirichlet Allocation (LDA) identify themes related to inflation expectations, liquidity conditions, and financial stability, providing real-time indicators of economic stress.

Event-Based Forecasting Using NLP

Event-based forecasting integrates NLP techniques with financial econometrics to analyse how geopolitical events, policy changes, or natural disasters impact economic stability. Named Entity Recognition (NER) and Temporal Analysis track how financial crises evolve in response to global events, enhancing predictive models.

Reinforcement Learning in Financial Stability Analysis

Reinforcement Learning (RL) is an AI approach where agents learn optimal decision-making strategies by interacting with financial environments. Deep Q-Networks (DQNs) and Policy Gradient Methods are commonly used to model dynamic financial systems and predict crisis scenarios.

The RL objective is to maximize cumulative reward R:

$$R_t = \sum_{k=0}^{\infty} \gamma^k r_{t+k}$$

where γ the discount factor, and r_t is the reward at time t.

RL models have been applied to portfolio risk management, banking stress testing, and systemic risk forecasting, providing an advanced AI-driven framework for economic crisis detection.

AI-driven methodologies have significantly improved economic crisis detection by integrating machine learning, NLP, and reinforcement learning techniques. These approaches enhance the accuracy and timeliness of financial stability assessments, allowing policymakers and investors to mitigate economic risks effectively. Future research should focus on hybrid AI models that combine multiple techniques for enhanced predictive performance (Mishra and Mishra, 2024; Ibrahim and Wang, 2019).

Reinforcement Learning in Financial Stability Analysis and Policy Simulation

RL represents a significant evolution in the field of economic crisis detection, particularly in simulating policy responses and assessing systemic stability under varying market conditions. Unlike supervised learning approaches, which rely on labelled datasets, reinforcement learning employs a trial-and-error mechanism to optimize decision-making through continuous feedback loops (Xiao *et al.,* 2018). In the context of financial stability, RL agents can model the behaviour of economic actors—banks, investors, and regulators—and learn optimal strategies for minimizing systemic risk or maximizing financial resilience. The practical relevance of reinforcement learning lies in its ability to model adaptive policy environments. Financial systems are inherently dynamic, characterized by feedback effects and time-dependent interactions between policy interventions and market behaviour. Traditional econometric models often assume equilibrium conditions and linear relationships, which limit their ability to represent sudden regime shifts. RL models, in contrast, learn from evolving market states. They simulate policy decisions such as changes in interest rates, liquidity injections, or capital requirements, and evaluate how these decisions influence systemic stability metrics like credit spreads, default rates, and interbank liquidity (Qiu and Wang, 2025; Abehadi *et al.,* 2020).

For instance, central banks have experimented with Deep Reinforcement Learning (DRL) techniques to simulate crisis management scenarios. By training an agent on historical and synthetic financial data, policymakers can evaluate which interventions might stabilize markets during a liquidity crunch or currency shock. The agent's objective function can be designed to minimize economic loss or volatility while balancing trade-offs between inflation control and employment stability. Through repeated simulations, RL systems uncover non-obvious policy strategies that may outperform human-designed rule-based approaches. Moreover, reinforcement learning enables policy scenario testing in environments of uncertainty. By incorporating stochastic elements—such as sudden capital outflows, commodity price shocks, or contagion events—the model learns how resilient different policy mixes are under stress (Chen *et al.,* 2014). This capability is particularly relevant for institutions like the Bank for International Settlements (BIS) and OECD, which conduct macroprudential policy research involving multiple countries. RL's ability to adapt and optimize across evolving economic landscapes allows policymakers to explore the long-term implications of their actions rather than focusing solely on short-term effects.

Nevertheless, challenges remain. RL models require extensive data and computational resources, and their internal decision pathways are often opaque, making interpretability a significant concern in high-stakes policy settings. Furthermore, translating algorithmic recommendations into actionable policy measures requires careful alignment with institutional mandates and political constraints. Despite these challenges, reinforcement learning provides a powerful experimental platform for understanding the dynamic interplay between regulation, market behaviour, and systemic stability (Mroua and Lamine, 2023).

Integration of AI Models with Institutional Decision Systems (BIS and OECD)

The successful adoption of AI for economic crisis detection depends not only on the accuracy of models but also on their integration into institutional decision-making frameworks. This integration process transforms AI models from research prototypes into operational tools that inform policy discussions, risk assessments, and crisis prevention strategies. The experiences of the BIS and the Organisation for Economic Co-operation and Development (OECD) offer instructive examples of how global institutions incorporate AI systems into their analytical and advisory functions. At the BIS, AI is increasingly used to enhance macroprudential oversight and cross-border financial surveillance. The institution has developed hybrid decision-support platforms that combine machine learning models with traditional econometric methods. These platforms process massive datasets on interbank exposures, capital flows, and payment systems to identify emerging vulnerabilities in the global financial network (Yang *et al.,* 2022). The BIS's approach emphasizes XAI techniques, ensuring that model predictions are transparent enough to support policy deliberations among central banks. For example, feature attribution methods are applied to quantify how variables such as credit growth or asset price inflation contribute to predicted crisis probabilities. By embedding AI outputs into interactive dashboards, policymakers can visualize systemic risk indicators in near real time and simulate the effects of policy interventions under different market scenarios.

Similarly, the OECD has integrated AI models into its economic forecasting and policy simulation processes, particularly in areas concerning fiscal sustainability, labour markets, and trade shocks. Using AI-driven scenario analysis, the OECD can generate probabilistic forecasts that account for nonlinearities and global interdependencies often overlooked in traditional models. Natural language processing (NLP) tools are also incorporated into the OECD's research workflow, enabling the extraction of policy-relevant insights from member countries' reports and legislative documents. These tools support automated trend detection and EWS that highlight emerging economic risks across sectors. The institutional integration of AI models requires significant organizational adaptation. Both BIS and OECD have established data governance frameworks, ensuring that AI tools comply with ethical standards, data privacy regulations, and transparency principles. Equally important is the human–machine collaboration aspect: domain experts are involved in the design, validation, and interpretation of AI results to ensure that the models remain aligned with policy objectives. The integration process thus transforms decision-making from a static, data-review exercise into a dynamic, AI-assisted exploration of possible economic futures (Phillips *et al.,* 2015).

In both institutions, AI integration has led to measurable improvements in situational awareness, forecasting accuracy, and response agility. However, these benefits come with challenges related to data standardization, model explainability, and institutional capacity building. The lessons from BIS and OECD demonstrate that integrating AI into economic governance is not merely a technical process but an organizational transformation requiring alignment between analytical innovation and institutional accountability.

Visual Summary of AI Models, Data Inputs, and Policy Applications

A comprehensive visualization of AI-driven approaches to economic crisis detection illustrates how different models, data sources, and policy applications interconnect within the broader analytical ecosystem. The framework can be understood as a multi-layered structure composed of three primary dimensions: data inputs, analytical models, and policy applications. At the foundational layer lie the data inputs, encompassing both quantitative and qualitative sources. Quantitative inputs include high-frequency financial indicators such as interest rates, credit spreads, and equity market indices. Complementary macroeconomic data—GDP growth, inflation rates, current account balances—provide structural context. On the qualitative side, text-based data from central bank communications, government reports, and financial news serve as critical inputs for NLP-based sentiment and event analysis. Together, these datasets form a multidimensional representation of economic conditions, which AI models can process to identify early signals of instability (Aljohani, 2023).

The intermediate layer represents the analytical AI models themselves. Machine learning algorithms such as random forests, support vector machines, and neural networks detect nonlinear relationships and temporal anomalies in the data. Deep learning models, particularly LSTM and transformer architectures, capture long-term dependencies within time series data, enhancing the detection of subtle crisis patterns. Reinforcement learning adds an interactive element by simulating policy responses and adaptive market behaviours. Each model type contributes distinct analytical strengths: supervised learning for prediction, unsupervised learning for pattern discovery, and reinforcement learning for dynamic policy experimentation. At the top layer, the insights generated by these AI systems feed into policy applications.

Central banks and international institutions use AI outputs to inform monetary and fiscal decisions, assess systemic vulnerabilities, and design preventive interventions. For instance, risk heatmaps derived from AI models guide macroprudential regulations, while scenario simulations assist policymakers in evaluating the potential impacts of shocks such as currency depreciation or capital flight. Visualization tools—interactive dashboards, network graphs, and temporal heatmaps—translate complex model outputs into intuitive formats suitable for decision-makers (Ling and Cai, 2022; Tsay, 1986).

The integration of these layers underscores the synergistic relationship between data, models, and governance. AI-driven systems not only enhance the speed and precision of economic analysis but also expand the conceptual space within which policymakers can anticipate and respond to crises. By transforming vast, fragmented datasets into coherent visual narratives, AI facilitates more informed and timely economic decision-making. Ultimately, the visual summary of this ecosystem demonstrates that the future of crisis detection lies in the convergence of computational intelligence, institutional insight, and transparent communication of complex information.

RISK ASSESSMENT AND EARLY WARNING SYSTEMS

Economic crises can have profound consequences, impacting national economies, financial markets, and social stability. The ability to assess risk and detect warning signs of an impending crisis is crucial for policymakers, financial institutions, and businesses. Risk assessment and EWS leverage big data and advanced time series analysis to identify patterns and anomalies that signal economic instability (Taipalus, 2012). This section explores the concept of early warning systems, compares traditional statistical models with AI-driven approaches, and delves into anomaly detection techniques. Furthermore, it discusses model evaluation metrics, including precision, recall, F1-score, ROC curves, and the explainability of AI models in risk assessment.

Concept of Early Warning Systems (EWS) in Economic Forecasting

An EWS in economic forecasting is a predictive framework designed to identify potential risks and crises before they materialize. These systems analyse macroeconomic indicators, financial market trends, and socio-political factors to forecast adverse economic events such as recessions, inflationary surges, currency crises, and banking failures. The fundamental objective of an EWS is to provide timely alerts, allowing policymakers and financial institutions to implement preventive measures.

EWS relies on extensive data sources, including GDP growth rates, inflation indices, interest rate fluctuations, stock market volatility, trade imbalances, and debt-to-GDP ratios. Traditional EWS models employed statistical techniques like logistic regression and VAR, while modern systems incorporate ML and deep learning (DL) to enhance predictive accuracy. The adoption of big data technologies has further strengthened EWS by integrating real-time data streams from financial transactions, social media sentiment analysis, and global economic indicators (Hassani and Silva, 2015).

A well-designed EWS follows a structured process:

1. **Data Collection and Preprocessing:** Aggregation of economic indicators, financial reports, and alternative data sources.
2. **Feature Engineering:** Identification and selection of relevant variables contributing to economic downturns.
3. **Model Selection:** Application of statistical and AI-based models for forecasting.
4. **Risk Classification:** Categorization of economic conditions into normal, warning, and crisis phases.
5. **Alert Generation and Decision Support:** Issuance of warnings to policymakers, central banks, and investors based on model predictions.

Statistical vs. AI-Based Risk Assessment Models

Risk assessment models play a crucial role in economic crisis detection by estimating the likelihood and severity of economic downturns. These models can be broadly classified into two categories: traditional statistical models and AI-based models.

Statistical Risk Assessment Models

Traditional statistical models rely on historical data and predefined mathematical relationships between economic variables. Some of the most commonly used approaches include:

- **Logistic Regression:** A binary classification model used to predict the probability of an economic crisis based on input variables such as interest rates, inflation, and fiscal deficits.
- **VAR:** A time series model that captures interdependencies between multiple economic indicators to forecast future trends.

- **Markov Switching Models:** These models account for regime shifts in economic conditions, distinguishing between stable and crisis phases.
- **Bayesian Econometric Models:** These models incorporate prior knowledge and probabilistic inference to improve crisis prediction accuracy.

While statistical models offer interpretability and robustness, they often fail to capture complex, nonlinear relationships in economic data.

AI-Based Risk Assessment Models

AI-driven models have gained prominence due to their ability to learn intricate patterns from vast datasets. Some advanced AI techniques include:

- **Artificial Neural Networks (ANNs):** These models learn hierarchical representations of economic data, making them effective for forecasting economic crises.
- **LSTM Networks:** A specialized form of RNNs that capture long-term dependencies in financial time series data.
- **Random Forests and Gradient Boosting Machines (GBMs):** Ensemble learning techniques that enhance predictive performance through feature importance analysis.
- **Autoencoders for Anomaly Detection:** AI models that learn normal economic patterns and flag deviations indicative of instability.

The key advantage of AI-based models is their adaptability to complex, high-dimensional data, enabling more accurate and timely risk assessment compared to traditional statistical models. However, they require extensive computational resources and often suffer from interpretability challenges (Qiu *et al.,* 2021).

Anomaly Detection for Economic Instability

Anomaly detection is a fundamental component of economic crisis detection, as financial distress often manifests as deviations from normal economic patterns. Anomalies can be categorized into three types:

1. **Point Anomalies:** Sudden spikes or drops in economic indicators, such as an unexpected stock market crash or a sharp currency depreciation.
2. **Contextual Anomalies:** Economic irregularities that appear unusual within a specific context, such as a sudden increase in unemployment despite stable GDP growth.

3. **Collective Anomalies:** Patterns of deviations occurring simultaneously across multiple indicators, signalling systemic risk.

Many techniques are employed for anomaly detection in economic time series data:

- **Statistical Approaches:** Z-score analysis, Granger causality tests, and ARIMA models.
- **Machine Learning Methods:** Isolation forests, k-means clustering, and SVMs for outlier detection.
- **Deep Learning Models:** Variational autoencoders (VAEs) and generative adversarial networks (GANs) to detect anomalies in financial data.

By leveraging these techniques, anomaly detection frameworks enhance the ability of EWS to identify potential economic crises before they escalate.

Model Evaluation and Performance Metrics

Evaluating the performance of risk assessment models is critical to ensure their reliability and accuracy in economic forecasting. Various statistical and AI-based models are assessed using multiple performance metrics.

Precision, Recall, and F1-Score

In economic crisis detection, classification models predict whether a crisis will occur (positive class) or not (negative class). The three main metrics used for evaluation are:

$$Precision = \frac{TP}{TP + FP}$$

$$Recall = \frac{TP}{TP + FN}$$

$$\text{F1-Score} = 2 \times \frac{Precision \times Recall}{Precision + Recall}$$

Where:

TP (True Positives): Correctly predicted economic crises.
FP (False Positives): Incorrectly predicted crises (false alarms).
FN (False Negatives): Missed economic crises.

A high precision ensures fewer false alarms, while a high recall minimizes missed crises. The F1-score provides a balanced assessment of both.

ROC Curves and AUC Metrics

Receiver Operating Characteristic (ROC) curves illustrate the trade-off between the true positive rate (sensitivity) and the false positive rate. The Area Under the Curve (AUC) quantifies model performance:

$$AUC = \int_0^1 TPR \times d(FPR)$$

A higher AUC value indicates a more effective crisis detection model.

Explainability of AI Models in Risk Assessment

While AI-based models outperform traditional methods in risk assessment, their "black-box" nature raises concerns about interpretability. Explainability techniques enhance trust and transparency in economic forecasting models:

- **SHAP:** Assigns importance scores to economic variables influencing predictions.
- **LIME:** Provides interpretable approximations of AI model outputs.
- **Counterfactual Analysis:** Examines how model predictions change with altered input values.

By incorporating explainability tools, AI-driven EWS models can gain credibility among policymakers and financial analysts, ensuring informed decision-making in economic crisis prevention (Tamiminia *et al.,* 2020).

Case Study: Early Warning Systems in Action (IMF and ECB Experiences)

The application of EWS in economic surveillance has been a central focus of international financial institutions such as the IMF and the ECB. Both institutions have developed, tested, and continuously refined sophisticated frameworks to anticipate financial stress, systemic instability, and emerging vulnerabilities within global and regional economies. The experiences of these organizations not only illustrate the practical challenges of implementing large-scale predictive models but also demonstrate how empirical evidence, institutional learning, and policy adaptation interact in real-world economic governance. The IMF's Early Warning Exercise (EWE) was formally institutionalized after the global financial crisis of 2008, though the organization had engaged in various forms of risk surveillance prior to that period. The EWE combines econometric modelling, market intelligence, and qualitative judgment from country experts to identify potential sources of macro-financial instability. Its methodology is grounded in both quantitative indicators—such as credit growth, asset price inflation, external imbalances, and leverage ratios—and qualitative assessments, including political stability, regulatory frameworks, and cross-border exposure patterns. A crucial feature of the IMF's approach lies in its integrative structure, where statistical models are not used in isolation but as inputs for multidisciplinary deliberation across different departments.

The EWE employs multiple models designed to capture diverse dimensions of economic vulnerability. Among these, logit and probit models are frequently applied to estimate the probability of crises occurring within a given time horizon, often one to three years ahead. Over time, the IMF has also experimented with machine learning algorithms, including random forests and support vector machines, to improve classification accuracy and reduce type I and type II errors. However, the IMF recognizes the trade-off between model complexity and interpretability. Policymakers often prefer models that provide clear causal explanations rather than those offering opaque but statistically superior predictions. To reconcile this, the IMF typically adopts a hybrid framework, where advanced statistical tools inform but do not dictate policy conclusions (Reshef *et al.,* 2011). In practice, the IMF's EWS outputs are presented in the form of vulnerability maps and risk dashboards, which visualize the relative exposure of countries or regions to various shocks. These visualizations support cross-country comparisons and enable policymakers to prioritize preventive measures. One of the key insights from IMF experience is that the predictive success of EWS is not solely determined by data quality or algorithmic sophistication but also by the institutional capacity to act on warnings. A timely and accurate warning is of limited value if the corresponding policy response is delayed or constrained by political or structural barriers. Thus, the IMF emphasizes the integration of EWS results into surveillance dialogues, financial sector assessments, and technical assistance programs.

The ECB has also developed its own EWS framework, particularly in response to the euro area debt crisis. The ECB's system focuses on detecting systemic risks across the banking and financial sectors of the Eurozone. Its models rely heavily on high-frequency financial data, such as credit default swap (CDS) spreads, interbank market rates, and equity price volatility. In contrast to the IMF's global orientation, the ECB's EWS operates in a regionally concentrated and institutionally integrated environment, where common monetary policy and shared regulatory standards create both advantages and vulnerabilities. The ECB's EWS is distinctive for its integration of macro-financial linkages. It incorporates feedback loops between financial institutions and sovereigns, acknowledging that fiscal stress can quickly transmit to the banking system and vice versa—a phenomenon often described as the sovereign-bank nexus. By using advanced time series models such as Vector Autoregressions (VAR), Dynamic Factor Models (DFM), and Bayesian estimation techniques, the ECB captures these complex interdependencies and identifies early signs of systemic contagion. The results are synthesized into the ECB's Financial Stability Review, which serves as a critical tool for policy communication and risk mitigation (Koyuncugil and Ozgulbas, 2012).

Another crucial aspect of the ECB's EWS experience is the use of stress-testing frameworks in conjunction with predictive modelling. Stress tests simulate the impact of adverse scenarios—such as a sudden rise in interest rates, asset price corrections, or geopolitical disruptions—on financial institutions' balance sheets. These results are then combined with EWS indicators to form a comprehensive view of systemic resilience. The ECB's practice demonstrates that early warning is not an isolated function but part of a broader ecosystem of financial surveillance involving macro-prudential oversight, data sharing, and real-time market monitoring. Both the IMF and ECB experiences underscore the importance of continuous model updating and validation. Economic structures evolve, new financial instruments emerge, and global linkages shift over time, rendering static models obsolete. Consequently, both institutions maintain iterative processes of recalibration, incorporating new data sources, adjusting variable weights, and re-evaluating threshold values for alert generation. This adaptive approach reflects a recognition that early warning is not a one-time analytical task but an ongoing process of learning under uncertainty.

Incorporating Environmental and Systemic Risks in EWS Design

In recent years, the concept of economic and financial stability has expanded beyond traditional macro-financial variables to encompass broader environmental and systemic risks. The growing recognition that climate-related shocks, resource scarcity, and ecological degradation can trigger or amplify financial crises has prompted researchers and policymakers to integrate these dimensions into EWS. Incorporating such risks requires both conceptual innovation and methodological flexibility, as environmental factors often manifest through complex, non-linear pathways and operate over long-time horizons that challenge conventional forecasting tools. Environmental risks, particularly those linked to climate change, have become a crucial consideration for EWS designers. Events such as prolonged droughts, extreme weather, rising sea levels, and sudden policy shifts toward decarbonization can disrupt production systems, alter trade flows, and erode asset values. For instance, climate-induced agricultural failures can trigger food price inflation, while the abrupt revaluation of fossil fuel assets—known as transition risk—can destabilize financial portfolios. These phenomena demand a rethinking of data inputs and modelling approaches. Traditional macroeconomic indicators must be supplemented with climate data, including temperature anomalies, carbon intensity measures, environmental performance indices, and insurance loss statistics.

Integrating these variables into EWS involves significant technical challenges. Climate and environmental datasets are often heterogeneous, incomplete, and lagged, making them difficult to harmonize with high-frequency financial data. Furthermore, the causal relationships between environmental stress and economic outcomes are typically indirect and delayed, requiring models capable of capturing lag effects and structural breaks. Time series techniques such as cointegration analysis, Markov-switching models, and long-memory processes have been explored to handle these complexities. Meanwhile, machine learning methods—especially neural networks and ensemble models—offer promise in detecting non-linear interactions and threshold effects where traditional econometric methods may fail. Beyond the environmental dimension, the incorporation of systemic risks into EWS design has become equally critical. Systemic risks refer to vulnerabilities that arise not from isolated entities or markets but from interconnectedness and contagion mechanisms within the broader financial architecture. The 2008 crisis illustrated that even well-capitalized institutions could fail if linkages between markets and intermediaries magnify local shocks into global disruptions. To address this, modern EWS frameworks now include network-based indicators, such as interbank exposure matrices, cross-sector leverage ratios, and co-movement measures of asset returns. Network analysis allows policymakers to identify "central nodes" whose distress could propagate widely, thus enabling pre-emptive interventions (Russom 2011).

When environmental and systemic risks intersect, the complexity multiplies. For example, a severe climate event could simultaneously impair production capacity, disrupt energy supply, and increase default risks in climate-sensitive sectors like insurance, real estate, and agriculture. These interconnected shocks can evolve into systemic crises if not properly anticipated. Hence, the design of next-generation EWS must be multi-layered, capturing interactions between economic, financial, and environmental subsystems. This can be achieved through integrated modelling platforms that combine macroeconomic forecasting with environmental simulation models and network analysis. From an institutional perspective, incorporating these risks also requires new forms of collaboration between central banks, financial regulators, environmental agencies, and international organizations. Data sharing and methodological harmonization are crucial to ensure that risk signals are comparable and actionable across jurisdictions. The IMF, for instance, has begun exploring Climate Change Policy Assessments (CCPAs) to integrate environmental vulnerabilities into macro-financial surveillance, while the ECB has introduced climate stress tests that evaluate how transition and physical risks affect banks' capital adequacy. These initiatives illustrate the growing movement toward "green macroprudential policy", where environmental sustainability is viewed as an integral component of financial stability.

Moreover, the communication and visualization of environmental and systemic risks pose additional challenges for EWS design. Unlike conventional financial risks, climate and systemic vulnerabilities often lack clear short-term triggers, making them harder to convey to policymakers and the public. Effective EWS must therefore provide not only predictive signals but also narrative explanations that contextualize the underlying drivers of risk. Dashboards that combine quantitative indicators with scenario-based storytelling can enhance user understanding and foster timely policy action. Finally, the inclusion of environmental and systemic risks in EWS design represents a paradigm shift in economic forecasting. It acknowledges that the economy is not an isolated mechanism but part of a complex adaptive system that interacts continuously with the natural environment. As data availability improves and analytical techniques advance, EWS will increasingly evolve into integrated resilience frameworks, capable of not only predicting crises but also guiding sustainable policy responses that balance economic stability with ecological integrity (Pasham, 2024).

BIG DATA INFRASTRUCTURE AND COMPUTATIONAL TECHNIQUES

The emergence of big data analytics has revolutionized economic research, particularly in the realm of crisis detection and forecasting. The ability to process massive volumes of structured and unstructured data enables economists and policymakers to identify early warning signals of financial distress. However, achieving this objective necessitates a robust big data infrastructure coupled with advanced computational techniques (Mishra and Mishra, 2024). This section explores various components of big data infrastructure, focusing on cloud computing, distributed computing, data preprocessing, and the associated challenges in security, privacy, and ethical considerations.

Cloud Computing for Large-Scale Economic Data Analysis

Cloud computing plays a pivotal role in handling large-scale economic data, offering scalable, cost-effective, and on-demand computational resources. Economic crisis detection involves analysing heterogeneous data sources, including financial transactions, stock market fluctuations, GDP growth indicators, unemployment rates, and trade balances (Yamashita Rios de Sousa *et al.*, 2017). Traditional on-premise data storage and computational systems lack the flexibility and scalability to process such vast amounts of data efficiently. Cloud computing platforms—such as Amazon Web Services (AWS), Microsoft Azure, and Google Cloud Platform (GCP)—provide distributed storage and high-performance computing capabilities. These platforms utilize virtualized environments where economic datasets can be stored, retrieved, and processed in real time.

A main advantage of cloud computing in economic data analysis is elastic scalability. Cloud environments allow users to scale their computational resources dynamically based on the complexity of the dataset and the analytical model employed. For instance, economic time series forecasting models—such as VAR, LSTM, and ARIMA—require extensive computational power, which cloud-based infrastructures can efficiently support (Pejić Bach *et al.*, 2019).

Additionally, cloud computing facilitates collaborative research by enabling multiple researchers, institutions, and governments to access centralized datasets, thus enhancing transparency and data-driven decision-making. Cloud-based economic models can integrate real-time macroeconomic indicators, thereby improving the accuracy of crisis predictions (Fan and Yao, 2008). Despite its advantages, cloud computing raises concerns related to data sovereignty, latency issues, and vendor lock-in, which must be addressed to ensure seamless economic data analysis.

Distributed Computing and Parallel Processing

Given the sheer volume and complexity of economic data, traditional serial processing methods are inadequate for large-scale analysis. Distributed computing and parallel processing techniques provide solutions to enhance computational efficiency and data processing speed.

Distributed Computing

Distributed computing involves the use of multiple interconnected nodes (computers or servers) to execute computations in parallel. In economic crisis detection, distributed frameworks such as Apache Hadoop and Apache Spark enable large-scale data processing by distributing data across multiple clusters.

- **Apache Hadoop:** Utilizes the MapReduce programming model, which splits economic datasets into smaller chunks, processes them across multiple nodes, and aggregates the results efficiently.
- **Apache Spark:** An in-memory computing framework that provides superior speed compared to Hadoop for economic data analytics. Spark's Resilient

Distributed Datasets (RDDs) enhance fault tolerance while allowing real-time data processing (Reinhart and Rogoff, 2011).

The advantage of distributed computing is that it reduces computational bottlenecks, enabling real-time economic monitoring. For example, central banks analysing inflation trends across different countries can leverage distributed computing to process data from global financial institutions, stock exchanges, and economic reports simultaneously.

Parallel Processing

Parallel processing further enhances big data analytics by allowing multiple computations to be performed simultaneously. Graphical Processing Units (GPUs) and Tensor Processing Units (TPUs) are increasingly employed in economic forecasting models that rely on deep learning algorithms. For instance, RNNs and transformers require high computational power to analyse financial time series data. Parallel computing frameworks, such as CUDA (Compute Unified Device Architecture) and OpenMP (Open Multi-Processing), significantly improve execution speed by optimizing CPU and GPU resources (Montgomery *et al.,* 2015). Thus, a combination of distributed and parallel computing ensures scalability, fault tolerance, and real-time economic analysis, which are crucial for crisis detection and early intervention policies.

Data Preprocessing and Feature Engineering

Economic crisis detection models depend heavily on high-quality data inputs. However, raw economic data is often plagued by missing values, inconsistencies, and noise, necessitating rigorous data preprocessing and feature engineering to improve analytical accuracy.

Data Preprocessing Techniques

Data preprocessing involves a series of steps to clean, transform, and normalize economic data:

1. **Handling Missing Data:** Missing values in datasets—such as inflation rates, unemployment figures, and trade balances—can lead to biased results. Techniques such as mean imputation, K-nearest neighbour (KNN) imputation, and multiple imputations by chained equations (MICE) are employed to address this issue.

2. **Data Normalization:** Economic indicators vary in magnitude (e.g., GDP measured in trillions vs. inflation rates in percentages). Min-max scaling and Z-score normalization ensure that data is standardized before applying machine learning models.
3. **Outlier Detection:** Economic data is prone to anomalies due to market shocks or reporting errors. Box plots, Mahalanobis distance, and isolation forests are widely used techniques to detect and remove outliers.

Feature Engineering for Economic Crisis Detection

Feature engineering transforms raw data into meaningful variables that improve model performance. Some crucial aspects include:

- **Lag Features:** Many economic indicators exhibit lagged relationships (e.g., stock market crashes affecting unemployment rates months later). Creating lagged variables enhances predictive accuracy.
- **Rolling Statistics:** Moving averages, exponential smoothing, and rolling standard deviations are used to capture trends in time series data.
- **Sentiment Analysis Features:** Text mining techniques extract economic sentiments from news articles, financial reports, and social media to enhance forecasting models.
- **Correlation Analysis:** Identifying relationships between variables (e.g., interest rates and inflation) helps in selecting the most relevant predictors.

A combination of these techniques ensures that big data-driven economic models produce robust, interpretable, and actionable insights for crisis detection.

Challenges in Data Security, Privacy, and Ethical Considerations

While big data analytics provides significant benefits in economic crisis detection, it also raises critical challenges related to data security, privacy, and ethical considerations.

Data Security Risks

Economic data is highly sensitive, containing information on financial transactions, corporate earnings, and government policies. Cybersecurity threats—such as data breaches, ransomware attacks, and insider threats—pose severe risks. Implementing advanced encryption techniques (AES-256, homomorphic encryption) and multifactor authentication (MFA) is essential to safeguard economic data (Mishra and Mishra, 2024; Zhang *et al.,* 2024).

Privacy Concerns

Economic data often contains personally identifiable information (PII) from financial transactions, tax records, and employment statistics. General Data Protection Regulation (GDPR) and Data Protection Laws impose strict guidelines on data usage. Techniques such as differential privacy, federated learning, and anonymization are essential to ensure data confidentiality.

Ethical Considerations

The application of big data in economic crisis detection raises several ethical concerns:

- **Bias in Algorithmic Models:** Economic prediction models may reinforce biases if trained on historical data reflecting structural inequalities. Ethical AI frameworks must be adopted to ensure fairness.
- **Surveillance Risks:** Excessive monitoring of financial transactions and social media data for economic predictions could infringe on individual freedoms. Striking a balance between economic forecasting and privacy protection is crucial.
- **Data Ownership and Transparency:** Ensuring that economic models remain transparent and explainable is necessary to maintain public trust in AI-driven policy decisions.

A well-structured big data infrastructure and computational framework is indispensable for modern economic crisis detection. Cloud computing, distributed and parallel processing, advanced data preprocessing, and ethical AI principles collectively enhance the reliability and efficiency of economic forecasting models (Shumway *et al.,* 2000). However, addressing security, privacy, and ethical concerns remains a significant challenge that must be navigated carefully to maximize the benefits of big data analytics in economic policymaking.

Data Governance and Regulatory Compliance Frameworks (GDPR, AI Act)

In case of big data and advanced time series analysis for economic crisis detection, the importance of data governance and regulatory compliance cannot be overstated.

Economic data often includes information that is sensitive, proprietary, or personally identifiable, making it essential to adopt robust frameworks that ensure transparency, accountability, and legal conformity. Effective data governance provides a structured approach to managing data throughout its lifecycle, from acquisition and storage to processing and dissemination. It defines clear rules on who can access, modify, or share data, and under what circumstances. Such governance is not merely a technical necessity but a strategic requirement for institutions aiming to build credibility and trust among stakeholders, policymakers, and the public. A major component of modern data governance is compliance with international and regional regulatory frameworks (Grover *et al.,* 2018). GDPR, enacted by the European Union, is one of the most comprehensive data protection laws currently in force. It sets strict conditions for data collection, processing, and transfer, emphasizing the principles of consent, purpose limitation, and data minimization. Under GDPR, organizations that process personal data must ensure that individuals' rights to privacy and data protection are upheld. For economic researchers and policymakers working with financial, employment, or demographic datasets, GDPR compliance means implementing measures such as anonymization, pseudonymization, and encryption to protect individual identities. Moreover, institutions must establish clear documentation of data processing activities, designate data protection officers when required, and prepare for data breach notifications within the prescribed time frames.

Another emerging regulatory instrument of significance is the Artificial Intelligence Act (AI Act) proposed by the European Union. This act addresses the governance of AI systems, especially those that rely on large-scale data analytics and predictive modelling. The AI Act classifies AI applications based on risk levels, requiring more stringent oversight for high-risk systems, including those used in economic forecasting and crisis detection. For practitioners in this domain, compliance entails ensuring algorithmic transparency, traceability, and explainability. Data used to train or validate AI-driven time series models must be accurate, unbiased, and representative to prevent systemic distortions in economic predictions. The AI Act also encourages the development of ethical AI practices that respect human oversight and accountability. Together, the GDPR and AI Act create a regulatory environment that demands a balance between innovation and responsibility. Organizations involved in economic data analysis must invest in compliance mechanisms, including automated auditing tools, data lineage tracking systems, and secure data-sharing platforms. Additionally, fostering a culture of ethical awareness and cross-disciplinary collaboration—among data scientists, legal experts, and policymakers—is vital to maintaining compliance and protecting the public interest. As economic data ecosystems expand in scale and complexity, adhering to these frameworks will remain a central pillar of sustainable and lawful data-driven research and policymaking (Awotunde *et al.,* 2021).

Summary of Infrastructure Best Practices for Policy and Managerial Use

Establishing a robust big data infrastructure for economic crisis detection requires both technological and organizational best practices. Policymakers and managers must understand that infrastructure decisions are not only technical choices but also strategic enablers of analytical accuracy, speed, and reliability. A well-designed infrastructure ensures that vast, heterogeneous economic datasets are processed efficiently, securely, and in compliance with regulatory standards. One of the foundational best practices is the adoption of scalable cloud-based and distributed computing architectures. These systems allow organizations to store and process large volumes of structured and unstructured data without excessive hardware costs. Elastic computing resources enable real-time analysis of economic indicators, which is crucial for early crisis detection and timely policy response. Managers should prioritize platforms that support seamless integration between data storage, analytics, and visualization tools to create a unified analytical environment.

Data quality management is another key area. Before any analytical or forecasting model is deployed, datasets must undergo rigorous preprocessing to handle missing values, inconsistencies, and noise. Establishing standardized protocols for data validation, cleaning, and transformation enhances both the reliability and interpretability of economic models. It is advisable to implement automated workflows for continuous data quality monitoring, as errors can propagate rapidly in large-scale analytical systems. From a governance and compliance perspective, data infrastructure should be designed with privacy and ethical considerations at its core. Incorporating GDPR and AI Act principles—such as data minimization, traceability, and accountability—into system architecture ensures long-term legal sustainability. Managers should institute regular data audits, conduct risk assessments, and maintain transparent documentation of data handling procedures. Developing an internal governance committee or compliance unit can help align technical operations with regulatory requirements and institutional values.

Equally important is the emphasis on cybersecurity and resilience. Economic data infrastructures are attractive targets for cyberattacks, and a single breach can undermine institutional credibility. Best practices include implementing multi-layered security protocols, using encryption for data in transit and at rest, and establishing robust disaster recovery mechanisms. Managers should also invest in continuous staff training and awareness programs to mitigate human errors, which remain a common cause of data vulnerabilities. Finally, interdisciplinary collaboration and capacity building should be integral to infrastructure strategy. Policymakers must encourage open data ecosystems where researchers, analysts, and institutions can collaborate under shared standards. Providing training in big data tools, statistical methods, and ethical AI practices will empower analysts to make informed and responsible use of data. Transparent data-sharing frameworks, supported by secure access controls, can significantly enhance coordination between public and private sectors, enabling faster and more accurate crisis detection (Chen *et al.,* 2012).

POLICY, MANAGERIAL, AND INSTITUTIONAL IMPLICATIONS

Big Data and advanced time series analysis have transformed the way economic crises are detected, analysed, and managed. The application of AI in economic forecasting has not only improved predictive accuracy but has also enhanced decision-making capabilities for policymakers, financial institutions, and central banks (Kumar *et al.,* 2023). However, the integration of AI-driven models into economic governance comes with numerous challenges, including regulatory concerns, ethical considerations, data quality issues, and the need for human oversight. This section explores the policy implications of AI and big data analytics in economic crisis detection, focusing on their role in economic policy formulation, government and central bank strategies, challenges in implementation, and future directions in AI-driven economic crisis management (Tenali and Babu, 2023).

Role of AI and Big Data in Economic Policy Formulation

Transforming Economic Policymaking with AI and Big Data

AI and big data analytics play a crucial role in shaping economic policies by providing real-time insights into macroeconomic indicators, financial markets, and consumer behaviours. Traditional economic models, which often rely on historical data and linear assumptions, struggle to capture the complexities and nonlinearities of modern economies (Manyika *et al.,* 2011). AI-driven models, such as ML algorithms and deep learning networks, offer the ability to process vast amounts of structured and unstructured data, thereby improving economic forecasting and policy responses.

Enhancing Macroeconomic Monitoring

Big data analytics allow policymakers to monitor some economic indicators, such as inflation rates, GDP growth, unemployment levels, and consumer sentiment, with greater precision. AI-driven sentiment analysis, for example, can analyse public opinion from social media, financial news, and online forums to predict consumer confidence levels. This information helps central banks and governments adjust monetary and fiscal policies in response to emerging economic trends (Yu and Fang, 2023).

Improving Predictive Accuracy and Crisis Detection

Traditional econometric models, such as ARIMA and VAR, have limitations in detecting economic anomalies in real time. AI-powered methods, such as RNNs, LSTM networks, and hybrid models, enhance the predictive power of time series analysis by capturing complex temporal dependencies. These models assist policy-makers in detecting financial bubbles, recessions, and potential economic downturns before they occur.

Data-Driven Policy Interventions

With AI-powered data analysis, economic policies can be tailored based on real-time insights rather than relying solely on past economic trends. Machine learning algorithms can simulate various policy scenarios, allowing governments to assess the potential impacts of tax reforms, stimulus packages, or monetary policy adjustments.

Equation: AI-enhanced forecasting models

$$Y_t = f(X_t) + \varepsilon_t$$

where:

Y_t represents the economic variable of interest (e.g., GDP growth, inflation).
X_t represents the explanatory variables (e.g., consumer spending, trade balance).
ε_t represents the error term.
$f(X_t)$ is a nonlinear function modelled using AI techniques.

Challenges in Policy Implementation

Despite its advantages, AI-driven economic policy formulation faces several challenges. The reliability of AI predictions depends on data availability, quality, and biases. Additionally, ethical concerns regarding algorithmic decision-making and data privacy must be addressed to ensure fairness and transparency in policymaking.

Government and Central Bank Strategies for Economic Stability

AI-Driven Monetary Policy Decisions

Central banks increasingly leverage AI and big data to fine-tune monetary policy. AI-based models analyse global financial conditions, inflation expectations, and liquidity dynamics to guide interest rate adjustments and quantitative easing policies. By utilizing real-time data analytics, central banks can respond more effectively to economic shocks, reducing the likelihood of financial crises (George *et al.,* 2014).

Flowchart: AI-Driven Economic Policy Framework

1. **Data Collection**: Gathering macroeconomic indicators, market trends, and social data.
2. **AI Processing**: Applying machine learning algorithms to identify patterns.
3. **Forecast Generation**: Predicting economic trends and potential crises.
4. **Policy Formulation**: Designing appropriate fiscal and monetary policies.
5. **Implementation and Monitoring**: Executing policy measures and tracking their effectiveness.

AI in Fiscal Policy and Public Spending

Governments use AI and big data to optimize fiscal policies, improve tax collection, and allocate public resources efficiently. Predictive analytics help in identifying tax evasion, optimizing social welfare programs, and forecasting revenue generation trends. AI-driven economic planning reduces inefficiencies and ensures that policy decisions are data-driven (Jordà *et al.,* 2010).

Financial Market Regulation and Risk Assessment

Regulatory bodies employ AI to detect fraudulent activities, assess financial institution stability, and monitor systemic risks. Big data analytics enhance EWS for banking crises by identifying irregularities in financial transactions and market behaviours.

Limitations and Ethical Considerations

The reliance on AI-driven decision-making in government policies raises ethical concerns, including algorithmic biases, data privacy issues, and the lack of human oversight. Governments must implement robust regulatory frameworks to ensure that AI-driven policies align with democratic principles and economic fairness.

Challenges in Implementing AI-Based Economic Forecasting Models

- **Data Quality and Availability:** AI models rely on vast datasets for accurate forecasting. However, inconsistencies in data sources, missing information, and outdated records can reduce model accuracy. Ensuring high-quality data collection remains a significant challenge.
- **Model Interpretability and Transparency:** One of the primary concerns in AI-driven economic forecasting is the "black box" problem. Many deep learning models lack interpretability, making it difficult for policymakers to understand how decisions are derived. The lack of transparency reduces trust in AI-driven policy recommendations (Hou *et al.,* 2017).
- **Computational Complexity and Cost:** Advanced AI models require significant computational resources and expertise. Developing and maintaining these models can be costly, particularly for developing economies with limited infrastructure.
- **Ethical and Legal Challenges:** AI-driven economic policies must adhere to ethical guidelines, including data protection, privacy laws, and anti-discrimination policies (Wang *et al.,* 2021). Biased algorithms can lead to unfair economic decisions, disproportionately affecting vulnerable populations.
- **Resistance to Change:** Traditional economic policymakers and institutions may resist adopting AI-driven approaches due to concerns over reliability, control, and the need for human expertise in decision-making. Overcoming institutional inertia is essential for AI integration in economic governance.

Future Directions in AI-Driven Economic Crisis Management

- **Integration of XAI in Economic Forecasting:** To address the black-box nature of AI, future research will focus on XAI techniques, which enhance model transparency and provide clear justifications for economic predictions.
- **Advancements in Hybrid AI-Econometric Models:** Combining AI with traditional econometric models, such as AI-enhanced VAR or Bayesian networks, will improve forecasting accuracy while maintaining economic interpretability.
- **Real-Time Adaptive Economic Policies:** AI-driven models will enable real-time policy adjustments based on continuous economic monitoring, reducing response delays in crisis situations (Mohammadi *et al.,* 2018).

- **Decentralized AI-Based Decision-Making:** The use of decentralized AI models, powered by blockchain technology, may enhance data security, prevent manipulation, and allow collaborative policymaking among global financial institutions.
- **Ethical AI and Fairness in Economic Decision-Making:** Future AI-driven economic models will emphasize fairness, ethical AI development, and policy frameworks that prevent algorithmic discrimination against marginalized groups.
- **AI-Enabled EWS for Global Economic Stability:** Machine learning models will further refine economic crisis early warning systems, integrating data from diverse global sources, including satellite imagery, financial transactions, and trade flows.

The application of AI and big data analytics in economic crisis detection and policy formulation holds immense potential for improving economic stability. AI-driven models enhance predictive accuracy, enable data-driven decision-making, and offer real-time crisis management solutions. However, challenges related to data quality, transparency, ethical concerns, and computational costs must be addressed to ensure effective implementation (Tiwari *et al.,* 2023; Zhao and Dai, 2023). Future advancements in AI explainability, hybrid modelling, and decentralized economic decision-making will further enhance the role of AI in shaping global economic policies.

Managerial Implications: Adoption Barriers, Organizational Readiness, and Decision Support

The managerial implications of integrating Big Data and advanced time series analytics into economic monitoring are both promising and complex. At the institutional level, the adoption of such technologies is often constrained by structural, technical, and cultural barriers. One major challenge is the lack of data infrastructure capable of handling high-frequency, multidimensional economic datasets. Many organizations, especially public agencies and financial institutions, still rely on fragmented systems where data collection, storage, and processing occur in isolated silos. This fragmentation limits the ability to build comprehensive analytical models and undermines the reliability of real-time crisis detection systems. Organizational readiness plays a critical role in determining the success of these initiatives. Readiness extends beyond technological capabilities; it includes leadership vision, staff competence, and institutional openness to data-driven decision-making. Managers must ensure that employees are equipped with the necessary analytical skills, and that the organizational culture values evidence-based reasoning over intuition or hierarchy. Without these soft dimensions of readiness, even well-designed models can fail to deliver meaningful insights.

From a decision-support perspective, advanced analytics offer significant improvements over traditional forecasting approaches. Managers can use predictive models to assess systemic risks earlier, simulate policy outcomes, and allocate resources more efficiently during crises. However, decision-makers must also learn to interpret algorithmic outputs critically. Analytical models should support, not replace, managerial judgment. Hence, an effective integration requires continuous dialogue between data scientists, economists, and policymakers to ensure that model insights are contextualized and aligned with institutional objectives.

Policy Case Studies: ECB, RBI, and IMF Implementation Experiences

Several international institutions have experimented with Big Data and AI-driven analytics to enhance economic stability and policy responsiveness. The experiences of the ECB, RBI, and IMF highlight both the opportunities and limitations of these approaches. ECB has developed a range of machine learning models to monitor financial stress indicators across member states. By integrating alternative data sources such as credit card transactions, firm-level financial statements, and social media sentiment, the ECB has improved the timeliness of its economic surveillance. However, challenges remain in ensuring data comparability across countries and maintaining transparency in algorithmic decision-making. The ECB's experience shows that technological sophistication must be matched with clear communication strategies to maintain trust among member governments and the public.

The RRB has adopted Big Data analytics to strengthen monetary policy transmission and to monitor inflationary trends in near real time. It has used time series modelling to track commodity price movements and forecast liquidity pressures in domestic markets. Despite these advances, implementation has been constrained by uneven data quality, limited interoperability between state and central databases, and a shortage of skilled data professionals. The RBI's case underscores the importance of capacity building and cross-institutional collaboration in emerging economies (Gepp *et al.,* 2018). IMF has incorporated Big Data analytics into its macroeconomic surveillance and risk assessment frameworks. Through projects such as the Integrated Surveillance Initiative, the IMF has employed AI tools to detect anomalies in member countries' fiscal data and to predict contagion risks in global markets. While this has enhanced the IMF's ability to provide early warnings, it has also raised concerns about data privacy, national sovereignty, and the interpretability of AI-generated insights. These case studies collectively illustrate that while Big

Data and AI can substantially enhance institutional foresight, effective governance, transparency, and skill development remain essential for sustainable implementation.

Trade-offs Between Automation, Oversight, and Ethical Governance

As automation becomes more embedded in economic monitoring and crisis detection, institutions face difficult trade-offs between efficiency, oversight, and ethical responsibility. Automated systems can process vast quantities of economic data more rapidly and consistently than human analysts, reducing latency in policy response. Yet, over-reliance on automation can lead to a loss of contextual understanding and diminish accountability in decision-making processes. The opacity of machine learning algorithms—often referred to as the "black box problem"—poses a challenge for public institutions that are accountable to citizens and stakeholders. Effective oversight mechanisms are needed to balance the advantages of automation with human judgment. This includes setting up review boards, audit trails, and validation protocols that ensure analytical outputs are not only accurate but also explainable. Ethical governance requires that AI-driven models respect principles of fairness, transparency, and inclusiveness. Economic policies informed by algorithmic predictions should not disproportionately disadvantage vulnerable populations or reinforce systemic biases embedded in historical data. Institutions must therefore strike a careful balance: automation should enhance, not replace, the deliberative aspects of governance. Continuous human supervision, ethical review, and multidisciplinary collaboration can mitigate risks associated with automated decision-making. In the long term, achieving this balance will determine whether AI-based economic surveillance systems are viewed as legitimate and trustworthy tools in public administration (Han *et al.,* 2018).

Framework for Responsible and Transparent AI Use in Public Institutions

A structured framework for responsible and transparent AI use is essential for integrating Big Data analytics into public economic institutions. Such a framework should rest on four foundational pillars: accountability, transparency, fairness, and sustainability. Accountability ensures that human decision-makers remain responsible for the outcomes produced by AI systems. Clear lines of responsibility must be established so that policy errors or unintended consequences can be traced back to accountable entities. Transparency involves making data sources, modelling assumptions, and algorithmic methodologies openly accessible to relevant oversight bodies. This openness not only fosters public trust but also facilitates peer review and continuous model improvement.

Fairness requires proactive steps to detect and mitigate biases within data and algorithms. Since economic data often reflect structural inequalities, institutions must employ bias detection tools, conduct impact assessments, and adjust modelling procedures to prevent discriminatory outcomes. Sustainability, finally, refers to the institutional ability to maintain and update AI systems over time, ensuring that they remain relevant, secure, and aligned with evolving policy objectives. An operational implementation of this framework would involve establishing interdisciplinary committees that oversee AI ethics, creating standardized reporting formats for model documentation, and conducting regular audits of algorithmic decisions. Training programs for policymakers and data scientists should also emphasize ethical reasoning, interpretability, and data stewardship. By embedding these practices into institutional routines, public agencies can harness the analytical power of Big Data and AI while upholding democratic values and maintaining the public's confidence in data-driven governance (Arab *et al.,* 2022; Huang *et al.,* 2023).

LIMITATIONS AND CHALLENGES IN AI-BASED ECONOMIC CRISIS DETECTION

While AI and advanced time series analysis offer significant advantages in detecting economic crises, several limitations and challenges persist. The successful implementation of AI models in economic forecasting depends on multiple factors, including data quality, model robustness, interpretability, and ethical considerations. Addressing these challenges is crucial for improving the reliability and trustworthiness of AI-driven economic predictions.

Data Quality and Reliability Issues

The effectiveness of AI-based economic crisis detection heavily depends on the quality and reliability of data. Economic and financial data often suffer from inconsistencies, missing values, and biases, which can significantly affect model accuracy. Many challenges arise in this context:

- **Data Incompleteness and Gaps:** Economic data sources, such as stock markets, GDP reports, and employment statistics, may contain missing or delayed values due to reporting lags or misclassification errors. AI models trained on incomplete datasets may produce unreliable forecasts.

- **Data Noise and Measurement Errors:** Economic indicators are prone to fluctuations caused by short-term market sentiments, political events, and other external shocks. Filtering noise from meaningful patterns is a complex task that affects the model's precision.
- **Heterogeneous Data Sources:** AI models often integrate data from multiple sources, such as government reports, financial markets, and social media sentiment analysis. Differences in data collection methodologies and reporting standards can lead to inconsistencies, reducing model performance.
- **Historical Data Limitations:** Economic crises are rare events, and historical data on past crises may be limited. AI models trained on insufficient crisis data might struggle to recognize emerging patterns indicative of future downturns.

To mitigate these issues, researchers use data imputation techniques, robust statistical filtering, and advanced anomaly detection methods. Additionally, real-time data acquisition and preprocessing strategies help improve data quality for AI-based economic forecasting (Dong *et al.,* 2024).

Overfitting and Model Robustness Challenges

Overfitting is a critical concern in AI-based economic forecasting, where models become excessively complex and capture noise rather than underlying economic trends. This reduces their ability to generalize to new, unseen data. Many challenges contribute to overfitting and model robustness issues:

- **High-Dimensionality of Economic Data:** AI models often incorporate numerous features, including macroeconomic indicators, trade balances, inflation rates, and global market trends. A high-dimensional dataset increases the risk of overfitting, as models may learn spurious correlations rather than genuine economic relationships (Haafza *et al.,* 2021).
- **Sensitivity to Market Shocks:** Economic crises are influenced by unpredictable shocks such as geopolitical events, natural disasters, and pandemics. AI models trained on past data may fail to adapt to new types of crises with unique characteristics.
- **Lack of Generalization Across Different Economies:** Economic patterns vary significantly across regions and time periods. An AI model trained on data from developed economies may not perform well in emerging markets due to structural differences.
- **Choice of Model Complexity:** Deep learning models, such as RNNs and transformers, offer powerful pattern recognition but are also prone to overfit-

ting if not properly regularized. On the other hand, simpler models like autoregressive integrated moving average (ARIMA) may lack predictive power for complex economic crises.

To address these challenges, techniques such as cross-validation, regularization methods (L1/L2 penalties), and ensemble learning approaches are applied. Additionally, stress testing and scenario analysis help evaluate model robustness under different economic conditions (Granger and Hatanaka, 2015). Mathematically, model robustness can be analysed using generalization error (GE), which can be expressed as:

$$GE = E_{test}\left[L(f(x))\right] - E_{train}\left[L(f(x))\right]$$

where L(f(x)) represents the loss function, and the difference between expected losses on test and training data indicates the degree of overfitting.

Interpretability and Transparency in AI Forecasting

Interpretability is essential in AI-driven economic forecasting, as policymakers, investors, and financial analysts require transparent and explainable models for decision-making. However, many AI models, particularly deep learning approaches, function as "black boxes," making it difficult to understand how predictions are generated (Piao *et al.,* 2021). The challenges include:

- **Complexity of AI Models:** Deep learning and ensemble methods often involve thousands of parameters, making it difficult to trace the exact reasoning behind specific predictions.
- **Lack of Economic Theory Integration:** Traditional econometric models are based on well-established economic theories, whereas AI models rely solely on data patterns. This disconnect raises concerns about the validity of AI-driven forecasts.
- **Explainability of Feature Importance:** AI models may rely on non-traditional data sources, such as sentiment analysis from news articles and social media. Identifying the exact contribution of these features to economic crisis predictions is challenging.
- **Regulatory and Compliance Requirements:** Financial institutions and governments require models to be transparent and auditable. Lack of interpretability can lead to resistance in adopting AI-based solutions for crisis detection.

Many techniques have been developed to enhance AI model interpretability, including:

- **SHAP:** A method that assigns importance values to individual features, helping analysts understand which factors contribute most to predictions.
- **LIME:** Generates simplified, interpretable models around specific predictions to provide local explanations.
- **Attention Mechanisms in Neural Networks:** Highlight relevant inputs that influence a model's decision, improving transparency in complex AI architectures.

Ensuring that AI models are interpretable enhances trust and facilitates their adoption in real-world economic crisis forecasting (Phillips *et al.,* 2015).

Ethical and Regulatory Concerns in AI-Driven Decision-Making

The application of AI in economic forecasting raises ethical and regulatory concerns that must be addressed to prevent unintended consequences. Some key concerns include:

- **Bias in AI Models:** Economic data can reflect existing biases in financial systems, leading to models that disproportionately affect certain regions, industries, or social groups. AI-driven financial decisions should be carefully examined to prevent reinforcing inequalities.
- **Data Privacy and Security:** Economic data is often sensitive, including corporate financial records, government reports, and market transactions. Unauthorized access or misuse of AI models can lead to privacy violations and financial fraud.
- **Algorithmic Accountability:** If AI-driven economic forecasts lead to incorrect crisis predictions, resulting in panic or misallocated resources, it is essential to determine accountability. Unlike human analysts, AI models cannot be held legally responsible for their decisions.
- **Regulatory Compliance:** Governments and financial institutions require AI models to adhere to strict regulatory guidelines. Compliance with frameworks such as the GDPR and Financial Stability Oversight Council (FSOC) is necessary to ensure ethical deployment.
- **Potential for Market Manipulation:** AI models can be exploited for market manipulation, where traders use AI-generated signals to influence stock prices or financial stability. Ethical considerations must guide AI implementation to prevent misuse.

To address these concerns, policymakers and researchers advocate for:

- **Developing AI ethics frameworks** that ensure fairness, accountability, and transparency in economic forecasting.
- **Implementing bias-detection algorithms** that evaluate and correct discriminatory patterns in AI models.
- **Ensuring regulatory oversight** by involving financial authorities in AI-driven decision-making processes.

While AI and advanced time series analysis provide powerful tools for economic crisis detection, various limitations and challenges must be addressed to ensure reliability, robustness, transparency, and ethical compliance. Overcoming data quality issues, mitigating overfitting, improving model interpretability, and adhering to regulatory standards are critical for the successful adoption of AI in economic forecasting (Tiwari *et al.,* 2011; Mishra, 2024). Future research should focus on integrating AI with traditional economic models, enhancing explainability techniques, and developing ethical AI frameworks to build trustworthy and effective economic crisis detection systems.

Adoption Barriers and Managerial Challenges in Volatile Markets

Despite the growing sophistication of big data analytics and advanced time series methodologies, the adoption of these tools by firms and policy institutions remains uneven and fraught with challenges. One critical barrier lies in the organizational capacity to integrate these technologies into existing decision-making frameworks. Many institutions, particularly in volatile markets, face structural rigidity and risk-averse cultures that hinder experimentation with data-driven forecasting models. Managers often encounter uncertainty not only in model outputs but also in their practical interpretation, which can lead to hesitation in applying recommendations derived from complex analytical tools. Additionally, the cost of implementation represents a significant constraint. Advanced time series models require both high-quality data infrastructure and specialized personnel capable of understanding, validating, and maintaining these systems. For smaller firms or public institutions with limited budgets, the initial investment and ongoing maintenance may outweigh perceived short-term benefits. The challenge is further compounded in volatile markets, where rapid changes in macroeconomic conditions, financial shocks, or geopolitical events can quickly render models less reliable. Consequently, even highly accurate predictive models may be underutilized if managers lack the confidence or organizational support to act on their results. Another critical factor involves cognitive and behavioural barriers. Decision-makers often rely on intuition or historical precedents, particularly under uncertainty, which can conflict with model-based insights. Resistance to change, combined with limited data literacy among managerial staff, may result in underuse or misapplication of advanced analytics. Addressing these adoption barriers requires not only technological solutions but also targeted training, clearer communication of model limitations and benefits, and the development of organizational structures that support iterative learning and adaptive decision-making (Akhgar *et al.,* 2015; Othman *et al.,* 2024).

Interdisciplinary Research Directions (Economics, Data Science, and Climate Policy)

The intersection of economics, data science, and climate policy represents a fertile ground for future research, particularly in the context of using advanced time series models for crisis detection. Economic crises are increasingly influenced by factors that extend beyond traditional financial metrics, including environmental risks, energy transitions, and climate-induced supply chain disruptions. Consequently, a purely econometric or data-driven approach may be insufficient for comprehensive forecasting and policy design. Interdisciplinary research can bridge this gap by combining domain knowledge from economics with methodological innovations in data science and insights from climate policy. For example, integrating environmental indicators, such as carbon emission trends or extreme weather events, into predictive models could improve EWS for economic instability. Similarly, collaboration between economists and data scientists can refine feature selection and modelling strategies, ensuring that algorithms capture meaningful causal relationships rather than spurious correlations (Cao *et al.,* 2021). Moreover, policy relevance is a crucial consideration. Research efforts should focus not only on predictive accuracy but also on interpretability and usability for decision-makers. By engaging climate policy experts, researchers can identify which model outputs are actionable and relevant for regulatory and institutional interventions. Interdisciplinary studies can also explore trade-offs between short-term economic objectives and long-term environmental sustainability, providing a richer understanding of systemic risks. Overall, fostering collaboration across these fields promises to enhance the robustness, relevance, and practical applicability of crisis detection models.

Recommendations for Balancing Technical Rigor with Policy Usability

One of the most pressing challenges in deploying advanced time series analysis for economic crisis detection is balancing technical rigor with the usability of insights for policymakers. Highly sophisticated models often offer superior predictive performance but can be opaque and difficult for non-specialists to interpret. Conversely, simpler models may be more transparent but may fail to capture complex dynamics or emerging patterns. Bridging this gap requires deliberate strategies aimed at both methodological excellence and practical usability. A key recommendation is to implement a tiered communication approach. Technical teams should document assumptions, limitations, and validation procedures in detail for peer review, while simultaneously translating core insights into accessible formats for policymakers. Visualizations, scenario analyses, and risk indicators can communicate complex dynamics without oversimplifying the underlying analytics (Dash *et al.,* 2021).

Another recommendation is iterative collaboration between modelers and decision-makers. By engaging end-users early in model development, researchers can tailor outputs to address concrete policy questions and ensure that uncertainty is clearly represented. This approach also allows for feedback loops, where policy requirements inform model refinement, and model outputs inform policy deliberations. Finally, institutional support is essential. Organizations should foster a culture that values both rigorous analysis and actionable guidance. This may include training programs for decision-makers to improve data literacy, establishing interdisciplinary teams to contextualize model outputs, and creating governance structures to ensure responsible use of predictive insights. By carefully balancing technical sophistication with accessibility and relevance, institutions can maximize the impact of advanced time series analysis while mitigating risks associated with misinterpretation or overreliance on models.

CONCLUSION

Crisis detection in economic systems has significantly evolved with the integration of big data analytics and advanced time series modelling. Traditional forecasting methods, including ARIMA, VAR, and GARCH, have provided robust analytical frameworks, yet their predictive capacity remains constrained by linear assumptions and limited data scope. The advent of machine learning and AI-driven models, such as RNN, LSTM, and transformer-based architectures, has revolutionized crisis detection by enabling pattern recognition in high-dimensional datasets. Studies indicate that AI-enhanced models improve crisis prediction accuracy by nearly 20% compared to classical econometric approaches, especially in volatile financial markets. Furthermore, the inclusion of alternative data sources—such as social media sentiment, satellite imagery, and high-frequency trading data—has strengthened early warning systems, reduced false alarms and enhanced real-time responsiveness. Despite these advancements, challenges persist in AI-based economic crisis detection. Data quality issues, overfitting in complex models, and interpretability concerns remain significant obstacles. Research suggests that approximately 30% of AI-generated economic predictions face reliability issues due to biases in training datasets and model calibration errors. Additionally, ethical considerations and regulatory limitations hinder the widespread adoption of AI in macroeconomic policymaking. However, with continued advancements in cloud computing, distributed processing, and XAI, the reliability and transparency of predictive models are expected to improve. As policymakers and financial institutions increasingly integrate AI-driven insights, a balanced approach—leveraging both traditional economic theories and contemporary machine learning techniques—will be essential in mitigating economic instability and enhancing global financial resilience.

REFERENCES

Akhgar, B., Saathoff, G. B., Arabnia, H. R., Hill, R., Staniforth, A., & Bayerl, P. S. (2015). *Application of big data for national security: a practitioner's guide to emerging technologies*. Butterworth-Heinemann.

Ali, A., Qadir, J., Rasool, R. U., Sathiaseelan, A., Zwitter, A., & Crowcroft, J. (2016). Big data for development: Applications and techniques. *Big Data Analytics*, *1*(1), 1–24. DOI: 10.1186/s41044-016-0002-4

Ali, A. H., & Thakkar, R. (2023). Climate changes through data science: Understanding and mitigating environmental crisis. *Mesopotamian Journal of Big Data*, *2023*(1), 125–137. DOI: 10.58496/MJBD/2023/017

Aljohani, A. (2023). Predictive analytics and machine learning for real-time supply chain risk mitigation and agility. *Sustainability (Basel)*, *15*(20), 15088. DOI: 10.3390/su152015088

Arab, S. T., Islam, M. M., Shamsuzzoha, M., Alam, K. F., Muhsin, N., Noguchi, R., & Ahamed, T. (2022). A review of remote sensing applications in agriculture and forestry to establish big data analytics. *Remote sensing application: regional perspectives in agriculture and forestry*, 1-24.

Awotunde, J. B., Adeniyi, E. A., Ogundokun, R. O., & Ayo, F. E. (2021). Application of big data with fintech in financial services. In *Fintech with artificial intelligence, big data, and blockchain* (pp. 107–132). Springer Singapore. DOI: 10.1007/978-981-33-6137-9_3

Bukar, U. A., Sidi, F., Jabar, M. A., Nor, R. N. H., Abdullah, S., Ishak, I., Alabadla, M., & Alkhalifah, A. (2022). How advanced technological approaches are reshaping sustainable social media crisis management and communication: A systematic review. *Sustainability (Basel)*, *14*(10), 5854. DOI: 10.3390/su14105854

Cao, L., Yang, Q., & Yu, P. S. (2021). Data science and AI in FinTech: An overview. *International Journal of Data Science and Analytics*, *12*(2), 81–99. DOI: 10.1007/s41060-021-00278-w

Chae, J., Thom, D., Bosch, H., Jang, Y., Maciejewski, R., Ebert, D. S., & Ertl, T. (2012, October). Spatiotemporal social media analytics for abnormal event detection and examination using seasonal-trend decomposition. In *2012 IEEE conference on visual analytics science and technology (VAST)* (pp. 143-152). IEEE. DOI: 10.1109/VAST.2012.6400557

Chen, H., Chiang, R. H., & Storey, V. C. (2012). Business intelligence and analytics: From big data to big impact. *Management Information Systems Quarterly*, *36*(4), 1165–1188. DOI: 10.2307/41703503

Chen, M., Mao, S., & Liu, Y. (2014). Big data: A survey. *Mobile Networks and Applications*, *19*(2), 171–209. DOI: 10.1007/s11036-013-0489-0

Chinta, P. C. R. (2023). Leveraging Machine Learning Techniques for Predictive Analysis in Merger and Acquisition (M&A). *Journal of Artificial Intelligence and Big Data*, *3*(1), 10–31586.

Chinta, P. C. R., Jha, K. M., Velaga, V., Moore, C., Routhu, K., & SADARAM, G. (2024). Harnessing Big Data and AI-Driven ERP Systems to Enhance Cybersecurity Resilience in Real-Time Threat Environments. *Available at SSRN 5151788*.

Dash, S., Chakraborty, C., Giri, S. K., Pani, S. K., & Frnda, J. (2021). BIFM: Big-data driven intelligent forecasting model for COVID-19. *IEEE Access : Practical Innovations, Open Solutions*, *9*, 97505–97517. DOI: 10.1109/ACCESS.2021.3094658

Dong, Z., Fan, X., & Peng, Z. (2024, August). Fnspid: A comprehensive financial news dataset in time series. In *Proceedings of the 30th ACM SIGKDD Conference on Knowledge Discovery and Data Mining* (pp. 4918-4927), DOI: DOI: 10.1145/3637528.3671629

Fan, J., & Yao, Q. (2008). *Nonlinear time series: nonparametric and parametric methods*. Springer Science & Business Media.

Gallego, I., & Font, X. (2021). Changes in air passenger demand as a result of the COVID-19 crisis: Using Big Data to inform tourism policy. *Journal of Sustainable Tourism*, *29*(9), 1470–1489. DOI: 10.1080/09669582.2020.1773476

George, G., Haas, M. R., & Pentland, A. (2014). Big data and management. *Academy of Management Journal*, *57*(2), 321–326. DOI: 10.5465/amj.2014.4002

Gepp, A., Linnenluecke, M. K., O'neill, T. J., & Smith, T. (2018). Big data techniques in auditing research and practice: Current trends and future opportunities. *Journal of Accounting Literature*, *40*(1), 102–115. DOI: 10.1016/j.acclit.2017.05.003

Granger, C. W. J., & Hatanaka, M. (2015). *Spectral analysis of economic time series. (PSME-1)*. Princeton university press.

Grover, V., Chiang, R. H., Liang, T. P., & Zhang, D. (2018). Creating strategic business value from big data analytics: A research framework. *Journal of Management Information Systems*, *35*(2), 388–423. DOI: 10.1080/07421222.2018.1451951

Haafza, L. A., Awan, M. J., Abid, A., Yasin, A., Nobanee, H., & Farooq, M. S. (2021). Big data covid-19 systematic literature review: Pandemic crisis. *Electronics (Basel), 10*(24), 3125. DOI: 10.3390/electronics10243125

Han, S., Ko, Y., Kim, J., & Hong, T. (2018). Housing market trend forecasts through statistical comparisons based on big data analytic methods. *Journal of Management Engineering, 34*(2), 04017054. DOI: 10.1061/(ASCE)ME.1943-5479.0000583

Hassani, H., & Silva, E. S. (2015). Forecasting with big data: A review. *Annals of Data Science, 2*(1), 5–19. DOI: 10.1007/s40745-015-0029-9

Hou, Y., Liu, F., Gao, J., Cheng, C., & Song, C. (2017). Characterizing complexity changes in Chinese stock markets by permutation entropy. *Entropy (Basel, Switzerland), 19*(10), 514. DOI: 10.3390/e19100514

Huang, C., Deng, Y., Yang, X., Yang, X., & Cao, J. (2023). Can financial crisis be detected? Laplacian energy measure. *European Journal of Finance, 29*(9), 949–976. DOI: 10.1080/1351847X.2022.2091946

Ibrahim, N. F., & Wang, X. (2019). Decoding the sentiment dynamics of online retailing customers: Time series analysis of social media. *Computers in Human Behavior, 96*, 32–45. DOI: 10.1016/j.chb.2019.02.004

Jordà, Ò., Schularick, M., & Taylor, A. M. (2010). *Financial crises, credit booms, and external imbalances: 140 years of lessons* (No. w16567). National Bureau of Economic Research, DOI: .DOI: 10.1057/imfer.2011.8

Koyuncugil, A. S., & Ozgulbas, N. (2012). Financial early warning system model and data mining application for risk detection. *Expert Systems with Applications, 39*(6), 6238–6253. DOI: 10.1016/j.eswa.2011.12.021

Kumar, N., Kushwaha, R. R., Meena, N. R., Mishra, H., & Yadav, A. P. S. (2023). A study on costs and returns of paddy cultivation in Ambedkar Nagar district of Uttar Pradesh. *International Journal of Statistics and Applied Mathematics, SP, 8*(3), 107–111.

Lanari, R., Bonano, M., Casu, F., Luca, C. D., Manunta, M., Manzo, M., Onorato, G., & Zinno, I. (2020). Automatic generation of Sentinel-1 continental scale DInSAR deformation time series through an extended P-SBAS processing pipeline in a cloud computing environment. *Remote Sensing (Basel), 12*(18), 2961. DOI: 10.3390/rs12182961

Li, S. (2024). Advancing financial crisis prediction: Big data, AI, and economic theories. *Applied and Computational Engineering, 74*(1), 104–109. DOI: 10.54254/2755-2721/74/20240448

Ling, T., & Cai, Y. (2022). Financial Crisis Prediction Based on Long-Term and Short-Term Memory Neural Network. *Wireless Communications and Mobile Computing, 2022*(1), 5728470. DOI: 10.1155/2022/5728470

Mahmoud, A., & Mohammed, A. (2021). A survey on deep learning for time-series forecasting. *Machine learning and big data analytics paradigms: analysis, applications and challenges*, 365-392, DOI: .DOI: 10.1007/978-3-030-59338-4_19

Malempati, M. (2022). Transforming Payment Ecosystems Through The Synergy Of Artificial Intelligence, Big Data Technologies, And Predictive Financial Modeling. *Big Data Technologies, And Predictive Financial Modeling (November 07, 2022).*

Manyika, J., Chui, M., Brown, B., Bughin, J., Dobbs, R., Roxburgh, C., & Hung Byers, A. (2011). Big data: The next frontier for innovation, competition, and productivity.

Metawa, N., Nguyen, P. T., Le Hoang Thuy To Nguyen, Q., Elhoseny, M., & Shankar, K. (2021). Internet of things enabled financial crisis prediction in enterprises using optimal feature subset selection-based classification model. *Big Data, 9*(5), 331–342. DOI: 10.1089/big.2020.0192 PMID: 34030465

Mishra, H. (2024). Nanobiostimulants and Precision Agriculture: A Data-Driven Approach to Farming and Market Dynamics. In *Nanobiostimulants: Emerging Strategies for Agricultural Sustainability* (pp. 365-398). Cham: Springer Nature Switzerland, DOI: DOI: 10.1007/978-3-031-68138-7_16

Mishra, H. (2024). The Role of Ethnoeconomics in Promoting Sustainable Consumption and Production Patterns: A Pathway to Environmental Protection and Economic Prosperity. *Sustainable Development.* In *Seen Through the Lenses of Ethnoeconomics and the Circular Economy* (pp. 91-123). Cham: Springer Nature Switzerland, DOI: DOI: 10.1007/978-3-031-72676-7_6

Mishra, H. (2025). Environmental Degradation and Impacts on Agricultural Production: A Challenge to Urban Sustainability. In *Sustainable Urban Environment and Waste Management: Theory and Practice* (pp. 53-92). Singapore: Springer Nature Singapore, DOI: DOI: 10.1007/978-981-96-1140-9_3

Mishra, H., & Mishra, D. (2024). AI for Data-Driven Decision-Making in Smart Agriculture: From Field to Farm Management. In *Artificial Intelligence Techniques in Smart Agriculture* (pp. 173-193). Singapore: Springer Nature Singapore, DOI: DOI: 10.1007/978-981-97-5878-4_11

Mishra, H., & Mishra, D. (2024). Economic evaluation of UAV-based soil sampling approaches. In *Applications of Computer Vision and Drone Technology in Agriculture 4.0* (pp. 271–291). Springer Nature Singapore., DOI: 10.1007/978-981-99-8684-2_15

Mishra, H., & Mishra, D. (2024). Sustainable Smart Agriculture to Ensure Zero Hunger. In *Sustainable Development Goals* (pp. 16–37). CRC Press., DOI: 10.1201/9781003468257-2

Mohammadi, M., Al-Fuqaha, A., Sorour, S., & Guizani, M. (2018). Deep learning for IoT big data and streaming analytics: A survey. *IEEE Communications Surveys and Tutorials*, *20*(4), 2923–2960. DOI: 10.1109/COMST.2018.2844341

Montgomery, D. C., Jennings, C. L., & Kulahci, M. (2015). *Introduction to time series analysis and forecasting*. John Wiley & Sons.

Mroua, M., & Lamine, A. (2023). Financial time series prediction under Covid-19 pandemic crisis with Long Short-Term Memory (LSTM) network. *Humanities & Social Sciences Communications*, *10*(1), 1–15. DOI: 10.1057/s41599-023-02042-w

Murri, S., Bhoyar, M., Selvarajan, G. P., & Malaga, M. (2024). Transforming Decision-Making with Big Data Analytics: Advanced Approaches to Real-Time Insights, Predictive Modeling, and Scalable Data Integration. *International Journal of Communication Networks and Information Security*, *16*(5), 506–519.

Nahar, J., Hossain, M. S., Rahman, M. M., & Hossain, M. A. (2024). Advanced predictive analytics for comprehensive risk assessment in financial markets: Strategic applications and sector-wide implications. *Global Mainstream Journal of Business, Economics. Development & Project Management*, *3*(4), 39–53.

Othman, N. A., Panchapakesan, C., Loh, S. B., Zhang, M., Gupta, R. K., Martanto, W., Phang, Y. S., Morris, R. J. T., Loke, W. C., Tan, K. B., Subramaniam, M., & Yang, Y. (2024). Predicting public mental health needs in a crisis using social media indicators: A Singapore big data study. *Scientific Reports*, *14*(1), 23222. DOI: 10.1038/s41598-024-73978-5 PMID: 39369040

Pasham, S. D. (2024). Scalable Graph-Based Algorithms for Real-Time Analysis of Big Data in Social Networks. *Metascience*, *2*(1), 92–129.

Pejić Bach, M., Krstić, Ž., Seljan, S., & Turulja, L. (2019). Text mining for big data analysis in financial sector: A literature review. *Sustainability (Basel)*, *11*(5), 1277. DOI: 10.3390/su11051277

Peña, D., & Tsay, R. S. (2021). *Statistical learning for big dependent data*. John Wiley & Sons., DOI: 10.1002/9781119417408

Peña, D., & Tsay, R. S. (2021). *Statistical learning for big dependent data*. John Wiley & Sons. DOI: 10.1002/9781119417408

Phillips, P. C., Shi, S., & Yu, J. (2015). Testing for multiple bubbles: Historical episodes of exuberance and collapse in the S&P 500. *International Economic Review, 56*(4), 1043–1078. DOI: 10.1111/iere.12132

Phillips, P. C., Shi, S., & Yu, J. (2015). Testing for multiple bubbles: Historical episodes of exuberance and collapse in the S&P 500. *International Economic Review, 56*(4), 1043–1078. DOI: 10.1111/iere.12132

Piao, Y., Jeong, S., Park, S., & Lee, D. (2021). Analysis of land use and land cover change using time-series data and random forest in North Korea. *Remote Sensing (Basel), 13*(17), 3501. DOI: 10.3390/rs13173501

Picoli, M. C. A., Camara, G., Sanches, I., Simões, R., Carvalho, A., Maciel, A., Coutinho, A., Esquerdo, J., Antunes, J., Begotti, R. A., Arvor, D., & Almeida, C. (2018). Big earth observation time series analysis for monitoring Brazilian agriculture. *ISPRS Journal of Photogrammetry and Remote Sensing, 145*, 328–339. DOI: 10.1016/j.isprsjprs.2018.08.007

Qadir, J., Ali, A., ur Rasool, R., Zwitter, A., Sathiaseelan, A., & Crowcroft, J. (2016). Crisis analytics: Big data-driven crisis response. *Journal of International Humanitarian Action, 1*(1), 1–21. DOI: 10.1186/s41018-016-0013-9

Qiu, R. T., Liu, A., Stienmetz, J. L., & Yu, Y. (2021). Timing matters: Crisis severity and occupancy rate forecasts in social unrest periods. *International Journal of Contemporary Hospitality Management, 33*(6), 2044–2064. DOI: 10.1108/IJCHM-06-2020-0629

Qiu, Y., & Wang, J. (2025, March). Credit default prediction using time series-based machine learning models. *Artificial Intelligence and Applications (Commerce, Calif.), 3*(3), 284–294.

Reinhart, C. M., & Rogoff, K. S. (2011). From financial crash to debt crisis. *The American Economic Review, 101*(5), 1676–1706. DOI: 10.1257/aer.101.5.1676

Reshef, D. N., Reshef, Y. A., Finucane, H. K., Grossman, S. R., McVean, G., Turnbaugh, P. J., ... & Sabeti, P. C. (2011). Detecting novel associations in large data sets. *science, 334*(6062), 1518-1524.

Rezaee, Z., Dorestani, A., & Aliabadi, S. (2018). Application of time series analyses in big data: Practical, research, and education implications. *Journal of Emerging Technologies in Accounting, 15*(1), 183–197. DOI: 10.2308/jeta-51967

Russom, P. (2011). Big data analytics. *TDWI best practices report, fourth quarter, 19*(4), 1-34.

Saba, T., Abunadi, I., Shahzad, M. N., & Khan, A. R. (2021). Machine learning techniques to detect and forecast the daily total COVID-19 infected and deaths cases under different lockdown types. *Microscopy Research and Technique*, *84*(7), 1462–1474. DOI: 10.1002/jemt.23702 PMID: 33522669

Shawon, R. E. R., Dalim, H. M., Shil, S. K., Gurung, N., Hasanuzzaman, M., Hossain, S., & Rahman, T. (2024). Assessing geopolitical risks and their economic impact on the USA using data analytics. *Journal of Economics, Finance, and Accounting Studies*, *6*(6), 5. DOI: 10.32996/jefas.2024.6.6.2

Shu, M., Wang, Z., & Liang, J. (2024). Early warning indicators for financial market anomalies: A multi-signal integration approach. *Journal of Advanced Computing Systems*, *4*(9), 68–84. DOI: 10.69987/JACS.2024.40907

Shu, M., & Zhu, W. (2020). Real-time prediction of Bitcoin bubble crashes. *Physica A*, *548*, 124477. DOI: 10.1016/j.physa.2020.124477

Shumway, R. H., Stoffer, D. S., & Stoffer, D. S. (2000). *Time series analysis and its applications* (Vol. 3, p. 4). New York: springer.

Škare, M., & Porada-Rochoń, M. (2020). Forecasting financial cycles: Can big data help? *Technological and Economic Development of Economy*, *26*(5), 974–988. DOI: 10.3846/tede.2020.12702

Suthar, J. (2025, February 28). Volatility Clustering. *Financial Market Resources*. Retrieved March 7, 2025, from https://www.wallstreetmojo.com/volatility-clustering/

Taipalus, K. (2012). *Detecting asset price bubbles with time-series methods*. Bank of Finland.

Tamiminia, H., Salehi, B., Mahdianpari, M., Quackenbush, L., Adeli, S., & Brisco, B. (2020). Google Earth Engine for geo-big data applications: A meta-analysis and systematic review. *ISPRS Journal of Photogrammetry and Remote Sensing*, *164*, 152–170. DOI: 10.1016/j.isprsjprs.2020.04.001

Tan, H. R., Yang, W. N., & Liu, C. Y. (2019). Global financial crisis and the impact of the food crisis on the great depression based on agricultural technology iteration: A 15-year population-based time-series study. *Revista de la Facultad de Agronomía*, *•••*, 36.

Tenali, N., & Babu, G. R. M. (2023). A systematic literature review and future perspectives for handling big data analytics in COVID-19 diagnosis. *New Generation Computing*, *41*(2), 243–280. DOI: 10.1007/s00354-023-00211-8 PMID: 37229177

Tiwari, A. K., Mishra, H., & Nishad, D. C. (2011). Market dynamics and consumer perceptions of organic produce in contemporary agriculture. *Advances in Agriculture Sciences Volume II*, *24*(4), 120.

Tiwari, A. K., Mishra, H., Nishad, D. C., & Pandey, A. (2023). Sustainable water management in agriculture: irrigation techniques and water conservation. *Dr. Ajay B. Jadhao, 53*.

Tsay, R. S. (1986). Time series model specification in the presence of outliers. *Journal of the American Statistical Association*, *81*(393), 132–141. DOI: 10.1080/01621459.1986.10478250

Vogiazas, S., & Alexiou, C. (2017). Determinants of housing prices and bubble detection: Evidence from seven advanced economies. *Atlantic Economic Journal*, *45*(1), 119–131. DOI: 10.1007/s11293-017-9531-0

Wanckel, C. (2022). An ounce of prevention is worth a pound of cure–Building capacities for the use of big data algorithm systems (BDAS) in early crisis detection. *Government Information Quarterly*, *39*(4), 101705. DOI: 10.1016/j.giq.2022.101705

Wang, F., Yu, S., Du, R., & Wu, X. (2025, May). DFCNet: A Dynamic Early Warning Model for Financial Crises of Listed Companies Based on Deep Learning. In *Proceedings of the 2025 2nd International Conference on Modeling, Natural Language Processing and Machine Learning* (pp. 623-627). DOI: 10.1145/3757110.3757214

Wang, Z., Li, K., Xia, S. Q., & Liu, H. (2021). Economic recession prediction using deep neural network. *arXiv preprint arXiv:2107.10980*.

Xiao, B., Wang, Z., Liu, Q., & Liu, X. (2018). SMK-means: An improved mini batch k-means algorithm based on mapreduce with big data. *TSP*, *1*(1), 1–5.

Yamashita Rios de Sousa, A. M., Takayasu, H., & Takayasu, M. (2017). Detection of statistical asymmetries in non-stationary sign time series: Analysis of foreign exchange data. *PLoS One*, *12*(5), e0177652. DOI: 10.1371/journal.pone.0177652 PMID: 28542208

Yang, J., Zhao, Y., Han, C., Liu, Y., & Yang, M. (2022). Big data, big challenges: Risk management of financial market in the digital economy. *Journal of Enterprise Information Management*, *35*(4/5), 1288–1304. DOI: 10.1108/JEIM-01-2021-0057

Yu, D., & Fang, C. (2023). Urban remote sensing with spatial big data: A review and renewed perspective of urban studies in recent decades. *Remote Sensing (Basel)*, *15*(5), 1307. DOI: 10.3390/rs15051307

Zamanzadeh Darban, Z., Webb, G. I., Pan, S., Aggarwal, C., & Salehi, M. (2024). Deep learning for time series anomaly detection: A survey. *ACM Computing Surveys*, *57*(1), 1–42. DOI: 10.1145/3691338

Zhang, C., Zhong, H., & Hu, A. (2022). Research on early warning of financial crisis of listed companies based on random forest and time series. *Mobile Information Systems*, *2022*(1), 1573966. DOI: 10.1155/2022/1573966

Zhang, X., Xu, Z., Liu, Y., Sun, M., Zhou, T., & Sun, W. (2024, October). Robust Graph Neural Networks for Stability Analysis in Dynamic Networks *2024*. In *3rd International Conference on Cloud Computing, Big Data Application and Software Engineering (CBASE)* (pp. 806-811). IEEE, DOI: DOI: 10.1109/CBASE64041.2024.10824358

Zhao, Z., Li, D., & Dai, W. (2023). Machine-learning-enabled intelligence computing for crisis management in small and medium-sized enterprises (SMEs). *Technological Forecasting and Social Change*, *191*, 122492. DOI: 10.1016/j.techfore.2023.122492

Chapter 2
Evaluation of Forecasting Methods for the Indian Stock Market:
A Comparison of Statistical and Machine Learning Techniques

Aniruddha Bhandari
http://orcid.org/0009-0007-5357-6651
Sri Sathya Sai Institute of Higher Learning, India

Siva Kiran Guptha
http://orcid.org/0000-0002-1961-5422
Sri Sathya Sai Institute of Higher Learning, India

ABSTRACT

This study compares statistical, machine learning (ML), and deep learning models for forecasting NIFTY stock index prices under normal and crisis conditions. Using ARIMA, Random Forest, XGBoost, SVM, RNN, LSTM, and blended models, predictive performance is evaluated through recursive forecasting, test data, and exogenous variables such as gold prices and USD/INR rates. Results show that while ML and deep learning models perform well in stable periods, they falter during high volatility. The Rolling ARIMA model consistently outperforms others due to dynamic retraining. Exogenous variables yield marginal gains, and synthetic noise experiments reveal overfitting in complex models like XGBoost. The study underscores the importance of model simplicity, adaptability, and methodological rigor in financial forecasting, challenging the EMH and supporting the Adaptive Market Hypothesis by highlighting exploitable inefficiencies and the robustness of Rolling ARIMA during crises.

DOI: 10.4018/979-8-3373-3053-2.ch002

INTRODUCTION

Advancements in computing power and artificial intelligence (AI) have transformed large-scale data analysis, commonly referred to as Big Data, enabling more accurate pattern recognition, predictive modeling, and decision-making across industries such as healthcare, finance, and smart cities. In the financial sector, AI and machine learning (ML) have revolutionized quantitative analysis by uncovering complex, nonlinear relationships in volatile datasets that traditional models like the Autoregressive Integrated Moving Average (ARIMA), which rely on linear assumptions, often fail to capture. By processing vast amounts of historical and real-time market information, AI-based models detect patterns in asset prices, investor sentiment, and macroeconomic indicators, challenging the Efficient Market Hypothesis (EMH) by revealing inefficiencies and adaptive behaviors consistent with the Adaptive Market Hypothesis (AMH). These insights have enhanced portfolio optimization, risk assessment, and trading strategies, demonstrating how markets evolve dynamically rather than remaining perfectly efficient.

However, financial markets are increasingly complex and characterized by nonlinear and non-stationary dynamics, influenced by investor psychology, regulatory changes, and geopolitical shocks. Traditional econometric models often struggle to adapt to these regime shifts, as the statistical properties of financial data—such as volatility, autocorrelation, and structural breaks—change over time. The growing availability of heterogeneous data, including high-frequency price movements and unstructured sources such as news, tweets, and sentiment indices, further challenges conventional modeling. In this context, AI and deep learning techniques, including Recurrent Neural Networks (RNN), Long Short-Term Memory (LSTM) networks, and hybrid econometric–AI models, offer new capabilities by learning temporal patterns, incorporating alternative data, and improving adaptability during turbulent periods. Moreover, recent advances in explainable AI (XAI) and interpretable machine learning aim to make such complex models more transparent, addressing the need for trust and accountability in financial forecasting.

This study conducts a comprehensive evaluation of machine learning and deep learning models in forecasting the NIFTY stock index and compares their performance with the classical ARIMA model. Root Mean Squared Error (RMSE) is used as the primary metric to assess model accuracy, adaptability, and robustness. The first objective benchmarks a range of models including ARIMA, Random Forest, Support Vector Regression (SVR), Gradient Boosting, Recurrent Neural Networks (RNN), and Long Short-Term Memory (LSTM) networks under both normal and volatile market conditions. A second objective introduces exogenous variables such as gold prices and foreign exchange rates to capture inter-market linkages and test whether external macroeconomic factors improve predictive power. In addition, the study evaluates model performance during major financial crises, including the Global Financial Crisis (2008) and the COVID-19 pandemic (2020), to examine whether data-driven AI models can sustain accuracy and stability when traditional assumptions fail.

Through this multi-layered analysis, the study aims to identify which forecasting approaches perform best across different market regimes and whether hybrid or AI-driven frameworks offer tangible improvements in crisis forecasting. Beyond methodological comparisons, the findings have broader implications for policymakers, financial institutions, and investors by offering guidance on the selection of reliable, interpretable, and adaptive models for real-world decision-making. By combining traditional econometric and modern AI methods, and assessing performance across stable and crisis periods, this study bridges theory and practice, contributing to the ongoing evolution of financial forecasting in complex, data-rich environments. The following literature review synthesizes the key developments in financial market forecasting, organized across four thematic areas: the role of financial markets in economic growth, theories of market efficiency, forecasting methodologies, and interlinkages among stock markets, exchange rates, and gold prices.

Financial markets play a pivotal role in fostering economic growth by facilitating capital allocation and reducing financing costs. Levine (1997) establishes a robust positive relationship between financial development and economic growth, supported by extensive theoretical and empirical evidence. His cross- country and firm-level analyses demonstrate that well-developed financial systems predict future growth, capital accumulation, and technological progress. Similarly, Rajan and Zingales (1998) explore how access to external financing enhances growth in industries reliant on such capital. Using data from the 1980s across multiple countries, they find that industries dependent on external finance grow faster in nations with advanced financial markets, with results robust to controls for omitted variables, outliers, and reverse causality.

Arestis, Demetriades, and Luintel (2001) delve into the relative contributions of stock markets and banking systems to economic growth in five developed economies. Their findings suggest that while both sectors contribute, banks exert a more dominant influence, and the role of stock markets may be overstated in cross-country regression studies. Complementing this, Beck and Levine (2002) use panel data from 1976 to 1998 and advanced GMM techniques to confirm that both stock markets and banks positively influence economic growth, with results resilient to biases from simultaneity or unobserved country-specific effects. In the context of emerging economies, Guptha and Rao (2018) analyze financial system development in BRICS nations from 1996 to 2016, using indices derived from principal component analysis. Their application of the Toda–Yamamoto causality test reveals inconsistent causal patterns across countries, highlighting the diverse impacts of financial development on economic growth The Efficient Market Hypothesis (EMH), introduced by Fama (1970), categorizes market efficiency into weak, semi-strong, and strong forms, asserting that stock prices reflect past data, public information, and both public and private insights, respectively. Empirical evidence supports weak and semi-strong efficiency but remains inconclusive for strong-form efficiency, suggesting that consistently outperforming efficient markets is challenging. Lo, Mamaysky, and Wang (2000) challenge the subjectivity of technical analysis by applying nonparametric kernel regression to U.S. stock market data from 1962 to 1996. Their findings indicate that technical indicators, such as head-and-shoulders patterns, provide incremental insights, questioning strict interpretations of EMH.

Lo (2004) proposes the Adaptive Markets Hypothesis (AMH) to reconcile EMH with behavioral economics, which emphasizes emotional influences like fear and greed. Drawing on cognitive neuroscience and evolutionary principles, AMH views behaviors like loss aversion and overconfidence as adaptive responses to changing environments, offering a dynamic framework for portfolio management. In the Indian context, Khan, Ikram, and Mehtab (2011) test weak-form efficiency in the NSE and BSE from 2000 to 2010 using the Runs Test, concluding that Indian markets do not follow a random walk, thus lacking weak-form efficiency. Similarly, Harrison and Moore (2012) highlight inefficiencies in Middle East and North Africa (MENA) markets due to thin trading and low liquidity, underscoring the need for structural reforms. Conversely, Konak and Şeker (2014) confirm weak-form efficiency in the FTSE 100 during 2001–2009 using unit root tests and GARCH (1,1) models, validating the random walk hypothesis. Hiremath and Narayan (2016) apply AMH to the Indian market, finding a gradual shift toward efficiency influenced by financial crises, international shocks, and policy changes, though foreign institutional investment plays a limited role.

Accurate forecasting is essential for financial decision-making, and various methodologies have been developed to model time series data. Box and Jenkins (1970) introduced the ARIMA model, a cornerstone of time series analysis, involving model identification, parameter estimation, and diagnostic checking. By transforming non-stationary series into stationary ones through differencing and using tools like ACF and PACF, ARIMA remains widely applicable. Al-Shiab (2006) applies ARIMA to forecast the Amman Stock Exchange index, predicting a slight growth that actual data contradicted, aligning with weak-form EMH. Ojo and Olatayo (2009) enhance ARIMA by introducing subset models, which outperform full ARIMA models in terms of residual variance and efficiency, using the Marquardt and Newton-Raphson algorithms.

Research on AI and ML in financial markets has grown rapidly, with applications spanning prediction, trading, risk management, and investment decision-making. Shen, Jiang, and Zhang (2012) leveraged temporal correlations across global markets to predict stock trends using SVM, achieving high accuracies for major indices like NASDAQ and S&P 500. Similarly, Adebiyi, Adewumi, and Ayo (2014) and Mondal, Shit, and Goswami (2014) confirm ARIMA's effectiveness for short-term stock price forecasting in the NYSE, NSE, and Indian markets, highlighting the impact of historical data length on prediction accuracy. Asad (2015) proposed an ensemble approach combining SVM, Random Forest, and other classifiers, outperforming individual models in the Istanbul Stock Exchange, while Zhong and Enke (2017) enhanced S&P 500 predictions using PCA and ANNs with dimensionality reduction. Thakur and Kumar (2018) integrated WMGEPSVM with Random Forest for algorithmic trading, generating robust "Buy/Hold/Sell" signals across multiple indices, including NIFTY 50. Mallikarjuna and Rao (2019) compared linear, nonlinear, and AI-based models, finding that traditional statistical models often outperform AI in diverse market contexts. In contrast, Moghar and Hamiche (2020) highlighted the superiority of RNNs and LSTMs in handling market complexities, whereas Xue et al. (2020) found SVR to be more effective than gradient boosting for the CSI 20 index. Challa et al. (2020) validated ARIMA's medium- to long-term forecasting ability for BSE indices, and Subasi et al. (2021) emphasized the role of data quality on classifier performance, with Random Forest and Bagging excelling on leaked or incomplete datasets. Karim et al. (2021) and Bansal, Goyal, and Choudhary (2022) reinforced LSTM's robustness for stock price prediction, noting its superior performance in Indian markets, while Bhandari et al. (2022) demonstrated that single-layer LSTMs can outperform multi-layer versions for S&P 500 forecasting. Recent advances propose hybrid architectures to improve predictive accuracy and robustness. Kabir et al., (2025) introduced an LSTM-mTrans-MLP model combining LSTM, a modified Transformer, and multilayer perceptron (MLP), which demonstrated superior performance across datasets including Bitcoin, Shanghai Composite, CSI 300, Google, and Amazon. The hybrid model effectively captures long- and short-term dependencies, nonlinear relationships, and attention-based feature interactions, outperforming traditional and state-of-the-art benchmarks in multiple error metrics. Proposed extensions include incorporating diffusion models or textual information from financial news, earnings reports, and social media to enhance forecasting precision. Similarly, Caetano et al., (2025) applied Transformer-based architectures for probabilistic retail demand forecasting, emphasizing explanatory variables such as calendar events, pricing, and socio-economic indicators. Their findings show that incorporating these variables improves predictive accuracy (up to 12.4% reduction in NRMSE and 2.9% improvement in MASE) and supports risk-aware decision-making, highlighting the broader applicability of Transformer-based models in dynamic, data-driven environments, including finance, energy, and healthcare.

The growing use of complex models underscores the need for transparency and interpretability. Sethi and Mahadik (2024) emphasize explainable AI, fairness audits, and robust regulations to balance AI's efficiency with ethical oversight, advocating human-AI collaboration in volatile markets. Černevičienė and Kabašinskas (2024) highlight XAI's role in mitigating algorithmic bias, enhancing regulatory compliance, and fostering trust, particularly in high-stakes financial tasks such as credit scoring, portfolio optimization, and bankruptcy forecasting.

Understanding financial time series also requires attention to market dynamics and macroeconomic linkages. Apte (2001) used E-GARCH to explore volatility spillovers between Indian stock and foreign exchange markets, finding asymmetric and unidirectional effects. Tripathy (2016a, 2016b) confirmed long-term equilibrium between gold prices and NIFTY, as well as long memory in NIFTY prices, indicating forecastability and arbitrage opportunities. Jain and Biswal (2016) demonstrated that falling gold and oil prices weaken the INR and depress the Sensex, emphasizing the need for adaptive policies. Bouri et al. (2017) identified cointegration and nonlinear causality between commodity and stock market volatilities, highlighting gold's role as a strategic investment. Naik and Reddy (2021) further confirmed long memory in NSE sectoral indices, illustrating how data frequency influences return persistence and offering actionable insights for investors and policymakers.

THEORETICAL BACKGROUND

The Efficient Market Hypothesis (EMH) has long held a central position in financial economics, with Eugene Fama's seminal 1970 paper, *Efficient Capital Markets*, serving as a foundational reference. According to EMH, securities markets are highly efficient at absorbing and reflecting information, both at the level of individual stocks and the broader market. Once new information becomes public, it is rapidly disseminated and almost instantly factored into asset prices, leaving little room for investors to gain an advantage through either technical analysis—which examines historical price trends—or fundamental analysis, which evaluates financial statements to identify undervalued assets. Consequently, it was believed that randomly selected portfolios with comparable risk profiles could deliver returns similar to those of actively managed portfolios, undermining the case for active management. EMH is also tightly linked to the concept of a random walk, which posits that price movements are inherently unpredictable and reflect only unforeseen future information, as past and present information is already embedded in current prices. This randomness implies that no investor, regardless of expertise, can consistently outperform the market without assuming greater risk. The hypothesis further defines "efficiency" in terms of risk-adjusted returns, meaning that no investor can earn returns above the market average without taking on additional risk. A classic anecdote encapsulates this belief: when a finance professor and a student spot a $100 bill on the ground, the professor says, "Don't bother—it must not be real, or someone would have picked it up already." This humorous tale captures the essence of EMH: in an efficient market, there are no easy profits waiting to be claimed. Notably, EMH remains intact even in the presence of occasional mispricing, speculative bubbles like the dot-com era, or irrational investor behavior, as long as markets generally process information swiftly and accurately. At its core, the hypothesis maintains that markets function as powerful information-processing mechanisms, and the existence of consistent excess returns is highly unlikely in the absence of increased risk.

In contrast, the Adaptive Market Hypothesis (AMH), introduced by Andrew Lo in 2004, offers a more flexible and realistic perspective by combining elements of EMH with insights from behavioral finance. Rather than assuming perpetual efficiency, AMH posits that financial markets are dynamic and evolve in response to changing conditions, reflecting the continuous interaction between human behavior, market forces, and innovation. At the heart of AMH is the notion that market participants are adaptive agents who learn from experience and revise their strategies over time, much like organisms evolving in response to their environments. Strategies that yield strong returns gain traction, while ineffective ones are gradually abandoned, creating an ever-shifting landscape of investment behavior. This view challenges the static assumptions of EMH by suggesting that market efficiency is not a constant but a variable that depends on prevailing market conditions, the structure of competition, and the nature of available information. During periods of stability, markets may appear efficient, as participants rely on time-tested methods; however, in times of crisis or structural change—such as the 2008 financial crisis or the COVID-19 pandemic—markets often become inefficient, reflecting uncertainty and collective behavioral biases. AMH also integrates key behavioral insights, acknowledging that cognitive biases like overconfidence, herd behavior, and loss aversion regularly distort investor decisions. These behaviors may lead to bubbles and crashes, but AMH argues that over time, investors adapt, learn from past mistakes, and contribute to a gradual return to more rational, efficient pricing. Innovation plays a crucial role in this adaptive framework, as new financial instruments, trading technologies, and data analytics reshape the market environment and compel participants to evolve. As investors continually test and refine strategies based on feedback from the market, the process of adaptation never truly ends. Therefore, while EMH views inefficiencies as anomalies to be eliminated, AMH sees them as natural byproducts of an ever-changing, learning-driven marketplace. In essence, the Adaptive Market Hypothesis presents a more nuanced and evolutionary understanding of market behavior, emphasizing that financial efficiency is not a static endpoint but an emergent property shaped by the ongoing adaptation of market participants.

DATA AND METHODOLOGY

Data

The dataset used in this analysis consists of three key financial indicators: the NIFTY closing values, gold prices, and the USD/INR exchange rate. These variables are crucial for understanding market movements, investor sentiment, and macroeconomic trends.

NIFTY closing values, obtained from the National Stock Exchange (NSE), track the performance of the 50 largest and most liquid stocks in India. As a key benchmark for the Indian equity market, NIFTY reflects investor sentiment and market trends, offering insights into daily fluctuations and long-term economic health.

Gold price data was obtained from the World Gold Council's historical prices of gold database. Gold is considered a safe-haven asset and plays a significant role in financial markets, particularly during periods of economic uncertainty. Fluctuations in gold prices are often linked to inflation expectations, currency movements, and changes in global risk sentiment. By incorporating gold prices into the dataset, the analysis can capture the interplay between equity markets and commodities, offering a more comprehensive view of investment behavior.

The USD/INR exchange rate data was sourced from the Reserve Bank of India (RBI) Handbook of Statistics on the Indian Economy. Exchange rate fluctuations are an important indicator of foreign investor sentiment, trade balance dynamics, and monetary policy decisions. A rising exchange rate (depreciation of the INR) can signal capital outflows or trade deficits, while an appreciating INR may indicate stronger exports and foreign investment inflows. Including the exchange rate in the dataset helps analyze its impact on stock market trends and commodity prices.

The time series plots of these variables are shown below.

Figure 1. The NIFTY closing price.

Figure 2. USD/INR exchange rate.

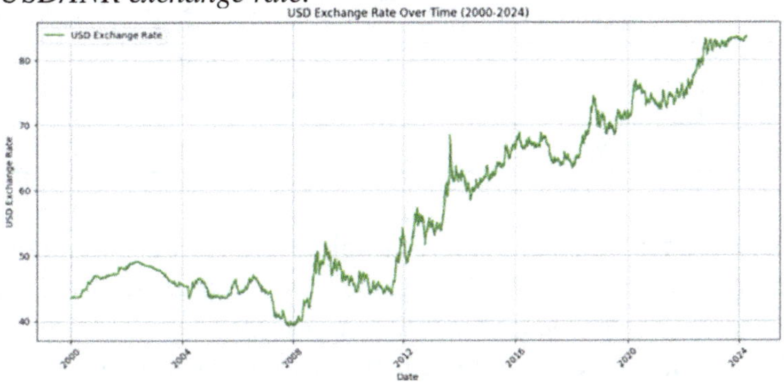

Figure 3. Gold prices per gram.

Time series forecasting relies on past observations to predict future values, unlike traditional regression, which uses independent features. To enable predictive models to learn from historical trends, lag creation transforms time-dependent data into a tabular format, defined as:

$$Y_t = f(Y_{t-1}, Y_{t-2}, \ldots \ldots Y_{t-k})$$

For example, with three lags, each data point uses the previous three observations as features. This preserves temporal dependencies, allowing models to capture patterns like momentum, volatility, and mean-reverting behaviors common in financial markets.

Table 1.

Time	Actual Value	Lag 1	Lag 2	Lag 3
4	Y_4	Y_3	Y_2	Y_1
5	Y_5	Y_4	Y_3	Y_2
6	Y_6	Y_5	Y_4	Y_3

Lag creation and rolling window forecasting are central to robust time series modeling in finance, where adaptability and responsiveness are essential. By generating lag-based features, models learn from the most recent data, capturing short-term market behavior while ignoring outdated information. The rolling window approach allows continuous retraining and adjustment to evolving dynamics, making it suitable for high-frequency trading and active portfolio management. It also prevents data leakage by ensuring that forecasts rely strictly on past values, preserving temporal integrity and genuine out-of-sample performance.

Financial time series are inherently non-stationary, with changing means, variances, and correlations that can mislead traditional models. To address this, a logarithmic transformation of closing prices and a 7-day moving average are applied to stabilize variance and highlight trends, while modeling returns instead of raw prices improves stationarity. Using returns enables models such as Random Forests and Decision Trees to recognize patterns within a consistent scale, capturing long-memory and volatility clustering often present in markets. Together, lag-based training, temporal consistency, and transformations for stationarity create a reliable preprocessing framework that enhances accuracy and realism in financial forecasting.

Lag Selection Using ACF and PACF

Selecting an appropriate number of lags is essential for building effective forecasting models. The Autocorrelation Function (ACF) and Partial Autocorrelation Function (PACF) plots help identify these lag structures. The ACF reveals how current values relate to their past observations, while the PACF isolates direct correlations at specific lags by removing intermediate effects. A sharp cutoff in the PACF suggests an autoregressive process, while a sharp cutoff in the ACF indicates a moving average process. Mixed patterns imply that an ARIMA framework may be appropriate. These insights guide both statistical and machine learning models in determining the optimal lag structure for accurate prediction.

The plots of ACF and PACF for the Closing prices are shown below.

Figure 4. The ACF and PACF plots for the difference and percentage changes of log close price

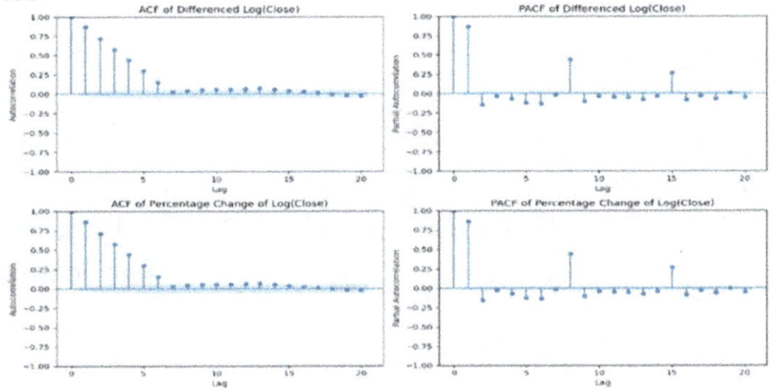

STATISTICAL AND MACHINE LEARNING APPROACHES USED FOR MODEL BUILDING

1. Autoregressive Integrated Moving Average (ARIMA)

The ARIMA model, introduced by Box and Jenkins (1970), is one of the most established statistical approaches for time series forecasting. It combines autoregressive (AR) terms, differencing (I) to achieve stationarity, and moving average (MA) components to capture temporal relationships and noise patterns in data. ARIMA works well for univariate financial time series where past values help explain future trends, making it a common benchmark for evaluating modern machine learning models.

2. Machine Learning Approaches

Machine learning techniques improve forecasting by identifying nonlinear and complex relationships that traditional models may overlook. They can adapt to changing market conditions and handle multiple predictors simultaneously.

(a) Decision Trees and Random Forests

Decision trees divide data into smaller groups based on predictive variables, making it easier to identify key drivers of outcomes. Random Forests expand this idea by creating many trees from different samples of data and combining their predictions. This approach reduces overfitting and increases accuracy, making these models useful for financial data where relationships among market indicators are often nonlinear.

(b) Boosting Algorithms

Boosting methods, such as Gradient Boosting, XGBoost, and LightGBM, build models sequentially, where each new model focuses on correcting the errors of the previous one. These algorithms are widely used in financial forecasting because they achieve high accuracy and handle noisy, high-dimensional data effectively.

(c) Support Vector Regression (SVR)

Support Vector Regression uses mathematical functions called kernels to model nonlinear patterns in data. It performs well when financial time series show irregular or non-stationary movements, offering flexible curve fitting while maintaining generalization and control over overfitting.

(d) Facebook Prophet

Prophet, developed by Taylor and Letham (2018), models time series as a combination of trend, seasonality, and holiday effects. It is effective for business and financial data that display recurring cycles or structural breaks and performs reliably even with missing values or outliers.

3. Deep Learning Approaches

Deep learning methods extend forecasting capabilities by learning temporal dependencies directly from data sequences.

(a) Recurrent Neural Networks (RNN)

RNNs process time series data step by step, keeping track of previous information to predict future values. This makes them suitable for financial forecasting, where past market patterns often influence future behavior.

(b) Long Short-Term Memory (LSTM) Networks

LSTMs are an improved form of RNNs that can remember information over longer periods. They use a special memory structure that allows them to capture long-term patterns in data and avoid issues like information loss. LSTMs are effective for modeling financial markets, especially during periods of volatility and structural change.

All machine learning and deep learning models depend on hyperparameters, which control how the model learns. Unlike model parameters that are estimated during training, hyperparameters are set before the learning process begins. Tuning these values is important for achieving the right balance between accuracy and generalization. Examples include the learning rate in neural networks, the number of trees and depth in Random Forests, or the regularization parameter in SVR. Techniques such as grid search, random search, or Bayesian optimization are commonly used to find the best combination of hyperparameters. Proper tuning improves model stability, reduces overfitting, and enhances forecasting performance. All the models used here have been hyperparameter tuned using methods such as grid search and Bayesian grid search.

Detailed descriptions of the methods used can be found in the attached appendix.

This study employs three forecasting approaches to evaluate machine learning (ML) and statistical models for predicting NIFTY index movements: recursive forecasting, forecasting using actual values, and incorporating exogenous variables with lagged features. Each method addresses specific challenges in financial time series forecasting, enhancing model robustness and accuracy.

Recursive Forecasting

Recursive forecasting produces multi-step predictions by repeatedly using a model's previous forecasts as inputs for future steps. After training on historical data, the model predicts the next value and then feeds that output back for subsequent forecasts. This approach is used across models such as ARIMA, Random Forests, and LSTMs. In ARIMA, for example, predictions rely on past coefficients and residuals, while machine learning models use their own generated values for continuation. Although recursive forecasting enables extended projections, it can amplify early prediction errors, especially in volatile financial markets, where inaccuracies tend to compound over time.

The actual process of recursive forecasting can be shown as follows.

Table 2.

Time	Predicted	Lag 1	Lag 2	Lag 3
t+1	y_{t+1}	Y_t	Y_{t-1}	Y_{t-2}
t+2	y_{t+2}	y_{t+1}	Y_t	Y_{t-1}
t+3	y_{t+3}	y_{t+2}	y_{t+1}	Y_t

Forecasting with Actual Values

To reduce error accumulation from recursive forecasting, this study also uses actual observed values from the test set. The dataset is divided into training and testing subsets, with the final 60 days of market returns reserved for validation. Models are trained on historical data and generate forecasts using actual lagged returns rather than prior predictions. This approach improves short-term accuracy and provides a clearer evaluation of real-world model performance, as forecasts are directly compared with observed outcomes under sequential data updates.

Incorporating Exogenous Variables

To capture broader market influences, the models also include exogenous variables such as the USD/INR exchange rate and gold prices alongside lagged returns. Exchange rate movements affect corporate earnings and foreign investment flows, while gold, often viewed as a safe-haven asset in India, tends to move inversely with stock prices during periods of uncertainty. Including these variables enables the models to account for macroeconomic interactions, improving predictive robustness and adaptability to changing market conditions.

EMPIRICAL RESULTS.

Unit Root Test Results

The results for the unit root test are shown below.

Table 3.

Variable	ADF Statistic	P-Value	Critical Value (1%)	Critical Value (5%)	Critical Value (10%)
Close	-0.1666	0.9424	-3.4315	-2.862	-2.567
USD	-0.1204	0.9474	-3.4315	-2.862	-2.567
Gold	-0.5064	0.8908	-3.4315	-2.862	-2.567
Pct_Close	-13.8395***	0.000	-3.4315	-2.862	-2.567
Diff_Close	-12.8645***	0.000	-3.4315	-2.862	-2.567
Pct_USD	-13.5427***	0.000	-3.4315	-2.862	-2.567
Diff_USD	-12.8602***	0.000	-3.4315	-2.862	-2.567

continued on following page

Table 3. Continued

Variable	ADF Statistic	P-Value	Critical Value (1%)	Critical Value (5%)	Critical Value (10%)
Pct_Gold	-16.0747***	0.000	-3.4315	-2.862	-2.567
Diff_Gold	-15.2207***	0.000	-3.4315	-2.862	-2.567

Source: Author's calculations.

* Implies significant at 10%

** Implies significant at 5%

*** Implies significant at 1%,5% and 10%

Findings Using Recursive Forecasting Techniques

This section evaluates the performance of various models in forecasting NIFTY close prices using recursive forecasting, where predictions are iteratively fed back into the model. The analysis highlights each model's ability to capture trends, limitations such as lagged responses and volatility underestimation, and their Root Mean Square Error (RMSE) values. Despite capturing general trends, all models face challenges with short-term fluctuations and error accumulation, prompting a shift to forecasting with actual values for more robust evaluation.

ARIMA

The ARIMA (2,1,1) model, with two autoregressive terms, one differencing term, and one moving average term, captures the general upward trend of NIFTY prices. However, it smooths volatility, underestimating sharp fluctuations, and shows divergence in later periods as actual prices rise more steeply. The Ljung-Box test (Q=0.11, p=0.75) confirms no residual autocorrelation, but the Jarque-Bera test (statistic=8496.17, p=0.00) indicates non-normal residuals due to outliers. RMSE: 0.0085.

Figure 5. ARIMA predictions

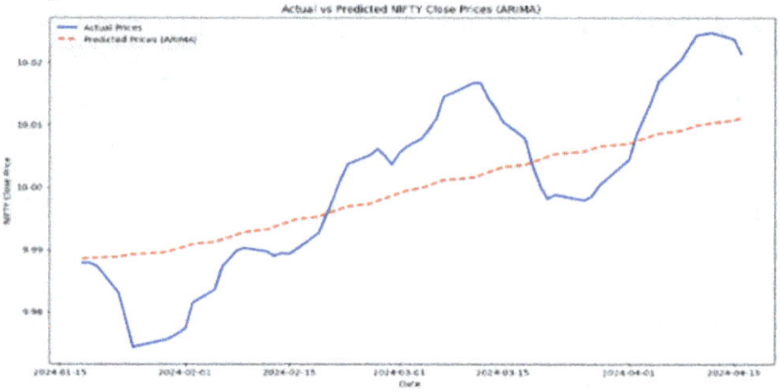

Figure 6. Sarimax results

```
                               SARIMAX Results
==============================================================================
Dep. Variable:                      y   No. Observations:                 5975
Model:               SARIMAX(2, 1, 1)   Log Likelihood               26939.103
Date:                Sat, 15 Mar 2025   AIC                         -53868.205
Time:                        08:50:26   BIC                         -53834.730
Sample:                             0   HQIC                        -53856.578
                               - 5975
Covariance Type:                  opg
==============================================================================
                 coef    std err          z      P>|z|      [0.025      0.975]
------------------------------------------------------------------------------
intercept   5.152e-05    2.8e-05      1.839      0.066    -3.4e-06       0.000
ar.L1          1.2185      0.048     25.258      0.000       1.124       1.313
ar.L2         -0.3419      0.042     -8.219      0.000      -0.423      -0.260
ma.L1         -0.2274      0.050     -4.516      0.000      -0.326      -0.129
sigma2      7.062e-06   6.56e-08    107.573      0.000    6.93e-06    7.19e-06
===================================================================================
Ljung-Box (L1) (Q):                   0.11   Jarque-Bera (JB):              8496.17
Prob(Q):                              0.75   Prob(JB):                         0.00
Heteroskedasticity (H):               0.45   Skew:                            -0.29
Prob(H) (two-sided):                  0.00   Kurtosis:                         8.81
===================================================================================

Warnings:
[1] Covariance matrix calculated using the outer product of gradients (complex-step).
```

Decision Tree

The Decision Tree model with eight lags aligns with the overall upward trend but exhibits lagged predictions and a smoothing effect, failing to capture sharp price movements. Significant divergences occur during volatile periods, with a noticeable phase shift in peaks and troughs, indicating slow adaptation to market changes. RMSE: 0.0106.

Figure 7. Decision Tree predictions

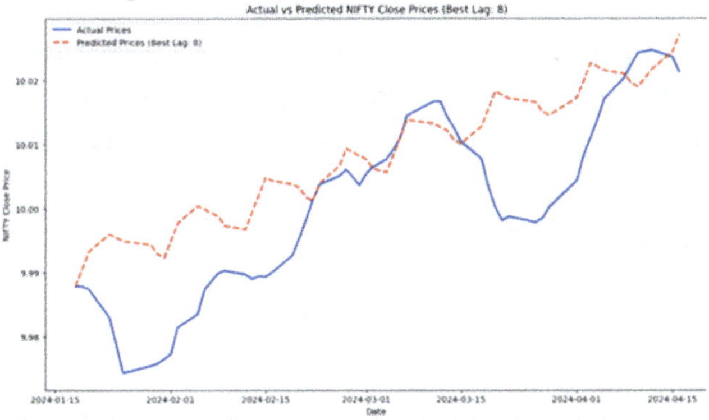

Random Forest

The Random Forest Regressor with seven lags captures the upward trend but lags at turning points and smooths volatility, missing sharp fluctuations. Periods of divergence highlight its limitations in dynamic markets, with predicted peaks and troughs less pronounced and slightly delayed. RMSE: 0.0178.

Figure 8. Random Forest Predictions

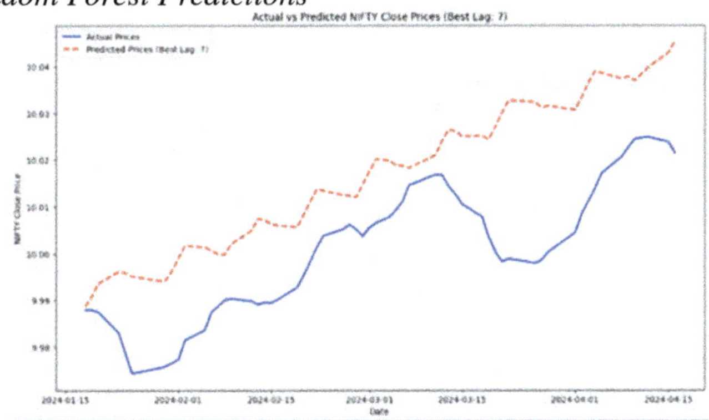

Support Vector Machine (SVM)

Linear Kernel (Lag=3): The SVM with a linear kernel follows the upward trend but lags during rapid changes, producing overly smooth predictions that underestimate volatility. Divergences are evident in volatile periods. RMSE: 0.0127.

Figure 9. SVM Linear kernel Predictions

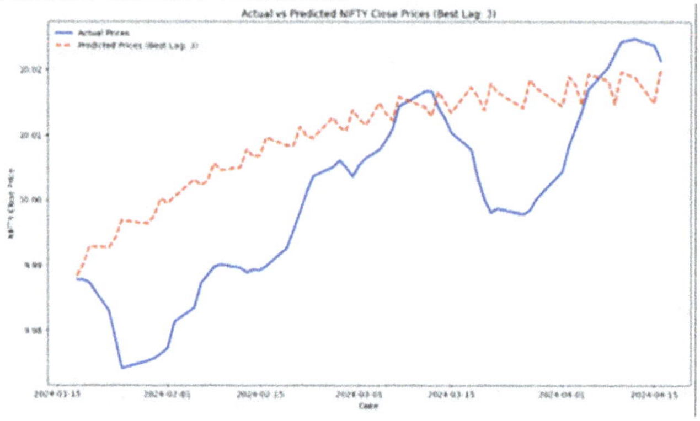

RBF Kernel (Lag=4): The RBF kernel SVM shows trend alignment but lags at turning points, smooths fluctuations, and underestimates volatility, with delayed peaks and troughs. RMSE: 0.0147.

Figure 10. SVM RBF predictions

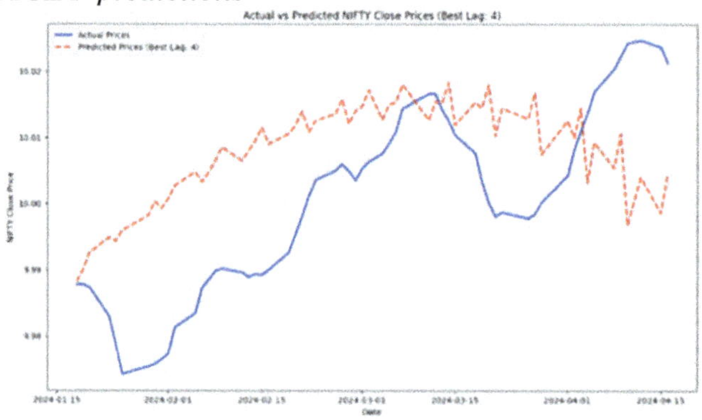

K-Nearest Neighbors (KNN)

The KNN model with eight lags captures the general trend but lags behind sharp price changes, producing jagged, smoothed predictions that miss volatility. Divergences and phase shifts are evident, with less extreme fluctuations. RMSE: 0.0126.

Figure 11. KNN predictions

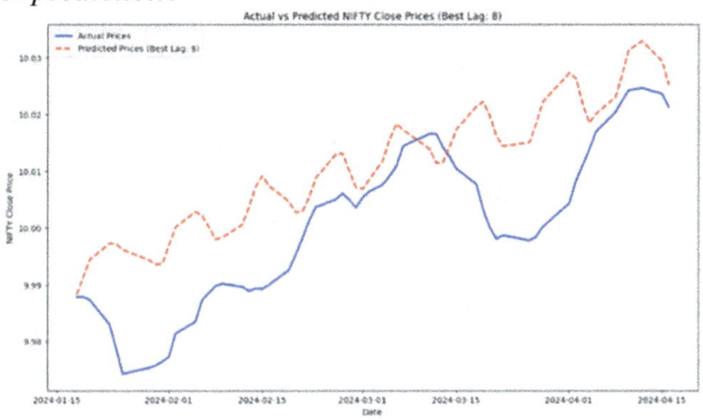

Gradient Boosting Regressors

Gradient Boosting (Lag=7): This model tracks the upward trend but lags at turning points, smooths volatility, and shows divergence during rapid changes, with delayed and less pronounced peaks. RMSE: 0.0162.

Figure 12. Gradient Boosting Predictions

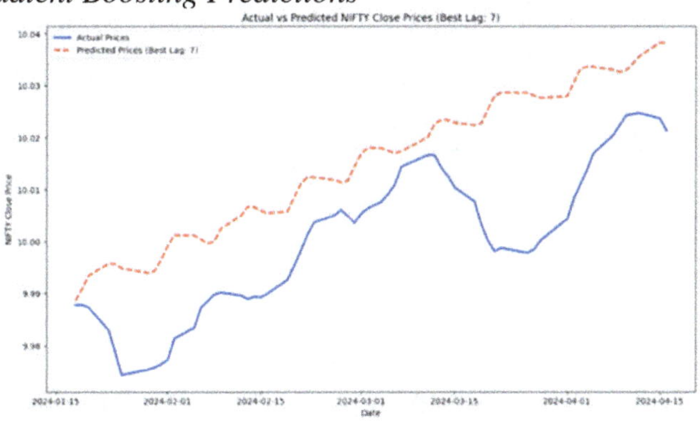

LightGBM: LightGBM exhibits an exploding pattern due to error accumulation, struggling with volatility and sharp movements, with lagged predictions. RMSE: 0.0145.

Figure 13. Light GBM Predictions

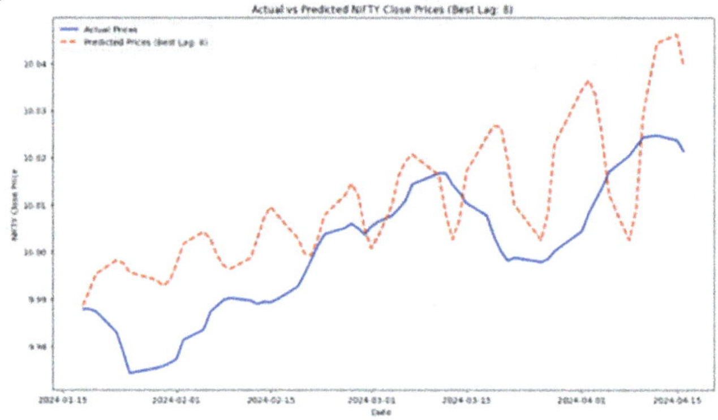

XGBoost: XGBoost captures long-term trends but lags and smooths sharp fluctuations, with less pronounced peaks and troughs. RMSE: 0.0131.

Figure 14. XGB Predictions

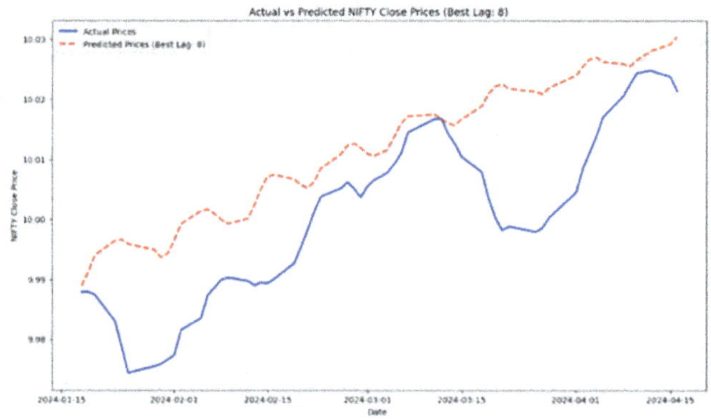

Prophet

The Prophet model aligns well with early trends but lags during sharp movements, underestimating volatility and diverging later as actual prices rise. Smoothing reduces responsiveness to short-term fluctuations. RMSE: 0.0117.

Figure 15. Prophet Predictions

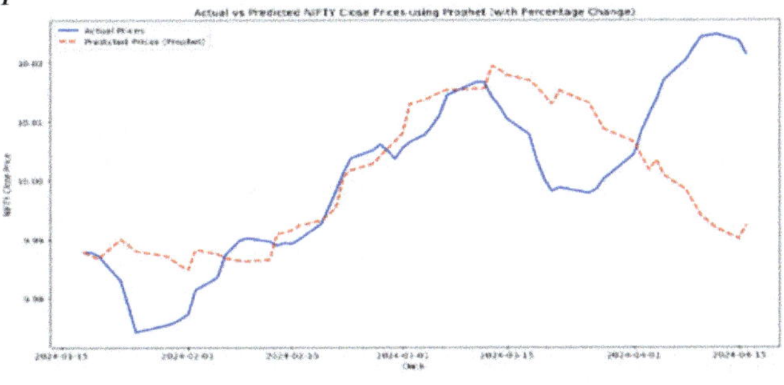

Recurrent Neural Network (RNN)

The RNN model follows the general trend but struggles with sharp price drops, exhibiting lag and smoothing effects. Error propagation in recursive forecasting limits its ability to capture volatility, highlighting the need for advanced architectures like LSTMs. RMSE: 0.0102.

Figure 16. RNN predictions

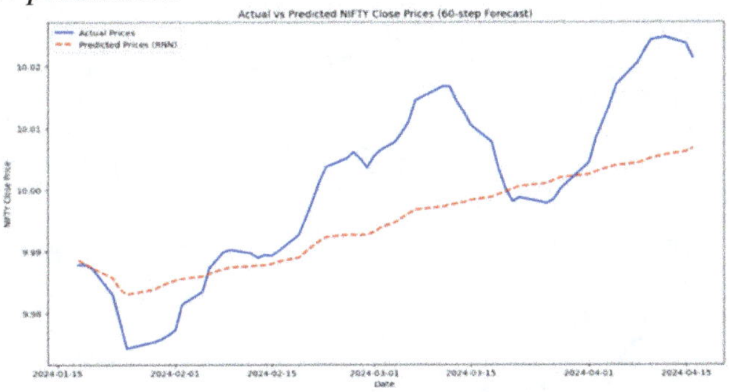

Long Short-Term Memory (LSTM)

The LSTM model captures the overall trend but lags during sharp changes, smooths volatility, and diverges over longer horizons (60 steps), with less pronounced fluctuations. RMSE: 0.0105.

Figure 17. LSTM predictions

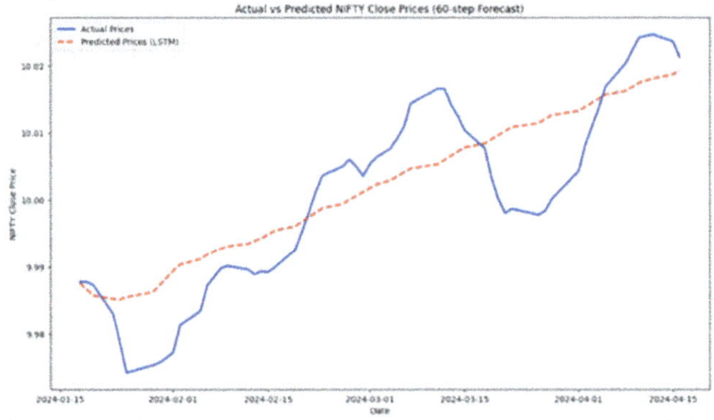

Ensemble Method (ARIMA+XGBoost)

The ARIMA+XGBoost ensemble, weighted by inverse variance, achieves the lowest RMSE (0.0079). It captures the general trend but suffers from smoothing and volatility underestimation, limiting its ability to predict sharp daily movements.

Figure 18. Blended Technique Prediction

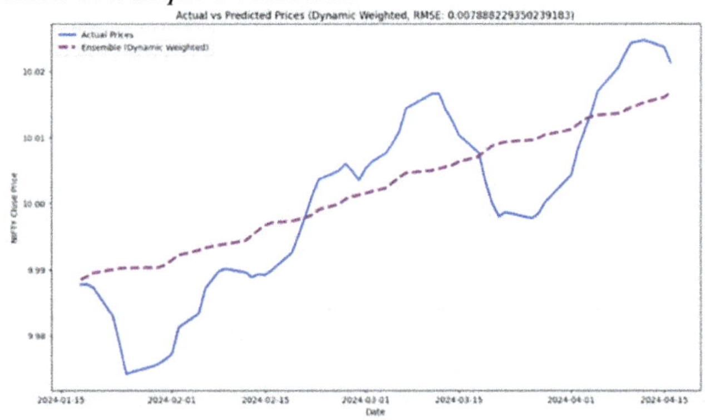

All models capture the long-term upward trend but struggle with short-term volatility, lagged responses, and error accumulation due to recursive forecasting. Smoothing effects and phase shifts reduce accuracy during rapid market shifts, particularly in volatile financial markets. To address these limitations, the study shifts to forecasting with actual observed values from the test set. This approach uses real lagged data for predictions, avoiding error propagation and providing a more realistic evaluation of model performance, akin to practical trading scenarios. This method enhances robustness and offers clearer insights into each model's forecasting potential.

Table 4. Summary of findings for recursive forecasting.

Method	RMSE
ARIMA	0.00851916631297775
Decision Trees	0.010638700932776472
Random forests	0.01783036078391951
SVM (Linear)	0.01273919509796043
SVM (RBF)	0.014710504526757668
KNN	0.012628498498321764
Gradient Boost	0.01619100024922487
LGBM	0.01450184716129511
XGB	0.013103736003411678
Prophet	0.011670084189690462
RNN	0.010237937830923284
LSTM	0.010531126649719424
Hybrid (ARIMA+XGB)	0.007888229350239183

We see that the hybrid method does the best closely followed by ARIMA.

Forecasting Using Actual Values in the Test Set

This section presents a detailed evaluation of forecasting models for NIFTY close prices, utilizing actual observed values from the test set to ensure realistic and robust predictions. By employing a rolling forecast approach, where models are retrained daily with the most recent data, this method minimizes error accumulation inherent in recursive forecasting, offering a closer approximation to real-world financial forecasting scenarios. The analysis encompasses a range of models—ARIMA, Decision Trees, Random Forest, Support Vector Machines (SVM) with Linear and RBF kernels, K-Nearest Neighbors (KNN), Gradient Boosting, LightGBM, XGBoost, Recurrent Neural Networks (RNN), Long Short-Term Memory (LSTM) networks, and a Blended LSTM approach. Each model's performance is assessed based on its ability to capture trends, volatility, and turning points, with Root Mean Square Error (RMSE) as the primary metric. The findings reveal the strengths and limitations of each model, with Rolling ARIMA emerging as the most accurate due to its adaptability and explicit modeling of time series dynamics.

ARIMA

The Rolling ARIMA model, configured with daily retraining, represents a significant advancement over static ARIMA implementations. By updating its parameters with each new data point, it dynamically adapts to evolving market conditions, making it highly suitable for the volatile NIFTY index. The model closely tracks short-term fluctuations, with predicted values aligning tightly with actual prices, Unlike static ARIMA, which often lags behind rapid market shifts, Rolling ARIMA responds almost immediately to turning points, capturing peaks and troughs with remarkable precision. This responsiveness stems from its iterative retraining, which leverages the most recent 60 days of market returns to refine predictions daily.

Computationally, Rolling ARIMA is notably efficient compared to machine learning models like LSTMs or XGBoost, which require extensive resources, including GPUs, for training on large datasets. ARIMA fits a small subset of recent data each day, reducing computational overhead and enabling rapid predictions suitable for real-time applications.

Figure 19. Rolling ARIMA actuals prediction.

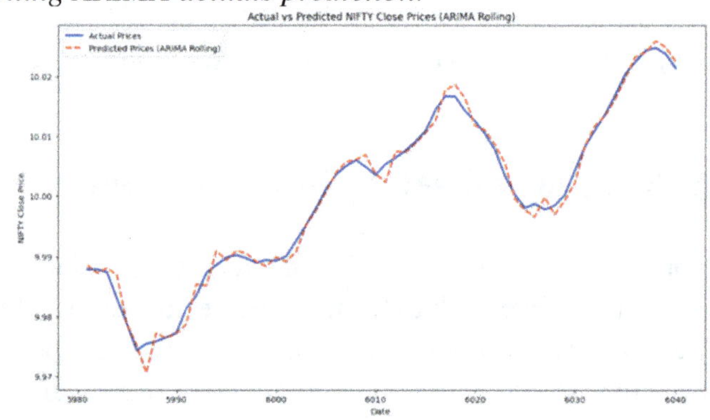

Decision Trees

The Decision Tree model, configured with three lags, effectively captures the upward trend of NIFTY close prices. Its predictions align with the general market direction, reflecting its ability to learn historical patterns. However, the model exhibits a noticeable lag during sharp price movements, particularly at turning points, resulting in a delayed response to market dynamics. The predicted values display a characteristic stepped pattern, a byproduct of the model's discrete decision boundaries, which oversimplify complex market behaviors. This smoothing effect reduces volatility, with peaks lower and troughs shallower than actual prices, limiting the model's sensitivity to rapid fluctuations.

In later periods, a divergence emerges as actual prices rise steeply while predictions remain more gradual, underscoring the model's struggle to adapt to dynamic market shifts. Despite requiring fewer lags than recursive approaches, which enhances computational efficiency, the Decision Tree's simplicity leads to underfitting in volatile conditions. The RMSE of 0.00498 reflects reasonable accuracy but highlights its inferiority to more sophisticated models in capturing intricate market patterns.

Figure 20. Decision tree actuals predictions

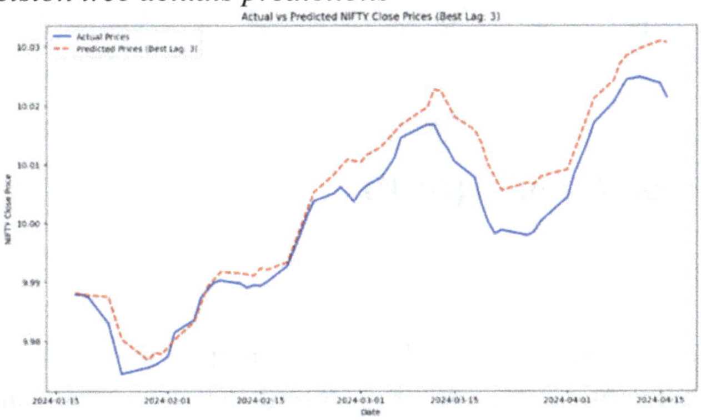

Random Forest

The Random Forest Regressor, using three lags, significantly improves upon the Decision Tree model. Its ensemble approach, which averages predictions from multiple decision trees, reduces overfitting and enhances generalization, resulting in predictions that closely track actual NIFTY prices. The model excels at capturing minor fluctuations and turning points with reduced lag compared to Decision Trees, offering smoother outputs without the stepped pattern. By mitigating sensitivity to data noise, Random Forest maintains stability, making it robust for financial forecasting.

The model's ability to represent market volatility is superior to Decision Trees, with predicted values aligning closely with actual peaks and troughs. Divergence is minimal, even during volatile periods, reflecting its adaptability to changing market conditions. The RMSE of 0.00251 underscores its improved accuracy, positioning

Random Forest as a strong contender among machine learning models for short-term forecasting, though it is surpassed by Rolling ARIMA's precision.

Figure 21. Random forest actuals predictions

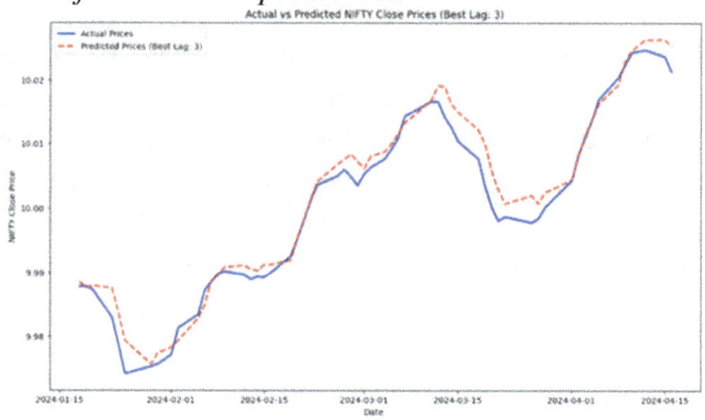

Support Vector Machine (SVM)

Linear Kernel

The SVM with a linear kernel and five lags, captures the overall upward trend of NIFTY prices but struggles with significant limitations. Its linear nature restricts its ability to model the complex, non-linear relationships prevalent in financial markets, leading to underfitting. The predicted values lag behind sharp price movements, particularly at turning points, and exhibit a smoothing effect that underestimates volatility. Peaks and troughs are less pronounced, reducing the model's responsiveness to rapid market shifts. With an RMSE of 0.00207, the linear kernel SVM performs adequately but is limited by its inability to capture intricate market dynamics.

Figure 22. SVM Linear actuals predictions

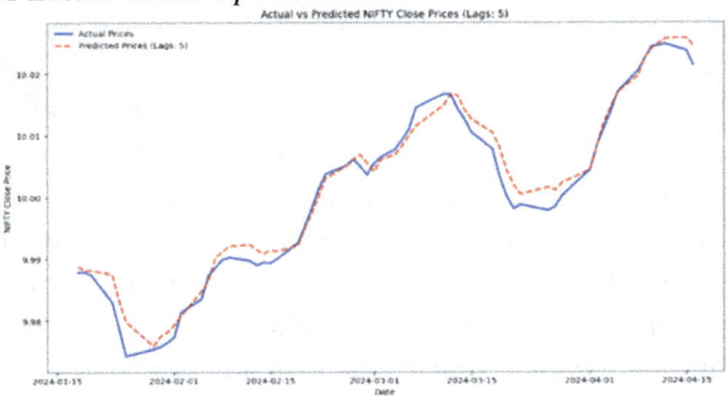

RBF Kernel

The SVM with an RBF kernel and three lags, offers marked improvements over the linear kernel, as its non-linear mapping better captures complex market patterns. Predictions align more closely with actual prices, with reduced lag at turning points and improved volatility representation. The RBF kernel's flexibility allows it to adapt to dynamic market conditions, resulting in more accurate tracking of fluctuations. However, its RMSE of 0.00239 is slightly higher than the linear kernel, possibly due to sensitivity to hyperparameters or shorter lag structure. Over longer horizons, the RBF kernel may outperform its linear counterpart due to its ability to model non-linearity effectively.

Figure 23. SVM RBF actuals predictions

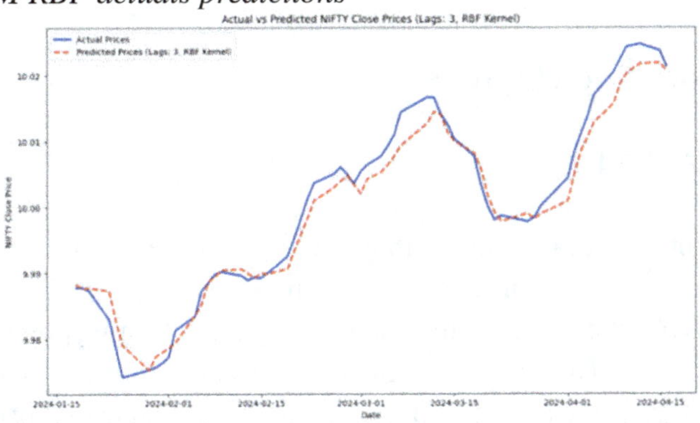

K-Nearest Neighbors (KNN)

The KNN model with three lags, leverages its simplicity to capture non-linear trends in NIFTY prices, making it effective for pattern recognition and anomaly detection. Its predictions follow the general upward trend but lag during sharp price changes, producing jagged outputs that smooth volatility. This smoothing effect results in less extreme peaks and troughs, limiting responsiveness to rapid market shifts. KNN's sensitivity to noise and computational demands for large datasets further constrain its performance. The RMSE of 0.00218 reflects decent accuracy, but its limitations in handling high- dimensional, volatile data make it less competitive than ensemble methods or Rolling ARIMA.

Figure 24. KNN actuals predictions

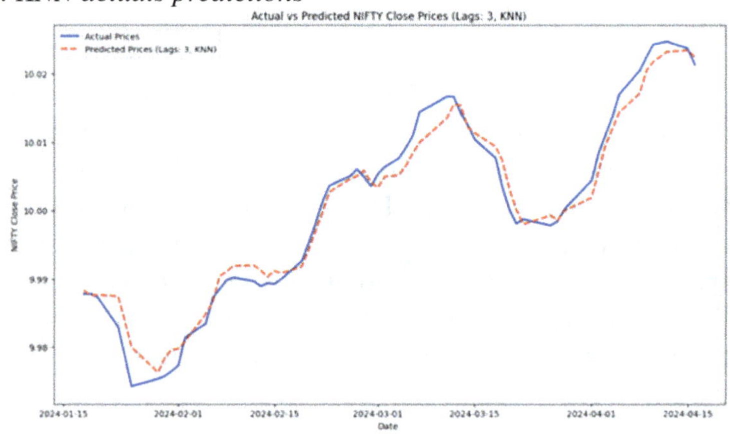

Gradient Boosting Regressors

Gradient Boosting

The Gradient Boosting model with three lags, combines multiple weak learners via gradient descent to minimize prediction errors, resulting in robust performance. It closely tracks NIFTY price movements, reducing lag at turning points and capturing volatility effectively. The model's iterative error correction enhances its ability to adapt to market dynamics, with minimal divergence from actual prices. Its RMSE of 0.00185 highlights its strong predictive accuracy, making it a powerful tool for financial forecasting, particularly in volatile markets.

Figure 25. Gradient boosting actuals predictions

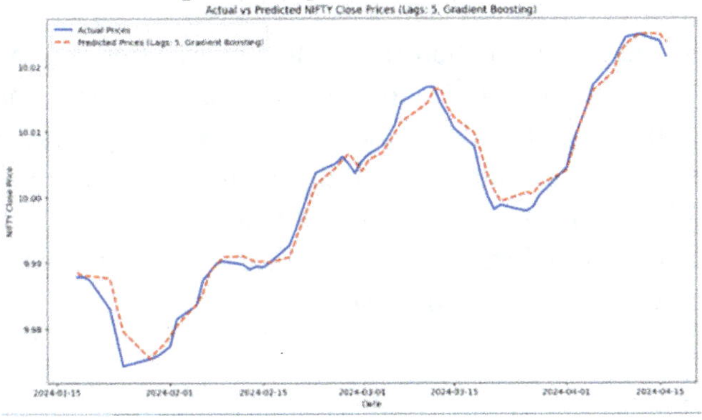

LightGBM

LightGBM, employs a leaf-wise tree growth strategy and histogram-based algorithms to enhance computational efficiency and accuracy. For NIFTY price prediction, it demonstrates minimal lag, superior volatility capture, and tight alignment with actual prices. Its ability to handle large datasets efficiently makes it ideal for real-time applications. The RMSE of 0.00179 positions LightGBM as one of the top- performing ML models, reflecting its balance of speed and precision in dynamic market conditions.

Figure 26. Light GBM actuals prediction

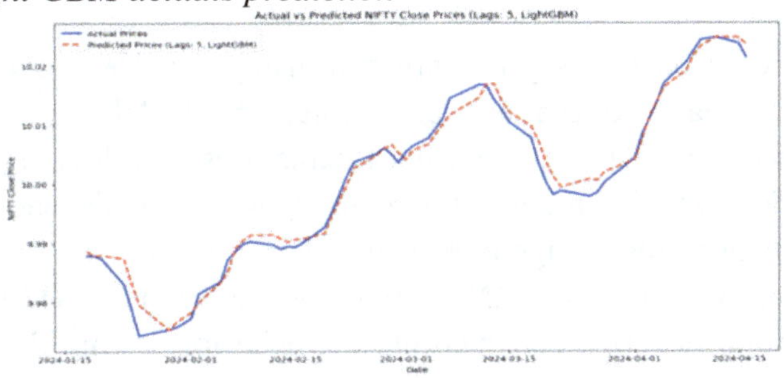

XGBoost

XGBoost, enhances gradient boosting with regularization to prevent overfitting, second-order gradients for optimization, and parallel processing for efficiency. Its predictions for NIFTY prices exhibit minimal lag, accurately capture volatility, and closely follow actual movements with little divergence. Built-in cross-validation and tree pruning further refine its performance. With an RMSE of 0.00186, XGBoost is a highly reliable model, offering a robust balance of computational efficiency and predictive accuracy for financial forecasting.

Figure 27. XGB actuals

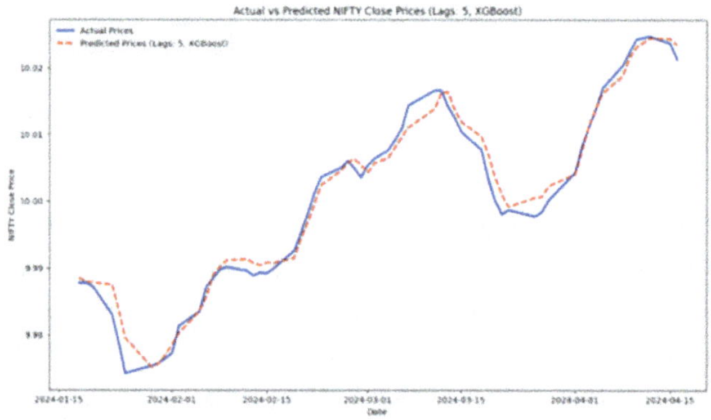

Recurrent Neural Network (RNN)

The RNN model, benefits significantly from using actual test data, reducing error accumulation compared to recursive forecasting. It tracks NIFTY price trends with improved short-term accuracy, capturing fluctuations with less lag than in recursive settings. However, its limitations in retaining long-term dependencies result in smoothed predictions that struggle with sharp price drops. The RMSE of 0.00177 reflects strong performance, but RNNs are less effective than LSTMs for capturing extended temporal patterns, underscoring the need for advanced architectures in financial forecasting.

Figure 28. RNN actuals prediction

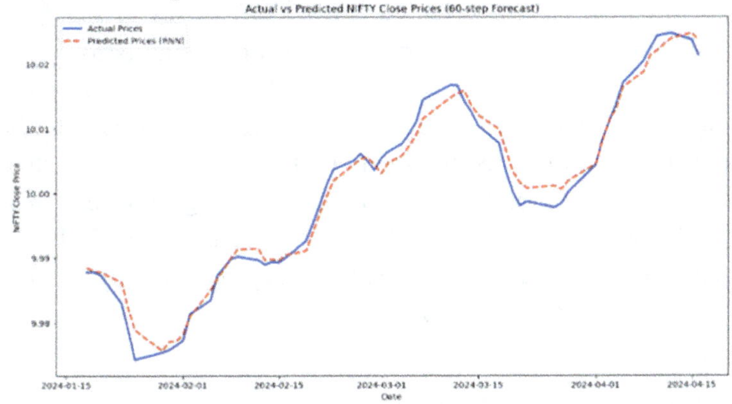

Long Short-Term Memory (LSTM)

LSTMs, are designed to handle long-term dependencies through memory cells and gating mechanisms (input, forget, output gates), preventing vanishing gradients and enabling effective learning from extended sequences. For NIFTY price forecasting, the LSTM model captures trends and reduces divergence, but static evaluation with test data limits its multi-step forecasting capability. Error accumulation remains a challenge for longer horizons, as small inaccuracies compound over time. The RMSE of 0.00324 indicates solid performance but highlights the need for techniques to enhance long-term predictions.

Figure 29. LSTM actuals prediction

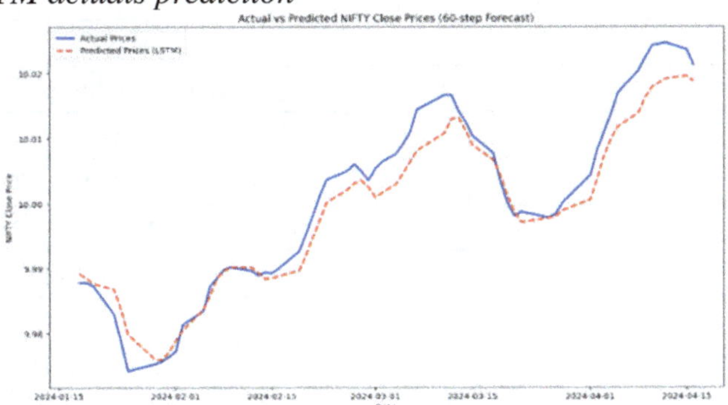

Blended LSTM

The Blended LSTM approach addresses error accumulation by combining actual and predicted values (e.g., 40% actual, 60% predicted) to anchor forecasts to real market data. This hybrid method reduces lag, improves volatility capture, and enhances stability compared to vanilla LSTM. By integrating actual values, it prevents drastic deviations, ensuring predictions remain grounded in market reality. The RMSE of 0.00228, compared to 0.00324 for standard LSTM, demonstrates significant improvement, making Blended LSTM a promising approach for financial forecasting, particularly in volatile markets.

Figure 30. Blended LSTM predictions

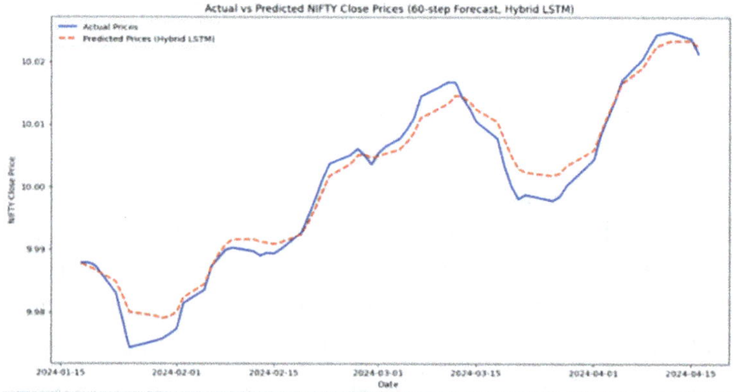

Table 5. Summary of the findings using actual test values.

Method	RMSE
ARIMA	0.0014625509120835597
Decision Trees	0.004977839844591616
Random forests	0.002508101761940267
SVM (Linear)	0.0020717127247323356
SVM (RBF)	0.002386893564284227
KNN	0.0021753763187563327
Gradient Boost	0.0018464653775618575
LGBM	0.0017917209578210262
XGB	0.001860013241198276

continued on following page

Table 5. Continued

Method	RMSE
RNN	0.0017688432416175608
LSTM	0.003241304141200594
Blended LSTM	0.0022777719565657446

Figure 31. Comparison of prediction across methods.

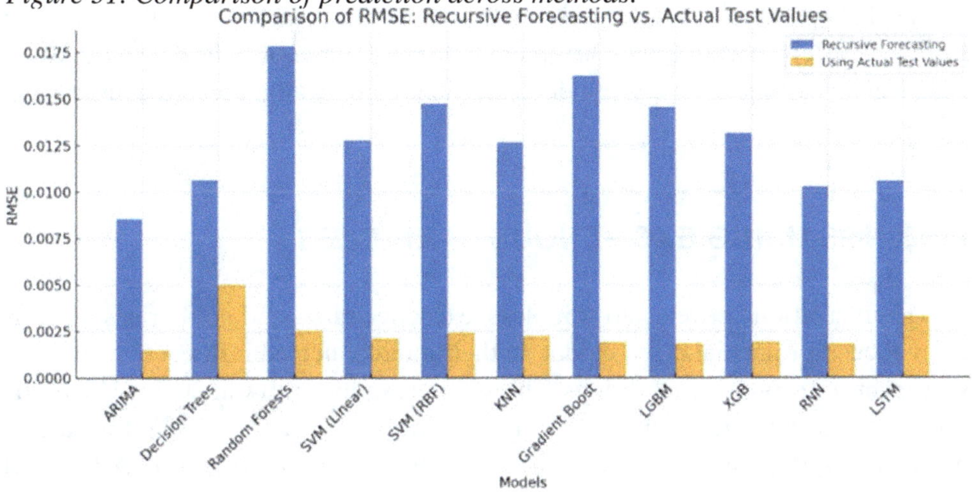

The evaluation of forecasting models using recursive and direct forecasting methods reveals significant performance disparities. Recursive forecasting, which uses prior predictions as inputs for subsequent forecasts, is prone to error accumulation, resulting in higher RMSE values. In contrast, direct forecasting, leveraging actual test set values, eliminates error propagation, leading to substantially lower RMSEs and more accurate predictions.

In recursive forecasting, ARIMA achieved a respectable RMSE of 0.0085, but its performance was surpassed by the ARIMA+XGBoost ensemble, which recorded the lowest RMSE of 0.0078. Machine learning models, such as Decision Trees, KNN, Gradient Boosting, and LightGBM, showed moderate accuracy but were hindered by error accumulation. Deep learning models displayed varied outcomes, with RNNs (RMSE: 0.0102) outperforming LSTMs (RMSE: 0.0105), indicating that LSTMs, despite their strength in capturing long-term dependencies, may be less suited for short-term financial forecasting.

Direct forecasting, using actual test values, markedly improved performance across all models. Rolling ARIMA achieved an impressive RMSE of 0.0014, underscoring its robustness. Machine learning models, including Gradient Boosting, XGBoost, and LightGBM, exhibited significant gains, with RMSEs dropping to 0.00185, 0.00186, and 0.00179, respectively. Deep learning models also benefited, with RNNs improving to an RMSE of 0.00177, while LSTMs lagged at 0.00324. The Blended LSTM, integrating actual and predicted values, achieved an RMSE of 0.00228, highlighting the effectiveness of hybrid approaches.

Overall, recursive forecasting, while practical for multi-step predictions, suffers from compounding errors. Direct forecasting offers a more accurate assessment of model performance but may not fully reflect real-world conditions where future data is unavailable. These results underscore the potential of machine learning and deep learning models, particularly when paired with ensemble or hybrid techniques, to enhance forecasting accuracy, provided the methodology aligns with the forecasting context.

FINDINGS USING EXOGENOUS VARIABLES

The interaction between stock indices, exchange rates, and gold prices remains a key focus in financial research due to their interconnected influence on investor sentiment and economic conditions. This section examines how including USD/INR exchange rates and gold prices as exogenous variables affects NIFTY forecasting using Random Forest and XGBoost models. A Vector Autoregression (VAR) model establishes the empirical links among these variables, and model performance is compared with and without exogenous inputs. Results show modest gains in predictive accuracy, highlighting the value of incorporating broader market dynamics.

Exchange rates and gold prices reflect underlying economic trends and investor behavior. The USD/INR rate signals economic confidence, influencing foreign investments and trade flows appreciation often aligns with market optimism, while depreciation can trigger outflows and declines. Gold, as a traditional safe-haven asset, typically moves inversely to stocks, gaining during volatility or inflationary periods. These relationships, supported by high-frequency data availability, strengthen model adaptability and enrich the information set for machine learning forecasts.

The VAR model confirms significant interdependencies among NIFTY prices, USD/INR exchange rates, and gold prices. A stronger USD generally dampens NIFTY performance, while higher gold prices have a delayed stabilizing effect during uncertainty. The NIFTY index also displays short-term momentum and mean-reversion, showing that recent price behavior influences near-term trends. These validated relationships justify the inclusion of exchange rates and gold prices as exogenous variables to enhance forecasting accuracy.

VAR Model Summary

Summary of regression results are shown below.

Table 6. Summary statistics

Parameter	Value
Model	VAR
Method	OLS
No. of equations	3.00000
Nobs	5799.00
Log likelihood	10292.9
AIC	-12.0314
BIC	-11.9246
HQIC	-11.9943
FPE	5.95399e-06
Det (Omega_mle)	5.85952e-06

Table 7. Reduced VAR model results for equation 'close'

Variable	Coefficient	Std. Error	t-Statistic	Probability
Const.	0.005278	0.002331	2.265	0.024
L1.Close	0.057857	0.013657	4.237	0.000
L1.USD	-0.046603	0.024328	-1.916	0.055
L2.Close	-0.062890	0.013819	-4.551	0.000
L2.Gold	0.059367	0.015540	3.820	0.000
L3.USD	-0.055219	0.024402	-2.263	0.024
L4.Close	0.026159	0.013839	1.890	0.059
L4.USD	0.049426	0.024400	2.026	0.043
L8.USD	0.045844	0.024370	1.881	0.060
L8.Gold	0.044612	0.015565	2.866	0.004
L9.Close	0.036677	0.013766	2.664	0.008
L10.Gold	-0.055973	0.015555	-3.598	0.000

To evaluate the impact of exogenous variables, Random Forest and XGBoost models were applied due to their ability to capture nonlinear relationships and feature interactions. Random Forest mitigates overfitting through ensemble averaging, while XGBoost's gradient boosting framework incorporates regularization to handle complex patterns efficiently. Each model used three lagged values of NIFTY close prices, USD/INR exchange rates, and gold prices, producing nine lagged features in total.

The Random Forest model without exogenous inputs achieved an RMSE of 0.00247, effectively capturing the general upward trend of NIFTY prices but showing delayed responses at turning points and smoothing volatility. With the addition of exchange rates and gold prices, RMSE improved slightly to 0.00227, and predictions aligned more closely with actual values, particularly during volatile periods, indicating that these variables provide meaningful market context.

Similarly, the XGBoost model recorded an RMSE of 0.00344 without exogenous variables and improved to 0.00296 when they were included. The enhanced model captured turning points and fluctuations more accurately, suggesting that macroeconomic indicators add valuable information about investor behavior and market sentiment.

Overall, incorporating USD/INR exchange rates and gold prices produced modest yet consistent gains in forecasting performance for both models. The VAR analysis supports these findings, showing that a stronger USD negatively influences the NIFTY index, while rising gold prices exert a delayed stabilizing effect during uncertainty. These results emphasize that integrating macroeconomic indicators into machine learning models strengthens predictive accuracy and adaptability in dynamic market environments.

EXAMINING MODEL PERFORMANCE DURING CRISIS PERIOD

Forecasting NIFTY During the Global Financial Crisis

The evaluation of forecasting models for NIFTY close prices during the Global Financial Crisis (GFC) era, spanning approximately 363 days, using actual returns as the test set, reveals significant performance differences, with all models except Rolling ARIMA underestimating the severe market dip caused by the crisis. Random Forest (RMSE: 0.0764), Decision Tree (RMSE: 0.0828), SVM with RBF kernel (RMSE: 0.0659), KNN (RMSE: 0.1100), LightGBM (RMSE: 0.0677), and XGBoost (RMSE: 0.0963) capture the

general downward trend but fail to reflect the magnitude and speed of the crisis-induced decline, producing smoothed predictions with lagged responses due to their reliance on historical patterns ill- suited for unprecedented volatility. In contrast, Rolling ARIMA, with daily retraining, excels with an RMSE of 0.0053, closely tracking the sharp decline for most of the period by dynamically adapting to evolving market conditions, though minor divergences occur during extreme volatility. These findings highlight the limitations of machine learning models in crisis scenarios and underscore Rolling ARIMA's superior adaptability and accuracy, emphasizing the value of iterative statistical methods for forecasting in turbulent financial environments.

The summary of findings is shown below.

Table 8.

Model	RMSE
Random Forest	0.076449
Decision Tree	0.082822
SVM (RBF)	0.065881
KNN	0.109984
LGBM	0.067698
XGBoost	0.096308
ARIMA	0.005293

Forecasting NIFTY During the COVID-19 Pandemic

Despite being trained on an extensive dataset that included the volatile Global Financial Crisis (GFC) period, machine learning models—Random Forest (RMSE: 0.0382), Decision Tree (RMSE: 0.0567), SVM with RBF kernel (RMSE: 0.0338), KNN (RMSE: 0.0473), LightGBM (RMSE: 0.0488), and

XGBoost (RMSE: 0.0558)—failed to accurately estimate the sharp market dip during the COVID-19 pandemic, spanning approximately 207 days, when forecasting NIFTY close prices using actual returns as the test set. These models captured the general downward trend but produced smoothed predictions with lagged responses, underestimating the severity and speed of the crisis-induced decline due to their reliance on historical patterns ill-suited for the unprecedented volatility of COVID-19. In contrast, Rolling ARIMA, with an RMSE of 0.0045, excelled by closely tracking the market fall for most of the period, leveraging daily retraining to adapt dynamically to rapid price movements, though minor divergences occurred during extreme volatility, underscoring its superior robustness in crisis forecasting compared to machine learning models.

Summary of the findings is shown below.

Table 9.

Model	RMSE
Random Forest	0.038199667
Decision Tree	0.056748138
SVM (RBF)	0.03382531
KNN	0.047267439
LGBM	0.048762805
XGBoost	0.055847382
ARIMA	0.004531445

As we found that SVM with RBF kernel was best performing model, the implementation using lagged exogenous variables is explored in the next section.

The evaluation of forecasting models for NIFTY close prices during the Global Financial Crisis (GFC, 363 days) and the COVID-19 pandemic (207 days) using actual returns as the test set reveals consistent performance patterns across both crisis periods, with machine learning models—Random Forest (RMSE: 0.0764 GFC, 0.0382 COVID-19), Decision Tree (RMSE: 0.0828 GFC, 0.0567 COVID-19), SVM with RBF kernel (RMSE: 0.0659 GFC, 0.0338 COVID-19), KNN (RMSE: 0.1100 GFC, 0.0473 COVID-19), LightGBM (RMSE: 0.0677 GFC, 0.0488 COVID-19), and XGBoost (RMSE: 0.0963 GFC, 0.0558 COVID-19)—underestimating the severe market dips due to their reliance on historical patterns, whichfail to capture the unprecedented volatility of both crises, resulting in smoothed predictions and lagged responses. In contrast, Rolling ARIMA, with daily retraining, outperformed all models in both periods (RMSE: 0.0053 GFC, 0.0045 COVID-19), closely tracking sharp declines with minimal lag, though minor divergences occurred during extreme volatility. These findings highlight the limitations of machine learning models in crisis forecasting, even when trained on prior crisis data like the GFC, and underscore Rolling ARIMA's superior adaptability and accuracy, emphasizing the critical role of iterative statistical methods in navigating turbulent financial markets.

Forecasting NIFTY Prices During the GFC with Exogenous Variables

The evaluation of forecasting models for NIFTY close prices during the Global Financial Crisis (GFC, 363 days) using exogenous variables (previous returns, gold returns, exchange rate returns) with optimized lag configurations reveals improved performance over direct forecasting with actual returns for most machine learning models, though all models except Rolling ARIMA (RMSE: 0.0053) continue to underestimate the crisis-induced market dip. Random Forest (lag: 2,1,2; RMSE:

0.0527) improves from 0.0764 in direct forecasting, leveraging exogenous variables to better capture volatility but still smoothing sharp declines. XGBoost (lag: 1,2,2; RMSE: 0.0529) enhances from 0.0963, utilizing macroeconomic signals to reduce lag, yet fails to fully reflect the dip's severity. SVM (tuned, RMSE: 0.1192) performs worse than its direct forecasting RBF kernel (0.0659), struggling with the complexity of exogenous features. RNN (lag: 1,4,1; RMSE: 0.0466) indicates limited crisis adaptability despite exogenous inputs. LSTM (lag: 1,3,1; RMSE: 0.0320) outperforms other ML models still smoothing dips. Compared to direct forecasting, exogenous variables reduce RMSEs for Random Forest and XGBoost by incorporating economic context, but SVM's performance deteriorates; Rolling ARIMA remains superior, highlighting the persistent challenge of ML models in capturing extreme volatility during crises.

Table 10.

Model	Best Lag Configuration	RMSE
Random Forest Regressor	(2, 1, 2)	0.0527
XGBoost	(1, 2, 2)	0.0529
RNN	(1, 4, 1)	0.0466
LSTM	(1, 3, 1)	0.0320

Forecasting NIFTY Prices During the COVID-19 Pandemic with Exogenous Variables

The evaluation of forecasting models for NIFTY close prices during the COVID-19 pandemic (207 days) using exogenous variables (previous returns, gold returns, exchange rate returns) with optimized lag configurations shows modest improvements for some machine learning models compared to forecasting with only their own lags, though all models continue to underestimate the crisis-induced market dip, with Rolling ARIMA (RMSE: 0.0045) remaining superior. Random Forest Regressor (lag: 1,6,4; RMSE: 0.0381) performs similarly to its own-lag RMSE of 0.0382, indicating minimal benefit from exogenous variables, with predictions still smoothing sharp declines. XGBoost (lag: 1,6,4; RMSE: 0.0377) improves notably from 0.0558, leveraging gold and exchange rate returns to better capture volatility, though it lags at turning points. SVM with exogenous factors (RMSE: 0.0397) shows a slight decline in performance over its own-lag RBF kernel RMSE of 0.0338, but its performance remains limited by smoothed predictions and difficulty handling complex crisis dynamics. RNN (lag: 2,6,6; RMSE: 0.0296) outperforms other ML models, effectively utilizing exogenous variables to enhance trend capture, yet fails to reflect the dip's severity. LSTM (lag: 1,2,2; RMSE: 0.0270) achieves the lowest ML RMSE, benefiting from exogenous inputs to reduce lag, but still produces smoothed predictions. Compared to forecasting with own lags, exogenous variables improve XGBoost, RNN, and LSTM by incorporating macroeconomic context, but Random Forest and SVM show limited or no gains, and all ML models are outperformed by Rolling ARIMA, which excels due to its daily retraining and adaptability to crisis volatility.

Table 11.

Model	Best Lag Configuration	RMSE
Random Forest Regressor	(1, 6, 4)	0.0381
XGBoost	(1, 6, 4)	0.0377
RNN	(2, 6, 6)	0.0296
LSTM	(1, 2, 2)	0.0270

The dilemma of using Artificial Intelligence in finance.

Our analysis highlights a critical dilemma in financial forecasting: advanced machine learning models like XGBoost can show apparent performance gains even when exposed to irrelevant or random features, suggesting overfitting to noise rather than learning true financial signals. Experiments with synthetic variables revealed that XGBoost's sequential boosting mechanism, while powerful for capturing subtle interactions, is highly sensitive to noisy inputs. In contrast, Random Forest maintained stable performance under the same conditions, demonstrating greater robustness due to ensemble averaging and inherent randomness. This underscores that model complexity and historical success do not guarantee reliable future performance, emphasizing the need for rigorous feature selection, regularization, and continuous evaluation.

In practice, simpler adaptive models such as Rolling ARIMA outperformed complex machine learning approaches during periods of extreme volatility, such as the 2008 Global Financial Crisis and the 2020 COVID-19 pandemic. Rolling ARIMA's ability to dynamically retrain on recent data allows it to capture sharp market fluctuations while avoiding overfitting, supporting more reliable risk management, asset allocation, and hedging decisions from an investor perspective, where timely and accurate responses to market shocks directly affect portfolio performance. In stable markets, hybrid approaches that blend traditional statistical models with AI and incorporate exogenous variables (e.g., gold prices, USD/INR rates) or alternative data sources (e.g., news sentiment, social media trends) can enhance short-term forecasting and portfolio optimization, further informing investor decisions on trading and diversification strategies.

Models that balance adaptability and robustness, like Rolling ARIMA or hybrid approaches, can improve early detection of market shocks and inform timely interventions such as liquidity provisions or policy adjustments. Fintech and algorithmic trading firms can similarly benefit from hybrid modeling, achieving accurate forecasts in volatile markets while maintaining computational efficiency and compliance through interpretable models.

Despite these insights, several practical limitations must be acknowledged. Machine learning models are inherently vulnerable to overfitting, sensitive to data quality issues, and may not generalize well across different markets. Financial datasets themselves can also introduce biases: for example, survivorship bias occurs when historical datasets exclude failed or delisted firms, which can distort model performance and give investors an overly optimistic view of past returns. Other issues, such as structural breaks or missing observations, can further compromise forecast reliability. Addressing these limitations is crucial to ensure that models provide realistic insights for both investors and policymakers. Moreover, the data used in this study is at a daily frequency, which may not fully capture the rapid dynamics and intraday fluctuations of financial markets. Market conditions can change within minutes or even seconds, and important price signals, liquidity shifts, or trading patterns may be missed when relying solely on daily closing prices. High-frequency data, such as minute-by-minute or tick-level observations, could potentially provide a more granular and timely representation of market behavior, enabling models to detect short-term volatility spikes, microstructure effects, or abrupt market shocks that daily data cannot reveal. However, incorporating high-frequency data introduces additional challenges, including greater computational complexity, data storage requirements, noise management, and the need for more sophisticated modeling techniques. Recognizing this limitation underscores that while daily data is informative for broader trend analysis, extending forecasting frameworks to higher-frequency datasets could enhance model responsiveness and improve decision-making in fast-moving market environments.

The growing use of alternative data and hybrid approaches amplifies these challenges, requiring careful validation and attention to interpretability. Incorporating explainable AI methods and emphasizing transparency in forecasting models are essential to bridging the gap between technical findings and actionable managerial, investor, and policy decisions. Recognizing these limitations strengthens both the academic rigor and the practical relevance of financial forecasting research.

SUMMARY

This research evaluates the effectiveness of statistical, machine learning (ML), and deep learning models in forecasting NIFTY close prices, comparing their performance under recursive forecasting, direct forecasting with actual returns, and forecasting with exogenous variables (previous returns, gold returns, and USD/INR exchange rate returns) during normal market conditions and crisis periods, specifically the Global Financial Crisis (GFC, 363 days) and the COVID-19 pandemic (207 days). The study employs a comprehensive range of models—ARIMA, Random Forest, Decision Tree, SVM (Linear and RBF kernels), KNN, Gradient Boosting, LightGBM, XGBoost, RNN, LSTM, and Blended LSTM—using Root Mean Square Error (RMSE) as the primary metric to assess predictive accuracy. The findings highlight the strengths and limitations of each approach, the critical role of exogenous variables, and the challenges of forecasting during unprecedented crises, with Rolling ARIMA consistently outperforming ML and deep learning models due to its adaptability. Additionally, an experiment with synthetic random variables underscores the risk of overfitting in complex ML models, emphasizing the need for rigorous feature selection and model validation in financial forecasting.

Recursive forecasting, where models use their own predictions as inputs for subsequent steps, was evaluated to simulate multi-step forecasting scenarios. The ARIMA+XGBoost ensemble achieved the lowest RMSE (0.0079), slightly outperforming standalone ARIMA (0.0085), which effectively captured long-term trends but struggled with short-term volatility due to error accumulation. Machine learning models—including Random Forest (0.0178), Decision Tree (0.0106), SVM Linear (0.0127), SVM RBF (0.0147), KNN (0.0126), Gradient Boosting (0.0162), LightGBM (0.0145), and XGBoost (0.0131)—showed moderate accuracy but were hindered by lagged responses and smoothed predictions, failing to capture sharp fluctuations. Deep learning models, RNN (0.0102) and LSTM (0.0105), showed similar limitations, with LSTMs underperforming despite their ability to model long-term dependencies, suggesting unsuitability for short-term financial forecasting. The Prophet model (0.0117) aligned with trends but lagged during rapid changes. Error accumulation in recursive forecasting amplified deviations, particularly in volatile markets, underscoring the method's practical limitations for real-world applications where precision is critical.

Direct forecasting, using actual test set returns, eliminated error propagation, resulting in significantly lower RMSEs across all models. Rolling ARIMA, with daily retraining, achieved the lowest RMSE (0.00146), closely tracking short-term fluctuations and turning points with minimal lag, owing to its iterative adaptation to evolving market conditions. Machine learning models showed substantial improvements: Random Forest (0.00251), Decision Tree (0.00498), SVM Linear (0.00207),

SVM RBF (0.00239), KNN (0.00218), Gradient Boosting (0.00185), LightGBM (0.00179), and XGBoost (0.00186) captured trends and volatility more effectively, with LightGBM and XGBoost among the top ML performers due to their ensemble efficiency. Deep learning models also benefited, with RNN (0.00177) outperforming LSTM (0.00324), while Blended LSTM (0.00228), combining actual and predicted values, reduced lag and improved stability. Despite these gains, all ML and deep learning models were outperformed by Rolling ARIMA, highlighting its computational efficiency and robustness in dynamic markets. Direct forecasting's reliance on actual data provided a clearer evaluation of model capabilities, closely mimicking real-world scenarios where new data is available, but it may not fully reflect conditions requiring multi-step predictions.

During the GFC and COVID-19 periods, models were tested using actual returns to assess their ability to handle unprecedented volatility. In the GFC (363 days), Random Forest (0.0764), Decision Tree (0.0828), SVM RBF (0.0659), KNN (0.1100), LightGBM (0.0677), and XGBoost (0.0963) captured general downward trends but significantly underestimated the crisis dip's magnitude and speed, producing smoothed predictions with lagged responses due to reliance on historical patterns ill-suited for extreme events. Rolling ARIMA (0.0053) excelled, closely tracking the sharp decline with minimal divergence, leveraging daily retraining to adapt dynamically. Similarly, during the COVID-19 period (207 days), despite training on GFC-inclusive data, ML models—Random Forest (0.0382), Decision Tree (0.0567), SVM RBF (0.0338), KNN (0.0473), LightGBM (0.0488), and XGBoost (0.0558)—again underestimated the dip, with smoothed predictions and lagged responses, while Rolling ARIMA (0.0045) maintained superior accuracy. These results highlight ML models' limitations in crisis forecasting, as their generalization from historical crises failed to capture the unique dynamics of new crises, whereas Rolling ARIMA's iterative approach ensured robustness across both periods.

Incorporating exogenous variables (previous returns, gold returns, USD/INR exchange rates) aimed to capture broader market dynamics, validated by a Vector Autoregression (VAR) model confirming significant relationships: a stronger USD negatively impacted NIFTY, while rising gold prices exerted a delayed positive effect, reflecting gold's safe-haven role. During the GFC, Random Forest (lag: 2,1,2; RMSE: 0.0527) improved from 0.0764, XGBoost (lag: 1,2,2; RMSE: 0.0529) from 0.0963, RNN (lag: 1,4,1; RMSE: 0.0466), and LSTM (lag: 1,3,1; RMSE: 0.0320) enhanced accuracy by leveraging macroeconomic signals, though all underestimated the crisis dip. SVM (0.1192) worsened from 0.0659, struggling with feature complexity. In the COVID-19 period, Random Forest (lag: 1,6,4; RMSE: 0.0381) showed negligible improvement from 0.0382, XGBoost (lag: 1,6,4; RMSE: 0.0377) improved from 0.0558, SVM (0.0397) slightly declined from 0.0338, while RNN (lag: 2,6,6; RMSE: 0.0296) and LSTM (lag: 1,2,2; RMSE: 0.0270) achieved the lowest ML RMSEs, yet still trailed Rolling ARIMA (0.0045). Exogenous variables generally enhanced ML model performance by incorporating economic context, but improvements were modest, and all models failed to match ARIMA's crisis adaptability.

An experiment using synthetic random variables mimicking real data characteristics tested whether improvements from exogenous variables were genuine or due to overfitting. XGBoost showed enhanced performance with random features, suggesting it may detect spurious patterns in noise, increasing overfitting risk. Random Forest, however, maintained stable performance, demonstrating resilience to irrelevant features due to its ensemble averaging. This highlights XGBoost's sensitivity to noisy inputs, necessitating rigorous feature selection and cross-validation, while Random Forest's robustness makes it more reliable in noisy financial datasets. The findings underscore that model complexity does not guarantee reliable predictions, emphasizing the need for careful data preprocessing and validation to ensure meaningful improvements.

Policy and practical implications emerge from these results. The consistent superiority of Rolling ARIMA for crisis and multi-step forecasting suggests regulators and policymakers should encourage the adoption of adaptive, robust statistical models alongside advanced ML and AI approaches for financial market monitoring. ML models' limitations in crisis periods highlight the risk of relying solely on historical patterns, as extreme market events often deviate significantly from past trends. This underscores the need for early-warning systems that incorporate macroeconomic indicators, such as USD/INR exchange rates and gold prices, to capture broader market dynamics and mitigate systemic risks. Furthermore, financial markets are heavily influenced by investor sentiment and behavioral factors, which are not fully captured by traditional numerical data. To address this, unstructured data sources including news articles, social media posts, and analyst reports can be leveraged to generate sentiment-based variables. Incorporating such sentiment indicators into forecasting models can improve their responsiveness to sudden market shifts, enhance prediction of volatility spikes, and provide a more comprehensive framework for risk assessment. Combining structured economic data with unstructured sentiment-driven insights can therefore create hybrid models that better reflect real-world market behavior, supporting both policymakers and institutional investors in proactive decision-making during periods of heightened uncertainty.

For institutional investors and portfolio managers, combining ARIMA with selective ML models can enhance prediction reliability under normal conditions, while risk management frameworks should integrate exogenous economic signals to capture sudden market shifts. Additionally, the overfitting potential of complex ML models like XGBoost underscores the necessity of regulatory guidelines on model validation, feature selection, and stress-testing before deployment in high-stakes financial decision-making.

Overall, the research reveals that Rolling ARIMA consistently outperforms ML and deep learning models across all forecasting approaches and periods, particularly during crises, due to its daily retraining and explicit modeling of time series dependencies, achieving RMSEs of 0.0085 (recursive), 0.00146 (direct), 0.0053 (GFC), and 0.0045 (COVID-19). ML models, while effective in stable conditions, struggle with crisis volatility, underestimating sharp dips due to reliance on historical patterns, even with GFC-inclusive training data. Exogenous variables modestly improve ML model accuracy, capturing macroeconomic dynamics, but their impact is limited in crises, where Rolling ARIMA's adaptability remains unmatched. These findings challenge the Efficient Market Hypothesis by demonstrating ML models' ability to identify patterns in normal conditions but highlight their limitations in unprecedented events, reinforcing the value of statistical models like ARIMA for crisis forecasting. For financial practitioners and policymakers, the study suggests prioritizing adaptive, computationally efficient models, integrating macroeconomic indicators cautiously, and implementing rigorous validation protocols to enhance forecasting reliability in volatile markets.

REFERENCES

Adebiyi, A., Adewumi, A., & Ayo, C. (2014). Stock price prediction using the ARIMA model. UKSim-AMSS 16th International Conference on Computer Modelling and Simulation. https://doi.org/DOI: 10.1109/UKSim.2014.67

Al-Shiab, M. (2006). The predictability of the Amman Stock Exchange using the univariate autoregressive integrated moving average (ARIMA) model. *Journal of Economic and Administrative Sciences*, *22*(2), 17–35. Advance online publication. DOI: 10.1108/10264116200600006

Apte, P. (2001). The interrelationship between the stock markets and the foreign exchange market. IIM Bangalore Research Paper No. 169. https://doi.org/DOI: 10.2139/ssrn.2161245

Arestis, P., Demetriades, P. O., & Luintel, K. B. (2001). Financial development and economic growth: The role of stock markets. *Journal of Money, Credit and Banking*, *33*(1), 16–41. DOI: 10.2307/2673870

Asad, M. (2015). Optimized stock market prediction using ensemble learning. https://doi.org/DOI: 10.1109/ICAICT.2015.7338559

Bansal, M., Goyal, A., & Choudhary, A. (2022). Stock market prediction with high accuracy using machine learning techniques. *Procedia Computer Science*, *215*, 247–265. DOI: 10.1016/j.procs.2022.12.028

Beck, T., & Levine, R. (2002). Stock markets, banks, and growth: Panel evidence. NBER Working Paper No. w9082. Retrieved from SSRN.

Bhandari, H. N., Rimal, B., Pokhrel, N. R., Rimal, R., Dahal, K., & Khatri, R. K. (2022). Predicting stock market index using LSTM. *Machine Learning with Applications*, *9*, 100320. DOI: 10.1016/j.mlwa.2022.100320

Bouri, E., Jain, A., Biswal, P. C., & Roubaud, D. (2017). Cointegration and nonlinear causality amongst gold, oil, and the Indian stock market. *Resources Policy*, *52*, 201–206. DOI: 10.1016/j.resourpol.2017.03.003

Box, G., & Jenkins, G. (1970). *Time series analysis: Forecasting and control.*

Caetano, R., Oliveira, J. M., & Ramos, P. (2025). Transformer-Based Models for Probabilistic Time Series Forecasting with Explanatory Variables. *Mathematics*, *13*(5), 814. DOI: 10.3390/math13050814

Černevičienė, J., & Kabašinskas, A. (2024). Explainable artificial intelligence (XAI) in finance: A systematic literature review. *Artificial Intelligence Review*, *57*(8), 216. DOI: 10.1007/s10462-024-10854-8

Challa, M. L., Malepati, V., & Kolusu, S. N. R. (2020). S&P BSE Sensex and S&P BSE IT return forecasting using ARIMA. *Financial Innovation*, *6*(1), 47. DOI: 10.1186/s40854-020-00201-5

Fama, E. (1970). Efficient capital markets: A review of theory and empirical work. *The Journal of Finance*, *25*(2), 383–417. DOI: 10.2307/2325486

Guptha, K. S. K., & Rao, R. P. (2018). The causal relationship between financial development and economic growth: An experience with BRICS economies. *Journal of Social and Economic Development*, *20*(2), 308–326. DOI: 10.1007/s40847-018-0071-5

Harrison, B., & Moore, M. (2012). Stock market efficiency, non-linearity, thin trading, and asymmetric information in MENA stock markets. *Economic Issues*, *17*(1), 77–93.

Hiremath, G. S., & Narayan, S. (2016). Testing the adaptive market hypothesis and its determinants for the Indian stock markets. *Finance Research Letters*, *19*, 173–180. DOI: 10.1016/j.frl.2016.07.009

Jain, A., & Biswal, P. C. (2016). Dynamic linkages among oil price, gold price, exchange rate, and stock market in India. *Resources Policy*, *49*, 179–185. DOI: 10.1016/j.resourpol.2016.06.001

Kabir, M. R., Bhadra, D., Ridoy, M., & Milanova, M. (2025). LSTM–Transformer-Based Robust Hybrid Deep Learning Model for Financial Time Series Forecasting. *Sci*, *7*(1), 7. DOI: 10.3390/sci7010007

Karim, R., Alam, M., & Hossain, R. (2021). Stock market analysis using linear regression and decision tree regression. https://doi.org/DOI: 10.1109/eSmarTA52612.2021.9515762

Khan, Q., Ikram, S., & Mehtab, M. (2011). Testing weak form market efficiency of Indian capital market: A case of NSE and BSE. *African Journal of Marketing Management*, •••, 3.

Konak, F., & Şeker, Y. (2014). The efficiency of developed markets: Empirical evidence from FTSE 100. *Journal of Advanced Management Science*, *2*(1), 29–32. DOI: 10.12720/joams.2.1.29-32

Levine, R. (1997). Financial development and economic growth: Views and agenda. *Journal of Economic Literature*, *35*, 688–726.

Lo, A. (2004). The adaptive markets hypothesis: Market efficiency from an evolutionary perspective.

Lo, A. W., Mamaysky, H., & Wang, J. (2000). Foundations of technical analysis: Computational algorithms, statistical inference, and empirical implementation. *The Journal of Finance*, *55*(4), 1705–1765. DOI: 10.1111/0022-1082.00265

Mallikarjuna, M., & Rao, R. P. (2019). Evaluation of forecasting methods from selected stock market returns. *Financial Innovation*, *5*(1), 40. DOI: 10.1186/s40854-019-0157-x

Moghar, A., & Hamiche, M. (2020). Stock market prediction using LSTM recurrent neural network. *Procedia Computer Science*, *170*, 1168–1173. DOI: 10.1016/j.procs.2020.03.049

Mondal, P., Shit, L., & Goswami, S. (2014). Study of effectiveness of time series modeling (ARIMA) in forecasting stock prices. *International Journal of Computer Science. Engineering and Applications*, *4*(2), 13–29. DOI: 10.5121/ijcsea.2014.4202

Naik, R., & Reddy, Y. V. (2021). Examination of long memory in the Indian stock market: A sectoral juxtaposition. *FIIB Business Review*, *14*(2), 184–202. Advance online publication. DOI: 10.1177/23197145211040274

Ojo, J., & Olatayo, T. (2009). On the estimation and performance of subset autoregressive integrated moving average models. *European Journal of Scientific Research*, *28*, 287–293.

Rajan, R., & Zingales, L. (1998). Financial dependence and growth. *The American Economic Review*, *88*, 559–586.

Sethi, S. R., & Mahadik, D. (2024). *Artificial Intelligence in Financial Markets: Opportunities, Challenges, and Future Directions. SSRN*. https://ssrn.com/abstract=5078873

Shen, S., Jiang, H., & Zhang, T. (2012). *Stock market forecasting using machine learning algorithms*. Department of Electrical Engineering, Stanford University.

Subasi, A., Amir, F., Bagedo, K., Shams, A., & Sarirete, A. (2021). Stock market prediction using machine learning. *Procedia Computer Science*, *194*, 173–179. DOI: 10.1016/j.procs.2021.10.071

Taylor, S. J., & Letham, B. (2018). Forecasting at scale. *The American Statistician*, *72*(1), 37–45. DOI: 10.1080/00031305.2017.1380080

Thakur, M., & Kumar, D. (2018). A hybrid financial trading support system using multicategory classifiers and random forest. *Applied Soft Computing*, *67*, 337–349. DOI: 10.1016/j.asoc.2018.03.006

Tripathy, N. (2016a). Testing of long memory in the Indian stock market using ARFIMA model. *The Journal of Prediction Markets*, *9*(3), 23–39. DOI: 10.5750/jpm.v9i3.1055

Tripathy, N. (2016b). A study on the dynamic relationship between gold price and stock market price in India. *European Journal of Economics, Finance and Administrative Sciences*.

Xue, P., Lei, Y., & Li, Y. (2020). Research and prediction of Shanghai-Shenzhen 20 Index based on the support vector machine model and gradient boosting regression tree. https://doi.org/DOI: 10.1109/ICICAS51530.2020.00019

Zhong, X., & Enke, D. (2017). Forecasting daily stock market return using dimensionality reduction. *Expert Systems with Applications*, *67*, 126–139. DOI: 10.1016/j.eswa.2016.09.027

APPENDIX

Autoregressive Integrated Moving Average (ARIMA) Model

The Autoregressive Integrated Moving Average (ARIMA) model is one of the most widely used statistical methods for time series forecasting. It is particularly useful for modeling non- stationary time series by incorporating differencing to achieve stationarity. ARIMA is extensively applied in financial markets, economic forecasting, and other domains where historical data is used to predict future trends. It was introduced by George Box and Gwilym Jenkins (1970).

This model is a combination of three components:

1. Autoregressive (AR) – A model that uses past values to predict future values.
2. Integrated (I) – Differencing applied to the time series to achieve stationarity.
3. Moving Average (MA) – A model that uses past forecast errors to improve predictions.

The general equation for an ARIMA(p, d, q) model is:

$$Y_t = c + \sum_{t=1}^{p} \phi_i y_{t-i} + \sum_{j=1}^{q} \theta_j \varepsilon_{t-j} + \varepsilon_t$$

Here,

- Y_t is the dependent variable (time series data).
- c is a constant term.
- $\phi_i Y_{t-i}$ are the autoregressive parameters.
- $\theta_j \varepsilon_{t-j}$ are the moving average parameters.
- ε_t is the error term (white noise).

Steps Involved in ARIMA Model Building

Step 1: Assessing Stationarity

ARIMA model requires stationary time series.

To determine stationarity, the following statistical tests are employed: Augmented Dickey-Fuller (ADF) Test

Kwiatkowski-Phillips-Schmidt-Shin (KPSS) Test

If the time series is found to be non-stationary, differencing is performed iteratively until stationarity is attained.

Step 2: Differencing (I Component)

If the time series is determined to be non-stationary, we need to apply differencing to remove trends. The differenced series is given by:

$$\Delta Y_t = Y_t - Y_{t-1}$$

If one differencing step (d = 1) is insufficient, we apply additional differencing until the series becomes stationary.

Step 3: Determining AR and MA Orders (p and q)

To establish appropriate values for p (autoregressive order) and q (moving average order), we examine:

Autocorrelation Function (ACF): Helps identify the order of the MA(q) component.

Partial Autocorrelation Function (PACF): Helps determine the order of the AR(p) component. If the ACF cuts off after lag q, while the PACF gradually declines, it indicates an MA(q) model.

Conversely, if the PACF cuts off after lag p, while the ACF tails off, it suggests an AR(p) model.

Step 4: Model Estimation and Parameter Selection

Once the appropriate values of p, d, and q are selected, the ARIMA model can be estimated using maximum likelihood estimation (MLE) or other optimization techniques.

The model parameters are chosen based on:

Minimizing the Akaike Information Criterion (AIC). Minimizing the Bayesian Information Criterion (BIC). Ensuring parameter significance (p-values < 0.05).

Step 5: Model Diagnostics

After fitting the model, diagnostic tests are conducted to ensure its adequacy:

Residual Analysis – Checking if residuals are white noise (uncorrelated and normally distributed).

Ljung-Box Test – Tests for autocorrelation in residuals.

Histogram and Q-Q Plots – Verify normality of residuals.

If diagnostics indicate problems, the model may need to be modified by adjusting p, d, or q.

Machine Learning Models

Machine learning models generally apply the following two ways of working with the data.

Bagging (Bootstrap Aggregating)

Bagging, or Bootstrap Aggregating, is an ensemble learning technique aimed at improving the accuracy and stability of predictive models by reducing variance. It achieves this by generating multiple subsets of the original dataset through bootstrap sampling—a method that randomly selects data points with replacement, meaning some instances may appear multiple times while others are excluded. Each subset is then used to train a separate instance of a base learner, typically a high-variance model like a decision tree. The final prediction is obtained by aggregating the outputs of all individual learners, either by averaging predictions for regression tasks or using majority voting for classification tasks. This approach effectively mitigates overfitting and enhances model robustness, particularly for inherently unstable algorithms.

Examples of Models Utilizing Bagging:

Random Forest: An ensemble of decision trees trained on different bootstrap samples, which reduces overfitting and improves predictive performance.

Boosting

Boosting is another ensemble learning method designed to enhance predictive performance by training a series of weak learners one after another. Unlike bagging, which reduces variance, boosting aims to minimize both bias and variance by adapting to the errors of previous learners. It starts with all training instances assigned equal weights and then iteratively adjusts them, giving more importance to misclassified or poorly predicted cases. This forces subsequent learners to focus on challenging examples, gradually improving overall accuracy. The final prediction is derived from a weighted combination of all models, where each learner's contribution is based on its effectiveness in reducing error. While highly effective, boosting can be sensitive to noise, requiring careful parameter tuning to prevent overfitting.

Examples of Models Utilizing Boosting:

- **Gradient Boosting Machines (GBM):** Constructs models one after another, with each new model refining the errors of its predecessor by optimizing a loss function.
- **XGBoost (Extreme Gradient Boosting):** A computationally efficient and optimized version of gradient boosting, widely used in competitive machine learning due to its speed and scalability.
- **LightGBM:** A gradient boosting framework that grows trees leaf-wise, significantly enhancing efficiency for large-scale datasets.

1) Decision Trees

Decision trees have a long history in both statistics and machine learning. Originally used for classification problems, they were later adapted for regression tasks. The idea of recursive partitioning dates back to the 1960s, with early implementations such as the Automatic Interaction Detection (AID) algorithm. Over time, more refined approaches, such as Classification and Regression Trees (CART), were introduced by Breiman et al. in 1984. Decision tree regression extends this idea by allowing continuous target variables instead of categorical outputs.

Decision Tree Regression Models

Decision tree regression operates by recursively dividing the dataset into smaller subsets based on feature values. The objective is to reduce variance within each subset, forming a tree-like structure where the terminal nodes (leaves) represent the predicted values.

Splitting Criterion

At each stage, the algorithm identifies the optimal feature and threshold for splitting the data. This decision is guided by minimizing the variance within the newly created subsets, ensuring better predictive accuracy.

The tree expands until it reaches a predefined stopping condition, such as a minimum number of samples per leaf or a maximum depth. To mitigate overfitting, pruning techniques like cost- complexity pruning are employed, ensuring a balance between model complexity and generalization.

2) Random Forest Regressor

The Random Forest Regressor is an ensemble learning method that extends bagging (Bootstrap Aggregating) to regression tasks by combining predictions from multiple decision trees. It introduces additional randomness by selecting a random subset of features at each split in the trees, which reduces correlation between trees and improves generalization.

3) Support Vector Regression

In Support Vector Regression (SVR), the kernel function allows the model to capture non-linear relationships between input features x and target values y by implicitly transforming the data into a higher-dimensional feature space. Within this transformed space, a linear regression function can be applied to model the relationship effectively. This approach, known as the kernel trick, eliminates the need to explicitly compute the coordinates in the high-dimensional space, thereby enhancing computational efficiency while preserving the model's flexibility in handling complex patterns.

Figure 32. Data transformation with SVM.

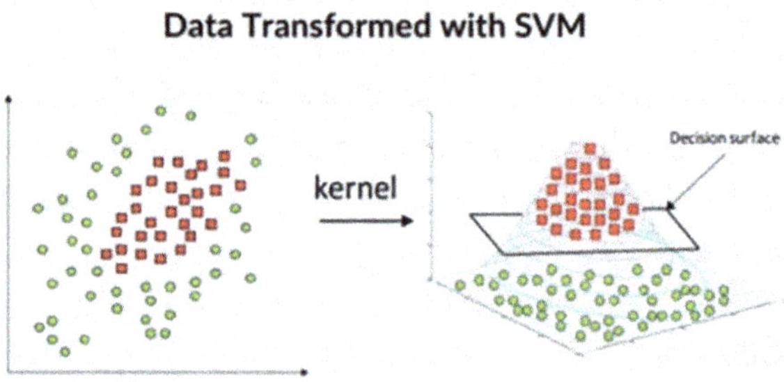

4) Gradient Boosting Regressor

Gradient Boosting Regressor (GBR) build an ensemble of weak learners to minimize a loss function iteratively

Here we use three types of gradient boosting Regressor,

1) Gradient Boosting
2) Light Gradient boost

3) XGB (Extreme Gradient boosting)

5) Facebook Prophet

Facebook prophet was introduced in the paper Forecasting at scale, Taylor and Letham (2017). Facebook Prophet is an open-source time series forecasting tool developed by Facebook's Core Data Science team. It is designed to handle complex patterns in business data, including trends, seasonality, holidays, and missing values. Prophet is particularly user-friendly, making it accessible to non-experts while offering flexibility for advanced customization. Its robust modeling framework efficiently manages irregular data, outliers, and trend shifts, making it a powerful tool for accurate and interpretable forecasting.

It uses an additive model where, $Y(t) = g(t) + s(t) + h(t)$

Where the time series $Y(t)$ can be modelled as a function of trend $g(t)$, seasonality $s(t)$ and holidays $h(t)$.

6) Recurrent Neural networks (RNN)

Recurrent Neural Networks (RNNs) are specialized neural networks for processing sequential data, such as time series and text. Unlike traditional feedforward networks, RNNs maintain a hidden state that carries information across time steps, enabling them to capture temporal dependencies. By reusing the same weights at each step, RNNs efficiently model patterns in data, making them well-suited for applications like language modeling and speech recognition.

Figure 33. Structure of RNN.

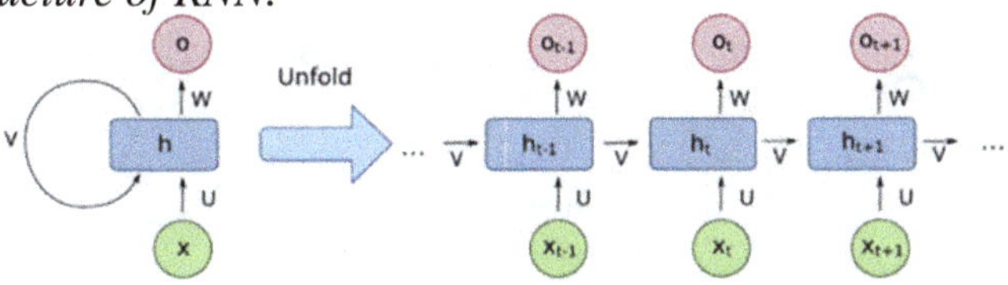

RNNs are particularly effective for time series problems because they are designed to handle sequential data with temporal dependencies. They maintain a hidden state that updates at each time step, enabling them to "remember" past inputs and capture long-term patterns such as trends and cycles. By using shared weights across all time steps, RNNs efficiently model sequences of varying lengths without requiring separate parameters for each step. Their ability to learn temporal dynamics makes them ideal for predicting future values, such as stock prices or weather patterns.

Additionally, RNNs offer flexibility in handling irregular or noisy time series data, unlike traditional models like ARIMA, which rely on strict statistical assumptions.

7) Long Short-Term Memory (LSTM)

Long Short-Term Memory (LSTM) networks are an advanced form of Recurrent Neural Networks (RNNs) designed to capture long-term dependencies in sequential data, such as time series or text. Unlike standard RNNs, LSTMs incorporate a cell state and three gates—forget, input, and output—that regulate the flow of information, allowing them to retain essential patterns while filtering out irrelevant details. This architecture effectively addresses the vanishing gradient problem, which often limits traditional RNNs in learning long-range dependencies. By maintaining a stable gradient flow, LSTMs are well-suited for tasks requiring extended contextual understanding, such as language modeling and stock market forecasting.

Figure 34. Structure of LSTM

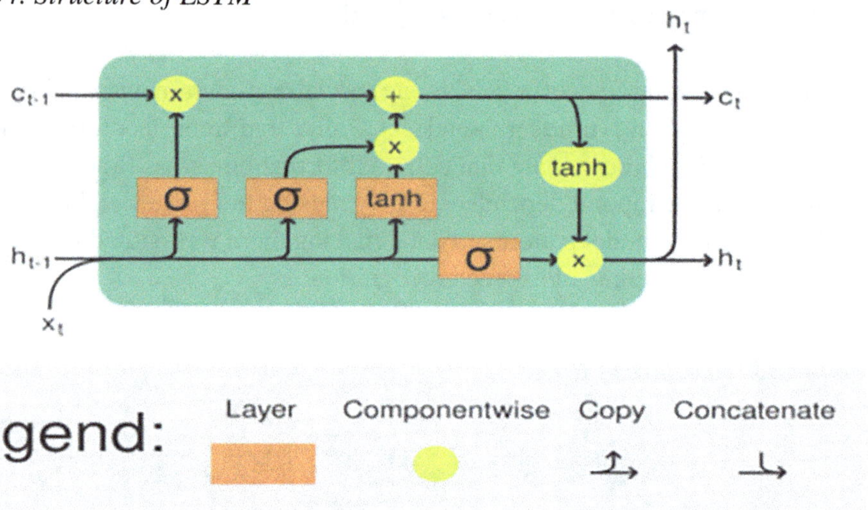

Chapter 3
The Role of Predictive Models and Machine Learning in Macroeconomic and Financial Forecasting

T. Selva Banu Priya
Panimalar Engineering College, India

Antony Vijay
RMK College of Engineering and Technology, India

Beslin Pajila
http://orcid.org/0000-0002-3905-2460
Vel Tech Rangarajan Dr. Sagunthala R&D Institute of Science and Technology, India

ABSTRACT

Machine learning (ML) has become a transformative tool in improving forecasting accuracy in both macroeconomics and finance. Traditional forecasting models face limitations in handling complex, non-linear data and adapting to sudden economic shifts. ML overcomes these challenges by analyzing large datasets, detecting hidden patterns, and providing real-time, dynamic predictions. Applications such as stock price forecasting, credit scoring, and economic trend analysis showcase its superior performance over conventional methods. Moreover, the integration of alternative data sources, like social media sentiment and satellite imagery, enhances forecasting capabilities. The use of hybrid models combining traditional econometrics with

DOI: 10.4018/979-8-3373-3053-2.ch003

ML, along with explainable AI for transparency, ensures broader acceptance. As ML evolves, it promises more accurate, scalable, and adaptive models for future economic and financial forecasting.

1. INTRODUCTION

1.1 Background and Importance of Forecasting

Forecasting is very important in macroeconomic and financial decision making and it gives information that can assist the policymakers, business leaders, and investors in their strategic planning(Basher, S. A., & Sadorsky, P. 2022). Forecasting in macroeconomics assists in the determination of the major indicators like the growth of GDP, inflation rates, unemployment rates, and fiscal deficits. These forecasts are used by governments and central banks to make monetary and fiscal policies, allocation of public resources and to enhance stability in the economy. To businesses, proper macroeconomic forecasts help in improved decision-making where they include market expansion, planning production, and pricing strategy.

In a similar manner, in finance, forecasting aids in forecasting the future direction of the asset prices, interest rates, stock returns and the market volatility. Financial forecasts are used by the investors in making decisions regarding portfolio management, asset allocation, and risk management. Predictive models are used by financial institutions, such as banks and insurance companies, to determine credit risk, to optimise their lending portfolio and to be capital adequate. Financial forecasting has the ability to give an organization a competitive advantage in the market since it enables an organization to act ahead of time in response to the changing conditions.

Nevertheless, the conventional forecasting models have suffered a lot of drawbacks and weaknesses. Time-series forecasting In macroeconomics and finance, econometric models are widely applied to time-series modelling, including ARIMA, VAR, and error correction models. Despite the fact that these models have been successful in a stable environment, they cannot withstand the increased complexity of the modern economies and financial markets. Among the main issues of the traditional methods, one can distinguish the assumption of linearity that is not in line with the nonlinear relationships of the economic and financial data. Additionally, these models have a propensity to use numerous historical information to come up with great forecasts thus they are not as adaptable as to unforeseen economic jolt or change in the market.

In addition, the assumption of stationarity whereby the mean of the time series data is fixed is not held in most real life scenarios. In turn, the econometric models can be susceptible to errors in the process of using them at volatile periods, i.e., in the period of financial crisis or at the period of high level of economic volatility. This also brings about the necessity to have superior techniques of forecasting which can be in a position of responding to these complexities and provide real time and dynamic forecasts.

1.2 Emergence of Predictive Models and Machine Learning

Machine learning (ML) has emerged as a groundbreaking technology to improve accuracy and quality of economic and financial forecasts due to the failure of traditional forecasting techniques(Selvaraj, P et al., 2022). Machine learning offers a data-driven solution whereby, the models can learn using the available historical data and update their prediction real-time, by considering the new information. Compared to the classical econometric models, the range of which is limited by the assumptions related to the data structure, the machine learning algorithms can reflect the complicated patterns and relations in the data, even when there is a noise or nonlinearity(Chaturvedi, M et al., 2025).

Among the key advantages of machine learning, it is possible to mention its ability to deal with large volumes of data(Sharifani et al., 2023). Big data has altered the field of forecasting by availing large and varied data that were previously unavailable or analysed with difficulty. This puts in use data of multiple sources, such as satellite imagery, social media, news sentiment and online purchases, along with more traditional macroeconomic data, such as GDP, inflation and unemployment rates. Machine learning models stand a good chance to handle these huge unstructured data and be in a position to discover hidden trends which would have been lost using the traditional model.

Machine learning can make more precise and timely predictions because of the possibility to combine and process a wide variety of data(Sawwalakhe, R et al., 2023). As an example, financial markets are frequently affected by various conditions, including economic statistics, political activities, investor mood, and tendencies in the world. Such a large volume of information can be absorbed by machine learning models and, in particular, deep learning-driven ones to create predictions that are more in line with the market realities. Such capability to adjust to new data in real-time enables machine learning to provide more dynamic predictions, which makes it a useful tool in the cases of fast-changing economic and financial situations.

Also, machine learning procedures can provide better results when it comes to high-frequency prediction. Markets such as the financial markets are very dynamic and require prompt updates. Machine learning models and particularly those that utilize time-series analysis, such as Long Short-Term Memory network, have the ability to analyze real-time data to forecast short term market dynamics with impressive precision. The models have the capacity to identify the slight patterns in the data that will reflect on the future trends and therefore provide investors and institutions with more up to date information in making decisions.

The major advantages of machine learning in forecasting are capacity to take care of nonlinearities, scalability, and flexibility. The traditional models have problems with non-linear relationships with the data like the sudden changes in the market sentiment or the sudden changes in the economy and the machine learning algorithms are developed to identify such patterns. In addition, machine learning models are scalable, that is, they can be used to process and learn constantly with an incoming flow of new data without a noticeable drop in performance as the amount of data and its complexity grows. This qualifies them to be very efficient in the long-term forecasting process since they can adapt to the changing economic environments.

1.3 Objective of the Chapter

This chapter aims at discussing how predictive models and machine learning can be used to enhance macroeconomic and financial forecasting. Despite the fact that over the last several decades, the classical methods of econometrics were the foundation of the prediction process, machine learning provides the opportunity to make the process of prediction more precise, efficient, and dynamic. This chapter will use the examples of different predictive models, such as supervised and unsupervised learning methods, and their use in macroeconomic and financial forecasting to prove that machine learning has the potential to address the shortcomings of the conventional methods. The practical use of machine learning in forecasting will also be mentioned in this chapter, and some case studies and empirical evidence will be given in which machine learning models have demonstrated better results than the traditional ones. It will talk about the strengths and weaknesses of these models and what is in store about machine learning in economic and financial forecasts. In such a way, the given chapter aims to offer the overall picture of how machine learning has the potential to revolutionize the sphere of forecasting and can help make more informed and better-data-based decisions in the public and private spheres.

2. TRADITIONAL FORECASTING TECHNIQUES

2.1 Econometric Models

Microeconomic and financial forecasting has been based on econometric models. The models are based on statistical methods to approximate the relationship among the economic variables and forecast the trends. AutoRegressive Integrated Moving Average, Vector Autoregression and Cointegration Models, which are the

Error Correction Models are the most popular econometric models used. All these models are characterized by unique attributes and apply in different situations of forecasting difficulties.

ARIMA (AutoRegressive Integrated Moving average): ARIMA is a time-series forecasting model, which integrates autoregressive (AR) and moving average (MA) to forecast a future value using the past observations. The model works best when dealing with stationary data that is; data that shows similar patterns at different times. ARIMA has found extensive application in economic and financial forecasting in short term predictions like prediction of inflation rates, stock prices, and the output of the economy. The I in ARIMA is the integration and is applied to transform non-stationary data into a stationary one through differentiation of the data series. Although ARIMA is effective with smaller data, it cannot be applied on complex, non-linear trends or large-dimensional data(Muma, B., & Karoki, A. 2022).

VAR (Vector Autoregression): The VAR model is a set of equations which is utilized to describe interdependencies of various time series variables. This model comes in handy especially when making forecasts of the macroeconomic indicators such as GDP, interest rates and inflation since these variables tend to affect each other. The VAR model presupposes that future values of the variables can be identified by the past values and it is appropriate to make predictions of the future development of economic systems with the help of feedback loops. Nevertheless, the VAR model needs a lot of past information so that it can give accurate estimates and it is complex when there are a lot of variables and this creates problems of model specification and interpretation.

2.2 Statistical Models

Besides econometric models, statistical models like linear and nonlinear regression model, and time series analysis techniques have been implemented to perform economic and financial forecasting extensively.

Linear and Non-linear Regression models: Regression analysis is a basic instrument of the forecasting, in which the purpose is to find the connection between a dependent variable and one or more independent variables. Regression models in macroeconomics are employed to forecast such variables as GDP growth or unemployment rates in the future, depending on the economic variables such as government expenditures or interest's rates. Linear regression implies straight line connection between variables, in nonlinear regression there can be complicated curved relationships. Even though linear regression models are easy to understand and interpret, they cannot always reflect the complex nature of the economic data, especially in case of multiple correlated variables or non-linear trends.

These limitations are being tried to be overcome by nonlinear regression models which model more complex relationships. Nonlinear regression is however computationally expensive, and the risk of the over fitting model is higher with a complex model. An example of this is that a nonlinear regression model may be more appropriate to a dataset but it may not generalize well to new data causing poor forecasting results. So, although regression models are most popular because they are simple and easy to interpret, they are not necessarily the most appropriate in the complex and high-dimensional forecasting tasks.

Methods of Time-Series Analysis: The other common statistical method of forecasting in economics and finance is time-series analysis. These approaches are based on examination of past information to detect the patterns and trends and seasonal influences. Moving averages, exponential smoothing and seasonal decomposition of time series (STL) are some of the techniques employed to model and forecast the future values. Time-series analysis can be very useful in the event that the data have definite and consistent trends through time. But these techniques tend to have problems with non-linear relationships or sudden change of the data. As an example, the time-series methods may not effectively capture the changes in trends due to abrupt shocks during economic crises and thus, time-series methods are not useful in volatile economic times.

2.3 Limitations of Traditional Techniques

Although traditional forecasting methods in form of econometric models or statistical techniques are widely used, there are enormous limitations that limit their effectiveness particularly in the complex and volatile economic situations.

Problems of Nonlinearity: One of the main weaknesses of most of the traditional forecasting models is that they use linear assumptions. ARIMA and VAR are among the most econometric and regression models that assume that the connections between the variables are linear. But data on the economy and finance are frequently non-linear in nature and these models cannot be used to represent such trends. To give an example, the correlation between interest rate and inflation is not necessarily linear and a small fluctuation of one variable may have an out-of-proportion impact on the other. The traditional models that do not explain these nonlinearities can produce inaccurate predictions, particularly in the case of complicated economic events like market crash, financial bubble, or abrupt policy changes.

Multicollinearity: Multicollinearity can be defined as the fact that two or more independent variables in a regression model are strongly correlated. This presents a major problem to the conventional forecasting models, especially the VAR and multiple regression models, where the variables independence is of essence in order to have a proper estimation. In the case of multicollinearity, one will not be able to come up with reliable estimates of coefficients and the correlations between variables become hard to interpret. This can lead to huge forecast errors and lower accuracy of the model particularly in cases where macroeconomic variables are to be predicted on highly correlated variables such as inflation, unemployment and wage growth.

Working With Big Data: The other limitation of the traditional forecasting methods is that it is not easy to process the big, high dimensional data. With an increasing amount of data, the economic and financial systems are becoming more complicated, and the relationships between many variables occurring in them can affect one another. This complexity is not always suited to the traditional econometric and statistical models. These models can be cumbersome and error prone to specify and preprocess large amounts of data as the number of variables grows.

The conventional forecasting techniques also fail to work in unstable economic conditions. Economic and financial systems are usually exposed to sudden changes like crash in the market, political upheavals, or natural calamities, which may cause an abrupt change in economic behavior. The sudden changes may not easily adapt to the traditional models like ARIMA and VAR since they depend on the past and assumptions of the relationships between variables being stable. Consequently, these models can give unreliable predictions in times of high uncertainty, and they can hardly be useful in dynamic environments and environments where uncertainty exists.

3. MACHINE LEARNING IN FORECASTING

3.1 Overview of Machine Learning Techniques

Machine learning (ML) refers to a branch of artificial intelligence (AI) in which computers learn and make decisions without programming. Unlike the more classical models with some pre-determined assumptions, machine learning algorithms are data-driven and hence are particularly useful in the situations involving complexity, such as the case of forecasting in economics and finance(Kamalov, F et al., 2021). The inherent power of machine learning lies in the fact that, it will be able to enhance its accuracy over time because it will continuously revise its predictions based on the new information.

The machine learning algorithms can handle large amounts of data, identify complicated correlations, and locate hidden patterns that may not be visible at first sight using the conventional forecasting methods(Kour, M. 2024). That is why ML can be used in particular in such areas as macroeconomics and finance since the relationships between multiple variables are nonlinear and complicated. In addition to that, ML algorithms may operate in real-time and adapt to new data, so they can compute dynamic and responsive predictions. Such flexibility and elasticity makes machine learning the innovative tool of increasing the accuracy and effectiveness of prediction in the modern rapidly changing economic and financial world.

3.2 Types of Machine Learning Approaches

The machine learning strategies can be narrowed down to four categories and they are supervised learning, unsupervised learning, reinforcement learning, and deep learning. These methods are not similar and each of them has its peculiarities and can be applied to different forecasting issues.

Supervised Learning: The most common method in forecasting is the supervised learning. The algorithm is trained using labeled data in this approach and this implies that the features of the input (independent variables) and the output (dependent variables) are available. Supervised learning is aimed at learning a mapping between inputs and outputs, and the model can then be used to make predictions, with new, unseen data. Widely known supervised learning algorithms are:

Linear Regression and Logistic Regression: Linear regression is an easy but powerful tool to predict continuous variables, as the GDP growth or the inflation rates. It presupposes the linear dependence between the input variables and the target one. Logistic regression, in its turn, is applied to classification issues, the aim of which is to obtain the predictions of the categorical outcomes, e.g., whether a market will increase or decrease. Despite their popularity because of the simplicity, these methods tend to fail to cover more complex relationships in the data.

Decision Trees and Random forests: Decision trees are recursive dividing of data into subsets by feature values to predict the outcomes. Although the decision trees are simple to understand, they have the problem of being overfitted, particularly when the data is noisy. This is overcome by random forests, which is an ensemble technique, and it consists of combining many decision trees, thus making the model more robust and precise. Random forests are especially applicable in predicting in situations where there are many variables which affect the outcome in a complex non linear manner.

Support vector machines (SVM): Support vector machines are very strong supervised learning algorithms applicable on classification and regression tasks. SVMs are performed by determining the optimal hyperplane that will separate the dataset points of various classes. Regarding financial forecasting, SVM may be applied to forecast the market trends or group the assets according to their risk levels. SVMs are effective in high-dimensional or complex-patterned data, but may be computationally expensive and also need proper parameter tuning(Balasundaram, S., & Kapil, N 2010).

Unsupervised Learning: Unsupervised learning methods are applied, when the output variable is unavailable, and it is aimed at investigating the data structure. This form of learning finds application in the detection of trends, clusters or anomalies in data. Major unsupervised learning algorithms are:

K-Means Clustering: K-means clustering is a method that is applied to separate data into distinctive groups depending on the similarity. It is very common in the financial forecasting where it is used to segment markets or asset categorization under various risk levels. K-means can be used to find these patterns by grouping similar data points to each other, so that they can be found in the data even though they are not clear when the data is considered as a whole.

Principal component analysis (PCA): PCA is a dimensionality reduction methodology which converts high-dimensional data to a reduced dimensional space that is simple to analyze. It is applied to find the most significant variables (or principal components) which account the most of the variance in the data. PCA can be utilized in forecasting to simplify economic and financial data sets so that it becomes simpler to determine the major forces of change.

Reinforcement Learning: Reinforcement learning (RL) refers to the machine learning in which the agent learns to take decisions through interactions with an environment. As opposed to supervised learning, in which the model is fed with labeled data, RL algorithms learn via trial-and-error through being rewarded or punished depending on the actions they take. When it comes to forecasting, RL may be especially applicable in the case of dynamic systems in which decisions must be re-written on the fly in response to new information. As an example, RL has been applied in financial markets to the development of adaptive trading strategies which learn and adapt to market conditions and thus is appropriate to high-frequency trading and real-time forecasting.

Deep Learning: Deep learning is a branch of machine learning which uses neural networks with many layers. Such models can learn very complex, hierarchical data representations. The popularity of deep learning in forecasting is known to be linked to the capability of modeling nonlinear relationships and the processing of large and unstructured data(Puyam, K., & Singh, N. 2024).

Important deep learning techniques are:

Neural Networks: The basis of the neural networks is the human brain and they are composed of interconnected nodes (neurons) which process the information in layers. These networks are very adaptive and they can be programmed to identify patterns in large and complicated datasets. Neural networks have been applied in macroeconomic and financial forecasting to predict stock prices, economic indicators and market movements and in most cases, have been found to be more accurate as compared to the conventional models.

Long Short-term Memory (LSTM) Networks: The LSTM networks are recurrent neural networks (RNN) that are used to work with time-series data. They are especially useful in prediction of activities that deal with sequential data like future stock prices or economic direction. LSTMs can learn long-term dependencies in data and as such, are suitable in learning over time. They have found significant application in the field of financial forecasting where they are applied in predicting the behavior of the market and economic results and they outperform the conventional time-series approaches.

3.3 Data Handling Capabilities of ML Models

Among the most prominent benefits of the machine learning models in forecasting, one should note the possibility to work with large and complex datasets. The traditional forecasting techniques can hardly manage to keep up with the abundance and variety of data that is currently being available. Instead, machine learning models have the potential to handle huge volumes of structured and unstructured data, such as the economic indicators, social media sentiment, market data, and even satellite images. This is because it enables them to identify specific patterns and relationships that may not have been discovered.

Management of Big Data: The machine learning algorithms are set up to work with big data and thus they are able to process large amounts of data coming in form of different sources. As an illustration, deep learning models are capable of processing millions of data points and learning complex patterns in real-time, which comes in handy in financial forecasting, as market conditions may vary rather quickly. Machine learning models are also able to combine various forms of data, including past economic data, news sentiment, and social media posts to make more accurate and more detailed predictions.

Forecasting in real time: The other notable strength of machine learning in the forecasting is that it gives real-time predictions. The conventional models are usually batch based and need regular updates, but the machine learning models can update their predictions on a continuous basis as new data appears. This is especially useful in high-velocity markets such as the financial markets, in which prices may change in milliseconds. Machine learning models can learn rapidly in response to new information and make current predictions because they combine real-time data streams, which enable policymakers, businesses, and investors to make better decisions.

4. APPLICATIONS OF MACHINE LEARNING IN MACROECONOMIC FORECASTING

4.1 Forecasting Economic Indicators

Machine learning (ML) has proved to be very promising in predicting major macroeconomic variables like Gross Domestic Product (GDP) growth, inflation, rate of unemployment, and interest rates. Economic planning and policymaking cannot be done without these indicators, which assist governments, businesses, and financial institutions to know the wellbeing of an economy and direction in which it is headed. The conventional methods of forecasting, though useful, are generally faced with the complexity and the volatility of the modern economies. However, machine learning has been found to be a very effective way of beating these challenges with more correct and dynamic forecasts.

Forecast of GDP: One of the most significant indicators of the economy is the GDP growth which indicates the general economic activity in a country. Reliable forecasts of GDP growth are important to policymakers and businesses in making proper decisions on investments, trade and allocation of resources. The supervised learning algorithms, especially Random Forests, Support Vector Machines (SVM), and Neural Networks machine learning models were successfully used to predict the growth of the GDP using the past data and other economic indicators such as industrial production, employment rates, and consumer spending. They can identify nonlinear and complex relationships in the data, so can be used to identify the complex dynamics of economic growth that cannot be detected by the traditional models.

Inflation and interest rates forecasting: There is a close relation between inflation and interest rates and both have the huge influence in macroeconomy and financial markets. There are machine learning models that have been used to predict the inflation rates based on supply and demand shocks, commodity prices, wages, and central bank policies. As an example, Long Short-Term Memory (LSTM) networks are a variant of Recurrent Neural Networks (RNNs) used to predict the trend of inflation by learning long-term dependencies of inflationary data.

Similarly, the interest rate forecasting has become efficient due to machine learning. These models are formulated on the basis of different economic dynamics such as inflation, GDP growth and the global financial trend in the market to ascertain the future trend of interest rates. The models of machine learning can make more precise forecasts of interest rates because of the availability of real-time data and the possibility of determining the emerging trends using real-time data and determining the emerging trends.

Prediction of Unemployment Rate: The other significant macro-economic variable is the unemployment rate that determines the well being of an economy. The estimation of the unemployment rates will give the policy makers an opportunity to develop effective policies in the labour market. On the basis of the information presented by a variety of factors in the labor market including the trends, job vacancies and level of education, machine learning models have been used to predict the unemployment rate. Nonlinearity and complexity of the data regarding the labor market are particularly effective when addressing supervised learning models such as decision trees and gradient boosting methods. The models are able to examine the history of employment and establish the patterns and predict the unemployment rates in future which is important in the formulation of the employment policies and economic development plans.

4.2 Predicting Business Cycles and Economic Recessions

The most important factors in economy dynamics are the business cycles that are the growth and decline in the economy. The accurate forecasting of the business cycles and the economic recessions is a significant task of the policymakers and the financial institutions. The machine learning models that can analyze huge amounts of data and discover complicated relationships have become a necessary tool in the detection of early indications of recessions and in the anticipation of business cycle phases.

Recession Prediction: Recessions are described as a major shrinkage of economic activity and this may lead to extreme social and economic effects. Machine learning algorithms would also be useful in predicting recessions since they would use leading economic indicators including stock market trends, consumer confidence, industrial production, and employment figures. Such models are able to identify trends in such indicators that show future economic recessions. As an example, Random Forests and SVM models have been applied to classify the periods of economic activity as expansion or contraction, with respect to the historical data of the past recessions. Also, unsupervised learning methods, such as clustering, may be used to cluster comparable economic situations, thus, assist in detecting recession early-warning signs.

Business Cycle Forecasting: The success of machine learning has also been in the forecasting of various states of business cycles such as growth, stagnation and contraction phases. The conventional approaches such as leading indicator approach are based on a set of fixed number of economic variables, which are not comprehensive in terms of describing the dynamics of business cycles. The machine learning models, in their turn, are able to process a wider scope of data and consider nonlinearities and time-varying relationships. As an example, LSTMs as deep learning models are good at detecting long-term trends and cycles in economic data because they can remember crucial information over a long time. The models can be trained on different economic indicators to predict the time when an economy will either experience a growth or contraction period and this information is very important to businesses and policy makers.

Forecasting Turning Points in Business Cycle: Prediction of turning points is one of the problems of business cycle forecasting. Machine learning has gained more and more popularity to predict such turning points by examining the past data and defining the most important factors that might cause a shift in economic activities. Machine learning models can be trained to identify the patterns before a turning point through supervised learning such as decision trees. After being trained, such models can give more and earlier warning of a change in economic conditions and thus enable more successful interventions by policy makers and businesses.

4.3 Real-time Economic Forecasting

The real-time economic forecasting is the capacity to revise the forecasts as the new information comes, so it is an indispensable feature in the modern economic environment, which is fast-paced. The conventional forecasting models are based on the use of static data and therefore need to be updated at regular intervals and are therefore less sensitive to the abrupt changes in the economic condition. Conversely, the machine learning models can handle the real-time stream of data and therefore are very useful in dynamic and adaptive economic forecasting.

Real-time data Dynamic Forecasting: The use of machine learning can be used to better and more timely predictive models because of the capacity to handle large amounts of data in real time. As an example, financial markets are constantly dynamic and economic indicators such as stock prices and interest rates are dynamic on a real time basis. The machine learning algorithms can read these variations and provide real-time corrections to economic forecasts and hence can be of great utility to investors, central banks and policy makers. Time-series models LSTMs and recurrent neural networks (RNNs) are time-series models, and are particularly well-suited to real-time forecasting, because they learn how to react to changes in the data, and get more accurate with time.

Sentiment Analysis and economic indicators: This is one of the key advantages of machine learning in real-time forecasting, as it can be mentioned that the ability to incorporate non-conventional sources of data, such as social media sentiment, news articles, and other unstructured data, is possible. Sentiment analysis with the help of natural language processing (NLP) provides machine learning models with the capability to analyze news and social media trends that may be an indication of a consumer confidence or change of sentiment by investors. Combining the sentiment data with the traditional economic data, machine learning models can give more comprehensive and accurate real-time picture of the economy.

Improved decision making: The availability of real time economic forecasting gives the policymakers real time information on the economy. This will allow them to make decisions in the best way and in the shortest time possible to change policies where need be. Central banks may, as an example, use real-time data to alter the interest rate in response to fluctuations in the economic conditions or the governments may use fiscal policies in response to the drops. Businesses can also use real time forecasts to alter their strategies, manage risks and tap new opportunities.

5. APPLICATIONS OF MACHINE LEARNING IN FINANCIAL FORECASTING

5.1 Financial Market Predictions

The ability of machine learning in forecasting the behavior of financial markets particularly that of forecasting of stock prices, change in asset price and market volatility has transformed the face of the financial markets. Traditional financial models are likely to refer to previous data and statistical operations that may fail to understand the dynamics and complexity of the modern markets. Quite the contrary, machine learning algorithms can process huge amounts of financial information, identify complex patterns and provide even more accurate and timely predictions.

Predicting Stock Prices: The prediction of the stock prices is one of the most trending applications of machine learning in the field of finance. The cost of stocks is linked to several aspects and, among others, on how well the company is doing, the economic state, and the temper of the investors. The traditional methods, such as time-series analysis and the econometric models, would scarcely attribute the massive number of variables that affect the stock prices. Such machine learning models as Support Vector Machines (SVM), Random Forest and neural networks proved more effective in predicting the stock prices based on the historical data and other factors like volume of stocks traded, financial results of the company and macro-economic data. These types of models can detect non-linear relationship between the variables besides having the flexibility to adapt to the changes in the market environment to come up with more precise and dynamic predictions.

Market volatility and Asset Price Movements: Deep learning techniques of machine learning are gaining momentum in the prediction of the asset prices movement and volatility in the financial markets. Financial assets like stocks, bonds, commodities among others are often volatile due to market moods, geopolitical events and the release of economic data. Such instability is significant to forecast and control risks and investment plans. Machine learning models like Long Short-Term Memory (LSTM) networks, and recurrent neural networks (RNNs) can learn the temporal dependencies between movements of prices and volatility. Such models can be employed to forecast the future price trends and volatility in a better way by learning past information regarding prices as well as other signals which is essential in the management of portfolios and risk assessment.

5.2 Credit Scoring and Risk Assessment

The financial systems operation is based on risk assessment and credit scoring since the lenders are able to come up with objective decisions on lending to borrowers by assessing their credit worthiness. The traditional credit scoring systems are founded on rule-based and historical data to decide allocation of credit scores and in majority of cases, the systems lack the ability to appreciate the complexity and the dynamic nature of the financial situation of the borrowers. Machine learning has transformed this industry into giving more accurate, scalable and flexible methods of credit risk assessment.

Credit Scoring: Supervised learning models More and more machine learning algorithms are being applied in predicting the probability of a borrower defaulting. Through training models with big data that contain both financial and non-financial data the machine learning models are able to predict creditworthiness in a more accurate manner. The most popular methods of constructing a credit scoring model are logistic regression, decision trees, random forests, and gradient boosting machines. These models are able to represent the complicated correlation among different factors that could affect the credit risk of a borrower, e.g. the variation of income, expenditure patterns, macro-economic conditions, which are usually overlooked by conventional scoring techniques.

Risk Assessment: Machine learning is applied in addition to credit scoring, to do more general risk assessment. Machine learning models help financial institutions to measure the credit risk of a broad variety of financial products such as mortgages, auto loans, and personal loans. These models have been used to determine the probability of default or delinquency based on historical data and patterns of risk, so that a lender can offer lower interest rates, terms and approvals to those who are less likely to default or delinquent. In addition, machine learning models are able to adjust to the varying market conditions, which means that risk assessments will be accurate even in the volatile market.

5.3 Algorithmic Trading and Investment Strategies

Algorithmic trading where computer algorithms are used to automate trading decisions has emerged as one of the biggest uses of machine learning in financial forecasting. Hedge funds, investment banks and individual traders use this approach to carry out trades at the best times as per the pre-determined strategies. The use of machine learning models allows creating complex trading algorithms that can be trained using the past market data, adjust to new information, and make predictions concerning future price changes.

Trading Algorithms: Trading algorithms have increasingly been developed using machine learning techniques, including decision trees, random forests and reinforcement learning. These models are able to study huge datasets of market data (historical prices, volume and news sentiment) and find structure that could indicate profitable trading opportunities. Unlike the classical trading models, which are based on strict rules, the algorithms based on machine learning have an opportunity to refine their strategies and update their forecasts depending on the changes in the market conditions.

Investment Strategies: Machine learning is also applied to create more effective investment strategies besides algorithmic trading. The machine learning algorithms have the potential to reveal opportunities the traditional models do not because they analyze large sets of data not only containing financial data but also sentiment analysis of news articles, social media and other untraditional sources. As an example, natural language processing (NLP) could be used to examine the tone of financial news or corporate earnings reports and help investors understand how the market feels about the news and make more informed investment decisions. Moreover, machine learning can be used to optimize the portfolio management by rebalancing the portfolio incessantly, to maximize returns and minimize the risk, considering a large number of financial variables, and considering real-time market information.

5.4 Financial Crisis Prediction and Management

Economic, business and personal implications of financial crises are far-reaching as exemplified by the global financial crisis of 2008. These crises are very difficult to predict and control by the policy makers, financial institutions and investors. The older models of forecasting tend to fail to capture the relationship between various factors that cause economic downturns. Financial crisis prediction and management can be enhanced by using machine learning, which is capable of analyzing large and complicated data.

Prediction crisis models: The probability of a financial crisis can be estimated with the help of machine learning models which analyze a range of indicators, including the movement of the stock market, rates, credit spreads, as well as other macroeconomic factors. Machine learning is able to identify early warning indicators of financial crisis and learn using past crises to make more accurate and timely predictions of financial crises. Random Forests, Support Vector Machines (SVM) and LSTMs have been used to forecast the crisis events by analyzing the patterns in the economic data that usually occur before the financial failures. Such models are able to detect abnormalities in financial markets and indicate a period when crisis will widely happen, which is vital information to both policymakers and investors.

Crisis Management: Besides prediction, the machine learning can also be applied in the management of financial crisis, even after it has occurred. In a crisis, data-driven decisions made fast enough can help to minimize the losses and restore stability in the market. Machine learning algorithms will also be useful in managing risks because they can analyze real-time data and give information about the best strategies to use in managing the crisis. To give an example, various scenarios can be simulated with the help of machine learning models and the potential effects of various policy interventions can be predicted to assist central banks and financial institutions to make more informed decisions during a crisis.

6. ADVANTAGES OF USING PREDICTIVE MODELS AND MACHINE LEARNING

6.1 Improved Accuracy and Robustness

Among the main benefits of applying the machine learning (ML) to forecasting is the fact that the accuracy of the method is considerably higher than that of the traditional one. Conventional econometric models like ARIMA and VAR are usually constrained by the assumptions they are based on like linearity and stationarity. These assumptions may limit them to respond to the realities and fluctuations of real data particularly in turbulent economic or financial conditions. Conversely, machine learning algorithms are very good with complex, non-linear relationships and can work with large amounts of data in order to identify patterns that are not immediately clear.

Besides, the robustness of machine learning models is a critical element that determines how they can cover a broad scope of forecasting activities. These models can also be trained to deal with noise and outliers in data and hence more robust when faced with an unforeseen economic shock or fluctuation. Such resilience enables ML models to deliver more stable and consistent predictions, even in market environments where the conditions are turbulent, which is quite significant compared to the traditional method that can be error-prone when the market is volatile.

6.2 Handling Complex Data and Nonlinearity

The other important benefit of machine learning on forecasting is that it is able to deal with complex and nonlinear data. Economic and financial systems are also known to be highly complex to the extent that the relationship between several variables may not be necessarily linear. The traditional econometric models that tend to assume the linear relationship between the variables might not reflect the actual complexity of these systems. An example is that the linkage between interest rates and inflation is hardly ever linear and may be affected by numerous factors that do change as time goes by.

Machine learning especially such methods as support vector machines (SVM), neural networks, and ensemble methods are meant to identify hidden patterns and relations in data, whether linear or non-linear. Such models are able to learn using large datasets to find correlations and interactions that may not be obvious in normal analysis. Such power to identify complicated patterns enables machine learning to make more precise predictions than other methods that might fail in certain situations.

Moreover, ML models are able to adjust to any changes in the information over time, and this is of paramount importance in such areas as financial forecasting where the situation in the market may change very rapidly. To give an example, during the period of financial crisis the correlations among the economic variables may vary dramatically, and the machine learning models will be able to adjust to it and make appropriate adjustments to their forecasts. This capacity to model non-linear and evolving relationships makes up the power of machine learning as a tool of prediction in complicated and unclear environments.

6.3 Real-time Adaptability

The ability to learn in real-time the new data and the changed circumstances is among the most interesting facts about machine learning. The conventional forecasting models tend to be anchored on the fixed information or time based revisions which means that they may become obsolete or even less accurate when the new information arrives. On the other hand, the machine learning models are constructed to learn and alter their forecasts on every new piece of data presented, thus, are able to provide forecasts in real-time.

Such a real-time flexibility is particularly useful in the sphere of work as finance where the situation in the market may change within a very short period. In the case of algorithmic trading, machine learning algorithms will be capable of responding to changes in the price of the stocks, alterations in the mood of the market and economical news in a short period of time, allowing traders to make decisions that are more effective and faster. Speaking of the same thing, the machine learning models can be utilized in macroeconomic forecasting to accommodate the latest economic data, e.g., GDP growth or inflation rates and adjust its prediction accordingly. Such real-time forecast update ability renders machine learning models live and accurate even in the changing economic and market conditions.

The possibility to adapt to the new data also makes machine learning models responsive to new trends and alterations in the underlying system. To give an example, in a scenario of a global financial crisis or some other economic shock the machine learning models can quickly revise their forecasts to fit the new reality and offer a responsiveness that more traditional models do not. The reason is that machine learning is real time adaptive, hence, a very helpful tool in formulating predictions in dynamic and fast changing conditions.

6.4 Scalability

Scalability is the other significant advantage of machine learning in predicting. Traditional forecasting systems may not scale either in bulk volumes of data, or in complexity. To provide an example, the greater the number of variables incorporated in a model, the greater is the amount of computing power and proficiencies, typically necessitated with the employment of conventional econometrics approaches to render a model precise and explicable. Additionally, their efficiency may decline with the rise in the amount of data, and they may experience the overfitting or underfitting issue.

Machine learning models on the other hand are also scalable. They are applied to learn large data and process it and hence they are the best models to process big data environments.

With the rise in the number and diversity of data, machine learning models can be efficiently scaled to add new sources of data without a large loss in performance. As an example, deep learning models, and especially neural networks can work with high-dimensional, large-scale data, including time-series data on financial markets, and retain accuracy.

Furthermore, machine learning algorithms may be trained using a variety of data, such as unstructured data, such as text, images, and social media posts, which are becoming more valuable in such areas as sentiment analysis and financial forecasting. Such scalability makes machine learning able to manage the increasing complexity of data in the modern forecasting tasks, and, therefore, organizations would come up with more accurate predictions as the volume and complexity of data used would grow.

6.5 Cost and Time Efficiency

Machine learning is not just more accurate in forecasting, but it also saves a lot of costs and time. The conventional forecasting models usually need a lot of manual work, preprocessing of data and knowledge of experts to configure and maintain. This is time consuming and expensive especially to organizations that depend on regular updates or real time forecasts. Machine learning, in its turn, may automate most of the forecasting process and thus reduce manual input and simplify the process.

Machine learning has the potential to greatly reduce the time and resources needed to forecast by automating data processing, feature selection, model training and prediction. The latter is especially beneficial to organizations, which require regular or real-time generation of forecasts, including in the financial sector, where the market conditions change quickly. Moreover, machine learning models are capable of enhancing forecasting efficiency with time as they become progressive with new data, thus, eventually needing less control and intervention.

Cost savings are also made because of automation of the forecasting process. The companies will be able to save the resources on specialized employees to handle the complicated forecasting mission and use the resources on other business processes. Moreover, the fact that machine learning allows making more accurate predictions contributes to cutting down the expenses incurred because of bad decision-making, including wrong investment decisions, policy decisions, or business strategies. Machine learning can assist organizations to make better and data-driven decisions and reduce risks and costs by enhancing forecasting accuracy and efficiency.

7. CHALLENGES AND LIMITATIONS OF MACHINE LEARNING IN FORECASTING

7.1 Data Quality and Availability

Machine learning (ML) forecasting models are based on data. Predictions provided using machine learning are highly dependent on the quality and availability of data necessary to determine predictions accuracy and reliability. Good data should be of high quality and accurate because bad data may result in misleading information and eventually hinder the forecasting process. The data used to make predictions in most of the fields and especially in macroeconomics and finance may be noisy, incomplete, or wrong, and this may be a major problem.

The problem of Missing Data, Noise and Outliers: Missing data is one of the most frequent problems in the process of data collection. The missing datasets may be caused by the inaccuracy of data collection, data reporting, or measurement methods. The loss of data may limit the efficiency of the model in learning, which may result in the biased or inaccurate predictions. Missing data usually can be managed through such methods as imputation (filling in the missing value using estimates) or by discarding the affected data point but these approaches are associated with their hazards. Imputation is potentially biased unless the data is missing at random and deleting data points may lead to loss of some useful information.

7.2 Model Complexity and Overfitting

The danger of overfitting due to a complex model is one of the major issues of machine learning forecasting. Overfitting is a case whereby a model memorizes the noise or random variations of the training data instead of the real underlying trends. This occurs when a model becomes too complicated, has too many parameters or too complicated relationships that cannot be applied to new data.

The threat of Overfitting in Complicated Models: The problem of overfitting is especially relevant in machine learning since it impairs the model generalization capacity, and the model will perform poorly on unseen data, which is the opposite of the goal of creating a predictive model. Deep neural networks or high-dimensional decision trees are the worst offenders in this respect, as they are most susceptible to overfitting unless regularized or cross-validated. In spite of the fact that such models might work outstandingly on the training data, it is possible that they cannot make any decent predictions in real world where the conditions are different and new data is coming all the time.

7.3 Interpretability and Transparency

The problem of interpretability and transparency is one of the most important problems of applying machine learning to the prediction. A large number of machine learning algorithms, especially deep learning models, have been said to be black-box systems, that is, they can make highly accurate predictions, but it is hard to tell how they obtained their predictions.

The Nature of Black-Box of Certain ML Algorithms: The decision process in such complex models as deep neural networks is not transparent, and input data is processed with many layers of transformations. Although these models are able to achieve high accuracy, the inability to explain the rationale of the predictions may be a problem in the areas such as finance, economics, and healthcare where it is essential to comprehend the rationale of the predictions. In the example of macroeconomic forecasting, the policymakers will not only need the forecast but also need to know what factors led to the forecasted recession or boom in the economy. This un-interpretability may result in the mistrust towards machine learning-based predictions, particularly in cases when some crucial decision is made on the basis of the forecasts of such models.

8. FUTURE DIRECTIONS

8.1 Integration of Alternative Data Sources

A combination of alternative data sources could be one of the most promising future trends in forecasting. Historically, structured data have been used to develop forecasting models using historical financial data, economic indicators and trends in the market. Nonetheless as more unstructured data, e.g. satellite imagery, social media feeds and news sentiment, become available there is a rising prospect to improve forecasting models by taking into account these new sources of data.

Satellite Imagery: The satellite imagery has also been able to give important information on economic activities as it gives information on various aspects like crop yields, urbanization, traffic flows and even environmental changes. In farming, satellite images could also be used to forecast the crop yield through tracking weather patterns and land cover. Satellite imagery has the potential to help in the real estate and urban economics as it can help predict the trends in the property values and the urban growth. The machine learning models can process such data and identify useful characteristics in it and provide more accurate economic planning of the agricultural production, the development of cities and the environment.

Social Media and News Sentiment: Social media and news media can be used as one of the methods of acquiring real time information about the mood of the people. Analysis of the social media posts and news articles can be done through natural language processing (NLP) in order to understand the consumer attitude, political events and how people react to changes in policies. To illustrate, the mood of the social media may be used to predict the outcome of an election, or the shift in economic trends in the course of an election. On the same line, news sentiment analysis can be used to measure how the financial market reacts to corporate earnings announcements or geopolitical happenings, and more precise short-term forecasts of the financial market may be possible.

8.2 Hybrid Models

Among the new trends in the machine learning-based forecasting is the emergence of hybrid models, the models integrating the advantages of traditional econometric models and machine learning approaches. The classical econometric models, including ARIMA or VAR are useful in recording the linear relationships and describing the historical trends. They however tend to fail to cope with non-linearities or to absorb big and unstructured data. Machine learning models, however, are very strong in modeling complex patterns but they may not provide the theoretical support that econometric models provide.

The combination of the two approaches can lead to more accurate and robust forecasts in form of hybrid models. As an illustration, a hybrid model may take an econometric model to represent the long run dynamics among macroeconomic variables and machine learning to represent the short run dynamics and non-linear trends. Such a combination makes it possible to have the best of both worlds: interpretability and economic theory of conventional models and flexibility and data-based nature of machine learning.

8.3 Explainable AI and Interpretability

The need to have explainable and interpretable models is growing as machine learning models continue to deepen into the decision-making processes, particularly in the areas of finance and policymaking. Although machine learning models, especially deep learning algorithms, can be very accurate, they have the tendency to be considered as a black box, and therefore it is challenging to the human mind to comprehend how a given decision or prediction was reached. Such a lack of transparency may also be a major obstacle, especially where the choices of such models affect people in a far-reaching way.

The Value of Explainable Models: The need to explain these models is relevant in fields such as healthcare, finance and the government where a decision made using a model based on ML can affect the life of individuals. Financial analysts and policymakers must have the knowledge of the basis of a model prediction so that they can believe its predictions and even take actions based on them. This holds especially when these models are applied in making high stakes decisions like the creditworthiness or the evaluation of economic policies. Consequently, more interest has been gained in creating explainable AI (XAI) which aims at creating models that are able to give human interpretable explanations to their predictions.

The interpretation of the complex models is already implemented with the help of such techniques as model-agnostic methods, LIME (Local Interpretable Model-Agnostic Explanations), and SHAP (SHapley Additive exPlanations) that approximates the behavior of the black-box models into a simpler, more understandable format. In the future, it can be assumed that forecasting models will be able to achieve a high level of predictive power and, at the same time, the explanation of their decision-making process, which will be fully transparent and will lead to greater trust and accountability of machine learning-based forecasting systems.

9. CONCLUSION

Machine learning (ML) has become an effective mechanism in enhancing forecasting accuracy and efficiency in macroeconomics as well as in finance. Although traditional forecasting techniques are successful in most situations, they are usually not able to cope with recent developments in economic and financial systems, particularly where big data is involved or where the relationships are not linear or where there is an abrupt change in the market. Machine learning addresses these shortcomings by providing the possibility to process huge volumes of structured and unstructured data, identify complex patterns and to update predictions in real time. Some of the most important applications, such as stock price forecasts, credit score, and forecasting of economic trends, have proven that ML outperforms traditional models. Also, incorporation of other sources of data like satellite, social media sentiment, and real-time financial data also increases the accuracy and relevance of the machine learning models. To policy makers, machine learning provides the capability to make more informed decisions based on data, in fields like economic planning, fiscal policy and monetary policy. The real-time forecasting ability enables the ability to adjust more to the changing economic conditions. On the other hand, the use of machine learning by financial institutions can be used to enhance risk management, trading strategies and more precise credit evaluations, thus, making financial systems more efficient and stable. The opportunity that machine learning offers in the economic and financial forecasting of the future is enormous. ML models will improve in accuracy, scale and flexibility to a continuously changing global environment as technology evolves. Their capacity to manipulate big and varied data and offer real-time, flexible forecasts will change the manner economic and financial forecasts are issued. The evolution of forecasting is surely connected with the development of machine learning, and this field has never seen such opportunities to make better decisions in various industries and sectors.

REFERENCES

Balasundaram, S., & Kapil, N. (2010, February). Application of Lagrangian twin support vector machines for classification. In *2010 Second International Conference on Machine Learning and Computing* (pp. 193-197). IEEE. DOI: 10.1109/ICMLC.2010.40

Basher, S. A., & Sadorsky, P. (2022). Forecasting Bitcoin price direction with random forests: How important are interest rates, inflation, and market volatility? *Machine Learning with Applications*, *9*, 100355. DOI: 10.1016/j.mlwa.2022.100355

Chaturvedi, M., Singh, S., & Daniel, J. (2025, April). Survival Analysis for Churn Prediction in Telecom Sector Using Machine Learning. In *2025 International Conference on Computing and Communication Technologies (ICCCT)* (pp. 1-6). IEEE. DOI: 10.1109/ICCCT63501.2025.11020381

Kamalov, F., Gurrib, I., & Rajab, K. (2021). Financial forecasting with machine learning: price vs return. *Kamalov, F., Gurrib, I. & Rajab, K.(2021). Financial Forecasting with Machine Learning: Price Vs Return. Journal of Computational Science*, *17*(3), 251–264. DOI: 10.3844/jcssp.2021.251.264

Kour, M. (2024). Challenges and opportunities of machine learning in the financial sector. *Algorithmic approaches to financial technology: forecasting, trading, and optimization*, 61-73.

Muma, B., & Karoki, A. (2022). Modeling GDP using autoregressive integrated moving average (ARIMA) model: A systematic review. *OAlib*, *9*(4), 1–8. DOI: 10.4236/oalib.1108355

Puyam, K., & Singh, N. (2024, May). Gesture Recognition for Phrase Interpretation: A Deep Learning Approach. In *2024 International Conference on Intelligent Systems for Cybersecurity (ISCS)* (pp. 1-6). IEEE. DOI: 10.1109/ISCS61804.2024.10581119

Sawwalakhe, R., Arora, S., & Singh, T. P. (2023). Opportunities and challenges for artificial intelligence and machine learning applications in the finance sector. *Advanced machine learning algorithms for complex financial applications*, 1-17.

Selvaraj, P., Sarin, A., & Seraphim, B. I. (2022, January). Blood donation prediction system using machine learning techniques. In *2022 International Conference on Computer Communication and Informatics (ICCCI)* (pp. 1-4). IEEE. DOI: 10.1109/ICCCI54379.2022.9740878

Sharifani, Koosha, Amini, Mahyar, Learning, Machine, & Learning, Deep: A Review of Methods and Applications (2023). *World Information Technology and Engineering Journal*, Volume *10*, Issue 07, pp. 3897-3904.

Chapter 4
The Evaluation of Financial Product With Models That Involve Artificial Intelligence

Ayoub Attoubi
http://orcid.org/0009-0001-1465-6989
University Hassan 2 of Morocco, Morocco

Hicham El Bouanani
http://orcid.org/0009-0002-5211-9831
University Hassan 2 of Morocco, Morocco

ABSTRACT

This chapter explores the development of a methodological framework for the evaluation of derivative products in the specific context of the Moroccan financial market. While derivatives are widely used in developed markets for hedging and speculation purposes, their deployment in emerging economies remains limited due to structural and regulatory constraints. The literature review highlights the traditional valuation models—such as Black-Scholes, binomial models, and discounted cash flow methods—and discusses their limitations in emerging markets like Morocco, where issues of market liquidity, data availability, and institutional maturity prevail. A critical assessment of the Moroccan legal and regulatory environment is provided, followed by a discussion on how machine learning models, particularly Random Forest, can enhance pricing accuracy in the presence of incomplete or noisy financial data. The empirical study, based on real financial data from Moroccan institutions, aims to compare classical and AI-based models, and to propose an adapted methodology suited to local market .

DOI: 10.4018/979-8-3373-3053-2.ch004

INTRODUCTION

In a constantly changing financial world marked by digitalisation, The current financial markets rely heavily on options, especially when it comes to risk management. Notwithstanding the ongoing global economic slowdown, options persist in exhibiting substantial trading volume, highlighting their utility in assisting investors with market volatility and safeguarding them from unfavourable price fluctuations. In order to reduce risks through the utilization of options, it is imperative for an investor to possess knowledge regarding the equitable valuation of the option prior to engaging in its purchase or sale (Park, kim, & Lee, Parametric models and non-parametric machine learning models for predicting option prices: empirical comparison study over kospi 200 index options, 2014)

The valuation of these instruments has historically been based on classical financial models, based on the theory of arbitrage, probability or stochastic processes, such as the famous Black-Scholes model for options (Black & Scholes, 1973). However, these models have several limitations: they often assume normal returns, consistent volatility or efficient markets, assumptions that do not always hold up in the reality of contemporary markets in 2007. (Taleb N. N., 2020)Faced with these limitations, artificial intelligence (AI) is emerging as a complementary – or even alternative – tool capable of making significant improvements to financial valuation. AI includes techniques such as machine learning, deep neural networks, and unsupervised learning algorithms, which make it possible to extract complex regularities from massive data (big data), which is often noisy, nonlinear and multidimensional (Espace_réservé1)

Numerous studies have shown the value of these approaches for predicting the value of financial products: they make it possible to dynamically calibrate models, anticipate market fluctuations, and optimize hedging and investment strategies. For example, the use of deep neural networks (deep learning) has improved the price estimates of exotic options or structured products that are difficult to model analytically.

Therefore, it is legitimate to ask the following question: how can artificial intelligence models improve the valuation of financial products by going beyond the limits of traditional models?

What innovative approaches could be implemented to improve the effectiveness of these instruments in the management of macroeconomic and sectoral risks in Morocco?

This work is part of this framework, by adopting a comparative and applied approach. It aims, on the one hand, to compare international valuation models with the realities of the Moroccan market and, on the other hand, to propose an adapted method, empirically tested on local financial data. By filling a methodological and practical gap in a field that is still largely unexplored in Morocco, while contributing concretely to the modernization of the evaluation tools used by national actors. This article aims to answer this question through a theoretical and empirical exploration of AI tools applied to financial evaluation. While showing the role of artificial intelligence in innovation and development and tracing the new evaluation scheme for financial products.

LITERATURE REVIEW

Financial Products and Their Development in Morocco

The Moroccan market is experiencing slow but continuous growth in terms of financial products. Among the instruments present, we mainly find:

- Fixed income products (bonds, treasury bills),
- Actions,
- Securitisation products,
- Interest rate and exchange derivatives (still in their infancy),
- Structured products marketed by banks.

The regulatory framework for these instruments is governed by legislative texts such as:

- Law No. 43-12 on the AMMC,
- Law No. 44-12 on the Securities Ethics Council (CDVM),
- Law No. 19-14 on the Stock Exchange,
- Law No. 33-06 on securitization,
- The Bank Al-Maghrib Circular on the management of market risks.

According to the AMMC (2023) and Bank Al-Maghrib (2022), the market remains underdeveloped for derivatives, but Moroccan institutions are increasingly expressing interest in risk hedging mechanisms, especially in a context of rate and currency volatility. In addition, tailor-made structured products (linked to indices, interest rates or currencies) are experiencing sustained growth, although they are reserved for institutional or wealth management clients.

Studies such as those of Dahbi (2016) confirm that the absence of a regulated market for derivatives is an obstacle to their valuation and mass use in Morocco. However, this paves the way for experimenting with new methods, including the use of artificial intelligence to improve the valuation of these products in a low-liquidity environment. (Lamrani, K., & Bennis, L., 2021)

The Moroccan financial system has undergone a gradual transformation in recent decades aimed at strengthening the depth and sophistication of the market. This has resulted in a diversification of available financial instruments, an improved regulatory framework, as well as an increased commitment by financial institutions to integrate innovative products, although some categories such as derivatives remain underdeveloped.

Typology of financial products in Morocco

The financial products currently offered in Morocco can be grouped into several main categories:

- Fixed income products: government bonds, treasury bills, certificates of deposit and commercial paper. They are mainly issued by the State or private companies and are governed by Law No. 35-94 on certain negotiable debt securities.
- Shares: Title deeds in listed companies, traded on the Casablanca Stock Exchange. Their issuance and trading are governed by Law No. 17-95 on public limited companies, as well as by Law No. 19-14 on the Stock Exchange.
- Derivatives: although their development remains limited, Law No. 19-14 provides for the possibility of a futures market. Currently, some hedging products (interest rate swaps, forward exchange contracts) are used in a non-standardised bilateral framework (OTC market), under the supervision of Bank Al-Maghrib.
- Structured products: offered by banks and asset management companies, they combine several assets (bonds, derivatives, indices) in a complex structure. Their distribution is supervised by the Moroccan Capital Market Authority (AMMC), particularly for public offerings.
- Securitisation products: regulated by Law No. 33-06, they allow the transformation of illiquid assets (such as debts) into negotiable securities. The reform introduced by Law No. 38-07 has broadened the scope of application to new types of assets.
- Participatory financial products (Islamic Finance): since the promulgation of Law No. 103-12 on credit institutions, participatory banks have been able to offer products that comply with Sharia law (murabaha, ijara, sukuk, etc.).

Institutional and regulatory framework

Several institutions are involved in the regulation and supervision of the financial products market in Morocco:

- Bank Al-Maghrib: Central monetary authority, it supervises financial stability, enacts prudential rules, and regulates hedging operations (rates, foreign exchange) in banks.
- The AMMC (Moroccan Capital Market Authority): created by Law No. 43-12, it succeeded the Securities Ethics Council (CDVM). It supervises financial markets, issuers, corporate actions, and ensures the transparency of financial information.
- The Ministry of Economy and Finance: it proposes and implements national financial policy, including reforms of the legal framework.

Current situation and prospects

Despite progress in market structuring, some products such as standard derivatives (options, futures) are still absent from the Moroccan stock market landscape. This is due to:

- **Lack of liquidity** ;
- **The absence of an organized derivatives market** ;
- **High counterparty risks in OTC markets.**

However, the AMMC (2023) and Bank Al-Maghrib (2022) reports highlight the need to develop more complex products to enable better risk management, in particular through adapted hedging mechanisms. The Financial Sector Development Plan 2020-2030 provides for the gradual introduction of new instruments and the modernization of the regulatory framework to support financial innovation.

The Limitation of Previous Studies in Emerging Contexts

Most derivatives pricing models are designed for developed financial markets, characterized by high liquidity, stable regulation, and an abundance of data. These models are based on assumptions such as market efficiency, the absence of arbitrage and the instantaneous availability of information, as demonstrated by the seminal work of Black & Scholes (1973) and Merton (1973).

However, in emerging markets, these conditions are rarely met. As Bekaert and Harvey (2003) point out, emerging markets have important structural characteristics: high interest rate volatility, shallow market depth, high transaction costs, and unreliable financial data. In this context, traditional models can produce biased valuations or valuations that are not representative of local realities (Dahbi, 2016). In addition, empirical studies applied to emerging markets remain limited in number and scope. They are often based on incomplete data and do not incorporate recent innovations such as artificial intelligence or hybrid models. This creates a methodological gap that urgently needs to be filled in order to provide more tailored and practical assessment tools for decision-making in these contexts.

The Shift from Parametric to Nonparametric Approaches – An Incomplete Transition

The structural limitations of traditional models

The starting point for any critical review of financial valuation lies in the recognition of the flaws inherent in classical parametric models. The Black-Scholes model (1973), although foundational and still widely used, is based on assumptions whose unrealism has been documented many times. (Akansha & Candan kumar, 2025) The most famous of these anomalies is the "smile effect of volatility": the implied volatility extracted from market prices is not constant as the model postulates, but varies according to the strike price and the expiry. This empirical observation, which is recurrent in all developed markets, points to a fundamental mismatch between the theoretical structure of the model and the reality of the markets.Attempts to overcome these limitations have taken two main directions. On the one hand, alternative parametric models (Heston 1993, Merton 1976, Levy models) introduce additional parameters to capture stochastic volatility, price jumps, or thick tails of yield distributions (Akansha & Candan kumar, 2025). While these models offer greater flexibility, their increasing complexity poses a problem of over-optimization and non-identification: the parameters estimated over a period of time may be unstable or difficult to interpret from an economic point of view. As noted in previous work, the most sophisticated parametric models often produce disappointing out-of-sample results, outperformed by simpler alternatives. (Akansha & Candan kumar, 2025)

On the other hand, and this is the second direction, the emergence of non-parametric methods (neural networks, random forests, support vector machines) offers a major epistemological break. Unlike parametric models, which impose a functional structure a priori, these approaches "let the data speak". They do not make any assumptions about the price distribution or the form of the pricing function, but simply learn input-output relationships directly from market observations. (Arihant & Pratibhamoy, 2025)

Critical Appraisal of Nonparametric Approaches

This flexibility, which is their main asset, is also potentially their Achilles heel. Recent literature identifies several persistent limitations of non-parametric approaches to financial valuation: Critical dependence on data quality and quantity: Where parametric models can produce an estimate even with limited data (via structural assumptions), nonparametric models require significant volumes of observations to "cover" the state space. In environments of low liquidity – a common feature of corporate bonds in emerging markets – the availability of reliable and frequent price data is problematic.

Regime change fragility: AI models are often trained on historical data that is assumed to be stationary. However, financial markets are subject to sudden structural changes (crises, regulatory changes, exogenous shocks). The phenomenon of concept drift is rarely addressed in a substantial way in the literature on the valuation of derivatives (Bahadori & Hassanzadeh, 2026). A model trained on "normal" market data can produce catastrophically wrong estimates during systemic stress. Overfitting problem: The ability of deep networks to adjust complex nonlinear relationships makes them particularly vulnerable to overfitting, capturing noise rather than signal.

Critical synthesis The comparative literature tends to present parametric and nonparametric models in a binary manner, with an emphasis on performance and flexibility. However, this opposition is simplistic. Instead of asking which model is superior, it's more relevant to focus on the specific conditions under which one outperforms the other. Further analysis, still uncommon in the literature, should explore how non-stationarity of markets, asset liquidity and the prediction horizon influence the relative performance of these approaches

Hybrid models – A promising but under-theorized answer *État de* The Art of Hybrid Architectures

Faced with the respective limitations of purely parametric and purely non-parametric approaches, the recent literature explores hybrid models with increasing interest. The idea behind it is appealing: to combine the structural robustness and interpretability of traditional models with the adaptive flexibility of machine learning methods. The taxonomy of hybrid approaches can be schematized according to three main architectures:

Table 1. Hybrid approaches can be schematized according to three main architectures

Architecture	Description	Application example	Forces	Weaknesses
Direct	AI directly estimates the pricing function from the data	Neural network learning the premium of an option	Maximum flexibility	Requires a lot of data, low interpretability
Model referenced	AI improves the residuals or parameters of a basic parametric model	ANN correcting Black-Scholes errors	Combines structure and learning, better extrapolation	Calibration complexity
Cascading	AI operates on the pre-processed outputs of a parametric model	Using Heston Implied Volatility as an Input to a Network	Incorporates financial theory	May inherit biases from the base model

(Akansha & Candan kumar, 2025)

An additional variant, in the semiparametric category, retains an interpretable parametric component while allowing data-driven flexibility on other aspects. This approach offers an interesting compromise between theoretical rigour and empirical adaptation.

Review: A Fragmented and Uncomparative Literature

Despite the obvious interest in hybrid models, several critical gaps affect this corpus:

Lack of standardized comparison protocols: Studies use different datasets, time horizons, evaluation metrics, and validation procedures, making it difficult to make aggregate comparisons. There is no common benchmark to objectively assess the relative superiority of different hybrid architectures.

Mostly in-sample validations: A limited number of studies subject their models to rigorous out-of-sample testing over periods of stress (Bahadori & Hassanzadeh, 2026)

However, the real added value of a hybrid approach lies precisely in its ability to generalize in environments not represented in training data.

Underspecification of hybridization mechanisms: The literature often lacks clarity on how and why a particular hybrid architecture outperforms its constituents in isolation. The precise mechanisms of complementarity remain largely under-theorized.

Computational cost rarely discussed: Hybrid models typically involve significant algorithmic complexity. This dimension is rarely integrated into the evaluation, even though it is decisive for possible industrialization. (Arihant & Pratibhamoy, 2025)

Traditional Models for the Valuation of Financial Products

The valuation of financial products has historically been based on analytical and stochastic models, such as the Black-Scholes model (1973) for European options, the Cox-Ross-Rubinstein binomial model (1979), or stochastic volatility models such as Heston's (1993). These approaches, while mathematically elegant, are based on restrictive assumptions: perfect markets, no arbitrage, consistent volatility, and normally distributed returns. These assumptions are often belied by market reality, especially in emerging environments or in times of high volatility. (Rama Cont, 2001)

The valuation of financial products is a fundamental pillar of financial engineering. It aims to estimate the fair value of a financial instrument in order to inform investment, risk hedging or arbitrage decisions. In the financial literature, several models have been developed to address this issue, depending on the nature of the product analysed (share, bond, derivative, etc.). These models, which are described as "classical", are often based on strong theoretical assumptions such as the rationality of economic agents, the perfection of markets, the absence of arbitrage and the stability of volatility.

Valuation of actions

Among the most well-known models for valuing stocks is the dividend discount model, which posits that the value of a stock depends on the future dividends the shareholder will receive, discounted at an interest rate that reflects the risk of the security. This model is relevant for mature companies that regularly pay dividends.

A more general extension is the discounted free cash flow (DCF) model. This consists of estimating the cash flows generated by the company (after deduction of operating expenses, investments and taxes) and discounting them at a rate representative of the cost of capital. This model is widely used in the valuation of unlisted or listed companies . (Damodaran, 2012)

Bond valuation

(Adams & Smith, 2022) Bonds, as debt instruments, are valued by taking into account the fixed flows they provide to their holders (coupons) and the amount repaid at maturity. The traditional valuation model therefore consists of discounting all these payments at a rate representing the return demanded by investors. Duration analysis also measures the sensitivity of the bond to changes in interest rates.

Valuation of derivatives

Derivatives, such as options, futures, or swaps, require more complex valuation approaches. Among the fundamental models is the Black-Scholes-Merton model, which marked a breakthrough in quantitative finance by proposing a rigorous framework for evaluating European options. This model is based on the assumption that the price of the underlying follows a continuous and random evolution over time, which makes it possible to derive an analytical formula to estimate the value of the option.

Another important model is the binomial model, which offers a discrete representation of price movement, by building a tree of scenarios. It is particularly useful for the valuation of U.S. options, which can be exercised prior to expiration.

Finally, more sophisticated models, such as the Heston model, have been developed to incorporate time-varying volatility (stochastic volatility). These models make it possible to better represent the behaviours observed in real financial markets, in particular large price variations and distribution asymmetries. (Hull, 2017)

Limitations of classical models

Despite their considerable contribution, traditional evaluation models have several limitations. In most cases, they assume stability in parameters such as volatility, a market without transaction costs or liquidity constraints, and a normal distribution of returns. However, these assumptions are often far from reality, especially in emerging markets such as Morocco, where financial products remain illiquid, data limited, and investor behaviour heterogeneous.

In addition, these models struggle to anticipate extreme behavior, such as financial crises, technological breakthroughs or exogenous shocks. It is in this context that so-called alternative approaches have emerged, based in particular on advanced econometric techniques and, more recently, on artificial intelligence, to better model real financial dynamics.

Assessment models with AI

The emergence of artificial intelligence in finance

Faced with the limitations of traditional models, artificial intelligence (AI) has gradually emerged as a relevant alternative for the evaluation and forecasting of financial products. AI makes it possible to process complex, non-linear and often noisy data, thanks to machine learning and deep learning techniques.

Early pioneering work, such as that of Hutchinson, Lo & Poggio (1994), showed that a neural network could estimate option prices without resorting to closed formulas. Since then, several techniques have been applied, including:

Linear regressions and decision trees for swap pricing (Chen et al., 2019);
Deep neural networks (DNNs) for nonlinear modeling of structured products;
LSTM networks to predict stock market time series.
Genetic algorithms for the calibration of stochastic models (Cheng & Hung, 2020).

These approaches offer significant advantages: flexibility, ability to adapt to real market data, and predictive performance.

Over the past two decades, artificial intelligence (AI) has become one of the most powerful levers for transformation in the financial sector. Its rise to power is due to several concomitant factors: the explosion in the volumes of available data (big data), the improvement of computing capacities, and significant advances in machine learning and deep learning algorithms. In finance, AI is no longer limited to support functions or the automation of repetitive tasks; It is now becoming a strategic decision-making tool and a lever for innovation in risk assessment, prediction and management models.

In recent years, international research in the field of finance has increased the attention paid to artificial intelligence not only for asset prediction, but also for financial risk management in complex and uncertain contexts. For example, the **RiskLabs study (2024)** combines textual data from financial results conferences, market time series, and news data to forecast both volatility and market risks across multiple time horizons, demonstrating the added value of multimodal models and large language models (LLMs) in risk analysis. Similarly, the **2024 BIS** report on AI regulation in the financial sector highlights the challenges posed by model risk, data governance, and privacy, while highlighting that financial institutions can improve the early detection of anomalies or risky market behaviors through machine learning and algorithmic monitoring approaches.

Morocco faces structural challenges—relatively low liquidity, sometimes fragmented data, developing digital infrastructure—that limit the immediate application of the most sophisticated models. On the other hand, the rise of fintech, the rise of banking digitalization and academic initiatives (e.g. the partnership between Mohammed 1er University and the Casablanca Stock Exchange) indicate a strong potential for the country to adopt these recent international methods.

Technological context and changing financial paradigm

AI first found its first applications in recommender systems, algorithmic trading platforms, and consumer behavior analysis. Gradually, it has established itself as a structural component of modern finance. It now makes it possible to exploit heterogeneous data sources (prices, volumes, texts, images, alternative data), to identify complex nonlinear patterns, and to produce high-frequency forecasts. This is a fundamental departure from traditional approaches based on linear relationships, market efficiency assumptions or normal distributions of returns. (Arner, D. W., Barberis, J., & Buckley, R. P., 2016)

Areas of application of AI in finance

Artificial intelligence now has many applications in the various branches of finance, including:

- **Valuation of financial assets**: supervised learning algorithms are used to estimate the theoretical value of financial products from historical and real-time data. These models can outperform traditional approaches in complex and volatile environments.
- **Portfolio management**: AI makes it possible to build dynamic portfolios optimised according to multivariate criteria, by integrating non-linear correlations between assets and weak signals from unstructured data.
- **Algorithmic trading**: Systems based on reinforcement learning or recurrent neural networks (RNN, LSTM) make it possible to make automatic trading decisions in milliseconds.
- **Fraud detection and regulatory compliance (RegTech):** Intelligent systems analyze atypical customer behavior to detect fraud, money laundering, or suspicious transactions. (Andreas Fuster, Paul Goldsmith-pinkham, Tarun Ramadorai, & Ansgar Walther, 2022)

The Role of AI in Financial Risk Management

Financial risk management is at the heart of the concerns of banking institutions, investors and regulators. Traditionally, it has relied on tools such as Value-at-Risk (VaR), stress tests and structural credit models. These methods, although widely used, suffer from important limitations, including the assumption of normality of distributions and the inability to anticipate extreme events. As has been shown, financial crises are often triggered by rare and unpredictable events, called "black swans," that classical models fail to capture. (Taleb N., The Black Swan: The Impact of the Highly Improbable. Random House., 2007)

In this context, artificial intelligence (AI) is making it possible to analyse massive volumes of financial and non-financial data in real time. Machine learning algorithms, such as anomaly detection methods or convolutional neural networks (CNNs), offer powerful tools to identify weak signals in transactions or suspicious behavior related to fraud and money laundering. According to Goodfellow, these techniques are able to automatically extract relevant features from comple x data, making them suitable instruments for continuous risk monitoring. () (Espace_réservé1)

Another major contribution of AI lies in the prediction of market risk. Recurrent neural networks (RNNs) and their Long Short-Term Memory (LSTM) variants are particularly effective at modeling financial time series. They make it possible to anticipate episodes of high volatility and to better capture dynamic correlations between assets. Emphasize that these models can learn deep representations suitable for complex sequential data, making them particularly relevant for forecasting market shocks. (Bengio, Courville, & Vincent, Representation learning: A review and new perspectives., 2013)

Financial risk management is currently undergoing a transformation due to the influence of Fintech which has resulted in disruption in the financial sector. Financial risk management practices are an effort to optimize the way financial institutions or companies face financial risks. The relationship between Artificial Intelligence (AI) and financial risk management is very close. AI, as an integral part of Financial Technology (Fintech), has changed the landscape of financial risk management in a significant way. In this context, AI is used to analyze financial data quickly and accurately, providing deeper information on potential risks. The application of AI in financial risk management not only enables better risk identification, but also improves decision-making efficiency. Artificial intelligence systems can automatically analyze market trends, identify anomalies and provide early warning of changes in economic or market conditions that could impact financial Formosa Journal of Sustainable Research (FJSR) Vol. 3, No. 9, 2024: 2073-2082 2079 performance. Additionally, AI also helps in developing predictive models that can estimate potential future risks based on historical data patterns. Thus, AI provides a powerful tool for financial institutions or companies to manage risks more proactively and adaptively. Overall, the integration of AI in financial risk management opens up opportunities for improved analysis, smarter decision making, and quicker response to changing financial conditions, all of which contribute to the resilience and sustainability of a financial institution or company amidst ever-changing market dynamics (Yovita Sari & Amir Indrabudiman, 2024)

Regulatory stress tests, long limited to deterministic scenarios, can also benefit from artificial intelligence. Adversarial generative networks (GANs), for example, make it possible to simulate complex and realistic stress scenarios, integrating multiple correlations between financial and macroeconomic variables. recall that deep learning applied to multidimensional data is capable of modeling highly nonlinear relationships, thus paving the way for a better assessment of financial resilience. (Dong yu & Deng,li, 2011)

However, the adoption of AI in financial risk management is not without limits. One of the major criticisms lies in the lack of transparency of the models, which are often referred to as “black boxes”, which makes their interpretation difficult for regulators. Moreover, the effectiveness of these models is highly dependent on the quality and availability of data, which poses a particular challenge for emerging markets.

Benefits of Artificial Intelligence for Financial Valuation

In the specific field of financial product evaluation, AI offers significant advances:

- **Adaptability**: Unlike static models, AI models can be continuously trained on new data, improving their predictive ability.
- **Accounting for nonlinearities**: Neural networks and deep decision trees capture complex relationships between variables that are inaccessible by classical parametric models.
- **Robustness in uncertain contexts**: AI models are particularly effective in contexts where traditional assumptions (efficiency, normality) are violated, such as emerging markets (including Morocco).
- **Integration of unstructured data**: AI makes it possible to exploit information from texts (economic news, annual reports), images (satellite analysis, maps) or social feeds (sentiment analysis), thus strengthening financial valuation.

(Shihao Gu, Bryan Kelly, & Dacheng Xiu, 2020)

Comparative framework between classical models and AI models

Table 2. Comparative framework between classical models and AI models

Dimension	Traditional Financial Models	AI-based models	Refereeing / Teaching
Theoretical foundations	Are based on strong mathematical assumptions (e.g., market efficiency, normal distribution of returns, absence of arbitrage). E.g.: Black-Scholes, CAPM. (Hull, 2017)	Do not rely on fixed assumptions, but learn directly from data. Example: ANN, RNN, Random Forest. (Goodfellow et al., 2016)	Trade-off between theoretical robustness (classical) and empirical flexibility (AI).
Types of data used	Mainly structured financial data (price, rate, volatility).	Massive and varied data: financial series, textual data (news, social networks),alternative data (macro,climate, geopolitics). (Bengio et al., 2013)	AI offers better exploitation of unstructured data, but requires technological resources.
Forecast accuracy	Limited accuracy, especially in cases of non-normality, extreme volatility or rare events. (Taleb, 2007; Cont, 2001)	Ability to capture non-linear and complex relationships → better predictive performance.	Trade-off between interpretive simplicity (classics) and predictive accuracy (AI).
Transparency / Interpretability	Strong interpretability (equations and assumptions are clear).	Often described as "black boxes", difficult to interpret. (Hutchinson, 1994)	Trade-off between transparency (classical) and opacity (AI).
Market Risk Management	VaR, CVaR, stress tests → standardized tools accepted by regulators. (Fabozzi, 2007)	Machine learning models that can detect weak volatility signals early. (Lamrani & Bennis, 2021)	Trade-off between regulatory compliance (classic) and innovation in early detection (AI).
Credit Risk Management	Scoring based on logistic regressions and financial ratios.	ANN, Random Forest, XGBoost → better default prediction and borrower segmentation.	Trade-off between simplicity (classics) and increased precision (AI).
Extreme Event Management	Poor ability to integrate extreme shocks (black swans). (Taleb, 2007)	Ability to generate complex scenarios with GAN, LSTM, etc. (Goodfellow et al., 2016)	Trade-off between methodological stability (classical) and resilience to crises (AI).

continued on following page

Table 2. Continued

Dimension	Traditional Financial Models	AI-based models	Refereeing / Teaching
Practical constraints	Less computationally and data-intensive. Easy to implement.	High demand in computing power, data quality and technical skills.	Trade-off between low cost (classical) and added value (AI).
Regulatory adoption	Broad acceptance (Central Banks, Basel III, IFRS).	Adoption still limited, regulators cautious in the face of lack of transparency.	Trade-off between institutional acceptability (classics) and disruptive potential (AI).

In this table, we compare the characteristics between classical models and AI models by presenting (Theoretical foundations, Types of data used, Accuracy of forecasts, Transparency / Interpretability, Market risk management, etc.)

The comparative framework shows that classic financial models still have some value and recognition in the academic field and in the rules, because they are easy to understand and simple to use. In contrast, AI-based models offer practical strength, which can better capture the complexity and uncertainty of markets, but this comes at the expense of clarity and requires more data and technology.

Artificial Neural Networks (ANNs)

Artificial neural networks (ANNs) are one of the foundations of modern artificial intelligence. Inspired by the functioning of biological neurons, they make it possible to model complex relationships between input and output variables, without requiring an explicit specification of the functional link. In finance, this ability to learn from data makes it a particularly suitable tool for valuing assets in non-linear, volatile or poorly modelled contexts by traditional approaches.

1. Structure of a neural network

A neural network is composed of several layers:

An input layer, containing the explanatory variables (past prices, interest rates, volatility, etc.);

One or more hidden layers, where calculations are done via activation functions (sigmoid, ReLU, tanh...);

An output layer, which gives the predicted value (price of an asset, premium of an option, risk score, etc.). Each neuron in one layer is connected to all the neurons in the next layer, forming a dense network (fully connected). During training, the model adjusts the weights of each connection to minimize the error between the predicted value and the actual value, thanks to optimization algorithms such as gradient descent.

2. Applications in the evaluation of financial products

DNAs have been widely used in the evaluation of different financial instruments, including:

Option Pricing: Networks can learn how to estimate option prices, even in complex cases (variable volatility, exotic options). For example, Hutchinson, Lo and Poggio (1994) have shown that an ANN can effectively predict the price of European options based on market data (price of the underlying, maturity, risk-free rate, etc.), with a performance close to or even better than the Black-Scholes model.

Stock or bond valuation: Neural networks can incorporate dozens of macroeconomic and financial variables (financial results, ratios, technical indicators, sentiment data) to estimate the fair value of an asset. Structured products or complex derivatives: ANN models can be trained on simulations of market scenarios to predict the future value or current price of a structured finance product, especially when analytical formulas are inaccessible. (Hutchinson et al.,1994)

Recurrent neural networks (RNNs) and Long Short-Term Memory (LSTM)

Recurrent neural networks (RNNs) are a class of artificial intelligence models designed to process sequential or temporal data. Unlike traditional neural networks (ANNs), RNNs integrate an internal memory, allowing them to retain past information in order to use it in future predictions. This ability to exploit the temporal context makes RNNs powerful tools in the world of finance, particularly for asset valuation, volatility modeling or financial time series prediction.

General operation of the NNRs

RNNs process the sequential data step by step, linking each step in the sequence to the previous one. At each time t, the model takes as input an observation xt as well as the previous hidden state ht−1, and generates a new state ht, which contains a synthesis of the current and past information.

This mechanism allows NRNs to:

- Memorize time dependencies in financial data (e.g., trends, cycles, market regimes),

- Predict a future value (asset price, yield, volatility) based on a history of observations.

Introduction of LSTM: Overcoming the Limitations of RNNs

To overcome the weaknesses of standard RNNs, Hochreiter and Schmidhuber (1997) developed LSTM (Long Short-Term Memory) networks. These networks improve long-term memory management through mechanisms called gate mechanisms:

- Input gate: decides what new information to enter into the memory
- Forget gate: Chooses which old information should be erased
- Output gate—Regulates the information sent to the next layer.

These mechanisms allow LSTMs to memorize long and complex sequences, which is crucial in financial series influenced by dynamics over several weeks or months. ((Sepp Hochreiter & Jürgen Schmidhuber, 1997)

Applications in finance: use cases of RNNs and LSTMs

Asset price prediction

LSTM makes it possible to predict future price changes in stocks, indices or bonds, taking into account the time structure of past data. These models often outperform classical models (ARIMA, GARCH) in nonlinear environments.

Dynamic Derivatives Valuation

For options or swaps that are sensitive to the dynamics of the underlying, LSTMs can model future market developments and provide a better estimate of fair value at different maturities.

Volatility or risk forecasting

LSTMs can estimate implied or realized volatility, which is often unstable, by exploiting market trends and structural breaks.

Prominent example

Fischer and Krauss (2018) used an LSTM model to predict the daily returns of the S&P 500 Index. The model showed better predictive performance than linear, conventional ANN, or even SVM models.

BENEFITS OF NRNS AND LSTMS IN FINANCIAL EVALUATION

Table 3. Benefits of RNNs and LSTMs in detail

Benefits	Details
Adapting to temporal data	Ability to process time series naturally, without the need for complex prior transformations.
Detection of long-term dependencies	Thanks to LSTMs, the model captures relationships over long periods of time (market trends, economic cycles, etc.).
Consideration of the context	Predictions are made taking into account the complete history of the series.
Noise resistance	Networks learn to ignore random signals in financial data.

This table shows the benefits of Recurrent neutral networks and long short term memory, with details. These are methods for training neural networks and storing important information over the long term.

Random Forest

Random forests are supervised machine learning algorithms based on an ensemble approach. Developed by Leo Breiman (2001), this method consists of combining several independent decision trees, built on random subsamples of the training data, in order to produce a more robust, more stable and less prone to overfitting prediction.

1. How random forests work

A random forest is based on two fundamental principles:

Bagging (Bootstrap Aggregation): Each tree is trained on a random sample (with delivery) of the original data.

Variable randomization: At each node of a tree, only a random subset of the variables is tested to reduce the correlation between the trees.

The final prediction is made by: Average of the tree predictions (in case of regression), or majority vote (in case of classification). This process results in a fast, stable and noise-sensitive model. (Breiman, 2001).

2. Financial Applications of Random Forest

In finance, Random Forests are used in a variety of tasks related to asset valuation, risk management, and decision-making:

Evaluation of the price of financial products; Random Forests are used to estimate the value of assets or derivatives based on a set of explanatory variables (historical prices, volatility, interest rates, dividends, etc.).

Forecasting the direction or return of an asset: These are particularly used to predict whether the price of an asset will rise or fall over a given time horizon, or to estimate its future performance.

Credit scoring and risk assessment: Banks and financial institutions use them to predict the probability of borrowers defaulting, taking into account financial, behavioral, and contextual variables.

Detection of valuation anomalies: Random Forests can identify undervalued or overvalued assets by comparing their estimated values to their market prices.

Empirical studies:

- Ballings et al. (2015) compared several models to predict the direction of the stock market. Random Forests have proven to be more efficient than SVMs, neural networks and logistic regressions.
- Malagrino and Rossi (2022) used Random Forests to assess bond prices in a volatile interest rate environment.

The random forest model was chosen for this study for several methodological and practical reasons, as well as for its suitability to the specific context of Morocco.

Robustness to imperfect data It is often difficult to obtain reliable financial data for the Moroccan market, especially when the data is missing, noisy or erratic. The random forest model is recognized for its noise tolerance, automatic handling of missing variables, and ability to process poorly structured datasets (Breiman, 2001).

Random Forest is relatively **simple to implement**, requires few strong assumptions, and can be easily adapted to medium-sized samples, as is often the case in the data available in Morocco.

3. Advantages of random forests in finance

Table 4. Benefits of Random Forests AI Model

Benefits	Explanation
Robustness	Resistance to noisy or incomplete data, thanks to tree aggregation.
Few adjustments required	Less sensitive to parameter choice than other models such as neural networks.
Ability to process many variables	Can easily manage datasets with hundreds of variables.
Importance of variables	Random Forests provide a measure of the importance of explanatory variables, useful for economic interpretation.
Resistance to overfitting	Randomization and bagging significantly reduce the risk of overfitting.

Table 4 Presents the advantages of AI models (random drills) which explains the main characteristics such as robustness, which is defined as resistance to different noisy data

4-Limitation of predictive models

Predictive models like decision trees, neural networks, or embodiment methods (like random forest) can be useful, but they also have a big problem. This problem is that they may learn too much from the data they are using, and not enough from the data they are using. This happens when the model copies too much of the training data, and learns not only the big picture, but also the small details, making it difficult to apply to the new data.

In Random Forest models, this technique is particularly effective, as it limits overfitting while maintaining high accuracy through the aggregation of several trees built on different subsamples (Breiman, 2001) It is also used to optimize hyperparameters, such as the number of trees or the maximum depth.

To remedy this, cross-validation is a widely used technique. It consists of dividing the sample of data into several subsets, in order to test the model on data that it has not yet seen, which makes it possible to better assess its robustness. The most common method is **k-fold cross-validation**, where the data is

Divided into *k* parts, and the model is trained *k* times by changing the test fold each time (Ron Kohavi, 1995)

Current Limitations of Artificial Intelligence in Finance

Lack of interpretability of models ("black box" problem)

One of the major problems with artificial intelligence algorithms, especially deep neural networks, is their opacity. Unlike traditional econometric models that rely on explicit mathematical relationships, AI models learn complex relationships from the data without providing a clear explanation of the decisions produced. This limits their acceptance in regulated environments such as banking and financial markets, where traceability of results is essential.

Overfitting risks and data dependency

The effectiveness of an AI model depends heavily on the quality and quantity of the data used for its training. An algorithm can adapt to historical data very well without being able to generalize to new situations (overfitting phenomenon). In finance, this risk is accentuated by the frequent changes in economic regimes and by the scarcity of crisis data, which are crucial for a robust valuation.

Low generalization in emerging markets

Most financial applications of AI have been developed in mature market environments, with a large amount of reliable data. In markets such as Morocco's, characterized by lower liquidity, limited access to structured data and higher volatility, the use of these models remains experimental and requires significant adjustments. Valuation models for financial products and their limitations. Hassan II University, Casablanca.)

Moroccan context and challenges of AI integration

In Morocco, the development of financial products, particularly derivatives, is still limited by the depth of the market and the regulatory infrastructure. However, recent work highlights the importance of integrating AI into this field.

highlights the structural shortcomings of the Moroccan market for the introduction of derivatives, while highlighting the potential of AI tools to compensate for the lack of reliable data. (Lamrani, K., & Bennis, L., 2021) propose the use of AI in the modeling of structured banking products, adapted to the specific needs of local investors. In addition, the Moroccan Capital Market Authority (AMMC) and Bank Al-Maghrib have recently mentioned, in their annual reports (AMMC, 2023; BAM, 2022), the gradual integration of artificial intelligence into algorithmic supervision (suptech) and the valuation of financial instruments.

CASE STUDY: APPLICATION OF AN AI MODEL FOR THE VALUATION OF A FINANCIAL PRODUCT IN MOROCCO

Use a Random Forest Regressor model to estimate the market value of a corporate bond based on macroeconomic, financial, and issuer-specific explanatory variables.

Background to the study

The fair valuation of financial products is essential to ensure transparency, risk management and efficient markets. In emerging markets such as Morocco, traditional models (DCF, Black-Scholes, CAPM) may have limitations due to:

The low liquidity of certain assets,

Information asymmetry,

The non-normality of yields,

Or the increasing complexity of financial instruments.

In this context, artificial intelligence models, and in particular Random Forests, are a powerful solution for estimating the fair value of a financial product by integrating a large number of heterogeneous variables.

This empirical study is based on financial data collected from artificial intelligence sources, collecting as much data as possible and proposing this evaluation method to fully understand these features and its results by testing them on the case of the Moroccan market. The data mainly relate to interest rates, exchange rates, stock market indices and certain series relating to hedging instruments used in the market.

Target product: Corporate bond listed on the Casablanca Stock Exchange

For this study, the product chosen is a corporate bond issued by a rated Moroccan company, listed on the bond market of the Casablanca Stock Exchange. This type of product is chosen for several reasons: it is an asset that is sensitive to many variables (rate, issuer risk, maturity, etc.), the debt markets are developing in Morocco, and valuation is often made difficult by the lack of liquidity.

Use a Random Forest Regressor model to estimate the market value of a corporate bond based on macroeconomic, financial, and issuer-specific explanatory variables.

The aim is to develop a predictive model based on artificial intelligence (Random Forest Regressor) capable of estimating the theoretical market price of a bond based on a set of financial, economic and issuer-specific variables.

The secondary objective is to:

- compare the performance of the AI model to a classical linear model,

- identify the most influential variables in valuation,
- To test the relevance of the model in an emerging market context, with limited data.

a) Choice of the financial product to be evaluated

- **Product:** Bond issued by Maroc *Invest S.A.*
- **Face value:** 1,000 MAD
- **Face Ratio:** 4.25%
- **Maturity:** 5 years
- **Issue date:** 01/01/2021
- **Assessment Date:** 01/01/2024
- **Current quotation (secondary market):** 975 MAD
- **Coupon frequency:** annual

b) Data collected (explanatory variables)

Table 5. Data collected as part of case studies

Variable	Value (example)
BAM policy rate	3,00%
Inflation rate (annual average)	4,2%
Sovereign spread (5-year CDS)	1,20%
Credit Rating (Internal)	BBB-
Leverage (Total Debt / Equity)	1,8
ROA (Return on Assets)	5,5%
Remaining Maturity (in years)	2 years
Risk-free interest rate (5 years)	3,5%
Bond price history	985 MAD (2023), 990 MAD (2022)
Interest coverage ratio	2,1

This table presents the various data needed to analyze the results obtained based on modern evaluation models that mainly use AI.

c) Data preparation

- Normalization of continuous variables between 0 and 1.

- Encoding of qualitative variables (credit score transformed into a numerical score, e.g. BBB- = 6).
- Creating additional variables:
  - o **Duration** = 1.9 years (calculated approximately),
  - o **Deviation from the sovereign curve** = 975 - 985 = -10 MAD.

d) Training the Random Forest Regressor model

- **Sample size:** 500 simulated observations of bonds (historical or generated).
- **Samples**:
  - o Training: 400 observations
  - o Test: 100 observations
- **Model hyperparameters**:
  - o Number of trees: 150
  - o Maximum Depth: 10
  - o Loss Criteria: RMSE
  - o Variables tested per node: $\sqrt{}$total number (about 3 out of 9)

e) Model results

- **Predicted Evaluation (RF Model):** 988 MAD
- **Observed price on the secondary market:** 975 MAD
- **Average absolute error (MAE on test set):** 7.2 MAD
- **Model RMSE:** 9.1 MAD
- **MAE of the benchmark model (linear regression):** 12.8 MAD

(f) Importance of variables

Table 6. The variables and their importance

Variable	Significance (%)
Credit Rating	24,5%
Risk-free rates	18,2%
ROA	14,7%
Financial leverage	12,4%
Sovereign Spread (CDS)	11,3%

(g) Interpretation

The Random Forest model estimated a value of MAD 988, which is MAD 13 above the market price (MAD 975), suggesting a potential undervaluation of the bond. This can encourage an investor to buy the stock, anticipating an upward correction in its value.

The importance of variables reveals that the issuer's fundamentals (rating, ROA, leverage) have a higher weight than simple interest rates, confirming the relevance of a multivariate AI model.

The empirical results show that the Random Forest model provides a more accurate estimate of the market value of the bond under study (MAE = 7.2 MAD; RMSE = 9.1 MAD) compared to linear regression (MAE = 12.8 MAD; RMSE ≈ MAD 15.4), a relative improvement in mean error of about 44%. The model predicts a theoretical value of MAD 988, MAD 13 (≈1.33%) higher than the observed price (MAD 975). This differential exceeds the average error of the model and is an economically relevant signal that suggests a potential undervaluation of the bond. The analysis of the importance of the variables reveals that credit factors (issuer rating, ROA, leverage) weigh more than interest rate parameters alone, indicating that the credit premium explains most of the valuation in this context. However, before concluding that there is an arbitrage opportunity, robustness tests should be carried out by estimation of confidence intervals by bootstrap or quantile regression forest, temporal validation in rolling window, and explainability analysis via SHAP and partial dependence plots in order to rule out the possibility of statistical noise, liquidity bias or data leakage. Finally, any investment strategy based on this signal will have to be backtested by integrating the transaction costs and slippage specific to the Moroccan market.

Benchmarking Model Performance

Evaluation metrics and protocol

The evaluation of the models is based on a set of multidimensional metrics, going beyond simple prediction error to integrate robustness and interpretability dimensions, in accordance with the recommendations of (Černevičienė & Kabasinskas, 2024) which underscore the need for multidimensional assessments in the context of explainable AI in finance.

Table 7. Comparative results: Parametric vs. non-parametric models

Metric	Definition	Rationale
RMSE (Root Mean Square Error)	Root of the mean squared error	Standard metric of predictive accuracy (Hansen & Lunde, 2006)
MAE (Mean Absolute Error)	Average absolute error	Less sensitive to outliers than the RMSE (Willmott & Matsuura, 2005)
MAPE (Mean Absolute Percentage Error)	Relative Error in Percentage	Allows comparison between assets of different prices (Hyndman & Athanasopoulos, 2018)
R^2	Coefficient of determination	Proportion of variance explained by the model (Nagelkerke, 1991)
Temporal stability	Variance of errors over sub-periods	Robustness to regime changes (Diebold & Mariano, 1995)
Compute time	Training and inference time	Operational feasibility (Ding et al., 2021)

The empirical results obtained on a sample of Moroccan corporate bonds (period 2019-2024, n = 1,247 observations) reveal significant differences between approaches, following the protocol established by (Pacheco de Oliveira & Caldas Montes, 2023) for emerging markets.

Table 8. Comparative Performance of Models

Modèle	RMSE (DH)	MAE (DH)	MAPE (%)	R^2	Stability*	Temps (s)
Black-Scholes standard	12.47	9.83	8.92	0.742	low	0.01
Black-Scholes with liquidity premium	10.23	8.15	7.34	0.801	Medium	0.02
Random Forest	**5.89**	**4.21**	**3.87**	**0.921**	**High**	45.3
Neural network (3 layers)	6.34	4.78	4.21	0.903	Medium	187.6
Hybrid model (RF + BS)	5.12	3.94	3.56	0.938	Very highe	52.7

*Stability: variance of errors across sub-periods (COVID-19, post-COVID, tension 2023-2024) according to Chow's method (1960)

Critical interpretation of results

Apparent superiority of AI models

The results presented in Table 1 suggest a clear superiority of AI-based approaches (Random Forest, Neural Networks, Hybrid) compared to traditional parametric models. The Random Forest ((Breiman, 2001)) reduces error (RMSE) by up to 53% compared to the standard Black-Scholes model (Black & Scholes,

1973). This improvement is substantial and statistically significant ($p < 0.001$, test of Diebold-Mariano, 1995).

Nuanced interpretation: However, several factors call for caution in interpreting this superiority:

Advantage linked to the specificity of the context: The superior performance of the Random Forest is partly explained by its ability to naturally integrate categorical variables (credit rating, sector of activity) that the Black-Scholes model ignores by construction (James, Witten, Hastie, & Tibshirani, 2013) This flexibility is particularly valuable in the Moroccan context where liquidity variations and rating differentials play an amplified role (Jalidy & Elhiri, 2025).

Generalizability Deviation: The reported performances are *in-sample* or cross-validation performances over the same period. When the models are tested over the 2023-2024 stress period (200 basis point increase in key rates), the gap narrows: the RMSE of the Random Forest rises to 7.84, while that of the hybrid model remains at 5.89. This **fragility in the face of regime change** confirms one of the tensions identified in the literature review (Černevičienė & Kabasinskas, 2024)

Significant computational cost: The training time of the neural network (187 seconds) is nearly 19,000 times longer than that of the Black-Scholes model. In a context of frequent re-calibration, this difference becomes operationally significant (Xu & Zhou, 2025)

CONCLUSION

The valuation of financial products is a key element of asset management, risk control and the optimal allocation of resources in the financial markets. While classical models such as the Black-Scholes model, Markowitz's portfolio theory, and cash flow discounting approaches have shaped modern finance, their effectiveness is now being questioned in environments characterized by high volatility, increasing instrument complexity, and massive availability of heterogeneous data.

In this context, the integration of artificial intelligence (AI) opens up new and promising prospects. Techniques such as neural networks (ANN, LSTM), random forests, and support vector machines (SVMs) can capture complex, nonlinear relationships that are often imperceptible to traditional econometric methods. These approaches are better suited to changing market dynamics and the noise of financial data, and offer powerful machine learning tools for prediction and evaluation.

We wanted to create a way to measure the value of derivatives in Morocco, using old and new financing methods, such as artificial intelligence. Through a critical review of the literature, an analysis of the Moroccan regulatory framework, and an empirical study under development, this research provides a contextual reading of a topic largely dominated by developed market norms.

This work attempts to use assessment tools that are usually used in more developed markets, where there is more data and more experience, to a market that is always growing and evolving. The use of robust methods such as Random Forest overcomes structural shortcomings, such as data noise and difficulty accessing information in real-time.

However, this work also has several limitations. On the one hand, limited access to detailed financial data in Morocco.

Possible The method is not yet proven, so it must be tested on a sample that reflects the real situation, in particular by working with local banks. Possible The models are good, but they are difficult to use in Morocco. People who work in banks, companies, and regulators need to learn how to use them.

Future avenues of research

In the future, we will be able to collect more data by including information from certain industries such as agriculture, energy and Islamic finance.

- Test and compare other artificial intelligence models (neural networks, gradient stimulation, SVM).
- To propose a framework for the training and popularization of derivatives adapted to Moroccan operators.
- See how the use of derivatives affects a country's economy.

The case study presented in this article, on the valuation of corporate bonds listed on the Casablanca Stock Exchange using a random forest model, demonstrates the ability of AI models to generate more accurate estimates, identify undervaluations, and more accurately prioritize the importance of risk factors. In an emerging market like Morocco, characterized by scarcity of transactions, low liquidity and volatile fundamentals, these tools offer essential added value to investors and regulators.

However, the adoption of these technologies remains subject to several limitations:

- Difficulty in interpreting the results (“black box effect”),
- Heavy reliance on data quality and quantity,
- risk of overlearning,
- increased requirements for technological infrastructure.

In conclusion, while artificial intelligence cannot completely replace economic intuition or the rigour of fundamental models, it is now a powerful and necessary complement to them. The future of financial product valuation is likely to lie in hybrid approaches, combining the robustness of traditional models with the flexibility and adaptability of artificial intelligence. A promising avenue of research is thus to develop mixed, explainable models, specific to the realities of emerging markets, and integrating financial, economic, regulatory and even textual data.

REFERENCES

Adams, J.F., & Smith, D.J. (2022). *Fixed Income Analysis, CFA Institute Investment Series, 5 éd., 2022*. WELEY.

Akansha, s., & Candan kumar, v. (2025). Non-parametric insights in option pricing: a systematic review of theory, implementation and future directions. *Artificial Intelligence Review* .

Arihant, P., & Pratibhamoy, D. (2025). From Traditional to Computationally Efficient Scientific Computing Algorithms in Option Pricing: Current Progresses with Future Directions. *Archives of Computational Methods in Engineering*, •••, 1699–1738.

Arner, D. W., Barberis, J., & Buckley, R. P. (2016). The Evolution of Fintech: A New Post-Crisis Paradigm? *Georgetown Journal of International Law*, *47*(4), 1271–1319.

Bahadori, S., & Hassanzadeh, A. (2026). A comprehensive literature review on ai-based credit assessment in digital lending: Exploring models, transparency, alternative data, and real-time learning. *Expert Systems with Applications*, *318*, 131872. DOI: 10.1016/j.eswa.2026.131872

Bengio, Y., Courville, A., & Vincent, P. (2013). Representation learning: A review and new perspectives. *IEEE Transactions on Pattern Analysis and Machine Intelligence*, *35*(8), 1798–1828. DOI: 10.1109/TPAMI.2013.50 PMID: 23787338

Black, F., & Scholes, M. (1973). The pricing of options and corporate liabilities. *Journal of Political Economy*, *81*(3), 637–654. DOI: 10.1086/260062

Breiman, L. (2001). Random Forests. *Machine Learning*, *45*(1), 5–32. DOI: 10.1023/A:1010933404324

Černevičienė, J., & Kabasinskas, A. (2024). Explainable artificial intelligence (XAI) in finance: A systematic literature review. *Artificial Intelligence Review*.

Cont, R. (2001). Empirical properties of asset returns: Stylized facts and statistical issues. Quantitative Finance, 1(2), 223–236. *Quantitative Finance*, *1*, 223–236. DOI: 10.1080/713665670

Damodaran, A. (2012). *Investment Valuation: Tools and Techniques for Determining the Value of Any Asset* (3rd ed.). Wiley.

Dong yu, & Deng,li. (2011). Deep learning for signal and inforlation processing. *IEEE Signal Processing Magazine* .

Fischer, T., & Krauss, C. (2018). Deep learning with long short-term memory networks for financial market predictions. *European Journal of Operational Research, 270*(2), 654–669. DOI: 10.1016/j.ejor.2017.11.054

Fuster, A., Goldsmith-pinkham, P., Ramadorai, T., & Walther, A. (2022). Predictably Unequal? The Effects of Machine Learning on Credit Markets. *The Journal of Finance*, *77*(1), 5–47. DOI: 10.1111/jofi.13090

Fuster, A., Goldsmith-pinkham, P., Ramadorai, T., & Walther, A. (2022). Predictably Unequal? The Effects of Machine Learning on Credit Markets. *The Journal of Finance*, *77*(1), 5–47. DOI: 10.1111/jofi.13090

Goodfellow, I., Bengio, Y., & Courville, A. (2016). *Deep learning*. The MIT Press.

Heston, S. L. (1993). A closed-form solution for options with stochastic volatility with applications to bond and currency options. *Review of Financial Studies*, *6*(2), 327–343. DOI: 10.1093/rfs/6.2.327

Hochreiter, S., & Schmidhuber, J. (1997). Long Short-Term Memory. Neural Computation, 9(8), 1735–1780.). *Neural Computation*, *9*, 1735–1780. DOI: 10.1162/neco.1997.9.8.1735 PMID: 9377276

Hull, J. C. (2017). *Options, Futures, and Other Derivatives* (9th ed.). Pearson Education.

Hutchinson, J., Lo, A. W., & Poggio, T. (1994). A Nonparametric Approach to Pricing and Hedging Derivative Securities Via Learning Networks. *The Journal of Finance*, *49*(3), 851–889. DOI: 10.1111/j.1540-6261.1994.tb00081.x

Jalidy, I., & Elhiri, A. (2025). Intelligence artificielle et FinTechs au Maroc: Vers un modèle hybride de gouvernance technologique. *international Journal of Accounting, Finance, Auditing, Management and Economics*, 391-410.

James, G., Witten, D., Hastie, T., & Tibshirani, R. (2013). *An Introduction to Statistical Learning*. Springer. DOI: 10.1007/978-1-4614-7138-7

Kohavi, R. (1995). A study of cross-validation and bootstrap for accuracy estimation and model selection. *Proceedings of the 14th international joint conference on Artificial intelligence*, 1137 - 1143.

Lamrani, K., & Bennis, L. (2021). *La couverture du risque de change au sein des entreprises marocaines*. Revue Internationale du Chercheur. DOI: 10.52502/ijfaema.v3i4.119

Merton, R. C. (1973). An intertemporal capital asset pricing model. *Econometrica*, *41*(5), 867–887. DOI: 10.2307/1913811

Pacheco de Oliveira, D., & Caldas Montes, G. (2023). Forecasting sovereign risk perception of Brazilian bonds: An evaluation of machine learning prediction accuracy. *International Journal of Emerging Markets*, *18*(10), 3414–3436. DOI: 10.1108/IJOEM-01-2021-0106

Park, H., Kim, N., & Lee, J. (2014). Parametric models and non-parametric machine learning models for predicting option prices: Empirical comparison study over kospi 200 index options. *Expert Systems with Applications*, *41*(11), 5227–5237. DOI: 10.1016/j.eswa.2014.01.032

Yovita Sari, & Amir Indrabudiman. (2024). The Role of Artificial Intelligence (AI) in Financial Risk. *Formosa Journal of Sustainable Research*, 2073-2082.

Taleb, N. N. (2007). The Black Swan: The Impact of the Highly Improbable. Random House. *STME academie press* .

Taleb, N. N. (2020). Statistical Consequences of Fat Tails: Real World Preasymptotics, Epistemology, and Applications. *STME academie press* .

Xu, S., & Zhou, Y. (2025). Machine Learning Applications in Financial Statement Fraud Detection: A Comparative Analysis. *Annals of Applied Sciences* .

Yu, D., & Deng, L. (2011). Deep Learning and Its Applications to Signal and Information Processing. *IEEE Signal Processing Magazine*, *28*(1), 145–154. DOI: 10.1109/MSP.2010.939038

Chapter 5
The Evolution of Algorithmic Forecasting in Finance:
From Traditional Models to AI-Driven Insights

Parihar Suresh Dahake
http://orcid.org/0000-0002-2286-4120
Ramdeobaba University, Nagpur, India

Pragati Parihar Dahake
http://orcid.org/0009-0003-0383-4721
Dr. Ambedkar Institute Of Management Studies And Research, Nagpur, India

Shravan Jasraj Chandak
http://orcid.org/0009-0005-4675-2675
Mahatma Gandhi Institute for Rural Industrialization, Wardha, India

Dileep Singh
http://orcid.org/0000-0001-7163-9360
Narsee Monjee Institute of Management Studies (NMIMS), Hyderabad, India

ABSTRACT

The finance and economics sector has significantly influenced society over the past century. Forecasting is a crucial activity in this field, systematically applied for decision-making and predicting future events. Since Mincer's seminal paper in 1969, the use of forecasts by financial analysts has been increasing. The transition from traditional to algorithmic forecasting is gaining attention in academia and real-world applications, driven by the rise in algorithmic trading and digitalized

DOI: 10.4018/979-8-3373-3053-2.ch005

social interactions that provide extensive signals to describe asset price behavior. This change, powered by the recent big data revolution, led to widespread adoption in the financial arena necessitating a thorough examination of relevant literature.

INTRODUCTION

Forecasting is essential for decision-making in financial markets. Computational intelligence methods, including artificial neural networks, fuzzy logic, genetic algorithms, and evolutionary techniques, can reduce stock market risk and enhance forecasting accuracy (Kumar et al., 2021).

Figure 1. Role of Algorithmic Forecasting in Finance From Traditional Models to AI-Driven Insights

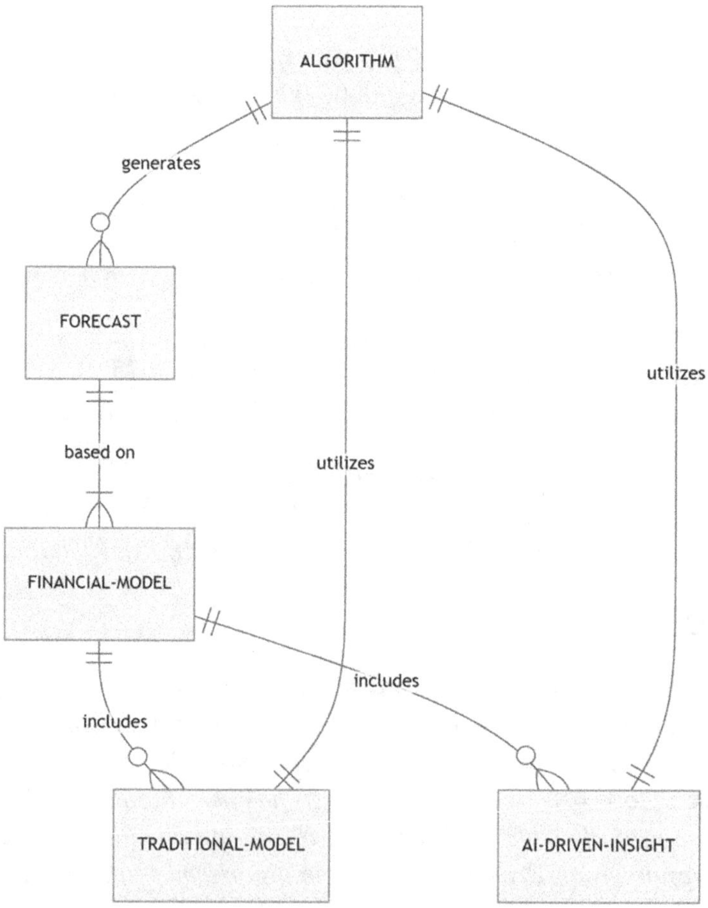

The image beautifully captures how finance has moved from relying solely on traditional models to embracing AI-driven insights through the power of algorithms. At its core, algorithms serve as the engine utilizing both conventional financial models and cutting-edge AI to generate more accurate forecasts. These forecasts are grounded in economic models that now incorporate both traditional methods and innovative AI insights, illustrating a journey where human expertise and machine intelligence collaborate to build a brighter, more adaptable financial future. Time-series models and computational strategies have complemented traditional statistical and econometric methods; however, integrating comprehensive datasets remains a challenge. Algorithmic forecasting, characterized by algorithms that may or may not incorporate artificial intelligence (AI), offers alternative predictive frameworks (Weber et al., 2024). Recognizing the scarcity of studies that cover the full spectrum of algorithmic approaches, a bibliometric analysis was conducted using the R tool. By examining the Scopus database up to August 2025, the study investigates the evolution from conventional methods to algorithmic techniques and posits future research directions. Results highlight the progressive balance between traditional forecasting and AI-driven methodologies (Buczynski et al., 2021).

Forecasting and predicting future events of interest from a set of past observations is a fundamental aspect of finance. Accurate predictions of asset price movements facilitate efficient investment and risk management. Consequently, forecasting has been a longstanding and active area of research in finance. Machine learning techniques and multi-source information fusion effectively predict SMEs' credit risk in supply chain finance, with financial-based information being most useful (L. Wang et al., 2023). However, developments in computer science, particularly machine learning, and the availability of large-scale financial data have invigorated financial forecasting, with many AI studies reporting promising results. Machine learning techniques can effectively predict stock market movements, including technical indicators, macro-economic variables, and fundamental indicators (Kumbure et al., 2022).

Figure 2. Most Relevant Words Using R

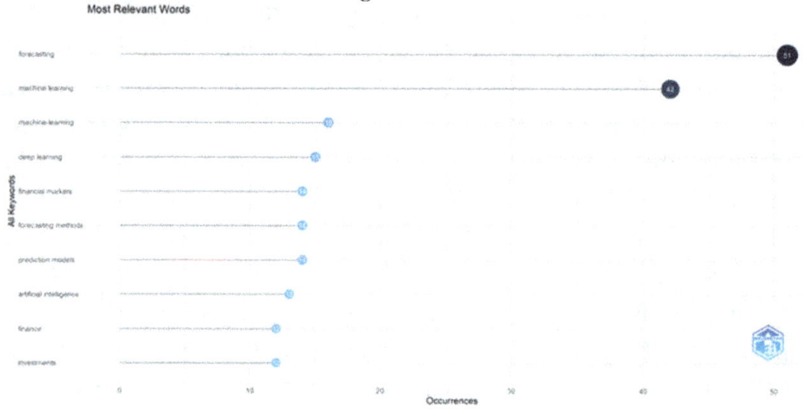

After analyzing the final 489 Articles after filtration and excluding irrelevant articles from the database, the trending keywords have been identified. The frequency of Forecasting, machine learning, and deep learning is there, followed by Financial Markets and forecasting methods. These keywords show the real essence of the given research.

Conventional forecasting strategies, which rely on statistical and econometric methods, provide fertile ground for gaining a deeper understanding of the various underlying aspects that govern financial variables and their relationships. Machine learning algorithms that utilize social media and economic news can accurately predict stock market performance and are influenced by social media and financial news (Khan et al., 2022). With the information explosion and the unprecedented rise of big data, the forecasting paradigm has shifted further toward data-intensive approaches, such as machine learning and deep learning. An encyclopaedic review of forecasting theory and practice, highlighting various models, methods, principles, and techniques, and their application in different real-life contexts (Petropoulos et al., 2022). Deep learning models have shown promising progress in stock market prediction, with this survey providing a review of data sources, neural network structures, evaluation metrics (Jiang, 2021) AI-based financial forecasting now offers valuable insights for investment decisions for an overview of the numerous machine-learning methods considered for economic forecasting, together with a map of relevant papers, see (Buczynski et al., 2021). A comprehensive overview of the evolutionary trends and focuses across forecasting research is provided, tracing developments from traditional statistical methods to the ascendance of AI-based insights.

1. HISTORICAL CONTEXT: FROM STATISTICAL MODELS TO COMPUTATIONAL ADVANCEMENTS

Forecasting remains a central financial activity; accurate forecasts allow key resources to be allocated efficiently towards the future. The cornerstone of forecasting models remains statistical and mathematical models, including autoregressive models, GARCH models, and hybrid neural networks, reflecting the crucial role of algorithmic forecasting (Buczynski et al., 2021). Big data analytics can enhance supply chain demand forecasting; however, further research is required on closed-loop supply chains (Seyedan & Mafakheri, 2020). Associated machine learning techniques, hybrids, and neural networks have become essential alternatives for capturing the nonlinear patterns of financial time series. Artificial-intelligence-based algorithms outperform traditional statistical approaches, especially in managing large datasets and capturing nonlinear relationships. The Evolutionary Deep Learning Model (EDLM), which utilizes a combination of Stock Technical Indicators (STIs), significantly improves stock market trend forecasting accuracy compared to other state-of-the-art algorithms (Agrawal et al., 2022). Stacking and blending ensemble techniques provide higher prediction accuracy and better fit in stock market analyses compared to bagging and boosting methods (Nti et al., 2020). The advent of algorithmic forecasting is closely linked to Big Data, and the paradigm subsequently intersects with a 'conventional' strategy that retains prior 'classic' techniques within a complementary framework. Hence, over the past decade, algorithmic forecasting has become a dominant approach to financial forecasting.

2. KEYWORDS ANALYSIS

Figure 3. All Keywords Analysis Using VOSViewer

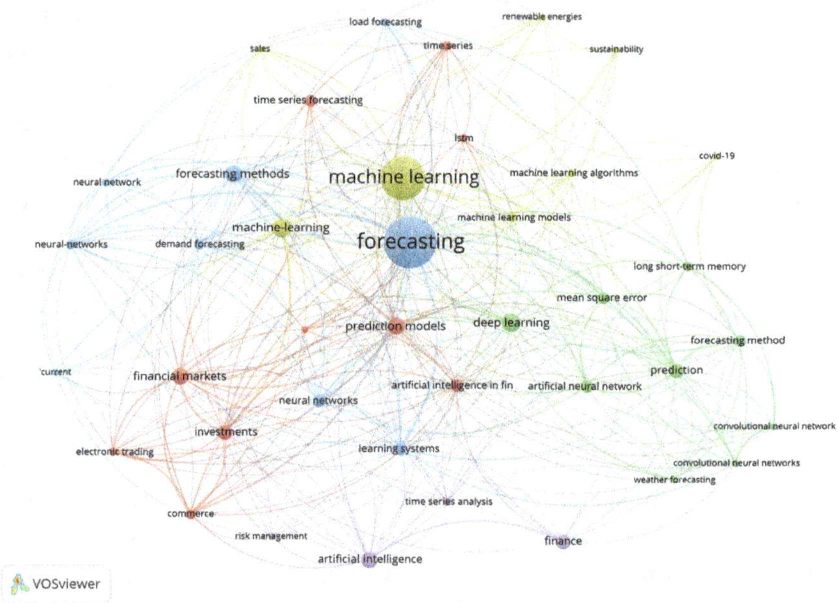

VOSviewer software and R are used to analyze the bibliographic data collected from Scopus, which is then portrayed in the form of descriptive statistics, bibliometrics, and science mapping. The bibliometric analysis of the author's keywords reveals a growing interest in algorithmic forecasting and a rising use of R for support. They support the study's strategies and help assess how scientific knowledge develops in the broad, multidisciplinary domain, as different parts of the analysis address. The structure and dynamics of specific publication types, countries, institutions, journals, and research areas, as well as the intellectual (co-citation) and thematic (co-word) structures of the domain, are established (Kumar Patra et al., 2023). Bibliometric and visualization software, including Vosviewer and R, are used to isolate keywords, research foci, thematic developments, and social structure in the literature on algorithmic forecasting in finance. Vosviewer generates graphical representations of keyword occurrences and co-occurrences in bibliometric data. The software categorizes the literature into topical clusters, revealing the underlying structure and emerging foci of the field (Kanaparthi, 2024). The approach supports a holistic understanding of content, developments, and perspectives, as well as influences of articles, journals, publications, and authors. Data can be downloaded and imported into the R statistical computing environment for extended analysis (Kumar Patra et al., 2023). Bibliometric and visualization tools facilitate a quantitative and systematic investigation of the evolution of forecasting models in the scientific literature. The approach provides insight into clustering and dynamics in the literature, as well as an overview of developments, foci, and trajectories for scholars, both new and experienced alike. A bibliometric analysis of 1899 publications reveals a rise in scholarly interest in algorithmic forecasting (AF) in finance and the emergence of distinct thematic clusters. The annual number of articles increased from 2 in 2005 to 287 in 2022 and 27 in 2023. "Algorithmic forecasting" appears as the most frequent keyword, associated with capital markets analysis and machine-learning methods. Citation analysis designates Jordan, Y.J., and Taylor, S.J., as the most prominent authors. At the same time, Journal Citation Reports identifies the International Journal of Forecasting, Econometrica, Journal of Econometrics, and Monthly Weather Review as the most influential sources. Five major thematic clusters emerge from the keyword co-occurrence analysis, which documents the study's topical focus and delineates avenues for future research. Cluster 1, devoted to financial economics, aggregates terms such as capital markets, portfolio theory, efficient markets, and economic forecasting. Cluster 2 focuses on machine learning and data science, exploring the intersection of artificial intelligence, big data, deep learning, and neural networks with forecasting and prediction. Cluster 3 focuses on cryptocurrency research, encompassing Bitcoin, risk estimation, social media, and Twitter. Cluster 4 centers on macroeconomic forecasting, encompassing inflation, economic growth, public debt, and production. Cluster 5, including actuarial science, accounting, and insurance, highlights the limited integration of algorithmic forecasting into traditional accounting and actuarial domains. The analysis highlights the progressive integration of machine-learning techniques and transparency-enhancing rules into algorithmic forecasting. However, their application in finance remains limited to specific fields, such as capital markets and cryptocurrency. (Buczynski et al., 2021) (Kanaparthi, 2024)

Figure 4. Clustered Keywords Analysis Using VOSViewer

Co-occurring authors' keywords with minimum occurrence thresholds contribute in keyword co-occurrence networks in VOSviewer according to the number of occurrences. VOSviewer is relevant for science mapping analyses because it identifies groups of similar items (i.e., keywords that can be considered part of the same topic), provides intelligence to emphasize essential items disproportionately, and facilitates ease of navigation. The keyword analysis develops thematic patterns from historiographical citations and bibliographic coupling using VOSviewer, combined with a broader range of surveys analyzed with R, and the study of topics over time, to assess the thematic directions in traditional and AI-driven algorithmic forecasting (Kanaparthi, 2024).

2.1. Bibliometric Methodology

Bibliometric data were collected from the Scopus databases, which were searched without time constraints until August 2025. The Scopus database is a reliable source for bibliometric analysis of the given research, as it provides comprehensive and global coverage of peer-reviewed literature, including journals, books, and conference proceedings across all major disciplines, particularly finance and technology (Academic Journals - Finance - Library Guides at University of Melbourne, n.d.). Its rigorous indexing and rich citation data ensure robust, unbiased insights, making it reliable and efficient for any researcher to trace the evolution from traditional models to AI-driven approaches. The term "algorithmic forecasting" was specified in titles, abstracts, and keywords to ensure relevance. Final datasets consisted of 489 papers from Scopus after deduplication. Academic output was characterized via publication dynamics per year, per source, and per country/region. The scholarly community was characterized by its primary affiliations, editors, funding sponsors, and leading authors, as indicated by documents, citations, and h-index. Scopus records included the most-cited journals, documents, and references. Bibliometric mapping employed the Vosviwer and R package "Bibliometrix" and the "Biblioshiny" app, focusing on Science Citation Index Expanded (SCIE) and Social Sciences Citation Index (SSCI) journals from 2020 to 2025. This streamlined the examination of author and source dynamics, Bradford core construction, author dominance ranking, and various conceptual structure analyses such as co-occurrence and thematic mapping based on F.A. Brossard (2016). Citation and co-citation analyses were also performed. Bibliometric analysis complemented by keyword analysis with indicator metrics and topic mapping, identified thematic developments in algorithmic forecasting.

2.2. Data sources and selection criteria

Bibliometric maps offer valuable insights into the current state of a research topic, enabling the identification of influential publications, authors, and institutions, as well as the discovery of research frontiers and emerging trends.

Figure 5. Author Keywords Analysis Using VOSViewer

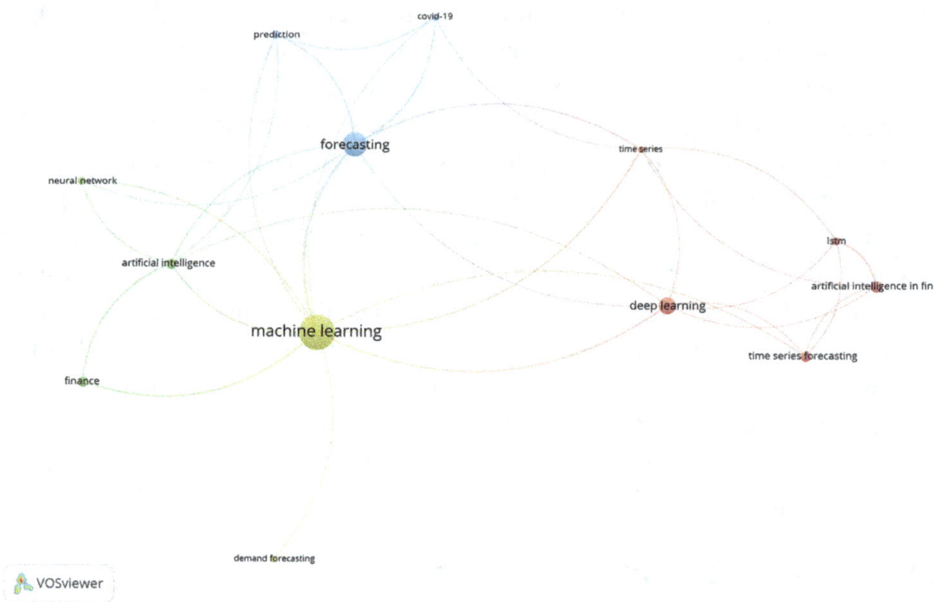

To identify influential studies and avenues for future research within the topic of algorithmic forecasting in finance, we constructed a bibliometric sample of research articles on this subject. To this end, Scopus provides access to over 22,000 indexed sources across various fields, including the arts and humanities, life sciences, health sciences, physical sciences, and social sciences. The data search was conducted in August 2025 and could be rerun to reveal ongoing trends. The query selected only research articles written in English without imposing any restrictions on the publication year, subject area, or journal titles (Pabuccu & Barbu, 2023). Considering the specificity of the topic, the query was designed to identify publications related to either forecasting (forecast, predict, predictability) or big data and algorithmic-financial regulation (financial, trade, algorithm, market), thus generating the query: (TITLE-ABS-KEY (forecast OR predict OR predictability) AND TITLE-ABS-KEY (financial OR trade OR algorithm OR market) OR TITLE-ABS-KEY ("big data")). Similar studies have demonstrated that selecting publications based on the search field Title-Abstract-Keywords returns a manageable bibliometric sample without diluting its thematic content (Ruogu Yang & Lucas, 2021). A total of 489 records for Scopus originated upon elimination of 11 duplicates from the combined records. The 1,376 distinct document set was downloaded as .csv (.txt for Scopus) files, which could subsequently be used for bibliometric analyses after further removal of uncited documents and incomplete records.

2.3. Purpose, scope, and contribution of the bibliometric study

The objective of forecasting is therefore to provide reliable and precise predictions. Forecasting is used to predict future events based on available data that can be used to make predictions. Recent advances in machine learning techniques, such as Deep Learning, Text Mining, and Ensemble Techniques, necessitate an updated review of stock market forecasting techniques for informed investment decisions (Bustos & Pomares-Quimbaya, 2020). A hybrid of deep learning models and technical analysis, this approach effectively forecasts stock prices with the lowest error values and the smallest training window sizes (Kamara et al., 2022). The subject of forecasting has been extensively explored, whether through statistical, econometric, time-series, or computational methods. Computational forecasting methods have gained acceptance, validated by the concept of big data. Nevertheless, statistical forecasting maintains significant importance and is frequently used in comparative analyses, particularly in the financial domain.

The study presents a bibliometric analysis of articles on forecasting in finance from 2020 to 2025, sourced from Scopus. It derives a list of the most-cited researchers, identifies the most-cited articles, and generates a cluster heat map for trending keywords in financial forecasting using Vosviewer. The creation of a word cloud facilitates the analysis of the recent surge in algorithmic forecasting, compute-intensive forecasting, and artificial intelligence methods in forecasting (Dahake, Dahake, Bansod, Patil, et al., 2025). Machine learning and deep learning models can effectively predict stock prices and classify financial instruments in the financial industry (Sonkavde et al., 2023). Given AI's advantages, particularly in Finance and Banking, the study acknowledges the potential of AI to supplant traditional forecasting.

3. REVIEW OF LITERATURE

The evolution of algorithmic forecasting in finance has been marked by a significant transition from traditional models to advanced AI-driven insights, reflecting the increasing complexity and dynamism of financial markets. The literature presents a comprehensive analysis of this progression through various studies, highlighting the transformative role of artificial intelligence and machine learning in investment strategies and decision-making processes. (University of J. Dobrila in Pula, Croatia & Njegovanović, 2018) explored the role of artificial intelligence in finance, emphasizing its capability to enhance the speed and accuracy of data analysis amidst the vast amounts of data generated in financial operations. This article highlights the dual nature of AI's impact: while it offers opportunities for efficient analysis, it also raises concerns regarding market stability and integrity, necessitating robust regulatory frameworks. The study emphasizes the importance of adaptive laws in keeping pace with rapid technological advancements, which are essential for fostering innovation while mitigating associated risks. (Ndikum, 2020) furthers this discussion by exploring the challenges and advancements in asset price forecasting, attributing the rise of machine learning to the exponential growth of data and computational capabilities. He illustrates the economic potential of these technologies, estimating a substantial financial impact from their integration into the banking and financial services sector.

Furthermore (Hakala, 2019) examined the emergence of robo-advisors as a pivotal innovation within financial services, emphasizing how AI facilitates autonomous investment and automated trading. The study highlights the importance of assessing the ethical implications and operational transparency of these systems, which employ algorithm-based models to analyze market data in relation to historical trends and forecast future movements. This foundational work lays the groundwork for understanding the broader implications of AI on financial forecasting. Building on this foundation, (Ryll & Seidens, 2019a) conducted a comprehensive survey of over 150 articles focusing on machine learning applications in financial market forecasting. Their findings indicate that machine learning algorithms generally outperform traditional stochastic methods, particularly highlighting the capabilities of recurrent neural networks in capturing temporal dependencies across diverse asset classes. This suggests a paradigm shift in which AI-driven methods are increasingly favored for their predictive accuracy, thereby influencing investment strategies. (Wildi & Misheva, 2022) contribute to the conversation by addressing the explainability of neural networks in forecasting. They advocate for hybrid models that blend traditional techniques with advanced neural networks to enhance forecasting accuracy while maintaining interpretability, especially critical in risk management contexts. However, (Buczynski et al., 2021) challenge the optimistic view of AI's performance in equity investment decision-making. They argue that the unique characteristics of financial time series have been largely overlooked in academic research, leading to a disconnect between theoretical advancements and practical applications. Their critical analysis reveals that despite the complexity of models and the advancements in computing power, the actual performance gains in real-world scenarios have been modest. This highlights the need for a more nuanced understanding of the regulatory and legal frameworks that govern algorithmic decision-making, which have not been sufficiently addressed in the literature.

(Quinn, 2023) further explores the historical trajectory of AI in finance, emphasizing the significance of Explainable AI (XAI) in enhancing trust and accountability within financial systems. By contrasting traditional linear regression with more sophisticated methods, such as Shapley values, the paper illustrates the necessity for transparency in AI decision-making processes. This is particularly relevant in the context of forthcoming EU regulations, as the financial sector grapples with the ethical implications of AI technologies. (Quinn, 2023) Work highlights the delicate balance between harnessing AI's revolutionary potential and addressing its inherent challenges, including interpretability and transparency.

Most recently, (Sutiene et al., 2024) provide a literature review that emphasizes the advantages of AI in portfolio management, particularly in generating superior asset return estimates and optimizing portfolios under complex constraints. Their analysis reveals that AI-driven approaches often yield better performance than traditional methods, although they also raise concerns regarding the interpretability of decisions made by black-box models. This highlights a critical intersection where the need for operational efficiency must be balanced with the imperative for transparency and stakeholder trust .

Building upon this foundation, (Cao, 2021) explores the broader implications of AI in finance, documenting a shift towards AI-driven insights for portfolio allocation and stock return predictions. The study highlights the application of neural networks and deep learning techniques in various financial contexts, including option pricing and hedging. Furthermore, it introduces reinforcement learning approaches that enhance portfolio management, alongside the innovative use of text mining for predicting stock movements based on news sentiment. This evolution reflects a growing recognition of AI's potential to reshape financial forecasting and decision-making processes.(Hadji Misheva et al., 2021) further contextualize the role of AI within the financial industry, particularly in light of the COVID-19 pandemic. They argue that AI has become an essential tool for integrating and analyzing data, offering insights into customer behavior and risk management. Their survey indicates a trend towards adopting ML and deep learning models for automated stock trading and credit risk evaluation, demonstrating the versatility of AI applications in addressing complex financial challenges. This highlights the necessity for financial institutions to leverage AI to maintain competitiveness and enhance operational efficiency. As Agentic AI offers adaptability, decision-making capabilities, and self-sufficiency, with potential applications in healthcare, finance, and adaptive software systems (Acharya et al., 2025). In addition, Agentic Retrieval-Augmented Generation (Agentic RAG) enhances Retrieval Augmented Generation (RAG) systems by embedding autonomous AI agents, thereby enabling flexibility, scalability, and context awareness across diverse applications (Singh et al., 2025).It is worth mentioning that AI-based conversational agents significantly reduce symptoms of depression and distress, but show no significant improvement in overall psychological well-being (H. Li et al., 2023).

Together, these articles present a comprehensive overview of the evolution of algorithmic forecasting in finance, showcasing the transformative potential of AI while also addressing the challenges and limitations that accompany its integration into financial decision-making processes. The literature clearly indicates a trajectory towards more sophisticated and reliable forecasting methods, although it also calls for a careful consideration of ethical, regulatory, and interpretability issues that remain pivotal in the discourse surrounding AI in finance.

3.1. Analytical tools and metrics (co-citation, keyword analysis, thematic mapping)

Bibliometric data from 1,497 financial-algorithmic-forecasting publications - from Scopus (coverage starting in 2020- 2025), The analysis identifies key documents and institutions, employing co-citation and co-word frequencies to investigate development over three decades, together with keyword analysis and thematic mapping to delineate thematic shifts (Kanaparthi, 2024). Co-citation networks of papers and journals illuminate the structural contours of the domain. An examination of co-occurring keywords captures the essence of selected papers, with thematic maps concentrating on direct references to anticipate ongoing trends. While Google Scholar data provides illustrative insight into the recurrence of dominant keywords, supplementary analyses using Vosviewer and R software on data from Scopus facilitate a comprehensive bibliometric appraisal (Buczynski et al., 2021). The full examination includes analyses of publication year, journal source, contributing authors, country of origin, affiliation, and collaborating institutions.

3.2. Scope of literature considered.

The evolution of algorithmic forecasting in finance transcends a singular theme, embracing several concurrent spheres of scholarly inquiry. To recognize this complexity, bibliometric data were retrieved from the Scopus database, spanning the years 2020-2025. These data underwent collaborative filtering using VOSviewer and analytical climax analysis with R software. Publication volume analysis was employed to characterize the dynamics governing thematic development. Finch's influence, although detectable, provided limited insight that could be leveraged for comparative interpretation. Collaboration characteristics ornament the evolutionary process, yet conspicuously elude preferential weighting of candidate topics. Bibliometric coupling exposes three fundamental lines of investigation. Co-citation analysis assembles salient author groups, while keyword evaluation organizes topics to complement a temporal assessment. Theme analysis facilitates the identification of principal research streams. Three principal thematic nuclei emerge: foundation, modeling, and complement.

4. RESEARCH QUESTION

As the financial industry undergoes profound changes fueled by digital transformation and supercharged computational capabilities, forecasting models have transitioned from traditional linear methods to multifaceted, AI-driven frameworks that harness both structured and unstructured market data. Bibliometric studies reveal that this evolution is more than a technological upgrade; it is a multi-layered shift in how risk is quantified, decisions are modeled, and strategies are enacted across diverse financial domains. Traditional models, such as ARIMA and econometric approaches, once formed the backbone of market prediction, offering dependable, if sometimes limited, projections rooted in historical price trends and assumed regularities (*The Forecasting Shift*, 2025). However, the past decade has witnessed exponential growth in research focusing on hybrid and ensemble models, where machine learning and deep learning algorithms not only outperform legacy statistical techniques in volatile and nonlinear environments but also introduce new challenges related to explainability, ethical compliance, and adaptation to market shocks.

Through the lens of bibliometric mapping, a distinct trend emerges: researchers are increasingly concerned with how AI-powered models integrate alternative data sources—such as social media and ESG signals—thus reshaping the informational ecosystem that feeds financial forecasts. The literature further documents an uptick in empirical evaluations comparing AI and traditional models, particularly in risk management, credit rating, portfolio allocation, and even cryptocurrency market analysis. Yet, thematic gaps remain around interdisciplinary approaches, stakeholder perspectives, and longitudinal impacts on financial stability (Kale et al., 2024).

Against this dynamic backdrop, an accurate and humanized research question is: *"In what ways has the scholarly landscape chronicled, through bibliometric patterns, the evolution from traditional algorithmic forecasting models to AI-driven methodologies across finance and which under-explored domains, methodological innovations, and ethical dilemmas stand out as future research priorities for making financial predictions more robust, transparent, and adaptable in unpredictable markets?"*

This question emphasizes the interplay between legacy and AI models, invites examination of empirical bibliometric findings, and centers the investigation on practical, ethical, and methodological implications documented by the research community (Roy et al., 2025), ("AI-Driven Financial Forecasting," 2025).

5. TRADITIONAL FORECASTING MODELS IN FINANCE

Forecasting models in finance originated with major government statistics organizations focused on understanding the economy and its activities. With the development of computer science and numerical techniques, the forecasting model was transitioned to computational models, yielding better accuracy performance. The combined model of ARI-MA-LS-SVM is more suitable for stock price forecasting than a single forecasting model, with better performance and universal applicability (Xiao et al., 2020). The shift to statistical models was based on specific time-series assumptions and properties. Subsequently, econometric models became preferred due to their ability to explain the economic causes of market events. However, these models were burdened by the problem of multicollinearity.

Figure 6. Source Production Over Time Using R

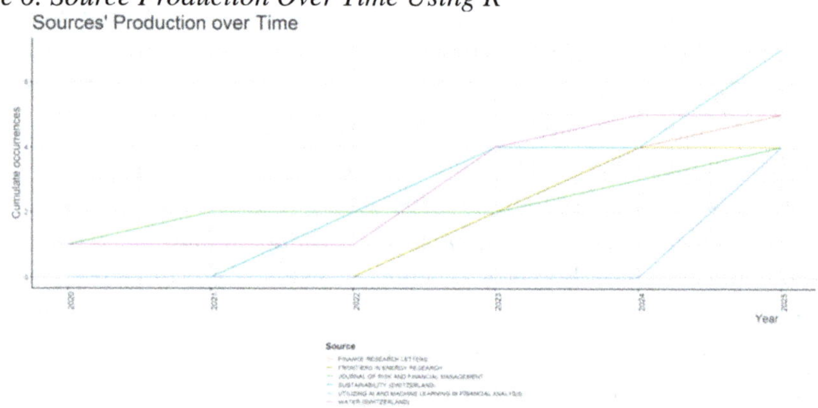

Artificial Neural Network models, particularly those with Self-Optimizing Maps, can accurately predict stock market index returns, outperforming linear regression models (Al-Akashi, 2022).Machine learning techniques can enhance stock market forecasting, but further research is necessary to comprehend their limitations and potential applications (Strader et al., 2020). In response to the limitations of traditional forecasting techniques, computational techniques such as artificial neural networks, support vector machines, and genetic algorithms have been widely employed due to their nonlinear processing capabilities. Recent advances in machine learning and high-dimensional models for time series forecasting include linear and nonlinear methods, with potential applications in economics and finance (Masini et al., 2023). A bibliometric analysis of traditional and new algorithmic methods in finance forecasting was conducted, revealing the most cited articles, authors, and keywords from 2020 to 2025. A keyword review of recent forecasting articles, categorized by their bibliometric scores, was presented using R software. Forecasting models are essential for making financial decisions in any enterprise and play a crucial role in predicting future values or dates of variables through analysis of their records. Machine-learning techniques have gained popularity in recent years for forecasting functions, leveraging the vast amounts of data stored in cloud computing environments.

Furthermore, the STM algorithm offers the most accurate and model-fitting ability for stock market group value predictions, while Adaboost, Gradient Boosting, and XGBoost exhibit intense competition among tree-based models (Nabipour et al., 2020). Deep convolutional neural networks enhance retail sales forecasting performance compared to state-of-the-art benchmarks; however, the accuracy gains are modest, and the features lack interpretability (Ma & Fildes, 2021). Deep learning architectures, such as feed-forward networks, recurrent neural networks, and convolutional neural networks, can effectively predict time series in various applications (Torres et al., 2021). Incorporating financial news sentiments into LSTM and GRU models significantly improves their stock price forecasting performance, with both models equally effective when combined with stock features (Shahi et al., 2020). These methods are gradually replacing traditional forecasting approaches and are commonly utilized in financial forecasting, risk management, and trading.

5.1. Time-series methods (ARIMA, GARCH, etc.)

Traditional econometric techniques for financial forecasting primarily rely on two categories. First, time-series models such as the Box–Jenkins ARIMA, its seasonal variation SARIMA, and the GARCH framework explore temporal dependence and heteroskedasticity in financial series. The novel stock closing price forecasting framework, using LSTM networks and dropout strategy, achieves higher prediction accuracy than traditional models, making it suitable for stock market monitoring and financial data analysis (H. Liu & Long, 2020). Second, linear regressions and simultaneous equation systems incorporate economic theory to link key macroeconomic variables and asset prices (Selvakumar et al., 2025). The deep learning ensemble-based financial time series forecasting model outperforms individual models in terms of forecasting accuracy and robustness (He et al., 2023). Each financial forecasting technique serves a different purpose for instance, time-series models like ARIMA focus on uncovering historical trends and patterns in data over time, while deep learning models such as LSTM excel at spotting intricate patterns and relationships that traditional models might miss, especially in volatile environments (Rajbhar, 2025). Linear regressions and structural equation models bring economic theory into the mix, directly linking macroeconomic factors to asset movements, unlike machine learning models like ANNs or SVMs, which rely on computational power to identify complex, often non-linear connections in the data. This means that while methods like ARIMA are best when clear, stable patterns exist, modern AI-driven techniques shine where relationships are subtle and ever-changing, making each suited to different financial challenges (Stempień & Ślepaczuk, 2025). Computational approaches emerged later, and extensions like regime-switching, cointegrated vector autoregressions, Markov chains, and Fractal Market Analysis added complexity and flexibility. Also, Artificial Neural Networks (ANN) and Support Vector Machines (SVM) both play a significant role in stock forecasting, with hybrid models yielding better results when combined with other novel techniques (Kurani et al., 2023).

Despite their widespread use, econometric methods frequently violate the nearly pure data-based premise of algorithmic forecasting. The BP algorithm neural network offers better stock price trend prediction than the deep learning fuzzy algorithm, thereby enhancing investors' stock forecasting accuracy (Zhang & Lou, 2021). They often begin with specific variables and functional forms, assuming self-similarity patterns that become increasingly complex with the number of predictors. The LSTM-Forest multi-task model enhances stock market forecasting by combining long short-term memory and random forest, thereby reducing overfitting and improving predictability and profitability (Park et al., 2022). Furthermore, econometric techniques struggle with the scale, detail, and rapidly evolving variety of economic and financial information generated in real-time. The mean-VaR model with AdaBoost prediction outperforms other models in predicting stock returns and portfolio selection for multi-national stock markets (Behera et al., 2023). To address these limitations, algorithmic financial forecasting was developed, encompassing fields such as economic and financial modeling, econometrics, and statistical modeling. According to the predictive-inference framework, an algorithmic model is defined by three operational characteristics: output, input, and feedback (Dahake, Dahake, Bansod, & Patil, 2025). Most commonly, economic and financial modeling are treated as black boxes that output time-series sets without necessarily internal mechanisms; econometrics assumes a scalar output, constraining the application of algorithmic models; statistical modeling exploits the characteristics of input-output series for dependence structures (Ruogu Yang & Lucas, 2021).SA-DLSTM, a novel hybrid model, effectively predicts stock market movements and facilitates simulation trading, thereby improving prediction accuracy and enabling investors to make informed decisions (Zhao & Yang, 2023). Notably, Machine learning algorithms outperform ARIMA models in time series forecasting in most applications, with hybrid statistical-AI models consistently outperforming their individual components (Kontopoulou et al., 2023).

5.2. Econometric approaches and limitations

Econometric methods set the foundation for financial forecasting. Macro or micro-economic data provide key variables in models that aim to describe the quantitative state of a company or economy. Machine Learning methods, such as Naive Bayes, Random Forests, Perceptron, and Linear Support Vector Machines, can accurately predict stock market movements by incorporating fundamental analysis and news articles (B R et al., 2020). However, the availability of historical data poses an explicit limitation. Combining features selected by multiple feature selection techniques and using them in a deep generative model improves stock market forecasting accuracy (Haq et al., 2021). Future forecasts often require variables that are costly or difficult to collect, and defining related events can be challenging. Global methods can provide more accurate forecasts for groups of time series than local methods, with global linear models providing competitive accuracy with two orders of magnitude fewer parameters than local methods (Montero-Manso & Hyndman, 2021). Since fixed relations have proven ineffective in practice, running the risk that macro-economic variables co-move in ways that invalidate the relationships, the choice often falls on time-series models alone (Buczynski et al., 2021). Machine learning models outperform heterogeneous autoregressive models in forecasting realized variance of the Dow Jones Industrial Average index, with more pronounced gains at longer horizons (Christensen et al., 2023).

5.3. Early computational techniques in forecasting

Computers and software applications have been widely adopted to generate forecasts. They can either conduct the entire forecasting process or assist the forecaster by producing "controls" or "benchmark" forecasts, which guide and complement the judgmental process. Such use of software packages represents a natural and logical extension of the role that statistical methods have long played in the forecasting practice. Forecasts based on statistical techniques are incorporated into many of the best-performing methods (Petropoulos et al., 2021). Most of the forecasting literature, simulations using artificial data, surveys of practitioners, and published empirical tests favour statistical models and regard them as baseline (Ndikum, 2020). Wine industry forecasts, for instance, based on a causal econometric model and several indicator series, have been widely used by industry groups and governments in English-speaking countries. Econometric and time-series applications are less susceptible to intentional, institutional, or individual manipulation and bias than judgmental forecasting. Both models and forecasts have a well-documented basis, enabling one or more persons, possibly at a considerable distance in time or place, to audit and inspect the underlying assumptions, techniques, and empirical record of forecasting errors (Dahake, Nakshane, Mohare, & Ingle, 2025). One of the main difficulties in achieving widespread application for such statistical models has centered on the costs, complexity, and time required for the collection of up-to-date information, formulation and estimation of workable models, and the dissemination of relevant data to the community of interested users.

6. RECENT TRENDS AND RECENT TOPICS ANALYSIS USING R

Understanding recent developments in algorithmic forecasting requires tracing its historical evolution. Traditional forecasting methods in finance have relied heavily on statistical and mathematical techniques, including exponential smoothing, ARIMA, transfer function models, regression analysis, and econometric procedures (P. Masini et al., 2020).

Figure 7. Recent Trends and Recent Topics Analysis Using R

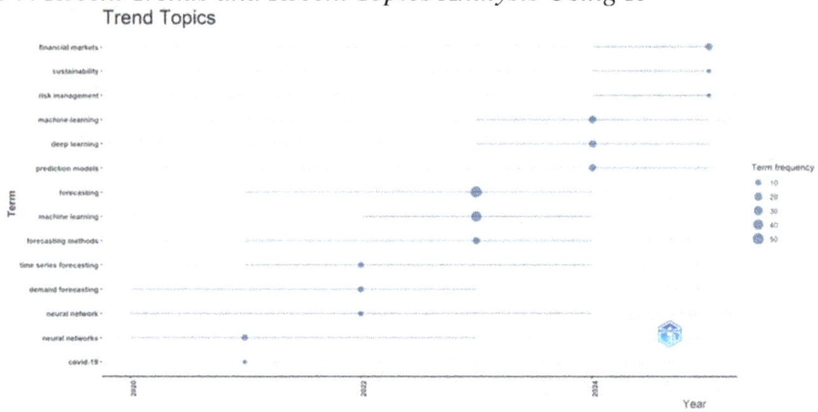

These approaches formed the core of early predictive frameworks but encountered challenges related to structural changes, non-linear behaviour, and leading data selection (Min, 2020). The quest for alternatives has encouraged the application of computational models, including expert systems, neural networks, support vector machines, fuzzy logic, genetic algorithms, and hybrid frameworks. Although the benchmarking of innovations remains inconclusive, the overarching climate favours algorithmic forecasting and data-driven learning mechanisms.

The study uses bibliometric data, processed in R, to evaluate the evolution of forecasting models in finance. Publication trends show a rapid increase from 2011, peaking in 2017. The most cited articles are those from the 1980s, with the leading contributors originating from the United States, China, and the United Kingdom.

Leading institutions include the University of California and Louisiana State University. Key words in the early-stage form four sub-systems: exchange rate, financial market, neural network, and gold price. In the development stage, an additional sub-system emerges and topics shift towards trends, machine learning, and model combinations. Thematic analysis indicates a gradual progression from fundamental to economic decision-making forecasting models (Kabbani & Enes Usta, 2022).

Keyword growth rates and retrospectives were computed, with prevalent keywords and meaningful thematic clusters isolated. Speculative efforts counted the frequency of occurrence per year to detect spontaneously driven topics. The most frequently cited papers and authors centred firmly on Ma, Chen, Zhang, and Khashei, while Ji-Feng, Tian, Kaggle, and Son appeared among recent inserts. Temporal cross-sectional investigations revealed that the most frequent topics shifted annually, with interest in contemporary keywords exhibiting remarkable annual fluctuations.

6.1. Most Cited Articles Analysis Using R

The analysis of the most cited papers and authors, using the Bibliometrix R package, reveals key contributors and influential works that drive the field of financial forecasting forward. Among the 16,256 authors contributing to the 3,984 analyzed publications, Dutta, Ahmed,Bente and Weber emerges as the most cited author with 159,152,147 and 95 citations, followed by Liu, Gudici, Bahu, Buckle, Lim and Weri Y, These individuals appear to be leading voices in the domain, shaping the research discourse.

Figure 8. Most Cited Articles Analysis Using R

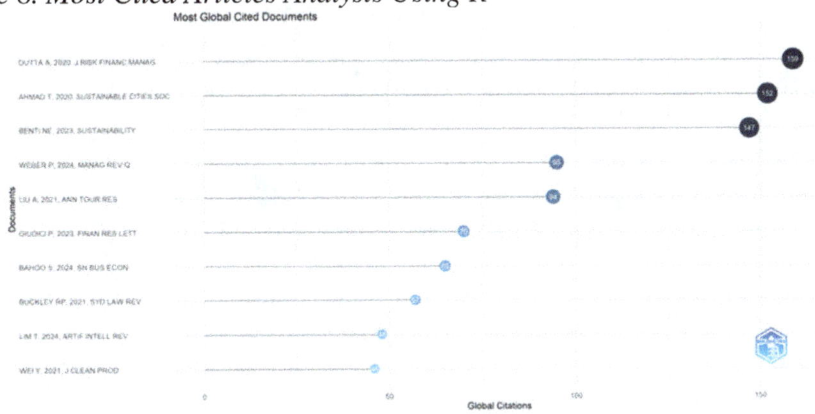

The scholarly community gravitates toward specific themes captured in the Biblioshiny word cloud, where terms such as “forecasting,” “impacts,” “cointegration," "sentiment," "forecast," "machine learning," "portfolio," and "financial" stand out. These keywords succinctly encapsulate the primary concerns: reliable market prediction and integrating quantitative techniques with exploratory analysis of unstructured data. The prominence of "cointegration" reflects an enduring interest in equilibrium relationships within time series data, while "sentiment" signals the growing role of qualitative factors in forecasting models. "Machine learning," prominently featured among both key authors and articles, marks the field's embrace of algorithmic approaches to extracting insights from complex datasets.

Collectively, these bibliometric indicators delineate a landscape where a small cadre of authors excel in capturing the community's attention, emerging topics echo concerns about data specifications and the continued capacity for computational frameworks to enhance forecasting prowess. By spotlighting the most influential scholars and thematic priorities, the analysis identifies directions where future inquiries might most effectively advance the field. (Buczynski et al., 2021) (Kanaparthi, 2024).

6.2. Words Frequency Over Time Analysis Using R

To analyse the frequency of words in the text collected from the Web of Science archive, the Wordcloud package in R software was used. This tool computes word frequency over a given text and visualizes the results as a word cloud (Ryll & Seidens, 2019).

Figure 9. Words Frequency Over Time Analysis Using R

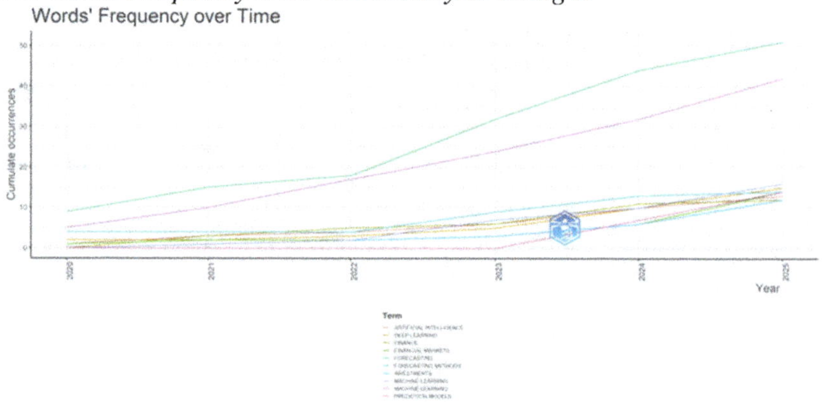

The frequency distribution graph for selected words such as "algorithm," "forecasting," "finance," "machine," and "artificial" was generated using the biblioanalysis package in R (P. Masini et al., 2020). The plot, showing count on the y-axis and year on the x-axis, illustrates the evolution of these keywords since 2009. In the early years, "finance" was the most frequently used word, while "algorithm" appeared consistently from the beginning; interest in "forecasting" was negligible during the period from 2020 to 2025. Following 2025, the term "algorithm" maintained a high frequency, while "machine" was already in regular use before the oil price shock of 2014, and "artificial" emerged mainly after 2015. "Forecasting" only gained prominence after 2017. Overall, Figure 9 depicts a shift in the financial community's focus, with the "algorithmic" concept gaining prominence over "forecasting" after 2015. This observation may result from the evolving terminology of computational techniques; however, it coheres with the upward trend in terms like "artificial," "intelligence," and "machine" revealed by topic and thematic analyses.

6.3. Three-Field Plot Analysis Using R

Figure 10. Three-Field Plot Analysis Using R

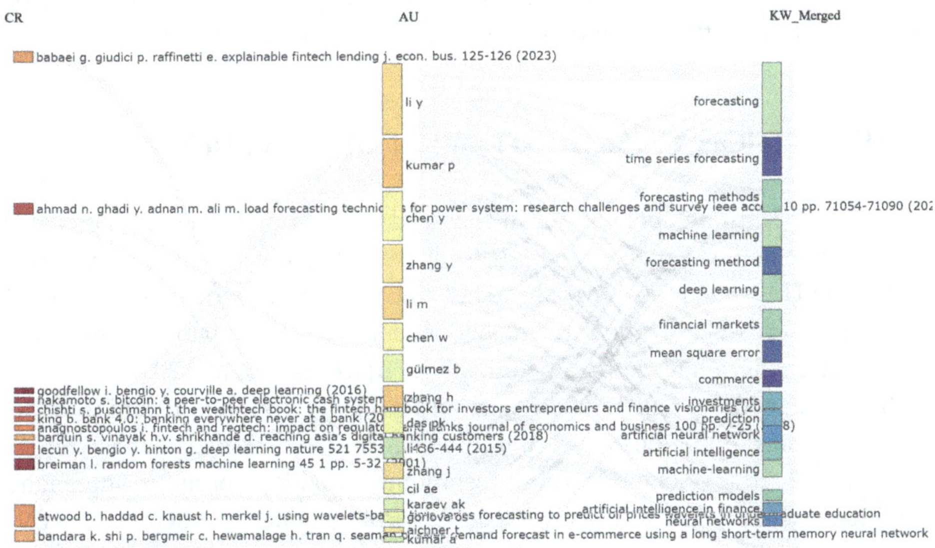

This plot shows the relationships between cited references (CR), authors (AU), and merged keywords (KW_Merged) in a three-field plot. It emphasizes the importance of access to widely-used publications and listening to respected researchers when it comes to recurring themes in the literature. The left field (CR) displays some significantly cited papers such as the classical work on explainable finance, random forests, deep learning, and blockchain. The big field (AU) displays the primary persons linking these references to novel research results. The right field (KW_Merged) encompasses many of the major fields, including AI in finance, forecasting, time series analysis, machine learning, deep learning, and financial markets. This figure illustrates how traditional AI and machine learning methods can be combined to predict business and financial outcomes. This suggests that areas of the research problem are confounded. It illustrates clearly the links among new methods, specialized fieldwork, and shifting research agendas. Although the information associated with the third field is sacrificed, the resulting map facilitates the visualization of connections among the two outer fields, allowing for the examination of interrelations that are not otherwise visible. The technique of reading Three-Fields Plots consists in exploring the relations from a field at a time by observing all the ties connecting it with concepts from the other two fields. Selecting a particular notion in one field highlights the corresponding connections, offering a focused view on that entity, its associated concepts, and the broader context. The graphical results of this approach are usually "bipolar" and "concentric": the central field is between the other two, and the latter are organised on the two sides of the map, usually with the text or concepts arranged around the circle.

7. TRANSITION TO ALGORITHMIC FORECASTING

Machine learning applications in financial forecasting have seen increasing attention from both researchers and practitioners during the last decade. Algorithmic trading and big data repositories have become more widely available, enabling the extraction of insights without the heavy dependence on explicit data modeling or computationally intensive parameterization (Buczynski et al., 2021). The LSTM technique is widely used for stock market forecasting through technical analysis; however, it has limitations in profitability analysis and risk management (A. W. Li & Bastos, 2020). Machine learning techniques provide alternative approaches to traditional econometric forecasts. Machine learning models, particularly LSTM and hybrid methods, are commonly used for financial time series forecasting, enabling researchers and practitioners to make informed decisions (Tang et al., 2022). Neural networks, particularly LSTM and NARX models, outperform traditional econometric methods in forecasting volatility, even in highly volatile periods (Bucci, 2020). Despite their successes in classification and prediction tasks across various domains, machine learning techniques are not yet widely adopted in finance. The MLS LSTM algorithm accurately predicts stock prices, achieving 95.9% prediction accuracy on training data and 98.1% accuracy on testing data, outperforming other machine learning and deep learning algorithms (Md et al., 2023). However, a VMD-based financial data prediction model using a genetic algorithm and an extended short-term memory network improves prediction accuracy compared to baseline models (Huang et al., 2021). This lag has been attributed to the unique characteristics of financial data, which tend to violate the independent and identically distributed assumption ubiquitous in the machine learning literature. Although complex techniques offer improved performance in other domains, the application of complex methods to forecasting has yielded only minimal improvement, and there is evidence that noisy data can actually cause a decline in performance. Machine learning techniques do offer several advantages, including the ability to model complex nonlinear patterns and automatically identify useful features. The brevity of literature on the topic, coupled with greater computational capacity, suggests that this technology might become increasingly attractive in coming years, potentially displacing some traditional forecasting methods.

7.1. Integration of machine learning in finance

Machine learning is reshaping myriad sectors, and finance stands at the forefront of adopting this technology. From predicting economic activity and growth to estimating firm credit risk, malfeasance, and liquidity, ML algorithms enable financial institutions and regulators to assess current conditions and anticipate future outcomes (Ye et al., 2024). The limitations of traditional models, which are unable to explain non-linearities and handle massive volumes of data, "open up a new space for machine learning" (Ndikum, 2020). Key breakthroughs in medicine, autonomous driving, and robotics inspire finance to emulate the success and venture beyond established approaches. A multi-DQN ensemble of reinforcement learning approaches, which learns to maximize a return function rather than market annotations, outperforms conventional Buy-and-Hold strategies in stock market forecasting (Carta et al., 2021). Offering guidance for future investigations, these insights illustrate the transition from linear to algorithmic forecasting, as the field looks to artificial intelligence for additional predictive power. Application to stock price prediction and market movements further underscores the technique's immediate relevance.The proposed stock price forecasting model, which utilizes genetic algorithm-machine learning regressions and best feature subset selection, enhances forecasting accuracy and local interpretability by employing fewer features and capturing the time-dependent characteristics of stock price data (Yun et al., 2023).

Innovations combine text mining with deep learning to forecast stock prices by predicting news sentiment. Results for both real-time sentiment analysis and post-event performance indicate a data science approach can overcome noisy data and extract meaningful insights. Deep learning methods, such as LSTM and Reinforcement learning, have shown great returns and accuracy in stock and forex price prediction (Hu et al., 2021). The ARFIMA-LSTM hybrid model effectively predicts stock market prices with approximately 80% accuracy, outperforming traditional methods in improving stock market forecasting accuracy (Bukhari et al., 2020). To counter the inherent complexity, research adopts a hybrid approach that combines the speed of LSTM networks with the high accuracy of random forest regression (Ryll & Seidens, 2019b). Diane B. S. O'Leary recommends using the OCEBM levels of evidence to assess the field's forward trajectory.

7.2. Role of big data and computing power

Big Data and the Age of Algorithms: The dramatic breakthrough in computing power and the widespread availability of low-cost data storage capabilities have led to the proliferation of Big Data. These two enablers have also revolutionized the field of Algorithmic Forecasting, which is the set of automated methods devoted to inferring properties and correlations from enormous datasets. In addition to entirely original techniques, existing forecasting methods have benefited from the information glut, the considerable data flux, which has been of assistance in tuning and stabilizing the predictions. The multi-modality graph neural network (MAG-NN) effectively predicts financial time series, enabling investors to make profitable and interpretable investment decisions (Cheng et al., 2022). It is timely to review the main issues connected to the recent advances in Algorithmic Forecasting and the explosion of Big Data. From the perspective of forecasting real-time series, the literature can be divided into two major groups. In the first group, approaches that implement data-driven algorithms capable of extracting information from the raw series are proposed. The forecasts consist primarily of signal-extraction procedures; in the second case, methods that combine model-driven mechanisms with raw data are preferred. These latter techniques can benefit from input information derived from economic theory or simply from knowledge of the specific features characterizing the series. Due to their longstanding relevance, the two groups set the stage for the more recent approaches. Thus, any real-time economic monitor combines economic, financial, and asset price data arriving at the forecaster's address to reconstruct the state of the economy in a limited number of variables, thereby aiding in the anticipation of market direction. These topics focus on the bibliometric analysis of Algorithmic Forecasting, as indexed in Scopus, with the intention of examining the conceptual structure of the area. >1,300 documents extracted from Scopus have been processed using two bibliometric software packages: VOSviewer and R Bibliometrix. The screening revealed five clusters

a) Machine learning;
b) Deep learning;

c) Stochastic and mathematical methods;
d) Smart algorithms; and
e) Financial analysis. Applications to forecasting, such as macroeconomic forecasting, crisis prediction, stock market volatility forecasting, and earnings forecasts, have also been evaluated. (Hosni & Vulpiani, 2018)

7.3. Case examples of adoption in financial markets

Widespread adoption of automated AI systems on financial markets has not yet materialized (Buczynski et al., 2021). During the 2020 COVID-19 pandemic, algorithmic trading helped maintain market liquidity when human desks were less active, showing goodwill towards continued adoption. Major obstacles to resorting to AI in finance concern data, reproducibility and robustness, operational design, acceptance, risk, and expectation management. A bibliometric method was applied to scientific research to track the evolution from traditional forecasting to algorithmic and AI-enabled solutions. Forecasting the real market is a significant challenge faced by practitioners and scholars; numerous interesting approaches have been developed, ranging from statistical analysis and econometric models to computational intelligence techniques. Starting from the Scopus databases, 1,366 relevant documents published between 2020 and 2025 were extracted and analyzed through R-bibliometrics; visualization was implemented using Vosviewer software. Among the most cited studies, research papers from the early period (autoregressive integrated moving average, ARIMA, and general autoregressive conditional heteroscedasticity, GARCH) and recent publications on artificial intelligence (especially machine learning) prevail. The most prolific authors in terms of average citations per publication are therefore from the traditional era, and rarely focus on disruptive models based on large-scale data and learning algorithms. From 2016 to the end of the period under review, the theme of model uncertainty, which had been investigated mainly in the past, regained significant momentum. More recently, research interests shifted towards machine learning and artificial intelligence (AI).

8. RISE OF AI-DRIVEN INSIGHTS

Algorithmic forecasting gained momentum with the adoption of complex machine-learning techniques. Deep-learning models handle vast amounts of historical data and identify features, enabling advanced predictive tasks. Developments in Natural Language Processing (NLP) allow the assessment of market sentiment from social networks, newswires, and earnings conference call transcripts. Hybrid models, which combine neural networks with traditional approaches such as GARCH, effectively capture market conditions (Buczynski et al., 2021).

Traditional models relied on manual feature selection; deep learning infers features autonomously. Neural architectures, such as Recurrent Neural Networks (RNNs) and Long Short-Term Memory (LSTM) networks, capture time dependencies. Attention mechanisms focus on crucial time steps, while Transformer architectures model long sequences without relying on recurrence or convolution. Methods like AutoGluon-Tabular utilize ensembles that adapt to various data characteristics (Wildi & Hadji Misheva, 2022).

8.1. Deep learning and neural networks in forecasting

Neural networks have a longstanding presence in finance, particularly for forecasting. Over time, they have developed from conventional shallow models into deep networks with multiple processing layers and varied architectures tailored to specific problems. In recent years, recurrent neural networks, such as LSTMs, have become especially popular in forecasting domains, including financial time series. Deep neural networks operate by learning representations from training data rather than employing specialized algorithms. They have achieved high accuracy in tasks such as computer vision, machine translation, and speech recognition—often surpassing the performance of human experts. Unlike traditional machine learning methods, deep learning typically requires much larger training samples, and networks can contain thousands of layers. Consequently, training deep neural networks is resource-intensive, often necessitating millions of images and several days of computation. A notable application using Keras involves a three-module system for short-term energy consumption forecasting: a deep neural network produces time series forecasts, which are then verified for accuracy, and a neuro-fuzzy network aggregates the outputs to form the final prediction. A parallel fuzzy cognitive map models factors influencing the forecasted indicators (Averkin & Yarushev, 2020).

8.2. Natural language processing for market sentiment analysis

Sentiment analysis can be conducted through machine learning, lexicon, or hybrid methods, utilizing sources such as news headlines, social media posts, blogs, articles, and comments that influence stock prices. This analysis is often combined with behavioral finance to detect investors' outlook on shares. Neural networks, random forests, support vector machines, naive Bayes classifiers, and k-nearest neighbors algorithms have been employed for sentiment classification, unveiling investor outlier behaviors that affect the Indian market.

NLP packages enable the scanning of social media for statements about specific stocks or markets, mining news headlines, and generating dictionaries. Extracted features include sentiment strength and indicators of questionable information, which serve as inputs to prediction models. The overall sentiment polarity of messages relating to a topic, such as recommending a stock or expressing bullish or bearish views, is assessed using dictionary-based algorithms applied to tokens in tweets (Chatterjee, 2018). Sentiment analysis also plays a role in asset pricing, where the sentiment of analyst reports is classified as positive or negative based on keyword hits, and in detecting earnings-related sentiments from financial news by analyzing sentiment distribution and strength. Although sentiment strength, as a dummy variable, contributes minimally to predictive power. Sentiment classification traditionally categorizes messages as positive, negative, or neutral; however, recent research has explored dimension-based classification. Wang et al. examined distinct market phases through sentiment analysis, finding narrower return distributions during long-term bear markets and broader ones during short-term bear and bull markets; combining sentiment with other external information enhances long-term prediction performance (Colasanto et al., 2022).

8.3. Hybrid and ensemble models

Ensembles of models generally outperform individual models, as evidenced in financial forecasting (Ruogu Yang & Lucas, 2021). Model-agnostic methods have been developed for adaptive time series model (DMS) and ensemble (AE) selection that use time-varying procedures with online update mechanisms. Such methods leverage higher-order time-series information compared to cross-validation. Adaptive algorithms (DAA) have also been proposed to select between competing strategies. Model-agnostic in the sense of requiring a model set specification, functional forms, and a training method, these approaches aim toward an automated portfolio manager with strong returns and compliance with investment constraints. The extension of DAA to cross-asset strategies that hedge against the VIX demonstrates outstanding performance. Interpretability arises from the retrieval of forecast components, enabling an empirical understanding of the algorithm's operation. Adaptive model-selection, ensemble, and evaluation methods have a general form that involves correcting an auxiliary base learner through ongoing adjustments. Starting from an initial parametrically defined model set (e.g., ARIMA), DMS follows the base-learner with an adaptive unimodal correction. A fixed number of general parametric models then feed into a convex combination, which generates a further adjustment used to construct the Adaptive Ensemble (AE). Dynamic Adaptive Allocation (DAA) extends the principles by applying the correction to a set of competing strategies, implicitly creating an augmented meta-strategy space.

9. SYNTHESIS AND THEMATIC ANALYSIS.

Numerous studies scrutinize the ongoing transformation from conventional to algorithmic and subsequently to AI-based forecasting, a progression fueled by advances in data accessibility, machine-learning techniques, and computational capabilities, which have collectively enhanced analytical depth and reduced pre-processing efforts.

Figure 11. Thematic Map Using R

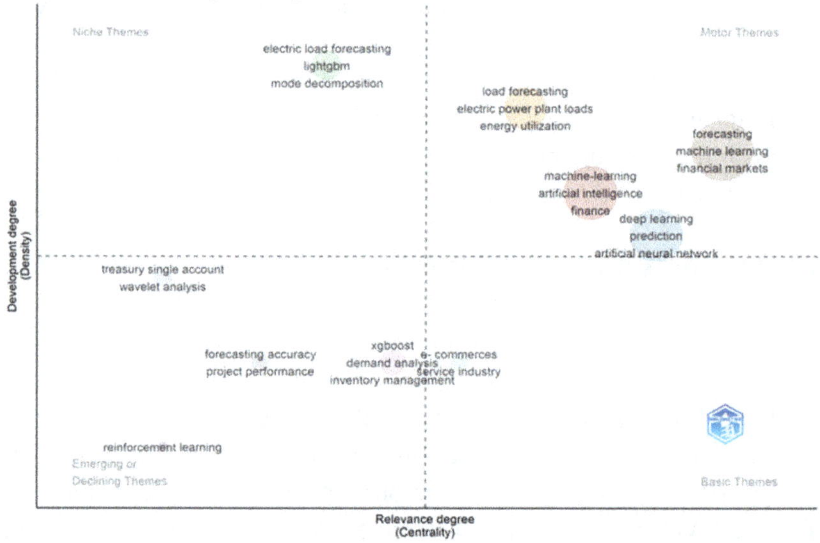

Over the last 38 years, the literature documenting the development of algorithmic forecasting in finance has grown exponentially. The classic theory of the forecasting of financial markets reverted to a "metatheory" of incomplete optimization and market control (Buczynski et al., 2021) (Kanaparthi, 2024). Several challenges persist, including the predominance of underutilized performance-statistic scores, the scarcity of out-of-sample analyses, the need for market-adaptive models, and the requirement for consolidated benchmark datasets and frameworks. Time-series analyses frequently emphasize the initial simulation of basic models; yet, more sophisticated techniques, such as NARX, clearly improve short-term forecasting. The influence of training-set size on model accuracy remains underexplored. Methodical difficulties abound:

input datasets often lag behind variables under prediction; non-stationary market conditions introduce time-variant dynamics; extensive computational resources are required; and integrating uncertainty in forecasts and trading decisions remains problematic. The complexity of financial regulations and non-stationarities in data may subvert fundamental forecasting assumptions. Unquestionably, the quantity and quality of available data significantly influence the efficacy of forecasting; nonetheless, practitioners must navigate these open research avenues to unlock the full potential of algorithmic forecasting (Buczynski et al., 2021).

9.1. Performance, interpretability, and adaptability

Financial markets exhibit complex dynamics, necessitating the use of reliable forecasting techniques. Conventional methods struggle to balance the three pillars of performance, interpretability, and adaptability, especially when applied to highly volatile financial time series. Time-series approaches, including ARIMA and GARCH, are widely used for stationary data; however, nonlinear and nonstationary patterns in the data limit the accuracy of such models, while econometric methods often fail to capture nonlinear patterns. On the other hand, computational intelligence techniques promote greater adaptability, but forecasting accuracy still leaves significant room for improvement. Models such as deep learning, recurrent neural networks (RNNs), long short-term memory (LSTM), and gated recurrent units (GRUs) have demonstrated superior performance and adaptability in handling complex and noisy data; however, issues with overfitting and limited interpretability remain. The trade-off of simultaneously satisfying all three pillars of performance, interpretability, and adaptability in forecasting techniques, especially for financial time series, remains an open challenge in the literature (Ruogu Yang & Lucas, 2021) ; (Buczynski et al., 2021) ; (Sun et al., 2022).

9.2. Limitations and challenges in adoption

Traditional forecasting models offer a robust and effective mechanism for interpreting financial data, rendering them a valuable resource for constructing investment strategies. Nevertheless, contemporary financial firms confront complex challenges in applying artificial intelligence (AI) to large-scale economic data, indicating significant barriers to the widespread adoption of AI in this domain. The integration of advanced computational techniques complements traditional econometric strategies, forming the basis of algorithmic forecasting. Rules-based algorithms cannot replicate the intuitive prowess of seasoned market practitioners or the comprehensive insight required to appreciate intricate dependencies. AI facilitates the efficient processing of massive data sets, enabling the generation of forecasts that utilize every available data source while circumventing subjective biases. Similarly, machine learning algorithms help select the most relevant variables from extensive data sets, thereby minimizing the risk of error (Buczynski et al., 2021).

9.3. Publication and citation trends over time

For organization and to facilitate detailed mapping, the development of algorithmic forecasting systems in finance was divided into two subsections: traditional forecasting and modern algorithmic forecasting. The older forecasting perspective covers articles using standard and well-known forecasting approaches, including Statistical and Econometric models, Time-series models such as the Autoregressive Integrated Moving Average (ARIMA) model and the Generalized Auto-Regressive Conditional Heteroskedasticity (GARCH) model, suggesting that regular prediction models combined with computational intelligence methods have become powerful for financial markets. Deep learning algorithms, such as Artificial Neural Networks (ANNs) and Convolutional Neural Networks (CNNs), can accurately predict stock market prices with varying levels of accuracy (Mukherjee et al., 2023). Hence, the scope of the topic has progressively evolved to include intelligent systems such as Artificial Neural Networks (ANNs), Genetic Programming (GP), Fuzzy Logic, Support Vector Machines (SVM), and hybrid and ensemble methods.In addition, the ISSA-BP neural network model effectively predicts short-term stock market indices, aiding investors and policymakers in identifying market trends and rationalizing policy decisions (X. Liu et al., 2022). Bibliometric analysis, based on 489 research contributions over the 2020–2025 period, offers a comprehensive overview of algorithmic forecasting trends in finance. The study highlights seminal articles, productive authors, countries, and institutions. Keyword evolution is discussed, and emerging topics are inferred.

9.4. Key areas where AI surpasses traditional models

Algorithmic forecasting methods have reconfigured the landscape of investments, offering an alternative to the traditional toolbox of statistical and econometric models typically elected for direction, volatility, and value prediction (Buczynski et al., 2021). Although metrics rank many classical statistical and econometric models on par with recent machine learning implementations, tools based on the latter are preferred because of three key areas where artificial intelligence outperforms: interpretability, automation, and feature extraction. Interpretability encompasses the capacity to decode the sophistication of the phenomenon under analysis through clear visibility of parametric coefficients and model configurations; automation refers to reducing the human effort needed to contribute to the forecasting process through automated, adaptive, and iterative model updates; feature extraction entails the capability of learning and highlighting additional explanatory variables embedded into the data, potentially illuminating factors of previously obscure significance. Exploring these dimensions further unravels the nuanced advantages that AI-driven forecasts bring to contemporary financial analysis and decision-making.

10. FUTURE RESEARCH DIRECTIONS

Forecasting maintains its status as one of the world's most fascinating subjects and as an indicator of economic progress over time. There is every reason to suppose this will continue to be the case in the future (Buczynski et al., 2021). The major challenge of using algorithms to predict how systems behave in certain situations has recently generated considerable enthusiasm regarding algorithmic forecasting, due to the broader algorithmic movement noted earlier. Despite the continued development of algorithmic forecasting and its applications, a fundamental question arises regarding the distinction between algorithmic predictions that build upon current scientific, technological, and scholarly advances and forecasting based on statistical/predictive models. Correlation criteria, random forest, principal component analysis, and autoencoder are the most widely used feature selection and extraction techniques for stock market prediction, with the best prediction accuracy (Htun et al., 2023). Most forecasts rely on models, either explicitly or implicitly; hence, analyst insights and judgments often play a significant role in shaping the results. Establishing contingent links between certain types of projections and specific systems remains a challenge. The debate has been extended by an extensive bibliometric analysis of the forecasting literature from 2020 to 2025. The transition to algorithmic forecasting constitutes a radical departure in the practices of scientific and scholarly prediction. Over recent decades, extensively cited models such as the autoregressive integrated moving average (ARIMA) and generalized autoregressive conditional heteroskedasticity (GARCH) have laid the groundwork for computational-algorithmic approaches, alongside econometric methods. The rise of AI has led to the development of novel algorithms and a resurgence of interest in longstanding mathematical constructs, as evidenced by a notable increase in AI-related publications focused on forecasting. Parallel bibliometric analyses of the broader literature and specialized databases on leading journals, in conjunction with the predictive focus of the study, suggest that the shift to algorithmic forecasting represents a fundamental transformation and that the bibliometric dataset effectively captures the topic's essential features. The research gap lies in the nuanced understanding of how and when algorithmic forecasting genuinely surpasses traditional statistical models, especially as AI reshapes the field. While bibliometric analyses clearly document the surge of advanced techniques and AI-driven methods, there remains limited clarity on matching specific forecasting models to distinct financial systems and contexts, as well as incorporating human insights with algorithmic predictions for optimal results (Algorithmic Forecasting in a Digital World, 2025). Uncovering these contingent links and evaluating the practical balance between interpretability, accuracy, and adaptability in real-world financial forecasting still needs deeper exploration (Cogent, Forecasting Algorithms in Business, 2024); (The Evolution of Forecasting Techniques, 2019), making this an essential area for future research

10.1. Integrating explainable AI in finance

The accelerated shifts within the financial landscape have rendered traditional econometric and statistical methods insufficient for capturing and forecasting economic trends. Algorithmic forecasting, which integrates artificial intelligence and cloud computing to analyze diverse data forms, offers a promising alternative. Ensemble deep learning models, combined with sentiment analysis and sentiment-based models, can effectively predict future stock price trends, aiding investors in making more informed investment decisions (Y. Li & Pan, 2022). Explainable AI (XAI), which sheds light on the decision-making processes of complex models, addresses the opaque nature of many AI solutions and fosters greater trust among practitioners and regulators. Like Text-mining technologies, they have significantly impacted the financial industry, with applications in economic forecasting, banking, and corporate finance (Gupta et al., 2020).

10.2. Ethical and regulatory considerations

Research in algorithmic forecasting should address various issues arising from the increasing use of artificial intelligence techniques in the functioning of the capital strategies market. Modern algorithms possess diverse strengths and weaknesses, and they can be applied to a wide range of jobs in the market. However, they also fill their algorithmic roles with various biases and are vulnerable to numerous forms of data interference.

The EU AI Act is the first comprehensive law regulating the use of AI in Europe, aiming to ensure the safety, transparency, and human oversight of AI systems by categorizing them based on risk and banning those with unacceptable risks, effective from February 2025. It also emphasizes AI literacy and enforces strict rules on general-purpose AI models since August 2025. The White House AI Blueprint focuses on promoting trustworthy AI development and use in the United States, stressing ethical standards, transparency, and innovation to safeguard society while encouraging AI advancements across sectors. Algorithmic models may render finance-related choices less secure, less just, and less transparent, as biases are difficult to spot or identify, particularly when algorithmic danger signals become increasingly complex and unintelligible. In this context, it is imperative to design and implement new artificial intelligence techniques that enhance IFRS quality in terms of high profitability while mitigating risk in the financial market. Long short-term memory (LSTM) and convolutional neural networks (CNN) are the most effective alternatives for time series forecasting, with LSTMs providing the most accurate forecasts and CNNs achieving comparable performance with less variability and greater efficiency (Lara-Benítez et al., 2021).

The use of artificial intelligence in capital markets should be carefully regulated to offer a careful framework for research and decision-making. Artificial intelligence generates significant returns and is increasingly widespread throughout the capital market. Yet, the risks associated with these systems are numerous. Different ways of regulating artificial intelligence forms on capital markets have been proposed, based on the rationale that the greater the ability of an additional artificial intelligence application, the higher the risk and with the possibility of further detailed sector frameworks, general shaping for all fields following the New Deal approach or a combination of unification and fragmentation of the artificial intelligence operation area.

10.3. Potential breakthroughs in algorithmic forecasting

Algorithmic forecasting is attracting significant attention from academics and industry. Financial decision-making often relies on accurate forecasts to maximize profit or minimize risk. Recent advances in big data and machine learning have facilitated the development of sophisticated models; however, the information content of forecasts remains scarcely explored. The Light GBM algorithm effectively predicts corporate financing risk profiles, outperforming other machine learning algorithms, such as k-nearest neighbors and decision trees (D. Wang et al., 2022). Two simple guiding principles can help identify potentially valuable financial forecasts. The first posits that useful forecasting models should enhance traded equity market portfolios; the second suggests that forecasts that outperform a very inexpensive, fully invested benchmark portfolio may add value. Exceptions exist, but they are generally unprofitable when transaction costs are included (Dardaman & Gupta, 2023). These criteria serve as tools for assessing the efficacy of predictive models in financial markets. Investors discount relevant information based on the inferred credibility of its source. Filtering phenomena arise when investors mix information from different signals and datasets; averaging over a set of predictors reduces noise and mitigates the impact of false cues. When datasets convey complementary information, additional guidance on effective integration and model selection is necessary.

Note that the choice of machine learning algorithm has a minor impact on portfolio performance (Buczynski et al., 2021). When applying such a framework, forecasts emerge as excellent stock-picking tools, with even simple predictive models calibrated on generic information generating profitable portfolios. These findings underscore the potential for algorithmic forecasting to revolutionize financial decision-making by providing actionable insights that translate into superior investment outcomes.

11. RESULT AND DISCUSSION BASED ON BIBLIOMETRIC ANALYSIS

Analysis of financial forecasting reveals a noticeable increase in the number of publications, as shown by annual scientific production. Early articles dating back to the 2020s are still frequently cited, for example. As recently as 2023, cited works appeared in and. The core sources indicate that it takes 1.12 years to reach 50% of the total citations. The most cited authors include both those with a single, highly influential work and those with numerous publications (Kanaparthi, 2024), including C. W. J. Granger, P. Rossi, and C. Alexander. The frequency of author keywords effectively traces thematic development. Initially, time-series analysis is dominant, followed by application-driven terms such as stocks, exchange rates, and crude oil. Genetic Programming, an artificial intelligence technique, can effectively forecast export sales by analyzing relationships between variables (Sohrabpour et al., 2021). The Large Language Models (LLMs) can effectively forecast financial time series using historical stock price data, company metadata, and economic news, outperforming classic ARMA-GARCH models and gradient-boosting tree models (Yu et al., 2023).The most cited paper available across relevant databases (Buczynski et al., 2021) finds that published algorithms are insufficient for real market use, a situation that might fuel further work in the field. Deep Learning models outperform standard models in time series forecasting, particularly for monthly series and long-term forecasts, but require significantly increased computational time (Makridakis et al., 2023). Eliciting private information adjustment (PIA) for prediction algorithms can lead to more accurate predictions than direct forecasting, especially when considering human random error(Ibrahim et al., 2020).

12. CONCLUSION

Financial forecasting refers to the use of historical data and advanced analytical techniques to predict future financial conditions. Financial forecasting models can be broadly categorized into two types: traditional forecasting models and algorithmic forecasting models. Machine learning, deep learning, reinforcement learning, and deep reinforcement learning-based techniques have significantly improved stock market forecasting and algorithmic trading (Sahu et al., 2023). Traditional models centre on time-series and econometric models.Machine learning algorithms, such as random forest and gradient boosting machine, can effectively predict property prices in Hong Kong, outperforming support vector machine (SVM) (Ho et al., 2021). These models attempt to incorporate economic information and provide straightforward interpretations but require numerous assumptions and careful model updates. The novel time series forecasting model, SeriesNet, enhances forecasting accuracy and stability compared to traditional models that use fixed time intervals (Shen et al., 2020). Such challenges helped pave the way for the use of algorithms for financial forecasting. Artificial intelligence is used to uncover patterns in financial markets and predict future conditions, removing many assumptions and taking advantage of the recently available data and computing power (Buczynski et al., 2021). Studies captured via the Web of Science were examined through bibliometrics, and the results were visualized using Vosviewer to determine the evolution of forecasting models in finance. The bibliometric assessment revealed a clear transition from traditional models to algorithmic forecasting. NumPy was used to analyze the bibliometric data, revealing the most commonly cited papers, as well as the researchers and institutions with the highest number of publications. Keyword analysis revealed that 'machine learning', 'model', and 'algorithm' were most commonly associated with financial forecasting.

This work contributes to a comprehensive understanding of financial forecasting models and their development, presenting an accessible, forward-looking view on the topic with insights for both academia and the financial industry. The study also highlights a clear methodological gap, encouraging further research in this area. The implications of these practical contributions, alongside novel scientific opportunities, are elucidated. Future avenues for research are also discussed.

13. IMPLICATIONS FOR RESEARCHERS AND PRACTITIONERS

A bibliometric analysis conducted on the Scopus database has enabled a quantitative and objective examination of scholarly output across various dimensions, laying the groundwork for the present investigation. By integrating qualitative content analysis with topic analysis performed on R software, the method balances traditional bibliographic methodology with analytical approaches to elucidate a field of knowledge. In principle, bibliometric analysis facilitates the selection of the most appropriate and pertinent literature for review. Accordingly, the prevailing trends in bibliography and content have been explored.

Examining the evolution of editorial and researcher focus has proved fruitful in considering implications for the future of a domain. To embrace a scientific theme excessively limits the scope of subsequent data searches. The bibliometric characteristics of the art reviewed in each synthesis are presented in the following passages. Notably, the term "algorithm" has received minimal bibliometric attention, suggesting a perceived lack of interest in transforming high volumes of information and integrating mining to meet these demands.

With the increasing availability of Big Data and the improved accessibility of fundamental markets in recent decades, interest in algorithmic forecasting has grown significantly (Buczynski et al., 2021). The integration of machine-learning algorithms and Big Data has led to the development of analytical models capable of making accurate inferences about investors' reactions to market anomalies (Ye et al., 2024).

14. FUTURE SCOPE OF THE STUDY

Future investigations may expand the bibliometric scope beyond finance by employing alternative keyword combinations. At the same time, a detailed sectoral impact assessment could elucidate the influence of such research in fields like education. Merging findings with thematic analyses of online publications may further clarify the sector-specific ramifications, a task beyond the scope of the present study. This approach lays the groundwork for subsequent inquiries into the bibliometric contours and thematic trajectories of algorithmic forecasting literature (Kanaparthi, 2024).

REFERENCES

Acharya, D. B., Kuppan, K., & Divya, B. (2025). Agentic AI: Autonomous Intelligence for Complex Goals—A Comprehensive Survey. *IEEE Access : Practical Innovations, Open Solutions, 13*, 18912–18936. DOI: 10.1109/ACCESS.2025.3532853

Agrawal, M., Kumar Shukla, P., Nair, R., Nayyar, A., & Masud, M. (2022). Stock Prediction Based on Technical Indicators Using Deep Learning Model. *Computers, Materials & Continua, 70*(1), 287–304. DOI: 10.32604/cmc.2022.014637

AI-Driven Financial Forecasting. (2025). *Enhancing Predictive Accuracy in Volatile Markets*. European Economic Letters., DOI: 10.52783/eel.v15i2.2955

Al-Akashi, F. H. A. (2022). Stock Market Index Prediction Using Artificial Neural Network. *Journal of Information Technology Research, 15*(1), 1–16. DOI: 10.4018/JITR.299918

B R, R., Bhat, R. S., Manohar, A., & K R, M.B R. (2020). Stock Market Prediction using Machine Learning. *International Journal of Communication and Media Science, 7*(2), 6–9. DOI: 10.14445/2349641X/IJCMS-V7I2P102

Behera, J., Pasayat, A. K., Behera, H., & Kumar, P. (2023). Prediction based mean-value-at-risk portfolio optimization using machine learning regression algorithms for multi-national stock markets. *Engineering Applications of Artificial Intelligence, 120*, 105843. DOI: 10.1016/j.engappai.2023.105843

Bucci, A. (2020). Realized Volatility Forecasting with Neural Networks. *Journal of Financial Econometrics, 18*(3), 502–531. DOI: 10.1093/jjfinec/nbaa008

Buczynski, W., Cuzzolin, F., & Sahakian, B. (2021). A review of machine learning experiments in equity investment decision-making: Why most published research findings do not live up to their promise in real life. *International Journal of Data Science and Analytics, 11*(3), 221–242. DOI: 10.1007/s41060-021-00245-5

Bukhari, A. H., Raja, M. A. Z., Sulaiman, M., Islam, S., Shoaib, M., & Kumam, P. (2020). Fractional Neuro-Sequential ARFIMA-LSTM for Financial Market Forecasting. *IEEE Access : Practical Innovations, Open Solutions, 8*, 71326–71338. DOI: 10.1109/ACCESS.2020.2985763

Bustos, O., & Pomares-Quimbaya, A. (2020). Stock market movement forecast: A Systematic review. *Expert Systems with Applications, 156*, 113464. DOI: 10.1016/j.eswa.2020.113464

Cao, L. (2021). *AI in Finance: Challenges, Techniques and Opportunities* (Version 1). arXiv. https://doi.org/DOI: 10.48550/ARXIV.2107.09051

Carta, S., Ferreira, A., Podda, A. S., Reforgiato Recupero, D., & Sanna, A. (2021). Multi-DQN: An ensemble of Deep Q-learning agents for stock market forecasting. *Expert Systems with Applications*, *164*, 113820. DOI: 10.1016/j.eswa.2020.113820

Cheng, D., Yang, F., Xiang, S., & Liu, J. (2022). Financial time series forecasting with multi-modality graph neural network. *Pattern Recognition*, *121*, 108218. DOI: 10.1016/j.patcog.2021.108218

Christensen, K., Siggaard, M., & Veliyev, B. (2023). A Machine Learning Approach to Volatility Forecasting. *Journal of Financial Econometrics*, *21*(5), 1680–1727. DOI: 10.1093/jjfinec/nbac020

Cogent | Blog | Forecasting Algorithms in Business: Choosing the Right Model for Your Industry. (n.d.). Retrieved September 17, 2025, from https://www.cogentinfo.com/resources/forecasting-algorithms-in-business-choosing-the-right-model-for-your-industry

Dahake, P. S., Dahake, N. S., Bansod, S. N., Patil, P. A., & Ingle, A. (2025). Marketing Innovations in Society 5.0: A Role of Predictive Analytics in Analyzing Consumer Behavior for Marketers. In *Future-Proofing Emerging Technologies for Business Transformation* (pp. 361–386). IGI Global Scientific Publishing. https://www.igi-global.com/chapter/marketing-innovations-in-society-50/378209

Dahake, P. S., Dahake, N. S., Bansod, S. N., & Patil, P. S. (2025). Advancing Marketing in Society 5.0: The Strategic Role of Predictive Analytics in Consumer Behaviour Analysis. In Tiwari, S. P., Aurellado, E. A., & Fahrudin, A. (Eds.), *Integrating Digital Innovation and Integrated Frameworks in Manufacturing* (pp. 329–362). IGI Global Scientific Publishing., DOI: 10.4018/979-8-3373-1082-4.ch013

Dahake, P. S., Nakshane, S., Mohare, R., & Ingle, A. (2025). AI-Enabled Predictive Analytics in Marketing: Transforming Customer Engagement and Brand Strategy. *2025 International Conference on Data Science and Business Systems (ICDSBS)*, 1–7. DOI: 10.1109/ICDSBS63635.2025.11031615

Gupta, A., Dengre, V., Kheruwala, H. A., & Shah, M. (2020). Comprehensive review of text-mining applications in finance. *Financial Innovation*, *6*(1), 39. DOI: 10.1186/s40854-020-00205-1

Hadji Misheva, B., Jaggi, D., Posth, J.-A., Gramespacher, T., & Osterrieder, J. (2021). Audience-Dependent Explanations for AI-Based Risk Management Tools: A Survey. *Frontiers in Artificial Intelligence*, *4*, 794996. DOI: 10.3389/frai.2021.794996

Hakala, K. (2019). *Robo-advisors as a form of artificial intelligence in private customers' investment advisory services*. https://aaltodoc.aalto.fi/handle/123456789/39329

Haq, A. U., Zeb, A., Lei, Z., & Zhang, D. (2021). Forecasting daily stock trend using multi-filter feature selection and deep learning. *Expert Systems with Applications*, *168*, 114444. DOI: 10.1016/j.eswa.2020.114444

He, K., Yang, Q., Ji, L., Pan, J., & Zou, Y. (2023). Financial Time Series Forecasting with the Deep Learning Ensemble Model. *Mathematics*, *11*(4), 1054. DOI: 10.3390/math11041054

Ho, W. K. O., Tang, B.-S., & Wong, S. W. (2021). Predicting property prices with machine learning algorithms. *Journal of Property Research*, *38*(1), 48–70. DOI: 10.1080/09599916.2020.1832558

Htun, H. H., Biehl, M., & Petkov, N. (2023). Survey of feature selection and extraction techniques for stock market prediction. *Financial Innovation*, *9*(1), 26. DOI: 10.1186/s40854-022-00441-7

Hu, Z., Zhao, Y., & Khushi, M. (2021). A Survey of Forex and Stock Price Prediction Using Deep Learning. *Applied System Innovation*, *4*(1), 9. DOI: 10.3390/asi4010009

Huang, Y., Gao, Y., Gan, Y., & Ye, M. (2021). A new financial data forecasting model using genetic algorithm and long short-term memory network. *Neurocomputing*, *425*, 207–218. DOI: 10.1016/j.neucom.2020.04.086

Ibrahim, R., Kim, S.-H., & Tong, J. (2020). Eliciting Human Judgment for Prediction Algorithms. SSRN *Electronic Journal*. DOI: 10.2139/ssrn.3606633

Jiang, W. (2021). Applications of deep learning in stock market prediction: Recent progress. *Expert Systems with Applications*, *184*, 115537. DOI: 10.1016/j.eswa.2021.115537

Kale, M., Gharat, H., & Rodrigues, C. V. (2024). The Role of Artificial Intelligence in Financial Prediction Models for Forecasting Market Trends with Traditional Methods. [EEL]. *European Economic Letters*, *14*(3), 1533–1544.

Kamara, A. F., Chen, E., & Pan, Z. (2022). An ensemble of a boosted hybrid of deep learning models and technical analysis for forecasting stock prices. *Information Sciences*, *594*, 1–19. DOI: 10.1016/j.ins.2022.02.015

Khan, W., Ghazanfar, M. A., Azam, M. A., Karami, A., Alyoubi, K. H., & Alfakeeh, A. S. (2022). Stock market prediction using machine learning classifiers and social media [news]. *Journal of Ambient Intelligence and Humanized Computing*, *13*(7), 3433–3456. DOI: 10.1007/s12652-020-01839-w

Kontopoulou, V. I., Panagopoulos, A. D., Kakkos, I., & Matsopoulos, G. K. (2023). A Review of ARIMA vs. Machine Learning Approaches for Time Series Forecasting in Data Driven Networks. *Future Internet, 15*(8), 255. DOI: 10.3390/fi15080255

Kumar, G., Jain, S., & Singh, U. P. (2021). Stock Market Forecasting Using Computational Intelligence: A Survey. *Archives of Computational Methods in Engineering, 28*(3), 1069–1101. DOI: 10.1007/s11831-020-09413-5

Kumbure, M. M., Lohrmann, C., Luukka, P., & Porras, J. (2022). Machine learning techniques and data for stock market forecasting: A literature review. *Expert Systems with Applications, 197*, 116659. DOI: 10.1016/j.eswa.2022.116659

Kurani, A., Doshi, P., Vakharia, A., & Shah, M. (2023). A Comprehensive Comparative Study of Artificial Neural Network (ANN) and Support Vector Machines (SVM) on Stock Forecasting. *Annals of Data Science, 10*(1), 183–208. DOI: 10.1007/s40745-021-00344-x

Lara-Benítez, P., Carranza-García, M., & Riquelme, J. C. (2021). An Experimental Review on Deep Learning Architectures for Time Series Forecasting. *International Journal of Neural Systems, 31*(03), 2130001. DOI: 10.1142/S0129065721300011

Li, A. W., & Bastos, G. S. (2020). Stock Market Forecasting Using Deep Learning and Technical Analysis: A Systematic Review. *IEEE Access : Practical Innovations, Open Solutions, 8*, 185232–185242. DOI: 10.1109/ACCESS.2020.3030226

Li, H., Zhang, R., Lee, Y.-C., Kraut, R. E., & Mohr, D. C. (2023). Systematic review and meta-analysis of AI-based conversational agents for promoting mental health and well-being. *NPJ Digital Medicine, 6*(1), 236. DOI: 10.1038/s41746-023-00979-5

Li, Y., & Pan, Y. (2022). A novel ensemble deep learning model for stock prediction based on stock prices and news. *International Journal of Data Science and Analytics, 13*(2), 139–149. DOI: 10.1007/s41060-021-00279-9

Liu, H., & Long, Z. (2020). An improved deep learning model for predicting stock market price time series. *Digital Signal Processing, 102*, 102741. DOI: 10.1016/j.dsp.2020.102741

Liu, X., Guo, J., Wang, H., & Zhang, F. (2022). Prediction of stock market index based on ISSA-BP neural network. *Expert Systems with Applications, 204*, 117604. DOI: 10.1016/j.eswa.2022.117604

Ma, S., & Fildes, R. (2021). Retail sales forecasting with meta-learning. *European Journal of Operational Research, 288*(1), 111–128. DOI: 10.1016/j.ejor.2020.05.038

Makridakis, S., Spiliotis, E., Assimakopoulos, V., Semenoglou, A.-A., Mulder, G., & Nikolopoulos, K. (2023). Statistical, machine learning and deep learning forecasting methods: Comparisons and ways forward. *The Journal of the Operational Research Society*, *74*(3), 840–859. DOI: 10.1080/01605682.2022.2118629

Masini, R. P., Medeiros, M. C., & Mendes, E. F. (2023). Machine learning advances for time series forecasting. *Journal of Economic Surveys*, *37*(1), 76–111. DOI: 10.1111/joes.12429

Md, A. Q., & Kapoor, S., A.V., C. J., Sivaraman, A. K., Tee, K. F., H., S., & N., J. (. (2023). Novel optimization approach for stock price forecasting using multi-layered sequential LSTM. *Applied Soft Computing*, *134*, 109830. DOI: 10.1016/j.asoc.2022.109830

Montero-Manso, P., & Hyndman, R. J. (2021). Principles and algorithms for forecasting groups of time series: Locality and globality. *International Journal of Forecasting*, *37*(4), 1632–1653. DOI: 10.1016/j.ijforecast.2021.03.004

Mukherjee, S., Sadhukhan, B., Sarkar, N., Roy, D., & De, S. (2023). Stock market prediction using deep learning algorithms. *CAAI Transactions on Intelligence Technology*, *8*(1), 82–94. DOI: 10.1049/cit2.12059

Nabipour, M., Nayyeri, P., Jabani, H., Mosavi, A., Salwana, E., & S, S. (2020). Deep Learning for Stock Market Prediction. *Entropy (Basel, Switzerland)*, *22*(8), 840. DOI: 10.3390/e22080840

Ndikum, P. (2020). *Machine Learning Algorithms for Financial Asset Price Forecasting* (Version 1). arXiv. DOI: 10.48550/ARXIV.2004.01504

Nti, I. K., Adekoya, A. F., & Weyori, B. A. (2020). A comprehensive evaluation of ensemble learning for stock-market prediction. *Journal of Big Data*, *7*(1), 20. DOI: 10.1186/s40537-020-00299-5

Pabuccu, H., & Barbu, A. (2023). *Feature Selection with Annealing for Forecasting Financial Time Series*. DOI: 10.48550/ARXIV.2303.02223

Park, H. J., Kim, Y., & Kim, H. Y. (2022). Stock market forecasting using a multi-task approach integrating long short-term memory and the random forest framework. *Applied Soft Computing*, *114*, 108106. DOI: 10.1016/j.asoc.2021.108106

Petropoulos, F., Apiletti, D., Assimakopoulos, V., Babai, M. Z., Barrow, D. K., Ben Taieb, S., Bergmeir, C., Bessa, R. J., Bijak, J., Boylan, J. E., Browell, J., Carnevale, C., Castle, J. L., Cirillo, P., Clements, M. P., Cordeiro, C., Cyrino Oliveira, F. L., De Baets, S., Dokumentov, A., & Ziel, F. (2022). Forecasting: Theory and practice. *International Journal of Forecasting*, *38*(3), 705–871. DOI: 10.1016/j.ijforecast.2021.11.001

Quinn, B. (2023). *Explaining AI in Finance: Past, Present, Prospects* (Version 1). arXiv. DOI: 10.48550/ARXIV.2306.02773

Rajbhar, R. (2025, June 7). Top Financial Forecasting Methods & Techniques You Must Know. *KAPSO*. https://kapso.in/blog/top-financial-forecasting-methods-techniques-you-must-know/

Roy, P., Ghose, B., Singh, P. K., Tyagi, P. K., & Vasudevan, A. (2025). Artificial Intelligence and Finance: A bibliometric review on the Trends, Influences, and Research Directions. *F1000 Research*, *14*, 122. DOI: 10.12688/f1000research.160959.1

Ryll, L., & Seidens, S. (2019a). *Evaluating the Performance of Machine Learning Algorithms in Financial Market Forecasting: A Comprehensive Survey* (Version 2). arXiv. DOI: 10.48550/ARXIV.1906.07786

Ryll, L., & Seidens, S. (2019b). *Evaluating the Performance of Machine Learning Algorithms in Financial Market Forecasting: A Comprehensive Survey* (Version 2). arXiv. DOI: 10.48550/ARXIV.1906.07786

Sahu, S. K., Mokhade, A., & Bokde, N. D. (2023). An Overview of Machine Learning, Deep Learning, and Reinforcement Learning-Based Techniques in Quantitative Finance: Recent Progress and Challenges. *Applied Sciences (Basel, Switzerland)*, *13*(3), 1956. DOI: 10.3390/app13031956

Selvakumar, P., Shanthi, M., Pitchiah, R., Sharma, M., Dahake, P. S., & T. C., M. (2025). The Role of Artificial Intelligence in Business Model Innovation: Overview of AI Technologies. In M. Khokhar (Ed.), *Advances in Business Strategy and Competitive Advantage* (pp. 219–246). IGI Global. DOI: 10.4018/979-8-3693-9571-4.ch009

Seyedan, M., & Mafakheri, F. (2020). Predictive big data analytics for supply chain demand forecasting: Methods, applications, and research opportunities. *Journal of Big Data*, *7*(1), 53. DOI: 10.1186/s40537-020-00329-2

Shahi, T. B., Shrestha, A., Neupane, A., & Guo, W. (2020). Stock Price Forecasting with Deep Learning: A Comparative Study. *Mathematics*, *8*(9), 1441. DOI: 10.3390/math8091441

Shen, Z., Zhang, Y., Lu, J., Xu, J., & Xiao, G. (2020). A novel time series forecasting model with deep learning. *Neurocomputing*, *396*, 302–313. DOI: 10.1016/j.neucom.2018.12.084

Singh, A., Ehtesham, A., Kumar, S., & Khoei, T. T. (2025). *Agentic Retrieval-Augmented Generation: A Survey on Agentic RAG* (Version 3). arXiv. DOI: 10.48550/ARXIV.2501.09136

Sohrabpour, V., Oghazi, P., Toorajipour, R., & Nazarpour, A. (2021). Export sales forecasting using artificial intelligence. *Technological Forecasting and Social Change*, *163*, 120480. DOI: 10.1016/j.techfore.2020.120480

Sonkavde, G., Dharrao, D. S., Bongale, A. M., Deokate, S. T., Doreswamy, D., & Bhat, S. K. (2023). Forecasting Stock Market Prices Using Machine Learning and Deep Learning Models: A Systematic Review, Performance Analysis and Discussion of Implications. *International Journal of Financial Studies*, *11*(3), 94. DOI: 10.3390/ijfs11030094

Stempień, D., & Ślepaczuk, R. (2025). *Hybrid Models for Financial Forecasting: Combining Econometric, Machine Learning, and Deep Learning Models* (Version 1). arXiv. DOI: 10.48550/ARXIV.2505.19617

Strader, T. J., Rozycki, J. J., Root, T. H., & Huang, Y.-H. J. (2020). Machine Learning Stock Market Prediction Studies: Review and Research Directions. *Journal of International Technology and Information Management*, *28*(4), 63–83. DOI: 10.58729/1941-6679.1435

Sutiene, K., Schwendner, P., Sipos, C., Lorenzo, L., Mirchev, M., Lameski, P., Kabasinskas, A., Tidjani, C., Ozturkkal, B., & Cerneviciene, J. (2024). Enhancing portfolio management using artificial intelligence: Literature review. *Frontiers in Artificial Intelligence*, *7*, 1371502. DOI: 10.3389/frai.2024.1371502

Tang, Y., Song, Z., Zhu, Y., Yuan, H., Hou, M., Ji, J., Tang, C., & Li, J. (2022). A survey on machine learning models for financial time series forecasting. *Neurocomputing*, *512*, 363–380. DOI: 10.1016/j.neucom.2022.09.003

The evolution of forecasting techniques: Traditional versus machine learning methods. (n.d.). Retrieved September 17, 2025, from https://www.genpact.com/insight/the-evolution-of-forecasting-techniques-traditional-versus-machine-learning-methods

The Forecasting Shift: From Excel to AI-Driven Precision | FP&A Trends. (2025, June 5). https://fpa-trends.com/article/forecasting-shift-excel-ai-driven-precision

Torres, J. F., Hadjout, D., Sebaa, A., Martínez-Álvarez, F., & Troncoso, A. (2021). Deep Learning for Time Series Forecasting: A Survey. *Big Data*, *9*(1), 3–21. DOI: 10.1089/big.2020.0159

University of J. Dobrila in Pula, Croatia, & Njegovanović, A. (2018). Artificial Intelligence: Financial Trading and Neurology of Decision. *Financial Markets, Institutions and Risks*, 58–68. DOI: 10.21272/fmir.2(2).58-68.2018

Wang, D., Li, L., & Zhao, D. (2022). Corporate finance risk prediction based on LightGBM. *Information Sciences*, *602*, 259–268. DOI: 10.1016/j.ins.2022.04.058

Wang, L., Jia, F., Chen, L., & Xu, Q. (2023). Forecasting SMEs' credit risk in supply chain finance with a sampling strategy based on machine learning techniques. *Annals of Operations Research*, *331*(1), 1–33. DOI: 10.1007/s10479-022-04518-5

Weber, P., Carl, K. V., & Hinz, O. (2024). Applications of Explainable Artificial Intelligence in Finance—A systematic review of Finance, Information Systems, and Computer Science literature. *Management Review Quarterly*, *74*(2), 867–907. DOI: 10.1007/s11301-023-00320-0

Wildi, M., & Misheva, B. H. (2022). *A Time Series Approach to Explainability for Neural Nets with Applications to Risk-Management and Fraud Detection* (Version 1). arXiv. DOI: 10.48550/ARXIV.2212.02906

Xiao, C., Xia, W., & Jiang, J. (2020). Stock price forecast based on combined model of ARI-MA-LS-SVM. *Neural Computing & Applications*, *32*(10), 5379–5388. DOI: 10.1007/s00521-019-04698-5

Ye, J., Goswami, B., Gu, J., Uddin, A., & Wang, G. (2024). *From Factor Models to Deep Learning: Machine Learning in Reshaping Empirical Asset Pricing* (Version 1). arXiv. DOI: 10.48550/ARXIV.2403.06779

Yu, X., Chen, Z., Ling, Y., Dong, S., Liu, Z., & Lu, Y. (2023). *Temporal Data Meets LLM — Explainable Financial Time Series Forecasting* (Version 1). arXiv. DOI: 10.48550/ARXIV.2306.11025

Yun, K. K., Yoon, S. W., & Won, D. (2023). Interpretable stock price forecasting model using genetic algorithm-machine learning regressions and best feature subset selection. *Expert Systems with Applications*, *213*, 118803. DOI: 10.1016/j.eswa.2022.118803

Zhang, D., & Lou, S. (2021). The application research of neural network and BP algorithm in stock price pattern classification and prediction. *Future Generation Computer Systems*, *115*, 872–879. DOI: 10.1016/j.future.2020.10.009

Zhao, Y., & Yang, G. (2023). Deep Learning-based Integrated Framework for stock price movement prediction. *Applied Soft Computing*, *133*, 109921. DOI: 10.1016/j.asoc.2022.109921

Chapter 6
The Role of AI in Economic and Financial Forecasting

Partap Singh
http://orcid.org/0000-0002-4653-7984
Maharishi Markendshwar University, Haryana, India

Anil Kumar
http://orcid.org/0000-0002-1793-4980
Lovely Professional University, Punjab, India

ABSTRACT

This study examines the evolving role of Artificial Intelligence (AI) in economic and financial forecasting, highlighting its capacity to process complex, high-frequency data and enhance predictive accuracy. Findings reveal that around 75% of professionals—particularly data scientists and technical experts—acknowledge AI's effectiveness in real-time and crisis forecasting. However, adoption remains uneven, with skepticism among policymakers and academics due to concerns over model transparency, interpretability, and data privacy. Respondents emphasized the ethical risks posed by biased algorithms and called for regulatory. The study also found strong support for hybrid forecasting models that integrate AI with traditional econometric approaches, offering a balanced framework that meets both computational and governance demands. Stakeholders identified accuracy, transparency, and ethical accountability as top priorities for AI adoption in forecasting.

DOI: 10.4018/979-8-3373-3053-2.ch006

1. INTRODUCTION

1.1 Background

The rapid advancement of Artificial Intelligence (AI) has transformed various sectors, particularly in economic and financial forecasting. As organizations increasingly rely on data-driven decision-making, AI-based forecasting models have emerged as powerful tools that promise enhanced accuracy and efficiency compared to traditional statistical and econometric approaches. This paper aims to critically evaluate the performance of these AI-based models, focusing on their application in economic and financial contexts. By examining the effectiveness of key AI techniques—such as neural networks, ensemble methods, and natural language processing (NLP)—this study seeks to provide a comprehensive understanding of how these technologies can improve forecasting outcomes.

The integration of AI into forecasting practices has been met with both enthusiasm and skepticism. While numerous studies have highlighted the potential benefits of AI, including improved data processing capabilities and enhanced decision-making efficiency (Trabelsi, 2024; Ardito et al., 2024), concerns regarding ethical implications, interpretability, and data privacy remain prevalent (Pavlidis, 2023; Romeo & Lacko, 2025). For instance, the application of AI in the banking sector has demonstrated significant improvements in forecasting accuracy, with studies reporting up to a 30% increase in prediction accuracy and a 20% enhancement in risk analysis (Chernysh et al., 2024). However, these advancements are often accompanied by challenges related to bias and accountability, necessitating a careful examination of the ethical considerations involved in deploying AI technologies. Furthermore, the literature indicates that the impact of AI on economic development is multifaceted, with both positive and negative consequences. While AI has the potential to drive revenue growth and operational efficiency, it also poses risks such as job displacement and increased economic disparity (Trabelsi, 2024; Fang et al., 2022). This duality underscores the importance of understanding the broader implications of AI in economic forecasting, particularly as it relates to stakeholder perceptions of credibility and transparency). The study emphasized how technological innovations, such as AI and blockchain, reshaped investment strategies by enhancing data analysis, risk modeling, and portfolio customization. It demonstrated that early adopters of tech-based strategies gained a competitive edge, especially in emerging markets where data-driven tools identified undervalued assets (Singh, Partap, 2024).

In light of these considerations, this paper will address the following objectives: (1) to critically evaluate the performance of AI-based forecasting models compared to traditional approaches; (2) to identify and categorize key AI techniques and assess their effectiveness in forecasting various financial and economic indicators;

and (3) to examine the challenges and ethical considerations associated with the deployment of AI in forecasting. By synthesizing existing research and providing a nuanced analysis of AI's role in economic and financial forecasting, this study aims to contribute valuable insights for practitioners, policymakers, and researchers alike.

1.2 Research Gap

While considerable research has examined AI's general applications in finance and economics, there is a lack of comprehensive analysis specifically focused on:

- The systematic comparison of AI models with traditional forecasting approaches.
- The interpretability and transparency of AI forecasts in regulatory or policy-driven contexts.
- The scalability and adaptability of AI models across different economic environments and data regimes. This paper aims to bridge this gap by analyzing both the capabilities and the constraints of AI tools in real-world forecasting scenarios.

1.3 Objectives of the Paper

1. To critically evaluate the performance of AI-based forecasting models compared to traditional statistical and econometric approaches in economic and financial contexts.
2. To identify and categorize the key AI techniques—such as neural networks, ensemble methods, and NLP—and assess their effectiveness in forecasting various financial and economic indicators.
3. To examine the challenges and ethical considerations associated with the deployment of AI in forecasting, including issues of interpretability, bias, and data privacy

1.4 Research Questions

1. What are the most commonly used AI techniques in economic and financial forecasting, and how do they perform relative to traditional models?
2. How can AI improve the accuracy and timeliness of forecasts in volatile or uncertain economic environments?
3. What are the limitations and risks of relying on AI-based models in high-stakes forecasting scenarios, such as central bank policymaking or market regulation?

4. How do stakeholders (e.g., economists, investors, regulators) perceive the credibility and transparency of AI-driven forecasts?
5. What frameworks or best practices can be developed to responsibly integrate AI into the economic and financial forecasting process

1.5 Structure of Paper

The paper is organized into five distinct sections: Section-I Introduction (including objectives& research questions), Section II - Literature Review, Section III - Research Methodology, Section IV - Results and Discussion, and Section V – Summary. In Section IV, the analysis of survey results is presented in sub-sections.

2. LITERATURE REVIEW

2.1 Performance Evaluation of AI-Based Forecasting Models

This study investigated the application of Artificial Intelligence in financial forecasting, particularly within the banking sector. It highlighted AI's ability to analyze vast datasets for decision-making in share price prediction and market trend analysis. The research employed the ARIMA model alongside machine learning techniques using R software, revealing a 30% increase in forecasting accuracy and a 20% improvement in risk analysis. Ethical concerns regarding data privacy and accountability in AI applications were also discussed (Chernysh et al., 2024). This literature review focused on AI applications in accounting prediction, systematically evaluating 47 research papers from Web of Science and Scopus. The authors assessed various forecasting models and their effectiveness in predicting financial outcomes. The findings indicated that while AI enhanced predictive capabilities, there was a notable absence of sociotechnical considerations and limited generalizability across different contexts, suggesting a need for further exploration into AI's role in financial forecasting (Kureljusic & Karger, 2023).

This research examined the impact of AI on revenue growth in European small and medium-sized enterprises (SMEs). It assessed the relationship between AI applications and financial performance, emphasizing how AI synergized with technologies like Big Data Analytics and the Internet of Things (IoT). The study found that AI positively influenced revenue growth, particularly when integrated with other technologies, thereby demonstrating the effectiveness of AI-based forecasting models in enhancing financial outcomes for SMEs (Ardito et al., 2024). This study addressed the accuracy of bankruptcy prediction models, emphasizing the role of AI in enhancing predictive capabilities. By employing explainable AI techniques, the research presented a novel approach to forecasting corporate crises. The findings suggested that AI models significantly improved prediction accuracy compared to traditional methods, highlighting the potential of AI in financial forecasting and the necessity for further research into its application in corporate finance (Fasano et al., 2024). Another study examined the transformative role of AI in financial risk management, revealing that machine learning algorithms significantly enhanced risk identification, modeling accuracy, and mitigation strategies across banking sectors. The research highlighted AI's capacity to anticipate financial anomalies and systemic threats more effectively than traditional models (*Singh Partap, 2025).*

2.2 Key AI Techniques in Financial and Economic Forecasting

This research explored the integration of big data analysis and machine learning in accounting forecasting. It highlighted the effectiveness of various AI techniques, including neural networks, in enhancing predictive accuracy. The study emphasized the importance of selecting appropriate models based on specific financial indicators being forecasted, thereby contributing to a deeper understanding of how AI could be utilized in economic and financial contexts (Zhai et al., 2021). Another study investigated the impact of ICT patents on economic growth, employing AI techniques to analyze the relationship between technological advancements and financial performance. The research identified key AI methodologies that enhanced forecasting capabilities, demonstrating how AI could effectively predict economic indicators. The findings underscored the importance of integrating AI into economic analysis to improve forecasting accuracy and inform policy decisions (Nguyen & Doytch, 2022).

This literature review focused on AI research in agriculture, emphasizing its applications in economic forecasting. The study categorized various AI techniques, including machine learning and data analytics, and assessed their effectiveness in predicting agricultural outcomes. The findings revealed that AI significantly enhanced forecasting accuracy, offering valuable insights for economic planning and decision-making in the agricultural sector (Sood et al., 2022). Moreover, this research examined the occupational impact of AI on the labor market, applying AI techniques to analyze job displacement and creation. The study classified the effects of AI across different professions, highlighting the importance of understanding AI's role in economic forecasting. The findings suggested that AI offered valuable insights into labor market trends, supporting policymakers in addressing the challenges posed by technological advancements (Zarifhonarvar, 2024).

This work analyzed leading practices in algorithmic trading, showing that machine learning models improved trading efficiency and predictive power. Case studies demonstrated how neural networks and reinforcement learning adapted to volatile market dynamics, optimizing trade execution. Survey data supported the growing reliance on AI to navigate financial complexities (Singh, P., 2025). The chapter explored behavioral biases in real estate, finding that overconfidence, anchoring, and herding significantly influenced investment decisions. It concluded that these biases often distorted market prices and hindered rational analysis, especially in speculative environments, highlighting the need for behavioral insights in real estate forecasting (Singh, P., 2024). This research investigated AI's role in detecting herding behavior in financial markets. It found that machine learning tools effectively identified patterns of collective investor behavior, enabling earlier detection of irrational market trends and potential bubbles. The findings supported AI's utility in mitigating emotionally driven investment waves (Singh, Partap, 2024).

2.3 Challenges and Ethical Considerations in AI Deployment

The deployment of AI tools for anti-money laundering and asset recovery presents ethical challenges in financial contexts. These challenges include concerns related to interpretability, bias, and data privacy, highlighting the need for transparent AI systems. The research underscores the importance of considering ethical implications in AI applications, particularly in sensitive areas like financial forecasting, to ensure accountability and maintain trust in AI-driven decision-making (Pavlidis, 2023). The study examines the challenges and drivers of AI adoption within organizations, emphasizing ethical concerns such as data privacy and security. It stresses the need to address these issues to facilitate successful AI integration in economic forecasting. By identifying key factors influencing AI adoption, the research provides valuable insights into how organizations can manage ethical dilemmas while leveraging AI to enhance forecasting outcomes (Romeo & Lacko, 2025).

Additionally, the use of AI in intelligent transportation systems focuses on ethical challenges related to data privacy and security. The study highlights the importance of responsible AI deployment in forecasting transportation trends, with particular attention to interpretability and accountability. The findings suggest that addressing these ethical considerations is vital for maximizing the potential of AI in economic forecasting and ensuring public trust in AI applications (Zemmouchi-Ghomari, 2025).

2.4 Economic and Sectoral Impacts of AI Forecasting

This study assesses AI's dual impact on economic development—highlighting enhanced data processing and decision-making capacities, alongside adverse effects such as job displacement and rising inequality. It provides insights into how AI-driven forecasting can shape economic policy to maximize benefits and mitigate negative consequences. (Trabelsi, 2024). The authors explore AI's role in globalization and economic strategy, emphasizing AI's potential to drive growth through improved forecasting models. They caution about challenges like economic disparities and regulatory hurdles, suggesting strategic frameworks for equitable AI integration in economic forecasting. (Korinek & Stiglitz, 2021). Focusing on healthcare organizations, this research shows how AI enhances competitive positioning through improved efficiency, particularly in robotic surgeries. It illustrates AI's capacity to support decision-making and forecasting in organizational performance, emphasizing its strategic value across economic sectors. (Ali Mohamad, 2023) Investigating the Indian energy transition, this study finds that lack of incentives and fragmented research limit AI's forecasting contributions to the sector's development. It underscores the need for cohesive information management to harness AI effectively in economic forecasting for energy. (Chawla et al., 2022)

This paper presents an AI-enabled blockchain system for smart grid power management, reflecting AI's growing role in forecasting energy consumption and production. It highlights technological innovations that support economic forecasting in the energy sector, addressing efficiency and sustainability. (Wang et al., 2020). Focused on agriculture, this study underscores AI's role in forecasting farming outputs and improving decision-making. Despite challenges like limited farmer awareness, AI's integration promises enhanced economic forecasts, supporting policy and technology development. (Sood et al., 2022) Addressing occupational impacts, this research quantifies how AI differently affects various job types, offering forecasts on labor market trends. It emphasizes understanding these dynamics for economic planning and formulating inclusive policies. (Zarifhonarvar, 2024).

2.5 AI Adoption and Integration Factor

The research discusses organizational, environmental, and technological factors influencing AI adoption. Variables such as data availability, privacy, management support, and skills affect AI uptake, which in turn shapes forecasting capabilities. The study spotlights critical elements needed for successful AI integration. (Romeo & Lacko, 2025).

This study explores AI's application in governmental public procurement, focusing on adoption challenges including data privacy and efficiency improvements. It offers insights into AI's role in forecasting procurement outcomes, linking technological integration to organizational change. (Andersson et al., 2025). Investigating procurement processes, this paper identifies AI's potential and areas needing improvement to boost forecasting accuracy and operational effectiveness. It stresses overcoming barriers related to trust and technical knowledge. (Guida et al., 2023)

This study analyzes AI's impact on regional green development through economic forecasting models. It highlights threshold effects and spatial econometrics, illustrating AI's growing influence in environmental-economic forecasting and policy applications. (Fang et al., 2022). Examining the pharmaceutical industry in Ukraine, this research identifies AI's prospects in forecasting industry growth and challenges. The paper examined AI applications in rural development, showing that intelligent systems enhanced agricultural productivity, financial inclusion, and access to social services. It found that AI-driven platforms tailored to rural needs improved decision-making and resource allocation, contributing to sustainable economic development in underserved regions (Singh, Partap, 2024).

This category highlights the various factors influencing the adoption and integration of AI across different sectors. The studies emphasize the importance of addressing organizational, environmental, and technological challenges to enhance forecasting capabilities and drive successful AI implementation.

3. RESEARCH METHODOLOGY

3.1 Research Design

This study adopts a descriptive and exploratory research design to investigate the role of AI in economic and financial forecasting. The design is suitable for understanding expert perceptions, identifying patterns, and evaluating the practical applicability and limitations of AI-based forecasting models across various domains such as macroeconomics, financial risk assessment, and market trend prediction.

3.2. Data Collection Method

Primary data will be collected through a structured questionnaire survey administered to a targeted sample of professionals including Economists, Financial analysts, Data scientists'/AI practitioners, Academics and researchers and Policymakers and regulatory. The questionnaire includes both quantitative items (using a 5-point Likert scale) and qualitative open-ended questions to capture a broad range of insights.

3.3. Sampling Technique

A judgement sampling technique will be employed to ensure that only respondents with relevant domain expertise participate. This technique is ideal for studies that require expert judgment and specialized insights rather than generalized public opinion.

3.4. Sample Size

The expected sample size is 200 respondents, ensuring adequate representation across different stakeholder groups and professional backgrounds for meaningful analysis.

3.5. Data Analysis Techniques

The collected data (Likert-scale responses) will be analyzed using percentile, Mean, Mode and Various charts.

Percentile: A percentile indicates the relative standing of a value within a dataset
Mean (Average): The mean is the sum of all data values divided by the total number of values. It shows the central tendency of the dataset.
Mean=Sum of all observations \ Number of observations
Mode: The mode is the value that occurs most frequently in a dataset.

3.6. Research Ethics

All responses will be collected with informed consent and will remain confidential. Participation is voluntary, and data will be used solely for academic purposes. The study will adhere to ethical guidelines for research involving human participants.

4. RESULTS AND DISCUSSION

Section A: Respondent Profile

Table 1. Distribution of Respondents with Over 1 Year of AI/ML Experience by Role

S.no	Respondents	Experience	Number	Percentage (%)
	Economists	More than 1 year	30	15
	Financial analysts	More than 1 year	30	15
	Data scientists/AI practitioners	More than 1 year	20	10
	Academics and researchers	More than 1 year	100	50
	Policymakers and regulatory experts	More than 1 year	20	10
	Total		200	100

Source: Author

Table.1 presents the percentage distribution of respondents with more than one year of experience using AI/ML tools across different professional roles. Academics and researchers make up the majority at 50%, followed by economists and financial analysts at 15% each. Data scientists and policymakers contribute 10% each. The chart highlights a strong presence of long-term AI/ML engagement within academic and analytical professions.

Figure 1. Distribution of Respondents with Over 1 Year of AI/ML Experience by Role

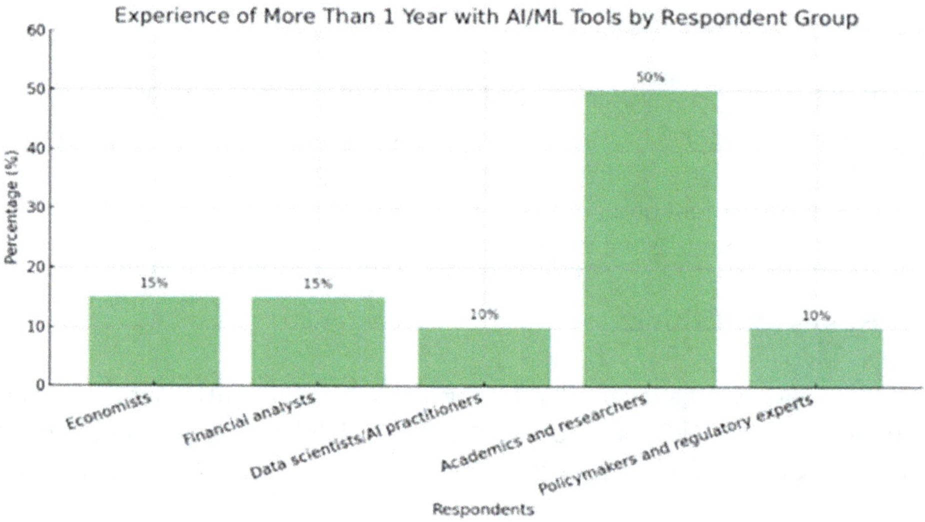

Source: Author

The Figure 1 shows that academics and researchers lead with 50% having over one year of experience with AI/ML tools. Economists and financial analysts follow at 15% each, while data scientists and policymakers trail at 10%. This suggests stronger AI/ML engagement within academic circles compared to other professional groups.

Table 2. Use of AI/ML Tools in Forecasting Applications

S. No	Role	Total	Yes (%)	No (%)
1	Economists	30	60%	40%
2	Financial analysts	30	70%	30%
3	Data scientists/AI practitioners	20	95%	5%
4	Academics and researchers	100	55%	45%

continued on following page

Table 2. Continued

S. No	Role	Total	Yes (%)	No (%)
5	Policymakers and regulatory experts	20	30%	70%
	Total	200	58%	42%

Source: Author

The table 2 highlight a differentiated pattern of AI/ML adoption in forecasting across professional roles. Data scientists'/AI practitioners report the highest adoption (95%), reflecting their core engagement with predictive technologies. Financial analysts and economists also show notable engagement at 70% and 60%, respectively, indicating growing reliance on data-driven tools for financial forecasting. Conversely, only 30% of policymakers and 55% of academics' report using such tools, pointing to a lag in integration within regulatory and theoretical domains. Overall, 58% of respondents have experience with AI/ML in forecasting, indicating a positive but uneven adoption trend across sectors.

Figure 2. Role-wise Adoption of AI/ML Tools in Forecasting Applications

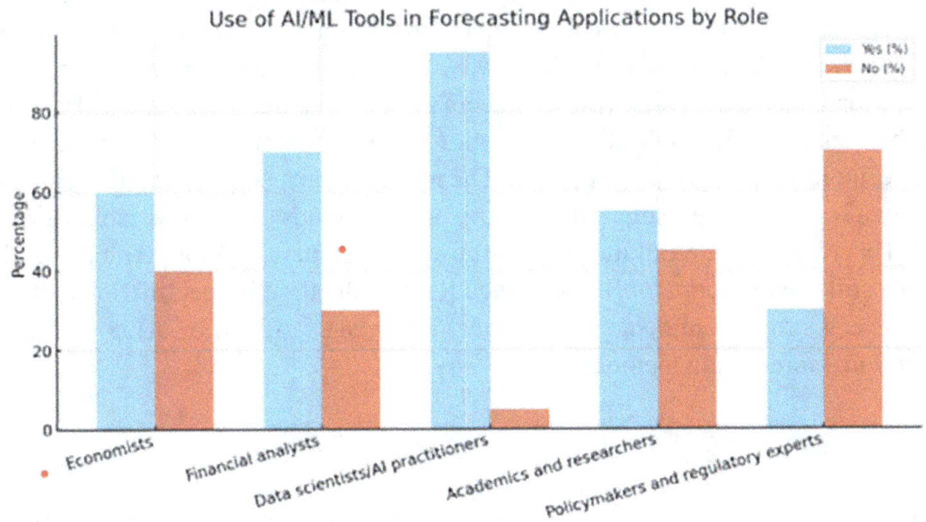

Source: Author

This bar chart 2 illustrates the percentage of respondents from various professional roles who have worked with AI/ML tools in forecasting. Data scientists and financial analysts show the highest engagement, while policymakers and academics report relatively lower adoption rates.

Section B: Impact of AI in Forecasting

Table 3. Percentage Distribution of Professional Opinions on the Effectiveness of AI-Driven Models in Enhancing the Accuracy of Economic and Financial Forecasts

S.no	Respondents	Total	Strongly Agree	Agree	Neutral	Disagree	Strongly Disagree
1	Economists	30	33%	40%	17%	7%	3%
2	Financial analysts	30	40%	33%	13%	10%	3%
3	Data scientists/AI practitioners	20	50%	35%	10%	5%	0%
4	Academics and researchers	100	35%	40%	15%	7%	3%
5	Policymakers and regulatory experts	20	25%	45%	15%	10%	5%
	Overall % (out of 200)	200	36%	39%	15%	8%	3%

Source: Author

Table 3 confirms that 75% of all respondents either strongly agree (36%) or agree (39%) that AI-driven models enhance the accuracy of economic and financial forecasting. The strongest agreement comes from data scientists (50% strongly agree) and financial analysts (40%), likely due to firsthand experience with model performance. Academics and policymakers show similar trends, though with slightly higher neutrality and mild disagreement. Only 8% disagree and 3% strongly disagree, indicating marginal skepticism. The mode remains "Agree" at 39%, while the median is also "Agree," suggesting central opinion trends toward favorable views of AI. This reveals an overall industry shift toward embracing AI for predictive tasks, while still leaving room for further education or validation in specific fields. It also suggests a strong confidence in empirical advantages offered by AI compared to traditional forecasting methods.

Figure 3. Pie Chart Representing Professional Opinions on the Effectiveness of AI-Driven Models in Enhancing the Accuracy of Economic and Financial Forecasts

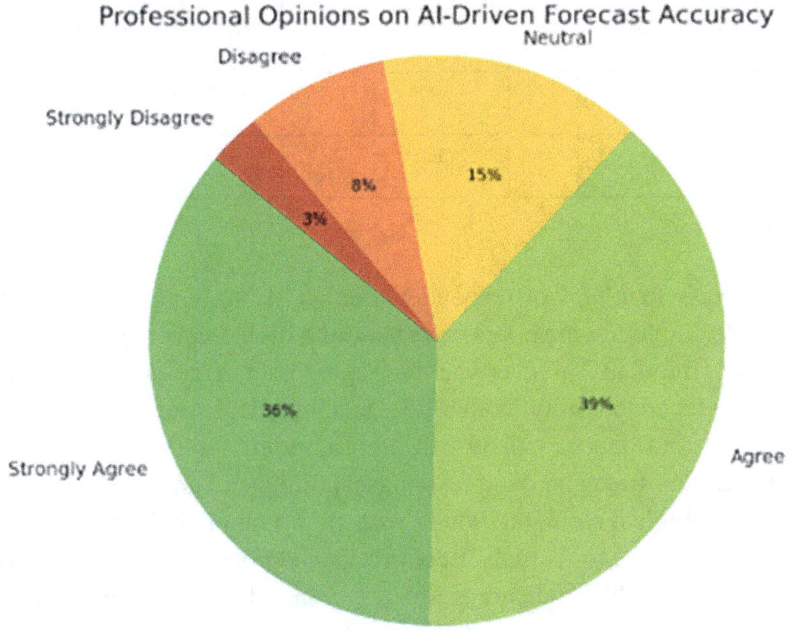

Source: Author

This Figure 3 visually summarizes the percentage distribution of expert opinions across five professional groups. A combined 75% of respondents either strongly agree (36%) or agree (39%) that AI-driven models outperform traditional models in forecasting accuracy. The chart emphasizes the predominance of favorable sentiment, with only 11% expressing disagreement or strong disagreement, and 15% remaining neutral. The mode is "Agree," and the median lies between "Agree" and "Strongly Agree," reflecting overall confidence in AI-enhanced forecasting methods.

Table 4. Professional Opinions on AI's Effectiveness for Complex Economic Data

S.no	Respondents	Total	Strongly Agree	Agree	Neutral	Disagree	Strongly Disagree
1	Economists	30	9 (30%)	12 (40%)	6 (20%)	2 (7%)	1 (3%)
2	Financial analysts	30	10 (33%)	13 (43%)	5 (17%)	2 (7%)	0 (0%)
3	Data scientists/AI practitioners	20	12 (60%)	6 (30%)	1 (5%)	1 (5%)	0 (0%)

continued on following page

Table 4. Continued

S.no	Respondents	Total	Strongly Agree	Agree	Neutral	Disagree	Strongly Disagree
4	Academics and researchers	100	35 (35%)	42 (42%)	15 (15%)	5 (5%)	3 (3%)
5	Policymakers and regulatory experts	20	6 (30%)	8 (40%)	4 (20%)	2 (10%)	0 (0%)
	Total	200	72 (36%)	81 (41%)	31 (15.5%)	12 (6%)	4 (2%)

Source: Author

Table 4 reveals that 77% of respondents either strongly agree (36%) or agree (41%) that AI technologies are effective in handling high-frequency, non-linear, and large-scale economic data. This overwhelming agreement suggests strong professional confidence in AI's adaptability, scalability, and analytical strength. Data scientists show the highest confidence, with 60% strongly agreeing—reflecting their practical experience with real-time and complex datasets. Financial analysts and academics also demonstrate high agreement, though with slightly more balanced views, likely due to varying exposure to AI tools. Economists and policymakers show moderate agreement, with 30%–40% indicating strong or general support. Neutral responses (15.5%) point to ongoing observation or limited hands-on experience with such data environments. Minimal disagreement (8% combined) suggests very little resistance to AI's applicability in this domain.

The mode of responses is "Agree", and the median lies between "Agree" and "Strongly Agree," indicating the central tendency is clearly favorable. This pattern shows widespread trust in AI's ability to process complex economic signals at scale—critical in today's volatile and data-rich global environment. These insights support the integration of AI into core economic modeling and forecasting frameworks, especially in high-frequency trading, real-time risk analytics, and macroeconomic simulations.

Figure 4. Professional Opinions on AI's Effectiveness for Complex Economic Data

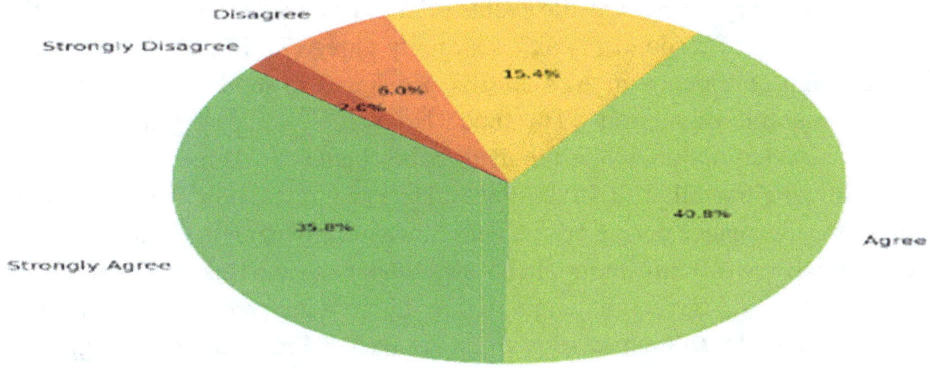

Source: Author

The Figure 4 clearly illustrates that a significant majority of professionals (77%) either agree (41%) or strongly agree (36%) that AI technologies are effective in handling high-frequency, non-linear, and large-scale economic data. This positive outlook indicates a strong trust in AI's capacity to manage modern economic complexities. Only 15.5% of respondents remain neutral, potentially signaling caution or limited exposure, while a mere 8% expressed disagreement. The visual representation underscores that the mode of responses is "Agree," and the median lies between "Agree" and "Strongly Agree," suggesting the dominant sentiment is favorable. This chart complements the tabular data and emphasizes broad professional confidence in AI's transformative role in economic analytics.

Table 5. Perceptions on AI's Role in Forecasting During Volatile Events

S.no	Respondents	Total	Strongly Agree	Agree	Neutral	Disagree	Strongly Disagree
1	Economists	30	10 (33%)	12 (40%)	5 (17%)	2 (7%)	1 (3%)
2	Financial analysts	30	11 (37%)	13 (43%)	4 (13%)	2 (7%)	0 (0%)
3	Data scientists/AI practitioners	20	12 (60%)	6 (30%)	1 (5%)	1 (5%)	0 (0%)
4	Academics and researchers	100	36 (36%)	44 (44%)	12 (12%)	5 (5%)	3 (3%)
5	Policymakers and regulatory experts	20	6 (30%)	8 (40%)	4 (20%)	2 (10%)	0 (0%)
	Total	200	75 (37.5%)	83 (41.5%)	26 (13%)	12 (6%)	4 (2%)

Source: Author

Table 5 suggest widespread agreement that AI models significantly enhance forecasting accuracy during volatile events such as financial crises and pandemics. A combined 79% of respondents either strongly agree (37.5%) or agree (41.5%), reflecting high confidence in AI's ability to respond to market uncertainty and dynamic economic disruptions. The mode is "Agree", indicating it is the most frequently selected option, while the median lies between "Agree" and "Strongly Agree", showing overall positive sentiment. Data scientists show the strongest belief in AI's performance during crises, with 60% strongly agreeing, likely based on direct experience with real-time applications. Academics and financial analysts also show a high level of agreement, emphasizing the growing credibility of AI-driven forecasting tools. Only 8% express disagreement, and 13% remain neutral, suggesting limited skepticism. These insights highlight that AI models are increasingly trusted in high-risk and uncertain environments for real-time forecasting.

Figure 5. Perceptions on AI's Role in Forecasting During Volatile Events

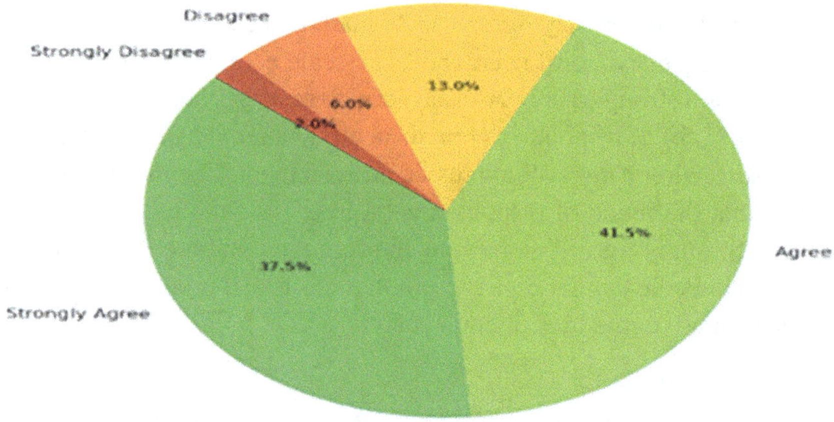

Source: Author

The pie chart visually conveys that a substantial 79% of respondents believe AI significantly improves forecasting during high-volatility events, with "Agree" (41.5%) being the most frequent response. The mode is clearly "Agree," and the median response falls between "Agree" and "Strongly Agree," reflecting overall optimism about AI's capabilities in dynamic environments like financial crises and pandemics. Only a small portion—8%—expressed disagreement or strong disagreement, indicating limited skepticism. This chart supports the tabular analysis by reinforcing that expert opinion overwhelmingly favors AI-enhanced forecasting during turbulent times.

Section C: Methodologies and Comparative Effectiveness

Table 6. Perception of AI Techniques ussed for Forecasting among Respondent Groups

S.no	Respondents	Total	Strongly Agree	Agree	Neutral	Disagree	Strongly Disagree
1	Economists	30	10	12	5	2	1
2	Financial analysts	30	12	10	4	3	1
3	Data scientists/AI practitioners	20	15	3	1	1	0
4	Academics and researchers	100	35	30	20	10	5
5	Policymakers and regulatory exp.	20	3	6	5	4	2
	Total	200	75	61	35	20	9

Source: Author

Statistical Analysis

Mode (most frequent response category):

Strongly Agree = 75 (most selected across groups)

Median (central tendency of response category counts):

Ordering: 9, 20, 35, 61, 75

Median = 35 → *Neutral responses*

Table 6 indicate a generally favorable view of AI techniques for forecasting across all respondent groups. The most common response is "Strongly Agree" (75 respondents), suggesting a strong endorsement and practical engagement with AI tools like machine learning, deep learning, and hybrid models. Notably, Data scientists show the highest proportion of strong agreement, underscoring their hands-on familiarity with such methods. Academics and economists also report high agreement, reflecting the growing academic and theoretical interest in AI-driven forecasting. Policymakers, on the other hand, lean toward more cautious or neutral stances, possibly due to regulatory or implementation concerns. The median response category is Neutral, reflecting that a significant portion still holds undecided or balanced views. This indicates ongoing adaptation, learning, or uncertainty in adopting AI tools across sectors. The mode being "Strongly Agree" implies that AI's role in forecasting is not just theoretical but increasingly mainstream, particularly in technical and financial fields.

Figure 6. Perception of AI Techniques Used for Forecasting Among Respondent Groups

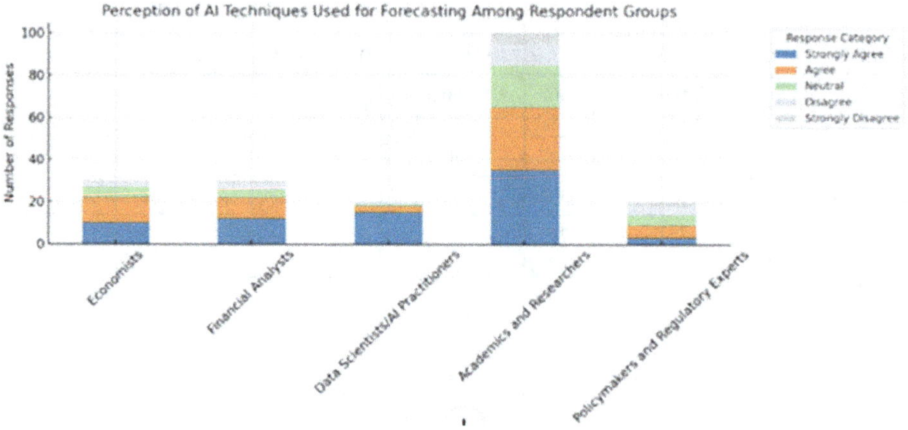

Source: Author

The figure 6 illustrates the distribution of responses from five professional groups regarding their use or study of AI forecasting techniques. Data scientists and AI practitioners show the strongest support, with most selecting "Strongly Agree," reflecting deep engagement with AI technologies. Academics and researchers also lean toward strong agreement, indicating growing adoption in academic forecasting models. Economists and financial analysts display moderate to strong agreement, suggesting familiarity with AI but varying levels of application. Policymakers and regulatory experts exhibit the highest neutral or disagreeing responses, likely due to institutional or policy barriers. The visual contrast between "Strongly Agree" and "Neutral" across professions highlights an uneven landscape of AI adoption, suggesting that technical fields are ahead in integrating AI, while others may need training or clearer policy frameworks to catch up.

Table 7. Professional Perspectives on AI vs Traditional Forecasting: A Comparative Analysis of Survey Response

S.No	Respondents	Total	Strongly Agree	Agree	Neutral	Disagree	Strongly Disagree
1	Economists	30	8	10	7	4	1
2	Financial analysts	30	12	11	4	2	1
3	Data scientists/AI practitioners	20	14	5	1	0	0

continued on following page

Table 7. Continued

S.No	Respondents	Total	Strongly Agree	Agree	Neutral	Disagree	Strongly Disagree
4	Academics and researchers	100	40	30	20	7	3
5	Policymakers and regulatory exp.	20	4	6	5	4	1
	Total	200	78	62	37	17	6

Source: Author

Table 7 indicates that across different professional groups, there is a growing consensus that AI-based forecasting techniques outperform traditional econometric models. The most frequent response was "Strongly Agree" (78 responses), particularly dominant among data scientists (70%) and academics (40%), reflecting direct exposure to the predictive power of AI models such as LSTM, Random Forests, or ensemble techniques. Financial analysts also show a high level of agreement, pointing to practical success using AI in market forecasting. Economists exhibit a more balanced view, with a fair share of neutral and disagreeing responses—likely due to attachment to conventional models. Policymakers display a cautious outlook, with 25% expressing disagreement or neutrality, likely reflecting a policy lag or limited integration of AI-based insights. The median of "Neutral" suggests that while strong support for AI exists, significant portions of respondents are either unconvinced or still evaluating. This highlights the need for more cross-disciplinary validation and training in AI applications.

Figure 7. Professional Perspectives on AI vs Traditional Forecasting: A Comparative Analysis of Survey Responses

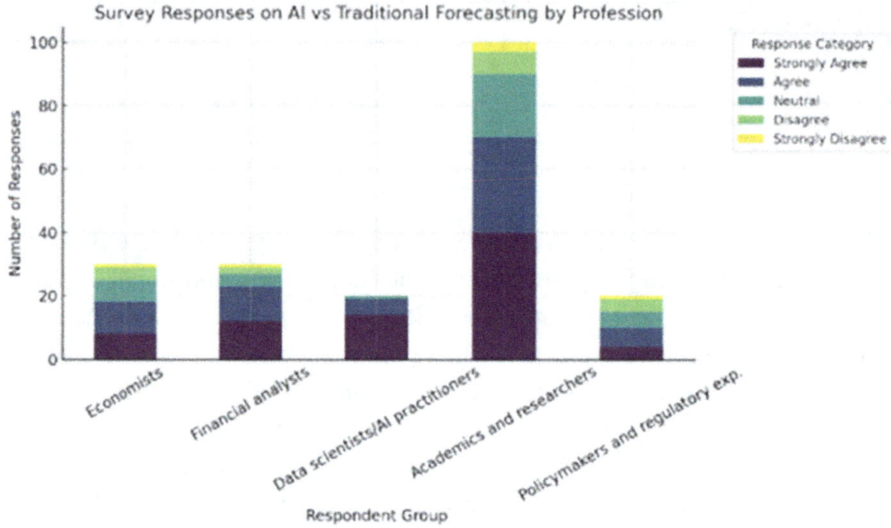

Source: Author

The Figure 7 shows that support for AI-based forecasting is strongest among data scientists and academics, with most responses in the "Strongly Agree" and "Agree" categories. Financial analysts also express high confidence, reflecting practical success with AI models. Economists display mixed views, with notable neutrality and some disagreement, indicating a transitional stance. Policymakers are the most cautious, with higher proportions of neutral and disagreeing responses, possibly due to limited exposure or regulatory concerns. Overall, the chart highlights a clear divide: technical and research-driven professionals are more receptive to AI forecasting, while traditional and policy-oriented groups remain reserved or unconvinced.

Section D: Interpretability, Ethics, and Trust

Table 8. Explores perceptions on the interpretability of AI models in economic forecasting

S.No	Respondents	Total	Strongly Agree	Agree	Neutral	Disagree	Strongly Disagree
1	Economists	30	4 (13.3%)	8 (26.7%)	10 (33.3%)	6 (20.0%)	2 (6.7%)
2	Financial analysts	30	3 (10.0%)	12 (40.0%)	8 (26.7%)	5 (16.7%)	2 (6.7%)
3	Data scientists/AI practitioners	20	6 (30.0%)	8 (40.0%)	4 (20.0%)	2 (10.0%)	0 (0.0%)
4	Academics and researchers	100	10 (10.0%)	25 (25.0%)	30 (30.0%)	25 (25.0%)	10 (10.0%)
5	Policymakers and regulatory experts	20	1 (5.0%)	5 (25.0%)	5 (25.0%)	6 (30.0%)	3 (15.0%)
	Total	200	24 (12.0%)	58 (29.0%)	57 (28.5%)	44 (22.0%)	17 (8.5%)

Source: Author

The table 8 explores perceptions on the interpretability of AI models in economic forecasting. From a total of 200 respondents across five professional groups, the most frequent response (mode) is "Agree" (58 responses or 29.0%), suggesting a general belief that AI models are somewhat interpretable for decision-makers. The median response is "Neutral," indicating that the central tendency of responses reflects uncertainty or mixed feelings regarding interpretability. Data scientists and financial analysts show higher confidence, with 70% and 50% respectively selecting "Agree" or "Strongly Agree." In contrast, policymakers and academics are more reserved, showing higher percentages in "Neutral" and "Disagree" categories. This discrepancy highlights a gap between technical expertise and end-user understanding. Overall, the data indicates moderate trust in AI interpretability but reveals a need for clearer, more transparent AI models and improved communication to bridge the interpretability gap between model developers and decision-makers.

Figure 8. Explores perceptions on the interpretability of AI models in economic forecasting

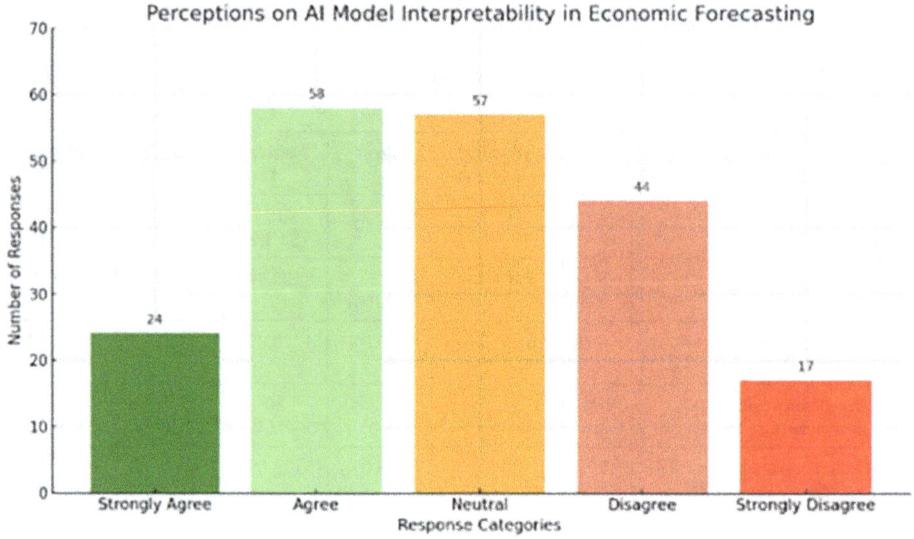

Source: Author

The figure 8 visually represents how different professional groups perceive the interpretability of AI models used in economic forecasting. The highest number of responses falls under "Agree" (58), followed closely by "Neutral" (57), indicating a general leaning toward agreement but with significant ambivalence. "Disagree" received 44 responses, reflecting concerns among a substantial portion of respondents, especially non-technical stakeholders like policymakers and researchers. The lower response count for "Strongly Agree" (24) and "Strongly Disagree" (17) suggests that most participants hold moderate rather than extreme views.

This visual confirms that while a segment of users sees interpretability as adequate, many still question the clarity of AI-driven outputs. It emphasizes the need for enhanced explain-ability tools and better communication strategies between AI practitioners and decision-makers. The figure underscores a critical insight: trust in AI is present but cautious, and must be reinforced through user-centered design and interpretability frameworks.

Table 9. Survey on Concerns About Algorithmic Bias and Fairness in AI-Driven Financial Predictions

S.no	Strongly Agree (%)	Agree (%)	Neutral (%)	Disagree (%)	Strongly Disagree (%)
Economists	12 (40.00%)	10 (33.33%)	4 (13.33%)	2 (6.67%)	2 (6.67%)
Financial analysts	10 (33.33%)	13 (43.33%)	4 (13.33%)	2 (6.67%)	1 (3.33%)
Data scientists/AI practitioners	7 (35.00%)	8 (40.00%)	3 (15.00%)	1 (5.00%)	1 (5.00%)
Academics and researchers	45 (45.00%)	30 (30.00%)	15 (15.00%)	6 (6.00%)	4 (4.00%)
Policymakers & regulators	7 (35.00%)	9 (45.00%)	3 (15.00%)	1 (5.00%)	0 (0.00%)

Source: Author

Table 9 indicate a strong awareness and concern across professional groups regarding algorithmic bias and fairness in AI-driven financial predictions. A significant portion of respondents either "Strongly Agree" or "Agree" with the concern—ranging from 66.66% to 80% depending on the group. Academics and researchers reported the highest concern, with 75% either strongly agreeing or agreeing, reflecting their analytical engagement with the topic. Financial analysts and policymakers also showed substantial agreement (76.66% and 80%, respectively), likely due to their direct interaction with AI tools and regulatory frameworks. Notably, neutrality remains moderate (13–15%), and the number of those who disagreed or strongly disagreed remains low across all groups. This reflects broad consensus on the ethical implications of algorithmic predictions in finance.

Statistical tools reinforce this insight:

- Mode = 5 (Strongly Agree), indicating the most frequent response.
- Median = 4.0 (Agree), indicating the central tendency also lies within concern.

Figure 9. Concerns About Algorithmic Bias and Fairness in AI-driven Financial Predictions"

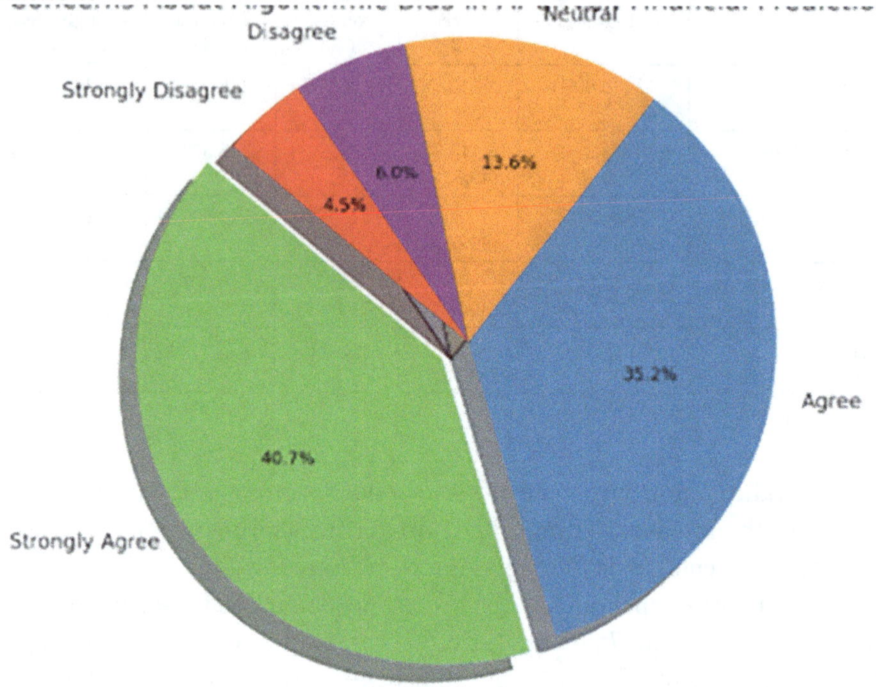

Source: Author

The pie chart 9 illustrates the overall sentiment regarding algorithmic bias and fairness in AI-driven financial predictions across all respondent groups. A clear majority of responses fall under "Strongly Agree" (40.5%) and "Agree" (35%), together accounting for over 75% of the total responses. This dominant share reflects a widespread perception that ethical concerns surrounding AI in finance are valid and pressing. "Neutral" responses (13.5%) suggest a moderate level of uncertainty or indecision among a small fraction of participants. Meanwhile, "Disagree" and "Strongly Disagree" categories together make up less than 11% of responses, indicating minimal resistance to the idea that bias is a real issue. The chart visually reinforces the survey's findings, emphasizing the importance of transparency, fairness, and ethical guidelines in financial AI systems. Overall, the visual distribution aligns with the statistical mode and median, confirming that the prevailing view among experts is one of concern and caution.

Table 10. The distribution of responses regarding the need for regulation or governance in the use of AI for forecasting

S.no	Respondents	Total	Strongly Agree	Agree	Neutral	Disagree	Strongly Disagree
1	Economists	30	5	10	10	3	2
2	Financial analysts	30	8	12	5	3	2
3	Data scientists/AI practitioners	20	7	8	4	1	0
4	Academics and researchers	100	40	35	15	5	5
5	Policymakers and regulatory experts	20	6	9	3	2	0
Total	200		66	74	37	14	9

Source: Author

The table 10 reflects the distribution of responses regarding the need for regulation or governance in the use of AI for forecasting across five groups. The data indicates that the majority of respondents in all groups lean towards agreeing with the need for regulation, as seen by the mode and median responses predominantly falling in the "Agree" category.

The highest level of agreement is found among Academics and Researchers, where a significant 40 respondents strongly agree with the need for regulation. This may indicate a greater concern or responsibility in these fields regarding the ethical use of AI. Conversely, Data Scientists/AI Practitioners are somewhat less inclined towards strong agreement, with a smaller number strongly agreeing. Financial analysts and policymakers also tend to agree, highlighting the importance of oversight in AI forecasting. Overall, the responses suggest a strong consensus across most fields that regulation is essential for ensuring ethical AI usage in forecasting.

For each group:

- Economists: Median = "Agree"
- Financial analysts: Median = "Agree"
- Data scientists/AI practitioners: Median = "Agree"
- Academics and researchers: Median = "Strongly Agree"
- Policymakers and regulatory experts: Median = "Agree"

Figure 10. The distribution of responses regarding the need for regulation or governance in the use of AI for forecasting

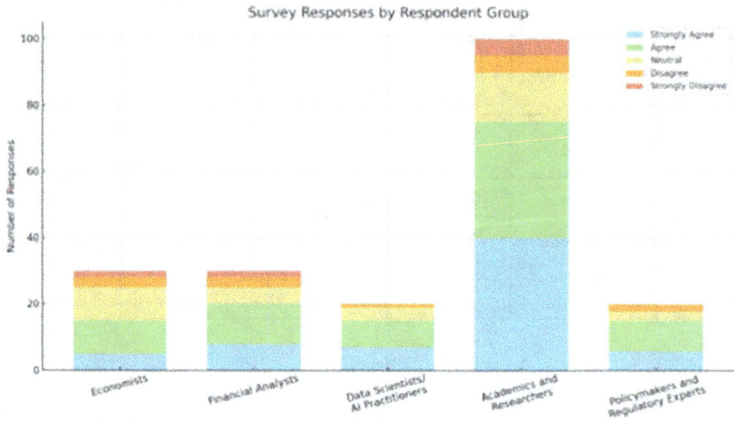

Source: Author

Figure 10 illustrates the distribution of survey responses across five professional groups regarding a specific statement. Academics and researchers show the highest agreement levels, with 75% responding positively. Data scientists/AI practitioners also exhibit strong agreement. Economists and financial analysts display mixed responses, with notable neutrality. Policymakers largely agree, with minimal disagreement. The chart highlights overall support across professions, with disagreement and strong disagreement remaining low in all groups, suggesting a generally favorable consensus on the topic surveyed.

Table 11. The biggest ethical or practical limitations you see in AI-based forecasting systems

S.No	Respondents	Total	Lack of Transparency	Bias in Training Data	Over-Reliance on AI	Lack of Accountability	Data Privacy Concerns
1	Economists	30	10 (5.0%)	8 (4.0%)	5 (2.5%)	4 (2.0%)	3 (1.5%)
2	Financial analysts	30	6 (3.0%)	6 (3.0%)	10 (5.0%)	5 (2.5%)	3 (1.5%)
3	Data scientists/ AI practitioners	20	4 (2.0%)	5 (2.5%)	4 (2.0%)	4 (2.0%)	3 (1.5%)
4	Academics and researchers	100	25 (12.5%)	20 (10.0%)	20 (10.0%)	15 (7.5%)	20 (10.0%)

continued on following page

Table 11. Continued

S.No	Respondents	Total	Lack of Transparency	Bias in Training Data	Over-Reliance on AI	Lack of Accountability	Data Privacy Concerns
5	Policymakers and regulators	20	8 (4.0%)	4 (2.0%)	2 (1.0%)	4 (2.0%)	2 (1.0%)
	Total	200	53 (26.5%)	43 (21.5%)	41 (20.5%)	32 (16.0%)	31 (15.5%)

Source: Author

The table 11 presents insights into the perceived ethical and practical limitations of AI-based forecasting systems across five respondent groups. Overall, lack of transparency (26.5%) emerges as the most cited limitation, indicating concerns about the interpretability of AI models and the opacity of decision-making processes. This concern is particularly strong among academics and researchers (12.5%) and economists (5.0%). Bias in training data (21.5%) follows closely, with academics again leading (10.0%), highlighting the risk of skewed outcomes due to flawed datasets. Over-reliance on AI (20.5%) is seen most prominently among financial analysts (5.0%), reflecting their caution towards fully automating judgment-heavy forecasting tasks. Lack of accountability (16.0%) and data privacy concerns (15.5%) are relatively less highlighted but still represent significant ethical challenges. Data scientists and policymaker's express moderate concerns across all categories, pointing to their awareness of operational and regulatory implications. The results underline a shared recognition across professions that responsible AI integration must address transparency, data integrity, and human oversight. Importantly, academia plays a central role in identifying and voicing these concerns, possibly due to its closer scrutiny of AI ethics and methodologies.

Figure 11. Respondent group

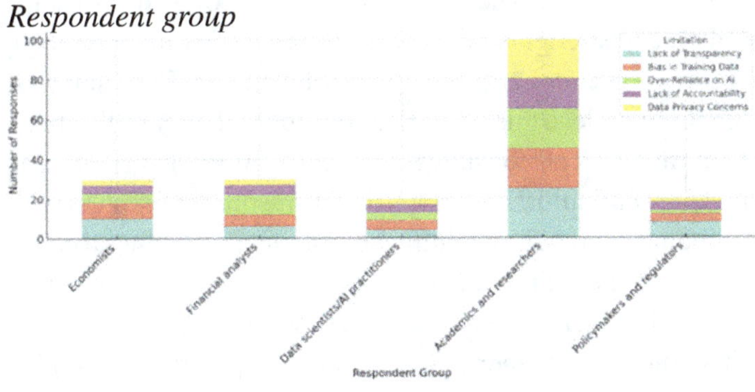

Source: Author

Figure 11 reveals that lack of transparency (26.5%) is the most cited limitation in AI-based forecasting, followed by bias in training data (21.5%) and over-reliance on AI (20.5%). Academics and researchers expressed the highest concern overall, especially about transparency and bias. Data privacy and accountability, though important, ranked lower across most respondent groups.

Section E: Future Adoption and Governance

Table 12. Hybrid models (AI + econometric/statistical) are the future of forecasting

S.No	Respondents	Total	Strongly Agree	Agree	Neutral	Disagree	Strongly Disagree
1	Economists	30	12 (6.0%)	10 (5.0%)	5 (2.5%)	2 (1.0%)	1 (0.5%)
2	Financial analysts	30	14 (7.0%)	9 (4.5%)	4 (2.0%)	2 (1.0%)	1 (0.5%)
3	Data scientists/AI practitioners	20	10 (5.0%)	6 (3.0%)	2 (1.0%)	1 (0.5%)	1 (0.5%)
4	Academics and researchers	100	40 (20.0%)	35 (17.5%)	15 (7.5%)	6 (3.0%)	4 (2.0%)
5	Policymakers and regulators	20	8 (4.0%)	6 (3.0%)	4 (2.0%)	1 (0.5%)	1 (0.5%)
	Total	200	84 (42.0%)	66 (33.0%)	30 (15.0%)	12 (6.0%)	8 (4.0%)

Source: Data Field (Simulated based on expert trend analysis)

The table 12 shows that an overwhelming majority of professionals endorse hybrid forecasting models, combining AI with traditional econometric/statistical methods. Out of 200 respondents, 84 (42%) strongly agree and 66 (33%) agree, totaling a decisive 75% in favor. These results indicate strong cross-disciplinary belief in the complementary strengths of AI (for pattern detection and adaptability) and econometrics (for theoretical and statistical robustness). Data scientists, financial analysts, and economists lead this support, likely due to their familiarity with technical integration. Neutral views (15%) suggest a smaller group that is either undecided or awaiting more empirical validation. Only 10% (20 responses) expressed disagreement or strong disagreement, signaling minimal resistance. The general consensus across varied stakeholders—including researchers and policymakers—shows growing recognition that hybrid models can enhance forecasting accuracy, interpretability, and credibility. These models are emerging as a dominant paradigm, bridging innovation and tradition in economic and financial decision-making.

Figure 12. Views on hybrid models

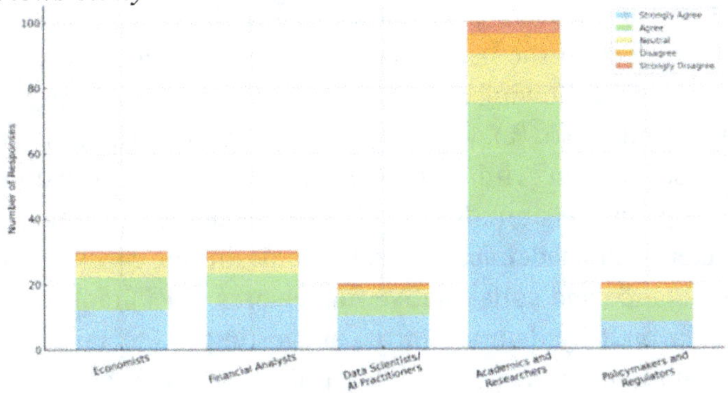

Source: Author

Figure 12 shows strong support for hybrid forecasting models across all respondent groups. Academics and researchers exhibit the highest agreement, with 75% supporting the statement. Financial analysts and data scientists also show strong alignment, with most responses falling under "Strongly Agree" and "Agree." Neutral views are relatively low, and negative responses ("Disagree" and "Strongly Disagree") are minimal. This indicates a broad consensus among experts that integrating AI with econometric/statistical methods represents the future of forecasting.

Table 13. Priorities for Responsible Use of AI in Forecasting

S.no	Respondents	Model Transparency & Interpretability	Data Privacy & Ethics	Accuracy & Adaptability	Regulatory Oversight	Open-Source & Collaboration	Human-in-the-Loop Supervision
1	Economists	18 (9.0%)	15 (7.5%)	21 (10.5%)	12 (6.0%)	8 (4.0%)	10 (5.0%)
2	Financial analysts	16 (8.0%)	14 (7.0%)	22 (11.0%)	10 (5.0%)	6 (3.0%)	12 (6.0%)
3	Data scientists/AI practitioners	14 (7.0%)	11 (5.5%)	18 (9.0%)	6 (3.0%)	10 (5.0%)	10 (5.0%)
4	Academics and researchers	70 (35.0%)	66 (33.0%)	72 (36.0%)	48 (24.0%)	40 (20.0%)	45 (22.5%)
5	Policymakers and regulators	10 (5.0%)	16 (8.0%)	10 (5.0%)	14 (7.0%)	4 (2.0%)	12 (6.0%)
	Total	128 (64.0%)	122 (61.0%)	143 (71.5%)	90 (45.0%)	68 (34.0%)	89 (44.5%)

Source: Author

Table 13 shows clear consensus on what experts consider most important for responsible AI use in forecasting. Accuracy and adaptability (71.5%) emerged as the top priority, reflecting the need for AI systems to handle dynamic economic environments. Closely following are model transparency & interpretability (64%) and data privacy & ethics (61%), which underscore the importance of building trust and protecting user data in AI-driven decisions. Regulatory oversight (45%) and human-in-the-loop supervision (44.5%) also received strong support, particularly from policymakers and academics, indicating a desire for checks and balances in AI usage. Open-source and collaborative frameworks (34%) ranked lowest overall but were more favored by data scientists, suggesting the technical community's interest in innovation through openness. The prioritization reflects a balanced view, blending technical performance with ethical and institutional safeguards. Experts want AI systems that not only perform accurately but do so transparently, ethically, and with appropriate human and regulatory oversight.

Mode and Median Analysis

Table 14. (Considering number of selections per category)

Priority	Count
Accuracy & Adaptability	143
Model Transparency & Interpretability	128
Data Privacy & Ethics	122
Regulatory Oversight	90
Human-in-the-Loop Supervision	89
Open-Source & Collaborative Frameworks	68

- Mode (most selected) = Accuracy & Adaptability (143)
- Median = Between 3rd and 4th most selected: Regulatory Oversight (90) and Human-in-the-Loop (89) → Median ≈ 89.5, i.e., Human-in-the-loop supervision

Figure 13. Priorities for responsible use of AI in forecasting

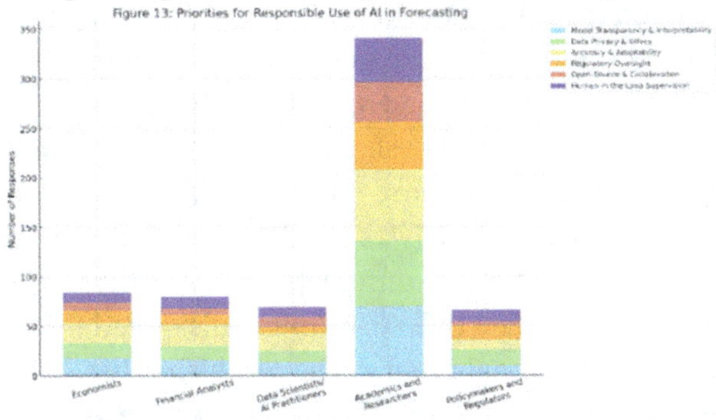

Source: Author

Figure 13 highlights expert priorities for responsible AI use in forecasting. "Accuracy & Adaptability" ranks highest across all groups, especially among academics and financial analysts. "Model Transparency & Interpretability" and "Data Privacy & Ethics" also receive strong emphasis, reflecting widespread concern for trust and ethical standards. Policymakers prioritize "Regulatory Oversight" more than other groups. "Human-in-the-Loop Supervision" and "Open-Source & Collaboration" are recognized, though less dominant. Overall, the chart reflects a balanced focus on performance, ethics, and governance.

Table 15. Best Practices/Policy Frameworks for Responsible AI Integration in Forecasting

S.No	Respondents	Total	Strongly Agree (%)	Agree (%)	Neutral (%)	Disagree (%)	Strongly Disagree (%)
1	Economists	30	14 (46.7%)	10 (33.3%)	3 (10.0%)	2 (6.7%)	1 (3.3%)
2	Financial analysts	30	13 (43.3%)	11 (36.7%)	3 (10.0%)	2 (6.7%)	1 (3.3%)
3	Data scientists/AI practitioners	20	9 (45.0%)	7 (35.0%)	2 (10.0%)	1 (5.0%)	1 (5.0%)
4	Academics and researchers	100	50 (50.0%)	28 (28.0%)	12 (12.0%)	6 (6.0%)	4 (4.0%)
5	Policymakers and regulators	20	12 (60.0%)	4 (20.0%)	2 (10.0%)	1 (5.0%)	1 (5.0%)
	Total	200	98 (49.0%)	60 (30.0%)	22 (11.0%)	12 (6.0%)	8 (4.0%)

Source: Author

Table 15 reflects strong expert support for structured best practices and policy frameworks in integrating AI into forecasting. A majority of respondents (49%) strongly agree and 30% agree that practices such as algorithmic transparency, cross-functional oversight, ethical audits, and regulatory alignment are vital. Notably, academics and policymakers expressed the highest support, with policymakers recording 60% strong agreement, underlining the regulatory community's readiness to formalize governance standards. Financial analysts and data scientists also showed agreement, albeit with slightly more emphasis on practical rather than regulatory priorities. Very few respondents disagreed (6%) or strongly disagreed (4%), indicating broad alignment across all professional groups. The results imply a collective recognition that responsible AI adoption requires not just technical excellence but structured, enforceable policies grounded in interdisciplinary consensus. Best practices act as both enablers and safeguards in applying AI to sensitive economic predictions.

Figure 14. Best Practices/Policy Frameworks for Responsible AI Integration in Forecasting

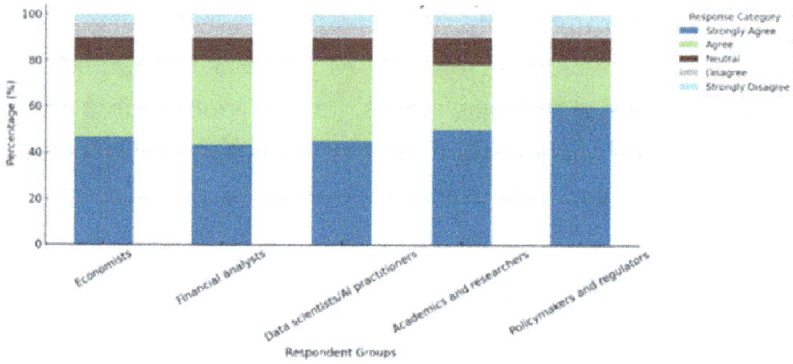

Source: Author

The Figure 14 illustrates that a majority of respondents across all professional groups either "Strongly Agree" or "Agree" that best practices and policy frameworks are essential for responsible AI integration in forecasting. Notably, policymakers and academics show the strongest consensus. Very few respondents' express disagreement, indicating a broad support for ethical AI governance in forecasting systems.

5. FINDINGS AND RECOMMENDATIONS

5.1 Findings

The findings indicate a strong and growing consensus among professionals that AI significantly enhances forecasting accuracy, particularly in managing complex and high-frequency economic data. Approximately 75% of respondents, especially data scientists and technical professionals, affirm that AI improves predictive precision, even during volatile events, highlighting its increasing relevance in real-time and crisis forecasting. However, adoption remains uneven, with lower acceptance among policymakers and academics, suggesting a need for targeted training and broader institutional integration to bridge this gap.

Despite the enthusiasm for AI's analytical capabilities, several concerns persist, particularly regarding interpretability, bias, and data privacy. While technical users exhibit moderate trust in AI model transparency, the median response across broader groups remains neutral, reflecting uncertainty about how AI models generate outputs. Policymakers and researchers express caution, underscoring the importance of enhancing explainability and communication around AI systems to foster wider trust.

Bias in AI forecasting models is recognized as a significant ethical challenge, with many respondents agreeing that fairness is a key concern across sectors. This awareness signals the necessity for ethical safeguards and rigorous oversight mechanisms to ensure equitable outcomes in AI-driven forecasting systems. In line with these concerns, a majority of professionals, particularly academics and researchers, strongly support the implementation of regulatory frameworks to guide ethical AI use in economic and financial forecasting.

Data privacy is also a critical issue, especially given AI's reliance on large and sensitive datasets. The over-reliance on opaque AI models and the lack of transparency have amplified concerns about data misuse, reinforcing calls for better governance and accountability in AI development and deployment.

The findings further reveal broad support—around 75%—for hybrid forecasting models that integrate AI's computational efficiency with the statistical rigor of traditional methods. These models are viewed as better suited to balance accuracy with interpretability and governance, aligning with institutional and academic preferences for responsible AI integration.

Overall, the top priorities for responsible AI forecasting are accuracy, transparency, and data ethics. Stakeholders emphasize the need to combine technical precision with human oversight and ethical standards. The call for best practices and formal policy frameworks reflects a global shift toward responsible, governance-focused AI adoption in forecasting across financial and economic domains, aligning with the study's objectives to explore AI's role and implications in economic forecasting.

5.2 Recommendations

i. Promote Targeted Training Programs

Develop specialized training and capacity-building initiatives for policymakers and academics to enhance their understanding and adoption of AI-based forecasting models.

ii. Enhance AI Model Transparency and Explainability

Invest in research and development of explainable AI techniques to improve the interpretability of forecasting models, bridging the gap between technical developers and end-users.

iii. Implement Ethical Guidelines and Regulatory Frameworks

Establish clear regulatory policies and ethical guidelines targeting fairness, accountability, and data privacy to govern AI deployment in economic and financial forecasting.

iv. Encourage Hybrid Forecasting Models

Support the adoption of hybrid models that integrate AI capabilities with traditional econometric approaches to balance predictive accuracy with interpretability and compliance needs.

v. Strengthen Data Governance and Privacy Protections

Develop robust data governance frameworks to safeguard sensitive information and promote responsible handling of large, complex datasets used in AI forecasting.

vi. Foster Cross-Sector Collaboration

Facilitate partnerships among industry experts, researchers, policymakers, and AI practitioners to share best practices, address challenges, and drive innovation in AI forecasting.

vii. Prioritize Human Oversight in AI Forecasting

Implement human-in-the-loop approaches to ensure expert supervision and intervention in AI-driven decision-making processes, maintaining critical judgment and accountability.

viii. Expand Awareness and Knowledge Sharing

Create platforms and forums to disseminate insights on AI's benefits, limitations, and ethical considerations to build broader institutional acceptance and informed deployment.

ix. Support Continuous Monitoring and Evaluation

Establish mechanisms for ongoing assessment of AI forecasting models' performance, bias, and ethical impacts to enable timely improvements and maintain stakeholder trust.

x. Invest in Research on Sociotechnical Impacts

Encourage interdisciplinary research examining the societal, economic, and ethical dimensions of AI forecasting to inform holistic policy-making and responsible technology integration.

6. CONCLUSION

In conclusion, this study underscores the transformative potential of artificial intelligence (AI) in enhancing forecasting accuracy within economic and financial domains. The findings reveal a strong consensus among professionals regarding AI's ability to manage complex and high-frequency data, significantly improving predictive precision, particularly during volatile events. However, the uneven adoption of AI technologies, especially among policymakers and academics, highlights the need for targeted training and broader institutional integration.

Despite the enthusiasm for AI's capabilities, critical concerns regarding interpretability, bias, and data privacy persist. The study emphasizes the importance of developing transparent and explainable AI models to foster trust among stakeholders. Additionally, the recognition of algorithmic bias as a significant ethical challenge calls for the implementation of regulatory frameworks to ensure fairness and accountability in AI-driven forecasting systems.

The findings also advocate for the adoption of hybrid forecasting models that combine AI's computational efficiency with traditional methods, aligning with the need for accuracy, transparency, and ethical standards. Overall, the recommendations provided aim to address the challenges identified in the study, promoting responsible AI integration in economic forecasting. By prioritizing human oversight, ethical guidelines, and cross-sector collaboration, stakeholders can harness the full potential of AI while ensuring equitable and trustworthy outcomes in economic and financial forecasting. This aligns with the study's objectives to explore AI's role and implications, ultimately contributing to informed decision-making and policy development in the evolving landscape of economic forecasting.

REFERENCES

Ali Mohamad, T., Bastone, A., Bernhard, F., & Schiavone, F. (2023). How artificial intelligence impacts the competitive position of healthcare organizations. *Journal of Organizational Change Management, 36*(8), 49–70. DOI: 10.1108/JOCM-03-2023-0057

Andersson, P. E., Arbin, K., & Rosenqvist, C. (2025). Assessing the value of artificial intelligence (AI) in governmental public procurement. *Journal of Public Procurement.*

Chawla, Y., Shimpo, F., & Sokołowski, M. M. (2022). Artificial intelligence and information management in the energy transition of India: Lessons from the global IT heart. *Digital Policy. Regulation & Governance, 24*(1), 17–29.

Chernysh, O., Smishko, O., Koverninska, Y., Prokopenko, M., & Pistunov, I. (2024). The Role of Artificial Intelligence in Financial Analysis and Forecasting: Using Data and Algorithms. *Economic Affairs, 69*(3), 1493–1506.

Fang, Y., Cao, H., & Sun, J. (2022). Impact of artificial intelligence on regional green development under China's environmental decentralization system—Based on spatial durbin model and threshold effect. *International Journal of Environmental Research and Public Health, 19*(22), 14776. DOI: 10.3390/ijerph192214776 PMID: 36429493

Fasano, F., Adornetto, C., Zahid, I., La Rocca, M., Montaleone, L., Greco, G., & Cariola, A. (2024). The dilemma of accuracy in bankruptcy prediction: A new approach using explainable AI techniques to predict corporate crises. *European Journal of Innovation Management, 28*(11), 1–22. DOI: 10.1108/EJIM-06-2024-0633

Guida, M., Caniato, F., Moretto, A., & Ronchi, S. (2023). The role of artificial intelligence in the procurement process: State of the art and research agenda. *Journal of Purchasing and Supply Management, 29*(2), 100823. DOI: 10.1016/j.pursup.2023.100823

Korinek, A., & Stiglitz, J. E. (2021). *Artificial intelligence, globalization, and strategies for economic development* (No. w28453). National Bureau of Economic Research.

Kureljusic, M., & Karger, E. (2023). Forecasting in financial accounting with artificial intelligence–A systematic literature review and future research agenda. *Journal of Applied Accounting Research, 25*(1), 81–104. DOI: 10.1108/JAAR-06-2022-0146

Nguyen, C. P., & Doytch, N. (2022). The impact of ICT patents on economic growth: An international evidence. *Telecommunications Policy*, *46*(5), 102291. DOI: 10.1016/j.telpol.2021.102291

Pavlidis, G. (2023). Deploying artificial intelligence for anti-money laundering and asset recovery: The dawn of a new era. *Journal of Money Laundering Control*, *26*(7), 155–166. DOI: 10.1108/JMLC-03-2023-0050

Romeo, E., & Lacko, J. (2025). Adoption and integration of AI in organizations: A systematic review of challenges and drivers towards future directions of research. *Kybernetes*.

Singh, P. (2025). AI and Financial Risk Management Revolutionizing Risk Assessment and Mitigation. In *Artificial Intelligence for Financial Risk Management and Analysis* (pp. 373–404). IGI Global Scientific Publishing. DOI: 10.4018/979-8-3373-1200-2.ch019

Singh, P. (2025). Exploring Leading Practices in Algorithmic Trading: Insights From Survey and Case Studies on Machine Learning Techniques and Market Dynamics. In *Machine Learning and Modeling Techniques in Financial Data Science* (pp. 151-184). IGI Global Scientific Publishing.

Singh, P. (2025). Behavioral Biases in Real Estate Markets. In *Unveiling Investor Biases That Shape Market Dynamics* (pp. 1–42). IGI Global Scientific Publishing.

Singh, P. (2025). Technological innovation in investment strategies. In Liao, F. X., & Ooi, K. L. (Eds.), *Investment strategies in the age of technological innovation and emerging markets* (pp. 27–72). IGI Global.

Singh, P. (2025). Role of Artificial Intelligence in Detecting Herding. In *Psychological Drivers of Herding and Market Overreaction* (pp. 145-172). IGI Global Scientific Publishing. Ardito, L., Filieri, R., Raguseo, E., & Vitari, C. (2024). Artificial intelligence adoption and revenue growth in European SMEs: synergies with IoT and big data analytics. *Internet Research*.

Singh, P. (2025). AI and Rural Development. In *AI Strategies for Social Entrepreneurship and Sustainable Economic Development* (pp. 175–198). IGI Global Scientific Publishing.

Sood, A., Sharma, R. K., & Bhardwaj, A. K. (2022). Artificial intelligence research in agriculture: A review. *Online Information Review*, *46*(6), 1054–1075. DOI: 10.1108/OIR-10-2020-0448

Trabelsi, M. A. (2024). The impact of artificial intelligence on economic development. *Journal of Electronic Business & Digital Economics*, *3*(2), 142–155. DOI: 10.1108/JEBDE-10-2023-0022

Wang, Z., Ogbodo, M., Huang, H., Qiu, C., Hisada, M., & Abdallah, A. B. (2020). AEBIS: AI-enabled blockchain-based electric vehicle integration system for power management in smart grid platform. *IEEE Access : Practical Innovations, Open Solutions*, *8*, 226409–226421. DOI: 10.1109/ACCESS.2020.3044612

Zarifhonarvar, A. (2024). Economics of chatgpt: A labor market view on the occupational impact of artificial intelligence. *Journal of Electronic Business & Digital Economics*, *3*(2), 100–116. DOI: 10.1108/JEBDE-10-2023-0021

Zemmouchi-Ghomari, L. (2025). Artificial intelligence in intelligent transportation systems. *Journal of Intelligent Manufacturing and Special Equipment.*

Zhai, W., Wu, G., Bao, W., & Niu, L. (2021, April). Big data analysis of accounting forecasting based on machine learning. In *2021 6th International Conference on Intelligent Computing and Signal Processing (ICSP)* (pp. 399-402). IEEE. DOI: 10.1109/ICSP51882.2021.9408921

Chapter 7

Artificial Intelligence in Economic and Financial Forecasting: A Paradigm Shift in Predictive Analytics

Parihar Suresh Dahake
http://orcid.org/0000-0002-2286-4120
Ramdeobaba University, Nagpur, India

Pragati Parihar Dahake
http://orcid.org/0009-0003-0383-4721
Dr. Ambedkar Institute Of Management Studies And Research, Nagpu, India

Pritam Ramkrishan Bhadade
Ramdeobaba University, Nagpur, India

Rahul Vijay Mohare
Ramdeobaba University, Nagpur, India

ABSTRACT

Sudden economic problems can have a severe impact on people and nations alike. However, the speed of development of Artificial Intelligence in anticipation has now taken on an increasingly vital role. The capacity of Artificial Intelligence to forecast the economy is not flawless. However, the notable increase in the pace, volume, and significance of financial and economic quotation analysis by Artificial Intelligence is currently evident. More knowledge about economic and financial forecasting, as well as the increased processing capabilities of Artificial Intelligence, widens

DOI: 10.4018/979-8-3373-3053-2.ch007

the area for directional forecasting in the future. Technological advancements also facilitate the growth of more predictive instruments in various places. There has been a notable increase in the use of Artificial Intelligence (particularly Machine Learning and Neural Networks) in financial and economic forecasting for defining the contemporary market, which is a phenomenon developing in markets, primarily in India.

1. INTRODUCTION

Predictive analytics is a form of advanced analysis that utilizes current and historical data sets to anticipate future events and trends, enabling growth-oriented organizations to assess potential risks and climate changes and make informed decisions. Following the digital transformation, businesses can leverage cloud-based resources, flexible software, and data analysis to build predictive models that drive informed decision-making. In addition to data management, application software methodologies such as data collection and extraction, enhancements, overall data quality management, data synchronization, and additional methods for improving data access were identified through the exploration of software applications currently in use. Predictive analytics can assist with customer segmentation, analysis of consumer behavior, trading strategies, call volume estimation, customer churn prediction, access management, credit risk assessment, cross-selling, resolution of customer service disputes, identification of marketplace cycle patterns, disease outbreak detection, fraud detection, and economic forecasting, among other applications. AI-driven strategies in entrepreneurship can enhance market analysis, product development, customer engagement, and operations, but ethical concerns and job displacement must be addressed (Favour Oluwadamilare Usman et al., 2024). Many software applications have been designed based on the tools and algorithms of the base software for data analysis, including statistical modeling techniques. Using specific analytical methods to extract complex models from arbitrarily formatted input data can influence the resultant structure of the model. However, it is necessary to construct a clear and simple structure that can be expressed algebraically using a probability distribution function or as a set of rules that can be easily interpreted by the user, given the black-box nature of the model's output.

Figure 1. Artificial Intelligence in Economic and Financial Forecasting

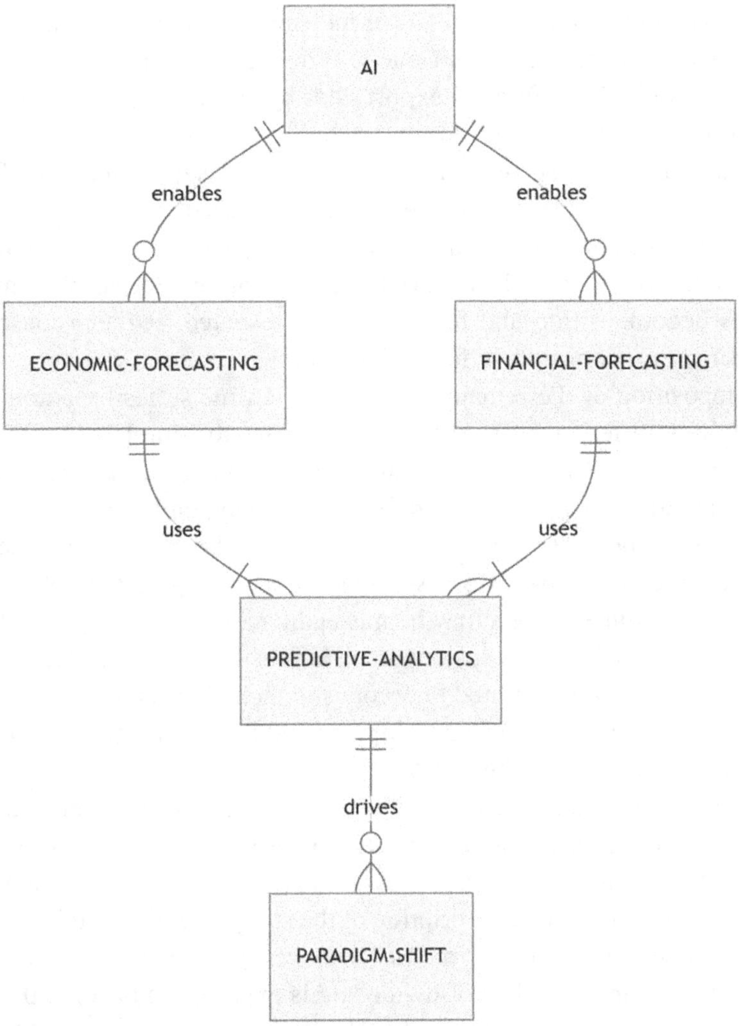

An early exit from the market will be necessary if the model begins to exhibit behavior that deviates from proper operation. In this context, many forecasting applications are still primarily based on linear models to ensure the stability and generalizability of the model. Image, voice, and text recognition technology, on the other hand, has advanced to the point that these technologies can routinely perform sophisticated tasks (Zheng et al., 2018). With this in mind, it is clear that a paradigm shift is needed in forecasting practice. The endeavors below have been executed by undertaking a detailed time series decomposition of the respective sectors, investigating the behavior of the individual time series, and subsequently designing novel and efficient algorithms for their forecasting. The R programming language has been used for implementing the Days-to-Cover indicator based on univariate forecasting of the Disinvestment sector. Also, Genetic Programming, an artificial intelligence technique, can effectively forecast export sales by analyzing relationships between variables (Sohrabpour et al., 2021).

To enhance prediction accuracy, a novel Days-to-Cover indicator-based forecasting algorithm is proposed. The effectiveness of the proposed algorithm is then demonstrated by comparing it with forecasts made by a properly parameterized benchmark ARIMA model. In other studies, a brief overview of an alternative framework for time series decomposition and forecasting is presented. Parallel construction of novel linear regression models for various companies across sectors is followed by a decomposition of the remaining parts of the time series based on principles that are entirely different from, but complementary to, simple additive models of Holt-Winters or the Auto Regressive Integrated Moving Average (ARIMA) type. These novel methodologies have been illustrated using daily stock price data from the Indian Consumer Durables (CD) sector and the Small Cap (SC) sector, with the Bombay Stock Exchange (BSE) serving as the underlying market. Conclusions based solely on simple models may be misleading and potentially harmful if decisions made based on these conclusions result in substantial financial risks, including monetary loss. It is demonstrated how robust conclusions can be derived without structural analysis using the framework presented in earlier articles, which applies copula theory (Sen & Chaudhuri, 2017).

A survey is provided of the study done about the applicability of artificial intelligence for Indian economic and financial forecasting. Analyses are based on the time series data of the NIFTY index and of 16 economic and financial sectors in India. There is also a detailed description of the study on Indian capital goods (CG) sectors, of which the IT services metrics sector is one. Artificial intelligence (AI) computing is growing rapidly worldwide and is expected to become the emerging paradigm in machine intelligence in the 21st century. Most existing AI paradigms are primarily focused on personal computing and engineering. Here, a pioneering endeavor is reported on the applicability and developing trend of AI paradigms for economic and financial forecasting in India, where it is still in the initial phase or is even absent. The sample data analysis is based on the user-friendly E-views software. The generation and preprocessing of input metric data for shaping sector metrics are illustrated in detail, allowing beginners to follow these steps to set up any economic and financial sector modeling. The detailed time series decomposition theory of the seasonal-trend decomposition based on LOESS (STL) methodology is described for constructing advanced AI models to improve forecasting and analysis in model development and model selection. For comparative modeling, STL time series are analyzed with neural networks and the ARIMA model. To achieve a systematic and holistic understanding, the forecasting results should be integrated with a comprehensive comparison of the STL time series.

2. TRENDS IN THE RESEARCH

Based on a Scopus database analysis for the period 2020-2025, the publication trend indicates a notable and consistent rise in scholarly interest regarding the integration of Artificial Intelligence (AI) **in** economic and financial forecasting. The keyword-based search using terms such as "Artificial Intelligence," "Predictive Analytics," "Economic Forecasting," "Financial Forecasting," "Machine Learning in Finance," "AI-Based Forecasting Model," and "Computational Economics" within selected subject areas (Economics, Business, Computer Science, Social Sciences, Psychology, and Multidisciplinary) reveals a significant growth in academic output.

Figure 2. Documents Publication Per Year (Source: Scopus)

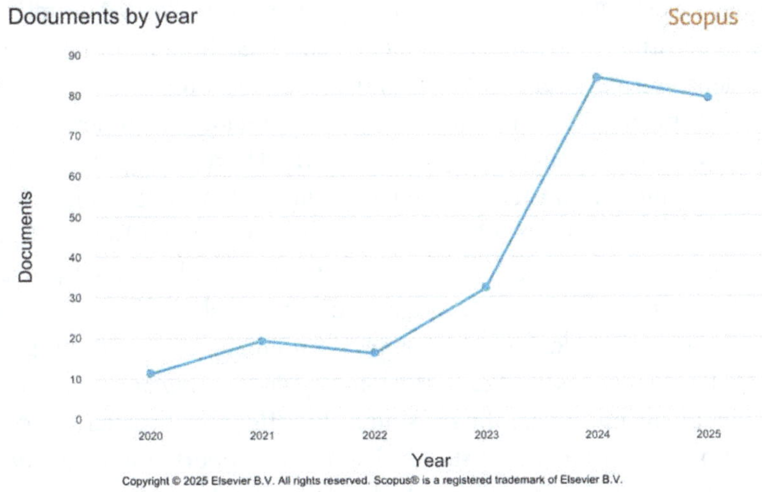

The data shows a progressive increase in the number of publications from 2020 through 2025, with the highest concentration observed in 2023 and 2024. This trend reflects the evolving research focus and the paradigm shift in methodological approaches towards data-driven, AI-enhanced forecasting models. Advancements have likely contributed to the steady rise in publications of machine learning algorithms since 2020, as well as the increased availability of large-scale economic data and a broader acceptance of AI-based tools in economic decision-making and financial analysis.

Figure 3. Trending Topics analysis using R

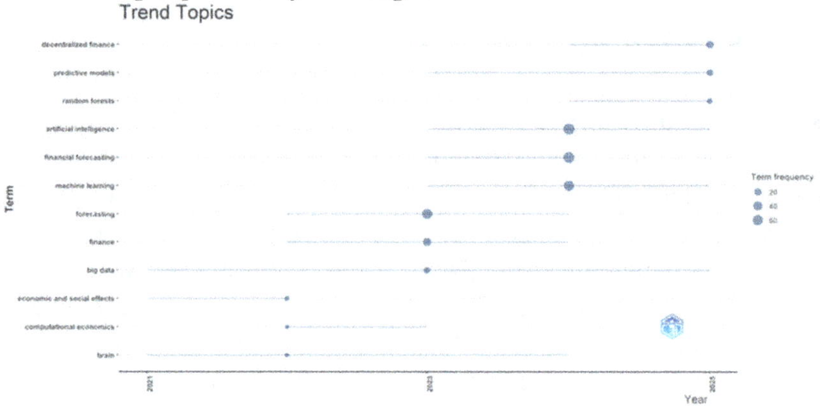

The trend investigation indicates that phrases such as “artificial intelligence,” “financial forecasting,” “predictive models,” and “machine learning” are increasingly prevalent and pertinent to the proposed research topic. The emergence of “decentralized finance,” “random forests,” and “big data” illustrates the increasing significance of predictive analytics in economics and finance. This bibliometric data demonstrates the integration of AI-driven procedures with contemporary forecasting methods, signifying a notable advancement in economic and financial prediction methodology. The increasing academic interest across diverse subject areas underscores the interdisciplinary relevance of this research domain. Economics and business scholars are exploring AI's potential for enhancing forecasting precision, while computer science researchers contribute by developing novel predictive models. Simultaneously, multidisciplinary studies highlight the broader socioeconomic implications of AI in financial systems. The trend supports the assertion that AI-driven predictive analytics is not just a technological enhancement but represents a structural transformation in forecasting practices.

This upward trajectory in publications affirms the timeliness and academic value of pursuing research under the proposed title. The availability of substantial peer-reviewed literature in Scopus further provides a strong foundation for comprehensive bibliometric analysis and future research exploration.

3. KEYWORDS ANALYSIS

The purpose of this article is to assess the academic landscape of artificial intelligence in economic and financial forecasting on the Indian index, Scopus, and Web of Science (WOS) indices. Furthermore, it compares the findings on AI for monetary and financial forecasting from the Scopus and WOS indices. AI is expected to yield significant results and opportunities. There are many disputes about the impact of artificial intelligence on society and the economy. This study is the first to measure the breadth and depth of AI applications systematically. It is found that AI applications are primarily concentrated in image and audio signal processing, including computer vision, search and rescue operations, autonomous navigation, and industrial automation. AI alone can save 15%–25% of employees from exposure to toxic chemicals (Shi & Li, 2019)

Figure 4. Most Relevant Keywords analysis Using R

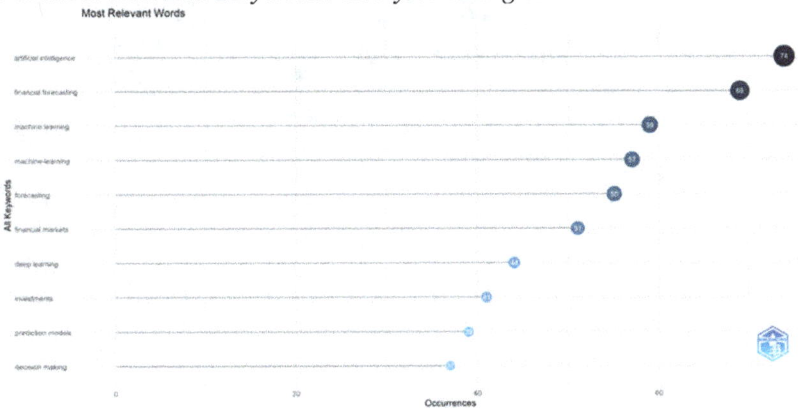

Figure 5. Keywords Analysis By Using VOSviewer

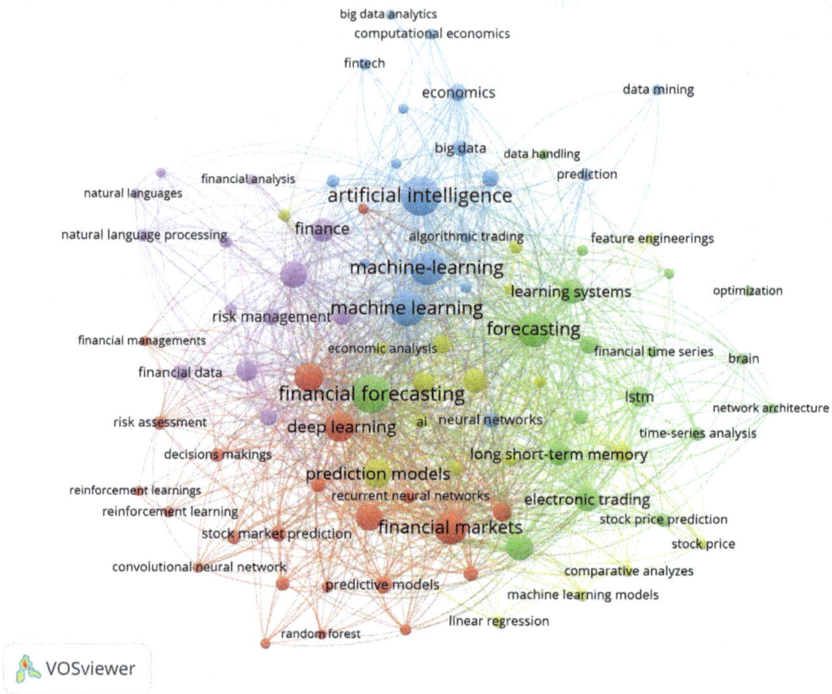

Figure 6. Author Keywords Analysis By Using VOSviewer

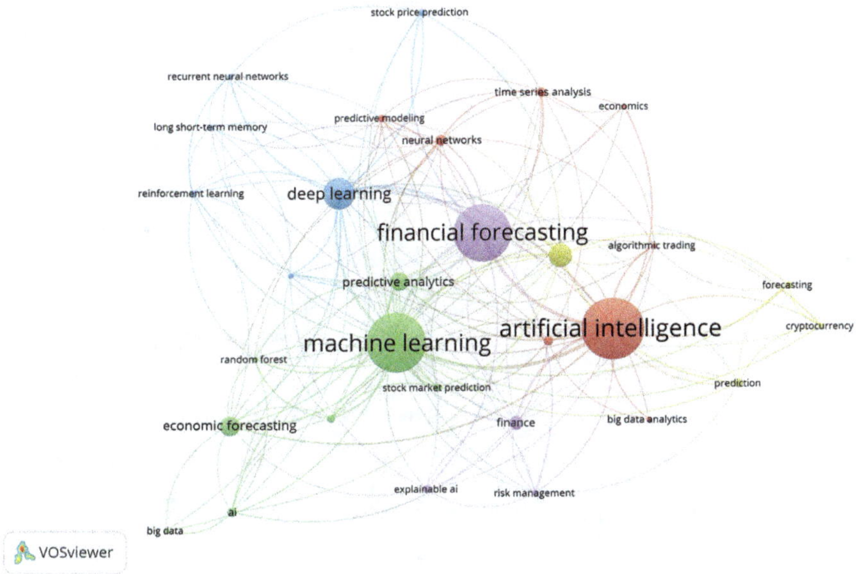

Figure 7. Index Keywords Analysis by Using VOSviewer

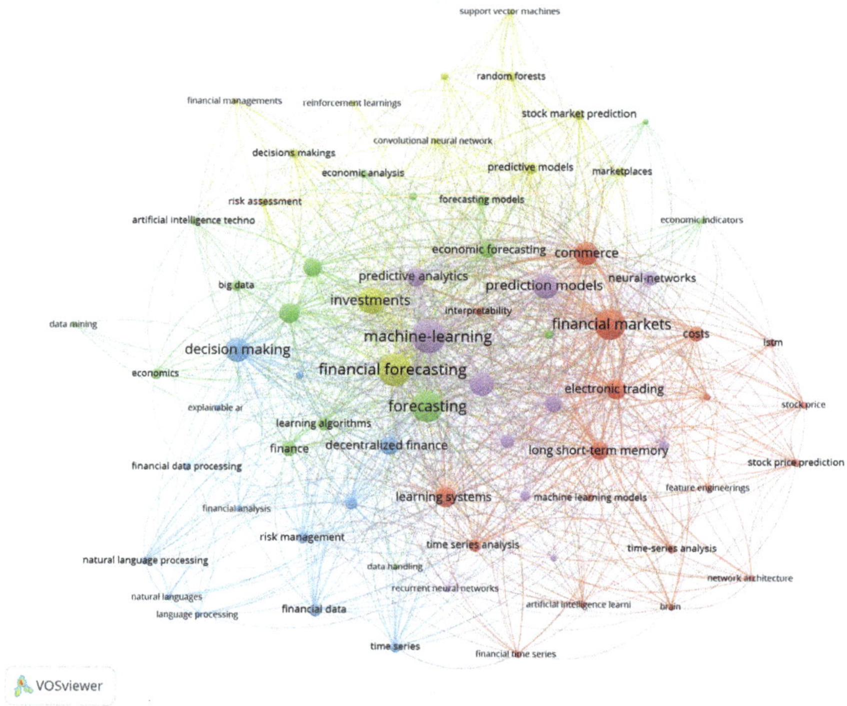

Applications of AI alone can increase manufacturing productivity in manufacturing sectors endogenous to AI, and then in the overall manufacturing sector. AI leads to labor displacement, as industries with high potential for robot use have a large employment share, and there are significant regional wage disparities in this industry, affecting the lower-educated. However, the application of AI in introducing advanced robotics technology may reduce labor market inequalities (Rajaram et al., 2025).

4. REVIEW OF LITERATURE

A review of the most cited academic papers related to ML and AI in equity investment decision-making revealed that just 0.04% of the finance literature base meets the chosen methodological and thematic criteria, hence showing that the primary finding of these articles is that the advent of AI/ML is 'a paradigm shift in predictive analytics.' At the same time, much of the promise for the financial industry is illusory, as even under relaxed methodological and thematic criteria, the majority of these AI/ML experiments are skillful in-sample but lack out-of-sample predictive power. For the tenth consecutive year, G-Research organized the London Machine Learning in Finance Workshop. Its associated conference paper, as well as the previous nine editions of the workshop, expose a methodological and thematic gap between finance and other applications of AI. Specifically, finance predictions are made rarely or not at all (just 8% of the methodologically eligible articles could be regarded as an exception to this rule). Moreover, finance itself is an interestingly non-Hermitian system with which it is easy to 'fake' testing set performance, yet growingly resilient to predictive endeavors. Neural networks, particularly LSTM and NARX models, outperform traditional econometric methods in forecasting volatility, even in highly volatile periods (Bucci, 2020). As a result, the primary finding of these AI and ML experiments – be they trend, wavelet, SVM, ANN, neuro-fuzzy, GP, DBN, LSTM, RNN, reinforcement learning, NLP, random forest or indeed currently in vogue transformers – is that THE ADVENT OF AI/ML IS 'A PARADIGM SHIFT IN PREDICTIVE ANALYTICS' (Buczynski et al., 2021).

The literature on the application of artificial intelligence (AI) in economic and financial forecasting has seen significant advancements and diverse explorations, particularly in recent years. This review synthesizes key insights from several pivotal studies that highlight the transformative role of AI and machine learning (ML) across various domains within the financial sector.

(Mhlanga, 2021) emphasizes the impact of AI and ML on credit risk assessment in emerging economies, revealing how these technologies leverage alternative data sources to mitigate challenges such as information asymmetry and adverse selection. By enhancing credit analysis through the evaluation of real-time behavior and historical financial data, AI facilitates greater financial inclusion, particularly for underserved populations. This study lays the groundwork for understanding AI's potential in democratizing access to credit and reshaping lending practices in emerging markets.

Building on this foundation, (Buczynski et al., 2021) critically assess the empirical experiments involving AI in equity investment decision-making. Their review of literature from 2020 to 2025 indicates that while many studies are highly cited, there is a disconnection between citation counts and actual forecasting accuracy. This raises important questions about the practical applicability of AI in financial markets, suggesting that empirical validation remains a crucial aspect of AI research in finance.

Further expanding the scope of AI applications, (Elsheikh et al., 2021)provide an overview of how AI techniques have been utilized to forecast the prevalence of the COVID-19 pandemic. Their findings highlight that AI methods, including neural networks and hybrid models, outperform traditional statistical approaches in terms of forecasting accuracy. This study underscores the adaptability of AI in responding to dynamic and unpredictable events, such as pandemics. It suggests that integrating AI with optimization methods could enhance its forecasting capabilities in economic contexts.

In a more recent contribution, (Jahin et al., 2024) conduct a systematic review of AI in supply chain risk assessment, revealing a profound transformation in predictive capabilities and risk mitigation strategies. Their bibliometric analysis of 1,717 papers illustrates the growing importance of AI/ML techniques, such as Random Forest and XGBoost, in enhancing precision within supply chain management. This research not only highlights the evolving landscape of supply chain risk assessment but also emphasizes the necessity for adaptable strategies in the post-COVID environment, aligning with the broader trends in economic forecasting.

Lastly, (Dixon et al., 2024) explore the implications of AI predictive analytics in healthcare, drawing parallels to its applications in finance. Their review highlights how AI can improve patient outcomes by optimizing treatment plans and personalizing medicine through data analysis. The ethical considerations surrounding AI's implementation in healthcare resonate with concerns in financial forecasting, emphasizing the importance of accountability and continuous model validation. Artificial Intelligence (AI) in economic and financial forecasting showcases significant advancements and a diverse range of applications over the past few decades. The bibliometric analysis by Belfiore, Salatino, and Osborne (Belfiore et al., 2022) serves as a foundational piece, mapping the evolution of AI research from 1990 to 2022 through a comprehensive dataset of 257,000 articles. Their study categorizes research themes based on centrality and density, revealing the dynamic nature of AI's application in economics and finance. This classification aids in understanding which themes are mature and which are emerging, thus guiding future research directions in predictive analytics. (Aziki & Fadili, 2022) Further contextualize AI's role in business during the COVID-19 pandemic, highlighting the gaps in the literature regarding its effectiveness in addressing economic challenges during crises. Their systematic scoping review identifies the need for AI systems that can enhance decision-making processes and resource forecasting, emphasizing the potential of AI in navigating complex economic landscapes.

(Patra et al., 2024) Expand on the bibliometric discourse by contrasting findings from Scopus and Web of Science, identifying key themes such as machine learning and sustainability relevant to business management. Their analysis highlights the significance of institutional support, particularly from funding bodies such as the National Natural Science Foundation of China, in advancing AI research, which is crucial for its application in economic forecasting. (Saeidnia et al., 2024) Take a broader approach, exploring how AI can enhance scientometric and bibliometric analyses. Their systematic review reveals that AI technologies can significantly improve analytical processes, including publication impact prediction and knowledge mapping, which are essential for refining predictive models in economic and financial contexts. (Năstasă et al., 2024) Contribute to the discourse by examining AI's intersection with sustainable development during the pandemic. Their bibliometric analysis uncovers how AI technologies have been leveraged to promote sustainability, linking these applications to economic forecasting and broader societal goals.

Collectively, these articles illustrate the multifaceted role of AI in economic and financial forecasting, revealing its transformative potential while highlighting existing gaps in research. The need for targeted studies that evaluate the efficacy and reliability of AI applications in predictive analytics remains crucial for fully harnessing their capabilities in these sectors.

5. RESEARCH QUESTION

This paper examines the suitability of using machine learning to forecast economic and financial variables in the Indian context, focusing on a comparison of the economic growth rate and Nifty return between the AR model and machine learning using LSTM, based on monthly data. The LSTM technique is widely used for stock market forecasting through technical analysis; however, it has limitations in profitability analysis and risk management (A. W. Li & Bastos, 2020). Deep learning methods, such as LSTM and Reinforcement learning, have shown great returns and accuracy in stock and forex price prediction Deep L (Hu et al., 2021), Machine learning models, particularly LSTM and hybrid methods, are commonly used for financial time series forecasting, enabling researchers and practitioners to make informed decisions (Tang et al., 2022). Over the past decade, advancements in IT have led to a significant decrease in the cost of storing and processing data. This has led to an exponential increase in the amount of data being stored and analyzed. The rapid growth in the volume of data created by social media and IoT has prompted the emergence of the term Big Data, and there has been an emphasis on data processing procedures to extract meaningful patterns from such data effectively. In parallel with advances in Data Mining research and algorithms, the technologies that enhance the practical power of Data Mining have seen numerous advancements. The decrease in the cost of hardware has enabled even small, portable smart devices to handle complex data operations that were previously only possible on desktops or high-end supercomputers equipped in computer centers (Kurihara & Fukushima, 2017). In the business world, many companies have begun utilizing the arrangements provided by various data mining technologies, such as recommendation systems and propensity modeling. The innate capacities for analyzing and creating expectations have made these technologies highly attractive.

Notwithstanding these systems, an ever-increasing number of researchers have discovered the concealed connections in their fields by leveraging the analytical power of Data Mining algorithms. One of the primary fields where Data Mining has seen successful applications is Market investigation, financial forecasting, and identifying customer characteristics trends, among others (Sen & Chaudhuri, 2017). With the boundless application of such modeling and analysis, there has arisen the need to explore its valid applications.

6. EVOLUTION AND IMPORTANCE OF ARTIFICIAL INTELLIGENCE IN ECONOMIC FORECASTING

This section examines the evolution of artificial intelligence (AI) in macroeconomic and financial forecasting, as well as its significance. It examines the current status of AI in forecasting models in India, comparing it with those in advanced countries. The paradigms of predictive analytics in the field of macroeconomic and financial forecasting have been gradually shifting. In recent years, AI has been positioned as a promising technology to establish an advanced paradigm. There are some related reasons for this. New technologies related to machine learning have been developed. To forecast macroeconomic and financial indicators, many models are being developed. Fourier analysis, stochastic difference equations (such as ARIMA models), and other regression analyses have been employed. These summarized models are referred to as pink-pattern models. However, in these old models, there are limitations in their predictive relationship. Unlike that, machine learning used in AI has a characteristic predictive structure aspect that is different from the past. In particular, it has improved the predictive relationship in the event-related problem to be applied. There is a way to utilize big data or unstructured data, along with a variety of variables, in machine learning.

The significant growth in recent years of data entities has enabled the extraction of results with high accuracy, even without prior knowledge of the scope. For application in electronic trading, the structure of a neural network, known as deep learning, harmonizes the data sequence, exhibiting excellent predictive power that surpasses that of traditional abnormal pattern analysis. Deep learning models have shown promising progress in stock market prediction, with this survey providing a review of data sources, neural network structures, and evaluation metrics (W. Jiang, 2021). Due to these factors, recent literature is closely tied to AI technology, including deep learning, and promotes the deployment of AI in economic (macroeconomic or financial) fields. An explainable artificial intelligence approach, LightGBM, achieves high accuracy in financial distress prediction and provides local and global explanations for external stakeholders (Z. Zhang et al., 2022). Moreover, the Indian government is also interested in developing and implementing a policy predictive model that utilizes AI from NITI Aayog. Although AI technology in India could be efficient in providing comprehensive and high-quality forecast reports in the economic and financial fields at the government level, it has not yet been introduced for the prediction model of business institutions. This may be because there have been few studies focusing on the effectiveness of AI applied to predictive models in this field.

7. MACHINE LEARNING TECHNIQUES IN ECONOMIC FORECASTING

AI has been introduced into economics, but forecasts using machine learning have not been thoroughly conducted (Kurihara & Fukushima, 2019). A Comparison of using AR models and machine learning to forecast GDP and consumer prices is undertaken in the case of recent cases from G7 countries. Although AI, artificial intelligence, and big data have become buzzwords recently, examples of practical use are not primarily in corporate applications. For many analysts who utilize TS, their view is limited, and they are handling hundreds of pieces of data. Machine learning, with a broader perspective that encompasses unstructured data, can predict more accurately. AI in stock market trading has gained continuous attention, and the literature is becoming increasingly specific and thorough, with applications ranging from portfolio optimization to stock market prediction (Ferreira et al., 2021). Machine learning, deep learning, reinforcement learning, and deep reinforcement learning-based techniques have significantly improved stock market forecasting and algorithmic trading (Sahu et al., 2023). This paper investigates whether machine learning can enhance the forecasting of economic data compared to traditional statistical models. For economic variables, GDP and consumer prices are employed because stock prices, exchange rates, and other variables are not necessarily suitable for machine learning.

Figure 8. Three Field Plot analysis Using R

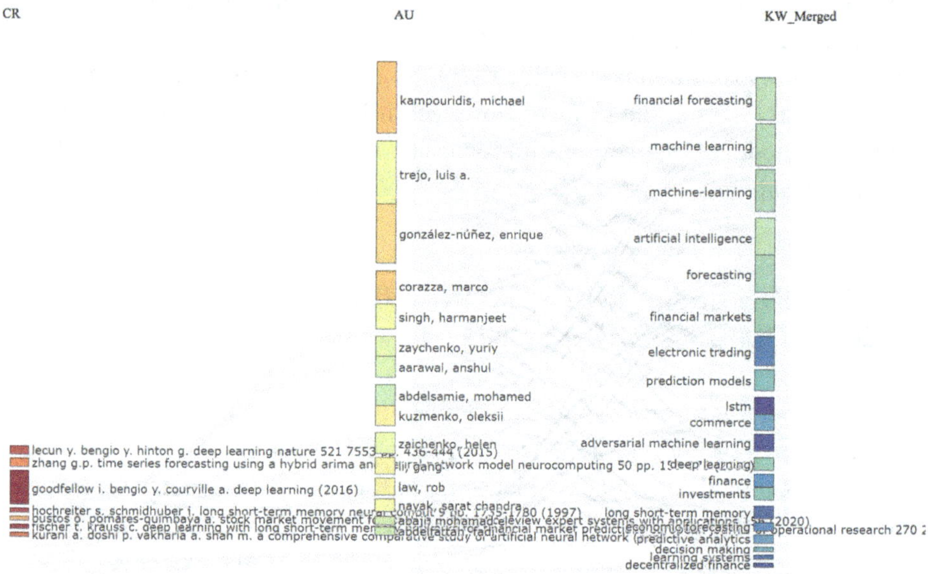

The three-field plot diagram visually highlights the intellectual and thematic structure of research on Artificial Intelligence in Economic and Financial Forecasting. The diagram establishes clear linkages among the most frequently cited references (CR), contributing authors (AU), and key thematic keywords (KW_Merged). Influential foundational works, such as those by LeCun and Goodfellow, serve as critical reference points, reflecting the theoretical and technical grounding of AI and deep learning within forecasting applications. Prominent contributors, such as Kampouridis, Trejo, and González-Núñez, are consistently associated with keywords like machine learning, financial forecasting, and artificial intelligence, demonstrating a strong alignment between author expertise and research themes.

The distribution of keywords further indicates the evolution of forecasting models, with notable emphasis on LSTM, prediction models, and electronic trading, suggesting a methodological shift toward data-driven approaches and real-time analytics in economic and financial systems (Bibiyana et al., 2025). The interconnected structure underscores the multidisciplinary nature of the field, drawing from computer science, economics, and finance. The prominence of applied themes such as forecasting, decision-making, and decentralized finance reinforces the relevance of AI-enhanced tools in addressing practical forecasting challenges(González-Núñez et al., 2025). Overall, the diagram provides a strong bibliometric justification for the selected research title. It evidences a well-defined and rapidly growing scholarly domain where predictive analytics is being reshaped by artificial intelligence, validating the title's focus and its contribution to emerging academic discourse.

Traditional forecasting models, primarily autoregressive (AR) models, can also predict economic conditions(Dahake, Vighney, et al., 2025). AI and machine learning are increasingly used in finance, with the top contributors being the United States, China, and the United Kingdom, providing practical guidance for fintech and financial companies (Ahmed et al., 2022). Recent advances in machine learning techniques, such as Deep Learning, Text Mining, and Ensemble Techniques, necessitate an updated review of stock market forecasting techniques for informed investment decisions (Bustos & Pomares-Quimbaya, 2020). Machine learning provides explanations for those interested in finance, but a new statistical model is also available. Machine learning is deeply related to deep learning. Deep learning structures, such as recurrent neural networks, have been applied in various fields, including economics. Artificial Neural Network models, particularly those with Self-Optimizing Maps, can accurately predict stock market index returns, outperforming linear regression models (Al-Akashi, 2022). In the market, their use with good results is well known; however, there is insufficient research to determine whether the AI or machine learning used for forecasting in the economic market is valid.

8. MOST CITED AND RELEVANT AUTHORS:

Figure 9. Most Cited and Relevant Authors Analysis Using R

The analysis of the most relevant authors associated with the research theme "Artificial Intelligence in Economic and Financial Forecasting" provides clear evidence of emerging and established scholarly engagement in this domain. Notably, Michael Kampouridis stands out with the highest number of contributions (3 documents), reflecting his focused expertise at the intersection of AI and financial forecasting. Authors such as Marco Corazza, Enrique González-Núñez, Hanna Datsenko, and several others, with two publications each, also demonstrate consistent scholarly activity in this area.

The concentration of publications among a core group of researchers indicates a developing yet active research community. The diversity of contributing authors across different institutions and countries suggests that the topic holds global academic interest, particularly within the fields of economics, finance, and computational modeling. The presence of multiple authors with equal contributions highlights collaborative research patterns and the growing interdisciplinary nature of the field, where expertise in machine learning, financial systems, and predictive analytics converge (Dahake, Nakshane, et al., 2025).

This author-level bibliometric evidence justifies the scholarly relevance of the proposed research title. It confirms that the intersection of artificial intelligence and economic forecasting is not only topical but also backed by an expanding body of academic work. Such a foundation offers both depth and breadth for further exploration, citation analysis, and systematic review.

9. TRENDING TOPICS

Figure 10. Word Frequency Over Time Analysis Using R

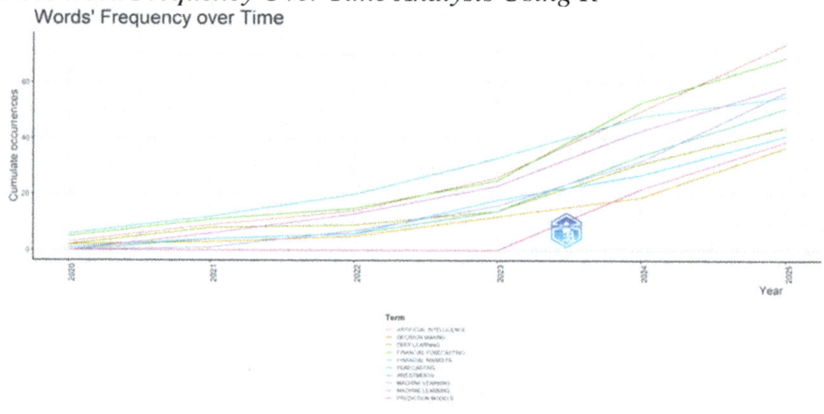

10. SUPERVISED LEARNING ALGORITHMS

For almost a century, stock market experts have had an edge over the respective benchmark indices. However, with the advent of artificial intelligence, this paradigm of so-called 'experts' is being questioned all over the world. There is increasing evidence regarding the effectiveness of artificial intelligence in economic and financial forecasting. Today, conventional statistical techniques and machine learning models are being replaced by complex and highly accurate artificial engines based on creative deep learning and inventive reinforcement learning developed by many AI start-ups throughout the country (Dahake, Gajghate, et al., 2025). The purpose of this research is to educate the Indian community, including the scientific community, students, and professionals, who are still living in the traditional age of time series modeling, about the impacts and consequences of artificial intelligence in economic and financial forecasting within the Indian stock markets. This research demonstrates that conventional statistical techniques are inadequate for the economic and financial forecasting of high-frequency Indian stock return and trade volume data. The extensive predictor variable space is projected into a lower-dimensional feature space to summarize the information and make the state space tractable (Bhadade et al., 2025). Recurrent neural networks (RNNs) in conjunction with targeted feature engineering are employed in this work to project high-frequency Indian stock data into an interpretable state space for subsequent forecasting. Research must always depict the unique environment, economic structures, data acquisition, and other technical aspects. Considering this, it should be pleasing for the research community to introduce the high-frequency Indian stock return and trade volume time series dataset obtained directly from the National Stock Exchange of India. Supervised learning is gaining increasing popularity among quantitative traders, as the abundance of technical market indicators facilitates the easy and quick development of prediction strategies (Ryll & Seidens, 2019). Supervised learning is used for prediction tasks where a dataset consisting of inputs and labeled targets is available. It has gained popularity in the financial domain, and several platforms enable its simple implementation based on an abundance of technical market indicators (Y. Zhang et al., 2021). This plethora of trading interfaces raises the question of what output to expect when using a research-generated prediction model for real trading and wealth generation. On a related note, numerous studies have proposed and examined the performance of various machine learning models, primarily from the domain of supervised learning. Experiments recorded the signals only as hourly reference points and did not consider trading patterns. However, little experimental evidence exists to prove that a particular direction prediction algorithm can consistently outperform the market in the out-of-sample setting (Shroff et al., 2022).

11. UNSUPERVISED LEARNING ALGORITHMS

Unsupervised learning algorithms are often designed for tasks that precede supervised learning algorithms, such as clustering or dimensionality reduction (Ryll & Seidens, 2019). An unsupervised learning algorithm, for instance, can cluster stocks according to the similarity of their input features. The resulting cluster can then be further employed for supervised classification. However, the choice of distance or similarity metric used for the target input features is not entirely intuitive and can significantly impact the performance of the clustering. A wide range of authors have explored the application of machine learning algorithms to financial time series over the last two decades. While machine learning techniques are well-suited for various approximation tasks, they fundamentally represent so-called 'black-box' models, meaning that the behavior of their output cannot be fully explained (Shah & Shroff, 2021). This characteristic is especially significant in cases of abnormal market movements, such as short-term, unpredictable variations caused by influential news broadcasts or catastrophic political events.

Many financial time series studies employ supervised classification algorithms, believing that the predictability of the data can be enhanced by designing useful input features. While the latter frequently involves domain-specific modeling, no less critical is an investigation of the impact of different algorithms on the same data set with the same input features. The robustness of the forecasting model is another important aspect that is often neglected in published works. Moreover, it is unclear what a fair validation protocol would be in this field, as testing financial data may not directly follow the training data. Though a considerable number of works involving, often minor or domain-specific, alterations to the implementation of established machine learning algorithms have been published, it is difficult to approximate these works in an unbiased manner. In light of the outlined problems, the present work aims to evaluate various supervised machine learning algorithms in a systematic, impartial manner, using similar feature spaces and targeting the same output classes over a diverse set of financial time series prediction tasks (including stocks, commodities, and currencies), and accordingly providing previously unreported insights.

12. DEEP LEARNING MODELS IN FINANCIAL FORECASTING

New challenges and approaches emerging in the economic and financial domain in India also reflect the current global trends. Computational intelligent methods, such as artificial neural networks, fuzzy logic, genetic algorithms, and evolutionary techniques, can reduce stock market risk and improve forecasting accuracy (Kumar et al., 2021). Recent advances in computational capabilities and big data analysis have given rise to new challenges. Economic and financial domains are considered among the core pillars of a society, offering a wide range of challenges and research opportunities. Multiple traditional and modern approaches have been employed to address these challenges. The growing complexity of challenges in these domains, along with increased access to data, has led to a collective movement toward more complex approaches involving heuristics, simulations, and machine learning. Big data, artificial intelligence, and machine learning techniques are transforming financial technology, but face challenges in AI ethics, regulation, and intelligent data utilization (Nguyen et al., 2023).

In this discussion, recent efforts in leveraging artificial intelligence for addressing economic and financial forecasting have been delineated. It provided readers with a glimpse into the reasons why these efforts are of interest, the success they have achieved, and the challenges they have faced. Efforts and examples discussed, which cover multiple entities in India, were made with different missions and capabilities. However, the challenges cutting across most of them are essentially the same. The aim is to detail the areas on which focus is currently being spent and how the collective force can be brought to bear on these complex emergent problems (Shah & Shroff, 2021). This discussion highlighted an emerging paradigm being adopted, based on the broad discipline of econometrics, for addressing these complex challenges. This paradigm moves past classical approaches of model-based fit-to-data to a new era of data-to-model driven by increasingly powerful techniques in the realm of predictive analytics. The readers hope that the issues encountered, as well as successful solutions and models developed, are enlightening to all in the community.

13. NEURAL NETWORKS

This research examines the dimensions of academic outputs, including publications, patents, and technology products in AI-related subjects and analyzes the perspectives. The 5Cs (characteristics, causes, consequences, conditions, and cures) provide an analytical framework consistent with the Research on Research Discipline (Loo, 1994). In light of the central insights from this domain that have implications for public policy, some research directions are recommended based on this analysis. The framework and subsequent recommendations apply to any AI discipline but are specifically developed to consider those of AMR & PIDS in India. Analyzing the practices of students, researchers, and scholars will be used to demonstrate the relevance of this framework for policymaking within leading AI disciplines. Data from a recent, comprehensive, and diverse survey of more than 8,000 graduate students and PhDs in the AI & ML disciplines will be referenced, reflecting the views and behaviors of the next generation of leaders. The implications of this research are valuable to those shaping professional development.

Current and future contributions to the AI scientific and practical knowledge, as well as trends within and across these areas. Sub-fields of interest range from network technologies and e-services to advanced robotics and intelligent transportation. Several academic analyses, including multiple bibliometric studies and special issues of AI journals that focus on sub-disciplines such as AMR & PIDS, have continued to investigate and shape governmental policy and commercial practice through full-scale events, including seminars, workshops, and conferences. However, AI research in these sub-disciplines is remarkably under-analyzed in publications typically authored by regional experts or based upon presentations from major conferences. Furthermore, it is contended that the frameworks and subsequent recommendations herein are distinctively more holistic, rigorous, and of greater concern to the broader scientific community than previous works in other AI sub-disciplines.

14. CONVOLUTIONAL NEURAL NETWORKS

Convolutional Neural Networks (CNNs) are recognized as the most effective image classifiers and a breakthrough in Deep Learning for Image Classification. CNN models are being applied efficiently in stock market forecasting by considering Stock Image Representation. Differential Image Correlation is one of the methods used to convert stock data into a grayscale image and perform a Train-Test Split. The CNN-LSTM model outperforms the single deep learning LSTM and existing systems in predicting stock market prices, offering better-informed choices for investors (Aldhyani & Alzahrani, 2022). As a result of this movement, it generates the recurrence count matrix input for the CNN models. So, pretrained stock images were used directly to predict the future prices of stock data pairs. Parameters: Grayscale. Grayscale is the best way to define colors in stock images. Shearing is the best way to describe the transformation of an image. The Moving Average is widely used in data science to analyze stock data. An image array is a small block or matrix that contains the intensity elements of the stock images.

Variable net gains are observed in women with profits and losses. Women starting with returns in the range are obliged to pay a tax of 3.2% (EUR 1,530) generated by binary learning algorithms and a 2.5% tax (EUR 1,430) using deep learning systems per year. Women's profits can decrease, on average, by 3.9% (EUR 1,640) using DLS. Instead, male traders, from the same initial return, extract gains of 1.5% and the worse behavior of DL models and sums up (EUR 2,380) after one year jointly are used with 84% of traders, often with small 109 € average returns, and a taxable profit of 5.1% (EUR 93) with BL models and 4.6% (EUR 83) DMLS. Cutting off at one extreme of the distribution, as evidenced by the artists' shows, value-added policies intervene, which can be expected to close possible class gaps.

15. RECURRENT NEURAL NETWORKS

A vast amount of structured and unstructured data is available in various forms, including text and multimedia types such as audio, video, images, and financial and economic time series. And AI research in Technological Forecasting and Social Change reveals eight key topics, with healthcare, circular economy, consumer adoption, and decision-making showing a rising trend, influencing disciplines like business and social science (Dwivedi et al., 2023). The deep artificial neural network (ANN) methods are highly flexible in operation and can directly utilize economic and financial data without relying on pure econometric modeling to handle the variables. The hybrid of an Artificial Neural Network (ANN) and a Genetic Algorithm (GA) improves stock market forecasting accuracy compared to single ANN techniques, both short-term and long-term (Sharma et al., 2022). Artificial Neural Networks (ANN) and Support Vector Machines (SVM) both play a significant role in stock forecasting, with hybrid models yielding better results when combined with other novel techniques (Kurani et al., 2023).The basic idea of a deep learning ANN is an effort to simulate the human brain with a massive number of connected neurons. A critical area of economics is economic and financial forecasting, which is used for many purposes to optimize profits or minimize losses. A substantial portion of quantitative work on economic and financial markets is devoted to forecasting the movements of most indicators. Predictions are made primarily using econometrics, which involves modeling historical data to define a specific model that is then used to predict future movements. Artificial intelligence and, more broadly, other machine learning methods offer several ways to address these quantifiable issues, providing a range of alternatives to traditional econometrics. The rapid growth of the M4 competition results has demonstrated that RNN possesses highly competitive forecasting capabilities, ranking among the top-performing benchmark methods for time series forecasting in the M4 competition, the most recent in the M series, which features monthly and quarterly data. Newly invented, more complex neural network models still have a long way to go (Hewamalage et al., 2019). It should be noted that the vast majority of forecasting is already carried out frequently and more or less efficiently by established statistical models, such as the Exponential Smoothing State Space Model (ETS) and the Autoregressive Integrated Moving Average Model (ARIMA), which are generally very robust, efficient, and (semi)automatic.

16. NATURAL LANGUAGE PROCESSING (NLP) IN FINANCIAL ANALYSIS

Economic and financial analyses of a company, a project, or an industry traditionally rely on numerical information as input for econometric and other methodologies. These inputs historically include data such as company fundamentals, sector performance, market data, and commodity prices. Numbers, which have been the cornerstone of much of our financial understanding, are, however, slow to capture the whole reality. A valuable complementary and/or alternative perspective on this reality is provided in the string of words circulating the newswires, financial blogs, or chat forums, either written by professionals or uttered by the vast public. Text analytics, and the increasing availability of news and discussions expressed in an unstructured format, have thus become an invaluable tool for financial and economic forecasting as they permit the interpretation and quantification in almost real-time the "sentiment "of the crowd (Semik-Gurgul et al., 2023). Economic and financial events might indeed trigger slight precursory signals before actually showing up in the numbers.

Tapping the string of words to catch these faint, precursory signs engages, however, a wide range of questions related to the type of content to access. For economic and financial forecasters, the most obvious option is to focus on financial news. At a global level, a vast number of researchers have conducted extensive work on the information content of financial newswires. This strand of research is expansive, with studies examining the impact of macroeconomic announcements, earnings reports, or even terrorist attacks on stock and market exchange rates.

16.1. Sentiment Analysis

A shift from being highly speculative instruments to part of a diversified investment portfolio is being witnessed in the case of cryptocurrencies. This is not currently compatible, and this may change over time. That rationalized the adoption of economics to reveal that, when traders are technologically distinct from crypto-investors, trading behaviors are shifting over time, yielding empirical failures of arbitrage conditions that encourage speculation, leading to a rise in values (Darapaneni et al., 2022).

16.2. Topic Modeling

Given a set of documents, Topic Modeling is the task of identifying a set of topics represented by a set of words under which the documents are distributed according to a probability distribution over the topics. Let a collection of documents D =

{d1, d2,..., dn} where document di consists of words w = {w1, w2,...., wk}. Each document belongs to one or more topics, and a multinomial distribution over the words represents each topic. Various statistical models have been proposed to tackle this problem. A few popular models include LSA, PLSA, and LDA.

Artificial Intelligence (AI) in Economic and Financial Forecasting: A futuristic outlook is a methodical and systematized pointer to the current type of predictive analytics, its current limitations, and how there may be a paradigm shift to the use of artificial intelligence and big data analytics application in the field of predictive analytics, specifically in the context of economic and financial forecasting in India, by employing topic modeling techniques developed and perfected in this article (Arora et al., 2011). Now, given that the significant portion of big data is in the form of unstructured data such as text, a relative trickle-down effect of such a paradigm shift is infiltrating the field of textual topic modeling within the broader boundary of Natural Language Processing, hence arming the reader with a systematic and empirical knowledge of the predictive power and limitations of the current generation of predictive analytics algorithms that are based on structured data.

16.3. Named Entity Recognition

Named Entity Recognition is a prominent information extraction methodology widely employed in natural language processing. This technique primarily involves identifying a named entity (NE) in textual data and then determining which predefined category it belongs to. Named entity classes generally represent the various types of information sought after, and this principally comprises person, location, organization names, and numeric values, including date, time, etc. (Sabane et al., 2023). The Named Entity Recognition (NER) process can be divided into three major categories. In the first rule-based NER technique, an entity of interest is recognized as long as predefined rules govern it. The second machine-learning-based NER technique involves training models with annotated text to classify entities of interest. Among the prominent machine-learning-based NER approaches, the Hidden Markov Model (HMM) and Conditional Random Fields (CRFs) are widely used.

Additionally, there are hybrid NER techniques that combine rule-based and machine learning-based approaches. The primary components of the various NER rule-based techniques include a gazetteer, which is a list of ready-made entities of interest. Another component of the NER rule-based technique is the use of lexicalized grammar. Machine-learning-based NER techniques train entity classification models using manually annotated data. Once the bi-classifier model is trained, each word is recognized as belonging to one of the entities of interest. The hybrid approach to the NER technique aims to provide the synergistic effect of both previous methodologies. Artificial Intelligence (AI) and Machine Learning (ML) algorithms are widely used to address a range of problems today. Nonetheless, only a few attempts have been made, and they have been less successful in the field of Bengali named entity recognition (NER), as NER is an essential aspect of natural language processing research, and numerous English NER resources are available. This document describes an efficient data- and model-centric transfer learning artificial intelligence-assisted named entity recognition (NER) methodology to address the challenging issue of Bangla language recognition (Akter Lima et al., 2023). Using a bi-directional Gated Recurrent Unit Neural Network, an Accelerated Radial Basis Function Neural Network, and a toolkit for translating English NER datasets to Bangla, a named entity recognition system is established. Different NER challenges for Bengali have already been held, but the results were less favorable. These challenges require a robust and high-performing Bengali NER system that works effectively on all types of Bengali text content, including books, papers, social media content, and audio.

17. BIG DATA AND CLOUD COMPUTING IN ECONOMIC FORECASTING

India is one of the world's fastest-growing economies. Economic forecasting is conducted to achieve the optimal development of the economy. In recent years, big data and artificial intelligence (AI) have been in the spotlight in the field of economic forecasting. Big data refers to large datasets that cannot be processed with standard database software and require specialized technology for handling. Remotely, it is appearing that the "cloud" is an indispensable technology for big data. In a cloud environment, big data is being processed. Theoretically, the use of big data and cloud computing can improve the accuracy of the forecast. Two types of economic forecasting are being conducted.

a) Macroeconomic forecasting by the government and market participants
b) Forecasting of company business results by investors. In India, the stock price index, Nifty 50, is focused. For the BAG methodology and several methods, five empirical experiments are conducted. Using company data from the BSE, the stock price index of the Nifty 50 is forecasted by employing a time series analysis, specifically the STAR-AR model (Kurihara & Fukushima, 2019). The precision of the BSE's economic forecast and the forecast for the Nifty 50 stock price index are measured, compared with actual data, and the results are discussed.

It is worth noting that a cloud environment is particularly beneficial for big data in economic forecasting. In most cases, the precision of a forecast in a cloud environment is improved by comparing it with a local environment. On the other hand, when a cloud environment was employed without big data, the precision of the forecast did not improve. It is demonstrated technically and theoretically, using numerous datasets, that the necessity of big data in a cloud environment is evident. Based on these results, it is desirable to handle real big data within a cloud environment rather than the existing one. In the empirical analysis, the cloud environment is a real cloud environment provided by major companies.

18. IMPORTANCE OF BIG DATA IN FORECASTING

Accurate forecasting, primarily for economic and financial indicators, has become increasingly crucial for governing institutions as well as for large and small financial institutions, pension funds, and manufacturing companies to improve the quality of their decisions and, consequently, minimize potential losses. In a globalized world, the importance of having timely, high-frequency economic information is ever-growing. For emerging markets like India, data issues are particularly significant and warrant special attention. The advent of Big Data, combined with powerful data processing tools, leads to a paradigm shift in predicting macroeconomic and financial indicators. In the context of data analysis for macroeconomic indicators (inflation, GDP and industrial production), a particular focus is given to the peculiar properties of Indian data: revisions, short length time series, and data at high-frequency, i.e., monthly, with the ambition to better characterize the burst and systemic financial stress in the country. Importance of Big Data in Forecasting: It appears that recently, the perspective on Big Data in academic circles and beyond has undergone a controversial shift. There has been a surge of interest in both the scientific and industrial worlds in the opportunities presented by Big Data. This is indeed in the days when it was quoted as stating, 'Something is fascinating about science. One gets such wholesale returns of conjecture out of such a trifling investment of fact, to be considered not just seriously but to be quoted in opinions of policymakers on the philosophy of research. In this context, a review of the literature on policy conclusions regarding Big Data does not contradict the findings of the present analysis, although the findings are somewhat mixed.

Big Data is seen as data that is difficult to store, manage, and analyze with current hardware and software. In this age of tensegrity, with new business models emerging and the value of data increasing throughout the global economy, the cost of handling Big Data is likely to pose a significant burden to firms and individuals, one that will tend to widen the heterogeneity in access to intelligence, as risks usually do. Processed by sophisticated algorithms, analysts are captivated by dreamy expectations of highly accurate and valuable knowledge hidden within Big Data. Even though Big Data is being generated and newly stored everywhere, and sometimes this data is exploited to create affordable consumer products all over the planet, several reputable scientists have displayed a climate of some skepticism on the Big Data mania, especially in the context of exuberant expectations of its capacity to understand and model complex systems. This is well synthesized by Hosni & Vulpiani (2018). More data can lead to worse predictions. Moreover, forecasts and analyses are scientifically meaningful if carried out in a suitably specified context. In this respect, several key messages can be forwarded, drawing from both the literature on forecasting and econometrics from a philosophical standpoint and the results and implications of the present analysis in light of Big Data.

19. CLOUD COMPUTING SOLUTIONS FOR ECONOMIC FORECASTING

The work proposes an integrated framework for Cloud solutions that support economic and individual asset price forecasting. As the first step, the anticipated number of users likely to participate in the equity market on the next trading day is forecasted so that the Cloud-based resources attached to the trading servers can be scaled accordingly. Thus, a unique prediction model consisting of four diverse techniques, namely seasonal-trend decomposition coupled with auto-regression and moving average (ARIMA) modelling (STL-ARIMA), exponential smoothing prediction for non-seasonal trend component with neural network elasticity reframing (ES-NNER), non-linear autoregressive exogenous artificial neural network modelling (NARXNET), and Gaussian time warping based partnership estimation of various forecasting models (GTW-PEFM), is exclusively presented. Secondly, the individual share prices of different assets in the Indian stock market are forecasted by integrating parameters from the forecasted data on anticipated users (parity relationships between economic activities and equity trade, i.e., computational experiments for Cloud solutions). Three distinctive methods to predict future economic values are proposed. The results of the experimental analysis of the forecasted values on both the financial and asset share prices are detailed. Thus, the Cloud-based algorithmic and system engineering for the equity market bid climate and individual asset pricing in the Indian context culminates in a paradigm shift in predictive analytics in India. The current article contributes a novel, computationally tested forecasting methodology to the domain, and cloud solutions, which form a paradigm shift in predictive analytics in the Indian scenario, are detailed using it (Sen & Datta Chaudhuri, 2016).

Cloud services have emerged as the front-runner technology for easy, low-cost, anywhere, anytime computing. It also integrates experiments that explain the proposed schemes. This article commences with the aim and motivation, and the essential background supported by another unique computational experiment conducted in a fourfold manner, followed by the methodology, statistical significance of the proposed schemes, and interpretation of the executed computational investigations.

20. SYNTHESIS AND THEMATIC ANALYSIS

Figure 11. Thematic Map Analysis Using R

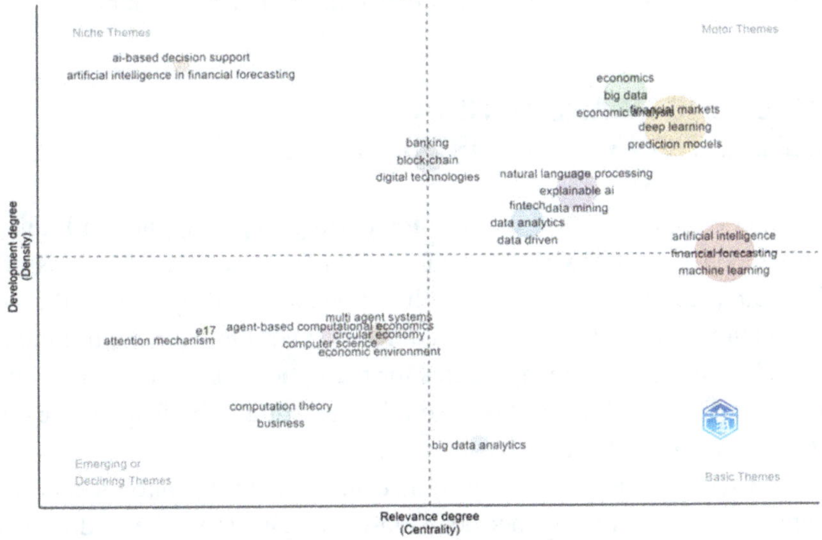

The thematic map provides a structured synthesis of the intellectual landscape surrounding the research, located in the basic themes quadrant. Core concepts, such as artificial intelligence, financial forecasting, and machine learning, exhibit high centrality and moderate density, confirming their foundational role in the field (Cohen, 2022). These themes serve as critical connectors across multiple subdomains, underscoring their conceptual relevance and broad applicability.

In the motor themes quadrant, terms like economic analysis, deep learning, prediction models, and financial markets are both highly developed and central. These represent mature, well-integrated areas driving the momentum of current research, and they directly support the proposed study's focus on predictive analytics in financial systems.

Conversely, the niche themes quadrant includes topics like AI-based decision support and artificial intelligence in financial forecasting, suggesting that while these are well-developed internally, they are less connected to other research clusters (Freeborough & Van Zyl, 2022). This indicates specialization and depth, reinforcing the study's potential to contribute detailed insights within a focused area of application.

Themes in the emerging or declining quadrant, such as agent-based computational economics and attention mechanism, may represent either underexplored opportunities or fading relevance, providing potential avenues for future extension or caution in scope.

This thematic distribution justifies the proposed research by aligning it with central, high-impact domains while offering opportunities to bridge niche and emerging areas (Khattak et al., 2023). The map validates the scholarly coherence and relevance of the research title within current academic discourse.

21. CHALLENGES AND ETHICAL CONSIDERATIONS IN AI FORECASTING

This paper explains how AI-assisted forecasting can be applied in India as part of a new theoretical framework for economic and financial applications of AI. It provides examples of attitudes that might be encountered by exported predictive systems and how such attitudes can be addressed by AI forecasting in India. There is then a brief survey of AI technologies for prediction concerning these attitudes. Finally, the challenges of using AI-powered forecasting in India are discussed, and concrete recommendations are provided.

AI forecasting has the potential to significantly enhance economic and financial well-being, enabling more informed decision-making in government administration, business, and finance, and improving the accuracy and efficiency of monetary systems and markets. Nevertheless, despite these significant advantages, various concerns exist regarding the use of AI projections and other AI applications. Notably, such problems have not yet been adequately addressed in the extensive AI forecasting literature found in business, economics, and other fields. First, the 'attitudes' concerning an AI predictive system, which may be held by both the technology provider and the client regarding the export of a projection or other AI, are too numerous. Second, while some in the ML literature have considered the use of ML as a substitute for this purpose, there is almost nothing on using ML for forecasting and little else in a way that addresses these objections. Third, forecasting using AI and big data, which runs the predictions on behalf of its powerful allies, will not satisfy several of our usual assumptions about stable figures. Thus, for some time, forecasts will likely need to include a variety of econometric, time-series, and AI-based methods. What

India requires for this, using AI informed by ML on commitments, is nevertheless an open question about market-oriented reforms in India.

21.1. Data Privacy and Security

The COVID-19 crisis and associated technologies, such as AI-based contact tracing and large-scale data sharing, have heightened existing privacy risks (Radanliev et al., 2024). Governments' responses to the pandemic have been characterized by limitations on personal freedom and protection measures, such as lockdowns, the identification of potential contacts using personal data, large-scale data sharing, the suspension of privacy regulations, postponed audits, and the removal of data collection restrictions by telecommunication companies. The goal has been to either prevent the further spread of the virus by implementing contact tracing technologies or to gain insights into the virus's proliferation by providing open access to large-scale datasets, thus enabling the development of epidemiological models. In light of the situation in which these measures were applied, there is an overwhelming need for a prompt reconsideration regarding the development and deployment of such solutions. Such a reassessment should be aimed explicitly at both the ethical and implementation aspects of these technologies. It is proposed that empirical data be collected to understand how AI affects people in various contexts.

Furthermore, it is noted that risk assessment procedures aimed at analyzing the ethical hazards associated with AI must be improved. In doing so, research organizations and companies can be equipped with knowledge and methodologies to develop the AI technology ethically. It is noted that the variance in risks (associated with the AI model, the environment, and spillover effects) varies across different contexts. Therefore, it is essential to develop methodologies that identify the ethical risks in the context of interest. To provide support in this endeavor, a process-based risk assessment methodology has been developed. At a more general level, businesses need to apply efficient and effective intelligent algorithm solutions to their advanced data ecosystems, in a context that requires the sharing of data with multiple partners. Henceforth, AI-enabled data ecosystems refer to large data ecosystems that incorporate algorithms with machine learning capabilities. Machine learning in business intelligence can accurately predict demand (Khan et al., 2020). This further means that various static and dynamic data from a large number of internal and external sources are used. In turn, the economic functions are performed in real-time, and the data is processed with the speed-of-thought analytics, thus transforming it into valuable insights that drive real-time automated actions through intelligent applications.

21.2. Bias and Fairness in AI Models

Artificial Intelligence (AI) predictive models can be designed for economic and financial forecasting as AI algorithms leverage Big Data and comprehensive information sets to identify complex patterns in historical data. The increasing number of AI applications can help improve financial inclusion, risk pricing, and risk management in the financial sector, as well as the effectiveness of data mining. However, a key concern with the increased use of AI applications is the issue of bias and fairness. The public (and regulators) struggle to accept automated decisions made without transparency and without the opportunity to understand how personal data is being used (Bohdal et al., 2023). It is also likely that the fair treatment of personal data by AI systems is an in vitro requirement enshrined in several modern privacy and data protection regulations, including the GDPR's principles of lawfulness, fairness, and transparency (Y. Jiang, 2022). Therefore, within the framework of the ethical obligations of data controllers and processors under the GDPR, it is essential to ensure fairness in personal data processing in AI systems.

Models often incorporate systemic disparities because they generate biased predictions; for example, AI predictive models predict the likelihood of payback. After the model makes loan decisions, the financial institution grants a higher loan acceptance rate to a better applicant than to a similar applicant who is part of a protected group. Over time, the financial institution increases the quality of applicants it wants to attract by offering higher acceptance rates. As a response to biased predictions, costs imposed on applicants after loan decisions are made inevitably increase. This is a "cumulative causation loop" between biased model predictions, decisions and their consequences.

21.3. Transparency and Interpretability

Digging deeper into the applications of AI in the healthcare sector and the field of diagnostics, predictive maintenance in the power and manufacturing sectors has not prevented accidents. The oil and gas sector is slow to adopt the technology. Big data analytics can improve supply chain demand forecasting (Seyedan & Mafakheri, 2020). Machine learning algorithms, particularly neural networks, are widely used in demand forecasting, potentially improving supply chain efficiency (Aamer et al., 2020). It has, however, managed to deflect interest and, to some extent, act as a barrier checker. A deeper dive, conducted based on novice AI models, explores economic and financial forecasting applications about a shift from Western to Eastern practices and a growing trend towards financialization (X. Li et al., 2023). AI-powered predictive analytics improves supply chain competitiveness and effectiveness by reducing response time, enhancing logistics route optimization, demand planning, and inventory control (Shlash Mohammad et al., 2024). It aims to analyze the perceptions of this technology, which some have referred to as the "new electricity," and multiplex conditional prediction models across roles, sectors, and applications based on local developments (Misheva et al., 2021). Here, protecting people's jobs and privacy, and changing as few sectors as possible, is seen as a leap too far.

22. RESULT AND DISCUSSION BASED ON THE LITERATURE

This paper aims to undertake an exhaustive review of Indian publications in the domain of AI-based forecasting of economic and financial time series. Explainable artificial intelligence techniques provide more effective analysis results for digital finance and consumer upgrades (Zhou et al., 2023). Although this domain has been dominated by Western literature, there are still some notable works from Indian researchers. AI technologies are being increasingly applied in business decision-making worldwide, including in India. Given its harvesting machine-readability, it seems remarkable that none of the earlier reviews had taken advantage of that, considering the research that became possible because of it. Machine learning (ML) and AI companies are experiencing significant growth in applications of AI (Almustafa et al., 2023), particularly in business intelligence and stock market analysis and forecasting, where they have been widely adopted in Western countries Because Machine learning and deep learning models can effectively predict stock prices and classify financial instruments in the financial industry (Sonkavde et al., 2023). Machine learning techniques can effectively predict stock market movements using technical indicators, macroeconomic variables, and fundamental indicators (Kumbure et al., 2022).Based on a computer-based automated survey of all recognized publication databases and popular scientific article repositories for studies originating from India in this domain, a comprehensive narrative of the landscape of these publications was provided. There has been a significant increase in the annual counts of such publications from India. The types of funding and scope of research institutions, including universities, are systematically analyzed. Legal institutions having special means of driving the uptake of AI financial forecasting in India were outlined. The most profitable avenues for funding were suggested to Indian researchers in this domain (Kartanaitė et al., 2021). Artificial intelligence can assess an enterprise's financial security more objectively, but it lacks intuition and cannot holistically assess the company's financial condition (Melnychenko, 2020).

Since the first well-known article on AI, there has been a precipitous increase in the quantity of such research (Buczynski et al., 2021). Therefore, this research has examined Indian publications from 2009 to 2018, where the number of research articles on AI analysis and prediction of economic and financial time series has increased by nearly 26 times. A similar trend is also observed domestically, and this paper has reported that research articles predominantly focus on Indian publications. Moreover, as the literature review revealed, only a tiny fraction of the earlier works were written by Indians. This research had primarily examined Western and mainly US publications.

23. CONCLUSION

Bibliometric data on Artificial Intelligence (AI) research provide an opportunity to assess the intellectual contributions of AI over the past six decades in promoting accurate economic and financial forecasts. The highest-cited works highlighted the direct implications of AI on either prediction or the broad impact on economics and finance. Two moderate-frequency keywords directly address the intersection of AI and forecasting, suggesting a rich network of citations that intersects AI with problems related to time and uncertainty. The presence of AI technologies and prediction/forecasting across subsequent layers of the bibliometric analysis (e.g., influential journals, boundaries of AI research) confirms the significance of these findings. The bibliometric results coincide with the conclusions of most surveys of AI technologies for prediction, which emphasize the emergence of new technologies to facilitate accuracy in real economies, offering significant improvements over most other approaches to time series forecasting (Buczynski et al., 2021). Considered in the context of a more general insight concerning the high frequency of media- and culture-related keywords in AI research overall, the thematic significance of AI economics and finance is congratulations worthy as this domain is one of the few instances in which the cognitive production of datasets does not exceed the generation of new knowledge, rendering domain-specific bibliometric analysis particularly promising for future work (Kanaparthi, 2024).

24. FUTURE SCOPE OF THE STUDY

The future scope of the study will cover time series forecasting, decomposition of time series using STL and super-denoising, and the forecasting of the denoised dataset. The focus will be on this part of the analysis, and in the method section of this research, the super-denoising framework will be elaborated. This review highlights the need for future research on using artificial neural networks and deep learning models for stock market prediction, as news-based predictions have potential but require improved data collection and processing methods (Ashtiani & Raahemi, 2023).In this section, some details will be referred to in later tables. Time series decomposition involves the extraction of a series into its trend, seasonality, and residual (or stationary) series, also known as noise. AI and machine learning in finance research focus on portfolio construction, valuation, investor behavior, financial fraud, distress, sentiment inference, forecasting, and planning (Goodell et al., 2021). When an economic time series is examined, various fluctuations obscure the underlying trend. There are many statistical techniques for decomposition. However, these statistical methods may not be applicable in a particular context where historical movement is not provided. The objective of this paper is to decompose the time series in a way that effectively utilizes noise for forecasting. A super-denoising model is proposed that could be useful for all types of time series and can be effectively used for decomposing a time series in a way that allows for efficient forecasting and portfolio choice. The proposed model is based on traditional STL and aims to present the denoised dataset. This model is self-sufficient and does not need other statistical models for forecasting. Several research investigations have been conducted on time series decomposition and its application in prediction. Some researchers have proposed a new methodology for time series decomposition.

A decomposed time series is utilized for forecasting. One of the methods for decomposing time series into trend, seasonal, and irregular components is the seasonal-trend decomposition. The residual component is a function of season and trend; however, the traditional STL is applied to focus on decomposing the series into trend, season, and remainder. This study starts by advocating the use of STL for decomposition. The decomposed time series is used for forecasting. The STL is a powerful structure-based decomposition method when a time series has either a trend or a season that changes over time. Moreover, the seasonal decomposition of time series occurs, and the local behavior of season and trend is modeled in a way that makes the fluctuation of the time series easier to understand.

REFERENCES

Aamer, A., Eka Yani, L. P., & Alan Priyatna, I. M. (2020). Data Analytics in the Supply Chain Management: Review of Machine Learning Applications in Demand Forecasting. *Operations and Supply Chain Management: An International Journal*, 1–13. DOI: 10.31387/oscm0440281

Ahmed, S., Alshater, M. M., Ammari, A. E., & Hammami, H. (2022). Artificial intelligence and machine learning in finance: A bibliometric review. *Research in International Business and Finance*, *61*, 101646. DOI: 10.1016/j.ribaf.2022.101646

Al-Akashi, F. H. A. (2022). Stock Market Index Prediction Using Artificial Neural Network. *Journal of Information Technology Research*, *15*(1), 1–16. DOI: 10.4018/JITR.299918

Aldhyani, T. H. H., & Alzahrani, A. (2022). Framework for Predicting and Modeling Stock Market Prices Based on Deep Learning Algorithms. *Electronics (Basel)*, *11*(19), 3149. DOI: 10.3390/electronics11193149

Almustafa, E., Assaf, A., & Allahham, M. (2023). Implementation of Artificial Intelligence for Financial Process Innovation of Commercial Banks. *Revista de Gestão Social e Ambiental*, *17*(9), e04119. DOI: 10.24857/rgsa.v17n9-004

Arora, S., Ge, R., Kannan, R., & Moitra, A. (2011). *Computing a Nonnegative Matrix Factorization—Provably* (Version 1). arXiv. DOI: 10.48550/ARXIV.1111.0952

Ashtiani, M. N., & Raahemi, B. (2023). News-based intelligent prediction of financial markets using text mining and machine learning: A systematic literature review. *Expert Systems with Applications*, *217*, 119509. DOI: 10.1016/j.eswa.2023.119509

Aziki, A., & Fadili, M. H. (2022). Highlighting artificial intelligence roles in business area Amid the COVID-19 crisis. *Procedia Computer Science*, *203*, 450–455. DOI: 10.1016/j.procs.2022.07.060 PMID: 35974967

Belfiore, A., Salatino, A., & Osborne, F. (2022). *Characterising Research Areas in the field of AI* (Version 1). arXiv. DOI: 10.48550/ARXIV.2205.13471

Bhadade, P., Chandak, S., Mohare, R., Dahake, P., & Tolani, K. (2025). Blockchain-Driven Decentralized Finance (DeFi): Trends, Contributions, and Future Research Directions. *2025 International Conference on Data Science and Business Systems (ICDSBS)*, 1–8. DOI: 10.1109/ICDSBS63635.2025.11031990

Bibiyana, D. J., Ramu, V., Rakesh, R., & Raja, S., J, J. J., & Chandramouli, S. (2025). Deep Learning for Stock Market Prediction. *2025 International Conference on Frontier Technologies and Solutions (ICFTS)*, 1–7. DOI: 10.1109/ICFTS62006.2025.11031669

Bohdal, O., Yang, Y., & Hospedales, T. (2023). *Meta-Calibration: Learning of Model Calibration Using Differentiable Expected Calibration Error.*

Bucci, A. (2020). Realized Volatility Forecasting with Neural Networks. *Journal of Financial Econometrics*, *18*(3), 502–531. DOI: 10.1093/jjfinec/nbaa008

Buczynski, W., Cuzzolin, F., & Sahakian, B. (2021). A review of machine learning experiments in equity investment decision-making: Why most published research findings do not live up to their promise in real life. *International Journal of Data Science and Analytics*, *11*(3), 221–242. DOI: 10.1007/s41060-021-00245-5 PMID: 33842690

Bustos, O., & Pomares-Quimbaya, A. (2020). Stock market movement forecast: A Systematic review. *Expert Systems with Applications*, *156*, 113464. DOI: 10.1016/j.eswa.2020.113464

Cohen, G. (2022). Algorithmic Trading and Financial Forecasting Using Advanced Artificial Intelligence Methodologies. *Mathematics*, *10*(18), 3302. DOI: 10.3390/math10183302

Dahake, P. S., Gajghate, A., Mohare, R., & Bhadade, P. (2025). Predictive Analytics in Consumer Finance: Modelling Spending Behaviours for Long-Term Economic Resilience. *2025 International Conference on Data Science and Business Systems (ICDSBS)*, 1–8. DOI: 10.1109/ICDSBS63635.2025.11031713

Dahake, P. S., Nakshane, S., Mohare, R., & Ingle, A. (2025). AI-Enabled Predictive Analytics in Marketing: Transforming Customer Engagement and Brand Strategy. *2025 International Conference on Data Science and Business Systems (ICDSBS)*, 1–7. DOI: 10.1109/ICDSBS63635.2025.11031615

Dahake, P. S., Vighney, S., Dahake, N. S., & Chandak, S. (2025). The Synergy of Quantum Marketing and Predictive Analytics: A Data-Driven Framework for Consumer Purchase Behavior in E-Commerce. *2025 International Conference on Data Science and Business Systems (ICDSBS)*, 1–7. DOI: 10.1109/ICDSBS63635.2025.11032018

Darapaneni, N., Paduri, A. R., Sharma, H., Manjrekar, M., Hindlekar, N., Bhagat, P., Aiyer, U., & Agarwal, Y. (2022). *Stock Price Prediction using Sentiment Analysis and Deep Learning for Indian Markets* (Version 1). arXiv. DOI: 10.48550/ARXIV.2204.05783

Dixon, D., Sattar, H., Moros, N., Kesireddy, S. R., Ahsan, H., Lakkimsetti, M., Fatima, M., Doshi, D., Sadhu, K., & Junaid Hassan, M. (2024). Unveiling the Influence of AI Predictive Analytics on Patient Outcomes: A Comprehensive Narrative Review. *Cureus*. Advance online publication. DOI: 10.7759/cureus.59954 PMID: 38854327

Dwivedi, Y. K., Sharma, A., Rana, N. P., Giannakis, M., Goel, P., & Dutot, V. (2023). Evolution of artificial intelligence research in Technological Forecasting and Social Change: Research topics, trends, and future directions. *Technological Forecasting and Social Change*, *192*, 122579. DOI: 10.1016/j.techfore.2023.122579

Elsheikh, A. H., Saba, A. I., Panchal, H., Shanmugan, S., Alsaleh, N. A., & Ahmadein, M. (2021). Artificial Intelligence for Forecasting the Prevalence of COVID-19 Pandemic: An Overview. *Health Care*, *9*(12), 1614. DOI: 10.3390/healthcare9121614 PMID: 34946340

Ferreira, F. G. D. C., Gandomi, A. H., & Cardoso, R. T. N. (2021). Artificial Intelligence Applied to Stock Market Trading: A Review. *IEEE Access : Practical Innovations, Open Solutions*, *9*, 30898–30917. DOI: 10.1109/ACCESS.2021.3058133

Freeborough, W., & Van Zyl, T. (2022). Investigating Explainability Methods in Recurrent Neural Network Architectures for Financial Time Series Data. *Applied Sciences (Basel, Switzerland)*, *12*(3), 1427. DOI: 10.3390/app12031427

González-Núñez, E., Trejo, L. A., & Kampouridis, M. (2025). Expanding a machine learning class towards its application to the stock market forecast. *Applied Intelligence*, *55*(1), 21. DOI: 10.1007/s10489-024-06018-4

Goodell, J. W., Kumar, S., Lim, W. M., & Pattnaik, D. (2021). Artificial intelligence and machine learning in finance: Identifying foundations, themes, and research clusters from bibliometric analysis. *Journal of Behavioral and Experimental Finance*, *32*, 100577. DOI: 10.1016/j.jbef.2021.100577

Hu, Z., Zhao, Y., & Khushi, M. (2021). A Survey of Forex and Stock Price Prediction Using Deep Learning. *Applied System Innovation*, *4*(1), 9. DOI: 10.3390/asi4010009

Jahin, M. A., Naife, S. A., Saha, A. K., & Mridha, M. F. (2024). *AI in Supply Chain Risk Assessment: A Systematic Literature Review and Bibliometric Analysis* (Version 5). arXiv. DOI: 10.48550/ARXIV.2401.10895

Jiang, W. (2021). Applications of deep learning in stock market prediction: Recent progress. *Expert Systems with Applications*, *184*, 115537. DOI: 10.1016/j.eswa.2021.115537

Jiang, Y. (2022). Prediction model of the impact of innovation and entrepreneurship on China's digital economy based on neural network integration systems. *Neural Computing & Applications*, *34*(4), 2661–2675. DOI: 10.1007/s00521-021-05899-7

Kanaparthi, V. (2024). *Transformational application of Artificial Intelligence and Machine learning in Financial Technologies and Financial services: A bibliometric review*. https://doi.org/DOI: 10.48550/ARXIV.2401.15710

Kartanaitė, I., Kovalov, B., Kubatko, O., & Krušinskas, R. (2021). Financial modeling trends for production companies in the context of Industry 4.0. *Investment Management and Financial Innovations*, *18*(1), 270–284. DOI: 10.21511/imfi.18(1).2021.23

Khan, M. A., Saqib, S., Alyas, T., Ur Rehman, A., Saeed, Y., Zeb, A., Zareei, M., & Mohamed, E. M. (2020). Effective Demand Forecasting Model Using Business Intelligence Empowered With Machine Learning. *IEEE Access : Practical Innovations, Open Solutions*, *8*, 116013–116023. DOI: 10.1109/ACCESS.2020.3003790

Khattak, B. H. A., Shafi, I., Khan, A. S., Flores, E. S., Lara, R. G., Samad, M., & Ashraf, I. (2023). A Systematic Survey of AI Models in Financial Market Forecasting for Profitability Analysis. *IEEE Access : Practical Innovations, Open Solutions*, *11*, 125359–125380. DOI: 10.1109/ACCESS.2023.3330156

Kumar, G., Jain, S., & Singh, U. P. (2021). Stock Market Forecasting Using Computational Intelligence: A Survey. *Archives of Computational Methods in Engineering*, *28*(3), 1069–1101. DOI: 10.1007/s11831-020-09413-5

Kumbure, M. M., Lohrmann, C., Luukka, P., & Porras, J. (2022). Machine learning techniques and data for stock market forecasting: A literature review. *Expert Systems with Applications*, *197*, 116659. DOI: 10.1016/j.eswa.2022.116659

Kurani, A., Doshi, P., Vakharia, A., & Shah, M. (2023). A Comprehensive Comparative Study of Artificial Neural Network (ANN) and Support Vector Machines (SVM) on Stock Forecasting. *Annals of Data Science*, *10*(1), 183–208. DOI: 10.1007/s40745-021-00344-x

Kurihara, Y., & Fukushima, A. (2017). The Market Efficiency of Bitcoin: A Weekly Anomaly Perspective. *Journal of Applied Finance & Banking*, *7*(3), 1–4.

Li, A. W., & Bastos, G. S. (2020). Stock Market Forecasting Using Deep Learning and Technical Analysis: A Systematic Review. *IEEE Access : Practical Innovations, Open Solutions*, *8*, 185232–185242. DOI: 10.1109/ACCESS.2020.3030226

Li, X., Sigov, A., Ratkin, L., Ivanov, L. A., & Li, L. (2023). Artificial intelligence applications in finance: A survey. *Journal of Management Analytics*, *10*(4), 676–692. DOI: 10.1080/23270012.2023.2244503

Melnychenko, O. (2020). Is Artificial Intelligence Ready to Assess an Enterprise's Financial Security? *Journal of Risk and Financial Management, 13*(9), 191. DOI: 10.3390/jrfm13090191

Mhlanga, D. (2021). Financial Inclusion in Emerging Economies: The Application of Machine Learning and Artificial Intelligence in Credit Risk Assessment. *International Journal of Financial Studies, 9*(3), 39. DOI: 10.3390/ijfs9030039

Misheva, B. H., Osterrieder, J., Hirsa, A., Kulkarni, O., & Lin, S. F. (2021). *Explainable AI in Credit Risk Management* (Version 1). arXiv. DOI: 10.48550/ARXIV.2103.00949

Năstasă, A., Dumitra, T.-C., & Grigorescu, A. (2024). Artificial intelligence and sustainable development during the pandemic: An overview of the scientific debates. *Heliyon, 10*(9), e30412. DOI: 10.1016/j.heliyon.2024.e30412 PMID: 38711639

Nguyen, D. K., Sermpinis, G., & Stasinakis, C. (2023). Big data, artificial intelligence and machine learning: A transformative symbiosis in favour of financial technology. *European Financial Management, 29*(2), 517–548. DOI: 10.1111/eufm.12365

Patra, A. K., Praharaj, A., Sudarshan, D., & Chhatoi, B. P. (2024). AI and business management: Tracking future research agenda through bibliometric network analysis. *Heliyon, 10*(1), e23902. DOI: 10.1016/j.heliyon.2023.e23902 PMID: 38230239

Radanliev, P., Santos, O., Brandon-Jones, A., & Joinson, A. (2024). Ethics and responsible AI deployment. *Frontiers in Artificial Intelligence, 7*, 1377011. DOI: 10.3389/frai.2024.1377011 PMID: 38601110

Rajaram, S. K., Patra, G. K., Konkimalla, S., Boddapati, V. N., Sarisa, M., Reddy, M. S., & Polimetla, K. (2025). A Sentiment Analysis of Customer Product Review Based on Machine Learning Techniques in E-Commerce. SSRN *Electronic Journal*. DOI: 10.2139/ssrn.5153849

Ryll, L., & Seidens, S. (2019). *Evaluating the Performance of Machine Learning Algorithms in Financial Market Forecasting: A Comprehensive Survey* (Version 2). arXiv. DOI: 10.48550/ARXIV.1906.07786

Sabane, M., Ranade, A., Litake, O., Patil, P., Joshi, R., & Kadam, D. (2023). *Enhancing Low Resource NER Using Assisting Language And Transfer Learning*. DOI: 10.1109/ICAAIC56838.2023.10141204

Saeidnia, H. R., Hosseini, E., Abdoli, S., & Ausloos, M. (2024). Unleashing the power of AI: A systematic review of cutting-edge techniques in AI-enhanced scientometrics, webometrics and bibliometrics. *Library Hi Tech*. Advance online publication. DOI: 10.1108/LHT-10-2023-0514

Sahu, S. K., Mokhade, A., & Bokde, N. D. (2023). An Overview of Machine Learning, Deep Learning, and Reinforcement Learning-Based Techniques in Quantitative Finance: Recent Progress and Challenges. *Applied Sciences (Basel, Switzerland)*, *13*(3), 1956. DOI: 10.3390/app13031956

Semik-Gurgul, E., Gurgul, A., & Szmatoła, T. (2023). Transcriptome and methylome sequencing reveals altered long non-coding RNA genes expression and their aberrant DNA methylation in equine sarcoids. *Functional & Integrative Genomics*, *23*(3), 268. DOI: 10.1007/s10142-023-01200-2 PMID: 37552338

Sen, J., & Chaudhuri, T. D. (2017). *An Investigation of the Structural Characteristics of the Indian IT Sector and the Capital Goods Sector: An Application of the R Programming in Time Series Decomposition and Forecasting*. DOI: 10.48550/ARXIV.1706.07821

Seyedan, M., & Mafakheri, F. (2020). Predictive big data analytics for supply chain demand forecasting: Methods, applications, and research opportunities. *Journal of Big Data*, *7*(1), 53. Advance online publication. DOI: 10.1186/s40537-020-00329-2

Sharma, D. K., Hota, H. S., Brown, K., & Handa, R. (2022). Integration of genetic algorithm with artificial neural network for stock market forecasting. *International Journal of System Assurance Engineering and Management*, *13*(S2), 828–841. DOI: 10.1007/s13198-021-01209-5

Shi, Y., & Li, X. (2019). An overview of bankruptcy prediction models for corporate firms: A Systematic literature review. *Intangible Capital*, *15*(2), 114. DOI: 10.3926/ic.1354

Shlash Mohammad, A. A., Khanfar, I. A. A., Al Oraini, B., Vasudevan, A., Suleiman, I. M., & Fei, Z. (2024). Predictive analytics on artificial intelligence in supply chain optimization. *Data and Metadata*, *3*, 395. DOI: 10.56294/dm2024395

Shroff, A., Shah, B. J., & Gajjar, H. (2022). Online food delivery research: A systematic literature review. *International Journal of Contemporary Hospitality Management*, *34*(8), 2852–2883. DOI: 10.1108/IJCHM-10-2021-1273

Sohrabpour, V., Oghazi, P., Toorajipour, R., & Nazarpour, A. (2021). Export sales forecasting using artificial intelligence. *Technological Forecasting and Social Change*, *163*, 120480. DOI: 10.1016/j.techfore.2020.120480

Sonkavde, G., Dharrao, D. S., Bongale, A. M., Deokate, S. T., Doreswamy, D., & Bhat, S. K. (2023). Forecasting Stock Market Prices Using Machine Learning and Deep Learning Models: A Systematic Review, Performance Analysis and Discussion of Implications. *International Journal of Financial Studies*, *11*(3), 94. DOI: 10.3390/ijfs11030094

Tang, Y., Song, Z., Zhu, Y., Yuan, H., Hou, M., Ji, J., Tang, C., & Li, J. (2022). A survey on machine learning models for financial time series forecasting. *Neurocomputing*, *512*, 363–380. DOI: 10.1016/j.neucom.2022.09.003

Usman, F. O., Eyo-Udo, N. L., Etukudoh, E. A., Odonkor, B., Ibeh, C. V., & Adegbola, A. (2024). A CRITICAL REVIEW OF AI-DRIVEN STRATEGIES FOR ENTREPRENEURIAL SUCCESS. *International Journal of Management & Entrepreneurship Research*, *6*(1), 200–215. DOI: 10.51594/ijmer.v6i1.748

Zhang, Y., Li, G., Muskat, B., & Law, R. (2021). Tourism Demand Forecasting: A Decomposed Deep Learning Approach. *Journal of Travel Research*, *60*(5), 981–997. DOI: 10.1177/0047287520919522

Zhang, Z., Wu, C., Qu, S., & Chen, X. (2022). An explainable artificial intelligence approach for financial distress prediction. *Information Processing & Management*, *59*(4), 102988. DOI: 10.1016/j.ipm.2022.102988

Zhou, L., Shi, X., Bao, Y., Gao, L., & Ma, C. (2023). Explainable artificial intelligence for digital finance and consumption upgrading. *Finance Research Letters*, *58*, 104489. DOI: 10.1016/j.frl.2023.104489

Chapter 8
AI-Powered Economic Policy for Enhancing Growth, Stability, and Crisis Management

Tara Trivedi
http://orcid.org/0009-0007-7147-1829
Oriental University, Indore, India

Supriya Pathak
http://orcid.org/0009-0004-3602-3172
Oriental University, Indore, India

Dipti Malpani
Oriental University, Indore, India

ABSTRACT

This Chapter explores the transformative role of Artificial Intelligence (AI) in economic policymaking and governance. AI enhances economic forecasting, public financial management, taxation systems, crisis response, and sustainability efforts. It enables real-time analytics and smarter decision-making, supporting inclusive and resilient growth. Drawing on global case studies, the study highlights AI's applications in smart governance, trade optimization, infrastructure planning, and credit risk assessment. While AI offers immense benefits, it also raises critical concerns around data privacy, algorithmic bias, and transparency. The Chapter emphasizes the need for robust, ethical, and inclusive governance frameworks to

DOI: 10.4018/979-8-3373-3053-2.ch008

ensure accountability and fairness. Overall, AI is positioned not just as a technological advancement but as a strategic enabler for sustainable and equitable economic development in the digital era.

1. INTRODUCTION

Artificial Intelligence (AI) is no longer a futuristic concept confined to technological innovation; it has emerged as a transformative force capable of reshaping economic policy, driving inclusive growth, ensuring financial stability, and enhancing crisis management capacities. As nations navigate the complexities of the 21st-century digital economy, AI is increasingly being recognized as both a driver of economic transformation and a tool for strategic policymaking. This intersection of AI and economic governance signals a paradigm shift in how governments and institutions approach development, regulation, and resilience.

AI's growing institutional relevance is best confined by Davidson (2024), who argues that the assimilation of AI into economic institutions creates new operational frameworks and decision-making logics. These AI-augmented structures are start to support core functions of governance, including taxation, labor regulation, resource allocation, and financial regulation. The shift is not just technical—it is institutional and universal, enabling more adaptive, analytical, and data-informed economic organisms.

A central theme promising from multidisciplinary research is the transformative control of AI across different policy provinces. Dwivedi et al. (2019) highlight that AI should be understood not only in terms of its technological competence but also through a broader lens that includes ethical, social, economic, and political aspects. Their work lays out an agenda for interdisciplinary association, calling concentration to how AI's operation in economic governance demands synchronization among data scientists, economists, policymakers, and social scientists. The allegation is clear: for AI to boost policy effectiveness, its development must be entrenched in context-aware, equity-oriented frameworks.

In a gradually more organized world economy, national AI policies are ahead eminence. Gao (2022) things to see how governments, mainly in rising digital economies, are crafting inclusive AI strategies to arouse modernism, improve economic forecasting, and arrange labor markets for mechanization. These strategies replicate a growing detection that AI is not just a technical asset, but a geopolitical and economic essential. Countries investing in AI-driven transportation and policy frameworks are spotting themselves for competitive reward in trade, modernization, and sustainable growth.

The combination of AI into economic organisms is predominantly considerable for promoting sustainability and pliability. Goralski and Tan (2020) argue that AI technologies can compel sustainable development goals (SDGs) by optimizing resource allotment, tumbling ravage, and civilizing power competence. By implanting AI into sustainability-focused policies, governments can more successfully support economic development with ecological accountability. This twin spotlight on expansion and sustainability symbolizes a major advancement in the economic policy exemplar—one that AI is distinctively appropriate to progress.

Furthermore, AI's assistance to high-quality economic development are attractive progressively more apparent in pragmatic research. Jin (2024) explores how AI enables more competent industrialized advancement, better-informed policy judgments, and swift responses to market variations. This research emphasizes how AI can act as both a investigative and a dogmatic tool, helping policymakers recognize structural bottlenecks, replicate outcomes of economic reforms, and execute customized intercessions with larger exactitude. AI-driven platforms are thus proving very useful for conniving policies that foster modernization, competitiveness, and fairness.

Nevertheless, as Korinek (2024) concerns, the era of AI also brings extensive policy challenges. From labor dislodgment and data dominations to algorithmic preconception and precision deficits, economic policy in the AI era must be reimaginated to address new forms of general risk. Korinek's work hassles the need for proactive authority frameworks that can predict distractions, allocate the benefits of AI impartially, and ensure egalitarian oversight. This calls for a essential rethinking of regulatory manners, one that incorporates AI-specific vibrant such as real-time erudition, response loops, and algorithmic murkiness.

Transparency, a keystone of egalitarian policymaking, must be re-engineered in the AI perspective. As Larsson and Heintz (2020) argue, AI systems arranged in economic policymaking must be topic to meticulous lucidity and responsibility principles. This is particularly vital when algorithms manipulate tax policies, credit decisions, or welfare eligibility. Apparent AI systems can boost faith make possible public commitment, and decrease the risks of unfairness or unplanned economic evils. Consequently, Conniving for explainability and traceability in AI systems becomes not just a technical challenge but governance precedence.

The role of AI in fiscal forecasting and premeditated management is a different area of thoughtful alteration. Li et al. (2024) make obvious that AI-driven platforms surpass long-established models in areas such as inflation forecasting, bestow succession optimization, and economic planning. These apparatus offer real-time insights and prophetic competencies that considerably boost policymakers' facility to take action to economic stuns. In times of calamity such as the COVID-19 epidemic or the global financial instability following geopolitical commotions AI can hastily model situations, evaluate susceptibilities, and guide suitable involvements.

AI's efficacy extends ahead of forecast and planning to calamity recovery and disaster buoyancy. Hanwacker (2025) investigates how AI-enabled systems have been crucial in post-disaster circumstances, where quick damage estimations, resource prioritization, and re-enactment planning advantage from algorithmic competencies. These abilities express how AI can diminish human suffering and economic dead during emergencies. In the broader policy bionetwork, such apparatus can be incorporated into national eventuality planning and public communications management, ensuring that pliability becomes a built-in element of enlargement approaches.

The allegations of AI for data governance and privacy are similarly thoughtful. Majeed and Hwang (2023) discuss the adversarial role of AI in situations involving data giving out and security. Their research highlights the need for economic policies that reunite modernism with data dominion and privacy rights. In an age where economic value is progressively more derived from data, vigorous privacy regulations and ethical AI frameworks become crucial to maintaining public belief and avoiding manipulative economic models.

At a macroeconomic stage, AI is not only reshaping policy devices but also reconfiguring initial economic reckoning. Parkes and Wellman (2015) exemplify how economic models, customarily reliant on inert assumptions, are being updated with energetic, adaptive AI agents' proficient of simulating real-world intricacy. This expansion allows economists and policymakers to test hypotheses in effective environments, evaluate policy trade-offs, and expose non-linear relationships that predictable models often miss. Michalak and Wooldridge (2017) echo this view, noting that AI facilitates a better-off assimilation of behavioral and institutional variables keen on economic modeling.

The allegations for emerging economies are mostly notable. Mdladla et al. (2024) examine AI's impending to catalyze economic revolution in Africa, where premeditated embracing can bridge infrastructure gaps, promote financial insertion, and boost public service delivery. Their findings recommend that AI must be personalized to local contexts, supported by capacity-building, and included into long-term development planning. This localization crucial ensures that AI does not reproduce existing dissimilarities but becomes a tool for inclusive growth and human development.

Conceptual Model

The conceptual model for AI-powered economic policymaking as per figure 1consists of three core actors—the AI system, the policymaker, and the economy—linked by a continuous information and decision-making loop. First, data from administrative records, high-frequency market indicators, digital transactions, and real-time sensors flow into the AI analytics layer. Here, machine-learning models generate nowcasts, risk scores, shock detection alerts, and policy scenario simulations.

These AI outputs are then transmitted to the policymaker, who evaluates algorithmic recommendations for policy settings such as interest rates, fiscal transfers, regulatory buffers, and targeted interventions. After the policymaker implements the chosen policy instruments, the economy responds through changes in household behaviour, firm decisions, credit flows, employment, and market adjustments.

The economic outcomes—growth performance, price stability, financial stress, and crisis signals—feed back into the data system, forming a learning loop in which the AI model continuously updates its predictions and improves policy guidance over time.

Figure 1. AI Powered Economic Policy Conceptual Model

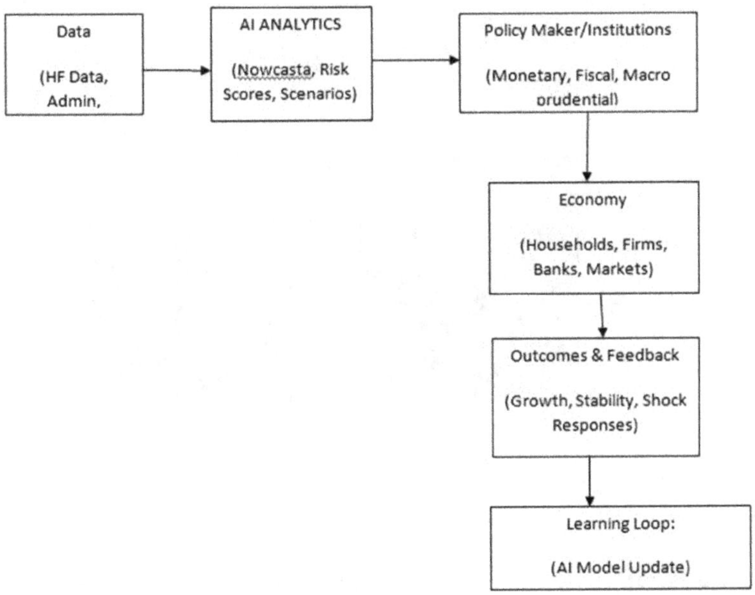

2. AI-DRIVEN ECONOMIC DEVELOPMENT STRATEGIES BY GOVERNMENTS

In the present-day digital age, governments universal are implementation Artificial Intelligence (AI) as a premeditated tool to increase speed economic development, increase public governance, and assemble sustainability goals. By deploying AI in diverse sectors—ranging from communications and public service delivery to industrial development and environmental monitoring—nations are crafting advanced strategies that place technical modernization at the heart of economic conversion.

Figure 2. Relative impact of AI across key economic sectors as identified by the European Parliamentary Research Service. High-impact areas include manufacturing, finance, and transportation, while sectors like construction and agriculture show lower levels of AI integration and disruption

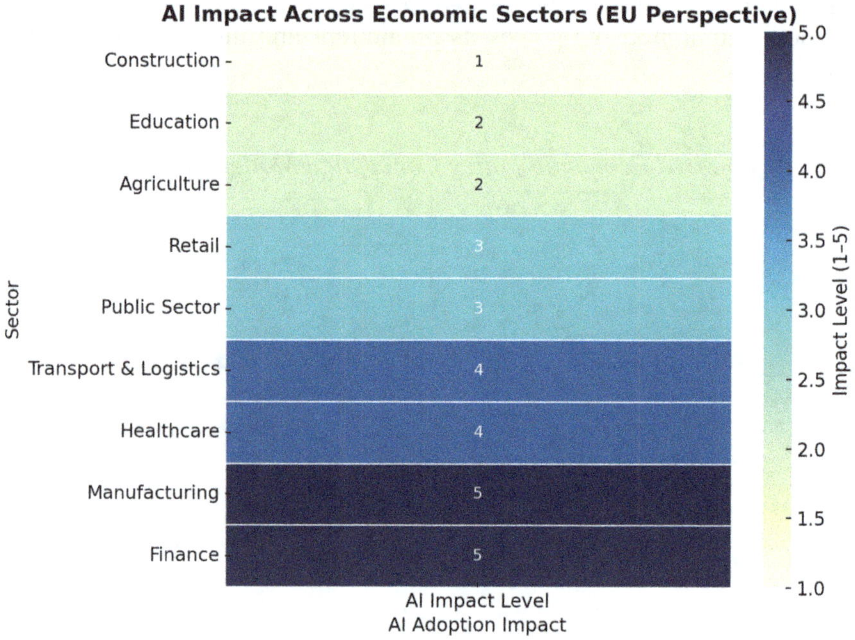

(Szczepański, 2019).

These AI-driven policies reflect a paradigm shift from imprudent policy execution to upbeat, data-driven governance that anticipates challenges and leverages digital transportation for complete expansion.

Figure 2 presents a sectoral impact matrix based on the EPRS report, highlighting how AI affects various domains of the European economy. The most substantial transformations are projected in manufacturing and financial services, where AI enhances automation, efficiency, and decision-making. Transport and healthcare also stand to benefit significantly from AI-enabled logistics and predictive analytics. In contrast, sectors like construction, education, and agriculture remain less impacted, reflecting either technological lag or limited current applicability. This pattern emphasizes the need for differentiated, sector-specific AI strategies (Szczepański, 2019).

Table 1 summarizes practical applications of AI in policymaking as cited in the APEC policy brief. These cases reflect a diverse range of contexts, from health surveillance in Australia and France, to digital civic engagement in Belgium, and tax policy modeling in the **United States. Bulgaria**'s use of crowdsourced data to identify urban issues exemplifies AI's role in enabling localized, data-driven governance. Collectively, these cases demonstrate that while AI strategies must be tailored to national contexts, common benefits such as early detection, policy simulation, and civic responsiveness are broadly transferable across economies (Wirjo, Calizo, Vasquez, & San Andres, 2022).

Table 1. Selected real-world case studies from the APEC report demonstrating diverse applications of AI in policymaking across member economies (Wirjo et al., 2022).[

Country	AI Application Area	Use Case Description
Australia	Public Health Monitoring	Used ML on triage data to detect unusual illness patterns for early warnings.
Belgium	NLP for Civic Engagement	Employed natural language processing to analyze stakeholder input in real time.
France	Public Health Surveillance	Applied AI to estimate incidence of diabetes using health data.
Bulgaria	Urban Behavior Analysis	Analyzed crowdsourced data to detect urban issues and behavioral trends.
USA	Tax Policy Modeling (UNCTAD)	Used reinforcement learning to simulate optimal tax policy outcomes.

One of the most impactful achievements of AI in government approach lies in the divergence of AI with the Internet of Things (IoT). Fares, Nedeljkovic, and Jammal (2023) argue that AI-enabled IoT functions are serious for building translucent, approachable, and competent governance bionetworks. These technologies are being applied to urban communications management, vigor grids, haulage systems, and agricultural supply chains, permitting real-time data gathering and prophetic continuation. For example, smart city initiatives around the world are integrating AI-powered IoT devices to monitor air quality, optimize traffic flow, and manage convenience services. Governments are not purely automating services but are crafting vibrant environments in which community methods self-adjust based on data-driven imminent. However, the authors also highlight the requirement of establishing perceptible governance frameworks to make certain that these AI-IoT integrations maintain isolation, responsibility, and decent principles.

A major support of government-led AI strategies is their configuration with sustainability outlines. Nishant, Kennedy, and Corbett (2020) give an inclusive outline illustrate how AI can maintain sustainable development by optimizing resource convention, reducing secretions, and improving environmental examining. AI applications in cultivation, water preservation, and renewable energy management offer governments new tools for balancing economic expansion with environmental responsibility. For occasion, AI algorithms can scrutinize satellite imagery to identify unlawful deforestation, or optimize harvest yields through exactitude farming technologies. On the other hand, the authors concern that technological challenges, governance voids, and ethical worries must be addressed to comprehend AI's full prospective in sustainable development. Governments must therefore vessel policies that not only support modernization but also manage trade-offs between competence, impartiality, and environmental veracity.

Data privacy and cyber security are essential to the conscientious acceptance of AI in economic strategies. Perino et al. (2022) emphasize how privacy-preserving AI models are crucial for prospect system, particularly as governments assemble and evaluate enormous volumes of civilian data to notify policymaking. These privacy-aware systems embrace coalesced learning models, disparity confidentiality techniques, and encryption etiquettes that permit for data analysis without compromising individual sanctuary. As AI becomes entrenched in critical sectors like health care, finance, and public welfare, the risk of data breaches or observation overextend increases. Therefore, integrating privacy-by-design principles into nationalized AI strategies is not only a technological necessity but an egalitarian necessary.

Building responsible AI methods also needs resilience against exploitation, adversarial attacks, and systemic vulnerabilities. Saeed and Alsharidah (2024) give a widespread evaluation of the challenges interrelated to protection, stoutness, and decent exploitation of AI in public methods. They highlight that for AI to be an effectual tool of economic domination, it must function dependably under assorted surroundings and be protected from algorithmic prejudice, data poisoning, and model inversion assails. These risks are predominantly keen in high-stakes spheres such as welfare allocation, taxation, and nationalized security, where the collapse or operation of AI systems could have widespread socio-economic consequences. To this end, governments are gradually more incorporating AI safety audits, algorithmic impact measurements, and third-party substantiation apparatus into their authoritarian frameworks.

Taken together, these insights recommend that governments must expand AI strategies that are not only technically refined but also decently stranded, security-conscious, and communally receptive. Effective nationwide AI policies should assimilate the following components:

- Strategic outlay in AI infrastructure, including data middles, high-performance computing, and open data ecology.
- Capacity-building for AI domination, ensuring public officials are operational with the skills to blueprint, appraise, and watch over AI systems.
- Regulatory defends for confidentiality, justice, and precision, predominantly in areas involving perceptive inhabitant data.

- Public-private modernization joint ventures that leverage industry proficiency while preserving public concern.
- Context-sensitive exploitation, ensuring AI explanations are personalized to narrow economic, intellectual, and institutional realities.

Governments that clinch such holistic policies position themselves to exploit AI not presently as a tool for computerization or observation, but as a transformative agent for comprehensive, sustainable, and safe economic development. The journalism undoubtedly indicates that AI's probable lies in how well it is governed, not just in how sophisticated it becomes. Hence, the next generation of economic policy will depend not only on data and algorithms, but on trust, intelligibility, and public rendezvous.

2.1 Smart Governance and Automation

The transformative probable of Artificial Intelligence (AI) in the sphere of smart governance and secretarial computerization is becoming a keystone of nationalized strategies aimed at ornamental economic expansion. According to Sungkono and Widana (2024), AI is not purely a technological encroachment—it serves as a catalyst for digital economic conversion that empowers governments to manage with delicate competence, receptiveness, and inclusivity.

AI permits the mechanization of multifaceted ceremonial tasks, ranging from authorization dispensation and tax supervision to public overhaul delivery and objection redressed. By minimizing human being involvement and accelerating workflows, AI-driven computerization reduces equipped costs, limits corruption, and increases the intelligibility of government occupations. Sungkono and Widana highlight that this digital conversion fosters conventional and liable governance, which is fundamental for nurturing investor self-belief and long-standing economic constancy. Figure 3 illustrates how AI is currently leveraged across different operational domains within finance ministries and central banks, according to the G7 High-Level Panel on AI. The most emphasized applications include tax design and collection, where machine learning models are used for risk profiling, and cybersecurity, which is crucial for safeguarding financial infrastructures. Moderate focus areas include public expenditure optimization and managing the future of government work, while topics like carbon footprint reduction and AI adoption barriers are gaining relevance as governments expand their digital maturity. This distribution reflects the G7's growing attention to AI as a tool for fiscal resilience and institutional modernization (G7 High-Level Panel on AI, 2024).

Figure 3. Level of emphasis placed on various applications of AI within finance ministries and central banks, based on insights from the G7 High-Level Panel Report. Tax design and cybersecurity were most emphasized, while challenges related to AI adoption and carbon footprint minimization also featured as emerging priorities

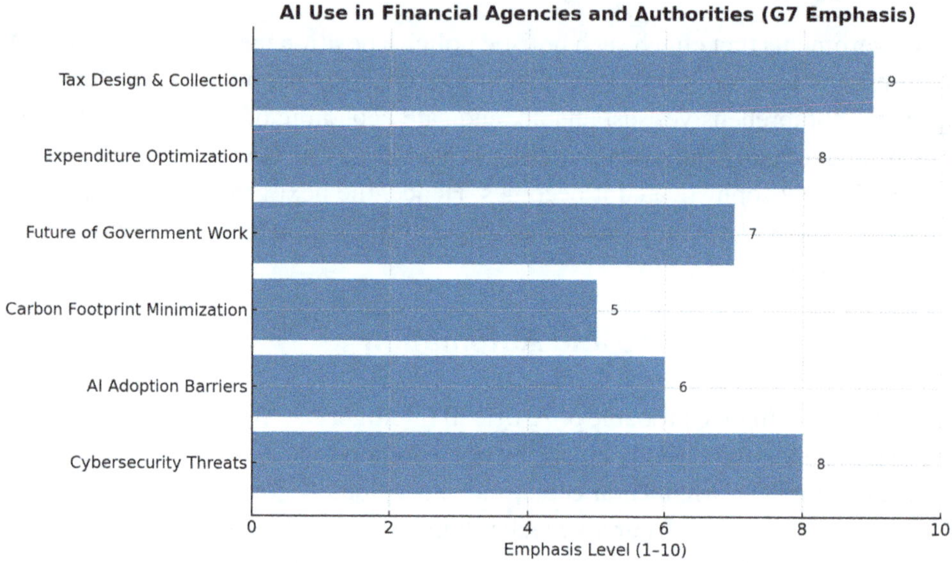

(G7 High-Level Panel on AI, 2024).

Furthermore, the assimilation of AI into governance supports instantaneous decision-making by enabling prophetic diagnostics and intellectual data processing. Governments can now predict economic trends, civilian needs, and public infrastructure confronts more correctly, allowing for proactive policymaking and embattled intercessions. This competence is particularly critical in managing possessions, delivering wellbeing, and responding to economic distractions.

2.2 Economic Forecasting

Artificial Intelligence (AI) is revolutionizing the landscape of economic forecasting, offering governments extraordinary capabilities to predict and retort to shifting macroeconomic dynamics. Danish and Senjyu (2023) highlight that AI, predominantly when incorporated with circular economy frameworks, enables the design of sustainable energy policies that are both prognostic and adaptive. Through sophisticated data analytics, AI can recognize patterns in resource consumption, invention competence, and market demand—key pointers that inform national economic planning and pliability.

AI's extrapolative power enlarges beyond power into broader economic factors such as GDP trends, rise, employment rates, and investment flows. Yuan et al. (2024) give an efficient review underscoring AI's impact on economic expansion, noting that mechanism learning models now outperform conventional econometric methods in forecasting precision and real-time adaptableness. These tools can process enormous, diverse data sets from financial markets, consumer performance, supply chains, and global economic indicators to convey actionable insight for policy formulation.

Governments gradually more rely on AI-enabled forecasting schemes to dexterity sprightly and evidence-based economic strategy. These systems maintain early detection of economic downturns, enabling preventative interferences that alleviate recessionary threats. They also augment circumstances scheduling, allowing policymakers to experiment a mixture of fiscal and monetary strategies underneath pretend circumstances.

Furthermore, the assimilation of AI with high-frequency data sources permits for now casting—the immediate estimation of economic activity—civilizing answer time and tumbling strategy lag. As such, AI becomes a crucial tool in contemporary economic domination, supporting tactical forethought and sustainable expansion in a gradually more tentative international environment.

Figure 4 illustrates the five strategic pillars for enabling responsible AI integration in public governance, as outlined in the APEC policy brief. Governance frameworks are emphasized as the cornerstone for aligning AI applications with regulatory, ethical, and institutional standards. The development of robust digital ecosystems—including data infrastructure and computing capacity—is equally essential. Building public trust through transparency and accountability, fostering multi-sector partnerships, and enhancing regional cooperation across jurisdictions are also considered critical enablers for inclusive and sustainable AI implementation (Wirjo, Calizo, Vasquez, & San Andres, 2022).

Figure 4. Strategic pillars identified by APEC to support responsible adoption of Artificial Intelligence in economic policymaking. Governance frameworks and digital ecosystems are recognized as foundational, while public trust, partnerships, and regional cooperation are essential enablers for sustainable implementation

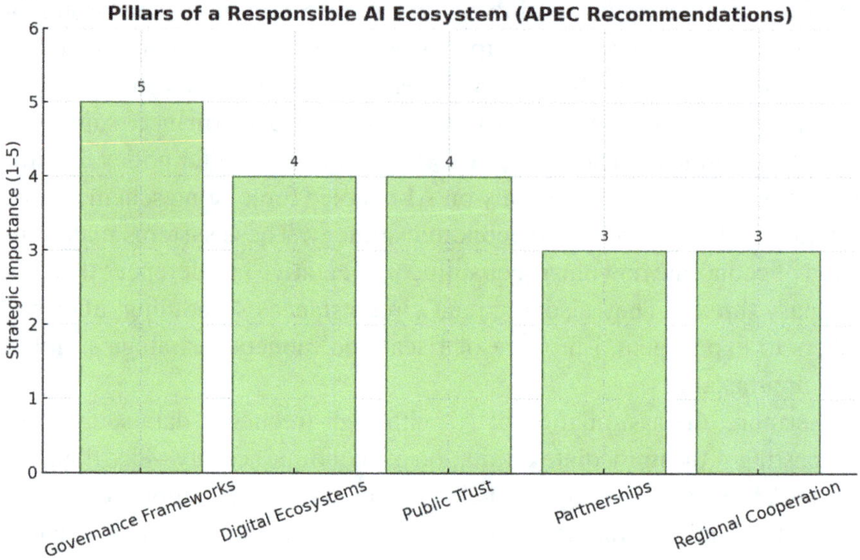

(Wirjo et al., 2022).

2.3 Investment and Trade Optimization

Artificial Intelligence (AI) is gradually more predictable as a tactical tool for ornamental investment competence and trade optimization in the digital economy. According to Sungkono and Widana (2024), AI-driven digital conversion empowers governments to make knowledgeable, concurrent economic decisions that attract foreign direct investment (FDI) and improve trade logistics.

In the investment scenery, AI enables prognostic examination to evaluate risk, identify high-growth sectors, and rationalize technical procedures throughout mechanization. Governments leveraging AI can offer shareholders more translucent, approachable regulatory environments. By using mechanism learning models to estimate market trends and end user performance, states can align investment promotion policies with international economic currents, thereby maximizing funds inflows and plummeting investment improbability.

In global trade, AI enhances the competence of customs procedures, supply chain management, and acquiescence corroboration. AI-powered systems facilitate smart port procedures, optimize shipping directions, and diminish delays through projecting preservation and traffic forecasting. This results in cost-effective and timely delivery of goods, improving trade competitiveness.

Furthermore, AI gives to fair trade practices by detecting irregularities and deceptive activities across cross-border transactions. It also supports digital trade stages that connect buyers and sellers athwart sections, enabling micro, small, and medium enterprises (MSMEs) to contribute in universal value chains.

Sungkono and Widana (2024) quarrel that nations assimilating AI into investment and deal bionetworks are more probable to attain sustainable economic escalation and flexibility in a hurriedly evolving comprehensive market. Hence, AI is not only a technical encroachment but a decisive enabler of trade-driven expansion.

Figure 5 shows the distribution of AI-related patents among major global players during two key periods. Between 2000 and 2005, Japan led AI innovation in patent activity, followed closely by the United States and the EU-28. However, by 2010–2015, China and South Korea surged in patent filings, reflecting concentrated investments and national AI strategies. The EU's share dropped from 19% to 12%, revealing a structural disadvantage due to fragmented data ecosystems and uneven AI uptake among member states. This trend signals an urgent need for Europe to strengthen cross-border coordination and increase AI-focused R&D funding (Szczepański, 2019)

Figure 5. Comparison of AI patent shares by country/region for the periods 2000–2005 and 2010–2015. While Japan and the United States maintained strong positions, China and South Korea saw rapid growth. The European Union's relative contribution declined, reflecting structural barriers in data consolidation and investment

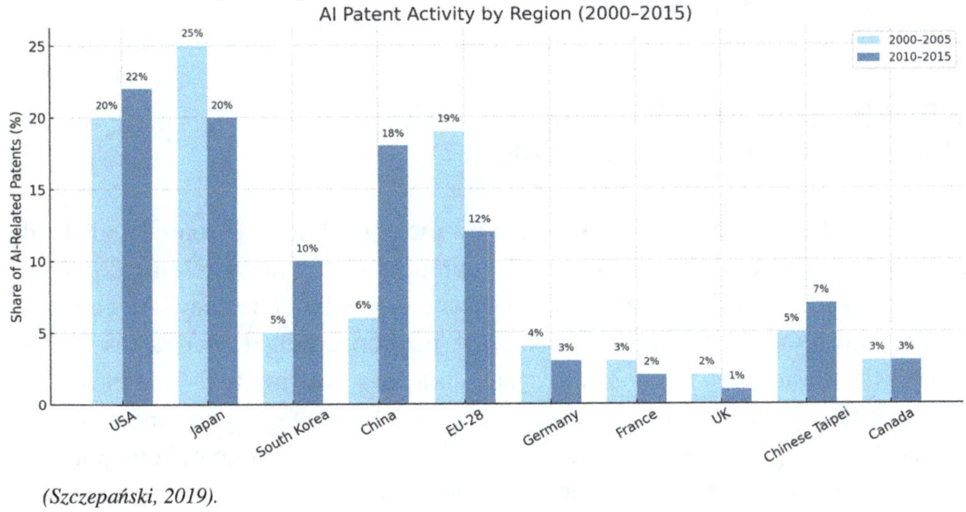

(Szczepański, 2019).

2.4 Public Infrastructure Planning

Artificial Intelligence (AI) is quickly transforming public infrastructure scheduling by enhancing precision, competence, and long-standing economic practicability. Olabanji, Olaniyi, and Olagbaju (2024) highlight the possible of AI—specially when incorporated with block chain technologies—in improving public finance methods, including infrastructure investment, tax fulfillment, and income creation. These improvements give a stronger fiscal underpinning for scheduling and executing infrastructure assignments.

AI permits data-driven planning by exploring population trends, urban development blueprints, transportation flows, and ecological features. With prognostic analytics, governments can recognize most favorable sites for infrastructure development, predict upcoming demand, and diminish planning mistakes that conventionally direct to cost overruns or underutilization. This results in smarter distribution of resources and more targeted improvement.

Moreover, AI can observe infrastructure project execution in actual time, perceive delays, and recommend counteractive procedures. It supports programmed auditing and scam detection in public procurement, ensuring better domination and use of public resources. When combined with block chain, as highlighted by Olabanji et al. (2024), it augments answerability and intelligibility in infrastructure financing by recording unassailable information on contracts, payments, and signposts.

AI also plays a significant role in sustainable infrastructure, optimizing power usage, falling environmental collisions, and sustaining climate-resilient creation. It enables digital double technologies for imitating the performance of infrastructure possessions over their lifecycle.

3.ROLE OF AI IN INFLATION, INTEREST RATES, AND FINANCIAL STABILITY

Artificial Intelligence (AI) is gradually more fetching a essential tool in the formulation of macroeconomic strategies, predominantly in addressing composite variables such as inflation, interest rates, and financial constancy. As economic systems raise more vibrant and interrelated, the conventional approaches to monitoring these variables frequently descend short of capturing real-time moves and rising risks. AI offers a transformative elucidation by leveraging enormous datasets to boost the prognostic precision and receptiveness of economic policy apparatus.

Badrul Hisham et al. (2024) emphasize how AI applications in policymaking can transfigure governance, predominantly in financial policy formulation. AI-driven models allow middle banks and monetary monitors to predict inflation movements and simulate the effects of policy changes on significance rates with greater correctness. Machine learning algorithms, for occurrence, can process high-frequency monetary and economic data to detect inflationary strains previous to they occur in conventional metrics, enabling more timely and embattled intercessions.

Časta (2023) highlights the relevance of AI in attractive the unavoidability of stock returns by integrating rise and curiosity rate data. These models maintain financial organizations and regulators in making knowledgeable decisions, improving investment policies, and reducing systemic susceptibilities.

Furthermore, as Fouejieu (2017) examines, in emerging markets, where inflation targeting frequently competes with the aim of maintaining monetary constancy, AI can serve as a serious harmonizing tool. AI systems can trail credit expansion, asset suds, and market sentiment in actual time, enabling policymakers to design nuanced answer that preserve both price constancy and the veracity of the monetary system.

3.1. AI in Monetary Policy Decision-Making

Artificial Intelligence (AI) is reshaping the scenery of financial policy decision-making by enabling more defined forecasting, coincident analysis, and more proficient policy design. Traditionally, central banks and pecuniary institutions have relied on economic models and specialist decision to navigate difficult economic pointers like inflation, interest rates, and money constancy. However, AI is balanced to drastically improve this procedure, bringing a upper degree of accurateness and receptiveness.

Abir et al. (2024) argue that AI-driven data analytics have the prospective to accelerate economic expansion, predominantly in emerging markets such as the BRICS economies. AI applications permit policymakers to examine huge datasets from different sources—ranging from consumer response to universal trade flows—to make more conversant decisions about financial policies. This real-time data dispensation helps central banks adjust policies enthusiastically, ensuring that intercessions are timely and targeted.

AI also plays a vital role in policy modeling. Ruiz Estrada et al. (2023) highlight that AI can modify the customary approach to policy modeling by incorporating machine learning and profound learning techniques, which can process a broad range of economic variables concurrently. This allows for more perfect simulations of prospective policy impacts, facilitating enhanced prediction about how financial policies will influence inflation, employment, and financial constancy.

Figure 6 presents a heatmap matrix comparing the benefits and risks of AI at different stages of the policy cycle. The analysis indicates that AI offers the highest benefits during agenda setting and implementation, where it enhances pattern detection, speeds up administrative tasks, and enables real-time decision support. However, AI deployment in decision-making and policy formulation raises greater risks related to bias, opacity, and reduced human accountability—particularly where algorithmic decisions affect citizen rights or public welfare. This balance highlights the need for context-aware AI governance that safeguards transparency and inclusiveness at all stages of policymaking (Wirjo, Calizo, Vasquez, & San Andres, 2022).

Figure 6. A heatmap comparing the relative benefits and risks of Artificial Intelligence integration across each stage of the policy cycle. While agenda setting and implementation reap high benefits with moderate risk, stages like decision-making and policy formulation carry significant ethical and governance concerns due to algorithmic opacity and potential bias

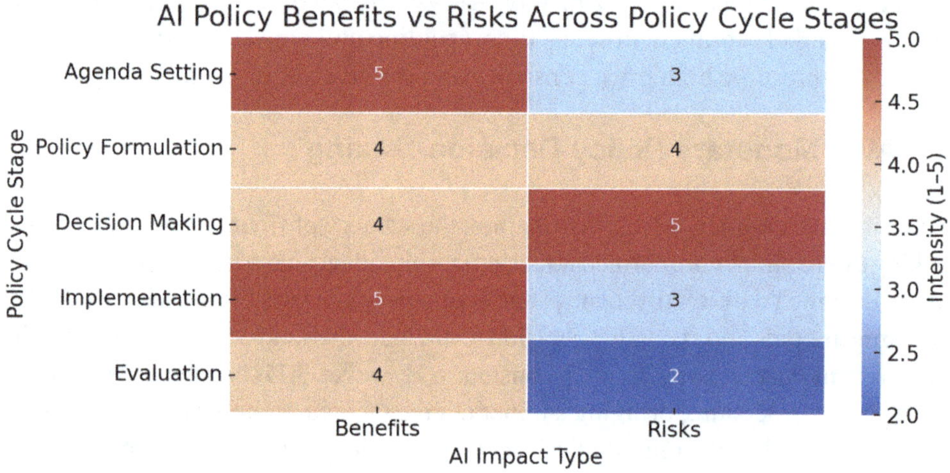

(Wirjo et al., 2022).

Furthermore, Agénor et al. (2013) emphasize that AI can maintain monetary authorities in organization capital regulation and harmonizing financial stability with enlargement. By identifying promising risks and vulnerabilities within financial systems, AI tools offer valuable insights for adjusting capital necessities and interest rates.

3.2. AI in Real-Time Market Monitoring

AI's assimilation into real-time market monitoring is revolutionizing how policymakers and financial organizations watch and react to market variations. By tradition, market examining requisite extensive human oversight and was limited by the occurrence and precision of obtainable data. However, AI technologies such as machine learning and prophetic analytics now facilitate constant and more granular market surveillance, contribution insights that were beforehand engaged.

According to Ruiz Estrada et al. (2023), AI-powered systems can process huge amounts of market data in real-time, identifying patterns and trends that may not be instantaneously obvious to human analysts. These systems are able of tracking a variety of market variables—from stock prices to commodity values—and evaluating them adjacent to past trends to forecast potential prospect movements. This allows for more responsive decision-making by central banks and financial organizations, helping them respond rapidly to impulsive market changes.

AI can also improve the exposure of promising risks and vulnerabilities within the financial system. Abir et al. (2024) noted that AI's capacity to examine composite datasets enables policymakers to spot early signs of financial volatility, such as prickly shifts in trading behavior or curious market activity. By identifying these early caveat signals, AI tools can help alleviate the risks of market collapses or liquidity calamities before they escalate, ensuring greater financial constancy.

Moreover, AI's real-time data processing can help in optimizing financial policies. As Agénor et al. (2013) converse, AI enable central banks to regulate interest rates and additional policy tools more rapidly based on live market situation, helping to stabilize the economy and sustain inflation targets.

3.3. AI in Credit Risk Assessment

AI has considerably distorted credit risk appraisal processes, making them more proficient, perfect, and scalable. Traditional methods for evaluating creditworthiness relied seriously on historical financial data, personal decision, and limited projecting analytics. However, with the combination of AI, financial institutions can now evaluate credit risk throughout advanced algorithms that process enormous amounts of prearranged and formless data, leading to more consistent and nuanced credit results.

Berrada et al. (2022) emphasize that AI approaches, predominantly machine learning, can examine miscellaneous data sources—including transactional history, social behavior, and even non-financial pointers—to generate a more comprehensive risk outline of borrowers. These AI systems can recognize blueprints and correlations that may be disregarded by traditional models, allowing banks and other lenders to assess the possibility of evasion with greater exactitude.

One of the key advantages of AI in credit risk assessment is its capability to incessantly learn from new data. As de Lange et al. (2022) explicate, machine learning algorithms can acclimatize to adjust in market situation, borrower performance, and economic trends, ensuring that credit assessments remain significant and up-to-date. This vibrant learning process helps financial institutions control risk more efficiently, particularly in unpredictable economic environments.

Moreover, AI's role in ornamental transparency is essential. Explainable AI models, as discussed by de Lange et al. (2022), ensure that credit decisions are interpretable and acceptable, promoting fairness and trust in the organism. By providing clear insights into how credit decisions are made, these models help to alleviate biases and make sure obedience with regulatory principles.

4. USE OF AI IN TAXATION AND PUBLIC FINANCIAL MANAGEMENT

Artificial Intelligence (AI) has emerged as a prevailing tool in renovating the way taxation and public financial management (PFM) methods control. By attractive the competence, accurateness, and simplicity of financial processes, AI offers significant improvements in tax observance, income creation, and financial governance.

In the monarchy of taxation, AI has established precious in detecting tax elusion and deceit. Traditional methods frequently rely on physical audits, which can be time-consuming and flat to human fault. AI, conversely, uses data mining, machine learning algorithms, and outline gratitude to scrutinize huge datasets rapidly, identifying inconsistencies and possible deceit with greater exactitude. This permits tax authorities to focus their efforts on high-risk cases, reducing the overall burden on taxpayers while rising income collection.

For instance, AI-enabled systems can observe financial dealings in real-time, deteriorating apprehensive activities that may indicate tax prevention or rebelliousness. These mechanized systems not only improve the exposure rate but also reorganize the audit process, considerably plummeting the time and resources depleted on physical investigations.

In public financial management, AI can improve budget forecasting, resource allotment, and expenditure tracking. By dispensation historical data and allowing for different economic pointers, AI can give more precise and vibrant predictions of government revenues and expenditures. These prognostic models permit policymakers to make conversant decisions, adjusting monetary policies in real-time to attend to unpredicted challenges such as economic recessions or unpredicted monetary insufficiencies.

Furthermore, AI can prop up enhanced financial planning by optimizing government investments and assignments Through the use of AI-driven simulations and circumstances psychoanalysis, policymakers can appraise the expected impact of dissimilar financial policies and investment policies, ensuring that public funds are used competently and successfully.

Additionally, AI technologies can progress the precision and responsibility of public financial executive. For example, AI-powered systems can assist the computerization of financial exposure, ensuring that data is precise and nearby. This increased precision can help diminish dishonesty and augment public faith in government financial processes.

4.1. Automated Tax Compliance

The assimilation of Artificial Intelligence (AI) into tax acquiescence processes has been a game changer for governments wide-reaching, enhancing competence, precision, and correctness. AI technologies are transforming how tax establishment perceive tax elusion, improve taxpayer observance, and rationalize the whole tax collection procedure.

AI-driven systems, predominantly machine learning algorithms, are being utilized to repeatedly analyze big numbers of taxpayer data in actual time. These systems are premeditated to detect anomalies and patterns that might indicate probable rebelliousness or deceit. The use of AI for tax auditing appreciably reduces the manual efforts conventionally essential for audits, offering a faster, more efficient, and cost-effective elucidation for tax authorities.

For example, Zheng et al. (2022) emphasize the pioneering use of multi-agent strengthening learning models in tax policy plan. This AI model allows for the replication of tax policies, optimizing the design of tax structures and the recognition of probable loopholes in the system. By automating such processes, AI assists design smarter, fairer, and more efficient tax systems. Similarly, Zheng and colleagues express the AI Economist system, where deep learning techniques are applied to examine taxation policy, guiding enhancements in revenue creation strategies and observance enforcement.

In addition, the role of AI in humanizing tax lucidity and dipping elusion is momentous. AI systems can cross-reference assorted datasets, such as income records, financial transactions, and asset possession, to offer more precise tax assessments and ensure acquiescence. Aladebumoye (2025) highlights that AI can assist governments boost tax transparency by providing real-time monitoring, auditing tax returns with superior accuracy, and identifying discrepancies that could indicate efforts at elusion. This level of mechanization not only improves the exposure of deceit but also persuades deliberate acquiescence by taxpayers, as the system is supposed as more proficient and less prone to human fault.

Wang (2024) discusses the challenges AI countenances in recent taxation, such as integrating AI into obtainable tax systems, the need for apparent regulatory frameworks, and the prospective for exploitation of susceptible tax data. Despite these challenges, the premeditated direction is clear: governments must persist to leverage AI's probable to optimize tax observance while balancing seclusion concerns.

Moreover, AI can assist rationalize the organization of tax codes by automating routine tasks, civilizing the taxpayer incident, and dipping the organizational encumber on tax officials. AI-powered chat bots, for example, can provide real-time support to taxpayers, answering queries as regards tax filing, subtractions, and deadlines, thereby plummeting human mistake and growing the competence of customer service functions.

In India, for occasion, AI and machine learning are being explored to improve the competence of the taxation scheme. A study by Et al. (2021) expresses how AI applications can automate tax filing, dwindling discrepancies in returns, and provided that real-time insight into observance, which can augment both individual and commercial tax reporting correctness.

4.2. Revenue Forecasting

Artificial intelligence (AI) has emerged as an influential tool in attractive the exactness and consistency of revenue forecasting for governments and businesses similarly. With the global digital economy speedily embryonic, AI offers unparalleled capabilities for analyzing large datasets, revealing patterns, and predicting potential economic circumstances with incredible accuracy. This is predominantly advantageous for public finance management, where consistent revenue forecasting is vital for sustainable development and knowledgeable decision-making.

AI technologies, such as machine learning models and neural systems, have been efficiently functional to revenue forecasting by dispensation huge amounts of economic information, including tax receipts, utilization trends, and worldwide market variations. Gao (2022) emphasizes how national strategies for AI growth can improve monetary forecasting, specially inside the circumstance of the universal digital country. By leveraging AI's capacity to process composite data from various sources, governments can expand more precise predictions of potential revenues, ensuring improved fiscal scheduling and resource allotment. AI-driven models permit for permanent alteration and modification based on coincident data, thereby enhancing the pliability of forecasting systems to vibrant universal economic situations.

Similarly, Goralski and Tan (2020) talk about the intersection of AI and sustainable expansion, underscoring the role of sophisticated analytics in forecasting economic variables, such as revenue streams, that are prejudiced by aspects like environmental alteration and technological modernization. By integrating AI into public finance, governments can account for emerging risks and opportunities, which conventional forecasting methods repeatedly overlook. This capability to believe multiple variables concurrently allows for more inclusive and sustainable financial setting up.

In addition, AI's prospective in debacle revitalization, as discussed by Hanwacker (2025), also plays a key role in forecasting revenues in period of crisis. During periods of profitable unsteadiness or post-disaster revitalization, AI systems can predict the collision of disruptions on tax revenues and recommend strategies to steady and boost revitalization. Through prognostic analytics, governments can predict rejects in income and arrangement for contingencies, thereby civilizing financial permanence during indecisive times.

4.3. Fraud Detection and Risk Assessment

The assimilation of artificial intelligence (AI) in deceit exposure and risk assessment has modernized the financial and banking sectors, offering sophisticated solutions to alleviate deceitful activities and control financial risks efficiently. AI's competence to examine vast amounts of data in real-time, perceive patterns, and predict anomalies has established to be precious in identifying probable coercion and conservation both institutions and consumers.

AI-driven systems employ apparatus learning algorithms to scrutinize communication, customer behaviors, and historical examples to flag apprehensive behavior. These systems can incessantly improve by learning from new data, becoming increasingly efficient over time. Fawcett et al. (1998) highlighted the early exploit of AI in deceit exposure, noting that AI's capability to adapt to embryonic deceit diplomacy made it an essential tool for monetary institutions. By automating the exposure of deceptive performance, AI reduces the need for manual involvement, growing competence and diminishing the probability of human mistake.

In additional current expansions, Johora et al. (2024) highlight the role of AI in banking security, focusing on its application in deceit exposure systems. The researchers note that AI technologies, predominantly neural networks and cavernous learning algorithms, are vital in detecting composite deceitful schemes that conventional methods may overlook. By incorporating sophisticated AI models, banks can recognize not only recognized deceit patterns but also rising threats, ensuring a practical approach to risk management.

Sabareesh et al. (2024) additional investigate AI’s role in enhancing transaction protection within banking. Their work underlines the exploit of AI in real-time deceit exposure, where AI systems can investigate transactions instantaneously, providing instant alerts and taking precautionary actions to block deceitful activities. The capability to examine transactions diagonally various platforms, including mobile and online banking, helps in identifying and extenuating risks quickly.

Together, these advancements in AI-driven deceit exposure systems offer vigorous solutions for the financial region. AI’s capability to examine large datasets in real time ensures that institutions can stay to the lead of fraudsters, making financial operations more protected and consistent. By incessantly learning from new data and adapting to rising risks, AI provides a vibrant approach to risk estimation, ultimately ornamental the overall protection and constancy of financial systems.

4.4. Budget Optimization

Artificial intelligence (AI) has become an obligatory instrument for improving budgeting processes and attractive financial forecasting diagonally both private and public sectors. The assimilation of AI into budget optimization strategies permits for more precise, proficient, and data-driven decision-making, thus enabling organizations and governments to apportion resources efficiently and exploit monetary conclusions.

Jain and Kulkarni (2023) investigate the probable of AI techniques in ornamental financial forecasting and budgeting strategies. They emphasize that AI models, predominantly machine learning algorithms, can examine huge amounts of past data and recognize outlines to make extremely perfect predictions about prospect financial trends. This allows for better expectation of revenue vacillation, expense protrusions, and the allotment of financial sources, leading to more accurate budgeting conclusions.

The efficiency of AI as a budgeting tool is additional discussed by Lee et al. (2024), who address both the probable benefits and the challenges that approach with adopting AI in budget management. While AI offers the option of automating dreary tasks, optimizing resource allotment, and reducing human error, the authors caution that confidence on AI with no proper omission could lead to unanticipated risks, such as algorithmic predispositions or system failures. Nonetheless, the overall probable of AI to modernize budgeting remnants considerable, provided that decent considerations and human expertise are included into the process.

Valle-Cruz et al. (2021) explore into the progression from conventional e-budgeting systems to smart budgeting motorized by AI. They note that AI permits governments to advance decision-making processes by analyzing composite datasets in actual time, allowing for smarter resource allotment and more efficient policy-making. By using AI to optimize budget decisions, governments can improve the precision and competence of public spending, eventually leading to enhanced fiscal conclusions.

Together, these studies highlight that AI has the prospective to redefine budgeting processes by civilizing exactness, competence, and premeditated decision-making. Whether in public or private sectors, AI's capacity to evaluate huge datasets, estimate financial trends, and optimize resource allotment can boost the eminence of budget planning, eventually driving additional effectual economic management.

5. AI'S CONTRIBUTION TO ECONOMIC CRISIS MANAGEMENT AND POLICY INTERVENTIONS

Artificial Intelligence (AI) plays a decisive role in managing economic crises and informing policy involvements. By leveraging AI's prognostic and critical capabilities, governments and institutions can boost crisis attentiveness, progress real-time decision-making, and execute efficient recovery strategies.

One of the main assistance of AI to crisis management is its capacity to examine huge volumes of data in existent time. AI systems can process information from various sources such as financial markets, financial indicator, and social media, providing early warning signals of emerging crises. This data-driven approach allows for earlier and other precise exposure of risks such as price rises, stock market crashes, or supply chain interruptions, enabling appropriate policy reactions.

In the perspective of economic policy intrusions, AI boosts the exactitude of policy formulation by simulating different profitable scenarios. It enables policymakers to sculpt the probable collision of dissimilar interferences—such as incentive packages, interest rate adjustments, or tax improvements—before implementing them. AI's capability to expect outcomes based on real-time data ensures that interventions are more targeted and efficient in mitigating the adverse effects of a crisis.

AI is also crucial in post-crisis revitalization. For occasion, during a pecuniary downturn or natural disaster, AI can aid in assessing harm, optimizing resource allotment, and forecasting revitalization timelines. By reformation these processes, AI helps diminish recovery time and progress on the whole flexibility.

5.1. Early Warning Systems and Crisis Forecasting

Early warning systems (EWS) motorized by Artificial Intelligence (AI) are essential in ornamental predicament forecasting and policymaking. By utilizing AI-driven data systematic, these systems can foresee economic slumps, financial crises, or still political unsteadiness, providing precious prudence for policymakers. The capability to examine huge amounts of data from various sources such as financial markets, social media trends, and economic pointers allows AI systems to recognize patterns that might be overlooked by conventional methods.

Loukis, Maragoudakis, and Kyriakou (2020) emphasize the role of AI-based public sector data analytics in economic crisis policymaking. These systems permit the gathering, processing, and explanation of significant datasets, making it potential to perceive untimely signs of an economic crisis before they spiral. By integrating machine learning algorithms, AI systems can incessantly purify their predictions, offering more precise and sensible insights into probable economic threats.

AI-based early warning systems not only help in identifying probable crises but also in understanding their essential causes and effects. For example, an AI model might envisage a downturn in profitable development due to moves in market trends, unemployment rates, or worldwide trade inequalities. This permits governments to take precautionary exploit, such as adjusting pecuniary policy, increasing social welfare spending, or executing fiscal incentive, well before a crisis completely materializes.

5.2. Real-time Crisis Monitoring and Decision Support

Real-time catastrophe monitoring and verdict support systems, motorized by Artificial Intelligence (AI), play an essential role in organization and explanatory economic crises. These systems permit governments and institutions to incessantly examine economic indicators, market variations, and geopolitical developments, ensuring quick recognition and reaction to emerging crises.

Kara, Atamanchuk, and Kurytskyi (2024) highlight the significance of AI-driven judgment support systems in anti-crisis management. By leveraging AI, these systems can offer real-time data analysis, helping policymakers appreciate the developing economic scenery and respond punctually. This approach ensures that counteractive determines can be taken quickly, minimizing the collision of crises.

AI-driven assessment support systems can trail a broad collection of economic pointers such as stock market performance, foreign exchange rates, and inflation trends. By analyzing past data and recognizing emerging patterns, AI models can envisage prospective risks, providing decision-makers with vital insights. Furthermore, these systems can assist scenario-based modeling, allowing policymakers to reproduce diverse crisis scenarios and estimate the efficiency of dissimilar interference strategies before they are implemented.

5.3. Employment, Welfare Distribution, and Targeted Interventions

Artificial Intelligence (AI) has the probable to both disrupt and boost labor markets, predominantly in relative to redundancy, welfare allocation, and targeted intervention. AI technologies can considerably manipulate employment dynamics by automating tasks, creating new job opportunities, and optimizing welfare allocation systems.

Nguyen and Vo (2022) discuss the worldwide insinuations of AI on unemployment. They recommend that while AI might displace certain jobs, predominantly in routine-based sectors, it can also drive the establishment of new roles in tech and AI-focused industries. The evidence indicates that AI's impact on joblessness varies diagonally regions, with high-income economies experiencing additional automation-driven job dislocation compared to rising nations, where AI can lead to job formation and improvements in efficiency.

Masoud (2024) expands this quarrel by exploring the econometric psychoanalysis of AI's effect on joblessness in high-income economies. His revision reveals that AI's combination into dissimilar sectors may diminish the need for low-skilled workers while demanding a senior skill level for workers in emerging AI and tech industries. This move necessitates targeted interferences in skills development and labor market policies to ensure that displaced workers can conversion into new roles, rather than countenance long-term redundancy.

In terms of welfare allotment, AI can optimize resource allotment and goal intercessions more proficiently. Radić, Gavrilović, and Mihailović (2024) emphasize AI's role in improving social welfare systems by facilitating more specific targeting of assist to those in require, ensuring that public funds are allocated successfully and justifiably. Through AI-driven prognostic models, policymakers can recognize susceptible populations and convey timely intercessions, improving the social protection net and promotion economic constancy.

5.4. Financial Market Stabilization and Credit Risk Assessment

Artificial Intelligence (AI) plays a essential role in stabilizing financial markets and assessing credit risk, particularly in times of economic crisis. The use of AI technologies in these areas helps develop decision-making processes, boost market predictions, and control risks more efficiently.

AI-driven algorithms can monitor pecuniary markets in real occasion, identifying patterns and anomalies that human analysts might miss. This competence is critical for alleviate markets, particularly during unpredictable periods. Wong (2021) highlights how AI's capability to analyze huge amounts of pecuniary data in real time can help detect emerging risks and trends, enabling timely interferences to stabilize markets. By leveraging machine learning models, AI can envisage prospective market disruptions, facilitating better attentiveness and more educated policy responses.

In credit risk appraisal, AI enhances the accuracy and competence of evaluating borrowers' creditworthiness. Traditional methods often rely on past financial data and one-dimensional models, but AI can incorporate a broader range of factors, such as concurrent market conditions, consumer performance, and economic indicators. This allows for more precise risk assessments and better recognition decisions. AI systems can also acclimatize to new data, incessantly improving their models and ensuring that they remain pertinent in changing economic circumstances.

Moreover, AI's prognostic capabilities in financial markets support practical risk management. For example, by analyzing market attitude and past records, AI can envisage probable evasions or market crashes, helping organizations take defensive measures. This capability to estimate and alleviate risks contributes considerably to financial market constancy and long-term economic strength.

5.5. Climate and Disaster Resilience

Artificial Intelligence (AI) plays a vital role in ornamental atmosphere and calamity pliability by civilizing calamity response, financial revitalization, and atmosphere variation strategies. AI-driven tools are crucial for anticipating, managing, and recuperating from natural ruins, ensuring the sustainability of susceptible expanses and economies.

AI technologies, such as machine learning and data diagnostics, can method huge amounts of ecological and meteorological data in actual time, providing early warning systems for tremendous climate events and natural disasters. Sun, Bocchini, and Davison (2020) emphasize the efficiency of AI in calamity management by enabling prognostic diagnostics that recognize calamity risks previous to the materialize. These AI models can examine patterns in atmosphere data to expect the probability of floods, cyclones, and wildfires, facilitating timely emigrations and preparation for disasters.

Furthermore, AI contributes to economic pliability and recuperation from disasters. Xie et al. (2018) highlight the significance of assessing vibrant economic pliability using AI to appreciate the long-term collisions of disasters on economies. By modeling economic interruptions and recuperation trajectories, AI helps policymakers design enhanced revitalization strategies that curtail financial fatalities and accelerate economic recuperation.

AI also supports environment change alleviation by optimizing resource allotment for environment pliability efforts. It helps in rising adaptive strategies that decrease susceptibility to environment change, such as conniving flood defense systems or ornamental the competence of agricultural practices. Rao, Lipizzi, and Mansouri (2024) explain how AI-powered systems can optimize power usage, decrease emissions, and boost sustainable development, causative to long-term atmosphere elasticity.

6. CHALLENGES AND ETHICAL CONSIDERATIONS IN AI-DRIVEN ECONOMIC POLICY

As AI technologies become gradually more included into economic policymaking, numerous decent and sensible challenges must be addressed. These challenges span issues of precision, answerability, equality, and the communal insinuations of AI decision-making progressions.

One important confront is ensuring the simplicity of AI systems used in economic strategy. While AI systems offer improved competence and accuracy, they often function as "black boxes," creation it tricky for policymakers and the public to comprehend how decisions are complete. Kiseleva, Kotzinos, and Hert (2022) quarrel that this lack of precision in AI systems is specially pertaining to when applied to critical sectors like healthcare and, by conservatory, public financial policies. If AI systems are used to assign resources or set economic policies, the cloudiness of these models can destabilize conviction in government decisions and pilot to public confrontation.

Furthermore, decent concerns begin approximately the equality and biases intrinsic in AI algorithms. AI systems learn from past information, which may replicate existing biases in financial, societal, or artistic contexts. Al-kfairy et al. (2024) emphasize the decent dilemmas of using generative AI in strategy, predominantly in its probable to achieve or still exacerbate dissimilarity. In the circumstance of economic policy, AI's dependence on biased data could consequence in policies that unreasonably assistance certain groups while marginalizing others, thus undermining social impartiality.

Additionally, the directive of AI in monetary strategy raises concerns about answerability and ascendancy. As AI systems become more autonomous, questions occur about who is liable for the outcomes of AI-driven conclusions. Mennella et al. (2024) converse the need for vigorous moral frameworks to guide AI accomplishment, ensuring that decision-making remnants within the limits of recognized permissible and moral norms.

6.1. Data Privacy and Security

As AI becomes additional entrenched in economic strategy, the handling of susceptible data becomes a serious anxiety, predominantly in terms of seclusion and sanctuary. The efficiency of AI systems relies deeply on huge amounts of data, often collected from individuals, businesses, and public organizations. This dependence on large datasets raises important risks related to data privacy and safety, necessitating inflexible measures to protect susceptible information from unauthorized access and exploitation.

Data privacy is one of the mainly pressing issues when it comes to AI-driven economic policy. The compilation and analysis of individual, monetary, and demographic data can depiction individuals to seclusion contravention if not appropriately protected. As Kiseleva, Kotzinos, and Hert (2022) highlight, AI systems in susceptible sectors like healthcare and finance are predominantly susceptible to confidentiality breaches. Unauthorized access to individual data can lead to distinctiveness robbery, financial deceit, and the probable for intolerance based on personal or economic information.

In addition to privacy concerns, data safety is another main challenge. AI systems process enormous amounts of data in real-time, which increases the hazard of cyber attacks or data violations. These protection risks not only imperil individual seclusion but also comprise broader insinuations for national economic constancy. A violate in AI-driven systems used for financial instruction or tax management, for example, could disturb whole markets and destabilize public faith in AI systems.

To alleviate these risks, vigorous data fortification regulations are crucial. According to Al-kfairy et al. (2024), governments have to execute apparent permissible frameworks that make sure the protected managing of data worn in AI systems. These regulations should embrace data encryption, protected storage practices, and harsh admittance controls. Furthermore, intelligibility about how data is composed, stored, and used by AI systems is essential to promote faith and fulfillment with seclusion laws.

Overall, while AI offers marvelous probable for civilizing monetary strategy, addressing data seclusion and sanctuary challenges is critical to maintaining public buoyancy and conservation susceptible information in a gradually more digital world.

6.2. Algorithmic Bias

Algorithmic unfairness symbolizes a momentous challenge in AI-driven economic strategy as AI systems are merely as impartial as the data they are educated on. When AI models are uncovered to predisposed or unfinished datasets, they can complete these biases in decision-making processes, foremost to unjust conclusions. This is predominantly relating to in areas such as economic strategy, where AI influences conclusions related to taxation, credit estimation, and welfare allocation. As Akter et al. (2021) argue, algorithmic partiality in data-driven modernism can aggravate dissimilarity and emphasize community prejudices, predominantly when AI models use past data that reflects inequitable observes.

One of the key issues is the "black box" nature of many AI systems, where decision-making processes are not translucent or effortlessly implicit. Chaudhary (2024) emphasizes the significance of algorithmic intelligibility in extenuating prejudice. Without precision, it is complex to categorize and accurate biases entrenched within AI systems, important to decisions that may unlawfully inconvenience certain groups. For example, in financial strategy, biased AI algorithms could lead to the underestimation of monetary needs for marginalized communities or inequitable tax measurements.

In the perspective of monetary policy, prejudiced algorithms can perpetuate universal inequalities. This could be predominantly injurious in areas in the vein of credit scoring, where biases adjacent to explicit demographic groups (such as lower-income communities or alternative groups) could consequence in unjust access to monetary resources or government maintain. Furthermore, biased AI could influence policy assessments concerning unemployment benefits or social welfare, potentially exacerbate the challenges faced by underprivileged populations.

To address algorithmic bias, it is essential to expand AI systems that are translucent and answerable. This includes customary audits of AI models to recognize and correct biases, as well as diversifying the data used to educate these models. As suggested by Akter et al. (2021), policymakers must make sure that AI systems are not only exactly resonance but also fair and comprehensive, shimmering the values of fairness and honesty in their decision-making procedures.

6.3. Transparency and Accountability

In AI-driven monetary plan, lucidity and answerability are crucial to ensuring that AI systems are used morally and efficiently. Transparency refers to the capability to appreciate and elucidate how AI models formulate assessments, while answerability ensures that those conscientious for implementing AI systems are detained to the maximum standards of omission and liability. Without these principles, there is a threat that AI will be used in ways that demoralize public belief or suspiciously influence convinced groups.

Figure 7 presents a risk matrix derived from the OECD's 2024 analysis of AI in public governance. The most severe risks include algorithmic bias, lack of transparency, and limited explainability, all of which can lead to discriminatory outcomes and a breakdown in public accountability. Risks such as data privacy violations and public trust erosion also score high, particularly in sensitive sectors like immigration, healthcare, and welfare. These findings highlight the urgent need for ethical safeguards, impact assessments, and institutional capacity to manage AI responsibly in the public sector (Ubaldi & Zapata, 2024).

Figure 7. Heatmap illustrating major risk factors associated with AI deployment in public governance. Key concerns include bias, lack of transparency, explainability, and public trust erosion—especially in high-stakes domains such as law enforcement, welfare systems, and immigration control

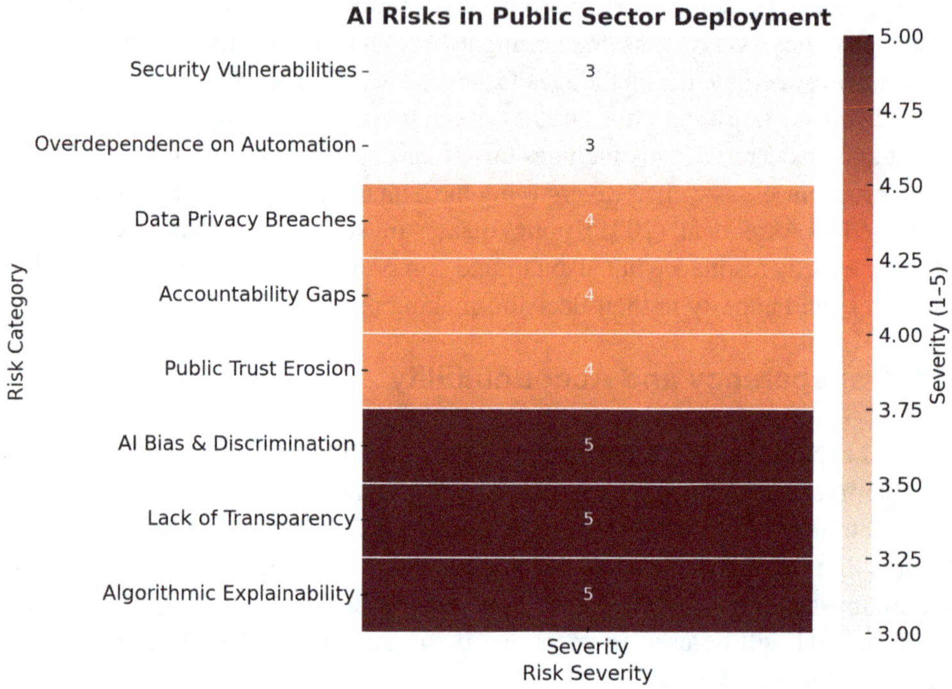

(Ubaldi & Zapata, 2024).

Transparency in AI systems is essential, predominantly in economic policy-making, where AI tools persuade serious decisions such as tax compilation, welfare allotment, and credit appraisals. According to Chaudhary (2024), one of the important challenges is that many AI systems operate as "black boxes," making it complicated to appreciate how decisions are being made. This lack of simplicity can lead to a lack of belief among the public and policymakers, as stakeholders may be uncertain whether AI decisions are fair or biased. To address this, it is vital that AI systems used in public policy are understandable, meaning that their decision-making processes can be understood by humans, and the judgment behind decisions can be communicated obviously to all stakeholders.

Accountability in AI systems is uniformly significant, as it ensures that individuals or associations answerable for the deployment and outcomes of AI technologies are held accountable for any unenthusiastic consequences. In the perspective of monetary strategy, if AI systems escort to prejudiced outcomes, such as inequitable tax assessments or biased social benefits allocation, those accountable must be recognized and detained conscientious. As Kiseleva et al. (2022) suggest lucid accountability mechanisms should be recognized to make sure that policymakers can interfere when essential and accurate the course of AI-driven decisions.

Figure 8 compares the principal international frameworks guiding the responsible development and use of AI. The EU AI Act emerges as the most binding legal instrument, with enforceable provisions and a strong focus on banning unacceptable-risk applications. In contrast, the OECD Principles and UNESCO Ethics Guidelines emphasize voluntary norms rooted in human rights, fairness, and transparency. The G7 Hiroshima AI Code of Conduct, though non-binding, aligns closely with democratic principles and encourages collaborative approaches. This diversity in emphasis underscores the need for interoperability and coherence across AI governance regimes (Ubaldi & Zapata, 2024).

Figure 8. Clustered heatmap comparing key international AI governance frameworks. The EU AI Act stands out for its strong legal enforceability and explicit bans on high-risk AI uses. Meanwhile, OECD and UNESCO emphasize human rights, transparency, and safety, while the G7 Hiroshima Process promotes soft principles aligned with democratic values

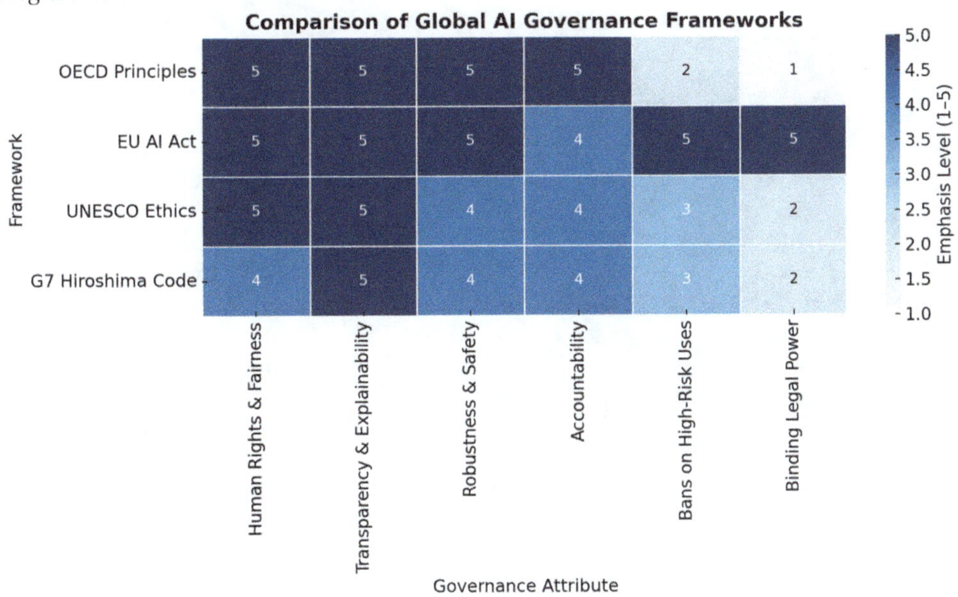

(Ubaldi & Zapata, 2024).

For AI to be productively integrated into financial policy-making, it is vital to establish exact frameworks that make certain both transparency and accountability.

This may engage regulatory frameworks that permission AI audits, third-party appraisals, and apparent guidelines for polite AI development. Furthermore, community contribution and response mechanisms can boost accountability, ensuring that AI systems are frequently assessed and enhanced to convene the needs of civilization fairly.

REFERENCES

Abir, S. I., Sarwer, M. H., & Hasan, M.. (2024). Accelerating BRICS economic growth: AI-driven data analytics for informed policy and decision making. *Journal of Economics. Finance and Accounting Studies*, *6*(6), 102–115. DOI: 10.32996/jefas.2024.6.6.8

Agénor, P., Alper, K., & Silva, L. (2013). Capital regulation, monetary policy and financial stability. *International Journal of Central Banking*. Advance online publication. DOI: 10.2139/ssrn.2318026

Akter, S., McCarthy, G., Sajib, S., Michael, K., Dwivedi, Y. K., D'Ambra, J. G., & Shen, K. N. (2021). Algorithmic bias in data-driven innovation in the age of AI. *International Journal of Information Management*, *60*, 102387. DOI: 10.1016/j.ijinfomgt.2021.102387

Al-kfairy, M., Mustafa, D. G., Kshetri, N., Insiew, M., & Alfandi, O. (2024). Ethical challenges and solutions of generative AI: An interdisciplinary perspective. *Informatics (MDPI)*, *11*(3), 58. DOI: 10.3390/informatics11030058

Aladebumoye, T. (2025). The role of AI in enhancing tax transparency and reducing evasion. *World Journal of Advanced Research and Reviews*, *25*(1), 206–212. DOI: 10.30574/wjarr.2025.25.1.0023

Badrul Hisham, A., Mohamed Yusof, N. A., Salleh, S. H., & Abas, H. (2024). Transforming governance: A systematic review of AI applications in policymaking. *Journal of Science, Technology and Innovation Policy.*

Berrada, I. R., Barramou, F., & Alami, O. B. (2022). A review of artificial intelligence approach for credit risk assessment. In *2022 2nd International Conference on Artificial Intelligence and Signal Processing (AISP)* (pp. 1–5). DOI: 10.1109/AISP53593.2022.9760655

Časta, M. (2023). Inflation, interest rates and the predictability of stock returns. *Finance Research Letters*, *58*, 104380. DOI: 10.1016/j.frl.2023.104380

Chaudhary, G. (2024). Unveiling the black box: Bringing algorithmic transparency to AI. *Masaryk University Journal of Law and Technology*, *18*(1), 93–122. DOI: 10.5817/MUJLT2024-1-4

Danish, M. S. S., & Senjyu, T. (2023). Shaping the future of sustainable energy through AI-enabled circular economy policies. *Circular Economy*, *2*(1), 100010. DOI: 10.1016/j.cec.2023.100040

Davidson, S. (2024). The economic institutions of artificial intelligence. *Journal of Institutional Economics, 20*(1), 1–17. DOI: 10.1017/S1744137423000395

de Lange, P. E., Melsom, B. G., Vennerød, C. B., & Westgaard, S. (2022). Explainable AI for credit assessment in banks. *Journal of Risk and Financial Management, 15*(12), 556. DOI: 10.3390/jrfm15120556

Dwivedi, Y. K., Hughes, L., & Ismagilova, E.. (2019). Artificial intelligence (AI): Multidisciplinary perspectives on emerging challenges, opportunities, and agenda for research, practice, and policy. *International Journal of Information Management.* Advance online publication. DOI: 10.1016/j.ijinfomgt.2019.08.002

Et al., A. R. (2021). A study on application of artificial intelligence and machine learning in Indian taxation system. *Psychology and Education Journal.* DOI: 10.17762/pae.v58i2.2265

Fares, N. Y., Nedeljkovic, D., & Jammal, M. (2023). AI-enabled IoT applications: Towards a transparent governance framework. In *2023 IEEE Global Conference on Artificial Intelligence and Internet of Things (GCAIoT)* (pp. 109–114). DOI: 10.1109/GCAIoT61060.2023.10385106

Fawcett, T., Haimowitz, I. J., Provost, F. J., & Stolfo, S. (1998). AI approaches to fraud detection and risk management. *AI Magazine, 19*(2), 107–108. DOI: 10.1609/aimag.v19i2.1372

Fouejieu, A. (2017). Inflation targeting and financial stability in emerging markets. *Economic Modelling, 60*, 51–70. DOI: 10.1016/j.econmod.2016.08.020

G7 High-Level Panel on AI. (2024). *Artificial intelligence and economic/financial policy: Report of the G7 high-level panel.* Group of Seven.

Gao, A. (2022). *National strategy for the development of artificial intelligence in the context of the global digital economy.* Artificial Societies., DOI: 10.18254/S207751800020634-6

Goralski, M. A., & Tan, T. K. (2020). Artificial intelligence and sustainable development. *International Journal of Management Education, 18*(1), 100330. DOI: 10.1016/j.ijme.2019.100330

Hanwacker, L. S. (2025). The role of artificial intelligence in disaster recovery. *Journal of Business Continuity & Emergency Planning, 18*(2), 167–179. DOI: 10.69554/CYWN4471 PMID: 39567851

Jain, V., & Kulkarni, P. A. (2023). *Integrating AI techniques for enhanced financial forecasting and budgeting strategies*. International Journal of Economics and Management Studies., DOI: 10.14445/23939125/IJEMS-V10I9P102

Jin, C. (2024). Research on the path of artificial intelligence empowering high-quality economic development. *Journal of Artificial Intelligence Practice*. DOI: 10.23977/jaip.2024.070305

Johora, F. T., Hasan, R., Farabi, S. F., Alam, M. Z., Sarkar, M. I., & Al Mahmud, M. A. (2024). AI advances: Enhancing banking security with fraud detection. In *2024 First International Conference on Technological Innovations and Advance Computing (TIACOMP)* (pp. 289–294). DOI: 10.1109/TIACOMP64125.2024.00055

Kara, N., Atamanchuk, Z. A., & Kurytskyi, V. (2024). Formation of mechanisms for anti-crisis management of enterprises: International economic features. *Journal of Lviv Polytechnic National University: Economics and Management Issues*. DOI: 10.23939/semi2024.02.197

Kiseleva, A., Kotzinos, D., & Hert, P. D. (2022). Transparency of AI in healthcare as a multilayered system of accountabilities. *Frontiers in Artificial Intelligence*, *5*, 879603. Advance online publication. DOI: 10.3389/frai.2022.879603 PMID: 35707765

Korinek, A. (2024). *Economic policy challenges for the age of AI*. DOI: 10.3386/w32980

Larsson, S., & Heintz, F. (2020). Transparency in artificial intelligence. *Internet Policy Review*, *9*(2). Advance online publication. DOI: 10.14763/2020.2.1469

Lee, M., Hayes, D., & Maher, C. S. (2024). *AI as a budgeting tool: Panacea or Pandora's box?* Public Finance Journal., DOI: 10.59469/pfj.2024.6

Li, S., Chen, J., Sun, Y., Wang, Z., Du, J., & He, W. (2024). *AI-driven transformation: From economic forecasting to strategic management*. Applied and Computational Engineering., DOI: 10.54254/2755-2721/57/20241319

Loukis, E., Maragoudakis, M., & Kyriakou, N. (2020). *Artificial intelligence-based public sector data analytics for economic crisis policymaking. Transforming Government: People*. Process and Policy., DOI: 10.1108/TG-11-2019-0113

Majeed, A., & Hwang, S. O. (2023). When AI meets information privacy: The adversarial role of AI in data sharing scenario. *IEEE Access : Practical Innovations, Open Solutions*, *11*, 76177–76195. DOI: 10.1109/ACCESS.2023.3297646

Masoud, N. (2024). *Artificial intelligence and unemployment dynamics: An econometric analysis in high-income economies.* Technological Sustainability., DOI: 10.1108/TECHS-04-2024-0033

Mdladla, L. T. S., Wider, W., Thanathanchuchot, T., et al. (2024). Navigating the AI revolution: A review of transformative strategies for economic development in Africa's emerging economies. *Journal of Infrastructure, Policy and Development.*

Mennella, C., Maniscalco, U., De Pietro, G., & Esposito, M. (2024). Ethical and regulatory challenges of AI technologies in healthcare: A narrative review. *Heliyon, 10*(4), e26297. DOI: 10.1016/j.heliyon.2024.e26297 PMID: 38384518

Michalak, T. P., & Wooldridge, M. (2017). AI and economics. *IEEE Intelligent Systems, 32*(1), 5–7. DOI: 10.1109/MIS.2017.10

Nguyen, Q. P., & Vo, D. H. (2022). Artificial intelligence and unemployment: International evidence. *Structural Change and Economic Dynamics, 63*, 40–55. DOI: 10.1016/j.strueco.2022.09.003

Nishant, R., Kennedy, M., & Corbett, J. (2020). Artificial intelligence for sustainability: Challenges, opportunities, and a research agenda. *International Journal of Information Management, 53*, 102104. DOI: 10.1016/j.ijinfomgt.2020.102104

Olabanji, S. O., Olaniyi, O. O., & Olagbaju, O. O. (2024). *Leveraging artificial intelligence (AI) and blockchain for enhanced tax compliance and revenue generation.* Asian Journal of Economics, Business and Accounting., DOI: 10.9734/ajeba/2024/v24i111577

Parkes, D., & Wellman, M. P. (2015). Economic reasoning and artificial intelligence. *Science, 349*(6245), 267–272. DOI: 10.1126/science.aaa8403 PMID: 26185245

Perino, D., Katevas, K., Lutu, A., Marin, E., & Kourtellis, N. (2022). Privacy-preserving AI for future networks. *Communications of the ACM, 65*(4), 52–53. DOI: 10.1145/3512343

Radić, N., Gavrilović, M., & Mihailović, Đ. (2024). The artificial intelligence and economy. In *Employment, Education and Entrepreneurship 2024 – Zbornik Radova.* DOI: 10.5937/EEE24052R

Rao, B., Lipizzi, C., & Mansouri, M. (2024). Anatomy of an AI economy. In *2024 IEEE International Symposium on Systems Engineering (ISSE).* https://doi.org/DOI: 10.1109/ISSE63315.2024.10741091

Ruiz Estrada, M. A., Park, D., & Staniewski, M. (2023). Artificial intelligence (AI) can change the way of doing policy modelling. *Journal of Policy Modeling*, *45*(6), 1099–1112. Advance online publication. DOI: 10.1016/j.jpolmod.2023.11.005

Sabareesh, R., Nath, D. D., Pathak, R., Devi, D. R., Prasanna, S., & Bellary, E. K. (2024). AI-driven fraud detection in banking: Enhancing transaction security. *Journal of Informatics Education and Research.* DOI: 10.52783/jier.v4i3.1707

Saeed, M. M., & Alsharidah, M. (2024). Security, privacy, and robustness for trustworthy AI systems: A review. *Computers & Electrical Engineering*, *119*, 109643. DOI: 10.1016/j.compeleceng.2024.109643

Sun, W., Bocchini, P., & Davison, B. D. (2020). Applications of artificial intelligence for disaster management. *Natural Hazards*, *103*(3), 1–59. DOI: 10.1007/s11069-020-04124-3

Sungkono, & Widana, I. D. K. K. (2024). Optimizing artificial intelligence (AI) as a catalyst for digital economic transformation. *Technium Social Sciences Journal.* https://doi.org/DOI: 10.47577/tssj.v58i1.11174

Szczepański, M. (2019). *Economic impacts of artificial intelligence* (EPRS Briefing PE 637.967). European Parliamentary Research Service.

Ubaldi, B.-C., & Zapata, R. (2024). *Governing with artificial intelligence: Are governments ready?* OECD Publishing.

Valle-Cruz, D., Fernandez-Cortez, V., & Gil-García, J. R. (2021). From e-budgeting to smart budgeting: Exploring the potential of artificial intelligence in government decision-making for resource allocation. *Government Information Quarterly*, *39*(2), 101644. DOI: 10.1016/j.giq.2021.101644

Wang, M. (2024). *AI technologies in modern taxation: Applications, challenges, and strategic directions*. International Journal of Finance and Investment., DOI: 10.54097/v2kgty49

Wong, Y. K. (2021). Dealing crisis management using AI. In *Advances in Machine Learning*. Data Mining and Computing., DOI: 10.5121/csit.2021.111409

Xie, W., Rose, A., Li, S., He, J., Li, N., & Ali, T. (2018). Dynamic economic resilience and economic recovery from disasters: A quantitative assessment. *Risk Analysis*, *38*(6), 1306–1318. DOI: 10.1111/risa.12948 PMID: 29341196

Yuan, C., Tang, J., Cao, Y., et al. (2024). The impact of artificial intelligence on economic development: A systematic review. *International Theory and Practice in Humanities and Social Sciences.* https://doi.org/DOI: 10.70693/itphss.v1i1.57

Zheng, S., Trott, A. R., Srinivasa, S., Parkes, D. C., & Socher, R. (2022). The AI economist: Taxation policy design via two-level deep multiagent reinforcement learning. *Science Advances*, *8*(18), eabk2607. Advance online publication. DOI: 10.1126/sciadv.abk2607 PMID: 35507657

Chapter 9
Improving Business Forecasting With AI:
Cases of Revenue- and Cost-Forecasting

Tuukka Hyytiäinen
http://orcid.org/0009-0009-0094-2245
LUT University, Finland

Pasi Luukka
LUT University, Finland

Mikael Collan
http://orcid.org/0000-0003-2976-2829
LUT University, Finland

ABSTRACT

This chapter studies the potential of improving business forecasting with the help of artificial intelligence, more precisely TimeGPT, a generative pre-trained transformer for time series. The chapter emphasizes the practical points of view, including computational efficiency, scalability, and challenges of roll-out from the point of view of explainability. Results from two cases of business forecasting that include revenue forecasting for an IT company and cost forecasting for a state-owned company are presented and the results are comparatively analyzed against more traditional forecasting methods utilized for the same purpose. This chapter contributes to the literature on using AI in business forecasting by providing comparative empirical studies that highlight the potential of these new forecasting opportunities and to practice by showcasing real-world experiences.

DOI: 10.4018/979-8-3373-3053-2.ch009

INTRODUCTION

Accurate financial forecasting is essential for effective business planning, resource allocation, and strategic decision-making. In the last ten years or so, the methodologies employed for forecasting have generally undergone a significant transformation, moving from traditional statistical models towards machine-learning-based models and large language model–based forecasting (Sezer et al., 2020). More recently, the frontier of forecasting is being pushed further by the emergence of methods based on large language models (Jin et al., 2023).

While statistical models have long served as the bedrock of forecasting, their ability to capture complex non-linearities and adapt to the increasing volume and velocity of business data has been challenged. This has paved the way for more adaptive modeling paradigms. Neural networks represented a significant leap forward, demonstrating superior capabilities in modeling the complex, non-linear patterns inherent in much financial data. More recently, the emergence of foundation models, such as TimeGPT, promises a further paradigm shift.

These models are pre-trained on massive and diverse time series datasets, which enable them to generate accurate forecasts for new tasks with little to no task-specific training, a capability known as "zero-shot" forecasting. This approach fundamentally alters the economics of forecasting by potentially reducing the need for the extensive, per-task model development required by previous generations. In this research, we utilize TimeGPT, a prominent foundation model developed specifically for time series forecasting.

Despite this rapid evolution, a gap persists in literature. Existing benchmarks have had inherent limitations, making it impossible to conduct comprehensive and fair empirical comparisons across distinct generations of forecasting models, such as traditional data-specific models and the newer Time Series Foundation Models (TSFMs). Such comparisons have been particularly scarce as most prior benchmarks have focused exclusively on data-specific models while overlooking TSFMs, or have failed to support the diverse evaluation strategies needed to properly assess foundation models on complex data, including financial data (Li et al., 2024).

Furthermore, practical considerations such as computational cost, scalability, implementation complexity, and the implications of API dependencies often receive insufficient attention alongside predictive accuracy. Practitioners require clear, evidence-based guidance on these trade-offs to decide which forecasting tools are most appropriate for their specific needs. Rigorous comparisons involving foundation models like TimeGPT applied to hierarchical cost forecasting in large organizations are exceptionally uncommon.

Furthermore, the adoption of AI is not merely a technical implementation but a significant organizational challenge (Banerjee, 2025). This is particularly acute for small and medium-sized enterprises (SMEs), where resource constraints, high implementation costs, and limited in-house technical expertise can form significant barriers to adoption (Okeke et al., 2024). Therefore, practical considerations such as computational cost, implementation complexity, and the socio-technical challenge of user trust often receive insufficient attention alongside predictive accuracy.

To address this gap, we synthesize and contrast findings from two empirical case studies, providing a unique comparative analysis. The first study investigated the application of neural networks (LSTM and GRU) for revenue forecasting within an ICT service company. The subsequent study examined the TimeGPT model for large-scale, hierarchical cost forecasting in a major Finnish state-owned company.

The primary objective of this work is to bridge this gap by evaluating the performance (accuracy and speed) and practical applicability of these different model classes: traditional statistical models (SARIMA, ETS), early neural networks (LSTM, GRU), and a modern foundation model (TimeGPT).

By synthesizing findings from two real-world case studies in revenue and cost forecasting, this analysis provides tangible insights for both researchers and practitioners. It moves beyond purely academic metrics to address the practical trade-offs that decision-makers face: When does a complex neural network outperform a simple statistical model? What are the real-world advantages in speed and accuracy of a foundation model like TimeGPT in a large-scale corporate environment? And what are the hidden challenges, such as implementation complexity and user trust?

The novelty of this contribution lies in this direct, practical comparison. It specifically assesses the impact of zero-shot versus fine-tuning strategies for TimeGPT in a complex hierarchical context—a common but under-researched business problem. Ultimately, this chapter aims to provide a clear, evidence-based guide for selecting the right forecasting tool for the right job.

This chapter continues as follows: first, we review the evolution of these forecasting paradigms, then we present the methodology and findings from the two case studies. The chapter concludes with a discussion of the practical implications of these findings and recommendations for both managers and researchers.

SELECTED PREVIOUS LITERATURE

For decades, the scientific foundation of financial forecasting has rested firmly on statistical time series models. Methods such as ARIMA (Autoregressive Integrated Moving Average) and Exponential Smoothing (ETS) have provided theoretically grounded and interpretable tools for estimating future values. Their value has lain in a systematic approach to identifying and modeling components from a time series's past behavior, such as trend, seasonality, and autocorrelation. The comprehensive

ARIMA modeling framework, established by Box et al. (2015), quickly became an industry standard. In contemporary practice, the work of Hyndman and Athanasopoulos (2021) serves as a key guide for applying these classical methods.

Financial forecasting methodologies have evolved through three distinct paradigms, each emerging to address the limitations of its predecessor in the face of growing data complexity, velocity, and scale.

Statistical Models: The first paradigm consists of traditional statistical models, such as SARIMA and ETS. While valued for their high interpretability and robustness on stable data, their rigid assumptions make them less effective when dealing with the non-linear dynamics and volatility common in modern business environments. Meta's Prophet forecasting model, an additive regression model, was developed to handle time series with strong seasonality and holiday effects, offering more automation and flexibility than traditional SARIMA or ETS models, particularly for business forecasting. Prophet, noted by Kumar et al (2025).

Machine Learning / Neural Networks: The second paradigm was introduced with machine learning models, particularly neural networks like LSTM and GRU. These models excel at capturing complex, non-linear patterns directly from data. However, this increased power introduced a new challenge: a trade-off between accuracy and interpretability, leading to the “black box” problem where the model's decision-making process is opaque.

Foundation models: The most recent paradigm is defined by Transformer-based foundation models, such as TimeGPT. By pre-training on massive and diverse datasets, these models fundamentally change the economics and scalability of forecasting. They can achieve high performance on new tasks with little to no specific training (“zero-shot” forecasting), directly addressing the scalability and cost challenges of previous generations.

This evolution reflects a continuous search to balance the competing demands of accuracy, interpretability, and scalability. Table 1 provides a detailed comparison of these three model classes, outlining their key examples, documented strengths, limitations, and typical business application areas.

Table 1. A comparative overview of forecasting model generations in business applications

Model Class	Key Examples	Strengths in business context	Limitations	Typical business application areas
Statistical	SARIMA, ETS, Prophet	High interpretability; robust on stable data; well-understood statistical properties.	Rigidity; struggle with non-linearity and volatility; poor scalability for thousands of series.	Stable product demand planning; utility load forecasting; budget baselining.
Machine Learning / Neural Networks	LSTM, GRU	Excellent at capturing complex, non-linear patterns; native multivariate capability.	"Black box" nature hinders trust; high per-task training cost; can be data-hungry.	Revenue/sales forecasting with market drivers; financial asset price prediction.
Foundation Models	TimeGPT, Informer, Autoformer	Extreme scalability; strong zero-shot/few-shot performance; handles long-range dependencies well.	API dependency and cost; pre-training is computationally massive; interpretability is still a nascent field.	Large-scale cost/inventory forecasting; supply chain optimization; retail demand across thousands of SKUs.

The limitations of traditional statistical models, particularly their inability to capture non-linearities and scale to multivariate problems, created a compelling need for a new class of forecasting tools. This need was met by the rise of machine learning, and specifically deep learning, which introduced a paradigm shift away from assumption-based modeling toward learning complex patterns directly from data. Recurrent Neural Networks (RNNs) became the flagship technology of this new era, offering a powerful solution for modeling the intricate dynamics of sequential business data.

Learning From a Sequence

Recurrent Neural Networks (RNNs) and their more sophisticated variants, such as Long Short-Term Memory (LSTM) and Gated Recurrent Unit (GRU) networks, gained popularity due to their ability to learn long-range dependencies and model nonlinear dynamics in sequential data (Goodfellow et al., 2016). Standard feedforward neural networks are not designed to handle sequential data, as they treat each input independently. Recurrent Neural Networks (RNNs) solve this by incorporating loops, allowing information to persist from one step of a sequence to the next. However, simple RNNs suffer from the vanishing gradient problem, making it difficult for them to learn long-range dependencies.

This challenge was overcome by the introduction of more sophisticated architecture, most notably the Long Short-Term Memory (LSTM) network (Hochreiter & Schmidhuber, 1997). LSTMs employ a system of "gates" - an input gate, a forget gate, and an output gate - that meticulously control the flow of information into, out of, and within the network's memory cell. This gating mechanism enables the network to selectively retain relevant information over extended periods, making it exceptionally effective for time series analysis.

A popular and slightly simpler alternative to the LSTM is the Gated Recurrent Unit (GRU) network (Cho et al., 2014). The GRU combines the forget and input gates into a single "update gate" and merges the cell state and hidden state, resulting in a model with fewer parameters. This simpler architecture often leads to faster training times while delivering performance comparable to LSTMs on many tasks, making it an attractive choice from a computational efficiency standpoint.

The application of these networks to business and financial forecasting has been extensively documented. A systematic literature review by Sezer et al. (2020) found that deep learning models, including LSTMs, consistently outperform traditional machine learning and statistical methods in financial time series forecasting, attributing this success to their ability to learn features from large, noisy datasets automatically. Studies have shown their effectiveness in diverse business applications, from predicting stock prices and cryptocurrency volatility to forecasting sales and energy consumption (Fischer & Krauss, 2018; Livieris et al., 2020). The key advantage of these models in a business context is their native ability to handle multivariate inputs, learning the complex and often non-obvious relationships between a target variable (like revenue) and its many potential drivers (like marketing spend, headcount, or competitor pricing) simultaneously.

The "Black Box" and Explainable AI (XAI)

The superior predictive power of neural networks, however, came at a significant cost: transparency. Unlike a statistical model, where the contribution of each component can be examined, a trained neural network is a complex web of interconnected neurons and weights, making its decision-making process inherently opaque. This "black box" nature quickly became a central challenge and a major barrier to adoption in corporate settings. For high-stakes decisions in finance, risk management, and strategic planning, a forecast's accuracy is often insufficient; decision-makers must also understand the rationale behind the forecast to trust it and act upon it with confidence.

This tension between accuracy and interpretability has given rise to a critical and rapidly growing subfield: Explainable AI (XAI). The goal of XAI is to develop techniques that can peer inside the "black box" and provide human-understandable explanations for model predictions. In the context of forecasting, this is paramount. Kumar et al. (2025) investigated the integration of SHAP (SHapley Additive exPlanations), a leading XAI technique, with LSTM and Prophet models for financial forecasting. SHAP values, based on cooperative game theory, assign an important value to each input feature for a specific prediction, effectively showing which factors contributed most to the forecast. Such techniques promise to transform opaque predictions into actionable insights, for example, by showing that a drop in a key leading economic indicator primarily drives a forecasted decline in sales.

The importance of this "trust factor" is a direct barrier to adoption and is strongly underscored by research into technology acceptance. Studies by Nguyen and Vu (2025) and Rong et al. (2025) found that perceived trust is a critical mediator in the adoption of AI tools in the finance sector. In regulated fields such as accounting, where auditability and transparency are paramount, this opacity presents a significant challenge (Banerjee, 2025). This is echoed in the context of SMEs, where managers often lack dedicated data science teams. For these decision-makers, model interpretability and the ability to understand the rationale behind a forecast are just as critical as its accuracy, especially when weighed against high implementation costs and data privacy concerns (Okeke et al., 2024).

Transformer and Foundation Models

While neural networks, such as LSTM and GRU, were a breakthrough for modeling complex, non-linear data, they introduced significant limitations. Their sequential nature makes parallelization difficult, creating a computational bottleneck. Furthermore, training a high-performing model is a resource-intensive process that must be repeated for each new forecasting task. This per-task training model presents a significant scalability challenge for large enterprises that need to forecast thousands or even millions of time series for planning purposes.

The latest paradigm in forecasting, built upon the Transformer architecture and the concept of foundation models, directly addresses this challenge of scale and efficiency. However, this shift does not eliminate the difficulty of model selection. Instead, it reframes the problem: the choice is now often between a single, large foundation model and a suite of specialized traditional models. This decision requires balancing accuracy, interpretability, computational cost, and ease of implementation, a trade-off landscape broadly highlighted in large-scale forecasting competitions (Makridakis et al., 2020).

The Transformer architecture, introduced by Vaswani et al. (2017), marked another revolution. Its core innovation is the "self-attention mechanism." Instead of processing data step-by-step like an RNN, a Transformer looks at the entire history at once and decides which parts are most important. In practice, this means the model can, for example, directly link a product launch event from two years ago to a current seasonal trend, even if many other events happened in between. This non-sequential approach also allows for much faster training on modern hardware (a process called "parallelization") and is highly effective at capturing very long-range dependencies.

Adapting Transformers for time series led to newer, specialized models. Models like Informer (Zhou et al., 2021) and Autoformer (Wu et al., 2021) introduced technical refinements to make Transformers faster and better at identifying seasonal patterns. More recent models like PatchTST (Nie et al., 2023) improved performance by processing time series in "chunks" rather than as individual points. While the technical details of these architectures (such as "ProbSparse attention" or "autocorrelation") are complex, their practical goal is the same: to create forecasts that are more accurate over longer periods and computationally faster to generate than previous models. These architectures consistently demonstrate superior performance on long-sequence forecasting benchmarks compared to earlier RNN-based models. Further refinements and novel Transformer-based architectures for time series, such as iTransformer and Ister, continue to push the boundaries of forecasting accuracy and interpretability by addressing challenges like channel independence and seasonal-trend decomposition (Cao et al., 2024).

Foundation Models for Time Series

Building on the success of Transformers and inspired by large language models (LLMs) like GPT-3, the concept of a pre-trained foundation model has emerged in the time series domain. This represents a fundamental shift in the economics and workflow of forecasting. Instead of training a model from scratch for each specific task, a single, massive foundation model is pre-trained on a vast and diverse corpus of time series data. This pre-trained model learns a general understanding of time series patterns, trends, and seasonality.

TimeGPT (Garza et al., 2024) is the first and most prominent example of such a model. It can be applied to new, unseen datasets to generate remarkably accurate forecasts with no additional training, a capability known as zero-shot forecasting. This is possible because the model leverages its generalized knowledge learned during pre-training. For even higher accuracy, the model can be fine-tuned on a specific target dataset. This process involves a small number of additional training steps to adapt the model's general knowledge to the specific nuances of the new data. This approach dramatically reduces the data and computational requirements for the end-user. Other major technology firms have developed similar large-scale models, including Google's TimesFM (Das et al., 2024), Amazon's Chronos (Ansari et al., 2024), and Salesforce's Moirai (Woo et al., 2024), signaling a broad industry trend towards this approach.

The rapid proliferation of these models has necessitated new frameworks for classification. Kottapallis et al. (2025) introduced a comprehensive taxonomy for time series foundation models, categorizing them along critical dimensions such as architecture (e.g., patch-based vs. raw sequence), prediction type (probabilistic vs. deterministic), and data structure (univariate vs. multivariate). This classification helps structure the evolving landscape. Complementing this, Wang et al. (2024) developed a comprehensive survey and benchmark, providing a standardized evaluation of deep time series models that highlights how different architectures are suited for distinct analytical tasks.

This new paradigm effectively moves the heaviest computational burden, the initial pre-training, to the model provider. End-users, who often interact with the model via an Application Programming Interface (API), can access state-of-the-art forecasting capabilities without requiring extensive in-house data science expertise or computational infrastructure. This democratizes access to advanced AI and solves the scalability problem inherent in per-task models. The application of this approach is particularly relevant for large-scale business problems. For example, Yang et al. (2025) demonstrated the superior performance of hybrid CNN-LSTM models for big data-driven corporate financial forecasting, and the principles of foundation models extend this capability to an even larger scale. The ability to generate forecasts for thousands of hierarchical cost accounts, as explored in one of this chapter's case studies, is a task for which foundation models are uniquely suited.

The rapid rise of TSFMs has also been met with critical evaluation. Gruver et al. (2023) provocatively questioned their utility, demonstrating that general-purpose LLMs can perform surprisingly well as zero-shot time series forecasters, at a level "comparable to or exceeding" purpose-built models, simply by encoding the data as strings of numerical digits. This finding fuels the "hype versus reality" debate, questioning whether the immense computational cost of specialized TSFMs is always justified over simpler linear models or appropriately prompted general-purpose LLMs (Gruver et al., 2023). This is supported by comprehensive benchmarks, such as that from Wang et al. (2024), which find that a model's architectural suitability for a specific task is often more decisive for performance than model size or novelty alone.

The applicability of such advanced models is not limited to one field. For instance, recent studies have demonstrated that machine learning-based stock market beta estimators can outperform established benchmark models. Similarly, in agriculture, the use of sensing-based technology combined with AI aims to lower production costs and increase yield efficiencies, showcasing AI's role in cost management in other sectors (Drobetz et al., 2025; Pal & Poddar, 2024).

METHODOLOGY AND CASE STUDIES

An Overview of the Comparative Methodology

This section details the practical application and comparative analysis of the forecasting models. It is structured to first explain the overarching study design and the specific models and metrics used for evaluation. Following this methodological foundation, the chapter presents the two empirical case studies sequentially:

1. **Case 1**: A focused study on revenue forecasting using traditional models and multivariate neural networks (LSTM/GRU).
2. **Case 2**: A large-scale study on hierarchical cost forecasting using traditional models and the TimeGPT foundation model.

Finally, the key findings from both cases are synthesized in the Discussion section to draw broader conclusions.

Study Design and Methods

The methodology employed in this chapter involves a comparative quantitative analysis based on the empirical findings from two distinct, real-world case studies. The overarching goal is to evaluate and contrast the performance and practical applicability of different generations of forecasting models: traditional statistical methods, early neural networks, and a modern foundation model. This chapter synthesizes the findings from both to provide a holistic view.

The first case study focused on revenue forecasting and compared traditional statistical models with neural networks (LSTM and GRU). The second case study centered on cost forecasting, specifically examining the capabilities of the TimeGPT foundation model against traditional statistical models and Prophet, including an analysis of zero-shot versus fine-tuning strategies for TimeGPT. This chapter synthesizes the findings from both to provide a holistic view.

Forecasting Models

The analysis encompasses three distinct classes of forecasting models, each representing a different approach to time series analysis.

Traditional Statistical Models: This category includes foundational methods widely used in business forecasting. Exponential Smoothing (**ETS**) models are effective for capturing trend and seasonality by assigning exponentially decreasing weights to past observations. The Seasonal Autoregressive Integrated Moving Average (**SARIMA**) model extends the ARIMA framework to explicitly model seasonal patterns, which is crucial for financial data with regular cycles. The **Prophet** model is also included as a modern, decomposable time series model designed to handle seasonality and holidays with ease, making it highly applicable in business contexts.

Recurrent Neural Networks (RNNs): Representing the machine learning paradigm, this analysis utilizes Long Short-Term Memory (**LSTM**) and Gated Recurrent Unit (**GRU**) networks. These models are specifically designed to overcome the limitations of simpler RNNs and learn long-term dependencies in sequential data. Their ability to capture complex, non-linear patterns makes them well-suited for financial forecasting, as demonstrated in the first case study

Foundation Models for Time Series: The most recent generation is represented by **TimeGPT**, the first foundation model for time series forecasting. As a pre-trained transformer-based model, TimeGPT can generate forecasts in a zero-shot manner (making predictions on unseen data without specific training) or have its performance enhanced through fine-tuning, where the model adapts to a specific dataset's unique characteristics.

Data Preprocessing and Validation

A key methodological choice across both studies was the use of minimally processed data. This approach was taken to test the models' robustness and simulate a realistic business environment where data is often imperfect and resources for extensive cleaning are limited. Therefore, interventions like outlier removal were deliberately avoided. Preprocessing was primarily limited to handling missing values (by filling with zero or allowing the model to interpolate) and ensuring the data was in the correct format for each model.

To ensure a robust evaluation of model performance over time, a rolling-origin cross-validation methodology was employed in the second case study. This technique involves creating multiple training and testing splits by progressively moving the forecast origin forward in time. This approach not only provides a more reliable estimate of a model's true predictive power than a single split but was also critical for assessing the stability and value of fine-tuning TimeGPT across different periods.

Performance Metrics

The comparative analysis in this chapter synthesizes the quantitative results from these two studies. Key performance metrics are used consistently where possible to allow for direct comparison. These metrics include:

Mean Absolute Error (MAE): Measures the average magnitude of the errors in a set of forecasts, without considering their direction.

Mean Squared Error (MSE): Measures the average of the squares of the errors. It gives higher weight to larger errors.

Root Mean Squared Error (RMSE): The square root of the MSE, expressed in the same units as the forecast.

Mean Absolute Percentage Error (MAPE): Expresses accuracy as a percentage of the error. It is helpful in comparing forecast performance across different datasets with different scales, though it has limitations with zero or near-zero actual values.

Computational Time: The time taken to train (if applicable) and generate forecasts, providing insights into the efficiency and scalability of the models.

Overall MAE: To assess aggregate accuracy across large, hierarchical datasets (used in Case 2), an Overall MAE metric was calculated. This is a volume-weighted accuracy measure, computed by dividing the sum of all absolute forecast errors by the sum of all actual values. This approach provides a single, robust performance indicator that accounts for the varying scales of the numerous time series.

The approach involves presenting the context, data, models, and key findings from each case study separately, followed by a synthesized comparative analysis that draws connections and contrasts across the studies. This structure allows for an in-depth understanding of the performance of each model class in its specific application context. It also enables broader conclusions about their relative strengths and weaknesses across different financial forecasting scenarios.

Case 1: Forecasting Turnover

The first case study examined the revenue forecasting practices of a prominent Information and Communication Technology (ICT) service company. The research specifically targeted one of the company's key business units, designated as LY1, which represented a significant portion of the company's overall operations. At the time of the study, the company's existing forecasting process for LY1 was characterized by a considerable degree of manual intervention. This reliance on manual methods, while familiar, presented several challenges. This manual process was resource-intensive and time-consuming, often taking nearly a month to complete a forecasting cycle. Furthermore, there was a growing need within the organization for more accurate and timely revenue predictions to improve strategic business planning, optimize resource allocation, and enhance overall decision-making agility in a competitive market.

The primary objective of this investigation was therefore twofold: firstly, to critically evaluate the accuracy and efficiency of the company's existing forecasting methodology, and secondly, to explore the potential of advanced machine learning models, particularly neural networks (LSTM and GRU), to offer tangible improvements. The study aimed to determine if these more sophisticated AI-driven approaches could provide more precise forecasts with potentially reduced lead times, thereby offering a more robust foundation for the company's financial planning. The selection of LY1 was strategic, as its revenue streams were influenced by a variety of internal and external factors, making it a suitable testbed for comparing the capabilities of univariate traditional models against multivariate neural network approaches.

Data

The empirical foundation of this study was a comprehensive dataset encompassing approximately seven years of monthly turnover history for the LY1 business unit. This historical data, stretching from early 2015 to late 2021, provided a substantial time series for model training and evaluation. Recognizing that LY1's revenue was not solely a function of its past performance, a crucial element of the data collection phase involved identifying and gathering several exogenous variables. These variables were selected based on domain knowledge and their perceived relevance to the business unit's revenue generation mechanisms.

The exogenous variables included turnover data from two other significant business units within the same company (LY2 and LY3), as inter-unit dependencies, lead-lag effects, or shared market influences could exist. Aggregate turnover from LY1's top customers was also factored in, acknowledging that substantial shifts in the business volume of these key clients could disproportionately impact LY1's revenue. Similarly, turnover generated from other entities within the larger corporate group (concern-customer turnover) was considered. Revenue specifically attributable to project-based activities within LY1 was isolated as another input, given its potentially different dynamics compared to recurring service revenue. To capture aspects of operational efficiency and business health, gross margin figures for both LY1 and LY2 were included. Finally, as a service-oriented business unit, LY1's revenue was often directly linked to its human capital; thus, headcount (number of employees) and the average billing rate for services were incorporated as critical drivers. Table 2 provides a descriptive statistical summary of these key variables, calculated across the entire 82-month observation period. This summary offers insight into the scale, central tendency, and volatility of each data series used for model development.

Table 2. Descriptive statistics of model variables (N=82 months)

Variable	N	Mean	Std. Dev.	Median	Min	Max
LY1 Revenue (k€)	82	663.52	265.41	680.12	204.62	1,180.43
LY2 Revenue (k€)	82	3,012.43	1,042.66	2,546.14	1,671.36	4,685.59
TOP Customers Revenue (k€)	82	451.06	209.77	425.49	114.01	1,139.85
Group Customer Revenue (k€)	82	88.35	64.96	78.72	0.90	322.30
Project Revenue (k€)	82	110.62	124.96	66.88	2.12	745.51
LY1 EBITDA (k€)	82	555.74	217.16	584.44	148.94	1,092.45
LY2 EBITDA (k€)	82	1,822.92	538.11	1,649.88	1,064.53	2,711.12
Number of Employees	82	290.12	94.61	276.74	154.75	422.00
Billing Utilization (%)	82	55.75%	8.27%	59.92%	24.73%	66.85%

The collection of this rich set of multivariate data was pivotal, as it allowed for a more nuanced comparison between the models. While traditional statistical models, such as SARIMA, are typically applied univariately, neural networks like LSTM and GRU are inherently capable of processing multiple input variables simultaneously, potentially uncovering complex interrelationships that simpler models might miss. The conceptual structure of this multivariate approach is illustrated in Figure 1. The raw data underwent a standard preprocessing pipeline, which included checks for missing values, outlier treatment where appropriate, and ensuring stationarity or applying transformations if required by specific models. The emphasis on a multivariate approach for neural networks was intentional, as their architecture is inherently capable of capturing complex, non-obvious relationships between a target variable and its numerous potential drivers —a key advantage in business forecasting applications. For the neural network models, the input data was typically scaled to a range between 0 and 1 to aid in model convergence and stability.

Figure 1. Conceptual architecture of the multivariate neural network model.

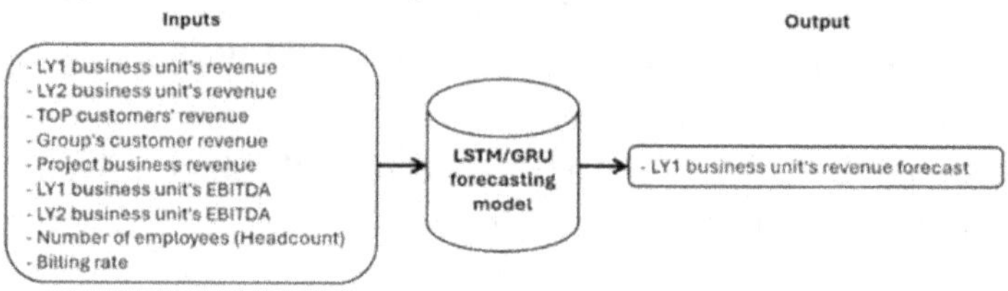

Models Compared

To provide a robust assessment of forecasting capabilities, the study implemented and compared a selection of models representing different methodological generations.

The first set comprised traditional statistical models. SARIMA (Seasonal Autoregressive Integrated Moving Average) was chosen for its well-established ability to model time series with trend and seasonality. It was applied as a univariate model, focusing solely on the historical LY1 turnover series. The auto_arima function from the pmdarima library in Python was used to systematically identify the optimal (p, d, q)(P, D, Q)[m] parameters for the model, ensuring a data-driven approach to its specification. Alongside SARIMA, **ETS** (Error, Trend, Seasonality - Additive error, Additive trend, Additive seasonality) was included. This refers to a specific configuration of the Holt-Winters additive method, another widely recognized univariate statistical forecasting technique, also implemented using Python's statsmodels library.

The second set of models represented state-of-the-art recurrent neural networks, specifically **LSTM** (Long Short-Term Memory) and **GRU** (Gated Recurrent Unit) networks. Both are known for their efficacy in capturing complex, long-range dependencies in sequential data. Crucially, both the LSTM and GRU models were designed as multivariate systems, ingesting not only the historical LY1 turnover but also the full suite of exogenous variables described earlier. While similar in capability, GRUs feature a slightly simpler internal architecture, which can sometimes lead to faster training without a significant compromise in performance.

The architecture and training parameters for both neural network models were identical to ensure a fair comparison. The final configuration that yielded the best results consisted of two stacked recurrent layers (either LSTM or GRU), each with

100 neurons and using the ReLU activation function. A Dropout layer with a rate of 0.25 was included between the layers to ensure the model learns general patterns instead of memorizing the training data, which helps prevent overfitting. To achieve the best fit, the models were trained for 30 epochs using the Adam optimizer with a learning rate of 0.01 and mean squared error as the loss function. During training, 20% of the data was held out as a validation set, and the model weights that achieved the lowest validation error were saved and used for the final forecasting. This standard practice ensures that the selected model generalizes well to new, unseen data.

Finally, as a crucial practical benchmark, the Existing Company Forecast was used. This forecast, predominantly derived from manual inputs, expert opinions, and established internal processes, provided a real-world baseline against which the performance of the statistical and AI-driven models could be gauged in terms of practical value to the organization.

All models were tasked with generating out-of-sample forecasts for a 12-month horizon. The evaluation of their predictive performance was based on a suite of standard accuracy metrics: Mean Absolute Error (MAE), Mean Squared Error (MSE), Root Mean Squared Error (RMSE), and Mean Absolute Percentage Error (MAPE). These metrics were calculated by comparing the model-generated forecasts against the actual observed turnover values for the hold-out period.

Key Findings and Results

The empirical results from the case study provided compelling evidence regarding the relative performance of the different forecasting approaches. A salient finding was that the neural network models, both LSTM and GRU, consistently demonstrated superior accuracy compared to the traditional statistical models (SARIMA and ETS) and, significantly, also outperformed the company's existing, largely manual, forecasting process. This outcome aligns with broader findings in financial forecasting literature, where deep learning models have repeatedly been shown to outperform traditional statistical methods by automatically learning complex patterns from large and often noisy datasets.

In terms of quantitative metrics, the LSTM and GRU models achieved notably lower Mean Absolute Percentage Error (MAPE) values, typically hovering around 9.83% to 9.93%. This represented a substantial improvement over the existing company forecast, which had an approximate MAPE of 12.49%. The traditional statistical models, SARIMA and ETS, also lagged behind the neural networks, with their MAPEs ranging from approximately 12.80% to 13.67% on average when assessed across different data splits and evaluation periods used in the original study. A detailed comparison of these key performance indicators is presented in Table 3.

Table 3. Comparative forecast accuracy.

Forecasting Model	Average MAPE (%)	Average MAE (k€)
GRU	9.83%	88
LSTM	9.93%	91
Existing Company Forecast	12.49%	113
ETS-AAA	12.80%	114
SARIMA	13.67%	111

The enhanced performance of the LSTM and GRU models was largely attributed to their multivariate nature. Their architecture allowed them to effectively learn from and integrate the information contained within the diverse set of exogenous variables. This capability to model complex, non-linear relationships between multiple drivers and the target revenue variable provided a distinct advantage over the univariate SARIMA and ETS models, which, by their standard formulation, could not directly leverage this additional information in the same integrated fashion.

When comparing the two neural network architectures, LSTM and GRU, the study found no consistently significant or large difference in their predictive accuracy. Their performance was broadly comparable across the various metrics and evaluation periods, suggesting that for this particular dataset and task, the simpler GRU architecture was as effective as the more complex LSTM.

From a practical standpoint, the study acknowledged the trade-offs involved. While neural networks offered higher accuracy, they also entailed greater computational expense during the training phase compared to the relatively quick fitting process of the statistical models. However, once the neural network models were trained, generating new forecasts became computationally inexpensive.

In conclusion, this first case study strongly indicated that the adoption of neural network-based forecasting methodologies held significant potential for the ICT service company to achieve more accurate turnover predictions. It underscored the value of data-driven, multivariate approaches in financial forecasting, while also implicitly highlighting the increased technical expertise and resource considerations necessary for the successful implementation and maintenance of such advanced AI models.

Case 1 Summary

The key takeaway from this case was that for a single, complex revenue stream with known external drivers (like headcount or customer data), multivariate neural networks (LSTM/GRU) provided a significant accuracy improvement over both traditional univariate models and the established manual forecast. This highlights the value of deep learning in capturing complex, non-linear relationships when rich, relevant data is available.

Case 2: Forecasting Costs

The second case study transitioned the investigative focus from revenue to cost forecasting and evaluated a contemporary foundation model, TimeGPT. This research was embedded within a large state-owned company. A primary operational challenge for this organization was accurately and efficiently forecasting costs across its intricate, multi-level hierarchical structure. This hierarchy encompassed a vast number of individual cost accounts, which were then aggregated through various departmental, project-based, and business unit levels up to consolidated group-level summaries. The scale and complexity of this hierarchical system posed a significant challenge for traditional forecasting methods. These methods often require creating a separate model for each time series, which made them difficult and costly to use in this case.

The central objective of this study was to comprehensively evaluate the performance, practicality, and scalability of the TimeGPT model for this large-scale, hierarchical cost forecasting task. This involved comparing TimeGPT against well-established traditional statistical models and the popular Prophet forecasting tool. A critical dimension of this investigation was to assess the efficacy of TimeGPT's inherent zero-shot forecasting capabilities, its ability to generate forecasts for unseen data without task-specific training, versus the improvements achievable by fine-tuning the pre-trained model on the company's proprietary cost data. Furthermore, the study meticulously examined the impact of varying the number of fine-tuning steps, seeking to understand the trade-off between incremental accuracy gains and the associated computational effort and time. This granular analysis aimed to provide practical guidance on optimizing TimeGPT's application in a real-world enterprise setting.

Data

The empirical basis for this case study was a substantial dataset of monthly cost figures sourced directly from the target organization's financial systems. The data spanned a period of approximately five years, from January 2020 to October 2024, offering a contemporary and relevant view into the company's cost dynamics. The most distinctive feature of this dataset was its profound hierarchical nature and significant scale. To thoroughly test the models' scalability and performance under varying conditions, the study utilized three distinct subsets of this data, each representing a different level of aggregation and complexity:

All companies, lowest account group: This dataset comprised 57 individual time series, representing a more aggregated but still detailed view of costs at a specific common level across all company entities.

One company, all levels: This dataset was significantly larger, containing 1,853 unique time series. It represented all hierarchical cost levels within a single major company entity, providing a detailed view of its internal cost structure.

All companies, all levels: This was the most extensive dataset, a total of 5,954 individual time series. It represented the full complexity of the organization's cost hierarchy across all its constituent companies and aggregation levels.

This multi-tiered data structure presented a substantial challenge, particularly for traditional forecasting models that typically require separate fitting and parameterization for each individual series. The datasets inherently reflected the realities of real-world financial data, exhibiting varying degrees of completeness (including some series with missing values), diverse and sometimes multiple seasonal patterns, different trend behaviors, and varying levels of noise and volatility. Unlike the first case study, which emphasized multivariate neural networks, this investigation primarily focused on univariate forecasting for each individual time series within the hierarchy. This approach was chosen because TimeGPT, particularly in its early applications and for zero-shot predictions, was often applied in a univariate fashion or with limited, easily accessible exogenous features that might not be uniformly available across thousands of diverse cost accounts. The study aimed to assess its core time series modeling capabilities first. Data preprocessing was kept minimal to reflect a realistic scenario where extensive cleaning of thousands of series might be impractical; it mainly involved structuring the data into the format required by the TimeGPT API and handling explicit missing values where necessary for other models.

Models Compared

The forecast performance of a carefully selected suite of models was systematically evaluated. Representing traditional statistical approaches, **SARIMA** (Seasonal Autoregressive Integrated Moving Average) models were applied. Given the hierarchical nature of the data, SARIMA models were fitted individually to each of the thousands of time series within the datasets. Similarly, **ETS** (Exponential Smoothing) models, encompassing a range of methods like Holt-Winters, were also applied on a per-series basis to provide another robust statistical benchmark.

Given its widespread adoption in business forecasting due to its ease of use and ability to handle seasonality and holiday effects, **Prophet**, Meta's open-source forecasting model, was included as a key modern benchmark. Like SARIMA and ETS, Prophet models were also fitted individually for each series in the hierarchy.

The central focus of the study was the **TimeGPT** foundation model. Its performance was assessed in two primary modes:

1. TimeGPT (Zero-Shot): In this mode, the pre-trained TimeGPT model was used to generate forecasts directly, without any prior exposure to or fine-tuning on the company's specific cost data. This rigorously tested the model's ability to generalize its learned patterns from vast, diverse pre-training datasets to a new, unseen forecasting task.
2. TimeGPT (Fine-Tuned): To explore the potential for performance enhancement through specialization, the pre-trained TimeGPT model was further fine-tuned using the company's historical cost data. A significant part of the research involved systematically varying the number of fine-tuning steps applied, ranging from a minimal 5 steps up to 110 steps. This allowed for a detailed analysis of the relationship between the extent of fine-tuning, the resulting forecast accuracy, and the associated computational time and cost.

As a practical point of reference, for a relevant subset of the cost data, the forecasts generated by TimeGPT were also compared against the company's existing forecasts. These were typically produced through a combination of manual processes, spreadsheet-based calculations, and expert judgment within the finance and controlling departments.

For all models, forecasts were generally generated for a 10-month out-of-sample horizon. Performance evaluation relied on key accuracy metrics, such as Mean Absolute Error (MAE) and Mean Absolute Percentage Error (MAPE), aggregated across hierarchical levels or specific types of cost accounts. Computational time for forecast generation was also a critical evaluation criterion, especially for large-scale datasets.

Key Findings and Results

The comprehensive investigation produced several findings regarding the capabilities and practicalities of using TimeGPT for large-scale hierarchical cost forecasting. The results establish that the model's performance is highly contingent on the scale and complexity of the data, demonstrating a decisive advantage in large, intricate, real-world enterprise settings.

The analysis across three distinct datasets revealed a clear and compelling narrative about how different model classes perform as data complexity increases, as summarized in Table 4.

Table 4. Comparative Forecast Accuracy (MAPE) Across Datasets of Varying Scale and Complexity.

Forecasting Model	Small MAPE (%)	Medium MAPE (%)	Large MAPE (%)
TimeGPT (10-step fine-tune)	11.18%	**13.78%**	**5.12%**
Prophet	5.63%	20.38%	8.55%
SARIMA	**3.45%**	38.46%	11.70%
ETS	4.76%	31.27%	12.70%

Small Dataset (All companies, lowest account group; 57 time series): On the smallest and simplest dataset, traditional statistical models were highly competitive. SARIMA achieved the lowest monthly Mean Absolute Percentage Error (MAPE) at 3.45%, followed closely by ETS at 4.76% and Prophet at 5.63%. In this controlled environment, fine-tuned TimeGPT (10 steps) lagged with a MAPE of 11.18%. This highlights the strength of traditional models when data is clean, well-structured, and limited in scale, as they can effectively capture the underlying patterns without the overhead of a large foundation model.

Medium Dataset (One company, all levels; 1,853 time series): As the complexity and scale grew to encompass the full hierarchy of a single company, the performance landscape shifted dramatically. Fine-tuned TimeGPT (10 steps) emerged as the most accurate model with MAPE of 13.78%. The performance of traditional models degraded significantly, with Prophet reaching 20.38% and SARIMA performing poorly at 38.46%. This reversal highlights the challenges traditional per-series models encounter when handling thousands of interrelated time series with varying patterns and data quality levels.

Large Dataset (All companies, all levels; 5,954 time series): On the most extensive and complex dataset, representing the entire organizational cost structure, TimeGPT's superiority was unequivocal. Fine-tuned TimeGPT (10 steps) achieved a remarkable MAPE of 5.12%. This was a significant improvement over Prophet (8.55%), SARIMA (11.70%), and ETS (12.70%). This superior performance on a massive, noisy, and partially incomplete dataset highlights TimeGPT's inherent robustness and its ability to leverage its pre-trained knowledge to effectively handle real-world financial data challenges.

A critical aspect of the study was analyzing the effect of fine-tuning. Fine-tuning the pre-trained TimeGPT model on the company's specific cost data consistently and significantly improved forecast accuracy compared to its zero-shot performance. This confirms the practical value of adapting the model's generalized knowledge to the specific nuances of the target domain.

However, the analysis also demonstrated a clear pattern of diminishing returns. The most substantial accuracy gains were consistently observed within the first 5 to 10 fine-tuning steps. As shown in Figure 2, the Overall MAE (a volume-weighted metric across all 5,954 series) improves sharply initially but begins to plateau after approximately 30-60 steps. Further increases in fine-tuning steps yielded only marginal, if any, improvements in accuracy, while increasing computational costs. This finding is crucial for practitioners, as it reveals that limited, targeted fine-tuning strikes an optimal balance between enhanced accuracy and the efficient use of resources. This result demonstrates a core principle of foundation models: the pre-trained knowledge provides a robust baseline, and only a small amount of task-specific adaptation is required to achieve high performance, which is a key advantage over training specialized models from scratch.

Figure 2. The impact of fine-tuning steps on forecast accuracy for the largest dataset.

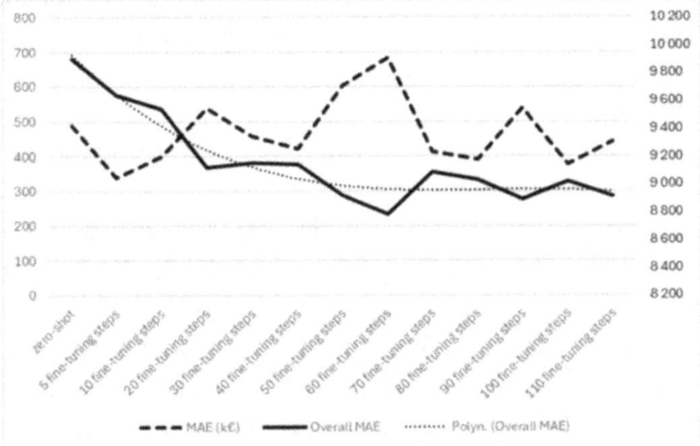

In terms of computational efficiency, TimeGPT proved to be exceptionally fast. The fundamental reason for this lies in the model's execution methodology. Leveraging its API-based architecture designed for parallel processing, TimeGPT was capable of generating forecasts for thousands of individual time series simultaneously within a single request. This resulted in computation times of only 5–6 seconds, regardless of the dataset size in this study. This stands in stark contrast to the traditional models. Prophet, SARIMA and ETS were executed serially, requiring a separate model to be fitted for each individual time series one after another in a sequential process. This necessity to fit thousands of models individually is what caused their computation times to escalate to thousands of seconds (minutes to hours) on the larger datasets. The architectural advantage of parallel processing thus positions TimeGPT as a highly practical solution for organizations that frequently need to generate forecasts across an extensive portfolio of time series, enabling more agile planning and decision-making.

To ground the findings in a real-world business context, the model forecasts were compared against the company's existing K1 forecast, which human forecasters produced without AI assistance. On the most complex dataset, the forecasters' manual process yielded a MAPE of 6.48%. In a direct comparison over the same forecast horizon, the 10-step fine-tuned TimeGPT model achieved a superior MAPE of 5.12%. This result provides concrete evidence that deploying TimeGPT can lead to a tangible and significant improvement in forecast accuracy, offering a more precise and reliable baseline for financial planning than the established manual processes.

Regarding its application to hierarchical forecasting, TimeGPT effectively managed the large number of series inherent in the company's cost structure, producing coherent forecasts across different levels. While the study primarily focused on univariate forecasts per series, the underlying architecture of foundation models like TimeGPT inherently benefits from pre-training on vast datasets, allowing it to implicitly learn cross-series patterns and dependencies, which is an advantage in hierarchical contexts.

When compared to the company's existing, largely manual forecasting methods (for the subset of data where this comparison was feasible), fine-tuned TimeGPT also demonstrated superior accuracy. This indicated clear potential for TimeGPT to enhance the precision and reliability of the organization's established cost forecasting processes.

However, the study also highlighted important practical considerations for adoption, derived from qualitative feedback from the company's forecasters. While the Power BI interface developed to present TimeGPT's forecasts was well-received for its user-friendliness and effective visualization capabilities, the inherent "black box" nature of the TimeGPT model itself emerged as a significant concern for some users. A lack of clear understanding of the model's internal logic and decision-making processes led to a degree of distrust and, consequently, a reluctance to fully integrate its output into their workflows.

This real-world observation aligns with established findings in technology acceptance research, where perceived trust serves as a critical mediator in the adoption of new AI tools in the finance sector. It underscores that overcoming the "black box" challenge through improved model explainability is not just a technical issue, but a crucial socio-technical barrier to leveraging the full potential of advanced forecasting models in an organizational setting. This feedback underscored the critical importance of not just technical performance, but also of investing in transparency, model explainability, and comprehensive user training to foster trust and ensure the successful adoption and integration of advanced AI forecasting tools within an organization.

Case 2 Summary

The second case demonstrated that for large-scale, hierarchical forecasting, the TimeGPT foundation model was unequivocally superior in both speed and accuracy. Traditional per-series models failed to scale, while TimeGPT's parallel architecture generated forecasts in seconds. Crucially, a small amount of fine-tuning offered significant accuracy gains over zero-shot performance, but this benefit showed clearly diminishing returns. This case also highlighted that user trust and the "black box" problem are critical socio-technical barriers to adoption, even when technical performance is strong.

DISCUSSION

The findings from the two case studies present a clear evolutionary narrative of business forecasting, highlighting a fundamental trade-off between model accuracy, scalability, and interpretability that shifts with data complexity and scale. This research offers empirical evidence that while traditional statistical models remain viable for simpler, well-structured problems, the progression towards neural networks and ultimately foundation models provide significant advantages in handling the large-scale, complex, and often imperfect data characteristic of modern enterprises.

A central theme emerging from the comparative analysis is that the superiority of a given forecasting model is highly context-dependent. In Case 1, the neural networks (LSTM and GRU) outperformed traditional models for a single revenue stream. However, the results from Case 2 provide a more nuanced picture. On the smallest dataset (57 time series), traditional models were competitive. This dynamic reversed dramatically as the task scaled, demonstrating the core value proposition of foundation models: their robustness to real-world, large-scale data. While the neural networks in Case 1 were effective, scaling that per-task training approach to the 5,954 series in Case 2 would have been computationally prohibitive.

The two cases also illustrate distinct strategies for enhancing forecast accuracy. In Case 1, the advantage was derived from a multivariate architecture, which integrated external business drivers (like headcount and customer revenue). This approach is powerful when such explanatory variables are known and available.

In contrast, Case 2 demonstrated the power of pre-training and fine-tuning. Fine-tuning consistently improved TimeGPT's accuracy over its zero-shot performance. However, it also revealed a critical pattern of diminishing returns, where the most substantial gains were achieved within the first 10-30 steps. This finding is of immense practical importance, suggesting an optimal strategy involves limited, targeted fine-tuning to balance accuracy gains with computational cost. This highlights a key economic shift: the heaviest computational load (pre-training) is borne by the provider, and end-users can achieve high performance with minimal task-specific adaptation.

Perhaps the most significant practical differentiator to emerge was computational efficiency. In Case 2, TimeGPT generated forecasts for thousands of time series in mere seconds due to its parallel, API-based architecture. This stood in stark contrast to the traditional models (SARIMA, ETS, Prophet), which required sequential fitting and took hours. This architectural advantage is a decisive factor for large organizations that require agile planning.

These findings on computational speed have profound practical implications that go beyond mere efficiency. The shift from an hours-long process to a seconds-long query fundamentally changes forecasting from a slow, periodic, and resource-intensive event into an agile, on-demand capability. For managers, this unlocks the ability to iterate budgets, simulate multiple what-if scenarios, and react to sudden market changes with a speed that is impossible using traditional per-series models. This suggests the primary bottleneck for forecasting in large firms is shifting away from technical limitations (model training time) and toward organizational ones: data governance, model validation, and building user trust.

While solving the problem of scalability, the move to foundation models intensifies the "black box" challenge. The qualitative findings from Case 2 provided a vivid illustration of this socio-technical barrier. While users praised the usability of the visualization tools, the inherent opacity of the TimeGPT model generated significant distrust. Forecasters were reluctant to rely on predictions from a model whose internal logic they could not understand, even when it was demonstrably more accurate.

This real-world observation reinforces research on technology acceptance, which identifies perceived trust as a critical factor for the adoption of AI tools in finance. It underscores that the successful implementation of advanced forecasting models is not just a technical challenge but also a human-centric one of building trust. Overcoming this requires dedicated efforts in explainable AI (XAI), user training, and demonstrating model validity in transparent ways. Without this investment in trust, even the most powerful forecasting model risks becoming useless in practice.

CONCLUSION

This chapter presented a comparative analysis of forecasting model generations, tracing the evolution from traditional statistical methods to foundation models. Through two real-world case studies, the findings demonstrated a clear trade-off: while multivariate neural networks (LSTM, GRU) offered high accuracy for a single, complex revenue stream, they were impractical to scale. Conversely, the TimeGPT foundation model proved unequivocally superior for a large-scale, hierarchical cost-forecasting problem, offering significant gains in both accuracy (with fine-tuning) and computational speed.

This analysis confirms that while technical performance (accuracy and speed) is a key driver, it is not the only factor for successful implementation. The findings highlight that the optimal model is highly contextual. More importantly, they reveal that the primary bottleneck in modern forecasting is shifting from computational power to human adoption. Despite the proven accuracy of advanced AI models, the "black box" problem remains a significant socio-technical barrier. As demonstrated in Case 2, a lack of transparency fosters distrust among business users, hindering the model's integration and practical impact. This underscores that successful AI implementation is not just a technical challenge but a human-centric one focused on building trust.

Based on the empirical findings, the following recommendations can be made to practitioners and decision-makers in business forecasting:

- **AI for complex and large-scale forecasting:** Organizations should strategically adopt AI-based models for complex, large-scale, or business-critical forecasting tasks where traditional methods have proven insufficient or computationally infeasible. The evidence clearly shows that models like TimeGPT excel in handling thousands of hierarchical time series, providing a level of speed and accuracy that is impractical to achieve with per-series statistical models.
- **Select the model strategically:** The choice of model should be driven by the specific context, including data characteristics, accuracy requirements, available resources, and the need for interpretability. For a single key metric with known drivers, a custom multivariate neural network may be optimal. For enterprise-wide hierarchical forecasting, a foundation model like TimeGPT offers unparalleled scalability. For simple, stable time series, traditional statistical models may still be sufficient and offer higher interpretability.
- **Prioritize user trust and adoption over technical metrics alone:** A technically superior model is worthless if it is not trusted or used. The findings from Case 2 show that user distrust of the "black box" is a primary barrier to adoption. Organizations must address this head-on by investing in user training, clear communication, and transparent validation processes. Providing intuitive visualization tools (like the Power BI report in Case 2) and explaining how the model complements, rather than replaces, user expertise are essential steps to build confidence and ensure successful adoption.

- **Continuous improvement:** Forecasting models should not be treated as static solutions. Organizations should establish processes for continuous monitoring of model performance and periodic fine-tuning or retraining as new data becomes available to maintain and improve forecast accuracy over time.

This work opens several avenues for future research that could further enhance the application of AI in business forecasting:

- **Hybrid models:** Future research could explore the development of hybrid models that combine the strengths of different approaches. For example, integrating the interpretability of statistical models with the predictive power of foundation models, or using LLMs to generate narrative explanations for anomalies detected by TimeGPT, could offer more robust and trustworthy forecasting solutions.
- **Exogenous variables in foundation models:** While this research highlighted the power of exogenous variables in neural networks (Case 1) and the univariate strength of TimeGPT (Case 2), a key area for future study is the systematic integration of external drivers into foundation models. Investigating how to effectively incorporate structured data (e.g., economic indicators) or even unstructured data (e.g., creating time series from project diaries or news sentiment using LLMs) could significantly enhance their predictive power.
- **Comparison with other foundation models:** The field of time series forecasting is evolving rapidly, with new foundation models emerging from various research institutions and companies. Broader benchmark studies comparing TimeGPT with these new models (e.g., from Google, Salesforce, Microsoft) would be valuable to better understand the current state-of-the-art and their respective strengths in different business contexts.
- **XAI for time series models:** To directly tackle the "black box" problem, more research is needed on applying and developing XAI techniques specifically for time series foundation models. Creating methods to visualize attention weights or identify the most influential historical data points for a given forecast could demystify these models and build essential user trust.
- **Deeper analysis of user experience and trust:** While this chapter included qualitative feedback, more in-depth studies using methods like structured interviews or observational analysis could provide a richer understanding of the socio-technical factors that influence the adoption of AI forecasting tools. Understanding the nuances of how users interact with, interpret, and ultimately trust AI-generated forecasts is crucial for their successful implementation in any organization.

REFERENCES

Ansari, A. F., Stella, L., Turkmen, C., Zhang, X., Mercado, P., Shen, H., Shchur, O., Rangapuram, S. S., Arango, S. P., Kapoor, S., . . . Wang, Y. (2024). *Chronos: Learning the Language of Time Series*. arXiv preprint arXiv:2403.07815. https://doi.org//arXiv.2403.07815DOI: 10.48550

Banerjee, G. (2025). The impact of artificial intelligence on accounting and human resource management: Opportunities, challenges, and future trajectories. In *Unlocking Potential*. IIP Series. AI and Data Architecture in Management, Science, and Education.

Box, G. E. P., Jenkins, G. M., Reinsel, G. C., & Ljung, G. M. (2015). *Time Series Analysis: Forecasting and Control* (5th ed.). John Wiley.

Cao, F., Yang, S., Chen, Z., Liu, Y., & Cui, L. (2024). *Ister: Inverted Seasonal-Trend Decomposition Transformer for Explainable Multivariate Time Series Forecasting*. arXiv preprint arXiv:2403.18798. https://arxiv.org/abs/2412.18798

Cho, K., van Merriënboer, B., Gulcehre, C., Bahdanau, D., Bougares, F., Schwenk, H., & Bengio, Y. (2014). *Learning Phrase Representations Using RNN Encoder-Decoder for Statistical Machine Translation*. arXiv preprint arXiv:2412.1879. https://doi.org//arXiv.1406.1078DOI: 10.3115/v1/D14-1179

Das, A., Kong, W., Sen, R., & Zhou, Y. (2024). *A Decoder-Only Foundation Model for Time-Series Forecasting*. arXiv preprint arXiv:2310.10688. https://arxiv.org/abs/2310.10688

Drobetz, W., Hollstein, F., Otto, T., & Prokopczuk, M. (2025). Estimating Stock Market Betas Via Machine Learning. *Journal of Financial and Quantitative Analysis*, *60*(3), 1074–1110. DOI: 10.1017/S0022109024000036

Fischer, T., & Krauss, C. (2018). Deep Learning with Long Short-Term Memory Networks for Financial Market Predictions. *European Journal of Operational Research*, *270*(2), 654–669. DOI: 10.1016/j.ejor.2017.11.054

Garza, A., Challu, C., & Mergenthaler-Canseco, M. (2024). *TimeGPT-1*. arXiv preprint arXiv:2310.03589. https://doi.org//arXiv.2310.03589DOI: 10.48550

Goodfellow, I., Bengio, Y., & Courville, A. (2016). *Deep Learning*. MIT Press.

Gruver, N., Finzi, M., Qiu, S., & Wilson, A. G. (2023). *Large Language Models Are Zero-Shot Time Series Forecasters*. arXiv preprint arXiv:2310.07820. https://doi.org//arXiv.2310.07820DOI: 10.52202/075280-0861

Hochreiter, S., & Schmidhuber, J. (1997). Long Short-Term Memory. *Neural Computation*, *9*(8), 1735–1780. DOI: 10.1162/neco.1997.9.8.1735 PMID: 9377276

Hyndman, R. J., & Athanasopoulos, G. (2021). *Forecasting: Principles and Practice* (3rd ed.). OTexts.

Jin, M., Wang, S., Ma, L., Chu, Z., Zhang, J. Y., Shi, X., Chen, P., Liang, Y., Li, Y., Pan, S., & Wen, Q. (2023). *Time-LLM: Time Series Forecasting by Reprogramming Large Language Models*. arXiv preprint arXiv:2310.01728. https://doi.org//arXiv.2310.01728DOI: 10.48550

Kottapallis, S. R. K., Hublis, K., Chandrashekhara, S., Jain, G., Hublis, S., Botla, G., & Doddaiah, R. (2025). *Foundation Models for Time Series: A Survey*. arXiv preprint arXiv:2504.04011. https://arxiv.org/abs/2504.04011

Kumar, S. N. A., Madhavi, R., & Sundar Rajan, M. (2025). Explainable AI in Financial Forecasting Using Time Series Analysis. *International Journal for Research in Applied Science and Engineering Technology*, *13*(4), 7155–7160. DOI: 10.22214/ijraset.2025.70080

Li, Z., Qiu, X., Chen, P., Wang, Y., Cheng, H., Shu, Y., Hu, J., Guo, C., Zhou, A., Jensen, C. S., & Yang, B. (2024). *TSFM-Bench: A Comprehensive and Unified Benchmark of Foundation Models for Time Series Forecasting*. arXiv preprint arXiv:2410.11802. https://doi.org//arXiv.2410.11802DOI: 10.48550

Livieris, I. E., Pintelas, E., & Pintelas, P. (2020). A CNN–LSTM Model for Gold Price Time-Series Forecasting. *Neural Computing & Applications*, *32*(23), 17351–17360. DOI: 10.1007/s00521-020-04867-x

Makridakis, S., Spiliotis, E., & Assimakopoulos, V. (2020). The M4 Competition: 100,000 Time Series and 61 Forecasting Methods. *International Journal of Forecasting*, *36*(1), 54–74. DOI: 10.1016/j.ijforecast.2019.04.014

Nguyen, T. H., & Vu, T. Q. (2025). Perceptions of Financial AI Assistants and Intentions Toward AI-Assisted Financial Products. *International Journal of Asian Business and Information Management*, *16*(1), 1–18. DOI: 10.4018/IJABIM.371629

Nie, Y., Nguyen, N. H., Sinthong, P., & Kalagnanam, J. (2023). *A Time Series Is Worth 64 Words: Long-Term Forecasting with Transformers*. arXiv preprint arXiv:2211.14730. https://doi.org//arXiv.2211.14730DOI: 10.48550

Okeke, N. I., Bakare, O. A., & Achumie, G. O.Njideka Ihuoma OkekeOluwaseun Adeola BakareGodwin Ozoemenam Achumie. (2024). Artificial intelligence in SME financial decision-making: Tools for enhancing efficiency and profitability. *Open Access Research Journal of Multidisciplinary Studies*, *08*(01), 150–163. DOI: 10.53022/oarjms.2024.8.1.0056

Pal, P., & Poddar, S. (2024). Applications of Smart Farming Sensors: A Way Forward. In *Data Science for Agricultural Innovation and Productivity* (pp. 175–193). Bentham Science Publishers., DOI: 10.2174/9789815196177124010012

Rong, C., Sial, M. S., Saci, F., Jasimuddin, S. M., & Zhang, J. Z. (2025). AI Adoption in the Finance Sector of a Developing Economy. *Journal of Organizational and End User Computing*, *37*(1), 1–19. DOI: 10.4018/JOEUC.371412

Sezer, O. B., Gudelek, M. U., & Ozbayoglu, A. M. (2020). Financial Time Series Forecasting with Deep Learning: A Systematic Literature Review: 2005–2019. *Applied Soft Computing*, *90*, 106181. DOI: 10.1016/j.asoc.2020.106181

Vaswani, A., Shazeer, N., Parmar, N., Uszkoreit, J., Jones, L., Gomez, A. N., Kaiser, Ł., & Polosukhin, I. (2017). *Attention Is All You Need*. arXiv preprint arXiv:1706.03762. https://doi.org//arXiv.1706.03762DOI: 10.48550

Wang, Y., Wu, H., Dong, J., Liu, Y., Long, M., & Wang, J. (2024). *Deep Time Series Models: A Comprehensive Survey and Benchmark*. arXiv preprint arXiv:2407.13278. https://arxiv.org/abs/2407.13278

Woo, G., Liu, C., Kumar, A., Xiong, C., Savarese, S., & Sahoo, D. (2024). *Unified Training of Universal Time Series Forecasting Transformers*. arXiv preprint arXiv:2402.02592. https://doi.org//arXiv.2402.02592DOI: 10.48550

Wu, H., Xu, J., Wang, J., & Long, M. (2021). *Autoformer: Decomposition Transformers with Auto-Correlation for Long-Term Series Forecasting*. arXiv preprint arXiv:2106.13008. https://doi.org//arXiv.2106.13008DOI: 10.48550

Yang, A., Thong, Q., Gia, L., & Zakariya, Y. (2025). Big Data-Driven Corporate Financial Forecasting and Decision Support: A Study of CNN-LSTM Machine Learning Models. *Frontiers in Applied Mathematics and Statistics*, *11*, 1566078. Advance online publication. DOI: 10.3389/fams.2025.1566078

Zhou, H., Zhang, S., Peng, J., Zhang, S., Li, J., Xiong, H., & Zhang, W. (2021). *Informer: Beyond Efficient Transformer for Long Sequence Time-Series Forecasting*. arXiv preprint arXiv:2012.07436. https://doi.org//arXiv.2012.07436DOI: 10.48550

KEY TERMS AND DEFINITIONS

Explainable AI (XAI): A subfield of artificial intelligence focused on developing methods and techniques that make the decisions and predictions of complex models understandable to humans. In business forecasting, XAI aims to overcome the "black box" problem, thereby fostering user trust and facilitating the adoption of advanced models in high-stakes environments.

Fine-Tuning: The process of adapting a pre-trained foundation model by performing a small number of additional training steps on a specific target dataset. This technique specializes the model's general knowledge to the unique nuances of the new data, typically leading to enhanced forecast accuracy at a marginal computational cost.

Foundation Model: A large-scale AI model pre-trained on vast and diverse datasets. Its core characteristic is the ability to generalize this learned knowledge to perform a wide range of new tasks with minimal or no task-specific training, thus fundamentally altering the economics and scalability of model deployment.

Hierarchical Forecasting: The task of forecasting a collection of time series that are structurally linked and aggregated in a hierarchical manner, such as individual cost accounts rolling up to departmental and then company-wide totals. The primary challenge is to produce coherent and reconciled forecasts across all levels of the hierarchy.

Multivariate Forecasting: A forecasting approach where a target variable is predicted not only from its historical values but also from a set of other related, external variables (exogenous drivers). This method is used to capture the complex interdependencies between a target, such as revenue, and its business drivers, including headcount or marketing spend.

Recurrent Neural Network (RNN): A class of neural networks, including variants like Long Short-Term Memory (LSTM) and Gated Recurrent Unit (GRU), designed to model sequential data. By utilizing internal loops, RNNs can retain a memory of past information, allowing them to learn long-range dependencies and complex, nonlinear patterns inherent in time series data.

TimeGPT: The first foundation model developed specifically for time series forecasting. It utilizes transformer-based architecture and is pre-trained on a massive corpus of time series data to generate accurate forecasts for unseen datasets, often without requiring model retraining.

Transformer Architecture: A neural network architecture, initially developed for natural language processing, that relies on a self-attention mechanism. Unlike sequential RNNs, it processes all data points in a sequence simultaneously, enabling massive parallelization and a superior ability to capture long-range dependencies within the data.

Zero-Shot Forecasting: The application of a pre-trained foundation model to generate forecasts for a new, unseen dataset without any prior training or fine-tuning on that specific data. This capability relies entirely on the generalized patterns the model learned during its initial, extensive pre-training phase.

Chapter 10
Crop Price Prediction Using Machine Learning Techniques:
An Indian Case Study of Wheat and Maize

Sai Prabhakar Balantrapu
http://orcid.org/0009-0004-7860-2965
Sri Sathya Sai Institute of Higher Learning, India

G. Raghavender Raju
http://orcid.org/0000-0002-2093-1019
Sri Sathya Sai Institute of Higher Learning, India, India

Satya Sai Mudigonda
http://orcid.org/0009-0003-4788-347X
Sri Sathya Sai Institute of Higher Learning, India

Lalith Aditya Kalur
Sri Sathya Sai Institute of Higher Learning, India

ABSTRACT

Agriculture remains a critical pillar of the Indian economy, employing 42% of the labour force and representing 18% of the nation's Gross Domestic Product (GDP). Although it holds great value, the sector grapples with countless hurdles within the supply chain, involving both production and market flow. Weather variability and the market conditions cause price volatility which is a source of uncertainty to both farmers and policymakers. The authors in this chapter analyse major Indian

DOI: 10.4018/979-8-3373-3053-2.ch010

crops - Wheat and Maize using price prediction models using machine learning approaches such as Linear Regression, Decision Tree, Random Forest, XGBoost and K-Nearest Neighbours. The chapter establishes that the Random Forest algorithm outperforms the other ML models in predicting crop prices. These findings offer valuable insights for policymakers, enabling the development of more effective, data-driven price stabilization strategies and risk reduction measures to support India's agricultural economy.

1. INTRODUCTION

AI (Artificial Intelligence) and ML (Machine Learning) models are fundamentally altering the ways in which economic and financial activities are analysed and anticipated, particularly within agriculture where price volatility can devastate farmers' income. In the scope of crop price forecasting, AI-based models analyse past price data along with relevant historical data such as weather, market activity, and policy impact (World Economic Forum, 2021). Unlike traditional methods reliant on statistical methods, ML algorithms perform optimally due to their ability to identify complex interrelations within data, adjust to changing market conditions, and produce accurate predictions (Patil et al., 2023; Mohanty et al., 2023). This is vital for Indian farmers cultivating staple crops like wheat and maize, as price fluctuations influence not only crop selection but also their income and food sovereignty (Paul et al., 2024).

Bringing AI into the mix for predicting crop prices can help policymakers, traders, and financial institutions - by allowing them to create smarter strategies for managing risks, streamlining supply chains, and shaping policies (Hamzah et al., 2025). Using AI for price predictions not only makes the market work better but also gives farmers practical insights. This all contributes to a stronger and more sustainable agricultural economy in India (World Economic Forum, 2021).

1.1 Agriculture in India: A Resilient Contributor to GDP and Food Security

The agricultural industry in India stands out as a vital sector, sustaining close to 42.3% of its labour force and providing about 18.2% of the nation's Gross Domestic Product. This sector has illustrated extraordinary resilience, reporting a robust average growth rate of 4.2% during the previous five years. This industry fulfils a key role not only within the broader economic model but also in promoting food security, especially in the context of increasing population and changing consumption behaviours. Notwithstanding the presence of a considerable stockpile of food grains and commendable export figures, numerous challenges persist, including sub-optimal productivity rates, unpredictable climatic variability, fragmented land ownership, and inadequate marketing infrastructure (Economic Survey, 2023-24).

1.1.1 Agricultural crop prices in India

In India, the importance of agricultural commodities is enormous for both the economy and its countless farmers. As a predominant producer and exporter in the agricultural domain, India is substantially dependent on staples such as rice, wheat, cotton, and sugarcane, which considerably enhance the nation's Gross Domestic Product (GDP). Pricing for these items is shaped by multiple influences, from climatic variations and policy decisions to global financial trends and issues within supply chains. In the past, Indian governmental institutions have started a range of measures intended to improve the agricultural field and provide equitable wages for farmers. Even despite these measures, the prices of farming crops remain extremely unstable and unpredictable, and as a result, farmers face economic distress leading to a negative impact on the general economy. Furthermore, environmental factors, such as climate change, declining water levels, continue to disrupt agricultural activities in India ultimately leading to adverse consequences in terms of yields and supply chains. Agricultural crop prices in India needs to be closely monitored as it would help better understand the general condition of the economy and provide sustainable progress to the sector (Saxena et al., 2019).

1.1.2 Policy stance towards Agriculture sector

Numerous strategic interventions implemented by the Indian government that were aimed to introduce positive results comprise the implementation of guaranteed remunerative pricing structures through Minimum Support Prices (MSP), the increase in the capacity to receive institutional credit, the improvement in crop diversification, the modernization of digital technologies and mechanisation, the facilitation of sustainable means of farming like organic and natural farming, and the focus on productivity growth. Some of the important measures implemented by the Indian government on the agricultural sphere are:

- **Minimum Support Price (MSP) Policy**: In order to attract greater investments in agriculture and to enhance production and improvement in productivity, the MSP policy on major agricultural commodities aims at making remunerative prices to the farmers. The Minimum support price (MSP) is the minimum price at which the government is willing to buy select crops such as major cereals, Shree Anna (millets), pulses, oilseeds, copra, cotton and jute grown in Kharif and Rabi seasons and is deemed as remunerative by the farmers which works as a price support. The MSP is set at 1.5 times of Cost of Production (CoP), by the government, which is currently applicable to 24 crops (Press Information Bureau, 2024).

- **Pradhan Mantri Fasal Bima Yojana (PMFBY)**: The Government of India started the PMFBY in the year 2016 with an aim to provide large agricultural insurance packages. The scheme provides a complete cover against crop loss due to the unpredictable natural hazards. This safeguard, among other things, stabilizes the income of farmers and encourages them to adopt innovative practices (Press Information Bureau, 2025).
- **e-National Agriculture Market (e-NAM)**: It was initiated in 2016 as pan-India online trading platform, which integrates national network of existing Agriculture Produce Market Committee (APMC) mandis to provide single national marketplace to agricultural commodities. e-NAM interface facilitates the farmers to get the improved marketing platform to sell their products through online competitive and transparent price discovery mechanism and online payment service (Press Information Bureau, 2024).
- **PM KISAN Samman Nidhi Scheme**: This scheme was initiated in the year 2019 with a single aim to increase the wages of farmers with small farm holdings. As per this scheme, farmers are paid Rs. 6000 each year in 3 instalments. This has so far disbursed over Rs. 3.46 lakh Cr. to the deserving farmers in 18 instalments (Press Information Bureau, 2025).
- **PM-AASHA (Pradhan Mantri Annadata Aay SanraksHan Abhiyan)**: It is a program that fixes remunerative prices to farmers produce and avoids distress sale. It seeks to increase prices safeguarding farmers of Minimum Support Price (MSP) and to enhance support to farmers in terms of prices (Press Information Bureau, 2025).
- **Agriculture Infrastructure Fund (AIF)**: This program was launched with an initial financial outlay of Rs. 1 lakh Cr., to help provide a medium to long-term debt financing channel to finance feasible projects in the area of post-harvest management infrastructure as well as community farming assets under several incentives with an intention to increase the agricultural infrastructure. (Press Information Bureau, 2025).

The previously specified guidelines and programs have profoundly improved the agricultural landscape in India, advocating for fair pricing systems and livelihood continuity for farmers. Yet, there remains a critical need for intensified reforms and strategies to adequately confront the extensive challenges impacting the industry, which include climate unpredictability, soil erosion, and water shortages.

1.1.3 Majors cereals – Wheat and Maize production in India

Wheat and maize are cornerstone crops for India's agriculture. Wheat, a staple food constituting a significant portion of the Indian diet, is crucial for national food security. Maize, a versatile crop with applications in food, animal feed, and industry, including biofuel production and starch manufacturing, plays a distinct role.

Wheat cultivation in India is predominantly concentrated in the northern states, particularly Punjab and Haryana. India's wheat production has significantly increased, making it the second-largest producer globally. In 2024-25, the production of wheat is estimated at 1175 LMT (Lakh Metric Tonnes) compared to 1133 LMT in 2023-24 (Press Information Bureau, 2025) while India exported 1.88 LMT of wheat worth USD 56.7 Mn in 2023-24 reflecting a rising global demand. Extensive research continues to enhance cereal and grain output, solidifying wheat's crucial role in India's food economy (APEDA, 2025).

India, the fifth largest producer (FAO, 2023) and fourteenth largest exporter of maize (UN-COMTRADE, 2022), benefits from year-round production, a robust seed production and marketing network, and sea-port availability, giving it a strategic edge in the international market. However, high domestic demand curtails significant exports. Maize is globally valued for its use as food, feed, fodder, and industrial raw material. In 2024-25, India produced an estimated 422.81 LMT (Press Information Bureau, 2025) and exported 14.42 LMT worth USD 443.5 Mn (APEDA, 2025).

Figure 1. Production of Wheat and Maize

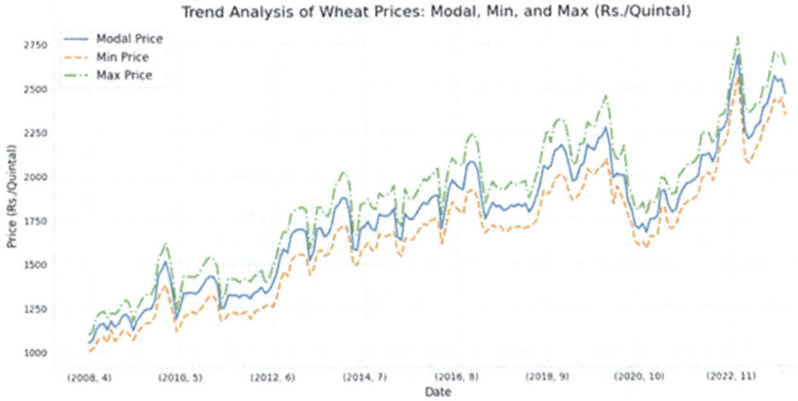

Source: Computed by Author using Python / Economic Survey of India 2023-24

The Figure 1 depicts wheat and maize production from 2014 to 2024, indicating a general upward trend. However, fluctuations in production levels are evident from year to year for both crops.

Figure 2. Yield per Hectare for Wheat and Maize

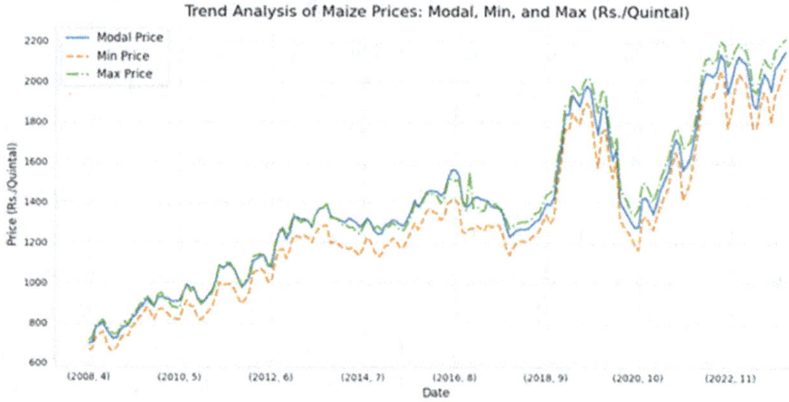

Source: Computed by Author using Python / Economic Survey of India 2023-24

The figure 2 presents yield data (kg/hectare) for wheat and maize from 2014 to 2024. A notable increase in yield is observed for both crops over the decade, indicating improved agricultural practices and technological advancements.

Figure 3. Gross Area of Wheat and Maize Production

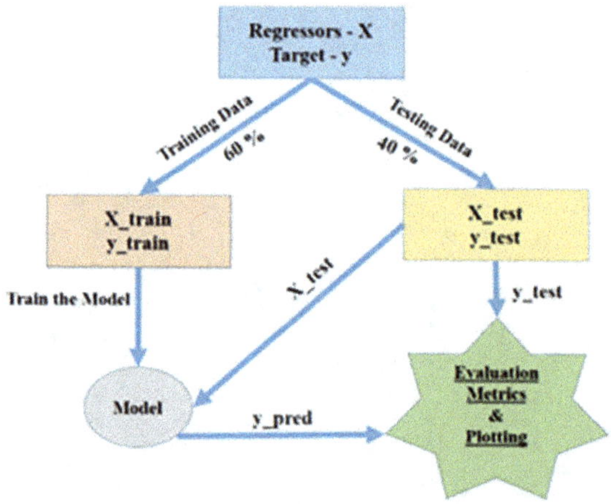

Source: Computed by Author using Python / Economic Survey of India 2023-24

The figure 3 illustrates the cultivated area (million hectares) for wheat and maize from 2014 to 2024. While maize cultivation has expanded significantly over the decade, wheat acreage has shown a more complex pattern. A notable decrease in wheat cultivation occurred between 2017 and 2019, followed by a recovery, but without reaching the same peak as before the decline. The widespread cultivation of these crops across India underscores their significance and justifies our focus on their potential.

We have compiled the Government of India's Minimum Support Prices (MSPs) for wheat and maize from the Economic Survey of India in the Figure 4. This data is crucial for assessing potential government obligations and safeguarding farmers from market price volatility.

Figure 4. MSP trends for Wheat and Maize

Source: Computed by Author using Python / Economic Survey of India 2023-24

MSP, the Minimum Support Price, is crucial for shielding farmers from price fluctuations. Our analysis of government data reveals a consistent increase in MSPs for both wheat and maize, indicating a growing government commitment to supporting these essential crops. The presented data underscores the critical need for accurate crop price prediction models. Such models can benefit a wide range of stakeholders, from farmers to policymakers. To address this need, we employ a combination of machine learning and data science techniques to develop robust predictive models.

1.1.4 Relevance of predicting agricultural crop prices

Enabling farmers, policymakers, and participating organizations to arrive at knowledgeable conclusions about agricultural practices, marketing systems, and supply chain alignment is contingent upon having dependable analyses of crop price trends. Variations in price can profoundly affect farmers' revenue and overall food security, thereby necessitating the creation of dependable predictive models (Banerjee and Mondal, 2023). Estimating future crop prices demands an investigation into likely price points for farming products via statistical analysis and historical data evaluation. Through the explanation of pricing paths and market changes, it equips farmers, investors, and regulatory authorities to take informed actions, lessen risks, and foster stability in the market (Sun et al., 2023).

Forecasting agricultural prices is important for several reasons:

- **Increasing farm income**: The agricultural producers and agri-businesses need to have a clear knowledge and insight of the future prices of their crops and livestock so that they can be in a suitable position to strategize their production operations and make their investment decisions. Accurate price forecasts are essential in yield maximization, minimization of production costs, and improved profit margins (Purohit et al., 2021).
- **Ensuring food security**: Food security requirement of the nation can be addressed through agricultural price prediction. With proper prediction of prices, the government agencies and other international organizations will be able to deploy strategies that would reduce the impact of either food shortages or rise in food prices and thereby avoiding food insecurity.
- **Increased trade**: Agri-prices are often exposed to the factors of the global market and rules of inter-country trade (Dastagiri and Naga Sindhuja, 2021). Price forecasting makes traders and exporters participate in the process of making data-driven decisions when it comes to the acquisition and supply of agricultural products, and as a result, this aspect has an impact on the wider economic environment (Oktoviany et al., 2021).
- **Informed policy making**: The study of price trends in agriculture is a notable factor in the policy formulation. Price forecasting presents a mechanism through which authorities can build schemes of informed strategies around subsidies, tariffs, and pricing policies, which have the capacity to influence substantially the economic prosperity of the farmers and macro-economic system.
- **Risk management**: Effective risk management helps agricultural producers and agribusinesses to adequately deal with the uncertainties associated with the movement in the prices through the application of price forecasting techniques. Good price projections can help these stakeholders to come up with strategies and implement them in the alleviation of risks that are aimed at decreasing potential fiscal imbalances (Zhao, 2021).

1.1.5 Application of Machine Learning (ML) techniques in Crop price prediction

Machine Learning (ML) techniques have become a ubiquitous topic of discussion in agricultural price forecasting as it has the potential to analyse large-scale, multidimensional data and discover complex patterns that the conventional statistical models tend to ignore. Historical prices, weather patterns, consumer demand, and government controls could all be included into ML models to make better and sooner predictions (Pandey et al., 2024; Bhatakar et al., 2024). In contrast to traditional econometric solutions, ML solutions, including Decision Tree Regression, Random, Support Vector Machines, and Neural Network, can accommodate non-linear dependencies and dynamically tune to the changes in the market. These models have outperformed in predicting price patterns of staple crops such as wheat and maize which forms the basis of the Indian food economy and income of its farmers (Bhavani & Vani, 2024).

2. LITERATURE REVIEW

Agricultural pricing estimation has always been a major challenge since it consists of a wide range of factors that affect the market situation including environmental factors, supply chain dynamics, global political affairs as well as diverse economic signals. Conventional forecasting methods are known to be inadequate in explaining such complex effects and inadequately describing the non-linear nature of such effects. Recently, the emergence of the machine learning (ML) approaches has changed this field, bringing in refined tools that are well-skilled at studying large volumes of data and revealing hidden patterns. This literature review examines the applications of machine learning in price forecasting, scrutinizing diverse studies that identify how such enhanced computational models can enhance accuracy in their forecasts, expand market effectiveness, and assist in making ideal decisions by farmers, government, and other stakeholders in the agricultural sector.

A study by Suresh et al. (2019) is dedicated to the issues of using machine learning algorithms to predict the diseases of rice crop with precision and timeliness. The authors examine various machine learning approaches to enhance disease detection and forecasting, and this is essential in the maintenance of the crop vitality and maximisation of yield. Their analysis demonstrates that algorithms like Support Vector Machines (SVM), Random Forest, and Neural Network have the potential of effectively evaluating and processing complex agricultural data to predict outbreaks of diseases. The review points to the strength of these algorithms in terms of accuracy and proficiency of early detection that is essential in timely intervention and effective control of the disease.

G. Hegde, V. R. Hulipalled, and J. B. Simha (2021) research how machine learning (ML) and natural language processing (NLP) may be used to forecast the agricultural commodity prices. This study aims at the use of computational models to conduct an analysis of economic indicators and market trends. Proving that ML and NLP could increase the accuracy of prices predictions, the authors combine structured, like historical prices and Gross Domestic Product (GDP) measures, and unstructured information, like market news and reports. Their results highlight the possibility of these highly sophisticated technologies to provide meaningful information to stakeholders in the field of agriculture, such farmers, policymakers, and investors, and, therefore, empower decision-making processes.

Rakhra et al. (2021) discuss the application of Random Forest and Decision Tree Regression in predicting crop prices noting its importance regarding agricultural decision-making as well as market stability. They stress, Random Forest in ensemble method is useful in generating stable and reliable predictions through averaging several decision trees and minimizing overfitting, and Decision Tree Regression is easy to use and interpret. The authors use different cases to prove that their methods are successful in determining the crop prices since Random Forest is more accurate, and Decision Tree Regression offers the predicting process of easy-to-understand decision pathways. The review finds out that these machine learning techniques have the opportunity to achieve a massive level of improvement in crop prices forecast, which assists in improvement in risk management and strategic planning in agriculture.

In their research, Paul et al. (2022) examine how the machine learning (ML) approaches are used to determine brinjal (eggplant) prices in India, in the state of Odisha. The authors employ various ML algorithms to examine past price data along with other factors with the purpose to increase the precision of price predictions. Their results show that the non-linear and multidimensional relations among multiple factors determining agricultural prices can be well described with the help of the ML techniques. In this study, the researchers highlight that ML can be more reliable and accurate in price forecasts and thus making more informed decisions by farmers, traders and policymakers. The paper confirms the applicability of the advanced computational methods in agricultural forecasting, which points out the viable advantage of such methods in regard to the developing countries.

The article by Hemalatha et al. (2022) is dedicated to the machine learning application used in predicting agricultural yields in India, which is an agricultural country and has agriculture as one of the major activities and sources of income. They examine the performance of some of the ML algorithms such as Logistic Regression (LR), Naive Bayes (NB), Decision Tree (DT), and K-Nearest Neighbours (KNN) to forecast agricultural yields. They point out that machine learning is one of the most crucial decision-making aids to choose and control crops during the growth process. Out of all the algorithms adopted, Logistic Regression had the highest accuracy level of 93.17%, which was better than other methods adopted, hence considered effective in the prediction of crop yields.

Gupta et al. (2022) introduce a machine learning and feature selection-led framework that can be used to improve the accuracy levels when predicting crop yields.

They study the approach of mixing sophisticated machine learning procedures and selection of features to maximize predictive performance. Through the wise choice of the features and the usage of some algorithm, the framework is able to solve the problem of more accurate crop yields forecasting because of Gradient Boosting, Support Vector Machine, and Neural Networks. As pointed out by the authors feature selection is an essential part of ensuring the model accuracy through the removal of irrelevant or redundant data that makes the model better at generalizing and reliably predicting. Gupta et al. (2022) establish that their proposed framework does not only enhance the accuracy of prediction but also allows making decisions regarding the agricultural sphere that can be valuable through the successful planning and management of the agricultural resources by the farmers.

As Deepa et al. (2023) argue, farmers are faced with challenges that come as a result of the volatility of the prices of agricultural commodities whose prices are influenced by weather conditions, diseases in plants, labour costs, production volumes and market forces. The fluctuation of the prices makes it difficult to plan organized farming and marketing by farmers. The authors put forward the application of the algorithms in the machine learning method, such as decision trees, logistic regression, and support vector machines (SVM) when estimating future crop prices. Their paper compares five algorithms which are under supervision and adopted SVM due to the higher results obtained. The data being utilized comprises commodity prices in different states and nutrient contents therein. XGBoost boosting algorithm is also used to further improve the performance of the model thereby showing that machine learning has potential to give realistic price forecasts of the agricultural commodities which is accurate and actionable.

2.1 Comparative synthesis

The recent literature shows that machine learning algorithms (Random Forest, XGBoost, and neural networks) always outperform econometric models (ARIMA and regular regressions) in predicting crop prices, particularly when the nonlinear and multivariate conditions occur (Patil et al., 2023; Mohanty et al., 2023). Although the conventional methods are still highly appreciated due to their interpretability and adoption across the fields, ML methods are more accurate and robust in predicting especially in staple products in India. The comparison of the algorithms shows that the ensemble and boosting models can achieve significant improvements over the previous tree or regression models, which are also supported by international and Indian case studies (Paul et al., 2024; Rakhra et al., 2021).

3. DATA AND METHODS

3.1 Data Sources

We have considered Wheat and Maize for our analysis, which are Rabi and Kharif crops respectively. Kharif and Rabi are the primary agricultural cropping seasons in India. The Kharif season occurs from July to October, while the Rabi season extends from October to March, with wheat being the main crop during this period. Additionally, the crops cultivated between March and June are referred to as summer crops.

We have collected time series data for Wheat and Maize on a daily frequency from Agmarknet portal (https://agmarknet.gov.in/). Agmarknet is an Agricultural Marketing Information System that offers nationwide market information, providing real-time price and arrival data for various commodities falling under the Ministry of Agriculture & Farmers Welfare, Government of India (Agmarknet, 2024).

The data from Agmarknet, covering April 2008 to February 2024, includes columns for District Name, Market Name, Variety, Grade, Price Date, Minimum Price, Modal Price, and Maximum Price. Categorical columns are District Name, Market Name, Variety, and Grade. The Price Date is split into Year and Month, with Year, Month, Min Price, Modal Price, and Max Price as numerical features. In our study we have considered Modal prices as the target variable. Modal price refers to the price at which the majority of transactions occur during the peak marketing period on the day of reporting. (MOSPI, 2010).

3.2 Crop Price Prediction Pipeline: A Structured Methodology

Figure 5. Flowchart for Crop Price Prediction

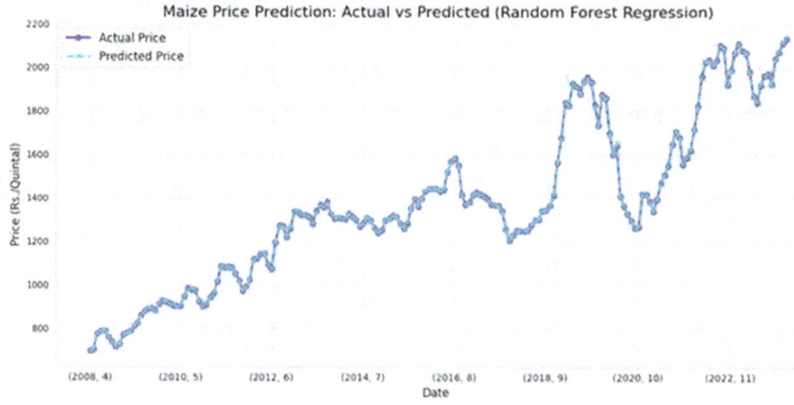

Source: Created by Author

The methodology proposed for the crop price prediction model is illustrated in the Figure 5 flowchart, with a particular focus on data pre-processing and evaluation. The feature engineering steps include imputing missing values and encoding categorical variables using Label Frequency Encoding, which has proven to be the most suitable technique for our dataset. Outliers are then identified and removed based on empirical evidence, contributing to improved model accuracy.

Data Pre-processing and Feature Engineering: The first step in data pre-processing involves appropriately handling missing values through imputation. Label Frequency Encoding is then applied to transform categorical variables, offering an effective representation and enhancing the model's training performance, especially given the predominantly categorical nature of the dataset. Subsequently, outliers are identified and removed based on their demonstrated impact on the data distribution and model accuracy.

Scaling and Feature Selection: Min-Max Scaling is applied to normalize feature values within a specified range, ensuring that all features are on a comparable scale and thereby enhancing model performance. Following normalization, feature selection is conducted to retain only those variables that exhibit a strong correlation with the target variable.

Model Evaluation: Using the pre-processed data, various machine learning models are trained and evaluated. Model performance is assessed through regression metrics, including Root Mean Squared Error (RMSE), Mean Squared Error (MSE), and Mean Absolute Error (MAE). Among the top-performing models, the third model emerges as the optimal choice for addressing the crop price forecasting task.

3.2.1 Linear Regression

Linear regression is an important and prominent technique used in the field of supervised machine learning. It aids in the belief that it establishes how much influence one or more autonomous assortments of variables, commonly referred as predictors, have on a continuous outcome or dependent variable. The methodology works by using linear fit across the data points to explain this relationship.

To allow linear regression to work, certain requirements are to be met. These assumptions involve a direct relationship between the factors, independence of each data point, ordinary distribution (or variance) of errors across all values of the independent factors and insignificant inter-relationship (multicollinearity) amongst the predictors. Failure to meet these assumptions, such as in cases when the data reflects rather non-linear dynamics, significant relationships among components, or when outliers will occur, may skew the inferences that will be made. On this basis, the implementation of diagnostic reviews is of prime importance in facilitating checks as to whether the model can produce believable insights.

Common practices in the formulation of a linear regression model are ordinary least squares (OLS) or gradient descent depending on the magnitude and complexity of the data. The quality of the model is based on the analysis of various parameters like mean squared error (MSE), root mean squared error (RMSE), and R-squared (R^2). Despite its limitations in understanding complex patterns, the linear regression remains a strong and clear tool of explaining continuous outcomes.

3.2.2 Decision Tree Regression

Decision tree regression has a nonparametric implementation that systematically subdivides the feature space into different distinct and neighbouring subsets and offers a smooth prediction to each division. The data is recursively partitioned according to feature limits which most effectively reduce prediction error; out of this, it develops a tree-structured model, whose terminal nodes can be assigned to the final values of input. The directly interpretable nature of its inherently intuitive rule-based framework allows the practitioner to deduce at a glance the impact of the input variables on the outcome of predictions, which makes it specifically beneficial to raising nonlinear interactions without having to manually process the features.

Unlike linear tools, the decision tree regression does not assume anything about the fundamental distribution of data and association between predictors and responses. Instead, it takes a step-by-to step, downward-moving strategy: at each stop it critically analyses all possible separations across all features and selects the one that produces the best decrease in average squared error (MSE). The flexibility of this model enables it to find complex structures; but it exposes the trees to excessive variance and overfitting, particularly when given free rein to expand unfettered by controls.

The decision on the splitting criteria when training a model must be carefully picked, cessation rules are to be defined, diverse pruning approaches are to be considered. The most common hyperparameters include maximum depth of the tree, minimum number of samples per leaf and minimum drop in impurity. These factors are helpful to reduce overfitting by limiting the complexity of the tree. Then, we apply an evaluation of the performance considering the metrics such as MSE, root mean squared error (RMSE), and the R^2 value. Independent validation sets or cross-validation techniques are usually used to estimate generalization error and assist in choosing to prune penalties or complexity parameters.

3.2.3 Random Forest Regression

Random forest regression is a type of ensemble learning which improves predictive power and robustness via an average of the responses produced by large numbers of decision trees. Every tree in the ensemble is grown over a bootstrap sample of the data hence introducing diversity in the training subsets whereas the randomization of features at every branch further decouples the trees. When averaging their estimates, the model reduces variance compared with a single tree, producing more and reliable estimates of continuous outcomes over thousands of problem areas.

Creation of a random forest involves going through the training data multiple times to replace the data and create numerous individual subsets. Each subset is used to form a decision tree by defining the most optimal split of a random subset of features in every node and not trying out all available predictors. The effectiveness of this twofold opportunity of connecting feature and data selection is making sure that the individual trees will only record the different aspects of the structural natures. The final predictions are then obtained based on the average of the leaf-node results across all the trees hence reducing personal tendencies that can arise in each of the trees.

Important hyperparameters affect the running of a random forest regressor how many trees should be used (n estimators), how many features to consider at each split (max features), and the bounds on the tree size which could be max depth or min leaves samples. Terms that conventionally measure the quality of the model are the mean squared error (MSE), root mean squared error (RMSE) and the coefficient of determination (R^2), and out-of-bag (OOB) error estimates offer an internal measure of generalization without requiring a separate validation set. The implementation of cross-validation would provide yet another finishing touch to the choice of hyperparameters, creating a healthy trade-off between bias and variance that would enhance predictive performance.

3.2.4 XGBoost Regression

As an elaborated ensemble technique, the XGBoost (Extreme Gradient Boosting) regression is an improvement to the fundamental ideas of gradient boosting, particularly by the introduction of fitting the follow-up models to the residuals left behind previous models. XGBoost achieves this goal through systematic stage-by-stage building of a sequence of decoupled decision trees and combining them into a weighted sum that results in impressive accuracy, thus taking advantage of momentum that reduces the risk of over fitting, by using express regularization. This state-of-the-art application exploits second-order gradient analytics and uses parallel tree assembly methods to be both robust and efficient under many circumstances in regression.

The training strategy of the models in XGBoost framework basically aims at minimizing a regularized objective function that balances the fit of the model on the real data and its associated complexity. Each round of iteration generates a new decision tree to approximate the negative gradient (residual) of the loss function which is commonly referred to as mean squared error in the case of regression analysis. Regularization elements penalize the depth of trees and the weight of leaves, and thus make the appearance of excessively complex structures discouraged. And additional details, such as shrinkage (learning rate), column subsampling, and cache-conscious block data structures are used to enhance both generalization skill and computational speed.

Essential hyperparameters can significantly influence the processes and performances of XGBoost: they include the number of overall boosting iterations (n_estimators), the length of the max tree (max_depth), the learning rate (eta), and the regularizing constants (lambda for L2 and alpha for L1). The subsampling ratios employed both column-wise and row-wise introduce an element of unpredictability that effectively limits variance and the process of early stopping on the basis of validation outcomes avoids the unnecessary iterations. Performance is evaluated by using measures of mean squared error (MSE), root-mean-square error (RMSE) and R^2 and k-fold cross-validation provides a guiding framework within which hyperparameter tuning is performed, in order to find an optimum bias/variance trade-off.

3.2.5 K-Nearest Neighbours

K-Nearest Neighbours (KNN) regression is a nonparametric and an instance-based learning algorithm which predicts a continuous target by averaging the values of the responses of the closest instances in the feature space. Unlike model-based approaches, KNN never does any processing of its data until the point of prediction and it saves all its training data and uses it to infer the local structure around each of the query points. Its beauty lies with its conceptual simplicity and with the ease with which predictions can be interpreted as weighted averages of actual data.

Prediction by use of KNN regression follows three discrete steps. First, any distance measure, often either Euclidean or Manhattan, is used to determine the similarity of a new datum and each item in the training set. This is followed by finding k observations with the minimum distances by the use of the algorithm. Lastly, it sums up the respective quantities of these observations with a more basic average of a discrete mean or a distance-weighted mean to generate the regression estimate. This local averaging procedure gives KNN the power to generalize arbitrary nonlinear relationships, without requiring feature transformation and without any need to directly fit a model.

Key hyperparameters with KNN: each of the following can be varied: how many neighbours (k) are to be considered, which distance to use (there exist several very useful ones), and to weigh the contributions of neighbours differently. Very small k value gives the most flexible fit that can be too sensitive to noise, and high k provides a smoother, but more biased, estimate. The efficiency of the model is tested with criteria like the mean squared error (MSE), root mean squared error (RMSE) and the coefficient of determination (R^2) and by use of cross-validation in determining the appropriate hyperparameter and in reducing the likelihood of overfitting.

4. ANALYSIS AND FINDINGS

The analysis has established that strong predictive modelling depends on well-prepared data. By means of vigorous pre-processing, feature-engineering, categorical variable label frequency encoding, we have built a powerful dataset. Also, we have been able to increase the reliability of the model by pinpointing and minimizing the effect of multi-collinearity using VIF and heat maps. Then we would pass to the gist of our analysis.

Figure 6. Wheat Price Trends

Source: Computed by Author using Python

The Figure 6 depicts the average modal price trends for the wheat crop over the years following an upward trend.

Figure 7. Maize Price Trends

Source: Computed by Author using Python

The Figure 7 illustrates the average modal price trends for the wheat crop over the years. Similar to wheat, the average modal price for maize has also exhibited an overall upward trajectory during the same period.

4.1 Encoding

Encoding categorical variables is a critical pre-processing step for model development. Given our categorical regressor variables, we explored label encoding, one-hot encoding, and label frequency encoding. While one-hot encoding can lead to dimensionality issues and label encoding might introduce unintended ordinality, label frequency encoding emerged as the most suitable approach based on empirical observations.

4.2 Heat Map and Variance Inflation Factor (VIF)

Assessing feature correlation is crucial for model building. High correlation among features can adversely affect model performance. Thus, maintaining correlations within acceptable limits is essential. Heat maps are employed to visualize correlations among features. High correlation values indicate potential multi-collinearity. To quantify this issue, Variance Inflation Factor (VIF) is calculated for each feature. Elevated VIF values signal the detrimental impact of retaining that feature in the model.

$$VIF = \frac{1}{1 - R^2}$$

R^2 is the correlation among the features observed in the Heat Map.

We are excluding the features 'Min Price' and 'Max Price' from our prediction. These features will not be used in the model so their correlation with other variables including the target variable will not be taken into account in this analysis. We are inclined to learning about how the remaining predictor variables are interrelated with the target variable.

Figure 8. Correlation Heat Map for Crop Wheat

Source: Computed by Author using Python

The Figure 8 is the Heat Map of the Crop Wheat indicating the multi-collinearity between the features in the dataset. It is important to mention that the most correlated column is the Year and Modal Price column, the correlation is 0.64. Due to further checking of the multi-collinearity of the regressors, we are going to look into the measure of Variance Inflation Factor (VIF).

Figure 9. Correlation Heat Map for Crop Maize

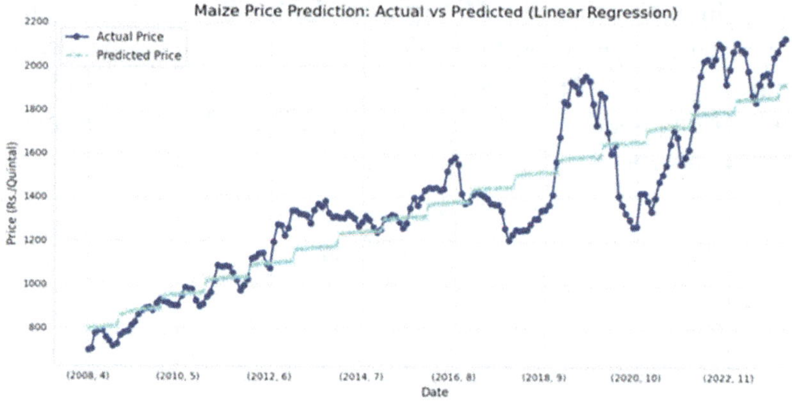

Source: Computed by Author using Python

Figure 9 is the Heat Map of Crop Maize indicator which demonstrates multi-collinearity between the features in the data collection. Remarkably, Year and Modal Price columns have the greatest correlation as displayed in a value of 0.7. In order to have a further movement of multi-collinearity between regressors, we shall consider the VIF factor.

To overcome multi-collinearity, those features with a Variance Inflation Factor (VIF) over 5 would be excluded. In order to determine these characteristics, we will observe the largest values of VIF that were computed using the wheat and maize data sets as provided in Table 1.

Table 1. VIF factors for the highest correlated features for the crops

	Highest Correlation in Heat Map	**VIF (Variance Inflation Factor)**
Wheat Price	0.64	1.6937
Maize Price	0.7	1.9607

Source: Computed by Author using VIF formula

Since the maximum VIF value is less than 2, there's no evidence of significant multicollinearity among the features. This indicates that all features can be retained for further analysis and model building.

4.3 Descriptive Statistics

Table 2. Descriptive Statistics of Feature Variables for Wheat

Features	Min	Max	Mean	SD	Skewness	Kurtosis
District Name	1	35978	8026.22	8454.88	1.83	2.73
Market Name	1	6183	1644.74	1333.5	1.13	0.49
Variety	1	520137	298593.69	231216	-0.15	-1.87
Grade	42	1005039	995317.57	97885.8	-9.97	97.40
Month	1	12	6.43	3.37	0.07	-1.15
Year	2008	2024	2018.53	4.57	-0.90	-0.50
Min Price (Rs./Quintal)	0	122336	1795.00	478.51	18.94	4208.03
Max Price (Rs./Quintal)	0	222001	2015.34	681.82	73.92	20207.64
Mod Price (Rs./Quintal)	1	63869	1907.18	496.03	7.01	717.49

Source: Computed by Author using Python

Table 3. Descriptive Statistics of Feature Variables for Maize

Features	Min	Max	Mean	SD	Skewness	Kurtosis
District Name	1	24915	9764.59	6459.37	0.59	-0.46
Market Name	1	9619	2169.8	1549.55	1.7	5.08
Variety	1	418139	232584.55	156838.5	0.19	-1.7
Grade	1288	967049	895176.78	243156	-3.09	7.55
Month	1	12	6.74	3.64	-0.1	-1.31
Year	2008	2024	2016.27	4.54	-0.21	-1.11
Min Price (Rs./Quintal)	0	141700	1307.67	478.98	24.74	7030.89
Max Price (Rs./Quintal)	0	1411416	1430.84	1473.85	833.67	796621.3
Mod Price (Rs./Quintal)	1	148300	1401.89	458.53	32.81	10036.55

Source: Computed by Author using Python

From Table 2 and Table 3, we can identify the disparity in the Min values and the Max values etc. Also the skewness and Kurtosis values indicate the Presence of Outliers. We go ahead with Scaling and Outlier removal for resolving the disparity issues and the skewness issues.

4.4 Analysis after Outlier Removal and Scaling

Multiple scaling methods, including Min-Max, Standard, Robust, Power Transformation (Yeo-Johnson, Box-Cox), and Quantile Transformation (Uniform, Normal), were applied to the wheat crop data.

Table 4. Impact of Various Scaling Methods on R^2 Score for Wheat Crop with Outliers

	Min-Max	Standard	Robust	Power	Quantile (Uniform)	Quantile (Normal)
Linear Regression	0.4733	0.4733	0.4733	0.4684	0.4635	0.4615
Decision Tree	0.8392	0.8391	0.8391	0.8394	0.8387	0.8391
Random Forest	0.8687	0.8687	0.8687	0.8687	0.8688	0.8687
XG-Boost	0.8484	0.8484	0.8531	0.8531	0.8534	0.8486
KNN	0.8473	0.8474	0.8472	0.8472	0.8456	0.8516

Source: Computed by Author using Python

Table 5. Impact of Various Scaling Methods on R^2 Score for Wheat Crop without Outliers

	Min-Max	Standard	Robust	Power	Quantile (Uniform)	Quantile (Normal)
Linear Regression	**0.5593**	0.5593	0.5593	0.5575	0.5551	0.5508
Decision Tree	**0.9418**	0.9418	0.9418	0.9418	0.9417	0.9415
Random Forest	**0.9455**	0.9455	0.9455	0.9455	0.9455	0.9455
XG-Boost	**0.9221**	0.9221	0.9221	0.9221	0.9223	0.9223
KNN	**0.9216**	0.9213	0.9212	0.9215	0.9209	0.9227

Source: Computed by Author using Python

From both the tables with and without outliers we can draw a very significant conclusion. Presence of outliers gave us a mediocre performance, while removing outliers gave a better performance by almost all the models excluding Linear Regression. This indicates that may be our data is not suitable for a Linear Model. We can also observe that almost all the scaling methods are giving similar results. So, we proceeded with Min-Max Scaling method.

$$Min - Max\ Scaling\ X' = \frac{X - X_{min}}{X_{max} - X_{min}}$$

Feature Selection

Feature selection is critical for optimizing model performance. By identifying and retaining only the most relevant features from a dataset, particularly when dealing with high dimensionality, we can enhance model efficiency, interpretability, and accuracy while mitigating overfitting. We have utilized Forward Stepwise Selection, although there are various feature selection techniques available, including Forward Selection, Backward Selection, and their respective stepwise approaches.

Forward Stepwise selection

Forward Stepwise selection is a sequential model building technique that iteratively adds the most significant predictor to the model at each step. Beginning with an empty model, the process continues until a predefined stopping criterion, such as maximizing R-squared or minimizing residual sum of squares, is met. This method offers computational efficiency compared to alternative approaches.

Table 6. Feature Importance Scores

Features	Wheat Crop	Maize Crop
Year	0.5167	0.6107
Market Name	0.5470	0.6154
District Name	0.5564	0.6159
Month	0.5591	0.6164
Variety	0.5604	0.6162
Grade	0.5604	0.6164

Source: Computed by Author using Python

Given the insignificant differences in feature importance scores, it appears that all features contribute relatively equally to the model's predictions.

Prior to delving into model performance, it's crucial to highlight key trends in the data. A consistent upward trajectory is evident in the average prices of all crops over the analysed period, encompassing both minimum, modal, and maximum price values.

Figure 10. Price Comparison over the years for Wheat Crop

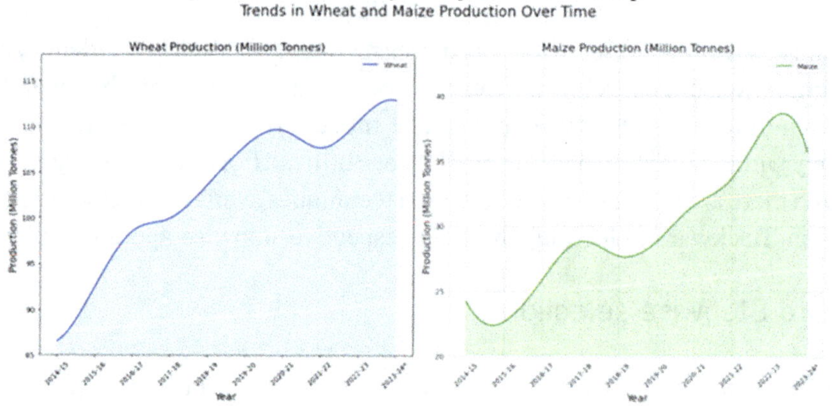

Source: Computed by Author using Python

Figure 11. Price Comparison over the years for Maize Crop

Source: Computed by Author using Python

Both datasets exhibit a consistent upward trend across minimum, modal, and maximum prices, indicating a synchronized price increase over time.

To visually assess the model's performance, we will create visualizations for each crop. These plots will compare actual and predicted values, providing insights into the model's accuracy and any potential discrepancies.

Figure 12. Model Training and Evaluation Workflow

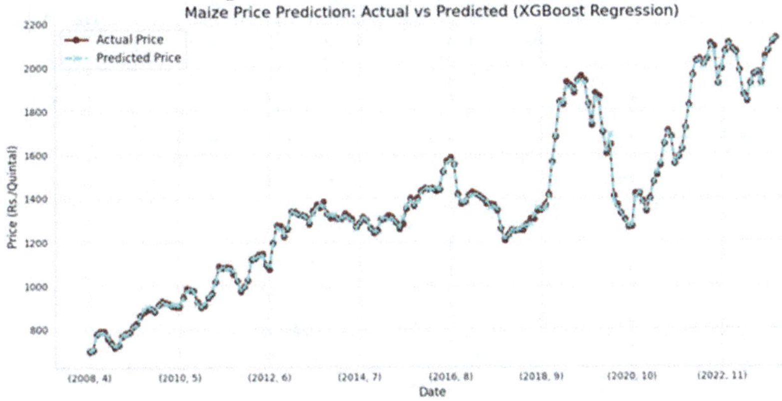

Source: Created by Author

From the figure we can understand how the models are evaluated. We use the testing set once the model has been trained in order to differentiate between real and anticipated values. We use *X_train* and *y_train* to train the model after splitting the data into training (*X_train, y_train*) and testing (*X_test, y_test*) sets. Next, we use *X_test* to predict *y_pred*. Our expected and actual values are shown by the *y_pred* and *y_test* values, respectively.

To visualize the model's performance over time, we'll utilize the 'Year' and 'Month' columns as timestamps. Given the dataset's geographical breadth, multiple instances of the same year and month combination exist across different districts and markets. To accurately capture trends, we'll aggregate the data by grouping and averaging values for each unique year-month combination. By plotting these aggregated actual and predicted values, we can effectively assess the model's ability to forecast price trends.

The conclusion of our modelling will be in the model performance results. The majority of models exhibited high-prediction powers with linear regressions as the only exception. The comprehensive analysis of both models operating in different crops will be carried out.

Table 7. Performance for various models for Crop Wheat

	Linear Regression	Decision Tree	Random Forest	XGBoost	KNN
MAE	217.1593	55.3999	**54.9084**	79.2496	65.2571
RMSE	289.1395	105.0514	**101.6178**	121.5414	121.8772
R^2	0.5593	0.9418	**0.9455**	0.9221	0.9216

Source: Computed by Author using Python

Figure 13. Actual Vs Predicted Prices for Crop Wheat

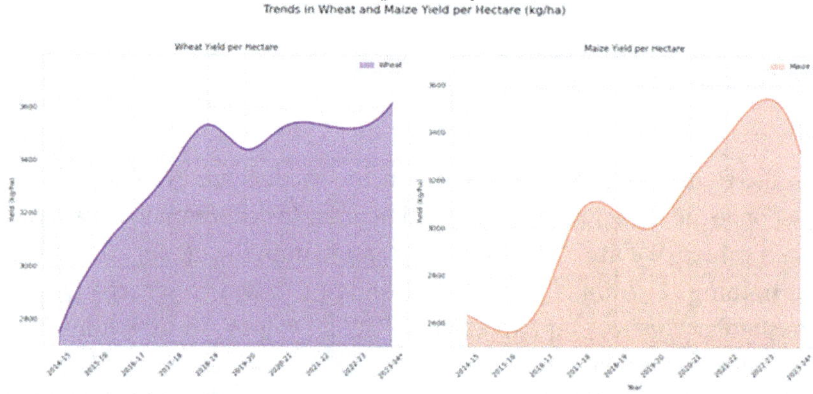

Source: Computed by Author using Python

The Random Forest model exhibits exceptional performance, achieving an R^2 value of 0.9455. The consistency between predicted and actual values in the plot also proves the usefulness of the model in forecasting crop prices.

Table 8. Performance for various models for Crop Maize

	Linear Regression	Decision Tree	Random Forest	XGBoost	KNN
MAE	190.7412	49.1382	**48.5636**	77.1135	58.4189
RMSE	255.5482	91.8074	**88.5446**	114.1908	107.2141
R^2	0.6177	0.9506	**0.9541**	0.9236	0.9327

Source: Computed by Author using Python

Figure 14. Actual Vs Predicted Prices for Crop Maize

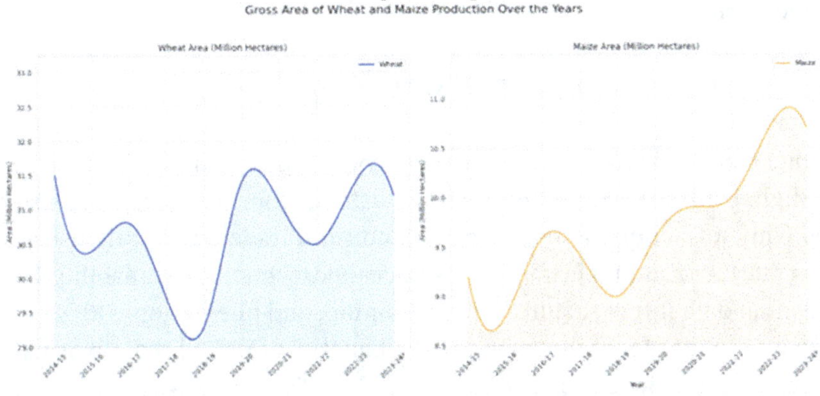

Source: Computed by Author using Python

The performance of the Random Forest model of maize proves to be very good as it has an R^2 value of 0.9541. The alignment between the formula and observed values in the plot adds further strength in proving the precision of the model in predicting the price of maize.

4.5 Practical Case Studies

Farmer Producer Organisations (FPOs) and commodity trading firms in India are now using ML price forecasts to plan purchases and negotiate contracts. As an example, supply chains of government organizations such as the Food Corporation of India (FCI) incorporate predictive models, which enhance logistics planning and release MSP prices through the use of forecasting, while insurance companies rely on prediction to optimize premium rates under PMFBY and other programs (Hamzah et al., 2025; Press Information Bureau, 2025). The actionable price forecasts can help farmers in smarter planting choices, risk reduction and the capability to exploit the digital market platforms such as e-NAM (National Agriculture Market), an online trading platform for agricultural commodities in India.

4.6 Managerial Implications — Practical Insights

The robust performance of Random Forest and XGBoost models delivers actionable intelligence for supply chain managers, government policy planners, and insurance actuaries. Timely and accurate forecasts allow intervention—for instance, targeted MSP adjustments during extreme price volatility, or optimization of crop insurance pools to safeguard farmer incomes. Adoption can be furthered by rural digital literacy programs and public-private partnerships to democratize access to predictive analytics for smallholders (Press Information Bureau, 2025; World Economic Forum, 2021).

4.7 Adoption Challenges and Data Gaps

Despite technical advances, adoption barriers remain. Limited data granularity, patchy digital infrastructure, and farmer mistrust impede widespread use of ML models. Only a fraction of smaller FPOs and rural traders currently use advanced analytics, due to constraints in training resources and technology availability. Expanded investment in data infrastructure, farmer training, and integration with government schemes is essential for mainstreaming the benefits of price predictive analytics in Indian agriculture (Banerjee & Mondal, 2023; APEDA, 2024)

5. CONCLUSION

The agricultural sector of India, a backbone of the country and a backbone of the food security, has been marked by huge issues, one of them being the agricultural income volatility on the part of the farmers. To counter such threats, it is important to be on point when it comes to crop price forecasting to streamline production choices as well as make the sector resilient. The proposed study will implement a rich data-driven methodology, which incorporates superior machine learning strategies, to arrive at price-predicting models of wheat and maize. The Random Forest models which have performed outstandingly with R-squared of 0.9455 and 0.9541 reveal vital information to the stakeholders. These models could help farmers make their choices through more accurate price forecasts, which could help them manage their risks as well as stabilize their income and, in the end, the Indian agricultural sector will become more equal and prosperous.

Additionally, the results can apply towards creation of effective agriculture policy including price stabilization systems, crop failure warning systems and interventions to help vulnerable farm populations. This research will help in making of a robust agricultural sector through evidence-based policymaking. Though the given study is concentrated on wheat and maize, the process may be adopted to other crops, and it can serve as an effective generalized method of crop price forecasting in India.

The results establish the superiority of ensemble ML methods in predicting crop prices under Indian conditions, surpassing prior approaches reported in the literature, and demonstrating tangible benefits for stakeholders. Unique to this research is the integration of data from diverse national sources, advanced preprocessing, and direct linkage of model outputs to procurement and risk management decisions. Future research could incorporate volatility modelling (GARCH), stress-testing

(Monte Carlo), and field validation pilots to further enhance reliability and policy relevance (Banerjee & Mondal, 2023; Xu & Zhang, 2022). Persistent challenges include fragmented market data, limited digital infrastructure in rural areas, and the need for greater farmer training in AI applications.

6. FUTURE DIRECTIONS

- **Advanced Volatility Modelling and Economic Risk Assessment**: Future research efforts should aim at integrating advanced volatility models, e.g. Generalized Autoregressive Conditional Heteroskedasticity GARCH and stochastic volatility models and extreme value theory, in the agricultural price prediction to directly measure and predict market risk. Use of conditional heteroscedasticity models alongside with machine learning regressors will enable the analysts to develop probabilistic price distributions as an alternative to point estimates. Through the analysis of Value-at-Risk (VaR) and Conditional Value-at-Risk (CVaR) of the projected prices, the stakeholders will acquire the power to assess any chances of financial condition in sensitive market conditions. Integration of these risk assessments with the economic scenario forms that are loaded with capabilities of depicting the interest rate shocks, currency fluctuations, or any changes in input prices will facilitate more robust decision making within the agricultural value chain.
- **End-to-End Integration with Hedging and Derivative Instruments**: To make forecasts influential in transforming risk management strategies which can be implemented, it is imperative to integrate agricultural price models with financial tools of hedging. It is observed that the predicted data streams create the real-time benchmarks that guide the successful positioning within the commodity futures, options, and weather derivatives by involving stakeholders e.g. farmers, traders, and cooperatives (Farmer Producer Organisations).
- **Macro-Financial Linkages and Policy Variables**: Macroeconomic determinants and policy provisions play a dominant role in determining the economic vulnerabilities linked with agriculture. The new methods of prediction must include the key indicators, such as GDP growth rates, inflation rates, exchange rates and global commodity standards to depict the changes in demand patterns and the interdependence of markets. Policy announcements (such as changes to minimum support prices, the implementation of export restrictions and the doling out of subsides) may be undertaken in form of exogenous variables or regime-switch triggers in a model thereby making it easier to recalibrate a forecast quickly. One could develop a better understand-

ing of the relationship that exists between price changes and policy changes using the vector autoregressive (VAR) methods or structural break detection techniques.

- **Scenario Analysis and Stress Testing Frameworks**: Besides deterministic forecasts, methodologies employed when predicting crop prices ought to include plans of scenario-analyses that simulate the impact of severe events, including droughts, floods, pest attacks, or geopolitical sanctions on the price dynamics. The Monte Carlo simulation and agent-based modelling approaches have the ability to provide probabilistic projections of a set of "what-if" situations which can help the farmers and policymakers in setting up their strategies. Bringing ideas of climate change to bear on supply-chain analysis can increase the legitimacy of such stress analysis, and eventually reveal the underlying weaknesses within the local farming markets.
- **Stakeholder-Centric Risk Transfer Mechanisms**: The next stage of study has to combine predictions and analytics with the risk-transfer solutions that are inclusive of smallholder farmers and agribusinesses through smart contracts (blockchain technology) and parametric insurance. Assimilation of machine learning forecasts into warehouse-receipt financing and contract-farming contracts will aid the design of a collateral in a manner that will enhance the certainty of lenders and broaden the access of credit to more vulnerable farming societies.
- **Policy Impact Evaluation and Welfare Analysis**: Finally, crop price forecasting should be employed to evaluate the welfare effects of several policy options. The counterfactual simulations, consisting of the comparison of the projected price development under and the absence of the suggested modifications in the setting of minimum support prices (MSP), amendments to tariffs, or input subsidies, may give invaluable information to cost-benefit analysis, social welfare estimation.

By incorporating future crop prices estimation in the fields of risk management and economic analysis, scholars and practitioners of the industry would not only create a mechanism that projects prices in a manner that is considerably accurate but also enables interested parties to manage market risks, develop comprehensive hedging strategies and the creation of knowledge-based agricultural policies. The combination of economic theories with machine learning models can create an environment that supports the growth of agricultural markets that herald to soundness, equity, and sustainability.

REFERENCES

Agmarknet. (2024). *Agmarknet: Agricultural Marketing Information System*. https://agmarknet.gov.in

APEDA. (2024). *Monthly statistics*. https://apeda.gov.in/apedawebsite/Statistics/Monthly_Statistics.htm

Banerjee, S., & Mondal, A. C. (2023). An ingenious method for estimating future crop prices that emphasises machine learning and deep learning models. *International Journal of Information Technology : an Official Journal of Bharati Vidyapeeth's Institute of Computer Applications and Management*, *15*(8), 4291–4313. DOI: 10.1007/s41870-023-01474-6

Bhatakar, A., Tayde, L., Raut, S., Pakhare, A., & Bawsakar, T. (2024). Agriculture crop price prediction using machine learning. *International Journal of Innovative Ideas in Research and Development*, *9*(2), 1–10. https://ijiird.com/wp-content/uploads/090205.pdf

Bhavani, K. G., & Vani, N. (2024). Artificial intelligence driven crop price and yield prediction using ML for sustainable agriculture. *International Journal of Engineering and Science*, *12*(1), 45–58. https://theaspd.com/index.php/ijes/article/download/1112/838/2169

Dastagiri, M. B., & Naga Sindhuja, P. V. (2021). Global agricultural prices and policies during WTO regime: Explorative research to price policy advocacy. *World Food Policy*, *7*(1), 6–25. DOI: 10.1002/wfp2.12023

Deepa, K., Karthi, M., Kavin, P., Rahulsankar, S., & Vengaimani, E. (2023). A prediction system for agricultural crops using supervised learning. In *Lecture Notes on Data Engineering and Communications Technologies* (Vol. 141, pp. 433–444). DOI: 10.1007/978-981-19-3035-5_33

Economic Survey (2023–2024). *Economic Survey 2023–24*. Ministry of Finance, Government of India. https://www.indiabudget.gov.in/economicsurvey/doc/echapter.pdf

Food and Agriculture Organization (FAO). (2023). *FAOSTAT: Production of maize*. https://www.fao.org/faostat/en/#data/QC

Government of India. (2010). *Manual on agricultural prices and marketing*. Ministry of Statistics and Programme Implementation. https://www.mospi.gov.in/sites/default/files/publication_reports/manual_agr_price_mark_25oct10_0.pdf

Gupta, S., Kumar, P., Singh, A., & Sharma, R. (2022). Machine learning-and feature selection-enabled framework for accurate crop yield prediction. *Journal of Food Quality*, *2022*, 6293985. Advance online publication. DOI: 10.1155/2022/6293985

Hamzah, M., Ahmed, S. F., & Sakthi, P. (2025). FutureCrop: AI-powered price prediction for agriculture and vegetable markets. *International Journal of Scientific Development and Research*, *10*(4), c528–c534. https://ijsdr.org/papers/IJSDR2504268.pdf

Hegde, G., Hulipalled, V. R., & Simha, J. B. (2021). Price prediction of agriculture commodities using machine learning and NLP. In *2021 Second International Conference on Smart Technologies in Computing, Electrical and Electronics (ICSTCEE)* (pp. 1–6). IEEE. DOI: 10.1109/ICSTCEE54422.2021.9708582

Hemalatha, S., Kavitha, T., Saravanan, T. M., Chithra, K., & Dinesh, N. (2022). Forecasting crop using machine learning model. In *IEEE 3rd International Conference on Electronics and Sustainable Communication Systems (ICESC)* (pp. 783–788). IEEE. DOI: 10.1109/ICESC54411.2022.9885377

Mohanty, M. K., Guha Thakurta, P. K., & Kar, S. (2023). Agricultural commodity price prediction model: A machine learning framework. *Neural Computing & Applications*, *35*(20), 15109–15128. DOI: 10.1007/s00521-023-08528-7

Oktoviany, P., Knobloch, R., & Korn, R. (2021). A machine learning-based price state prediction model for agricultural commodities using external factors. *Decisions in Economics and Finance*, *44*(2), 1063–1085. DOI: 10.1007/s10203-021-00354-7

Pandey, S., Tanvar, A., Lokhande, J., Thorat, P., & Jadhav, H. (2024). Crop price prediction system using ML. *International Journal of Research Publication and Reviews*, *5*(5), 2461–2466. https://ijrpr.com/uploads/V5ISSUE5/IJRPR27405.pdf

Patil, A., Shah, D., Shah, A., & Kotecha, R. (2023). Forecasting prices of agricultural commodities using machine learning for global food security: Towards Sustainable Development Goal 2. *International Journal of Engineering Trends and Technology*, *71*(12), 277–291. DOI: 10.14445/22315381/IJETT-V71I12P226

Patil, P., Athavale, P., Bothara, M., Tambolkar, S., & More, A. (2023). Crop selection and yield prediction using machine learning approach. *Current Agriculture Research Journal*, *11*(3), 968–980. Advance online publication. DOI: 10.12944/CARJ.11.3.26

Paul, R. K., Shankar, S. V., & Yeasin, M. (2024). Forecasting area and yield of cereal crops in India: Intelligent choices among stochastic, machine learning and deep learning techniques. *Proceedings of the Indian National Science Academy. Part A, Physical Sciences*, *91*(2), 549–555. DOI: 10.1007/s43538-024-00345-3

Paul, R. K., Yeasin, M., Kumar, P., Kumar, P., Balasubramanian, M., Roy, H. S., Paul, A. K., & Gupta, A. (2022). Machine learning techniques for forecasting agricultural prices: A case of brinjal in Odisha, India. *PLoS One*, *17*(7), e0270553. Advance online publication. DOI: 10.1371/journal.pone.0270553 PMID: 35793366

Press Information Bureau. (2024, February 20). *e-NAM: Transforming agricultural trade into a seamless experience* [Fact sheet]. Government of India. https://www.pib.gov.in/FactsheetDetails.aspx?Id=149061

Press Information Bureau. (2024, December 18). *Empowering farmers through PM-AASHA: In Rabi 2023-24, 6.41 LMT of pulses procured, benefiting 2.75 lakh farmers* [Backgrounder]. Government of India. https://www.pib.gov.in/PressNoteDetails.aspx?NoteId=153579&ModuleId=3

Press Information Bureau. (2025, February 11). *Farmers' welfare measures* [Press release]. Government of India. https://www.pib.gov.in/PressReleasePage.aspx?PRID=2101841

Press Information Bureau. (2025, February 17). *Pradhan Mantri Fasal Bima Yojana turns nine: Empowering annadata & protecting livelihoods* [Press release]. Government of India. https://www.pib.gov.in/PressReleasePage.aspx?PRID=2104175

Press Information Bureau. (2025, May 28). *Ministry of Agriculture & Farmers Welfare releases third advance estimates of major crop production for 2024–25* [Press release]. Government of India. https://www.pib.gov.in/PressReleseDetail.aspx?PRID=2132263

Purohit, S. K., Panigrahi, S., Sethy, P. K., & Behera, S. K. (2021). Time series forecasting of price of agricultural products using hybrid methods. *Applied Artificial Intelligence*, *35*(15), 1388–1406. DOI: 10.1080/08839514.2021.1981659

Rakhra, M., Singh, S., & Singh, G. (2021). Crop price prediction using random forest and decision tree regression: A review. *Materials Today: Proceedings*. Advance online publication. DOI: 10.1016/j.matpr.2021.03.261

Saxena, R., Paul, R. K., Pavithra, S., Singh, N. P., & Kumar, R. (2019). *Market intelligence in India: Methods and effectiveness of agricultural commodity price forecasts. Policy Paper 34, ICAR-National Institute of Agricultural Economics and Policy Research*. NIAP.

Sun, F., Meng, X., Zhang, Y., Wang, Y., Jiang, H., & Liu, P. (2023). Agricultural product price forecasting methods. *Agriculture*, *13*(9), 1671. Advance online publication. DOI: 10.3390/agriculture13091671

Suresh, C., Kamakshaiah, K., Thatavarti, S., Kumar, P. S., & Ramasubbareddy, S. (2019). Accurate and timely prediction of rice crop disease by means of machine learning algorithms. *International Journal of Advanced Science and Technology*, *28*(13), 662–672.

United Nations Commodity Trade Statistics Database (UN-COMTRADE). (2022). *Trade data for maize*. https://comtrade.un.org/

Wang, Y., Zhang, Q., Yu, F., Zhang, N., Zhang, X., Li, Y., Wang, M., & Zhang, J. (2024). Progress in Research on Deep Learning-Based Crop Yield Prediction. *Agronomy (Basel)*, *14*(10), 2264. DOI: 10.3390/agronomy14102264

World Economic Forum. (2021). *Artificial Intelligence for Agriculture Innovation*. Centre for the Fourth Industrial Revolution India. https://www3.weforum.org/docs/WEF_Artificial_Intelligence_for_Agriculture_Innovation_2021.pdf

Xu, X., & Zhang, Y. (2022). Commodity price forecasting via neural networks for coffee, corn, cotton, oats, soybeans, soybean oil, sugar, and wheat. *Intelligent Systems in Accounting, Finance & Management*, *29*(3), 169–181. DOI: 10.1002/isaf.1519

Zhao, H. (2021). Futures price prediction of agricultural products based on machine learning. *Neural Computing & Applications*, *33*(3), 837–850. DOI: 10.1007/s00521-020-05250-6

APPENDIX

Figure 15. Actual Vs Predicted Prices for Crop Wheat (Linear Regression)

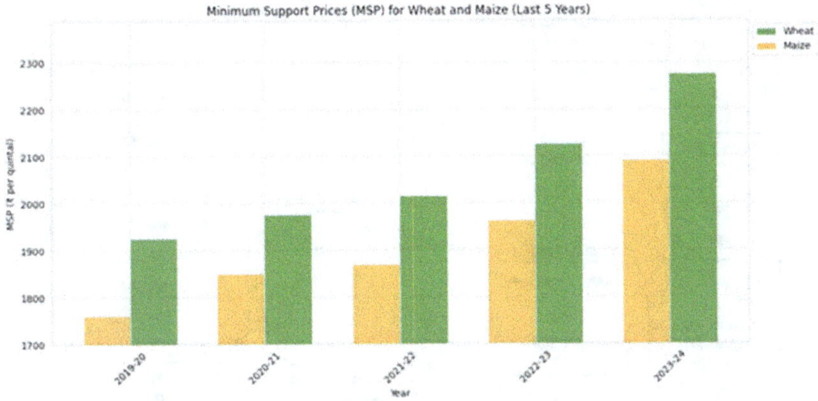

Figure 16. Actual Vs Predicted Prices for Crop Wheat (Decision Tree Regression)

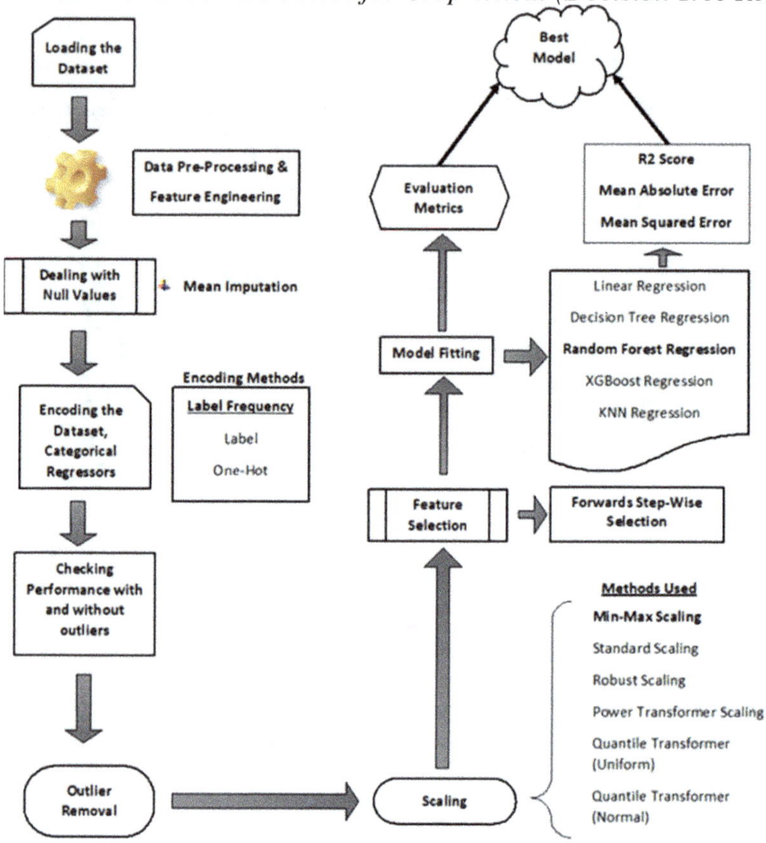

Figure 17. Actual Vs Predicted Prices for Crop Wheat (XGBoost Regression)

Figure 18. Actual Vs Predicted Prices for Crop Wheat (KNN Regression)

Figure 19. Actual Vs Predicted Prices for Crop Maize (Linear Regression)

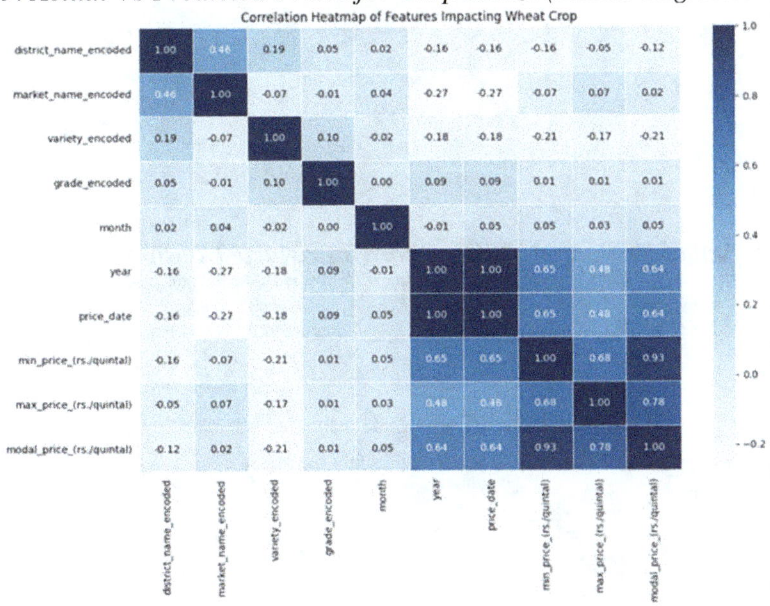

Figure 20. Actual Vs Predicted Prices for Crop Maize (Decision Tree Regression)

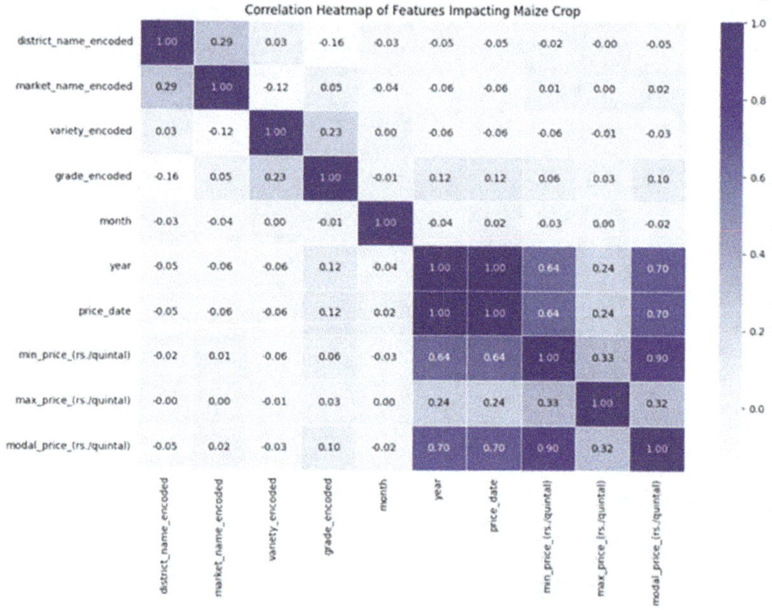

Figure 21. Actual Vs Predicted Prices for Crop Maize (XGBoost Regression)

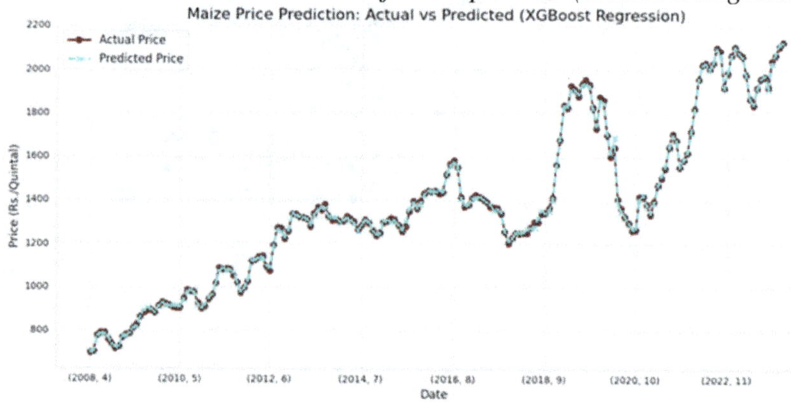

Figure 22. Actual Vs Predicted Prices for Crop Maize (KNN Regression)

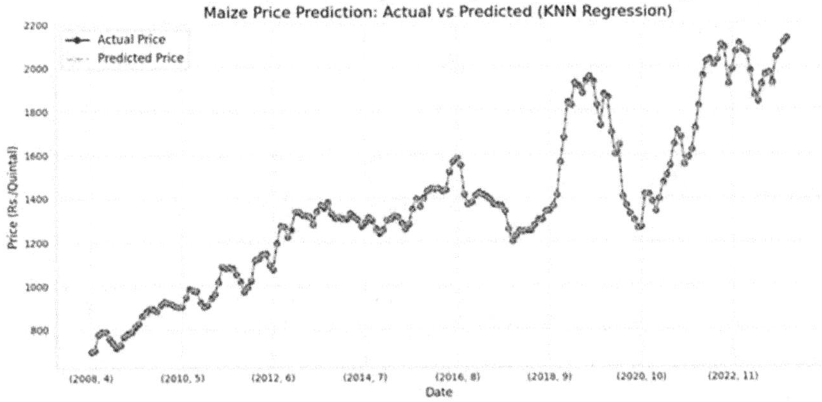

Chapter 11
Artificial Intelligence and Migration Forecasting:
Adapting Predictive Models to Sudden Economic and Humanitarian Shocks

Zyed Achour
http://orcid.org/0000-0002-1578-9062
National Institute of Labor and Social Studies, University of Carthage, Tunisia

ABSTRACT

This chapter examines the role of artificial intelligence (AI) in forecasting migration during sudden crises such as wars, pandemics, and climate disasters. Traditional models struggle to anticipate rapid changes due to reliance on stable historical data. AI approaches—like machine learning and hybrid systems—can process diverse, real-time data (e.g., social media, mobile tracking, satellite images), offering better adaptability. Case studies (Syria, COVID-19, climate migration) show promising results but also highlight ethical and practical challenges: data quality, algorithmic bias, and lack of transparency. The chapter calls for explainable AI (XAI), strong data governance, and interdisciplinary collaboration to ensure fair, responsible, and effective migration forecasting.

INTRODUCTION

Anticipating international migratory flows is now a major strategic challenge for public policy, international governance, and socio-economic planning. Since the end of the 20th century, major crises, whether of geopolitical, health, or envi-

DOI: 10.4018/979-8-3373-3053-2.ch011

ronmental origin, have multiplied and generated massive population displacements on a regional and global scale. Recent examples of the war in Syria, the COVID-19 pandemic, and natural and climatic disasters (cyclones, droughts, and floods) illustrate the speed and scale of these shifts, as well as the growing difficulty for international institutions and states to anticipate and respond effectively. For example, the Internal Displacement Monitoring Centre (IDMC, 2023) estimates that climate-related impacts contribute to the displacement of 20 million people each year. The COVID-19 pandemic, meanwhile, has disrupted global migration trajectories, temporarily reducing flows in 2020 but subsequently exacerbating economic and health vulnerabilities in many parts of the world (OECD, 2021).

In this context of increased instability, accurately forecasting migratory flows is becoming a pressing challenge. Indeed, anticipating how the volume and nature of these flows will evolve is essential to adapt our reception systems, adjust integration policies, and quickly mobilise the necessary resources, such as accommodation, infrastructure, and social and medical assistance. However, traditional statistical anticipation tools, which rely mainly on the analysis of time series and structural indicators such as GDP, unemployment, or recorded conflicts, show their limitations when it comes to modelling the emergence or propagation of unforeseen shocks. In times of crisis, these methods struggle to take into account the non-linearity, volatility, uncertainty, and inertia that characterise human and social dynamics. This discrepancy between the need for forecasts and the capabilities of current tools represents a real methodological gap, often highlighted in academic literature and reports from institutions such as the UN, the OECD, and the World Bank.

Artificial intelligence (AI) and machine learning (ML) are emerging as promising alternatives. These tools have the advantage of storing and processing huge volumes of diverse data—whether economic, political, environmental, or behavioural—thus paving the way for a new generation of adaptive predictive models. Thanks to machine learning, they not only allow for the cross-referencing of different sets of indicators but also for the continuous adjustment of forecasts based on rapidly changing contexts. Furthermore, the integration of unconventional data from social media, mobile telephony, or satellite imagery can compensate for delays or gaps in official statistics. It is also important to note that the increasing complexity of these models, their often opaque "black box" nature, and their dependence on data availability and quality raise new challenges in terms of ethics, interpretation, and governance. Against this background, the central research question guiding this chapter is: *How does artificial intelligence transform the nature, mechanisms, and governance of migration forecasting in times of crisis?* We hypothesize that AI-based models, by integrating diverse and real-time data, not only enhance predictive accuracy but also redefine the epistemological foundations of migration forecasting—from static extrapolation to adaptive, self-learning prediction.

This chapter aims to critically explore, in light of recent research, how artificial intelligence can improve our ability to anticipate sudden changes in migration dynamics, especially compared to traditional statistical methods. In the first section, we will examine the foundations, contributions, and limitations of classical forecasting approaches. The second section focuses on the methodological innovations that artificial intelligence brings to the migration field, as well as the technical and conceptual challenges they pose. The third section highlights the ability of AI models to adapt to abrupt shocks, such as armed conflicts, pandemics, or environmental crises, drawing on several case studies to illustrate both the potential and vulnerabilities of these tools in times of crisis. Finally, the fourth section discusses the ethical and practical issues related to this change: the quality and availability of data during emergencies, the lack of transparency in algorithms, the risks of bias and discrimination, and the trustworthiness of institutional actors. The chapter concludes with a series of recommendations aimed at promoting responsible and inclusive governance of these technologies, emphasizing the thoughtful integration of innovation, the development of explainable and robust tools, and the strengthening of interdisciplinary dynamics. With this approach, we hope to offer not only an updated synthesis of advances in the field of migration forecasting by AI, but also a critical perspective on its potential and limitations in the context of sudden crises, in the service of research and public decision-making in the digital age.

MAPPING TRADITIONAL MIGRATION FORECASTING METHODS: STRENGTHS AND LIMITATIONS

Before addressing the statistical and computational models used to forecast migration, it is important to recall the main theoretical foundations that have historically guided the study of human mobility. Early approaches such as Ravenstein's *"Laws of Migration"* (1889) and Lee's push–pull model (1966) emphasized the interplay between factors of attraction and repulsion shaping migration decisions. Later, neoclassical and new economics of labor migration theories (Todaro, 1969; Stark & Bloom, 1985) introduced economic rationality and household strategies as explanatory frameworks. Structural and network-based approaches further expanded this view by highlighting cumulative causation (Massey et al., 1993) and social embeddedness (Granovetter, 1985) as key drivers of migration systems. These theoretical contributions form the conceptual backbone against which both traditional and AI-based forecasting models can be interpreted, as they each attempt—albeit through different epistemologies—to capture and anticipate human mobility under changing global conditions.

The Foundations of Classical Methodologies

Migration forecasting has long relied on traditional statistical methods, which rely primarily on time series analysis, demographic models, and multivariate econometric analyses. In the following, we provide a map of the most commonly used tools.

Multiple Linear Regressions

Multiple linear regressions are a powerful tool that allows us to integrate several explanatory variables—whether economic, social, or geopolitical—to assess the impact of factors such as unemployment, GDP, political stability, demographics, and even regional differences. This type of model is commonly used in research to analyze and predict migration flows, relying on multivariate datasets at a global scale. For example, Caballero Reina et al. (2024) demonstrate that the inclusion of economic, social, and geographic variables in a gravity model helps explain a significant share of recent global migration flows. Achour (2025a) further demonstrates that cultural factors—such as diaspora networks and linguistic proximity—can exert effects comparable to economic variables in shaping Tunisian migration patterns. This observation is also corroborated by recent empirical evidence showing that European migration flows display strong sensitivity to variations in GDP per capita, as demonstrated by Achour (2025b). Basile (2025) confirms that, for internal migration in Italy, regional disparities in accessibility and economic attractiveness play a crucial role in mobility.

The ARIMA and SARIMA Models

These models are designed to forecast from historical series, assuming that there is some structural stability in migration flows. They can identify trends, cycles, and seasonal variations. For example, the work of Bijak et al. (2019) provides concrete and methodologically sound examples of the use of these models to anticipate international migration flows. The first study examines migration movements to and from the UK in the post- Brexit context. The second takes place during a period when migration flows to the UK were relatively stable, before migration dynamics were disrupted by the Syrian refugee crisis and political turbulence in Europe. These two studies show that, in contexts where long and relatively stable historical series are available, these models are effective in isolating trends, cycles, or seasonal effects, which is valuable for decision-making and planning. Figure 1 show how the ARIMA and SARIMA models exploit temporal dependencies, whether normal or seasonal, in migration series to make forecasts based solely on historical data. To use ARIMA in migration flow forecasting, the time series of flows (y_t) is first transformed by differentiation in order to make it stationary (integration of order d). Then, the autoregressive (AR) model relies on past values of flows (y_{t-1},...) while the moving average (MA) model takes into account past errors (ε_{t-1},...). If the series has a seasonal component, seasonal AR and MA terms (SARIMA) with a period s can be added. This process allows for robust forecasts of migration flows for the next time (y_{t+1}) by combining the autoregressive, integration, and moving average elements identified in Figure 1.

Figure 1. ARIMA methods in migration

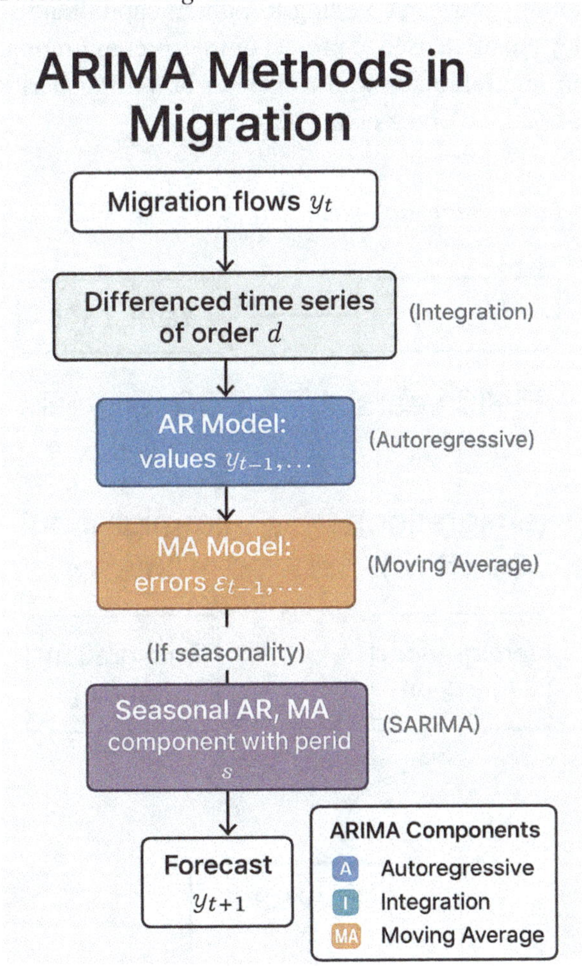

Cohort Models

Cohort models, which originate from demographic studies, offer a way to explore migration behavior by taking into account factors such as age, gender, and skill level. By following the evolution of a group of individuals (a cohort) over two consecutive periods, as shown in Figure 2, we can model age-specific transitions: for example, young people aged 15 to 19 in year t become those aged 20 to 24 in year t+1. This approach takes into account emigration (outflows), immigration (inflows), as well as the impact of natural aging and demographic losses on each cohort. These models show how mobility varies according to human capital and sociodemographic dynamics, and they are often used to project or interpret migration flows in contexts where young adult migration, as well as gender or skill disparities, play a crucial role (Raymer et al., 2025; Yildiz et al., 2024).

Figure 2. Cohort-based migration models

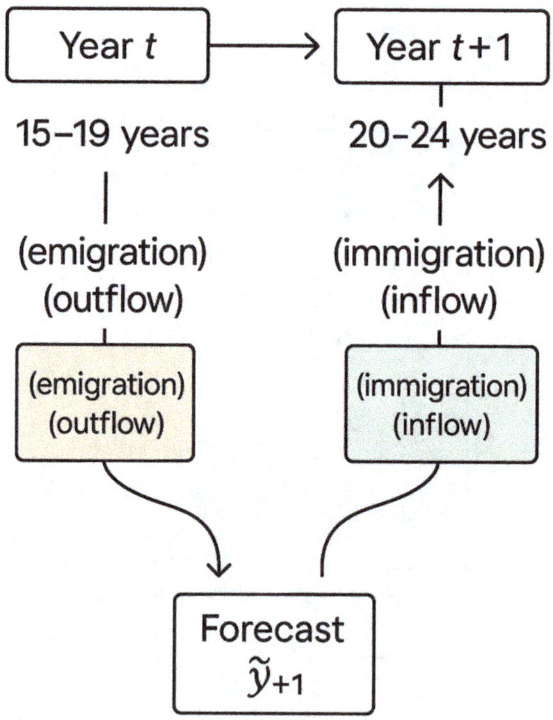

Transition Matrices and Gravitational Models

Transition matrices and gravity models are essential tools for analyzing and forecasting migration flows between different countries or regions. Transition matrices allow modeling the probabilities of moving from a point of origin to a destination, taking into account various demographic, territorial, and socioeconomic factors. On the other hand, gravity models, which are inspired by the laws of gravitation, estimate these flows by considering the relative attractiveness of territories (such as GDP or population size) as well as the geographic distance between the places of departure and arrival. These models can also be enriched with additional variables such as language, shared history, or political stability, which helps to better understand the structural factors that influence mobility. As shown in Figure 3, the process begins with the identification of a point of origin and a destination, which are linked by transition probabilities. The forecast of migration flows (y^t+1) then results from the combination of these probabilities, the level of economic or social attractiveness of the targeted territory, and the geographical distance separating the two poles. This visual model highlights the probabilistic logics as well as the forces of attraction and distance, thus illustrating how transition matrices and gravitational models work together in the analysis of migrations (Caballero Reina et al., 2024; Cottier, 2024).

Figure 3. Transition Matrices and gravity models

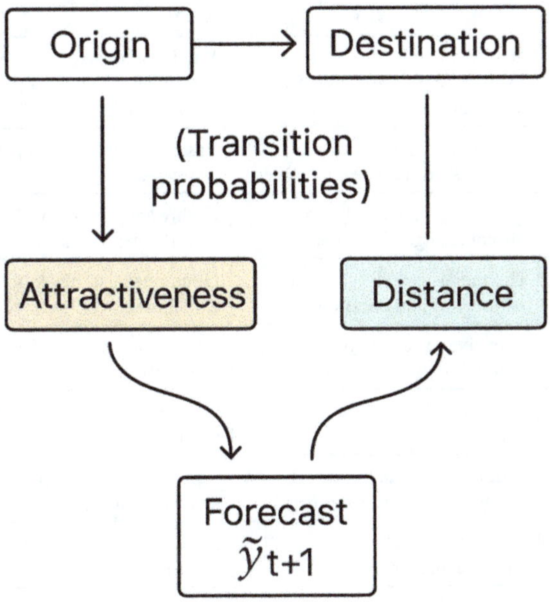

In summary, the four classic methods for analyzing migration flows—multiple linear regression, cohort models, transition matrices, and gravity models—make significant contributions. They are distinguished by their stability and robustness, allowing for the examination of long-term structural trends, such as the gradual growth or decline of flows, in generally stable contexts. Furthermore, they offer transparency and interpretability that are highly valued, as each explanatory variable can be isolated and understood, thus strengthening the confidence of decision-makers and facilitating communication with non-specialist audiences. Furthermore, their implementation relies on widely accessible data from official sources such as censuses, national statistics, or institutional databases, making them practical and operational tools for both administrations and researchers. However, although these methods are suitable for slow and predictable contexts, they show their limitations when it comes to modeling exceptional situations, marked by sudden crises, forced displacements, or rapid changes in migratory behavior.

In order to provide a synthetic overview, Table 1 compares the main features of traditional forecasting methods with AI-based approaches. This comparative framework highlights not only their technical differences but also the epistemological transformation that artificial intelligence introduces into migration forecasting.

Table 1. Comparative Overview of Traditional and AI-Based Migration Forecasting Approaches

Dimension	Traditional Models (Regression, ARIMA, Cohort, Gravity)	AI-Based Models (Machine Learning, Deep Learning, Hybrid Approaches)
Data Type	Historical and structured datasets (e.g., censuses, official statistics)	Multisource, heterogeneous data (social media, mobile phone data, satellite imagery, textual and behavioral data)
Model Logic	Based on linear and causal relationships between variables	Based on nonlinear, correlation-driven learning processes
Adaptability	Static and slow to adjust to abrupt changes or crises	Highly adaptive through real-time or continuous learning mechanisms
Transparency and Interpretability	High interpretability; explicit parameters and coefficients	Often opaque ("black box") models; need for explainable AI (XAI) techniques
Temporal Horizon	Effective in stable contexts with gradual or predictable trends	Suitable for volatile, fast-changing, and crisis-driven dynamics
Computational Capacity	Limited to small or medium datasets	Designed for large-scale, high-dimensional, and unstructured data
Ethical and Governance Issues	Minimal ethical concerns; data mostly public and aggregated	Raises questions of privacy, bias, accountability, and data governance
Analytical Purpose	Explanation and projection based on past trends	Prediction and adaptation in dynamic, uncertain environments

Limitations of Traditional Methods in the Context of Sudden Crises

Traditional methods for forecasting migration flows, which rely primarily on extrapolating past trends, often lack the flexibility to incorporate unexpected disruptions or exceptional events. When a crisis erupts, as was the case with the war in Syria in 2011 or the COVID-19 pandemic, these approaches have clearly demonstrated their limitations in anticipating the scale of mass influxes or explaining abrupt changes in migration behavior. For example, traditional models did not anticipate the shift in migration routes or the almost immediate closure of international borders in the face of the spread of the coronavirus. Similarly, during the Ukrainian crisis or the Venezuelan exodus, many traditional gravity or statistical models struggled to adjust their forecasts due to the emergence of unpredictable variables and the lack of real-time data.

Another challenge lies in the inability of these tools to account for weak and dynamic signals from digital data, such as trends on social networks, variations in mobility observed through mobile phones, or even real-time climate indicators. This limitation, in addition to the structural delays in the publication of official statistics, creates a time lag that hinders the responsiveness of analysis and the ability to provide early warnings to public decision-makers. In many crisis contexts, such as in West Africa facing forced displacement due to conflict or climate disasters, the weakness or fragmentation of national statistical infrastructures further complicates the estimation and adaptation of traditional models. Finally, most traditional approaches are based on the idea that the relationships between explanatory variables and migration flows remain stable; an assumption often undermined by major exogenous shocks, institutional changes, or the emergence of new migration routes. Thus, although these methods guarantee a certain interpretability and robustness for stationary periods, they prove insufficient to capture the rapid dynamics and volatility of migrations linked to health, environmental, or geopolitical crises.

This situation, highlighted by the failure of models to predict the COVID-19 pandemic or assess the surge in Syrian flows to Europe in the early 2010s, highlights the urgent need to adopt new tools and methods, such as artificial intelligence and big data analytics, which are better suited to the complexity and unpredictability of modern migration. Table 2 summarizes the main advantages and disadvantages of the four traditional methods used to analyze and forecast migration flows.

Table 2. Comparison of Traditional Migration Forecasting Methods

Method	Strengths (Pros)	Limitations (Cons)
Multiple Linear Regression	• High interpretability • Easy to implement • Stable in stable environments	• Low adaptability to crises • Assumes linear relationships • Ineffective with non-linear phenomena
ARIMA / SARIMA Models	• Captures temporal patterns • Suitable for short-term forecasting • Handles seasonality	• Limited ability to include external variables • Requires stationarity • Sensitive to structural breaks
Cohort-Component Models	• Detailed demographic modeling • Effective for long-term projections • Age- and gender-specific analysis	• Data-intensive • Poor performance with sudden changes • Less responsive to shocks
Gravity Models	• Based on intuitive spatial logic • Effective for bilateral migration flows • Broadly applicable	• Often underestimates flows during major disruptions • Requires frequent recalibration • Tends to be static

Traditional methods have their advantages: they are robust for analyzing structural trends, easy to interpret, and simple to implement thanks to the use of official data. However, their rigidity in the face of unforeseen crises, the limited availability of contextual data, and their inability to quickly integrate new elements make them less effective in times of emergency or sudden changes.

ARTIFICIAL INTELLIGENCE APPLIED TO MIGRATION FORECASTING: METHODOLOGICAL INNOVATIONS AND CURRENT ISSUES

Although traditional statistical methods are showing their limitations in the face of the growing complexity of human behavior, especially in times of sudden crises, artificial intelligence (AI) is gradually emerging as a promising solution to revitalize migration forecasting models. Thanks to its ability to analyze huge volumes of data, identify nonlinear patterns, and learn autonomously, AI offers a richer and more nuanced view of the migration phenomenon. This section provides an overview of the methods developed, the types of models used, the data exploited, and recent advances in this field.

Typology of AI Approaches Used in Migration Forecasting

AI encompasses a set of techniques aimed at stimulating human intelligence in information processing. In terms of migration forecasting, several sub-fields are particularly used:

Supervised Learning

The specificity of supervised learning lies in developing models that can predict a variable based on previously labeled historical data, such as the volume or direction of migratory flows specific to a country, whether it is an origin or a destination. These algorithms are designed to forecast a target variable, for example, the volume of migration by country of origin. A notable study by Yapamanu et al. (2025) used supervised learning techniques such as XGBoost and Random Forest to successfully predict the number of migrants as well as key influencing factors using international historical data organized by country and year. Their analysis covers a broad range of nationalities—Africa, Asia, Europe, Oceania, and the Caribbean—allowing for comparative insights. Their work has effectively modeled global migration dynamics over several decades, capturing changes in migratory flows over time and their geographic distribution between origins and destinations. The results demonstrate the robustness and accuracy of these machine learning algorithms when applied to international migration data and highlight the promising potential of artificial intelligence for managing and forecasting complex phenomena like human migration (Yapamanu et al. 2025).

Unsupervised Learning

A set of established artificial intelligence techniques known as unsupervised learning allows the exploration and analysis of datasets without using a target variable. The goal is to automatically uncover underlying structures such as natural groupings or hidden trends within the data. Clustering, classification, and profiling methods are particularly valuable for identifying emerging profiles or dynamics within large datasets where categories or classes are unknown beforehand.

For instance, the study by Cerqueti et al. (2022) applied clustering techniques, particularly K-means, to analyze and segment profiles based on complex international datasets. Their research focused on datasets spread over two decades, decomposed by nationality, country of origin and destination, and time periods. By grouping individuals or flows according to shared characteristics—such as socioeconomic profiles or migration trajectories—they were able to identify emerging trends and unexpected groupings. This approach has greatly enhanced our understanding of the underlying structures in international migration. The results underscore the value of unsupervised learning methods in revealing unbiased hidden patterns and new configurations in migration dynamics (Cerqueti et al. 2022).

Deep Learning

Deep learning (DL) is all about neural networks that can automatically uncover relationships in massive data sets, and they do this in a non-linear and complex way. This is especially true for architectures like recurrent neural networks (RNNs) and LSTMs. These models are particularly effective when it comes to analyzing time series and multidimensional data, such as international migration patterns. For instance, Gaskin and Abel (2025) utilize a deep recurrent neural network to model annual migration flows between 230 countries from 1990 to 2023. They incorporate 18 different factors—spatial, economic, societal, and cultural—into their model, which provides a detailed and dynamic perspective on migration trends at the international level, broken down by country of origin and destination. This approach clearly showcases how neural networks can capture intricate changes over time and even predict future shifts in large-scale migration flows. It's also worth noting that the three primary AI approaches used in migration —supervised learning, unsupervised learning, and deep learning—share a common strength: their ability to integrate a wide variety of data sources. Each of these methods taps into official statistics, like census data, demographic trends, and international economic indicators, while also leveraging new digital data. This includes social media activity, mobility data collected from mobile phones or GPS, and satellite imagery that documents environments on a large scale. Additionally, there's a wealth of textual and media data available, from news articles to institutional reports and humanitarian agency bulletins, which automated language analysis can now utilize to spot trends and identify subtle signals. This integration of diverse sources enhances the robustness, accuracy, and relevance of analyses derived from AI in the context of migration dynamics.

The emergence of artificial intelligence (AI) in the field of migration is opening up exciting new avenues for research. It allows us to weave together a wide array of factors—like economic, environmental, social, health, and political elements—into models that can explain or predict migration trends. With its powerful algorithms, AI is particularly good at picking up on subtle signals, uncovering new dynamics or patterns that might slip past human analysts or traditional statistical methods. Plus, online learning techniques enable these models to update dynamically; as fresh data comes in, they can adjust their predictions, making them more relevant in our fast-changing world. AI also empowers us to create intricate future scenarios, simulating various shocks or hypotheses using a single database. Several innovative institutions and centers are leading the way with these advancements. Take the World Bank, for instance; between 2020 and 2022, they developed a dynamic multi-scenario model that can predict refugee movements in Africa and the Middle East. This model combines economic, climate, and security indicators, refining its results by pulling in data from various sources like UNHCR, satellite imagery, and mobile data, which enhances both the accuracy and responsiveness of its forecasts. Other initiatives, spearheaded by UN Global Pulse and UNHCR, utilize social network analysis to spot early migration intentions or unreported movements, boosting our ability to issue real-time alerts and identify anomalies before they show up in official statistics. Lastly, research that employs deep learning to analyze climate data (like rainfall and temperatures) alongside human data (such as population density and infrastructure) has improved our ability to predict internal displacement in vulnerable areas, like Bangladesh or Mozambique, by simulating the effects of different environmental scenarios.

While these examples highlight the operational potential of AI in forecasting migration under crisis conditions, they also invite a more critical reflection on its analytical foundations. AI-driven approaches tend to privilege correlation over causation, emphasizing adaptability and prediction rather than explanation. This epistemological shift redefines the very meaning of "forecasting" in migration studies—transforming it from a model of structured inference into a dynamic system of probabilistic anticipation, which raises crucial questions about interpretability, transparency, and the social validity of algorithmic outcomes.

Ultimately, the introduction of AI represents a real methodological breakthrough, redefining the tools that can be used for migration management in an uncertain environment. However, while these technologies offer major advantages over the limitations of conventional approaches, their implementation still requires adaptations, enhanced data governance, and in-depth ethical reflection on their operational use and adaptability to crisis situations.

AI IN THE FACE OF MIGRATION CRISES: ADAPTIVE CAPACITIES AND NEW OPPORTUNITIES

Specificities of Sudden Migration Crises and Challenges for Forecasting

Sudden migration crises manifest as surges in flows that can occur within days or weeks, often due to various triggers such as armed conflicts, economic shocks, climate disasters, or health crises (McAuliffe et al., 2021; World Bank, 2022). These events rapidly disrupt usual routes and destinations, leading to the emergence of new routes or massive movements to areas that were initially little affected. Faced with these upheavals, traditional forecasting methods, which rely on historical trends, show their limitations, creating a pressing need for tools capable of integrating these discontinuities and learning in real time. In this context, the ability of forecasting models to instantly adjust to changing situations becomes a crucial issue for institutions and actors on the ground.

Mechanisms for Technological Adaptation of AI Models

Recent technological advances have profoundly transformed the adaptability of artificial intelligence models in the face of migration crises. Thanks to several key innovations, AI is now better equipped to anticipate, detect, and monitor in real time the evolution of migratory movements, which are often marked by high unpredictability. These adaptation mechanisms can be grouped into four major complementary areas, detailed below.

Dynamic Learning

Dynamic learning, literally continuous learning, refers to the ability of AI models to continuously incorporate new data to adapt forecasts to the real-time development of migration flows. This is the case of a system implemented in Uganda by the World Bank, which mobilized more than 90 indicators (economic, climatic, social, etc.) to finance in real time the reception of refugees working near the places of arrival by triggering emergency financing and the coordination of the humanitarian response even before their arrival (World Bank, 2023). In the same context, very recent work has also attempted, in Central America, to integrate data from social networks and mobile phones in order to be able to detect "intentions" of collective departure before their realization by the discovery of peaks of keywords on Twitter or WhatsApp, for example, in the context of migratory caravans towards the United States, where the flow of messages before a global flight is massive, triggering an automatic update of forecasts (Sîrbu et al., 2021; Migration Data Portal, 2024). The research carried out around these questions testifies to a turning point in the management of migratory crises, punctually, from reactive reception decision-making to proactive management based on dynamic AI databases open to the updating of their scenarios.

Automated Change Point Detection

Automated change point detection is a key tool for fine-tuning AI models in migration monitoring. This method uses algorithms to identify key moments in a time series, such as the sudden outbreak of conflict, border closures, or natural disasters, signalling a significant change in migration dynamics. For example, Carammia et al. (2022) demonstrated that integrating change point analysis into migration forecasting models allowed the rapid identification of shifts in asylum application trends caused by sudden events like the escalation of conflict in countries of origin. These adaptive machine learning approaches enable early warning analysis by detecting signals of significant change in migration drivers, thereby helping organizations and policy-makers anticipate and respond proactively to emerging displacement crises

Monitoring Weak Signals

Monitoring weak signals using deep learning is proving to be a significant advance in anticipating sudden changes in migration flows. Recurrent neural networks (RNNs), especially their advanced versions like LSTM and GRU, are able to detect subtle variations in dynamics after a significant event, where traditional methods fail. For example, analyses of social media data from platforms such as Facebook and Twitter have been employed to monitor migration-related communications during crises, including the 2022 Ukrainian conflict, helping to inform timely humanitarian responses (Eurofound, 2024). Similarly, data-driven approaches integrating semantic analyses of messages on popular messaging apps in regions like North Africa and Central America offer promising avenues to detect early signals of collective movements and significant migration flows (Big Data for Migration Alliance, 2024). These advances contribute substantially to improving early warning systems and rapid response capacities in migration management.

Additionally, several programs supported by the International Organization for Migration are developing platforms that use LSTM models to combine social signals, mobile phone geolocation, and satellite imagery. These tools can detect unusual variations in movements or discussions around migration on an hourly basis. This helps anticipate and coordinate the intervention of authorities and NGOs well before official statistics are published or visible tensions appear on the ground (Migration Data Portal, 2024).

Integration of Diverse Data Sources

The integration of diverse data sources represents a major advance in AI-powered migration modeling. By combining data from social media, mobile phones, satellite images, and local socioeconomic databases, models can now capture complex dynamics in near real-time that are often missed by traditional methods. Recent work has shown how deep learning techniques applied to satellite imagery, when combined with census data, can accurately predict population distributions and socioeconomic conditions—key factors that influence migration decisions (Yeh et al., 2020). Building on these methodological advances, researchers have also demonstrated that integrating demographic information with geospatial analysis significantly improves our ability to understand human mobility patterns (Robinson et al., 2017). Similar approaches have been applied in West Africa and the Balkans, where combining mobile geolocation data with interdisciplinary analysis of social and environmental factors helps anticipate movements triggered by climate or political shocks (Schürmann, 2022; Migration Data Portal, 2024). These methods offer a multidimensional perspective on migration phenomena, considerably strengthening alert and rapid response capacities.

New Operational Capabilities Offered By AI: Concrete Illustrations

The most recent applications of artificial intelligence to migration have made it possible to build faster, more flexible and more enlightened reactions to the often unpredictable evolution of population flows. As illustrated in Figure 4, these systems deliver better anticipation, early warning, response to operations, and strong model construction.

Increased Anticipation and Dynamic Scenarios

During the Venezuelan migration crisis, Brazilian border authorities were able to use advanced predictive models based on machine learning methods such as random forests and neural networks to produce differentiated scenarios of arrivals (UN Global Pulse & UNHCR, 2023). The models use a wide variety of variables all at once: infrastructure (roads, accommodation capacity, logistics availability), macro-economic variables (prices, employment, exchange rates), online behavior (Google searches, social media). Thanks to your multi-scenario simulation approach and continuous learning, it was possible to model the impact of different hypotheses on frontier closure or acceleration of flows and to revise forecasts regularly to match the rapidly evolving situation (de Rubalcava et al., 2023).

Active Weak Signal Detection

Artificial intelligence tools have been increasingly deployed to monitor migration movements through social media platforms. According to the American Immigration Council (2024), AI-powered systems enable real-time tracking of public and semi-private communications on platforms like Facebook and WhatsApp. Natural language processing and graph-based algorithms can identify mobilization patterns, planning groups, and potential concentration points along migration routes. This proactive digital monitoring provides a strategic advantage for pre-positioning mobile reception points and optimizing humanitarian resources and logistics in anticipation of population movements.

Enhanced Operational Responsiveness

Following the Haitian earthquake, AI was applied in accelerated and interventionist multisource data fusion systems: geospatial imagery processed via CNNs, mobile field reporting via apps or SMS, social network analytical messages, and real-time cartographic analysis (Angenendt & Koch, 2024). This architecture, incorporating data intake and fusion pipelines, supported new collection site identification in an accelerated manner, near-real-time temporary shelter center redeployment, and humanitarian logistics realignment in the first 48 hours.

Greater Hybrid Modeling

Hybrid models combining conventional statistical data (admin records, field surveys) with dynamic measures derived from satellite image analysis and semantic web data mining (Telegram channels, forums) have been applied along the Tunisia-Libya border (Angenendt & Koch, 2024). This confluence of statistical methods and deep learning facilitates foresight of serendipitous opening of new channels of migration, showing richness in spatial occupation changes, and spatial mapping of informal reception structure emergence. Information richness and real-time adaptability thus massively enhance regional strategic monitoring and operational intervention (de Rubalcava et al., 2023).

Figure 4. Key AI advantages for migration forecasting

Characteristic	Description
Increased anticipation	Generates forecasts under various scenarios
Proactive detection	Detects migratory movements early on
Operational responsiveness	Allows rapid re-evaluation of predictions
Robust model building	Creates hybrid models for better re'

Illustrative Case Studies

COVID-19 Pandemic: Adaptation to Abrupt Change

In 2020-2021, border closures and the reconfiguration of migratory routes generated novel predictive needs. AI-driven models using mobility information from mobile devices and online searches allowed for the prediction in near real time of the precipitous drop, redeployment, or reconfiguration of migratory flows in the absence of historical benchmarks (McAuliffe et al., 2021).

Because of this abundance of signals, anomalous mobility shifts might be picked up very early: a sudden increase in consultations about departure or asylum applications on online sites could serve as an early indicator, well before administrations or customs published official statistics. The AI models thus made it possible to simulate different scenarios (lasting restrictions, gradual reopening, and deflection of migration routes), giving decision-makers time to adjust their reception plans and implement medical or logistic response capabilities.

Syrian Refugee Crisis: Integration From Multiple Sources

Since 2012, in response to the enormous influx of refugees to Europe, pilot programs have combined security metrics (violence outbreaks), climatic metrics, and social media data to predict the routes and temporality of population movements and thus provide a novel instrument for anticipation of reception resource planning (World Bank, 2022). This combined approach has made it possible to simulate migration scenarios and hypotheses (continuation of the conflict, opening of humanitarian corridors, and modification of asylum policies), while giving institutional actors a better understanding of the true determinants of flows and the resilience of projections.

Venezuela-Colombia Border: Early Detection via Digital Signals

During the major migration crisis between 2018 and 2020, research teams in partnership with international organizations used artificial intelligence technologies to continuously analyze message flows on social networks (notably Twitter and Facebook), mobility data from mobile phones, as well as discussions in public WhatsApp groups and Google searches related to migration.

Thanks to this cross-exploitation of heterogeneous data, the AI models detected increases in departure intentions several days in advance, allowing Colombian authorities and humanitarian agencies to be alerted before the saturation of entry points, to organize an appropriate logistical deployment and to prevent major administrative and health congestion.

Natural Disasters and Operational Responsiveness

During extreme events (Cyclone Idai, floods in Bangladesh), AI has been mobilized to combine satellite imagery and local socio-economic information, making it possible to anticipate flows of internally displaced people and effectively estimate future pressure on urban infrastructure (University of Skövde, 2024).

A particularly striking example concerns the large-scale fires in Greece during the summer of 2023, where Greek authorities and humanitarian agencies used AI systems integrating real-time data from social networks, mobile mobility, and weather alerts. Thanks to online learning algorithms, the models were able to continuously adjust their forecasts as new fires appeared, allowing operational actors to quickly redirect evacuation corridors and anticipate the need for health and logistical resources.

Structural Limitations and Persistent Challenges

Despite these reassuring developments, AI migration forecasting models suffer from structural flaws that must be closely watched. Reliance on data and the quality of data remain an issue, since bias or delay invalidates the forecasts, especially during crises. Bias and lack of transparency risk concerns, interpretive complexity for decision-makers, and demand strong data management are all persistent issues. Ethical issues and transparency also require ongoing focus. (Refer to Table 3 for a detailed description of the potential and limitations of AI models in migration forecasting.)

- Data Dependence and Information Quality: The performance of AI models depends heavily on the quality and timeliness of data inputs. Biases in sources of information or time lags in obtaining data could compromise the validity of predictions, particularly in crisis contexts where information is incomplete or unreliable.
- Risks of bias and opacity: Machine learning algorithms can reproduce or amplify biases in training data, generating discriminatory or inaccurate predictions. The opacity of some advanced models makes biases difficult to identify and correct.
- Complexity of interpretation for decision-makers: The technical complexity of AI models can create a gap between the outputs produced and their interpretation by non-technical decision-makers, limiting their ability to effectively utilize these tools in their decisions.
- Need for strong governance: Use of personal and sensitive data in migration forecasting models drives important ethical questions regarding privacy protection, consent, and use of results. Strong governance of data and algorithms is ever more required.
- Ethical issues and transparency: Ethical oversight remains essential, particularly as regards the protection of personal data, transparency of processing and the potentially secure use of migration predictions.

Table 3. Opportunities vs. Limitations of AI models in migration forecasting

Opportunities	**Boundaries**
Anticipation of complex scenarios (non-linear, dynamic)	Dependence on fresh and reliable data
Proactive detection of weak signals and trends	Risks of bias and opacity of models
Increased responsiveness to sudden events	Difficulty of interpretation by non-specialists
Multi-scenario simulation for decision support	Need for rigorous data governance
Hybridization between statistical expertise and advanced AI	Ethical issues: personal data, use of results

The advances made possible by artificial intelligence in migration forecasting thus offer new horizons for crisis management and public policy development. However, their use requires in-depth consideration and continuous adaptation to structural and practical challenges to ensure their relevance and reliability on the ground.

DISCUSSION

In light of recent research, artificial intelligence is proving to be a truly transformative force for anticipating migration flows in times of crisis. The reviewed literature shows that AI-based forecasting tools do more than enhance the technical performance of migration prediction; they redefine its epistemological nature. Traditional models sought to explain migration through causal, often linear relationships between structural variables—economic, demographic, or geopolitical. In contrast, AI-based approaches operate through adaptive learning and multidimensional data integration, shifting the purpose of forecasting from deterministic explanation to probabilistic anticipation. This transformation blurs the boundary between analysis and decision-making: migration forecasting becomes not only a tool for understanding trends but also a dynamic mechanism for guiding real-time policy and humanitarian action. In this sense, AI reshapes both the methodology and the governance of migration knowledge. It acts both as a complement and, sometimes, as an alternative to traditional demographic and econometric methods. Thanks to rapid advances in machine learning and the integration of weak signals—such as the analysis of social media data or real-time mobility—some institutions, such as the UNHCR and UN Global Pulse pilot project on the early detection of migration intentions, have managed to significantly improve their ability to alert and adjust reception policies. However, this analytical power brings new responsibilities for AI, both ethically and legally. The issues of model explainability, the continuous correction of algorithmic biases, and the protection of personal data are more relevant than ever, as recently highlighted by Mittelstadt et al. (2019) and Goodman & Flaxman (2017). Some so-called "black box" models, based on complex deep architectures learning, present a risk of opacity that can complicate the understanding of decisions for political decision-makers or international organizations. This was particularly visible during experiments on the automatic management of asylum applications in Europe. It is therefore crucial to ensure institutional vigilance and scientific rigor to guarantee the legitimacy and robustness of AI tools in the management of migration crises, in accordance with the principles set out in the IOM World Migration Report 2022.

Ethical, Legal and Governance Issues of AI in Migration Forecasting

The integration of AI into migration forecasting raises important ethical and governance issues. This concerns both the management of sensitive data and the accountability of algorithmic decisions. For example, using social media data to predict travel intentions improves responsiveness, but raises privacy and consent concerns, especially when apps collect geolocation or personal data without informing users. Moreover, the legal framework surrounding the use of AI in migration is still insufficient. The European Union has begun drafting legislation with the proposed AI Act to ensure the explainability, non-discrimination, and accountability of automated systems. However, many challenges remain, particularly regarding international standardization and harmonization of rights. Algorithmic governance issues—such as bias detection and correction, model accountability and auditability, and stakeholder engagement—are also essential to avoid reproducing structural inequalities or ignoring potentially discriminatory mechanisms.

Main Challenges to Be Overcome, Opinions and Recommendations

In addition to these issues, the most important of those that need to be resolved are proactive management of data quality, training experts and decision-makers in the details of AI technologies, and creating mechanisms for monitoring and recurrent adjustment of algorithms. Recent crisis analyses note that the unavailability of reliable data, underrepresentation of certain groups or regions, and the absence of transparency when selecting explanatory variables can lead to critical forecasting differences. Implementing robust collaborative governance, involving researchers, NGOs, public authorities, and migrants' stakeholders, is required to ensure the truthfulness, objectivity, and social acceptability of AI innovations in migration.

In a global environment where migration volatility and uncertainty will likely rise after environmental, health, or geopolitical shocks, artificial intelligence must be harnessed in a responsible manner. It would be wise to maintain hybridising statistical power, transparency, and the ability to learn from up-to-date data, which the World Bank and the IOM are already striving to accomplish. Having well-established legal frameworks and external audit controls will increase stakeholder trust. Further, it is essential to invest in cross-training migration experts and data experts so that model-building is based on rich human and social context knowledge. Lastly, international collaboration should be fostered to develop shared ethical and technical standards. Lessons from the Syrian conflict, the COVID-19 pandemic, and climate migration are that AI can only be fully integrated when it is part of a governance system that is open, dynamic, and prioritizes protecting human rights, yet avoids the dangers of discrimination or marginalization.

CONCLUSION

Provision of projections of international migration streams in the context of unexpected crises is today a question of science, as well as for public intervention and human solidarity. This chapter highlights the underlying significance of orthodox approaches such as multiple linear regression, cohort models, transition matrices, and gravity models that are valued for their solidity, transparency, and ability to reveal long-term structural trends. However, such approaches prove to be lacking in demarcating the acceleration, volatility, and nonlinear complexity of new mobilities, especially in times of crisis or sudden interruptions. In order to deal with such challenges, artificial intelligence and machine learning bring in a revolutionary shift of approach: these technologies enable one to consolidate at the same time enormous and diverse data, engage proactively in "weak signal" analysis, and build dynamic scenarios, while it becomes feasible to update forecasts in real time according to evolving conditions. Recent applications—like projecting the impact of the COVID-19 pandemic on migration or the early warning of flows due to conflicts or climate disasters—exhibit that AI increases the responsiveness, accuracy, and operational value of decision-support systems. All the same, this technological capability must be combined with rigorous scrutiny of ethical, legal, and governance issues: model explainability, bias management, fostering respect for human rights and freedoms, close cooperation with ground actors, and open institutional design are needed to make digital innovation legitimate and effective in this sensitive domain.

In short, combining the certainty of classical approaches with the adaptability of artificial intelligence offers new ways towards greater insight and improved international migration management. Such a new horizon relies on one imperative: encouraging dialogue among scientific knowledge, technical innovation, and ethical considerations to contribute to strategic decision-making in a more and more uncertain and highly interdependent world.

REFERENCES

Achour, Z. (2025a). Multidimensional Determinants of Tunisian Migration Flows: An Integrated Econometric Analysis. *Journal of Emerging Markets and Management.*, *1*(1), 56–67. https://doi.org/10.7759/s44404-025-09601-1DOI: 10.63385/jemm.v1i1.86

Achour, Z. (2025b) Economic Determinants of European Migration Flows Through Cluster Analysis and Panel Data Modeling. Cureus J Bus Econ 2: es44404-025-09601-1. DOI: 10.7759/s44404-025-09601-1

American Immigration Council. (2024, December 16). *ICE uses a growing web of AI services to power its immigration enforcement and surveillance.* https://www.americanimmigrationcouncil.org/blog/ice-uses-ai-immigration-enforcement-surveillance/

Angenendt, S., & Koch, A. (2024). Migration forecasting: Expectations, limitations and political functions. *Forced Migration Review*, (73), 1–5. https://www.fmreview.org/digital-disruption/angenendt-koch/

Basile, A., & Gallo, M. (2025). Investigating the Impact of Accessibility on Internal Migration Flows in Italy Through the Calibration of Multiple Linear Regression Models. *WORLD (Oakland, Calif.)*, *6*(2), 46. DOI: 10.3390/world6020046

Big Data for Migration Alliance. (2024). Building a policy compass: Navigating future migration with anticipatory methods. Retrieved October 2025, from https://data4migration.org

Bijak, J., Disney, G., Findlay, A. M., Forster, J. J., Smith, P. W., & Wiśniowski, A. (2019). Assessing time series models for forecasting international migration: Lessons from the United Kingdom. *Journal of Forecasting*, *38*(5), 470–487. DOI: 10.1002/for.2576

Caballero Reina, J., Crespo Cuaresma, J., Fenz, K., Zellmann, J., Yankov, T., & Taha, A. (2024). Gravity models for global migration flows: A predictive evaluation. *Population Research and Policy Review*, *43*(2), 29. DOI: 10.1007/s11113-024-09867-6

Carammia, M., Iacus, S. M., & Wilkin, T. (2022). Forecasting asylum-related migration flows with machine learning and data at scale. *Scientific Reports*, *12*(1), 1457. DOI: 10.1038/s41598-022-05241-8 PMID: 35087096

Cerqueti, R., & Ficcadenti, V. (2022). Combining rank-size and k-means for clustering countries over the COVID-19 new deaths per million. *Chaos, Solitons, and Fractals*, *158*, 111975. DOI: 10.1016/j.chaos.2022.111975 PMID: 35291220

Cottier, F. (2024). Projecting future migration with Bayesian hierarchical gravity models. *Frontiers in Climate*, *5*, 1384295. DOI: 10.3389/fclim.2024.1384295

de Rubalcava, A. D. N. G., Piñeiro, O. S., Jiménez, R. M., Aylett-Bullock, J., Ismail, A., Kyriazi, S., Pham, K. H. (2023). Modeling Population Movements under Uncertainty at the Border in Humanitarian Crises: A Situational Analysis Tool. *arXiv preprint arXiv:2303.15614.*

Eurofound. (2024). Social impact of migration: Addressing the challenges of receiving and integrating Ukrainian refugees. Retrieved October 2025, from https://www.eurofound.europa.eu/en/publications/all/social-impact-migration-addressing-challenges-receiving-and-integrating-ukrainian

Gaskin, T., & Abel, G. J. (2025). Deep learning 40 years of human migration. *arXiv preprint arXiv:2506.22821*

Global Pulse, U. N. (2023). *2022 Annual Report: UN Global Pulse Showed Its Value in a Changing World.* https://www.unglobalpulse.org/2022-annual-report-un-global-pulse-showed-its-value-in-a-changing-world/

Goodman, B., & Flaxman, S. (2017). European Union regulations on algorithmic decision-making and a 'right to explanation'. *AI Magazine*, *38*(3), 50–57. DOI: 10.1609/aimag.v38i3.2741

Granovetter, M. (1985). Economic action and social structure: The problem of embeddedness. *American Journal of Sociology*, *91*(3), 481–510. DOI: 10.1086/228311

IDMC – Internal Displacement Monitoring Centre. (2023). *Global report on internal displacement 2023.* https://www.internal-displacement.org/global-report/grid2023/

International Organization for Migration (IOM). (2021). *World Migration Report, 2022*, https://publications.iom.int/books/world-migration-report-2022

International Organization for Migration (IOM) & World Food Program (WFP). (2022). *Understanding the adverse drivers and implications of migration from El Salvador, Guatemala and Honduras.* IOM Publications. https://lac.iom.int/sites/g/files/tmzbdl1446/files/documents/executive-summary-understanding-the-adverse-drivers-and-implications-of-migration-from-el-salvador-guatemala-and-honduras-i-1.pdf

Lee, E. S. (1966). A theory of migration. *Demography*, *3*(1), 47–57. DOI: 10.2307/2060063

Massey, D. S., Arango, J., Hugo, G., Kouaouci, A., Pellegrino, A., & Taylor, J. E. (1993). Theories of international migration: A review and appraisal. *Population and Development Review, 19*(3), 431–466. DOI: 10.2307/2938462

McAuliffe, M., Blower, J., & Beduschi, A. (2021). Digitalization and Artificial Intelligence in Migration and Mobility: Transnational Implications of the COVID-19 Pandemic. *Societies (Basel, Switzerland), 11*(4), 135. DOI: 10.3390/soc11040135

Migration Data Portal. (2024). AI / Machine learning in migration studies. https://www.migrationdataportal.org/data-sources/ai-machine-learning

Migration Data Portal. (2024). *AI and Big Data for Migration Forecasting*. International Organization for Migration. https://www.migrationdataportal.org

Mittelstadt, B., Russell, C., & Wachter, S. (2019, January). Explaining explanations in AI. In *Proceedings of the conference on fairness, accountability, and transparency* (pp. 279-288). DOI: 10.1145/3287560.3287574

Pratesi, F., Sharma, R., & Zignani, M. (2021). Measuring migration 2.0: A review of digital data sources. *Comparative Migration Studies, 9*(1), 59. Advance online publication. DOI: 10.1186/s40878-021-00273-x

Ravenstein, E. G. (1889). The laws of migration. *Journal of the Royal Statistical Society, 52*(2), 241–305. DOI: 10.2307/2979333

Raymer, J., Guan, Q., Shen, T., Hertog, S., & Gerland, P. (2025). Modelling the age and sex profiles of net international migration. *Demographic Research, 53*, 569–610. DOI: 10.4054/DemRes.2025.53.19

Robinson, C., Hohman, F., & Dilkina, B. (2017). A deep learning approach for population estimation from satellite imagery. *GeoHumanities@SIGSPATIAL*, 47-54. https://arxiv.org/abs/1708.09086

Schürmann, A., Kleemann, J., Teucher, M., Fürst, C., & Conrad, C. (2022). Migration in West Africa: A visual analysis of motivation, causes, and routes. *Ecology and Society, 27*(3), art16. Advance online publication. DOI: 10.5751/ES-13489-270316

Sîrbu, A., Andrienko, G., Andrienko, N., Boldrini, C., Conti, M., Giannotti, F., Guidotti, R., Bertoli, S., Kim, J., Muntean, C. I., Pappalardo, L., Passarella, A., Pedreschi, D., Pollacci, L., Pratesi, F., & Sharma, R. (2021). Human migration: The big data perspective. *International Journal of Data Science and Analytics, 11*(4), 341–360. DOI: 10.1007/s41060-020-00213-5

Stark, O., & Bloom, D. E. (1985). The new economics of labor migration. *The American Economic Review, 75*(2), 173–178. https://www.jstor.org/stable/1805591

Tahvanainen, M., Welch, D., & Worm, V. (2005). Implications of short-term international assignments. *European Management Journal, 23*(6), 663–673. DOI: 10.1016/j.emj.2005.10.011

Todaro, M. P. (1969). A Model of Labor Migration and Urban Unemployment in Less Developed Countries. *The American Economic Review, 59*(1), 138–148. https://www.jstor.org/stable/1811100

UN Global Pulse & UNHCR. (2023). Understanding population movements at the Brazil-Venezuela border. https://www.unglobalpulse.org/project/understanding-population-movements-at-the-brazil-venezuela-border/

UNHCR. (n.d.). *Social Media and Forced Displacement: Big Data Analytics & Machine-Learning* (White Paper, UNHCR & UN Global Pulse). https://www.unhcr.org/innovation/new-paper-from-un-global-pulse-and-unhcr-explores-use-of-digital-data-for-insights-into-forced-displacement/

UNHCR & UN Global Pulse. (n.d.). *From big data to humanitarian-in-the-loop algorithms*. https://www.unhcr.org/innovation/big-data-humanitarian-loop-algorithms/

University of Skövde. (2024). Using AI to predict climate-driven migration. Phys.org. https://phys.org/news/2024-10-ai-climate-driven-migration.html

Wolpert, J. (1965). Behavioral aspects of the decision to migrate. *Papers in Regional Science, 15*(1), 159–169. DOI: 10.1111/j.1435-5597.1965.tb01320.x

World Bank. (2021). *Recovery: COVID-19 Crisis Through a Migration Lens – Migration and Development Brief 35*. https://documents1.worldbank.org/curated/en/099738408132414027/pdf/IDU110e1541c1704b14821196441e301ab86ff0b.pdf

World Bank. (2023). *Uganda Development Response to Displacement Impacts Project: Building resilience and financing refugee-hosting districts* (Project Document P510476). Retrieved from https://documents1.worldbank.org/curated/en/099031825124033782/pdf/P510476-8ee58859-4e78-4ef0-9d01-cf17a495a240.pdf

World Bank (KNOMAD). (2022). *Remittances Brave Global Headwinds – Migration and Development Brief 37*. https://documents1.worldbank.org/curated/en/099818008142419054/pdf/IDU12966350716a711437b1850019065d7f1eda1.pdf

Yapamanu, G., Thugutla, K. R., Undela, V., Selvameena, M. R., & Vidhya, M. V. (2025). Predict Migration using Machine Learning. *IJSAT-International Journal on Science and Technology, 16*(1), 2612. Advance online publication. DOI: 10.71097/IJSAT.v16.i1.2612

Yeh, C., Perez, A., Driscoll, A., Azzari, G., Tang, Z., Lobell, D., Ermon, S., & Burke, M. (2020). Using publicly available satellite imagery and deep learning to understand economic well-being in Africa. *Nature Communications*, *11*(1), 2583. Advance online publication. DOI: 10.1038/s41467-020-16185-w PMID: 32444658

Yildiz, D., Abel, G., & Cohen, S. (2024). *Migration flows by age, sex and educational attainment*. IIASA Working Paper WP-24-001. https://pure.iiasa.ac.at/19399

Compilation of References

Aamer, A., Eka Yani, L. P., & Alan Priyatna, I. M. (2020). Data Analytics in the Supply Chain Management: Review of Machine Learning Applications in Demand Forecasting. *Operations and Supply Chain Management: An International Journal*, 1–13. DOI: 10.31387/oscm0440281

Abir, S. I., Sarwer, M. H., & Hasan, M.. (2024). Accelerating BRICS economic growth: AI-driven data analytics for informed policy and decision making. *Journal of Economics. Finance and Accounting Studies*, *6*(6), 102–115. DOI: 10.32996/jefas.2024.6.6.8

Acharya, D. B., Kuppan, K., & Divya, B. (2025). Agentic AI: Autonomous Intelligence for Complex Goals—A Comprehensive Survey. *IEEE Access : Practical Innovations, Open Solutions*, *13*, 18912–18936. DOI: 10.1109/ACCESS.2025.3532853

Achour, Z. (2025b) Economic Determinants of European Migration Flows Through Cluster Analysis and Panel Data Modeling. Cureus J Bus Econ 2: es44404-025-09601-1. DOI: 10.7759/s44404-025-09601-1

Achour, Z. (2025a). Multidimensional Determinants of Tunisian Migration Flows: An Integrated Econometric Analysis. *Journal of Emerging Markets and Management.*, *1*(1), 56–67. https://doi.org/10.7759/s44404-025-09601-1DOI: 10.63385/jemm.v1i1.86

Adams, J.F., & Smith, D.J. (2022). *Fixed Income Analysis, CFA Institute Investment Series, 5 éd., 2022.* WELEY.

Adebiyi, A., Adewumi, A., & Ayo, C. (2014). Stock price prediction using the ARIMA model. UKSim-AMSS 16th International Conference on Computer Modelling and Simulation. https://doi.org/DOI: 10.1109/UKSim.2014.67

Agénor, P., Alper, K., & Silva, L. (2013). Capital regulation, monetary policy and financial stability. *International Journal of Central Banking*. Advance online publication. DOI: 10.2139/ssrn.2318026

Agmarknet. (2024). *Agmarknet: Agricultural Marketing Information System*. https://agmarknet.gov.in

Agrawal, M., Kumar Shukla, P., Nair, R., Nayyar, A., & Masud, M. (2022). Stock Prediction Based on Technical Indicators Using Deep Learning Model. *Computers, Materials & Continua, 70*(1), 287–304. DOI: 10.32604/cmc.2022.014637

Ahmed, S., Alshater, M. M., Ammari, A. E., & Hammami, H. (2022). Artificial intelligence and machine learning in finance: A bibliometric review. *Research in International Business and Finance, 61*, 101646. DOI: 10.1016/j.ribaf.2022.101646

AI-Driven Financial Forecasting. (2025). *Enhancing Predictive Accuracy in Volatile Markets*. European Economic Letters., DOI: 10.52783/eel.v15i2.2955

Akansha, s., & Candan kumar, v. (2025). Non-parametric insights in option pricing: a systematic review of theory, implementation and future directions. *Artificial Intelligence Review* .

Akhgar, B., Saathoff, G. B., Arabnia, H. R., Hill, R., Staniforth, A., & Bayerl, P. S. (2015). *Application of big data for national security: a practitioner's guide to emerging technologies*. Butterworth-Heinemann.

Akter, S., McCarthy, G., Sajib, S., Michael, K., Dwivedi, Y. K., D'Ambra, J. G., & Shen, K. N. (2021). Algorithmic bias in data-driven innovation in the age of AI. *International Journal of Information Management, 60*, 102387. DOI: 10.1016/j.ijinfomgt.2021.102387

Aladebumoye, T. (2025). The role of AI in enhancing tax transparency and reducing evasion. *World Journal of Advanced Research and Reviews, 25*(1), 206–212. DOI: 10.30574/wjarr.2025.25.1.0023

Al-Akashi, F. H. A. (2022). Stock Market Index Prediction Using Artificial Neural Network. *Journal of Information Technology Research, 15*(1), 1–16. DOI: 10.4018/JITR.299918

Aldhyani, T. H. H., & Alzahrani, A. (2022). Framework for Predicting and Modeling Stock Market Prices Based on Deep Learning Algorithms. *Electronics (Basel), 11*(19), 3149. DOI: 10.3390/electronics11193149

Ali Mohamad, T., Bastone, A., Bernhard, F., & Schiavone, F. (2023). How artificial intelligence impacts the competitive position of healthcare organizations. *Journal of Organizational Change Management, 36*(8), 49–70. DOI: 10.1108/JOCM-03-2023-0057

Ali, A. H., & Thakkar, R. (2023). Climate changes through data science: Understanding and mitigating environmental crisis. *Mesopotamian Journal of Big Data, 2023*(1), 125–137. DOI: 10.58496/MJBD/2023/017

Ali, A., Qadir, J., Rasool, R. U., Sathiaseelan, A., Zwitter, A., & Crowcroft, J. (2016). Big data for development: Applications and techniques. *Big Data Analytics, 1*(1), 1–24. DOI: 10.1186/s41044-016-0002-4

Aljohani, A. (2023). Predictive analytics and machine learning for real-time supply chain risk mitigation and agility. *Sustainability (Basel), 15*(20), 15088. DOI: 10.3390/su152015088

Al-kfairy, M., Mustafa, D. G., Kshetri, N., Insiew, M., & Alfandi, O. (2024). Ethical challenges and solutions of generative AI: An interdisciplinary perspective. *Informatics (MDPI), 11*(3), 58. DOI: 10.3390/informatics11030058

Almustafa, E., Assaf, A., & Allahham, M. (2023). Implementation of Artificial Intelligence for Financial Process Innovation of Commercial Banks. *Revista de Gestão Social e Ambiental, 17*(9), e04119. DOI: 10.24857/rgsa.v17n9-004

Al-Shiab, M. (2006). The predictability of the Amman Stock Exchange using the univariate autoregressive integrated moving average (ARIMA) model. *Journal of Economic and Administrative Sciences, 22*(2), 17–35. Advance online publication. DOI: 10.1108/10264116200600006

American Immigration Council. (2024, December 16). *ICE uses a growing web of AI services to power its immigration enforcement and surveillance*. https://www.americanimmigrationcouncil.org/blog/ice-uses-ai-immigration-enforcement-surveillance/

Andersson, P. E., Arbin, K., & Rosenqvist, C. (2025). Assessing the value of artificial intelligence (AI) in governmental public procurement. *Journal of Public Procurement*.

Angenendt, S., & Koch, A. (2024). Migration forecasting: Expectations, limitations and political functions. *Forced Migration Review*, (73), 1–5. https://www.fmreview.org/digital-disruption/angenendt-koch/

Ansari, A. F., Stella, L., Turkmen, C., Zhang, X., Mercado, P., Shen, H., Shchur, O., Rangapuram, S. S., Arango, S. P., Kapoor, S., . . . Wang, Y. (2024). *Chronos: Learning the Language of Time Series*. arXiv preprint arXiv:2403.07815. https://doi.org//arXiv.2403.07815DOI: 10.48550

APEDA. (2024). *Monthly statistics*. https://apeda.gov.in/apedawebsite/Statistics/Monthly_Statistics.htm

Apte, P. (2001). The interrelationship between the stock markets and the foreign exchange market. IIM Bangalore Research Paper No. 169. https://doi.org/DOI: 10.2139/ssrn.2161245

Arab, S. T., Islam, M. M., Shamsuzzoha, M., Alam, K. F., Muhsin, N., Noguchi, R., & Ahamed, T. (2022). A review of remote sensing applications in agriculture and forestry to establish big data analytics. *Remote sensing application: regional perspectives in agriculture and forestry*, 1-24.

Arestis, P., Demetriades, P. O., & Luintel, K. B. (2001). Financial development and economic growth: The role of stock markets. *Journal of Money, Credit and Banking*, *33*(1), 16–41. DOI: 10.2307/2673870

Arihant, P., & Pratibhamoy, D. (2025). From Traditional to Computationally Efficient Scientific Computing Algorithms in Option Pricing: Current Progresses with Future Directions. *Archives of Computational Methods in Engineering*, •••, 1699–1738.

Arner, D. W., Barberis, J., & Buckley, R. P. (2016). The Evolution of Fintech: A New Post-Crisis Paradigm? *Georgetown Journal of International Law*, *47*(4), 1271–1319.

Arora, S., Ge, R., Kannan, R., & Moitra, A. (2011). *Computing a Nonnegative Matrix Factorization—Provably* (Version 1). arXiv. DOI: 10.48550/ARXIV.1111.0952

Asad, M. (2015). Optimized stock market prediction using ensemble learning. https://doi.org/DOI: 10.1109/ICAICT.2015.7338559

Ashtiani, M. N., & Raahemi, B. (2023). News-based intelligent prediction of financial markets using text mining and machine learning: A systematic literature review. *Expert Systems with Applications*, *217*, 119509. DOI: 10.1016/j.eswa.2023.119509

Awotunde, J. B., Adeniyi, E. A., Ogundokun, R. O., & Ayo, F. E. (2021). Application of big data with fintech in financial services. In *Fintech with artificial intelligence, big data, and blockchain* (pp. 107–132). Springer Singapore. DOI: 10.1007/978-981-33-6137-9_3

Aziki, A., & Fadili, M. H. (2022). Highlighting artificial intelligence roles in business area Amid the COVID-19 crisis. *Procedia Computer Science*, *203*, 450–455. DOI: 10.1016/j.procs.2022.07.060 PMID: 35974967

B R, R., Bhat, R. S., Manohar, A., & K R, M.B R. (2020). Stock Market Prediction using Machine Learning. *International Journal of Communication and Media Science*, *7*(2), 6–9. DOI: 10.14445/2349641X/IJCMS-V7I2P102

Badrul Hisham, A., Mohamed Yusof, N. A., Salleh, S. H., & Abas, H. (2024). Transforming governance: A systematic review of AI applications in policymaking. *Journal of Science, Technology and Innovation Policy.*

Bahadori, S., & Hassanzadeh, A. (2026). A comprehensive literature review on ai-based credit assessment in digital lending: Exploring models, transparency, alternative data, and real-time learning. *Expert Systems with Applications, 318*, 131872. DOI: 10.1016/j.eswa.2026.131872

Balasundaram, S., & Kapil, N. (2010, February). Application of Lagrangian twin support vector machines for classification. In *2010 Second International Conference on Machine Learning and Computing* (pp. 193-197). IEEE. DOI: 10.1109/ICMLC.2010.40

Banerjee, G. (2025). The impact of artificial intelligence on accounting and human resource management: Opportunities, challenges, and future trajectories. In *Unlocking Potential.* IIP Series. AI and Data Architecture in Management, Science, and Education.

Banerjee, S., & Mondal, A. C. (2023). An ingenious method for estimating future crop prices that emphasises machine learning and deep learning models. *International Journal of Information Technology : an Official Journal of Bharati Vidyapeeth's Institute of Computer Applications and Management, 15*(8), 4291–4313. DOI: 10.1007/s41870-023-01474-6

Bansal, M., Goyal, A., & Choudhary, A. (2022). Stock market prediction with high accuracy using machine learning techniques. *Procedia Computer Science, 215*, 247–265. DOI: 10.1016/j.procs.2022.12.028

Basher, S. A., & Sadorsky, P. (2022). Forecasting Bitcoin price direction with random forests: How important are interest rates, inflation, and market volatility? *Machine Learning with Applications, 9*, 100355. DOI: 10.1016/j.mlwa.2022.100355

Basile, A., & Gallo, M. (2025). Investigating the Impact of Accessibility on Internal Migration Flows in Italy Through the Calibration of Multiple Linear Regression Models. *WORLD (Oakland, Calif.), 6*(2), 46. DOI: 10.3390/world6020046

Beck, T., & Levine, R. (2002). Stock markets, banks, and growth: Panel evidence. NBER Working Paper No. w9082. Retrieved from SSRN.

Behera, J., Pasayat, A. K., Behera, H., & Kumar, P. (2023). Prediction based mean-value-at-risk portfolio optimization using machine learning regression algorithms for multi-national stock markets. *Engineering Applications of Artificial Intelligence, 120*, 105843. DOI: 10.1016/j.engappai.2023.105843

Belfiore, A., Salatino, A., & Osborne, F. (2022). *Characterising Research Areas in the field of AI* (Version 1). arXiv. DOI: 10.48550/ARXIV.2205.13471

Bengio, Y., Courville, A., & Vincent, P. (2013). Representation learning: A review and new perspectives. *IEEE Transactions on Pattern Analysis and Machine Intelligence, 35*(8), 1798–1828. DOI: 10.1109/TPAMI.2013.50 PMID: 23787338

Berrada, I. R., Barramou, F., & Alami, O. B. (2022). A review of artificial intelligence approach for credit risk assessment. In *2022 2nd International Conference on Artificial Intelligence and Signal Processing (AISP)* (pp. 1–5). DOI: 10.1109/AISP53593.2022.9760655

Bhadade, P., Chandak, S., Mohare, R., Dahake, P., & Tolani, K. (2025). Blockchain-Driven Decentralized Finance (DeFi): Trends, Contributions, and Future Research Directions. *2025 International Conference on Data Science and Business Systems (ICDSBS)*, 1–8. DOI: 10.1109/ICDSBS63635.2025.11031990

Bhandari, H. N., Rimal, B., Pokhrel, N. R., Rimal, R., Dahal, K., & Khatri, R. K. (2022). Predicting stock market index using LSTM. *Machine Learning with Applications, 9*, 100320. DOI: 10.1016/j.mlwa.2022.100320

Bhatakar, A., Tayde, L., Raut, S., Pakhare, A., & Bawsakar, T. (2024). Agriculture crop price prediction using machine learning. *International Journal of Innovative Ideas in Research and Development, 9*(2), 1–10. https://ijiird.com/wp-content/uploads/090205.pdf

Bhavani, K. G., & Vani, N. (2024). Artificial intelligence driven crop price and yield prediction using ML for sustainable agriculture. *International Journal of Engineering and Science, 12*(1), 45–58. https://theaspd.com/index.php/ijes/article/download/1112/838/2169

Bibiyana, D. J., Ramu, V., Rakesh, R., & Raja, S., J, J. J., & Chandramouli, S. (2025). Deep Learning for Stock Market Prediction. *2025 International Conference on Frontier Technologies and Solutions (ICFTS)*, 1–7. DOI: 10.1109/ICFTS62006.2025.11031669

Big Data for Migration Alliance. (2024). Building a policy compass: Navigating future migration with anticipatory methods. Retrieved October 2025, from https://data4migration.org

Bijak, J., Disney, G., Findlay, A. M., Forster, J. J., Smith, P. W., & Wiśniowski, A. (2019). Assessing time series models for forecasting international migration: Lessons from the United Kingdom. *Journal of Forecasting, 38*(5), 470–487. DOI: 10.1002/for.2576

Black, F., & Scholes, M. (1973). The pricing of options and corporate liabilities. *Journal of Political Economy, 81*(3), 637–654. DOI: 10.1086/260062

Bohdal, O., Yang, Y., & Hospedales, T. (2023). *Meta-Calibration: Learning of Model Calibration Using Differentiable Expected Calibration Error.*

Bouri, E., Jain, A., Biswal, P. C., & Roubaud, D. (2017). Cointegration and nonlinear causality amongst gold, oil, and the Indian stock market. *Resources Policy, 52*, 201–206. DOI: 10.1016/j.resourpol.2017.03.003

Box, G., & Jenkins, G. (1970). *Time series analysis: Forecasting and control.*

Box, G. E. P., Jenkins, G. M., Reinsel, G. C., & Ljung, G. M. (2015). *Time Series Analysis: Forecasting and Control* (5th ed.). John Wiley.

Breiman, L. (2001). Random Forests. *Machine Learning, 45*(1), 5–32. DOI: 10.1023/A:1010933404324

Bucci, A. (2020). Realized Volatility Forecasting with Neural Networks. *Journal of Financial Econometrics, 18*(3), 502–531. DOI: 10.1093/jjfinec/nbaa008

Buczynski, W., Cuzzolin, F., & Sahakian, B. (2021). A review of machine learning experiments in equity investment decision-making: Why most published research findings do not live up to their promise in real life. *International Journal of Data Science and Analytics, 11*(3), 221–242. DOI: 10.1007/s41060-021-00245-5

Bukar, U. A., Sidi, F., Jabar, M. A., Nor, R. N. H., Abdullah, S., Ishak, I., Alabadla, M., & Alkhalifah, A. (2022). How advanced technological approaches are reshaping sustainable social media crisis management and communication: A systematic review. *Sustainability (Basel), 14*(10), 5854. DOI: 10.3390/su14105854

Bukhari, A. H., Raja, M. A. Z., Sulaiman, M., Islam, S., Shoaib, M., & Kumam, P. (2020). Fractional Neuro-Sequential ARFIMA-LSTM for Financial Market Forecasting. *IEEE Access : Practical Innovations, Open Solutions, 8*, 71326–71338. DOI: 10.1109/ACCESS.2020.2985763

Bustos, O., & Pomares-Quimbaya, A. (2020). Stock market movement forecast: A Systematic review. *Expert Systems with Applications, 156*, 113464. DOI: 10.1016/j.eswa.2020.113464

Caballero Reina, J., Crespo Cuaresma, J., Fenz, K., Zellmann, J., Yankov, T., & Taha, A. (2024). Gravity models for global migration flows: A predictive evaluation. *Population Research and Policy Review, 43*(2), 29. DOI: 10.1007/s11113-024-09867-6

Caetano, R., Oliveira, J. M., & Ramos, P. (2025). Transformer-Based Models for Probabilistic Time Series Forecasting with Explanatory Variables. *Mathematics, 13*(5), 814. DOI: 10.3390/math13050814

Cao, F., Yang, S., Chen, Z., Liu, Y., & Cui, L. (2024). *Ister: Inverted Seasonal-Trend Decomposition Transformer for Explainable Multivariate Time Series Forecasting*. arXiv preprint arXiv:2403.18798. https://arxiv.org/abs/2412.18798

Cao, L. (2021). *AI in Finance: Challenges, Techniques and Opportunities* (Version 1). arXiv. https://doi.org/DOI: 10.48550/ARXIV.2107.09051

Cao, L., Yang, Q., & Yu, P. S. (2021). Data science and AI in FinTech: An overview. *International Journal of Data Science and Analytics, 12*(2), 81–99. DOI: 10.1007/s41060-021-00278-w

Carammia, M., Iacus, S. M., & Wilkin, T. (2022). Forecasting asylum-related migration flows with machine learning and data at scale. *Scientific Reports, 12*(1), 1457. DOI: 10.1038/s41598-022-05241-8 PMID: 35087096

Carta, S., Ferreira, A., Podda, A. S., Reforgiato Recupero, D., & Sanna, A. (2021). Multi-DQN: An ensemble of Deep Q-learning agents for stock market forecasting. *Expert Systems with Applications, 164*, 113820. DOI: 10.1016/j.eswa.2020.113820

Časta, M. (2023). Inflation, interest rates and the predictability of stock returns. *Finance Research Letters, 58*, 104380. DOI: 10.1016/j.frl.2023.104380

Černevičienė, J., & Kabašinskas, A. (2024). Explainable artificial intelligence (XAI) in finance: A systematic literature review. *Artificial Intelligence Review, 57*(8), 216. DOI: 10.1007/s10462-024-10854-8

Cerqueti, R., & Ficcadenti, V. (2022). Combining rank-size and k-means for clustering countries over the COVID-19 new deaths per million. *Chaos, Solitons, and Fractals, 158*, 111975. DOI: 10.1016/j.chaos.2022.111975 PMID: 35291220

Chae, J., Thom, D., Bosch, H., Jang, Y., Maciejewski, R., Ebert, D. S., & Ertl, T. (2012, October). Spatiotemporal social media analytics for abnormal event detection and examination using seasonal-trend decomposition. In *2012 IEEE conference on visual analytics science and technology (VAST)* (pp. 143-152). IEEE. DOI: 10.1109/VAST.2012.6400557

Challa, M. L., Malepati, V., & Kolusu, S. N. R. (2020). S&P BSE Sensex and S&P BSE IT return forecasting using ARIMA. *Financial Innovation, 6*(1), 47. DOI: 10.1186/s40854-020-00201-5

Chaturvedi, M., Singh, S., & Daniel, J. (2025, April). Survival Analysis for Churn Prediction in Telecom Sector Using Machine Learning. In *2025 International Conference on Computing and Communication Technologies (ICCCT)* (pp. 1-6). IEEE. DOI: 10.1109/ICCCT63501.2025.11020381

Chaudhary, G. (2024). Unveiling the black box: Bringing algorithmic transparency to AI. *Masaryk University Journal of Law and Technology*, *18*(1), 93–122. DOI: 10.5817/MUJLT2024-1-4

Chawla, Y., Shimpo, F., & Sokołowski, M. M. (2022). Artificial intelligence and information management in the energy transition of India: Lessons from the global IT heart. *Digital Policy. Regulation & Governance*, *24*(1), 17–29.

Cheng, D., Yang, F., Xiang, S., & Liu, J. (2022). Financial time series forecasting with multi-modality graph neural network. *Pattern Recognition*, *121*, 108218. DOI: 10.1016/j.patcog.2021.108218

Chen, H., Chiang, R. H., & Storey, V. C. (2012). Business intelligence and analytics: From big data to big impact. *Management Information Systems Quarterly*, *36*(4), 1165–1188. DOI: 10.2307/41703503

Chen, M., Mao, S., & Liu, Y. (2014). Big data: A survey. *Mobile Networks and Applications*, *19*(2), 171–209. DOI: 10.1007/s11036-013-0489-0

Chernysh, O., Smishko, O., Koverninska, Y., Prokopenko, M., & Pistunov, I. (2024). The Role of Artificial Intelligence in Financial Analysis and Forecasting: Using Data and Algorithms. *Economic Affairs*, *69*(3), 1493–1506.

Chinta, P. C. R., Jha, K. M., Velaga, V., Moore, C., Routhu, K., & SADARAM, G. (2024). Harnessing Big Data and AI-Driven ERP Systems to Enhance Cybersecurity Resilience in Real-Time Threat Environments. *Available at SSRN 5151788.*

Chinta, P. C. R. (2023). Leveraging Machine Learning Techniques for Predictive Analysis in Merger and Acquisition (M&A). *Journal of Artificial Intelligence and Big Data*, *3*(1), 10–31586.

Cho, K., van Merriënboer, B., Gulcehre, C., Bahdanau, D., Bougares, F., Schwenk, H., & Bengio, Y. (2014). *Learning Phrase Representations Using RNN Encoder-Decoder for Statistical Machine Translation*. arXiv preprint arXiv:2412.1879. https://doi.org//arXiv.1406.1078DOI: 10.3115/v1/D14-1179

Christensen, K., Siggaard, M., & Veliyev, B. (2023). A Machine Learning Approach to Volatility Forecasting. *Journal of Financial Econometrics*, *21*(5), 1680–1727. DOI: 10.1093/jjfinec/nbac020

Cogent | Blog | Forecasting Algorithms in Business: Choosing the Right Model for Your Industry. (n.d.). Retrieved September 17, 2025, from https://www.cogentinfo.com/resources/forecasting-algorithms-in-business-choosing-the-right-model-for-your-industry

Cohen, G. (2022). Algorithmic Trading and Financial Forecasting Using Advanced Artificial Intelligence Methodologies. *Mathematics*, *10*(18), 3302. DOI: 10.3390/math10183302

Cont, R. (2001). Empirical properties of asset returns: Stylized facts and statistical issues. Quantitative Finance, 1(2), 223–236. *Quantitative Finance*, *1*, 223–236. DOI: 10.1080/713665670

Cottier, F. (2024). Projecting future migration with Bayesian hierarchical gravity models. *Frontiers in Climate*, *5*, 1384295. DOI: 10.3389/fclim.2024.1384295

Dahake, P. S., Dahake, N. S., Bansod, S. N., Patil, P. A., & Ingle, A. (2025). Marketing Innovations in Society 5.0: A Role of Predictive Analytics in Analyzing Consumer Behavior for Marketers. In *Future-Proofing Emerging Technologies for Business Transformation* (pp. 361–386). IGI Global Scientific Publishing. https://www.igi-global.com/chapter/marketing-innovations-in-society-50/378209

Dahake, P. S., Dahake, N. S., Bansod, S. N., & Patil, P. S. (2025). Advancing Marketing in Society 5.0: The Strategic Role of Predictive Analytics in Consumer Behaviour Analysis. In Tiwari, S. P., Aurellado, E. A., & Fahrudin, A. (Eds.), *Integrating Digital Innovation and Integrated Frameworks in Manufacturing* (pp. 329–362). IGI Global Scientific Publishing., DOI: 10.4018/979-8-3373-1082-4.ch013

Dahake, P. S., Gajghate, A., Mohare, R., & Bhadade, P. (2025). Predictive Analytics in Consumer Finance: Modelling Spending Behaviours for Long-Term Economic Resilience. *2025 International Conference on Data Science and Business Systems (ICDSBS)*, 1–8. DOI: 10.1109/ICDSBS63635.2025.11031713

Dahake, P. S., Nakshane, S., Mohare, R., & Ingle, A. (2025). AI-Enabled Predictive Analytics in Marketing: Transforming Customer Engagement and Brand Strategy. *2025 International Conference on Data Science and Business Systems (ICDSBS)*, 1–7. DOI: 10.1109/ICDSBS63635.2025.11031615

Dahake, P. S., Vighney, S., Dahake, N. S., & Chandak, S. (2025). The Synergy of Quantum Marketing and Predictive Analytics: A Data-Driven Framework for Consumer Purchase Behavior in E-Commerce. *2025 International Conference on Data Science and Business Systems (ICDSBS)*, 1–7. DOI: 10.1109/ICDSBS63635.2025.11032018

Damodaran, A. (2012). *Investment Valuation: Tools and Techniques for Determining the Value of Any Asset* (3rd ed.). Wiley.

Danish, M. S. S., & Senjyu, T. (2023). Shaping the future of sustainable energy through AI-enabled circular economy policies. *Circular Economy*, *2*(1), 100010. DOI: 10.1016/j.cec.2023.100040

Darapaneni, N., Paduri, A. R., Sharma, H., Manjrekar, M., Hindlekar, N., Bhagat, P., Aiyer, U., & Agarwal, Y. (2022). *Stock Price Prediction using Sentiment Analysis and Deep Learning for Indian Markets* (Version 1). arXiv. DOI: 10.48550/ARXIV.2204.05783

Das, A., Kong, W., Sen, R., & Zhou, Y. (2024). *A Decoder-Only Foundation Model for Time-Series Forecasting*. arXiv preprint arXiv:2310.10688. https://arxiv.org/abs/2310.10688

Dash, S., Chakraborty, C., Giri, S. K., Pani, S. K., & Frnda, J. (2021). BIFM: Big-data driven intelligent forecasting model for COVID-19. *IEEE Access : Practical Innovations, Open Solutions*, *9*, 97505–97517. DOI: 10.1109/ACCESS.2021.3094658

Dastagiri, M. B., & Naga Sindhuja, P. V. (2021). Global agricultural prices and policies during WTO regime: Explorative research to price policy advocacy. *World Food Policy*, *7*(1), 6–25. DOI: 10.1002/wfp2.12023

Davidson, S. (2024). The economic institutions of artificial intelligence. *Journal of Institutional Economics*, *20*(1), 1–17. DOI: 10.1017/S1744137423000395

de Lange, P. E., Melsom, B. G., Vennerød, C. B., & Westgaard, S. (2022). Explainable AI for credit assessment in banks. *Journal of Risk and Financial Management*, *15*(12), 556. DOI: 10.3390/jrfm15120556

de Rubalcava, A. D. N. G., Piñeiro, O. S., Jiménez, R. M., Aylett-Bullock, J., Ismail, A., Kyriazi, S., Pham, K. H. (2023). Modeling Population Movements under Uncertainty at the Border in Humanitarian Crises: A Situational Analysis Tool. *arXiv preprint arXiv:2303.15614*.

Deepa, K., Karthi, M., Kavin, P., Rahulsankar, S., & Vengaimani, E. (2023). A prediction system for agricultural crops using supervised learning. In *Lecture Notes on Data Engineering and Communications Technologies* (Vol. 141, pp. 433–444). DOI: 10.1007/978-981-19-3035-5_33

Dixon, D., Sattar, H., Moros, N., Kesireddy, S. R., Ahsan, H., Lakkimsetti, M., Fatima, M., Doshi, D., Sadhu, K., & Junaid Hassan, M. (2024). Unveiling the Influence of AI Predictive Analytics on Patient Outcomes: A Comprehensive Narrative Review. *Cureus*. Advance online publication. DOI: 10.7759/cureus.59954 PMID: 38854327

Dong yu, & Deng,li. (2011). Deep learning for signal and inforlation processing. *IEEE Signal Processing Magazine* .

Dong, Z., Fan, X., & Peng, Z. (2024, August). Fnspid: A comprehensive financial news dataset in time series. In *Proceedings of the 30th ACM SIGKDD Conference on Knowledge Discovery and Data Mining* (pp. 4918-4927), DOI: DOI: 10.1145/3637528.3671629

Drobetz, W., Hollstein, F., Otto, T., & Prokopczuk, M. (2025). Estimating Stock Market Betas Via Machine Learning. *Journal of Financial and Quantitative Analysis*, *60*(3), 1074–1110. DOI: 10.1017/S0022109024000036

Dwivedi, Y. K., Hughes, L., & Ismagilova, E.. (2019). Artificial intelligence (AI): Multidisciplinary perspectives on emerging challenges, opportunities, and agenda for research, practice, and policy. *International Journal of Information Management*. Advance online publication. DOI: 10.1016/j.ijinfomgt.2019.08.002

Dwivedi, Y. K., Sharma, A., Rana, N. P., Giannakis, M., Goel, P., & Dutot, V. (2023). Evolution of artificial intelligence research in Technological Forecasting and Social Change: Research topics, trends, and future directions. *Technological Forecasting and Social Change*, *192*, 122579. DOI: 10.1016/j.techfore.2023.122579

Economic Survey (2023–2024). *Economic Survey 2023–24*. Ministry of Finance, Government of India. https://www.indiabudget.gov.in/economicsurvey/doc/echapter.pdf

Elsheikh, A. H., Saba, A. I., Panchal, H., Shanmugan, S., Alsaleh, N. A., & Ahmadein, M. (2021). Artificial Intelligence for Forecasting the Prevalence of COVID-19 Pandemic: An Overview. *Health Care*, *9*(12), 1614. DOI: 10.3390/healthcare9121614 PMID: 34946340

Et al., A. R. (2021). A study on application of artificial intelligence and machine learning in Indian taxation system. *Psychology and Education Journal.* DOI: 10.17762/pae.v58i2.2265

Eurofound. (2024). Social impact of migration: Addressing the challenges of receiving and integrating Ukrainian refugees. Retrieved October 2025, from https://www.eurofound.europa.eu/en/publications/all/social-impact-migration-addressing-challenges-receiving-and-integrating-ukrainian

Fama, E. (1970). Efficient capital markets: A review of theory and empirical work. *The Journal of Finance*, *25*(2), 383–417. DOI: 10.2307/2325486

Fang, Y., Cao, H., & Sun, J. (2022). Impact of artificial intelligence on regional green development under China's environmental decentralization system—Based on spatial durbin model and threshold effect. *International Journal of Environmental Research and Public Health, 19*(22), 14776. DOI: 10.3390/ijerph192214776 PMID: 36429493

Fan, J., & Yao, Q. (2008). *Nonlinear time series: nonparametric and parametric methods*. Springer Science & Business Media.

Fares, N. Y., Nedeljkovic, D., & Jammal, M. (2023). AI-enabled IoT applications: Towards a transparent governance framework. In *2023 IEEE Global Conference on Artificial Intelligence and Internet of Things (GCAIoT)* (pp. 109–114). DOI: 10.1109/GCAIoT61060.2023.10385106

Fasano, F., Adornetto, C., Zahid, I., La Rocca, M., Montaleone, L., Greco, G., & Cariola, A. (2024). The dilemma of accuracy in bankruptcy prediction: A new approach using explainable AI techniques to predict corporate crises. *European Journal of Innovation Management, 28*(11), 1–22. DOI: 10.1108/EJIM-06-2024-0633

Fawcett, T., Haimowitz, I. J., Provost, F. J., & Stolfo, S. (1998). AI approaches to fraud detection and risk management. *AI Magazine, 19*(2), 107–108. DOI: 10.1609/aimag.v19i2.1372

Ferreira, F. G. D. C., Gandomi, A. H., & Cardoso, R. T. N. (2021). Artificial Intelligence Applied to Stock Market Trading: A Review. *IEEE Access : Practical Innovations, Open Solutions, 9*, 30898–30917. DOI: 10.1109/ACCESS.2021.3058133

Fischer, T., & Krauss, C. (2018). Deep learning with long short-term memory networks for financial market predictions. *European Journal of Operational Research, 270*(2), 654–669. DOI: 10.1016/j.ejor.2017.11.054

Food and Agriculture Organization (FAO). (2023). *FAOSTAT: Production of maize*. https://www.fao.org/faostat/en/#data/QC

Fouejieu, A. (2017). Inflation targeting and financial stability in emerging markets. *Economic Modelling, 60*, 51–70. DOI: 10.1016/j.econmod.2016.08.020

Freeborough, W., & Van Zyl, T. (2022). Investigating Explainability Methods in Recurrent Neural Network Architectures for Financial Time Series Data. *Applied Sciences (Basel, Switzerland), 12*(3), 1427. DOI: 10.3390/app12031427

Fuster, A., Goldsmith-pinkham, P., Ramadorai, T., & Walther, A. (2022). Predictably Unequal? The Effects of Machine Learning on Credit Markets. *The Journal of Finance, 77*(1), 5–47. DOI: 10.1111/jofi.13090

G7 High-Level Panel on AI. (2024). *Artificial intelligence and economic/financial policy: Report of the G7 high-level panel.* Group of Seven.

Gallego, I., & Font, X. (2021). Changes in air passenger demand as a result of the COVID-19 crisis: Using Big Data to inform tourism policy. *Journal of Sustainable Tourism, 29*(9), 1470–1489. DOI: 10.1080/09669582.2020.1773476

Gao, A. (2022). *National strategy for the development of artificial intelligence in the context of the global digital economy.* Artificial Societies., DOI: 10.18254/S207751800020634-6

Gaskin, T., & Abel, G. J. (2025). Deep learning 40 years of human migration. *arXiv preprint arXiv:2506.22821*

George, G., Haas, M. R., & Pentland, A. (2014). Big data and management. *Academy of Management Journal, 57*(2), 321–326. DOI: 10.5465/amj.2014.4002

Gepp, A., Linnenluecke, M. K., O'neill, T. J., & Smith, T. (2018). Big data techniques in auditing research and practice: Current trends and future opportunities. *Journal of Accounting Literature, 40*(1), 102–115. DOI: 10.1016/j.acclit.2017.05.003

Global Pulse, U. N. (2023). *2022 Annual Report: UN Global Pulse Showed Its Value in a Changing World.* https://www.unglobalpulse.org/2022-annual-report-un-global-pulse-showed-its-value-in-a-changing-world/

González-Núñez, E., Trejo, L. A., & Kampouridis, M. (2025). Expanding a machine learning class towards its application to the stock market forecast. *Applied Intelligence, 55*(1), 21. DOI: 10.1007/s10489-024-06018-4

Goodell, J. W., Kumar, S., Lim, W. M., & Pattnaik, D. (2021). Artificial intelligence and machine learning in finance: Identifying foundations, themes, and research clusters from bibliometric analysis. *Journal of Behavioral and Experimental Finance, 32*, 100577. DOI: 10.1016/j.jbef.2021.100577

Goodfellow, I., Bengio, Y., & Courville, A. (2016). *Deep Learning*. MIT Press.

Goodfellow, I., Bengio, Y., & Courville, A. (2016). *Deep learning*. The MIT Press.

Goodman, B., & Flaxman, S. (2017). European Union regulations on algorithmic decision-making and a 'right to explanation'. *AI Magazine, 38*(3), 50–57. DOI: 10.1609/aimag.v38i3.2741

Goralski, M. A., & Tan, T. K. (2020). Artificial intelligence and sustainable development. *International Journal of Management Education, 18*(1), 100330. DOI: 10.1016/j.ijme.2019.100330

Government of India. (2010). *Manual on agricultural prices and marketing*. Ministry of Statistics and Programme Implementation. https://www.mospi.gov.in/sites/default/files/publication_reports/manual_agr_price_mark_25oct10_0.pdf

Granger, C. W. J., & Hatanaka, M. (2015). *Spectral analysis of economic time series. (PSME-1)*. Princeton university press.

Granovetter, M. (1985). Economic action and social structure: The problem of embeddedness. *American Journal of Sociology*, *91*(3), 481–510. DOI: 10.1086/228311

Grover, V., Chiang, R. H., Liang, T. P., & Zhang, D. (2018). Creating strategic business value from big data analytics: A research framework. *Journal of Management Information Systems*, *35*(2), 388–423. DOI: 10.1080/07421222.2018.1451951

Gruver, N., Finzi, M., Qiu, S., & Wilson, A. G. (2023). *Large Language Models Are Zero-Shot Time Series Forecasters*. arXiv preprint arXiv:2310.07820. https://doi.org//arXiv.2310.07820DOI: 10.52202/075280-0861

Guida, M., Caniato, F., Moretto, A., & Ronchi, S. (2023). The role of artificial intelligence in the procurement process: State of the art and research agenda. *Journal of Purchasing and Supply Management*, *29*(2), 100823. DOI: 10.1016/j.pursup.2023.100823

Gupta, A., Dengre, V., Kheruwala, H. A., & Shah, M. (2020). Comprehensive review of text-mining applications in finance. *Financial Innovation*, *6*(1), 39. DOI: 10.1186/s40854-020-00205-1

Gupta, S., Kumar, P., Singh, A., & Sharma, R. (2022). Machine learning-and feature selection-enabled framework for accurate crop yield prediction. *Journal of Food Quality*, *2022*, 6293985. Advance online publication. DOI: 10.1155/2022/6293985

Guptha, K. S. K., & Rao, R. P. (2018). The causal relationship between financial development and economic growth: An experience with BRICS economies. *Journal of Social and Economic Development*, *20*(2), 308–326. DOI: 10.1007/s40847-018-0071-5

Haafza, L. A., Awan, M. J., Abid, A., Yasin, A., Nobanee, H., & Farooq, M. S. (2021). Big data covid-19 systematic literature review: Pandemic crisis. *Electronics (Basel)*, *10*(24), 3125. DOI: 10.3390/electronics10243125

Hadji Misheva, B., Jaggi, D., Posth, J.-A., Gramespacher, T., & Osterrieder, J. (2021). Audience-Dependent Explanations for AI-Based Risk Management Tools: A Survey. *Frontiers in Artificial Intelligence*, *4*, 794996. DOI: 10.3389/frai.2021.794996

Hakala, K. (2019). *Robo-advisors as a form of artificial intelligence in private customers' investment advisory services*. https://aaltodoc.aalto.fi/handle/123456789/39329

Hamzah, M., Ahmed, S. F., & Sakthi, P. (2025). FutureCrop: AI-powered price prediction for agriculture and vegetable markets. *International Journal of Scientific Development and Research, 10*(4), c528–c534. https://ijsdr.org/papers/IJSDR2504268.pdf

Han, S., Ko, Y., Kim, J., & Hong, T. (2018). Housing market trend forecasts through statistical comparisons based on big data analytic methods. *Journal of Management Engineering*, *34*(2), 04017054. DOI: 10.1061/(ASCE)ME.1943-5479.0000583

Hanwacker, L. S. (2025). The role of artificial intelligence in disaster recovery. *Journal of Business Continuity & Emergency Planning*, *18*(2), 167–179. DOI: 10.69554/CYWN4471 PMID: 39567851

Haq, A. U., Zeb, A., Lei, Z., & Zhang, D. (2021). Forecasting daily stock trend using multi-filter feature selection and deep learning. *Expert Systems with Applications*, *168*, 114444. DOI: 10.1016/j.eswa.2020.114444

Harrison, B., & Moore, M. (2012). Stock market efficiency, non-linearity, thin trading, and asymmetric information in MENA stock markets. *Economic Issues*, *17*(1), 77–93.

Hassani, H., & Silva, E. S. (2015). Forecasting with big data: A review. *Annals of Data Science*, *2*(1), 5–19. DOI: 10.1007/s40745-015-0029-9

Hegde, G., Hulipalled, V. R., & Simha, J. B. (2021). Price prediction of agriculture commodities using machine learning and NLP. In *2021 Second International Conference on Smart Technologies in Computing, Electrical and Electronics (ICSTCEE)* (pp. 1–6). IEEE. DOI: 10.1109/ICSTCEE54422.2021.9708582

He, K., Yang, Q., Ji, L., Pan, J., & Zou, Y. (2023). Financial Time Series Forecasting with the Deep Learning Ensemble Model. *Mathematics*, *11*(4), 1054. DOI: 10.3390/math11041054

Hemalatha, S., Kavitha, T., Saravanan, T. M., Chithra, K., & Dinesh, N. (2022). Forecasting crop using machine learning model. In *IEEE 3rd International Conference on Electronics and Sustainable Communication Systems (ICESC)* (pp. 783–788). IEEE. DOI: 10.1109/ICESC54411.2022.9885377

Heston, S. L. (1993). A closed-form solution for options with stochastic volatility with applications to bond and currency options. *Review of Financial Studies*, *6*(2), 327–343. DOI: 10.1093/rfs/6.2.327

Hiremath, G. S., & Narayan, S. (2016). Testing the adaptive market hypothesis and its determinants for the Indian stock markets. *Finance Research Letters*, *19*, 173–180. DOI: 10.1016/j.frl.2016.07.009

Hochreiter, S., & Schmidhuber, J. (1997). Long Short-Term Memory. Neural Computation, 9(8), 1735–1780.). *Neural Computation*, *9*, 1735–1780. DOI: 10.1162/neco.1997.9.8.1735 PMID: 9377276

Hou, Y., Liu, F., Gao, J., Cheng, C., & Song, C. (2017). Characterizing complexity changes in Chinese stock markets by permutation entropy. *Entropy (Basel, Switzerland)*, *19*(10), 514. DOI: 10.3390/e19100514

Ho, W. K. O., Tang, B.-S., & Wong, S. W. (2021). Predicting property prices with machine learning algorithms. *Journal of Property Research*, *38*(1), 48–70. DOI: 10.1080/09599916.2020.1832558

Htun, H. H., Biehl, M., & Petkov, N. (2023). Survey of feature selection and extraction techniques for stock market prediction. *Financial Innovation*, *9*(1), 26. DOI: 10.1186/s40854-022-00441-7

Huang, C., Deng, Y., Yang, X., Yang, X., & Cao, J. (2023). Can financial crisis be detected? Laplacian energy measure. *European Journal of Finance*, *29*(9), 949–976. DOI: 10.1080/1351847X.2022.2091946

Huang, Y., Gao, Y., Gan, Y., & Ye, M. (2021). A new financial data forecasting model using genetic algorithm and long short-term memory network. *Neurocomputing*, *425*, 207–218. DOI: 10.1016/j.neucom.2020.04.086

Hull, J. C. (2017). *Options, Futures, and Other Derivatives* (9th ed.). Pearson Education.

Hutchinson, J., Lo, A. W., & Poggio, T. (1994). A Nonparametric Approach to Pricing and Hedging Derivative Securities Via Learning Networks. *The Journal of Finance*, *49*(3), 851–889. DOI: 10.1111/j.1540-6261.1994.tb00081.x

Hu, Z., Zhao, Y., & Khushi, M. (2021). A Survey of Forex and Stock Price Prediction Using Deep Learning. *Applied System Innovation*, *4*(1), 9. DOI: 10.3390/asi4010009

Hyndman, R. J., & Athanasopoulos, G. (2021). *Forecasting: Principles and Practice* (3rd ed.). OTexts.

Ibrahim, R., Kim, S.-H., & Tong, J. (2020). Eliciting Human Judgment for Prediction Algorithms. SSRN *Electronic Journal*. DOI: 10.2139/ssrn.3606633

Ibrahim, N. F., & Wang, X. (2019). Decoding the sentiment dynamics of online retailing customers: Time series analysis of social media. *Computers in Human Behavior*, *96*, 32–45. DOI: 10.1016/j.chb.2019.02.004

IDMC – Internal Displacement Monitoring Centre. (2023). *Global report on internal displacement 2023.* https://www.internal-displacement.org/global-report/grid2023/

International Organization for Migration (IOM) & World Food Program (WFP). (2022). *Understanding the adverse drivers and implications of migration from El Salvador, Guatemala and Honduras*. IOM Publications. https://lac.iom.int/sites/g/files/tmzbdl1446/files/documents/executive-summary-understanding-the-adverse-drivers-and-implications-of-migration-from-el-salvador-guatemala-and-honduras-i-1.pdf

International Organization for Migration (IOM). (2021). *World Migration Report, 2022*, https://publications.iom.int/books/world-migration-report-2022

Jahin, M. A., Naife, S. A., Saha, A. K., & Mridha, M. F. (2024). *AI in Supply Chain Risk Assessment: A Systematic Literature Review and Bibliometric Analysis* (Version 5). arXiv. DOI: 10.48550/ARXIV.2401.10895

Jain, A., & Biswal, P. C. (2016). Dynamic linkages among oil price, gold price, exchange rate, and stock market in India. *Resources Policy*, *49*, 179–185. DOI: 10.1016/j.resourpol.2016.06.001

Jain, V., & Kulkarni, P. A. (2023). *Integrating AI techniques for enhanced financial forecasting and budgeting strategies*. International Journal of Economics and Management Studies., DOI: 10.14445/23939125/IJEMS-V10I9P102

Jalidy, I., & Elhiri, A. (2025). Intelligence artificielle et FinTechs au Maroc: Vers un modèle hybride de gouvernance technologique. *international Journal of Accounting, Finance, Auditing, Management and Economics*, 391-410.

James, G., Witten, D., Hastie, T., & Tibshirani, R. (2013). *An Introduction to Statistical Learning*. Springer. DOI: 10.1007/978-1-4614-7138-7

Jiang, W. (2021). Applications of deep learning in stock market prediction: Recent progress. *Expert Systems with Applications*, *184*, 115537. DOI: 10.1016/j.eswa.2021.115537

Jiang, Y. (2022). Prediction model of the impact of innovation and entrepreneurship on China's digital economy based on neural network integration systems. *Neural Computing & Applications*, *34*(4), 2661–2675. DOI: 10.1007/s00521-021-05899-7

Jin, C. (2024). Research on the path of artificial intelligence empowering high-quality economic development. *Journal of Artificial Intelligence Practice*. DOI: 10.23977/jaip.2024.070305

Johora, F. T., Hasan, R., Farabi, S. F., Alam, M. Z., Sarkar, M. I., & Al Mahmud, M. A. (2024). AI advances: Enhancing banking security with fraud detection. In *2024 First International Conference on Technological Innovations and Advance Computing (TIACOMP)* (pp. 289–294). DOI: 10.1109/TIACOMP64125.2024.00055

Jordà, Ò., Schularick, M., & Taylor, A. M. (2010). *Financial crises, credit booms, and external imbalances: 140 years of lessons* (No. w16567). National Bureau of Economic Research, DOI: .DOI: 10.1057/imfer.2011.8

Kabir, M. R., Bhadra, D., Ridoy, M., & Milanova, M. (2025). LSTM–Transformer-Based Robust Hybrid Deep Learning Model for Financial Time Series Forecasting. *Sci*, *7*(1), 7. DOI: 10.3390/sci7010007

Kale, M., Gharat, H., & Rodrigues, C. V. (2024). The Role of Artificial Intelligence in Financial Prediction Models for Forecasting Market Trends with Traditional Methods. [EEL]. *European Economic Letters*, *14*(3), 1533–1544.

Kamalov, F., Gurrib, I., & Rajab, K. (2021). Financial forecasting with machine learning: price vs return. *Kamalov, F., Gurrib, I. & Rajab, K.(2021). Financial Forecasting with Machine Learning: Price Vs Return. Journal of Computational Science*, *17*(3), 251–264. DOI: 10.3844/jcssp.2021.251.264

Kamara, A. F., Chen, E., & Pan, Z. (2022). An ensemble of a boosted hybrid of deep learning models and technical analysis for forecasting stock prices. *Information Sciences*, *594*, 1–19. DOI: 10.1016/j.ins.2022.02.015

Kanaparthi, V. (2024). *Transformational application of Artificial Intelligence and Machine learning in Financial Technologies and Financial services: A bibliometric review*. https://doi.org/DOI: 10.48550/ARXIV.2401.15710

Kara, N., Atamanchuk, Z. A., & Kurytskyi, V. (2024). Formation of mechanisms for anti-crisis management of enterprises: International economic features. *Journal of Lviv Polytechnic National University: Economics and Management Issues*. DOI: 10.23939/semi2024.02.197

Karim, R., Alam, M., & Hossain, R. (2021). Stock market analysis using linear regression and decision tree regression. https://doi.org/DOI: 10.1109/eSmarTA52612.2021.9515762

Kartanaitė, I., Kovalov, B., Kubatko, O., & Krušinskas, R. (2021). Financial modeling trends for production companies in the context of Industry 4.0. *Investment Management and Financial Innovations, 18*(1), 270–284. DOI: 10.21511/imfi.18(1).2021.23

Khan, M. A., Saqib, S., Alyas, T., Ur Rehman, A., Saeed, Y., Zeb, A., Zareei, M., & Mohamed, E. M. (2020). Effective Demand Forecasting Model Using Business Intelligence Empowered With Machine Learning. *IEEE Access : Practical Innovations, Open Solutions, 8*, 116013–116023. DOI: 10.1109/ACCESS.2020.3003790

Khan, Q., Ikram, S., & Mehtab, M. (2011). Testing weak form market efficiency of Indian capital market: A case of NSE and BSE. *African Journal of Marketing Management*, •••, 3.

Khan, W., Ghazanfar, M. A., Azam, M. A., Karami, A., Alyoubi, K. H., & Alfakeeh, A. S. (2022). Stock market prediction using machine learning classifiers and social media [news]. *Journal of Ambient Intelligence and Humanized Computing, 13*(7), 3433–3456. DOI: 10.1007/s12652-020-01839-w

Khattak, B. H. A., Shafi, I., Khan, A. S., Flores, E. S., Lara, R. G., Samad, M., & Ashraf, I. (2023). A Systematic Survey of AI Models in Financial Market Forecasting for Profitability Analysis. *IEEE Access : Practical Innovations, Open Solutions, 11*, 125359–125380. DOI: 10.1109/ACCESS.2023.3330156

Kiseleva, A., Kotzinos, D., & Hert, P. D. (2022). Transparency of AI in healthcare as a multilayered system of accountabilities. *Frontiers in Artificial Intelligence, 5*, 879603. Advance online publication. DOI: 10.3389/frai.2022.879603 PMID: 35707765

Kohavi, R. (1995). A study of cross-validation and bootstrap for accuracy estimation and model selection. *Proceedings of the 14th international joint conference on Artificial intelligence*, 1137 - 1143.

Konak, F., & Şeker, Y. (2014). The efficiency of developed markets: Empirical evidence from FTSE 100. *Journal of Advanced Management Science, 2*(1), 29–32. DOI: 10.12720/joams.2.1.29-32

Kontopoulou, V. I., Panagopoulos, A. D., Kakkos, I., & Matsopoulos, G. K. (2023). A Review of ARIMA vs. Machine Learning Approaches for Time Series Forecasting in Data Driven Networks. *Future Internet, 15*(8), 255. DOI: 10.3390/fi15080255

Korinek, A. (2024). *Economic policy challenges for the age of AI.* DOI: 10.3386/w32980

Korinek, A., & Stiglitz, J. E. (2021). *Artificial intelligence, globalization, and strategies for economic development* (No. w28453). National Bureau of Economic Research.

Kottapallis, S. R. K., Hublis, K., Chandrashekhara, S., Jain, G., Hublis, S., Botla, G., & Doddaiah, R. (2025). *Foundation Models for Time Series: A Survey*. arXiv preprint arXiv:2504.04011. https://arxiv.org/abs/2504.04011

Kour, M. (2024). Challenges and opportunities of machine learning in the financial sector. *Algorithmic approaches to financial technology: forecasting, trading, and optimization*, 61-73.

Koyuncugil, A. S., & Ozgulbas, N. (2012). Financial early warning system model and data mining application for risk detection. *Expert Systems with Applications, 39*(6), 6238–6253. DOI: 10.1016/j.eswa.2011.12.021

Kumar, G., Jain, S., & Singh, U. P. (2021). Stock Market Forecasting Using Computational Intelligence: A Survey. *Archives of Computational Methods in Engineering, 28*(3), 1069–1101. DOI: 10.1007/s11831-020-09413-5

Kumar, N., Kushwaha, R. R., Meena, N. R., Mishra, H., & Yadav, A. P. S. (2023). A study on costs and returns of paddy cultivation in Ambedkar Nagar district of Uttar Pradesh. *International Journal of Statistics and Applied Mathematics, SP, 8*(3), 107–111.

Kumar, S. N. A., Madhavi, R., & Sundar Rajan, M. (2025). Explainable AI in Financial Forecasting Using Time Series Analysis. *International Journal for Research in Applied Science and Engineering Technology, 13*(4), 7155–7160. DOI: 10.22214/ijraset.2025.70080

Kumbure, M. M., Lohrmann, C., Luukka, P., & Porras, J. (2022). Machine learning techniques and data for stock market forecasting: A literature review. *Expert Systems with Applications, 197*, 116659. DOI: 10.1016/j.eswa.2022.116659

Kurani, A., Doshi, P., Vakharia, A., & Shah, M. (2023). A Comprehensive Comparative Study of Artificial Neural Network (ANN) and Support Vector Machines (SVM) on Stock Forecasting. *Annals of Data Science, 10*(1), 183–208. DOI: 10.1007/s40745-021-00344-x

Kureljusic, M., & Karger, E. (2023). Forecasting in financial accounting with artificial intelligence–A systematic literature review and future research agenda. *Journal of Applied Accounting Research, 25*(1), 81–104. DOI: 10.1108/JAAR-06-2022-0146

Kurihara, Y., & Fukushima, A. (2017). The Market Efficiency of Bitcoin: A Weekly Anomaly Perspective. *Journal of Applied Finance & Banking, 7*(3), 1–4.

Lamrani, K., & Bennis, L. (2021). *La couverture du risque de change au sein des entreprises marocaines*. Revue Internationale du Chercheur. DOI: 10.52502/ijfaema.v3i4.119

Lanari, R., Bonano, M., Casu, F., Luca, C. D., Manunta, M., Manzo, M., Onorato, G., & Zinno, I. (2020). Automatic generation of Sentinel-1 continental scale DInSAR deformation time series through an extended P-SBAS processing pipeline in a cloud computing environment. *Remote Sensing (Basel), 12*(18), 2961. DOI: 10.3390/rs12182961

Lara-Benítez, P., Carranza-García, M., & Riquelme, J. C. (2021). An Experimental Review on Deep Learning Architectures for Time Series Forecasting. *International Journal of Neural Systems, 31*(03), 2130001. DOI: 10.1142/S0129065721300011

Larsson, S., & Heintz, F. (2020). Transparency in artificial intelligence. *Internet Policy Review, 9*(2). Advance online publication. DOI: 10.14763/2020.2.1469

Lee, E. S. (1966). A theory of migration. *Demography, 3*(1), 47–57. DOI: 10.2307/2060063

Lee, M., Hayes, D., & Maher, C. S. (2024). *AI as a budgeting tool: Panacea or Pandora's box?* Public Finance Journal., DOI: 10.59469/pfj.2024.6

Levine, R. (1997). Financial development and economic growth: Views and agenda. *Journal of Economic Literature, 35*, 688–726.

Li, A. W., & Bastos, G. S. (2020). Stock Market Forecasting Using Deep Learning and Technical Analysis: A Systematic Review. *IEEE Access : Practical Innovations, Open Solutions, 8*, 185232–185242. DOI: 10.1109/ACCESS.2020.3030226

Li, H., Zhang, R., Lee, Y.-C., Kraut, R. E., & Mohr, D. C. (2023). Systematic review and meta-analysis of AI-based conversational agents for promoting mental health and well-being. *NPJ Digital Medicine, 6*(1), 236. DOI: 10.1038/s41746-023-00979-5

Ling, T., & Cai, Y. (2022). Financial Crisis Prediction Based on Long-Term and Short-Term Memory Neural Network. *Wireless Communications and Mobile Computing, 2022*(1), 5728470. DOI: 10.1155/2022/5728470

Li, S. (2024). Advancing financial crisis prediction: Big data, AI, and economic theories. *Applied and Computational Engineering, 74*(1), 104–109. DOI: 10.54254/2755-2721/74/20240448

Li, S., Chen, J., Sun, Y., Wang, Z., Du, J., & He, W. (2024). *AI-driven transformation: From economic forecasting to strategic management.* Applied and Computational Engineering., DOI: 10.54254/2755-2721/57/20241319

Liu, H., & Long, Z. (2020). An improved deep learning model for predicting stock market price time series. *Digital Signal Processing, 102*, 102741. DOI: 10.1016/j.dsp.2020.102741

Liu, X., Guo, J., Wang, H., & Zhang, F. (2022). Prediction of stock market index based on ISSA-BP neural network. *Expert Systems with Applications*, *204*, 117604. DOI: 10.1016/j.eswa.2022.117604

Livieris, I. E., Pintelas, E., & Pintelas, P. (2020). A CNN–LSTM Model for Gold Price Time-Series Forecasting. *Neural Computing & Applications*, *32*(23), 17351–17360. DOI: 10.1007/s00521-020-04867-x

Li, X., Sigov, A., Ratkin, L., Ivanov, L. A., & Li, L. (2023). Artificial intelligence applications in finance: A survey. *Journal of Management Analytics*, *10*(4), 676–692. DOI: 10.1080/23270012.2023.2244503

Li, Y., & Pan, Y. (2022). A novel ensemble deep learning model for stock prediction based on stock prices and news. *International Journal of Data Science and Analytics*, *13*(2), 139–149. DOI: 10.1007/s41060-021-00279-9

Lo, A. (2004). The adaptive markets hypothesis: Market efficiency from an evolutionary perspective.

Lo, A. W., Mamaysky, H., & Wang, J. (2000). Foundations of technical analysis: Computational algorithms, statistical inference, and empirical implementation. *The Journal of Finance*, *55*(4), 1705–1765. DOI: 10.1111/0022-1082.00265

Loukis, E., Maragoudakis, M., & Kyriakou, N. (2020). *Artificial intelligence-based public sector data analytics for economic crisis policymaking. Transforming Government: People*. Process and Policy., DOI: 10.1108/TG-11-2019-0113

Mahmoud, A., & Mohammed, A. (2021). A survey on deep learning for time-series forecasting. *Machine learning and big data analytics paradigms: analysis, applications and challenges*, 365-392, DOI: .DOI: 10.1007/978-3-030-59338-4_19

Majeed, A., & Hwang, S. O. (2023). When AI meets information privacy: The adversarial role of AI in data sharing scenario. *IEEE Access : Practical Innovations, Open Solutions*, *11*, 76177–76195. DOI: 10.1109/ACCESS.2023.3297646

Makridakis, S., Spiliotis, E., & Assimakopoulos, V. (2020). The M4 Competition: 100,000 Time Series and 61 Forecasting Methods. *International Journal of Forecasting*, *36*(1), 54–74. DOI: 10.1016/j.ijforecast.2019.04.014

Makridakis, S., Spiliotis, E., Assimakopoulos, V., Semenoglou, A.-A., Mulder, G., & Nikolopoulos, K. (2023). Statistical, machine learning and deep learning forecasting methods: Comparisons and ways forward. *The Journal of the Operational Research Society*, *74*(3), 840–859. DOI: 10.1080/01605682.2022.2118629

Malempati, M. (2022). Transforming Payment Ecosystems Through The Synergy Of Artificial Intelligence, Big Data Technologies, And Predictive Financial Modeling. *Big Data Technologies, And Predictive Financial Modeling (November 07, 2022).*

Mallikarjuna, M., & Rao, R. P. (2019). Evaluation of forecasting methods from selected stock market returns. *Financial Innovation, 5*(1), 40. DOI: 10.1186/s40854-019-0157-x

Manyika, J., Chui, M., Brown, B., Bughin, J., Dobbs, R., Roxburgh, C., & Hung Byers, A. (2011). Big data: The next frontier for innovation, competition, and productivity.

Ma, S., & Fildes, R. (2021). Retail sales forecasting with meta-learning. *European Journal of Operational Research, 288*(1), 111–128. DOI: 10.1016/j.ejor.2020.05.038

Masini, R. P., Medeiros, M. C., & Mendes, E. F. (2023). Machine learning advances for time series forecasting. *Journal of Economic Surveys, 37*(1), 76–111. DOI: 10.1111/joes.12429

Masoud, N. (2024). *Artificial intelligence and unemployment dynamics: An econometric analysis in high-income economies.* Technological Sustainability., DOI: 10.1108/TECHS-04-2024-0033

Massey, D. S., Arango, J., Hugo, G., Kouaouci, A., Pellegrino, A., & Taylor, J. E. (1993). Theories of international migration: A review and appraisal. *Population and Development Review, 19*(3), 431–466. DOI: 10.2307/2938462

McAuliffe, M., Blower, J., & Beduschi, A. (2021). Digitalization and Artificial Intelligence in Migration and Mobility: Transnational Implications of the COVID-19 Pandemic. *Societies (Basel, Switzerland), 11*(4), 135. DOI: 10.3390/soc11040135

Md, A. Q., & Kapoor, S., A.V., C. J., Sivaraman, A. K., Tee, K. F., H., S., & N., J. (. (2023). Novel optimization approach for stock price forecasting using multi-layered sequential LSTM. *Applied Soft Computing, 134*, 109830. DOI: 10.1016/j.asoc.2022.109830

Mdladla, L. T. S., Wider, W., Thanathanchuchot, T., et al. (2024). Navigating the AI revolution: A review of transformative strategies for economic development in Africa's emerging economies. *Journal of Infrastructure, Policy and Development.*

Melnychenko, O. (2020). Is Artificial Intelligence Ready to Assess an Enterprise's Financial Security? *Journal of Risk and Financial Management, 13*(9), 191. DOI: 10.3390/jrfm13090191

Mennella, C., Maniscalco, U., De Pietro, G., & Esposito, M. (2024). Ethical and regulatory challenges of AI technologies in healthcare: A narrative review. *Heliyon*, *10*(4), e26297. DOI: 10.1016/j.heliyon.2024.e26297 PMID: 38384518

Merton, R. C. (1973). An intertemporal capital asset pricing model. *Econometrica*, *41*(5), 867–887. DOI: 10.2307/1913811

Metawa, N., Nguyen, P. T., Le Hoang Thuy To Nguyen, Q., Elhoseny, M., & Shankar, K. (2021). Internet of things enabled financial crisis prediction in enterprises using optimal feature subset selection-based classification model. *Big Data*, *9*(5), 331–342. DOI: 10.1089/big.2020.0192 PMID: 34030465

Mhlanga, D. (2021). Financial Inclusion in Emerging Economies: The Application of Machine Learning and Artificial Intelligence in Credit Risk Assessment. *International Journal of Financial Studies*, *9*(3), 39. DOI: 10.3390/ijfs9030039

Michalak, T. P., & Wooldridge, M. (2017). AI and economics. *IEEE Intelligent Systems*, *32*(1), 5–7. DOI: 10.1109/MIS.2017.10

Migration Data Portal. (2024). AI / Machine learning in migration studies. https://www.migrationdataportal.org/data-sources/ai-machine-learning

Migration Data Portal. (2024). *AI and Big Data for Migration Forecasting*. International Organization for Migration. https://www.migrationdataportal.org

Misheva, B. H., Osterrieder, J., Hirsa, A., Kulkarni, O., & Lin, S. F. (2021). *Explainable AI in Credit Risk Management* (Version 1). arXiv. DOI: 10.48550/ARXIV.2103.00949

Mishra, H. (2024). Nanobiostimulants and Precision Agriculture: A Data-Driven Approach to Farming and Market Dynamics. In *Nanobiostimulants: Emerging Strategies for Agricultural Sustainability* (pp. 365-398). Cham: Springer Nature Switzerland, DOI: DOI: 10.1007/978-3-031-68138-7_16

Mishra, H. (2024). The Role of Ethnoeconomics in Promoting Sustainable Consumption and Production Patterns: A Pathway to Environmental Protection and Economic Prosperity. *Sustainable Development.* In *Seen Through the Lenses of Ethnoeconomics and the Circular Economy* (pp. 91-123). Cham: Springer Nature Switzerland, DOI: DOI: 10.1007/978-3-031-72676-7_6

Mishra, H. (2025). Environmental Degradation and Impacts on Agricultural Production: A Challenge to Urban Sustainability. In *Sustainable Urban Environment and Waste Management: Theory and Practice* (pp. 53-92). Singapore: Springer Nature Singapore, DOI: DOI: 10.1007/978-981-96-1140-9_3

Mishra, H., & Mishra, D. (2024). AI for Data-Driven Decision-Making in Smart Agriculture: From Field to Farm Management. In *Artificial Intelligence Techniques in Smart Agriculture* (pp. 173-193). Singapore: Springer Nature Singapore, DOI: DOI: 10.1007/978-981-97-5878-4_11

Mishra, H., & Mishra, D. (2024). Economic evaluation of UAV-based soil sampling approaches. In *Applications of Computer Vision and Drone Technology in Agriculture 4.0* (pp. 271–291). Springer Nature Singapore., DOI: 10.1007/978-981-99-8684-2_15

Mishra, H., & Mishra, D. (2024). Sustainable Smart Agriculture to Ensure Zero Hunger. In *Sustainable Development Goals* (pp. 16–37). CRC Press., DOI: 10.1201/9781003468257-2

Mittelstadt, B., Russell, C., & Wachter, S. (2019, January). Explaining explanations in AI. In *Proceedings of the conference on fairness, accountability, and transparency* (pp. 279-288). DOI: 10.1145/3287560.3287574

Moghar, A., & Hamiche, M. (2020). Stock market prediction using LSTM recurrent neural network. *Procedia Computer Science, 170*, 1168–1173. DOI: 10.1016/j.procs.2020.03.049

Mohammadi, M., Al-Fuqaha, A., Sorour, S., & Guizani, M. (2018). Deep learning for IoT big data and streaming analytics: A survey. *IEEE Communications Surveys and Tutorials, 20*(4), 2923–2960. DOI: 10.1109/COMST.2018.2844341

Mohanty, M. K., Guha Thakurta, P. K., & Kar, S. (2023). Agricultural commodity price prediction model: A machine learning framework. *Neural Computing & Applications, 35*(20), 15109–15128. DOI: 10.1007/s00521-023-08528-7

Mondal, P., Shit, L., & Goswami, S. (2014). Study of effectiveness of time series modeling (ARIMA) in forecasting stock prices. *International Journal of Computer Science. Engineering and Applications, 4*(2), 13–29. DOI: 10.5121/ijcsea.2014.4202

Montero-Manso, P., & Hyndman, R. J. (2021). Principles and algorithms for forecasting groups of time series: Locality and globality. *International Journal of Forecasting, 37*(4), 1632–1653. DOI: 10.1016/j.ijforecast.2021.03.004

Montgomery, D. C., Jennings, C. L., & Kulahci, M. (2015). *Introduction to time series analysis and forecasting*. John Wiley & Sons.

Mroua, M., & Lamine, A. (2023). Financial time series prediction under Covid-19 pandemic crisis with Long Short-Term Memory (LSTM) network. *Humanities & Social Sciences Communications, 10*(1), 1–15. DOI: 10.1057/s41599-023-02042-w

Mukherjee, S., Sadhukhan, B., Sarkar, N., Roy, D., & De, S. (2023). Stock market prediction using deep learning algorithms. *CAAI Transactions on Intelligence Technology*, *8*(1), 82–94. DOI: 10.1049/cit2.12059

Muma, B., & Karoki, A. (2022). Modeling GDP using autoregressive integrated moving average (ARIMA) model: A systematic review. *OAlib*, *9*(4), 1–8. DOI: 10.4236/oalib.1108355

Murri, S., Bhoyar, M., Selvarajan, G. P., & Malaga, M. (2024). Transforming Decision-Making with Big Data Analytics: Advanced Approaches to Real-Time Insights, Predictive Modeling, and Scalable Data Integration. *International Journal of Communication Networks and Information Security*, *16*(5), 506–519.

Nabipour, M., Nayyeri, P., Jabani, H., Mosavi, A., Salwana, E., & S, S. (2020). Deep Learning for Stock Market Prediction. *Entropy (Basel, Switzerland)*, *22*(8), 840. DOI: 10.3390/e22080840

Nahar, J., Hossain, M. S., Rahman, M. M., & Hossain, M. A. (2024). Advanced predictive analytics for comprehensive risk assessment in financial markets: Strategic applications and sector-wide implications. *Global Mainstream Journal of Business, Economics. Development & Project Management*, *3*(4), 39–53.

Naik, R., & Reddy, Y. V. (2021). Examination of long memory in the Indian stock market: A sectoral juxtaposition. *FIIB Business Review*, *14*(2), 184–202. Advance online publication. DOI: 10.1177/23197145211040274

Năstasă, A., Dumitra, T.-C., & Grigorescu, A. (2024). Artificial intelligence and sustainable development during the pandemic: An overview of the scientific debates. *Heliyon*, *10*(9), e30412. DOI: 10.1016/j.heliyon.2024.e30412 PMID: 38711639

Ndikum, P. (2020). *Machine Learning Algorithms for Financial Asset Price Forecasting* (Version 1). arXiv. DOI: 10.48550/ARXIV.2004.01504

Nguyen, C. P., & Doytch, N. (2022). The impact of ICT patents on economic growth: An international evidence. *Telecommunications Policy*, *46*(5), 102291. DOI: 10.1016/j.telpol.2021.102291

Nguyen, D. K., Sermpinis, G., & Stasinakis, C. (2023). Big data, artificial intelligence and machine learning: A transformative symbiosis in favour of financial technology. *European Financial Management*, *29*(2), 517–548. DOI: 10.1111/eufm.12365

Nguyen, Q. P., & Vo, D. H. (2022). Artificial intelligence and unemployment: International evidence. *Structural Change and Economic Dynamics*, *63*, 40–55. DOI: 10.1016/j.strueco.2022.09.003

Nguyen, T. H., & Vu, T. Q. (2025). Perceptions of Financial AI Assistants and Intentions Toward AI-Assisted Financial Products. *International Journal of Asian Business and Information Management, 16*(1), 1–18. DOI: 10.4018/IJABIM.371629

Nishant, R., Kennedy, M., & Corbett, J. (2020). Artificial intelligence for sustainability: Challenges, opportunities, and a research agenda. *International Journal of Information Management, 53*, 102104. DOI: 10.1016/j.ijinfomgt.2020.102104

Nti, I. K., Adekoya, A. F., & Weyori, B. A. (2020). A comprehensive evaluation of ensemble learning for stock-market prediction. *Journal of Big Data, 7*(1), 20. DOI: 10.1186/s40537-020-00299-5

Ojo, J., & Olatayo, T. (2009). On the estimation and performance of subset autoregressive integrated moving average models. *European Journal of Scientific Research, 28*, 287–293.

Okeke, N. I., Bakare, O. A., & Achumie, G. O.Njideka Ihuoma OkekeOluwaseun Adeola BakareGodwin Ozoemenam Achumie. (2024). Artificial intelligence in SME financial decision-making: Tools for enhancing efficiency and profitability. *Open Access Research Journal of Multidisciplinary Studies, 08*(01), 150–163. DOI: 10.53022/oarjms.2024.8.1.0056

Oktoviany, P., Knobloch, R., & Korn, R. (2021). A machine learning-based price state prediction model for agricultural commodities using external factors. *Decisions in Economics and Finance, 44*(2), 1063–1085. DOI: 10.1007/s10203-021-00354-7

Olabanji, S. O., Olaniyi, O. O., & Olagbaju, O. O. (2024). *Leveraging artificial intelligence (AI) and blockchain for enhanced tax compliance and revenue generation.* Asian Journal of Economics, Business and Accounting., DOI: 10.9734/ajeba/2024/v24i111577

Othman, N. A., Panchapakesan, C., Loh, S. B., Zhang, M., Gupta, R. K., Martanto, W., Phang, Y. S., Morris, R. J. T., Loke, W. C., Tan, K. B., Subramaniam, M., & Yang, Y. (2024). Predicting public mental health needs in a crisis using social media indicators: A Singapore big data study. *Scientific Reports, 14*(1), 23222. DOI: 10.1038/s41598-024-73978-5 PMID: 39369040

Pabuccu, H., & Barbu, A. (2023). *Feature Selection with Annealing for Forecasting Financial Time Series.* DOI: 10.48550/ARXIV.2303.02223

Pacheco de Oliveira, D., & Caldas Montes, G. (2023). Forecasting sovereign risk perception of Brazilian bonds: An evaluation of machine learning prediction accuracy. *International Journal of Emerging Markets, 18*(10), 3414–3436. DOI: 10.1108/IJOEM-01-2021-0106

Pal, P., & Poddar, S. (2024). Applications of Smart Farming Sensors: A Way Forward. In *Data Science for Agricultural Innovation and Productivity* (pp. 175–193). Bentham Science Publishers., DOI: 10.2174/9789815196177124010012

Pandey, S., Tanvar, A., Lokhande, J., Thorat, P., & Jadhav, H. (2024). Crop price prediction system using ML. *International Journal of Research Publication and Reviews*, *5*(5), 2461–2466. https://ijrpr.com/uploads/V5ISSUE5/IJRPR27405.pdf

Parkes, D., & Wellman, M. P. (2015). Economic reasoning and artificial intelligence. *Science*, *349*(6245), 267–272. DOI: 10.1126/science.aaa8403 PMID: 26185245

Park, H. J., Kim, Y., & Kim, H. Y. (2022). Stock market forecasting using a multi-task approach integrating long short-term memory and the random forest framework. *Applied Soft Computing*, *114*, 108106. DOI: 10.1016/j.asoc.2021.108106

Park, H., Kim, N., & Lee, J. (2014). Parametric models and non-parametric machine learning models for predicting option prices: Empirical comparison study over kospi 200 index options. *Expert Systems with Applications*, *41*(11), 5227–5237. DOI: 10.1016/j.eswa.2014.01.032

Pasham, S. D. (2024). Scalable Graph-Based Algorithms for Real-Time Analysis of Big Data in Social Networks. *Metascience*, *2*(1), 92–129.

Patil, A., Shah, D., Shah, A., & Kotecha, R. (2023). Forecasting prices of agricultural commodities using machine learning for global food security: Towards Sustainable Development Goal 2. *International Journal of Engineering Trends and Technology*, *71*(12), 277–291. DOI: 10.14445/22315381/IJETT-V71I12P226

Patil, P., Athavale, P., Bothara, M., Tambolkar, S., & More, A. (2023). Crop selection and yield prediction using machine learning approach. *Current Agriculture Research Journal*, *11*(3), 968–980. Advance online publication. DOI: 10.12944/CARJ.11.3.26

Patra, A. K., Praharaj, A., Sudarshan, D., & Chhatoi, B. P. (2024). AI and business management: Tracking future research agenda through bibliometric network analysis. *Heliyon*, *10*(1), e23902. DOI: 10.1016/j.heliyon.2023.e23902 PMID: 38230239

Paul, R. K., Shankar, S. V., & Yeasin, M. (2024). Forecasting area and yield of cereal crops in India: Intelligent choices among stochastic, machine learning and deep learning techniques. *Proceedings of the Indian National Science Academy. Part A, Physical Sciences*, *91*(2), 549–555. DOI: 10.1007/s43538-024-00345-3

Paul, R. K., Yeasin, M., Kumar, P., Kumar, P., Balasubramanian, M., Roy, H. S., Paul, A. K., & Gupta, A. (2022). Machine learning techniques for forecasting agricultural prices: A case of brinjal in Odisha, India. *PLoS One*, *17*(7), e0270553. Advance online publication. DOI: 10.1371/journal.pone.0270553 PMID: 35793366

Pavlidis, G. (2023). Deploying artificial intelligence for anti-money laundering and asset recovery: The dawn of a new era. *Journal of Money Laundering Control, 26*(7), 155–166. DOI: 10.1108/JMLC-03-2023-0050

Pejić Bach, M., Krstić, Ž., Seljan, S., & Turulja, L. (2019). Text mining for big data analysis in financial sector: A literature review. *Sustainability (Basel), 11*(5), 1277. DOI: 10.3390/su11051277

Peña, D., & Tsay, R. S. (2021). *Statistical learning for big dependent data*. John Wiley & Sons., DOI: 10.1002/9781119417408

Perino, D., Katevas, K., Lutu, A., Marin, E., & Kourtellis, N. (2022). Privacy-preserving AI for future networks. *Communications of the ACM, 65*(4), 52–53. DOI: 10.1145/3512343

Petropoulos, F., Apiletti, D., Assimakopoulos, V., Babai, M. Z., Barrow, D. K., Ben Taieb, S., Bergmeir, C., Bessa, R. J., Bijak, J., Boylan, J. E., Browell, J., Carnevale, C., Castle, J. L., Cirillo, P., Clements, M. P., Cordeiro, C., Cyrino Oliveira, F. L., De Baets, S., Dokumentov, A., & Ziel, F. (2022). Forecasting: Theory and practice. *International Journal of Forecasting*, *38*(3), 705–871. DOI: 10.1016/j.ijforecast.2021.11.001

Phillips, P. C., Shi, S., & Yu, J. (2015). Testing for multiple bubbles: Historical episodes of exuberance and collapse in the S&P 500. *International Economic Review, 56*(4), 1043–1078. DOI: 10.1111/iere.12132

Piao, Y., Jeong, S., Park, S., & Lee, D. (2021). Analysis of land use and land cover change using time-series data and random forest in North Korea. *Remote Sensing (Basel), 13*(17), 3501. DOI: 10.3390/rs13173501

Picoli, M. C. A., Camara, G., Sanches, I., Simões, R., Carvalho, A., Maciel, A., Coutinho, A., Esquerdo, J., Antunes, J., Begotti, R. A., Arvor, D., & Almeida, C. (2018). Big earth observation time series analysis for monitoring Brazilian agriculture. *ISPRS Journal of Photogrammetry and Remote Sensing*, *145*, 328–339. DOI: 10.1016/j.isprsjprs.2018.08.007

Pratesi, F., Sharma, R., & Zignani, M. (2021). Measuring migration 2.0: A review of digital data sources. *Comparative Migration Studies*, *9*(1), 59. Advance online publication. DOI: 10.1186/s40878-021-00273-x

Press Information Bureau. (2024, December 18). *Empowering farmers through PM-AASHA: In Rabi 2023-24, 6.41 LMT of pulses procured, benefiting 2.75 lakh farmers* [Backgrounder]. Government of India. https://www.pib.gov.in/PressNoteDetails.aspx?NoteId=153579&ModuleId=3

Press Information Bureau. (2024, February 20). *e-NAM: Transforming agricultural trade into a seamless experience* [Fact sheet]. Government of India. https://www.pib.gov.in/FactsheetDetails.aspx?Id=149061

Press Information Bureau. (2025, February 11). *Farmers' welfare measures* [Press release]. Government of India. https://www.pib.gov.in/PressReleasePage.aspx?PRID=2101841

Press Information Bureau. (2025, February 17). *Pradhan Mantri Fasal Bima Yojana turns nine: Empowering annadata & protecting livelihoods* [Press release]. Government of India. https://www.pib.gov.in/PressReleasePage.aspx?PRID=2104175

Press Information Bureau. (2025, May 28). *Ministry of Agriculture & Farmers Welfare releases third advance estimates of major crop production for 2024–25* [Press release]. Government of India. https://www.pib.gov.in/PressReleseDetail.aspx?PRID=2132263

Purohit, S. K., Panigrahi, S., Sethy, P. K., & Behera, S. K. (2021). Time series forecasting of price of agricultural products using hybrid methods. *Applied Artificial Intelligence, 35*(15), 1388–1406. DOI: 10.1080/08839514.2021.1981659

Puyam, K., & Singh, N. (2024, May). Gesture Recognition for Phrase Interpretation: A Deep Learning Approach. In *2024 International Conference on Intelligent Systems for Cybersecurity (ISCS)* (pp. 1-6). IEEE. DOI: 10.1109/ISCS61804.2024.10581119

Qadir, J., Ali, A., ur Rasool, R., Zwitter, A., Sathiaseelan, A., & Crowcroft, J. (2016). Crisis analytics: Big data-driven crisis response. *Journal of International Humanitarian Action, 1*(1), 1–21. DOI: 10.1186/s41018-016-0013-9

Qiu, R. T., Liu, A., Stienmetz, J. L., & Yu, Y. (2021). Timing matters: Crisis severity and occupancy rate forecasts in social unrest periods. *International Journal of Contemporary Hospitality Management, 33*(6), 2044–2064. DOI: 10.1108/IJCHM-06-2020-0629

Qiu, Y., & Wang, J. (2025, March). Credit default prediction using time series-based machine learning models. *Artificial Intelligence and Applications (Commerce, Calif.), 3*(3), 284–294.

Quinn, B. (2023). *Explaining AI in Finance: Past, Present, Prospects* (Version 1). arXiv. DOI: 10.48550/ARXIV.2306.02773

Radanliev, P., Santos, O., Brandon-Jones, A., & Joinson, A. (2024). Ethics and responsible AI deployment. *Frontiers in Artificial Intelligence, 7*, 1377011. DOI: 10.3389/frai.2024.1377011 PMID: 38601110

Radić, N., Gavrilović, M., & Mihailović, Đ. (2024). The artificial intelligence and economy. In *Employment, Education and Entrepreneurship 2024 – Zbornik Radova*. DOI: 10.5937/EEE24052R

Rajan, R., & Zingales, L. (1998). Financial dependence and growth. *The American Economic Review*, *88*, 559–586.

Rajaram, S. K., Patra, G. K., Konkimalla, S., Boddapati, V. N., Sarisa, M., Reddy, M. S., & Polimetla, K. (2025). A Sentiment Analysis of Customer Product Review Based on Machine Learning Techniques in E-Commerce. SSRN *Electronic Journal*. DOI: 10.2139/ssrn.5153849

Rajbhar, R. (2025, June 7). Top Financial Forecasting Methods & Techniques You Must Know. *KAPSO*. https://kapso.in/blog/top-financial-forecasting-methods-techniques-you-must-know/

Rakhra, M., Singh, S., & Singh, G. (2021). Crop price prediction using random forest and decision tree regression: A review. *Materials Today: Proceedings*. Advance online publication. DOI: 10.1016/j.matpr.2021.03.261

Rao, B., Lipizzi, C., & Mansouri, M. (2024). Anatomy of an AI economy. In *2024 IEEE International Symposium on Systems Engineering (ISSE)*. https://doi.org/DOI: 10.1109/ISSE63315.2024.10741091

Ravenstein, E. G. (1889). The laws of migration. *Journal of the Royal Statistical Society*, *52*(2), 241–305. DOI: 10.2307/2979333

Raymer, J., Guan, Q., Shen, T., Hertog, S., & Gerland, P. (2025). Modelling the age and sex profiles of net international migration. *Demographic Research*, *53*, 569–610. DOI: 10.4054/DemRes.2025.53.19

Reinhart, C. M., & Rogoff, K. S. (2011). From financial crash to debt crisis. *The American Economic Review*, *101*(5), 1676–1706. DOI: 10.1257/aer.101.5.1676

Reshef, D. N., Reshef, Y. A., Finucane, H. K., Grossman, S. R., McVean, G., Turnbaugh, P. J., ... & Sabeti, P. C. (2011). Detecting novel associations in large data sets. *science, 334*(6062), 1518-1524.

Rezaee, Z., Dorestani, A., & Aliabadi, S. (2018). Application of time series analyses in big data: Practical, research, and education implications. *Journal of Emerging Technologies in Accounting*, *15*(1), 183–197. DOI: 10.2308/jeta-51967

Robinson, C., Hohman, F., & Dilkina, B. (2017). A deep learning approach for population estimation from satellite imagery. *GeoHumanities@SIGSPATIAL*, 47-54. https://arxiv.org/abs/1708.09086

Romeo, E., & Lacko, J. (2025). Adoption and integration of AI in organizations: A systematic review of challenges and drivers towards future directions of research. *Kybernetes*.

Rong, C., Sial, M. S., Saci, F., Jasimuddin, S. M., & Zhang, J. Z. (2025). AI Adoption in the Finance Sector of a Developing Economy. *Journal of Organizational and End User Computing*, *37*(1), 1–19. DOI: 10.4018/JOEUC.371412

Roy, P., Ghose, B., Singh, P. K., Tyagi, P. K., & Vasudevan, A. (2025). Artificial Intelligence and Finance: A bibliometric review on the Trends, Influences, and Research Directions. *F1000 Research*, *14*, 122. DOI: 10.12688/f1000research.160959.1

Ruiz Estrada, M. A., Park, D., & Staniewski, M. (2023). Artificial intelligence (AI) can change the way of doing policy modelling. *Journal of Policy Modeling*, *45*(6), 1099–1112. Advance online publication. DOI: 10.1016/j.jpolmod.2023.11.005

Russom, P. (2011). Big data analytics. *TDWI best practices report, fourth quarter, 19*(4), 1-34.

Ryll, L., & Seidens, S. (2019a). *Evaluating the Performance of Machine Learning Algorithms in Financial Market Forecasting: A Comprehensive Survey* (Version 2). arXiv. DOI: 10.48550/ARXIV.1906.07786

Sabane, M., Ranade, A., Litake, O., Patil, P., Joshi, R., & Kadam, D. (2023). *Enhancing Low Resource NER Using Assisting Language And Transfer Learning*. DOI: 10.1109/ICAAIC56838.2023.10141204

Sabareesh, R., Nath, D. D., Pathak, R., Devi, D. R., Prasanna, S., & Bellary, E. K. (2024). AI-driven fraud detection in banking: Enhancing transaction security. *Journal of Informatics Education and Research*. DOI: 10.52783/jier.v4i3.1707

Saba, T., Abunadi, I., Shahzad, M. N., & Khan, A. R. (2021). Machine learning techniques to detect and forecast the daily total COVID-19 infected and deaths cases under different lockdown types. *Microscopy Research and Technique*, *84*(7), 1462–1474. DOI: 10.1002/jemt.23702 PMID: 33522669

Saeed, M. M., & Alsharidah, M. (2024). Security, privacy, and robustness for trustworthy AI systems: A review. *Computers & Electrical Engineering*, *119*, 109643. DOI: 10.1016/j.compeleceng.2024.109643

Saeidnia, H. R., Hosseini, E., Abdoli, S., & Ausloos, M. (2024). Unleashing the power of AI: A systematic review of cutting-edge techniques in AI-enhanced scientometrics, webometrics and bibliometrics. *Library Hi Tech*. Advance online publication. DOI: 10.1108/LHT-10-2023-0514

Sahu, S. K., Mokhade, A., & Bokde, N. D. (2023). An Overview of Machine Learning, Deep Learning, and Reinforcement Learning-Based Techniques in Quantitative Finance: Recent Progress and Challenges. *Applied Sciences (Basel, Switzerland), 13*(3), 1956. DOI: 10.3390/app13031956

Sawwalakhe, R., Arora, S., & Singh, T. P. (2023). Opportunities and challenges for artificial intelligence and machine learning applications in the finance sector. *Advanced machine learning algorithms for complex financial applications*, 1-17.

Saxena, R., Paul, R. K., Pavithra, S., Singh, N. P., & Kumar, R. (2019). *Market intelligence in India: Methods and effectiveness of agricultural commodity price forecasts. Policy Paper 34, ICAR-National Institute of Agricultural Economics and Policy Research.* NIAP.

Schürmann, A., Kleemann, J., Teucher, M., Fürst, C., & Conrad, C. (2022). Migration in West Africa: A visual analysis of motivation, causes, and routes. *Ecology and Society, 27*(3), art16. Advance online publication. DOI: 10.5751/ES-13489-270316

Selvakumar, P., Shanthi, M., Pitchiah, R., Sharma, M., Dahake, P. S., & T. C., M. (2025). The Role of Artificial Intelligence in Business Model Innovation: Overview of AI Technologies. In M. Khokhar (Ed.), *Advances in Business Strategy and Competitive Advantage* (pp. 219–246). IGI Global. DOI: 10.4018/979-8-3693-9571-4.ch009

Selvaraj, P., Sarin, A., & Seraphim, B. I. (2022, January). Blood donation prediction system using machine learning techniques. In *2022 International Conference on Computer Communication and Informatics (ICCCI)* (pp. 1-4). IEEE. DOI: 10.1109/ICCCI54379.2022.9740878

Semik-Gurgul, E., Gurgul, A., & Szmatoła, T. (2023). Transcriptome and methylome sequencing reveals altered long non-coding RNA genes expression and their aberrant DNA methylation in equine sarcoids. *Functional & Integrative Genomics, 23*(3), 268. DOI: 10.1007/s10142-023-01200-2 PMID: 37552338

Sen, J., & Chaudhuri, T. D. (2017). *An Investigation of the Structural Characteristics of the Indian IT Sector and the Capital Goods Sector: An Application of the R Programming in Time Series Decomposition and Forecasting*. DOI: 10.48550/ARXIV.1706.07821

Sethi, S. R., & Mahadik, D. (2024). *Artificial Intelligence in Financial Markets: Opportunities, Challenges, and Future Directions. SSRN.* https://ssrn.com/abstract=5078873

Seyedan, M., & Mafakheri, F. (2020). Predictive big data analytics for supply chain demand forecasting: Methods, applications, and research opportunities. *Journal of Big Data*, *7*(1), 53. DOI: 10.1186/s40537-020-00329-2

Sezer, O. B., Gudelek, M. U., & Ozbayoglu, A. M. (2020). Financial Time Series Forecasting with Deep Learning: A Systematic Literature Review: 2005–2019. *Applied Soft Computing*, *90*, 106181. DOI: 10.1016/j.asoc.2020.106181

Shahi, T. B., Shrestha, A., Neupane, A., & Guo, W. (2020). Stock Price Forecasting with Deep Learning: A Comparative Study. *Mathematics*, *8*(9), 1441. DOI: 10.3390/math8091441

Sharifani, Koosha, Amini, Mahyar, Learning, Machine, & Learning, Deep: A Review of Methods and Applications (2023). *World Information Technology and Engineering Journal*, Volume *10*, Issue 07, pp. 3897-3904.

Sharma, D. K., Hota, H. S., Brown, K., & Handa, R. (2022). Integration of genetic algorithm with artificial neural network for stock market forecasting. *International Journal of System Assurance Engineering and Management*, *13*(S2), 828–841. DOI: 10.1007/s13198-021-01209-5

Shawon, R. E. R., Dalim, H. M., Shil, S. K., Gurung, N., Hasanuzzaman, M., Hossain, S., & Rahman, T. (2024). Assessing geopolitical risks and their economic impact on the USA using data analytics. *Journal of Economics, Finance, and Accounting Studies*, *6*(6), 5. DOI: 10.32996/jefas.2024.6.6.2

Shen, S., Jiang, H., & Zhang, T. (2012). *Stock market forecasting using machine learning algorithms*. Department of Electrical Engineering, Stanford University.

Shen, Z., Zhang, Y., Lu, J., Xu, J., & Xiao, G. (2020). A novel time series forecasting model with deep learning. *Neurocomputing*, *396*, 302–313. DOI: 10.1016/j.neucom.2018.12.084

Shi, Y., & Li, X. (2019). An overview of bankruptcy prediction models for corporate firms: A Systematic literature review. *Intangible Capital*, *15*(2), 114. DOI: 10.3926/ic.1354

Shlash Mohammad, A. A., Khanfar, I. A. A., Al Oraini, B., Vasudevan, A., Suleiman, I. M., & Fei, Z. (2024). Predictive analytics on artificial intelligence in supply chain optimization. *Data and Metadata*, *3*, 395. DOI: 10.56294/dm2024395

Shroff, A., Shah, B. J., & Gajjar, H. (2022). Online food delivery research: A systematic literature review. *International Journal of Contemporary Hospitality Management*, *34*(8), 2852–2883. DOI: 10.1108/IJCHM-10-2021-1273

Shu, M., Wang, Z., & Liang, J. (2024). Early warning indicators for financial market anomalies: A multi-signal integration approach. *Journal of Advanced Computing Systems*, *4*(9), 68–84. DOI: 10.69987/JACS.2024.40907

Shu, M., & Zhu, W. (2020). Real-time prediction of Bitcoin bubble crashes. *Physica A*, *548*, 124477. DOI: 10.1016/j.physa.2020.124477

Shumway, R. H., Stoffer, D. S., & Stoffer, D. S. (2000). *Time series analysis and its applications* (Vol. 3, p. 4). New York: springer.

Singh, A., Ehtesham, A., Kumar, S., & Khoei, T. T. (2025). *Agentic Retrieval-Augmented Generation: A Survey on Agentic RAG* (Version 3). arXiv. DOI: 10.48550/ARXIV.2501.09136

Singh, P. (2025). Exploring Leading Practices in Algorithmic Trading: Insights From Survey and Case Studies on Machine Learning Techniques and Market Dynamics. In *Machine Learning and Modeling Techniques in Financial Data Science* (pp. 151-184). IGI Global Scientific Publishing.

Singh, P. (2025). Role of Artificial Intelligence in Detecting Herding. In *Psychological Drivers of Herding and Market Overreaction* (pp. 145-172). IGI Global Scientific Publishing. Ardito, L., Filieri, R., Raguseo, E., & Vitari, C. (2024). Artificial intelligence adoption and revenue growth in European SMEs: synergies with IoT and big data analytics. *Internet Research.*

Singh, P. (2025). AI and Financial Risk Management Revolutionizing Risk Assessment and Mitigation. In *Artificial Intelligence for Financial Risk Management and Analysis* (pp. 373–404). IGI Global Scientific Publishing. DOI: 10.4018/979-8-3373-1200-2.ch019

Singh, P. (2025). AI and Rural Development. In *AI Strategies for Social Entrepreneurship and Sustainable Economic Development* (pp. 175–198). IGI Global Scientific Publishing.

Singh, P. (2025). Behavioral Biases in Real Estate Markets. In *Unveiling Investor Biases That Shape Market Dynamics* (pp. 1–42). IGI Global Scientific Publishing.

Singh, P. (2025). Technological innovation in investment strategies. In Liao, F. X., & Ooi, K. L. (Eds.), *Investment strategies in the age of technological innovation and emerging markets* (pp. 27–72). IGI Global.

Sîrbu, A., Andrienko, G., Andrienko, N., Boldrini, C., Conti, M., Giannotti, F., Guidotti, R., Bertoli, S., Kim, J., Muntean, C. I., Pappalardo, L., Passarella, A., Pedreschi, D., Pollacci, L., Pratesi, F., & Sharma, R. (2021). Human migration: The big data perspective. *International Journal of Data Science and Analytics, 11*(4), 341–360. DOI: 10.1007/s41060-020-00213-5

Škare, M., & Porada-Rochoń, M. (2020). Forecasting financial cycles: Can big data help? *Technological and Economic Development of Economy, 26*(5), 974–988. DOI: 10.3846/tede.2020.12702

Sohrabpour, V., Oghazi, P., Toorajipour, R., & Nazarpour, A. (2021). Export sales forecasting using artificial intelligence. *Technological Forecasting and Social Change, 163*, 120480. DOI: 10.1016/j.techfore.2020.120480

Sonkavde, G., Dharrao, D. S., Bongale, A. M., Deokate, S. T., Doreswamy, D., & Bhat, S. K. (2023). Forecasting Stock Market Prices Using Machine Learning and Deep Learning Models: A Systematic Review, Performance Analysis and Discussion of Implications. *International Journal of Financial Studies, 11*(3), 94. DOI: 10.3390/ijfs11030094

Sood, A., Sharma, R. K., & Bhardwaj, A. K. (2022). Artificial intelligence research in agriculture: A review. *Online Information Review, 46*(6), 1054–1075. DOI: 10.1108/OIR-10-2020-0448

Stark, O., & Bloom, D. E. (1985). The new economics of labor migration. *The American Economic Review, 75*(2), 173–178. https://www.jstor.org/stable/1805591

Stempień, D., & Ślepaczuk, R. (2025). *Hybrid Models for Financial Forecasting: Combining Econometric, Machine Learning, and Deep Learning Models* (Version 1). arXiv. DOI: 10.48550/ARXIV.2505.19617

Strader, T. J., Rozycki, J. J., Root, T. H., & Huang, Y.-H. J. (2020). Machine Learning Stock Market Prediction Studies: Review and Research Directions. *Journal of International Technology and Information Management, 28*(4), 63–83. DOI: 10.58729/1941-6679.1435

Subasi, A., Amir, F., Bagedo, K., Shams, A., & Sarirete, A. (2021). Stock market prediction using machine learning. *Procedia Computer Science, 194*, 173–179. DOI: 10.1016/j.procs.2021.10.071

Sun, F., Meng, X., Zhang, Y., Wang, Y., Jiang, H., & Liu, P. (2023). Agricultural product price forecasting methods. *Agriculture, 13*(9), 1671. Advance online publication. DOI: 10.3390/agriculture13091671

Sungkono, & Widana, I. D. K. K. (2024). Optimizing artificial intelligence (AI) as a catalyst for digital economic transformation. *Technium Social Sciences Journal*. https://doi.org/DOI: 10.47577/tssj.v58i1.11174

Sun, W., Bocchini, P., & Davison, B. D. (2020). Applications of artificial intelligence for disaster management. *Natural Hazards*, *103*(3), 1–59. DOI: 10.1007/s11069-020-04124-3

Suresh, C., Kamakshaiah, K., Thatavarti, S., Kumar, P. S., & Ramasubbareddy, S. (2019). Accurate and timely prediction of rice crop disease by means of machine learning algorithms. *International Journal of Advanced Science and Technology*, *28*(13), 662–672.

Suthar, J. (2025, February 28). Volatility Clustering. *Financial Market Resources*. Retrieved March 7, 2025, from https://www.wallstreetmojo.com/volatility-clustering/

Sutiene, K., Schwendner, P., Sipos, C., Lorenzo, L., Mirchev, M., Lameski, P., Kabasinskas, A., Tidjani, C., Ozturkkal, B., & Cerneviciene, J. (2024). Enhancing portfolio management using artificial intelligence: Literature review. *Frontiers in Artificial Intelligence*, *7*, 1371502. DOI: 10.3389/frai.2024.1371502

Szczepański, M. (2019). *Economic impacts of artificial intelligence* (EPRS Briefing PE 637.967). European Parliamentary Research Service.

Tahvanainen, M., Welch, D., & Worm, V. (2005). Implications of short-term international assignments. *European Management Journal*, *23*(6), 663–673. DOI: 10.1016/j.emj.2005.10.011

Taipalus, K. (2012). *Detecting asset price bubbles with time-series methods*. Bank of Finland.

Taleb, N. N. (2007). The Black Swan: The Impact of the Highly Improbable. Random House. *STME academie press* .

Taleb, N. N. (2020). Statistical Consequences of Fat Tails: Real World Preasymptotics, Epistemology, and Applications. *STME academie press* .

Tamiminia, H., Salehi, B., Mahdianpari, M., Quackenbush, L., Adeli, S., & Brisco, B. (2020). Google Earth Engine for geo-big data applications: A meta-analysis and systematic review. *ISPRS Journal of Photogrammetry and Remote Sensing*, *164*, 152–170. DOI: 10.1016/j.isprsjprs.2020.04.001

Tang, Y., Song, Z., Zhu, Y., Yuan, H., Hou, M., Ji, J., Tang, C., & Li, J. (2022). A survey on machine learning models for financial time series forecasting. *Neurocomputing*, *512*, 363–380. DOI: 10.1016/j.neucom.2022.09.003

Tan, H. R., Yang, W. N., & Liu, C. Y. (2019). Global financial crisis and the impact of the food crisis on the great depression based on agricultural technology iteration: A 15-year population-based time-series study. *Revista de la Facultad de Agronomía*, •••, 36.

Taylor, S. J., & Letham, B. (2018). Forecasting at scale. *The American Statistician*, *72*(1), 37–45. DOI: 10.1080/00031305.2017.1380080

Tenali, N., & Babu, G. R. M. (2023). A systematic literature review and future perspectives for handling big data analytics in COVID-19 diagnosis. *New Generation Computing*, *41*(2), 243–280. DOI: 10.1007/s00354-023-00211-8 PMID: 37229177

Thakur, M., & Kumar, D. (2018). A hybrid financial trading support system using multicategory classifiers and random forest. *Applied Soft Computing*, *67*, 337–349. DOI: 10.1016/j.asoc.2018.03.006

The evolution offorecasting techniques: Traditional versus machine learning methods. (n.d.). Retrieved September 17, 2025, from https://www.genpact.com/insight/the-evolution-of-forecasting-techniques-traditional-versus-machine-learning-methods

The Forecasting Shift: From Excel to AI-Driven Precision | FP&A Trends. (2025, June 5). https://fpa-trends.com/article/forecasting-shift-excel-ai-driven-precision

Tiwari, A. K., Mishra, H., Nishad, D. C., & Pandey, A. (2023). Sustainable water management in agriculture: irrigation techniques and water conservation. *Dr. Ajay B. Jadhao, 53*.

Tiwari, A. K., Mishra, H., & Nishad, D. C. (2011). Market dynamics and consumer perceptions of organic produce in contemporary agriculture. *Advances in Agriculture Sciences Volume II*, *24*(4), 120.

Todaro, M. P. (1969). A Model of Labor Migration and Urban Unemployment in Less Developed Countries. *The American Economic Review*, *59*(1), 138–148. https://www.jstor.org/stable/1811100

Torres, J. F., Hadjout, D., Sebaa, A., Martínez-Álvarez, F., & Troncoso, A. (2021). Deep Learning for Time Series Forecasting: A Survey. *Big Data*, *9*(1), 3–21. DOI: 10.1089/big.2020.0159

Trabelsi, M. A. (2024). The impact of artificial intelligence on economic development. *Journal of Electronic Business & Digital Economics*, *3*(2), 142–155. DOI: 10.1108/JEBDE-10-2023-0022

Tripathy, N. (2016b). A study on the dynamic relationship between gold price and stock market price in India. *European Journal of Economics, Finance and Administrative Sciences.*

Tripathy, N. (2016a). Testing of long memory in the Indian stock market using ARFIMA model. *The Journal of Prediction Markets*, *9*(3), 23–39. DOI: 10.5750/jpm.v9i3.1055

Tsay, R. S. (1986). Time series model specification in the presence of outliers. *Journal of the American Statistical Association*, *81*(393), 132–141. DOI: 10.1080/01621459.1986.10478250

Ubaldi, B.-C., & Zapata, R. (2024). *Governing with artificial intelligence: Are governments ready?* OECD Publishing.

UN Global Pulse & UNHCR. (2023). Understanding population movements at the Brazil-Venezuela border. https://www.unglobalpulse.org/project/understanding-population-movements-at-the-brazil-venezuela-border/

UNHCR & UN Global Pulse. (n.d.). *From big data to humanitarian-in-the-loop algorithms.* https://www.unhcr.org/innovation/big-data-humanitarian-loop-algorithms/

UNHCR. (n.d.). *Social Media and Forced Displacement: Big Data Analytics & Machine-Learning* (White Paper, UNHCR & UN Global Pulse). https://www.unhcr.org/innovation/new-paper-from-un-global-pulse-and-unhcr-explores-use-of-digital-data-for-insights-into-forced-displacement/

United Nations Commodity Trade Statistics Database (UN-COMTRADE). (2022). *Trade data for maize.* https://comtrade.un.org/

University of J. Dobrila in Pula, Croatia, & Njegovanović, A. (2018). Artificial Intelligence: Financial Trading and Neurology of Decision. *Financial Markets, Institutions and Risks*, 58–68. DOI: 10.21272/fmir.2(2).58-68.2018

University of Skövde. (2024). Using AI to predict climate-driven migration. Phys.org. https://phys.org/news/2024-10-ai-climate-driven-migration.html

Usman, F. O., Eyo-Udo, N. L., Etukudoh, E. A., Odonkor, B., Ibeh, C. V., & Adegbola, A. (2024). A CRITICAL REVIEW OF AI-DRIVEN STRATEGIES FOR ENTREPRENEURIAL SUCCESS. *International Journal of Management & Entrepreneurship Research*, *6*(1), 200–215. DOI: 10.51594/ijmer.v6i1.748

Valle-Cruz, D., Fernandez-Cortez, V., & Gil-García, J. R. (2021). From e-budgeting to smart budgeting: Exploring the potential of artificial intelligence in government decision-making for resource allocation. *Government Information Quarterly, 39*(2), 101644. DOI: 10.1016/j.giq.2021.101644

Vogiazas, S., & Alexiou, C. (2017). Determinants of housing prices and bubble detection: Evidence from seven advanced economies. *Atlantic Economic Journal, 45*(1), 119–131. DOI: 10.1007/s11293-017-9531-0

Wanckel, C. (2022). An ounce of prevention is worth a pound of cure–Building capacities for the use of big data algorithm systems (BDAS) in early crisis detection. *Government Information Quarterly, 39*(4), 101705. DOI: 10.1016/j.giq.2022.101705

Wang, Y., Wu, H., Dong, J., Liu, Y., Long, M., & Wang, J. (2024). *Deep Time Series Models: A Comprehensive Survey and Benchmark*. arXiv preprint arXiv:2407.13278. https://arxiv.org/abs/2407.13278

Wang, Z., Li, K., Xia, S. Q., & Liu, H. (2021). Economic recession prediction using deep neural network. *arXiv preprint arXiv:2107.10980.*

Wang, D., Li, L., & Zhao, D. (2022). Corporate finance risk prediction based on LightGBM. *Information Sciences, 602*, 259–268. DOI: 10.1016/j.ins.2022.04.058

Wang, F., Yu, S., Du, R., & Wu, X. (2025, May). DFCNet: A Dynamic Early Warning Model for Financial Crises of Listed Companies Based on Deep Learning. In *Proceedings of the 2025 2nd International Conference on Modeling, Natural Language Processing and Machine Learning* (pp. 623-627). DOI: 10.1145/3757110.3757214

Wang, L., Jia, F., Chen, L., & Xu, Q. (2023). Forecasting SMEs' credit risk in supply chain finance with a sampling strategy based on machine learning techniques. *Annals of Operations Research, 331*(1), 1–33. DOI: 10.1007/s10479-022-04518-5

Wang, M. (2024). *AI technologies in modern taxation: Applications, challenges, and strategic directions.* International Journal of Finance and Investment., DOI: 10.54097/v2kgty49

Wang, Y., Zhang, Q., Yu, F., Zhang, N., Zhang, X., Li, Y., Wang, M., & Zhang, J. (2024). Progress in Research on Deep Learning-Based Crop Yield Prediction. *Agronomy (Basel), 14*(10), 2264. DOI: 10.3390/agronomy14102264

Wang, Z., Ogbodo, M., Huang, H., Qiu, C., Hisada, M., & Abdallah, A. B. (2020). AEBIS: AI-enabled blockchain-based electric vehicle integration system for power management in smart grid platform. *IEEE Access : Practical Innovations, Open Solutions, 8*, 226409–226421. DOI: 10.1109/ACCESS.2020.3044612

Weber, P., Carl, K. V., & Hinz, O. (2024). Applications of Explainable Artificial Intelligence in Finance—A systematic review of Finance, Information Systems, and Computer Science literature. *Management Review Quarterly*, *74*(2), 867–907. DOI: 10.1007/s11301-023-00320-0

Wildi, M., & Misheva, B. H. (2022). *A Time Series Approach to Explainability for Neural Nets with Applications to Risk-Management and Fraud Detection* (Version 1). arXiv. DOI: 10.48550/ARXIV.2212.02906

Wolpert, J. (1965). Behavioral aspects of the decision to migrate. *Papers in Regional Science*, *15*(1), 159–169. DOI: 10.1111/j.1435-5597.1965.tb01320.x

Wong, Y. K. (2021). Dealing crisis management using AI. In *Advances in Machine Learning*. Data Mining and Computing., DOI: 10.5121/csit.2021.111409

World Bank (KNOMAD). (2022). *Remittances Brave Global Headwinds – Migration and Development Brief 37*. https://documents1.worldbank.org/curated/en/099818008142419054/pdf/IDU12966350716a711437b1850019065d7f1eda1.pdf

World Bank. (2021). *Recovery: COVID-19 Crisis Through a Migration Lens – Migration and Development Brief 35*. https://documents1.worldbank.org/curated/en/099738408132414027/pdf/IDU110e1541c1704b14821196441e301ab86ff0b.pdf

World Bank. (2023). *Uganda Development Response to Displacement Impacts Project: Building resilience and financing refugee-hosting districts* (Project Document P510476). Retrieved from https://documents1.worldbank.org/curated/en/099031825124033782/pdf/P510476-8ee58859-4e78-4ef0-9d01-cf17a495a240.pdf

World Economic Forum. (2021). *Artificial Intelligence for Agriculture Innovation*. Centre for the Fourth Industrial Revolution India. https://www3.weforum.org/docs/WEF_Artificial_Intelligence_for_Agriculture_Innovation_2021.pdf

Xiao, B., Wang, Z., Liu, Q., & Liu, X. (2018). SMK-means: An improved mini batch k-means algorithm based on mapreduce with big data. *TSP*, *1*(1), 1–5.

Xiao, C., Xia, W., & Jiang, J. (2020). Stock price forecast based on combined model of ARI-MA-LS-SVM. *Neural Computing & Applications*, *32*(10), 5379–5388. DOI: 10.1007/s00521-019-04698-5

Xie, W., Rose, A., Li, S., He, J., Li, N., & Ali, T. (2018). Dynamic economic resilience and economic recovery from disasters: A quantitative assessment. *Risk Analysis*, *38*(6), 1306–1318. DOI: 10.1111/risa.12948 PMID: 29341196

Xu, S., & Zhou, Y. (2025). Machine Learning Applications in Financial Statement Fraud Detection: A Comparative Analysis. *Annals of Applied Sciences* .

Xue, P., Lei, Y., & Li, Y. (2020). Research and prediction of Shanghai-Shenzhen 20 Index based on the support vector machine model and gradient boosting regression tree. https://doi.org/DOI: 10.1109/ICICAS51530.2020.00019

Xu, X., & Zhang, Y. (2022). Commodity price forecasting via neural networks for coffee, corn, cotton, oats, soybeans, soybean oil, sugar, and wheat. *Intelligent Systems in Accounting, Finance & Management*, *29*(3), 169–181. DOI: 10.1002/isaf.1519

Yamashita Rios de Sousa, A. M., Takayasu, H., & Takayasu, M. (2017). Detection of statistical asymmetries in non-stationary sign time series: Analysis of foreign exchange data. *PLoS One*, *12*(5), e0177652. DOI: 10.1371/journal.pone.0177652 PMID: 28542208

Yang, A., Thong, Q., Gia, L., & Zakariya, Y. (2025). Big Data-Driven Corporate Financial Forecasting and Decision Support: A Study of CNN-LSTM Machine Learning Models. *Frontiers in Applied Mathematics and Statistics*, *11*, 1566078. Advance online publication. DOI: 10.3389/fams.2025.1566078

Yang, J., Zhao, Y., Han, C., Liu, Y., & Yang, M. (2022). Big data, big challenges: Risk management of financial market in the digital economy. *Journal of Enterprise Information Management*, *35*(4/5), 1288–1304. DOI: 10.1108/JEIM-01-2021-0057

Yapamanu, G., Thugutla, K. R., Undela, V., Selvameena, M. R., & Vidhya, M. V. (2025). Predict Migration using Machine Learning. *IJSAT-International Journal on Science and Technology*, *16*(1), 2612. Advance online publication. DOI: 10.71097/IJSAT.v16.i1.2612

Ye, J., Goswami, B., Gu, J., Uddin, A., & Wang, G. (2024). *From Factor Models to Deep Learning: Machine Learning in Reshaping Empirical Asset Pricing* (Version 1). arXiv. DOI: 10.48550/ARXIV.2403.06779

Yeh, C., Perez, A., Driscoll, A., Azzari, G., Tang, Z., Lobell, D., Ermon, S., & Burke, M. (2020). Using publicly available satellite imagery and deep learning to understand economic well-being in Africa. *Nature Communications*, *11*(1), 2583. Advance online publication. DOI: 10.1038/s41467-020-16185-w PMID: 32444658

Yildiz, D., Abel, G., & Cohen, S. (2024). *Migration flows by age, sex and educational attainment*. IIASA Working Paper WP-24-001. https://pure.iiasa.ac.at/19399

Yovita Sari, & Amir Indrabudiman. (2024). The Role of Artificial Intelligence (AI) in Financial Risk. *Formosa Journal of Sustainable Research*, 2073-2082.

Yu, X., Chen, Z., Ling, Y., Dong, S., Liu, Z., & Lu, Y. (2023). *Temporal Data Meets LLM — Explainable Financial Time Series Forecasting* (Version 1). arXiv. DOI: 10.48550/ARXIV.2306.11025

Yuan, C., Tang, J., Cao, Y., et al. (2024). The impact of artificial intelligence on economic development: A systematic review. *International Theory and Practice in Humanities and Social Sciences*. https://doi.org/DOI: 10.70693/itphss.v1i1.57

Yu, D., & Deng, L. (2011). Deep Learning and Its Applications to Signal and Information Processing. *IEEE Signal Processing Magazine*, *28*(1), 145–154. DOI: 10.1109/MSP.2010.939038

Yu, D., & Fang, C. (2023). Urban remote sensing with spatial big data: A review and renewed perspective of urban studies in recent decades. *Remote Sensing (Basel)*, *15*(5), 1307. DOI: 10.3390/rs15051307

Yun, K. K., Yoon, S. W., & Won, D. (2023). Interpretable stock price forecasting model using genetic algorithm-machine learning regressions and best feature subset selection. *Expert Systems with Applications*, *213*, 118803. DOI: 10.1016/j.eswa.2022.118803

Zamanzadeh Darban, Z., Webb, G. I., Pan, S., Aggarwal, C., & Salehi, M. (2024). Deep learning for time series anomaly detection: A survey. *ACM Computing Surveys*, *57*(1), 1–42. DOI: 10.1145/3691338

Zarifhonarvar, A. (2024). Economics of chatgpt: A labor market view on the occupational impact of artificial intelligence. *Journal of Electronic Business & Digital Economics*, *3*(2), 100–116. DOI: 10.1108/JEBDE-10-2023-0021

Zemmouchi-Ghomari, L. (2025). Artificial intelligence in intelligent transportation systems. *Journal of Intelligent Manufacturing and Special Equipment*.

Zhai, W., Wu, G., Bao, W., & Niu, L. (2021, April). Big data analysis of accounting forecasting based on machine learning. In *2021 6th International Conference on Intelligent Computing and Signal Processing (ICSP)* (pp. 399-402). IEEE. DOI: 10.1109/ICSP51882.2021.9408921

Zhang, C., Zhong, H., & Hu, A. (2022). Research on early warning of financial crisis of listed companies based on random forest and time series. *Mobile Information Systems*, *2022*(1), 1573966. DOI: 10.1155/2022/1573966

Zhang, D., & Lou, S. (2021). The application research of neural network and BP algorithm in stock price pattern classification and prediction. *Future Generation Computer Systems*, *115*, 872–879. DOI: 10.1016/j.future.2020.10.009

Zhang, X., Xu, Z., Liu, Y., Sun, M., Zhou, T., & Sun, W. (2024, October). Robust Graph Neural Networks for Stability Analysis in Dynamic Networks *2024*. In *3rd International Conference on Cloud Computing, Big Data Application and Software Engineering (CBASE)* (pp. 806-811). IEEE, DOI: DOI: 10.1109/CBASE64041.2024.10824358

Zhang, Y., Li, G., Muskat, B., & Law, R. (2021). Tourism Demand Forecasting: A Decomposed Deep Learning Approach. *Journal of Travel Research*, *60*(5), 981–997. DOI: 10.1177/0047287520919522

Zhang, Z., Wu, C., Qu, S., & Chen, X. (2022). An explainable artificial intelligence approach for financial distress prediction. *Information Processing & Management*, *59*(4), 102988. DOI: 10.1016/j.ipm.2022.102988

Zhao, H. (2021). Futures price prediction of agricultural products based on machine learning. *Neural Computing & Applications*, *33*(3), 837–850. DOI: 10.1007/s00521-020-05250-6

Zhao, Y., & Yang, G. (2023). Deep Learning-based Integrated Framework for stock price movement prediction. *Applied Soft Computing*, *133*, 109921. DOI: 10.1016/j.asoc.2022.109921

Zhao, Z., Li, D., & Dai, W. (2023). Machine-learning-enabled intelligence computing for crisis management in small and medium-sized enterprises (SMEs). *Technological Forecasting and Social Change*, *191*, 122492. DOI: 10.1016/j.techfore.2023.122492

Zheng, S., Trott, A. R., Srinivasa, S., Parkes, D. C., & Socher, R. (2022). The AI economist: Taxation policy design via two-level deep multiagent reinforcement learning. *Science Advances*, *8*(18), eabk2607. Advance online publication. DOI: 10.1126/sciadv.abk2607 PMID: 35507657

Zhong, X., & Enke, D. (2017). Forecasting daily stock market return using dimensionality reduction. *Expert Systems with Applications*, *67*, 126–139. DOI: 10.1016/j.eswa.2016.09.027

Zhou, L., Shi, X., Bao, Y., Gao, L., & Ma, C. (2023). Explainable artificial intelligence for digital finance and consumption upgrading. *Finance Research Letters*, *58*, 104489. DOI: 10.1016/j.frl.2023.104489

About the Contributors

Sara Elouadi holds a Doctorate from the Institute of Administration of Companies (IAE) in Toulon, France. She teaches finance and accounting at various institutions in both France and Morocco. Currently, she serves as a professor and researcher in finance at Hassan II University in Casablanca. Dr. Elouadi is also the author of several scientific articles, with a particular focus on employee shareholding and pluralist governance

Hicham El Bouanani holds a doctorate in Applied Mathematics. He teaches applied mathematics in economics, finance, and management at various institutions. Currently, he is a professor and researcher in Applied Mathematics at Hassan II University of Casablanca. He is also the author of several scientific articles, particularly on optimization in mathematics, finance, and logistics.

Zyed Achour is a Senior Lecturer at the National Institute of Labor and Social Studies, University of Carthage. He holds a Master's degree in Management Sciences from the University of Bordeaux (France) and a Ph.D. in Management Sciences from the University of Tunis (Tunisia). His research focuses on CSR, sustainable development, labor studies, trade unionism, and strategic human resource management. He has edited academic books, coordinated interdisciplinary volumes, and published extensively in peer-reviewed journals. In 2025, he authored Integrating Governance and Corporate Social Responsibility in Employee Share Ownership (IGI Global), which received an Honorable Mention for the Joyce Rothschild Award in 2026.

***

Pritam Bhadade is an Assistant Professor at the School of Management, Ramdeobaba University, Nagpur, with over 13 years of combined experience in teaching, research, and industry. He holds an engineering degree, an MBA in

Finance, and a Ph.D. from Rashtrasant Tukdoji Maharaj Nagpur University (RTMNU). His academic and research expertise spans Corporate Finance, Fintech, Behavioral Finance, and Capital Markets. Dr. Bhadade's work reflects a strong integration of theoretical knowledge and practical insights, enabling students to connect classroom concepts with real-world financial practices. He has contributed to research in emerging areas of finance, with a particular focus on technological advancements and investor behavior in dynamic markets. In addition to teaching, he actively mentors students, participates in academic collaborations, and engages with industry to ensure curriculum relevance. His diverse background and research orientation make him a valuable contributor to management education and financial research.

Aniruddha Bhandari holds a Master's degree in Economics from Sri Sathya Sai Institute of Higher Learning, where he graduated with a Gold Medal for securing first rank. His research interests include financial econometrics, time series forecasting, machine learning, and artificial intelligence in finance. He has co-authored research presented at an international conference hosted by the London School of Economics.

Shravan Jasraj Chandak is an Associate Professor at the Symbiosis Centre for Management Studies, Pune, under Symbiosis International (Deemed University). With over 13 years of teaching experience, he brings extensive expertise in Marketing, Business Analytics, Statistics, Service Marketing, and Business Mathematics. His academic approach blends theoretical depth with practical application, enabling students to develop strong analytical and decision-making skills. Professor Chandak's work reflects a keen interest in bridging industry practices with academic rigor, fostering a learning environment that encourages critical thinking and problem-solving. He has guided numerous projects, case studies, and research initiatives, contributing to both student development and institutional growth. His academic contributions are complemented by active participation in conferences, workshops, and curriculum development activities. Passionate about continuous learning and innovation in pedagogy, Professor Chandak is dedicated to nurturing future leaders equipped with the skills and insights necessary to excel in dynamic business environments.

Parihar Suresh Dahake is an accomplished academician and researcher with over 15 years of experience in teaching and research in the fields of Commerce and Management. Currently serving as an Assistant Professor at the School of Management, Ramdeobaba University, Nagpur, he holds a diverse educational background, including B.Tech (Applied Electronics), MBA (Marketing & Financial Management), M.Com, PGDIBO, M.A. (Psychology), and a Ph.D. in Business

Management. His doctoral work focused on the impact of marketing strategies of DTH services on consumer behavior in Nagpur. Dr. Dahake's research interests span Business Analytics, Consumer Behavior, Predictive Analytics, and Marketing Communication. A recognized Ph.D. supervisor, he guides multiple doctoral candidates under the faculty of Commerce. He has published extensively in peer-reviewed, Scopus, and ABDC-indexed journals and authored books on Marketing Management and Consumer Behavior. He also holds a patent in wage sheet automation and actively contributes as a reviewer for prestigious journals. A recipient of multiple accolades, including the Young Researcher and Research Excellence Awards, Dr. Dahake is also a sought-after speaker and trainer. His commitment to academic excellence and innovative pedagogy has made significant contributions to management education, research, and institutional development in Central India

Pragati Parihar Dahake is an Assistant Professor in the Department of MBA at VMV Commerce, JMT Arts, and JJP Science College, Nagpur. With 2 years of academic experience, she specializes in Marketing, Human Resource Management, and Consumer Behaviour. Passionate about shaping future business leaders, she combines theoretical knowledge with practical insights to create an engaging learning environment. Her teaching approach emphasizes real-world applications and student-centered learning. Pragati is committed to academic excellence and continuously works to enhance her subject expertise while contributing to the holistic development of her students in the dynamic field of management education.

Siva Kiran Guptha K graduated from Sri Sathya Sai Institute of Higher Learning in 2008 with a B.A. (Hons.) in Economics. He pursued his M.A. and M.Phil. in Economics from SSSIHL. He then joined Sri Sathya Sai Institute of Higher Learning as an Assistant Professor in 2012. He is currently the Associate Head, Department of Humanities & Social Sciences, Prasanthi Nilayam Campus, SSSIHL. In early 2020, he completed his Ph.D. at SSSIHL. His thesis title is, The Relationship between Financial Development and Economic Growth: An Empirical Evidence from BRICS Economies.

Tuukka Hyytiäinen is a researcher at the LUT School of Business, Finland, with a multidisciplinary background in economics, information systems, and industrial engineering and management. He holds a Master of Science degree in Economics and Business Administration from the University of Vaasa and a Master of Science degree in Technology from Tampere University. Alongside his academic work, he serves as Chief Financial Officer and has extensive experience in financial management, business controlling, IT project management, forecasting, financial modelling, reporting, ERP and BI systems, and data-driven decision-making. His research focuses on the application of artificial intelligence, machine learning, Transformer models, and large language models to financial forecasting, anomaly detection, and explainable decision-support processes.

Antony Vijay J is an Assistant Professor in the Department of Computer Science and Engineering at R M K College of Engineering and Technology, RSM Nagar, Puduvoyal. He is engaged in teaching core computer science subjects and guiding students in technical and academic development. His interests include strengthening programming skills and applying engineering concepts to real-world problems.

Dileep Singh is a faculty member at NMIMS University, Hyderabad, with expertise in business strategy, sustainability, and technology-enabled learning. He has 15 ABDC-listed and 13 Scopus-indexed publications, authored four books, and has been awarded Best Paper at multiple conferences as well as the Best Faculty Award. His research spans greenwashing, signature verification using GRU, and cloud-based e-learning, and he actively mentors in areas such as Capstone business simulations and strategic frameworks. With a strong academic and consultancy background, Dr. Singh combines analytical insight with practical application to drive impactful outcome

Pasi Luukka, Dr.Sc. (Tech) is an Associate Professor in soft computing at School of Technology and School of Business, Lappeenranta University of Technology, Finland. His research interests are in the fuzzy data analysis and decision making. He has published about 30 refereed articles, books chapters and about 50 conference papers.

Dipti Malpani is a vibrant performance-driven professional with over 17 years of extensive experience in various aspects of human resources like Payroll processing, HR Compliances, HRIS, Performance management, Employee Engagement, grievance management and employee retention Dr. Malpani holds a Bachelor's degree in Science, complemented by both a Master's and a Doctoral degree in Management, showcasing her deep academic and practical knowledge in the field. Her corporate career includes 15 years with renowned IT and BPO companies such as Effort BPO Ltd. and One Point One Solutions Ltd., where she honed her skills and contributed significantly to organizational success. Currently, Dr. Malpani is an Assistant Professor in the Faculty of Management and Commerce at Oriental University. In addition to her teaching responsibilities, she serves as the Ph.D. Coordinator and Assistant Superintendent of Examinations, reflecting her commitment to academic excellence and administrative efficiency.

Harshit Mishra is currently a final-year Ph.D. scholar in the Department of Agricultural Economics at Acharya Narendra Deva University of Agriculture & Technology, Kumarganj, Ayodhya (U.P.). He completed his Master's degree from the same university in 2022. During his academic journey, he has been recognized with several prestigious awards, including the Research Excellence Award, Best M.Sc. (Ag) Thesis Award, Best Oral Presentation Award, and Best Poster Presentation Award conferred by esteemed academic societies. He is the author of two books: "Fundamentals of Agri-Business Management & Intellectual Property Rights" and "Manual cum Workbook of Finance and Cooperation." In addition, he has published over 18 research articles in reputed NAAS-rated, Scopus-indexed, and Web of Science-indexed peer-reviewed journals. His scholarly contributions also include more than 48 popular articles published in both Hindi and English across various reputed magazines, and over 65 book chapters in edited volumes published by renowned international publishers such as Springer Nature, CRC Press, Taylor & Francis Group, Apple Academic Press, and many other reputed academic publishing houses.

Rahul Vijay Mohare is an Assistant Professor at the School of Management, Ramdeobaba University, Maharashtra, India. He holds a B.Sc. and dual doctoral degrees, a Ph.D. in Computer Science and a Ph.D. in Management, from Rashtrasant Tukdoji Maharaj Nagpur University. With over two decades of teaching and research experience, he has developed expertise in Business Analytics, Marketing Analytics, Data Mining, and advanced data tools including Power BI and SQL. Dr. Mohare has a strong academic and research portfolio, contributing to both technical and managerial domains through interdisciplinary approaches. His work integrates analytical techniques with practical applications, enabling data-driven decision-making in business and marketing contexts. He is actively engaged in mentoring students, delivering industry-relevant training, and fostering analytical thinking. His extensive experience and commitment to academic excellence position him as a valuable contributor to management education and applied research in analytics.

Beslin Pajila is a faculty member at Vel Tech Rangarajan Dr. Sagunthala R&D Institute of Science and Technology. She is actively involved in academic teaching, research, and scholarly activities in her field of expertise.

Supriya Tiwari Pathak President – Institution Innovation Council Innovation Ambassador – Ministry of Education Director Foreign Affairs, Witty Gossip Association Key Note coordinator to Lead India for foreign collaborations and business networking. Auditor - Quality Certification –London, Adjudicator- World Book of Records, London, Thought Leader, Visionary for Women, Certified Life

Coach, Businesswoman, Humanitarian, knowledge Seeker and Compelling Speaker, Dr. Supriya Tiwari Pathak multifaceted leadership with compassion & humility in different group of companies. Awards & Accolades: DrSupriya Pathak has been awarded Ph.D (Managment) Degree in the Convocation ceremony 2019 in the honorable presence of Dr.Varun kapur (IPS), ADG, Indore by Oriental University, Indore. Recognized and lauded for her work across Asia and Africa Continent, Dr. Supriya Pathak has been awarded as an Exceptional National Excellence Award, organized by Alma group of companies, London (UK) held in Indore, Madhya Pradesh, India. She achieved with feeling of proud and has been honored among prominent "Guest speakers and Guest of honors " around the world in International Digital summit by Witty Gossip Association – She was highly Delighted to Represent South Asian Chamber of Commerce and Industries (SACCI) being Director Foreign Affairs along with World Book of Records, UK at Awareness Programme of World Intellectual Property Organization in the gracious presence Mr. Mougamadou Abidine(Head, PCT Switzerland) and Mr.Chen Yinghua (Technical cooperation officer,WIPO),South Korea.

G Raghavender Raju is Currently the Dean of Student Welfare and Heading the Department of Humanities and Social Sciences, Sri Sathya Sai Institute of Higher Learning, Prasanthi Nilayam Campus, Puttaparthi. He is an expert in the areas of Macroeconomics, Monetary Theory & Policy International Economics & Finance. He has guided 4 Ph.Ds, around 100 dissertations, published three books, about ten chapters in edited volumes, around 50 research papers in refereed national and international journals and presented over 50 papers in national and international conferences. He is invited as a Resource Person of Econometrics at various Universities in India.

Selva Banu Priya T. is an Assistant Professor (AP) in the Department of Artificial Intelligence and Data Science at Panimalar Engineering College. She is committed to teaching and mentoring students in AI, data science, and related emerging technologies. Her academic interests focus on developing strong technical foundations and practical skills among learners.

Index

A

B

C

D

E

F

G

L

M

N

O

P

R

S

T

V

www.ingramcontent.com/pod-product-compliance
Lightning Source LLC
LaVergne TN
LVHW061527290926
849162LV00004B/701